THE WOMEN OF
KLIMT, SCHIELE AND KOKOSCHKA

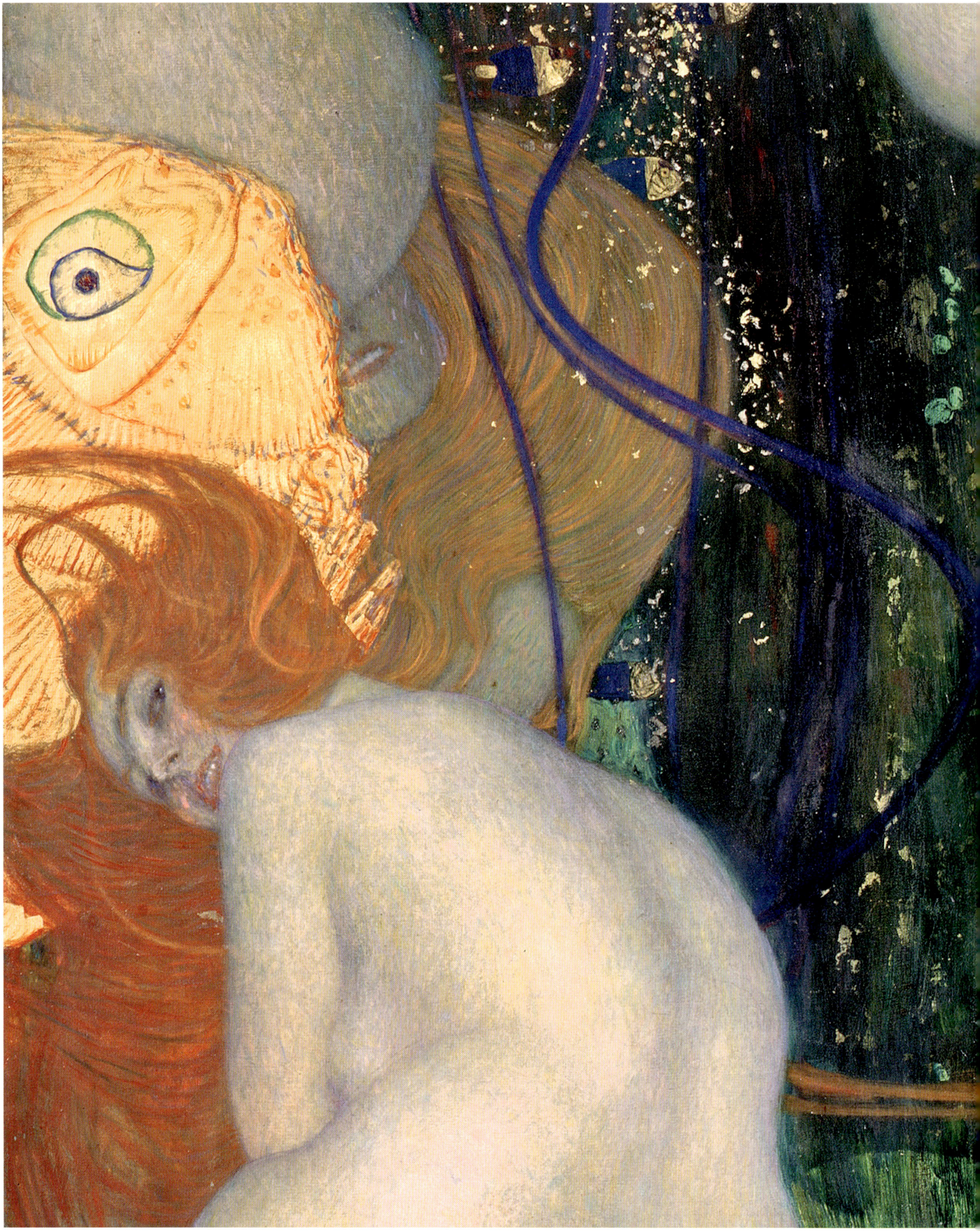

THE WOMEN OF KLIMT, SCHIELE AND KOKOSCHKA

Edited by Agnes Husslein-Arco,
Jane Kallir, and Alfred Weidinger

belvedere

PRESTEL
Munich • London • New York

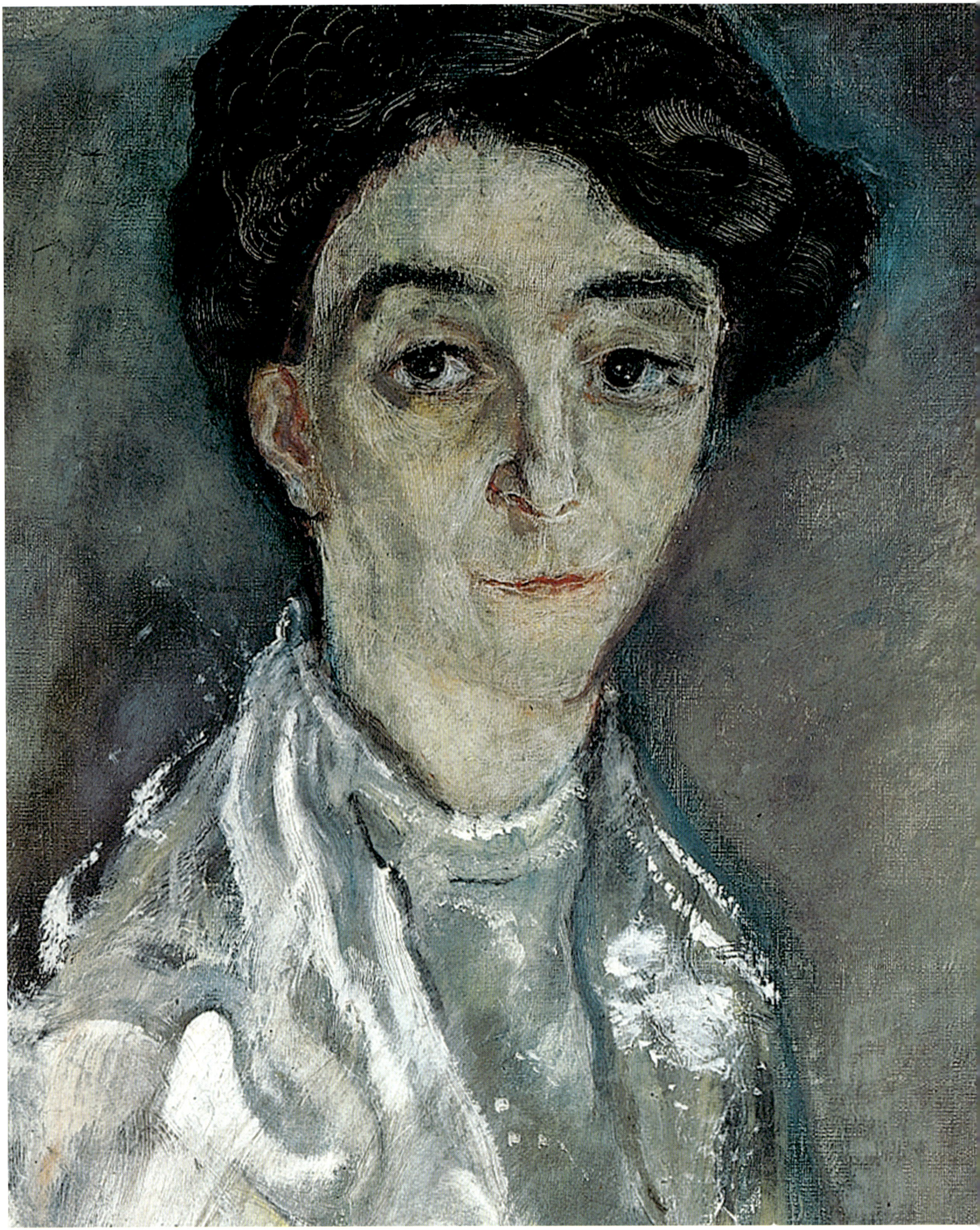

Content

Love, Psyche and Obsession. The Women of Klimt, Schiele and Kokoschka

Agnes Husslein-Arco

The exhibition "The Women of Klimt, Schiele and Kokoschka" at the Belvedere looks at one of the most pertinent and at the same time wide-ranging subject areas within the oeuvre of each of these three major Austrian artists.

The era before 1900 and the end of the Austro-Hungarian empire may be described as an epoch of historic change, something that also left its mark on the artists of the time. Science, particularly the field of psychology, was revolutionized, changing the direct understanding of the female psyche and generating a number of new types of women, which is also reflected in the works of these three artists. It is only retrospectively, however, that the significance of this development can be appreciated.

Over the centuries, art had established clear definitions of "women," which were adopted and taken for granted until well into the nineteenth century. Initially they were portrayed exclusively in a Christian context in biblical scenes, and in depictions of the Virgin Mary and saints. With the Renaissance and its orientation towards Antiquity, artists in the early modern period had possibilities, albeit limited, for showing the naked body in scenes from mythology. Women were depicted in a modest portrait format, and any suggestive innuendo could only be communicated through symbolic allusions. Obvious sexual content did not become a subject of visual arts until the late nineteenth century, pioneered by Gustave Courbet, whose lascivious paintings in the early 1860s culminated in *L'Origine du Monde* (p. 174, fig. 3). His unsparing picture was dismissed by the shocked visitors to the Paris Salon as pornography, but this revolutionary work of art can also be seen as a glorification of women, although Courbet's oeuvre also contains scenes of sexual interaction.

At the same time, rapid advances were being made in psychological research. Of particular interest were Pierre Janet's essays on hysteria and his experimental psychology at Hôpital de la Salpêtrière. His work may be contrasted with Sigmund Freud's ideas about psychoanalysis. Both approaches brought about a lasting change in the image of women, and Freud's theoretical writings in particular had a long-term impact. Together with Otto Weininger's *Sex and Character*, they offered a wide methodological spectrum, which was actively discussed in the Vienna art scene. Against this fascinating background, the Belvedere has put together an exhibition that sheds light on the image of women in Vienna Modernism. It focuses exclusively on works by its three main protagonists and offers a new way of looking at and comparing the works of Gustav Klimt, Egon Schiele, and Oskar Kokoschka.

A major part of the exhibition is devoted to portraits. Gustav Klimt especially painted many portraits on commission, and numerous examples of these are included. The members of Viennese high society were very fond of his compositions, notable for their perfect balance between the stylistic elements of Jugendstil and a realistic portrayal of the model. They may be contrasted with Egon Schiele's marked expressionist tendencies and the abstraction to be found in Oskar Kokoschka's works.

The lives of the artists are also interesting, since their intimate relationships influenced their creativity—Oskar Kokoschka and Alma Mahler, Egon and Edith Schiele, Gustav Klimt and Emilie Flöge. These women informed the artists' work to different degrees—as sources of inspiration, muses, or objects of obsession. They became the models of choice, and their treatment shifted constantly. This is particularly evident in the case of Schiele. While the portrait *Edith Schiele in a Striped Dress* (cat. 37) is relatively harmless, Schiele's drawings show a very different picture (see cat. 3, 4, 5, 9, 10, 91 etc.). Gustav Klimt had a much more respectful approach to nudes. Although he studied female masturbation intensively—and even attempted to establish the subject in the visual arts—he still maintained a certain distance from the model, even when painting the most intimate moments. Schiele's models, by contrast, were practically dissected; they make direct eye contact and present themselves face-on to the observer. These different approaches are also reflected in the choice of technique. Klimt's pencil drawings have a delicate, restrained character, while Schiele completed many drawings using firm pencil strokes and tempera paint to create a significant presence.

While many models were short-term sources of inspiration, Alma Mahler was the personification of the classic muse. Alongside numerous famous personalities like Gustav Mahler, Max Reinhardt, and Arnold Schönberg, she was also courted in her youth by Gustav Klimt. The Lower Belvedere features a temporary collection of works by Oskar Kokoschka tracing his relationship with her. They testify to desires and an all-consuming obsession. The six Fans for Alma Mahler, two of them are exhibited (cat. 103, 104), recall this intensive connection, which for Kokoschka became a passion. Initially he longed for family bliss and dearly wanted a child with Alma. When Alma radically put paid to these longings, she began to slip away from him. For a long time, Kokoschka refused to accept that the liaison was over, and this denial reached its climax with his idea of commissioning a life-size doll of Alma—a disappointing and lifeless substitute that finally brought Kokoschka to his senses.

The different approaches to women by these three artists are evident in their works. Kokoschka's depictions still contain Christian elements, which are nowhere to be found in the works of Klimt and Schiele, who show an increasing interest in the female body and essence. When comparing them directly, however, it becomes apparent that the depiction of women in early Modern art imposed great artistic demands, extending far beyond the popular *femme fragile* or *femme fatale* types. This exhibition shows mothers, girlfriends, couples, protectors, icons, and seductresses.

My sincere thanks go to the relevant experts Jane Kallir and Alfred Weidinger, who enthusiastically and knowledgeably developed this exhibition and the associated catalogue. The intensive preparations have led to a show that brings together a number of high-quality loans from museums and private collections. I am particularly grateful to all private lenders who have made these precious items available for the exhibition and to the museums that have agreed to lend the Belvedere major works from their collections. The result is a unique exhibition that highlights the role of women in Austrian art in the Vienna Modernist period, presenting great masterpieces together for the first time and offering perhaps the most intimate insight to date into the work of Klimt, Schiele, and Kokoschka.

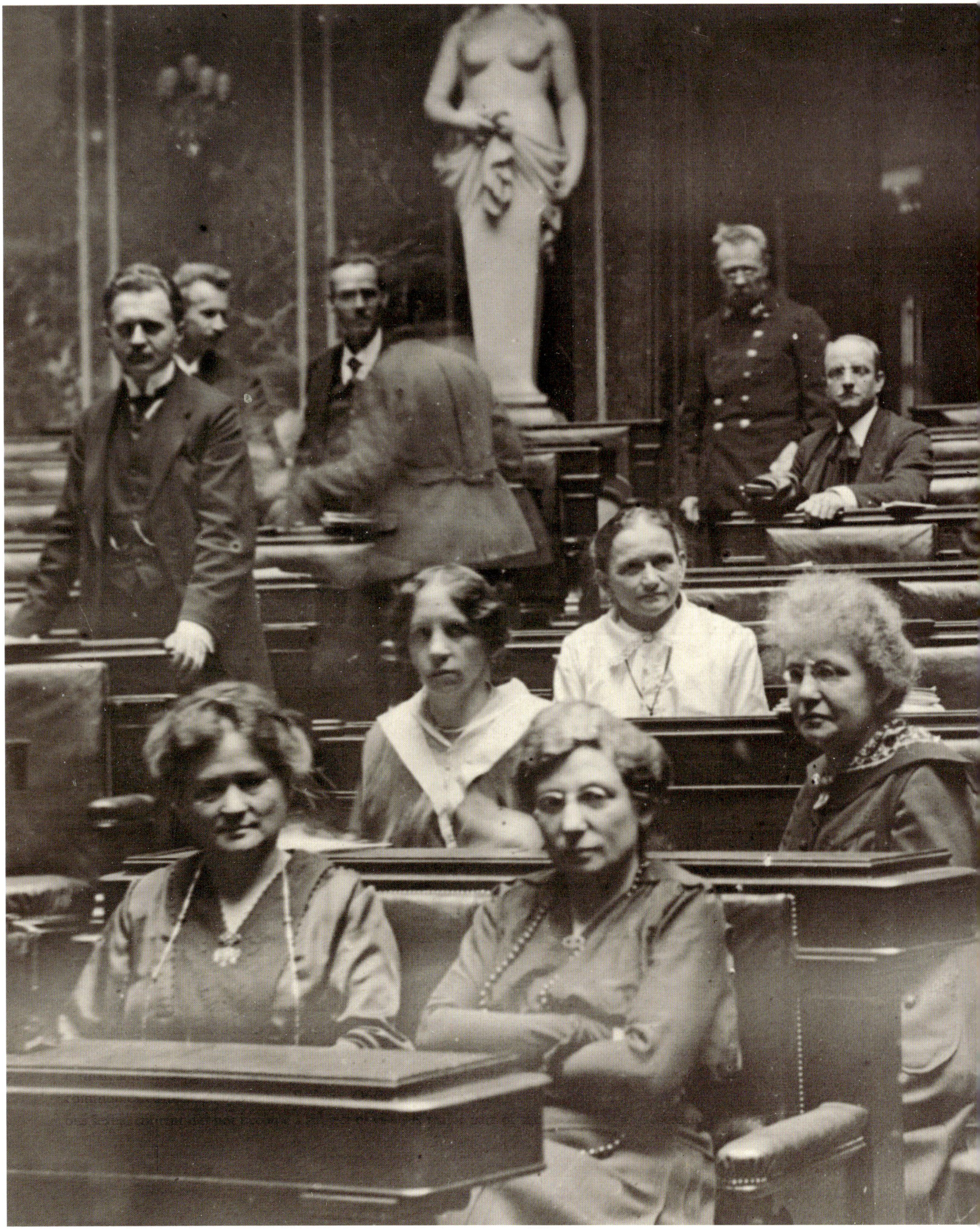

On the Women's Question in Vienna around 1900 Gender asymmetries, emancipation efforts, and uprisings

Luisa Ziaja

Fig. 1
Meeting of the constituting National Assembly in Parliament. Sector with women members of the Social Democratic Party from front l. Adelheid Popp, Therese Schlesinger, Anna Boschek, Emmy Freundlich, Maria Tusch, and Amalie Seidel, 1919
Österreichische Nationalbibliothek, Bildarchiv und Grafiksammlung

In 1901, the German writer and social democratic women's rights activist Lily Braun published an internationally acclaimed study entitled *Die Frauenfrage: Ihre geschichtliche Entwicklung und wirtschaftliche Seite (*The Woman Question: Its Historical Development and Economic Perspective*)*.[1] In the introductory remarks, she claims "From whatever point of view one regards this complex and multifaceted problem, the real conditions of existence for the female gender within society create—for the past as well as for the present—the guiding Ariadne's thread, without which my premise must fail. Only when the economic facts are given their due consideration, is the connection revealed between the woman question and the social question, of which the former is an integral component."[2]

Lily Braun is by no means the first woman writer to turn to the so-called "woman question"; her book must be seen in context with numerous previous publications on the theme, especially in the German-speaking world. Nor is the connection of the woman question with the highly virulent social question as a central line of argument particularly new.[3] However, her great achievement is a historical derivation of women's situation in society and its comprehensive description based on extensive empirical data in transnational comparison, which she then links with the demands of the women's rights movement. She is, as it were, the first to express gender relations in percentages.[4]

In the multitude of statistics quoted in this early benchmark work, one stands out in particular (and also seemed noteworthy to its contemporary reviewer, Mabel Atkinson): the share of women who were active in the proletarian workforce in the reference period around 1890. While this figure comprises close to 25 percent in the United States and around 37 percent in England and Wales, as well as in Germany, the share of working women in Austria was extremely high, at nearly 55 percent.[5] As a second table shows, however, the share of women in middle-class professions in Austria was a mere 12 percent, similar to Germany (19 percent in the United States, 22 percent in England and Wales).[6] These class-specific differences in gainful employment figures reflect not only fundamentally divergent lived realities—genuine hardship versus ennui—but also quite contradictory objectives and demands of the proletarian and the bourgeois women's rights movements, which will be discussed below.

As Lily Braun shows, factual asymmetries, rooted in a historically evolved inherent discrimination of women in all aspects of public and private life, converge in the woman question, and were challenged by the emancipation efforts for social, economic, and political equality. At the same time, attached to this omnipresent question[7] is a whole set of issues on the image of women, gender roles and morals, representations and attributions of femininity, as well as issues of sexuality, which accompany, pervade, and essentially determine these arguments. The fact that discrimination of women is a transnational phenomenon present in all modern societies in the second half of the nineteenth century is evident, but equally evident is that there are underlying specific regional and national features, both in terms of structural conditions and its discursive treatment. This essay illuminates the woman question in Vienna around 1900 against this backdrop, and pursues the theory that the (discursive) history of women's emancipation operates as a—paradoxical but nonetheless crucial—driving factor of Viennese modernism. After a brief epistemological summary of Vienna in 1900 in general, the second part deals with the situation of women in particular, with regard to education and work, political participation and representation, and intertwines these fields of activity with the aspect of organization within the women's movements of the time. A third part is devoted to the discursive "battle of the sexes" between (othering) misogynous ascription and defiant self-description, and references back to the "psychotopos" Vienna.[8]

1. Vienna around 1900

More than identifying a place and time, and beyond the "Golden Age"[9] proclaimed by city marketing, "Vienna around 1900" is a code for the farewell and departure of an outdated society transitioning to the Modern era—indeed, for the ambivalence and antimonies of the Modern era per se. In his publication *Hugo von Hofmannsthal and His Time*, Hermann Broch describes Vienna retrospectively as the oft-quoted "center of the European value vacuum,"[10] and those years as shaped by a spirited sense of approaching demise, a "joyful apocalypse."[11]
Spurred by the "(re-)discovery" of the Viennese *fin-de-siècle* via Carl E. Schorske's influential study in the early 1980s on the spirit and society of this epoch,[12] what has occupied cultural studies in a, by now, impenetrable flood of research projects and publications is the interaction between the creative innovation in art, architecture, music, literature, philosophy, and psychology on the one hand, and the anti-Modern societal conditions of clerical conservatism on the other—a political culture steeped in anti-Semitism, misogyny, and nationalism.[13] To its more liberal contemporaries, Vienna was not a center of Modernism, but rather a "bastion of everything that was archaic,"[14] characterized by political and economic crises, and a steady decline in its importance in competition with other major European cities.[15]
At the same time, the second half of the nineteenth century was a period of structural modernization and economic prosperity: the industrial revolution and expansion of the *Gründerjahre* enabled the bourgeoisie to advance socially and gain in political power, providing recruits for a liberal government from 1867. The influence of the empowered bourgeoisie became manifest outwardly in the buildings of the Ringstrasse, ultimately financed through the purchase of building lots. The public buildings, such as the city hall, parliament, university, and Burgtheater, were an expression of bourgeois liberal values, while the prestigious residential palaces meanwhile testified to the upper classes' endeavor to approximate aristocracy. At the same time, the development of the *glacis* and the former bastions and fortifications surrounding the city also signified a removal of the strict border between wealthy city center and poor suburbs, a convergence of middle classes and proletariat.[16]
Urban expansion projects, including the regulation of the Wien and Danube rivers as well as infrastructural renewal of public transportation and drinking water networks, and of the electricity and gas mains were key to the spectacular modernization surge and Vienna's rise to urban metropolis. In just a few decades, the city recorded an explosive growth in population, making Vienna the seventh largest city in the world—from 900,009 inhabitants in 1869 to 2,083,630 in 1910.[17] In addition to the incorporation of the suburbs in 1890, which turned thousands of workers and small traders into Viennese residents,

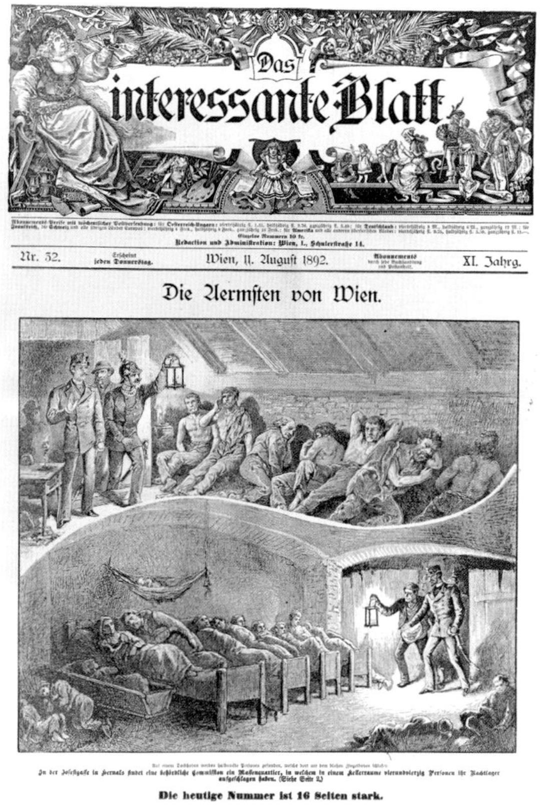
Das interessante Blatt
Redaction und Administration: Wien, I., Schulerstraße 14.
Nr. 32. Erscheint jeden Donnerstag. Wien, 11. August 1892. XI. Jahrg.
Die Aermsten von Wien.
In der Josefigasse in Hernals findet eine behördliche Commission ein Massenquartier, in welchem in einem Kellerraume vierundvierzig Personen ihr Nachtlager aufgeschlagen haben. (Siehe Seite 2.)
Die heutige Nummer ist 16 Seiten stark.

Fig. 2
Discovery of mass accommodation in an attic and basement in Hernals, Title page of the weekly magazine *Das interessante Blatt* of August 11, 1892
Österreichische Nationalbibliothek, Bildarchiv und Grafiksammlung

this growth was mainly due to the steady stream of immigrants, especially from the non-German-speaking eastern provinces of the Habsburg empire, principally from Bohemia, Moravia, Galicia, and Poland—including many Jews. This resulted in a socially differentiated and ethnically and culturally heterogeneous population. The flipside to the infrastructural urbanization and social modernization, the display of political emancipation described above, and to the social advancement of the liberal bourgeoisie while simultaneously upholding a moribund state apparatus, was the large-scale exploitation of the proletariat, whose living conditions, as a result of several interconnected factors, became extremely precarious. Material constraints, the daily battle for paid work, food, clothing, and fuel, and—not least—a roof over their head, dominated the social circumstances of working class Viennese families.[18]

The depression initiated by the stock market crash in 1873, which first dragged down the hitherto flourishing construction and railway industries, soon engulfed all sectors and resulted in mass unemployment. Combined with a series of crop failures in the following years, this led to a sustained agricultural crisis, land flight, supply shortages, and extreme inflation. The electrical industry emerged from the economic transformation in the 1890s as the most dynamic player, but was extensively backed by and dependent on foreign capital, without which recovery and continuous growth in general was no longer conceivable. This second economic surge set off heavy immigration from the crown lands, leading to Vienna's already mentioned population explosion. With housing already in short supply, this influx into the commercial-industrial outer districts and suburbs led to extreme densification. Rampant building speculation with tenement blocks whose *Gründerzeit* façades could only superficially conceal the misery behind gave rise to exorbitant rents, which in turn resulted in overcrowding and *Bettgehertum* (the subletting of beds). For even the most squalid quarters in basements and back buildings rents were being charged that exceeded the square-meter price of Ringstrasse palaces.[19]

Like most of its European counterparts, Vienna around 1900 was a city of contrasts: The wealth of the upper classes and relative prosperity of the bourgeoisie, in combination with appropriate access to education, stood against the proletariat's abject poverty and widespread illiteracy. Yet no matter how extensively the misery of suburban life was documented in journalistic contributions and social-reform writings—such as by Emil Kläger, who devoted himself to the housing shortage and homelessness, or by eyewitnesses like Alfons Petzold and Max Winter, who described the inhumane living conditions of dressmakers and assembly line workers, bricklayers and construction workers—the explosive nature of these social issues was not met with reforms.[20] Instead, the liberal government, along with the anti-progressive emperor and his court as well as the fossilized bureaucratic apparatus, ignored the exploitation and mass impoverishment of the proletariat.

In addition, the social question was eclipsed by the central problem of the national issue. Against the backdrop of ethnically and religiously heterogeneous immigration and the fear of foreign infiltration, nationalist movements gained strength and radicalized, targeting especially the Czech and Jewish populations with their call for a homogenized "German Vienna."[21] Rather than becoming a "cultural melting pot," the metropolis of Vienna, multicultural only in terms of demographics, developed into a "battlefield of national chauvinisms, of ethnic and social opposites, and ultimately, of all kinds of racisms and of anti-Semitism,"[22] Jacques Le Rider wrote. Meanwhile, the two major parties—Christian Socialists under Karl Lueger and Social Democrats under Victor Adler—replaced the liberal government, weakened by the economic crisis, and undertook to uphold the interests of the middle and working classes. The election of Lueger as mayor in 1897 accelerated the social disintegration, as he functionalized the growing anti-Semitism by turning it into a political agenda, thus aggravating the social and ethnic entrenchment.[23]

Parallel to the establishment of the mainstream political parties—and, in the case of the Social Democrats, partially in conflict to this, though still in close conjunction—women's associations, already in existence for several decades, organized into an umbrella organization to counter the dominance of men in all public areas of life and vehemently demand professional, social, and legal equality for women.[24] The patriarchal imagination, especially the bourgeois-male identity, was shaken—indeed, profoundly questioned—by the insistence of this new, major movement.

Jacques Le Rider's approach toward explaining the convergences of this era promptly defines the social and ideological crises as crises of individual identity, and conceives Viennese Modernism as a "resonance field" for the collective and individual awareness of crisis, the conflicting constructions of gender identity, and for the search for identity among the Jewish intellectual elite in an anti-Semitic environment.[25] Carl E. Schorske had previously interpreted *fin-de-siècle* Vienna, with its acutely felt tremors of social and political disintegration—and, one might add, disintegration of identity—as "one of the most fertile breeding grounds of our century's anti-historical culture."[26] With Allan Janik, one may describe Vienna around 1900 as the "birthplace of Modernity,"[27] precisely because it expresses the contradictions, discontinuities, and ambivalences of the contemporary modernization process. Social, national, and gender issues became so intertwined that the cohabitation of genders, nationalities, and classes became precarious. Social and political powers, meanwhile, responded insufficiently, losing their legitimacy as a result, and, ultimately, overall integration collapsed. Within the *fin-de-siècle* metaphors of dissolution, the erosion of traditional structures, institutions, and norms became a reality, together with the construction of new social, political, and cultural configurations.[28] Against the backdrop of this fragmentation and diversity, the insecurities, crises, and redefinitions of identities, and the aforementioned omnipresent debate of "the woman question," art and literature of the epoch discovered one of its key motifs in women, femininity, and female sexuality. Before discussing the male projections, fantasies of desire, and fears surrounding the femme fatale or, alternatively, the femme fragile, which were to fundamentally define contemporary discourse, we first need a depiction of the concrete situation of women in Vienna's *fin-de-siècle* society.

2. The situation of women in Vienna around 1900

The deeply-rooted thinking in social hierarchies was also decisive for the situation of women. Social status was linked to radically diverging lifestyles of women; but subordination within a patriarchal regime and the lack of political rights applied to all: Until 1918 women had neither suffrage nor the right of political assembly. The differences between bourgeois and proletarian life are probably best reflected in the areas of education and work.[29] As shown in the introductory statistics quoted from Lily Braun, the percentage of women in proletarian work in Austria around 1890 was exceptionally high, while that of women in middle-class work corresponded with the low European average. Whereas for working-class women the issue was everyday survival under cruel working conditions with wages even lower than those of their male colleagues and in precarious housing situations, combined with the additional burden of caring for home and family, the role of the bourgeois married woman did not really foresee any employment, as the man was expected to provide

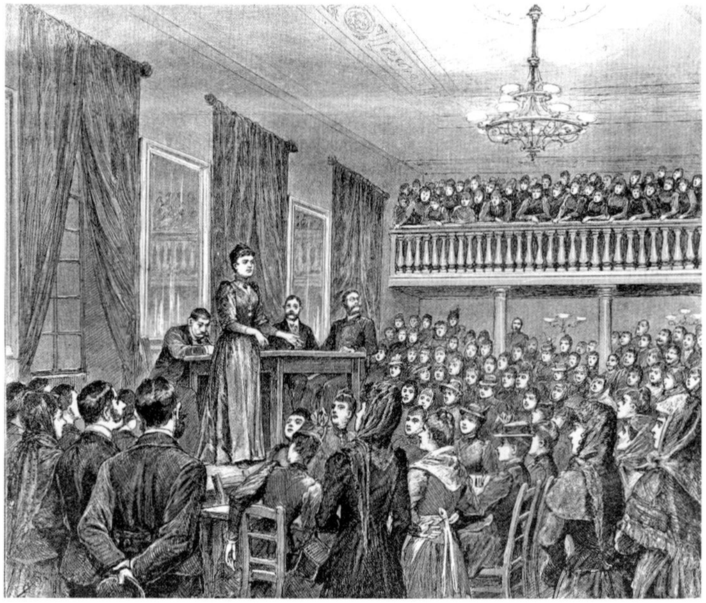

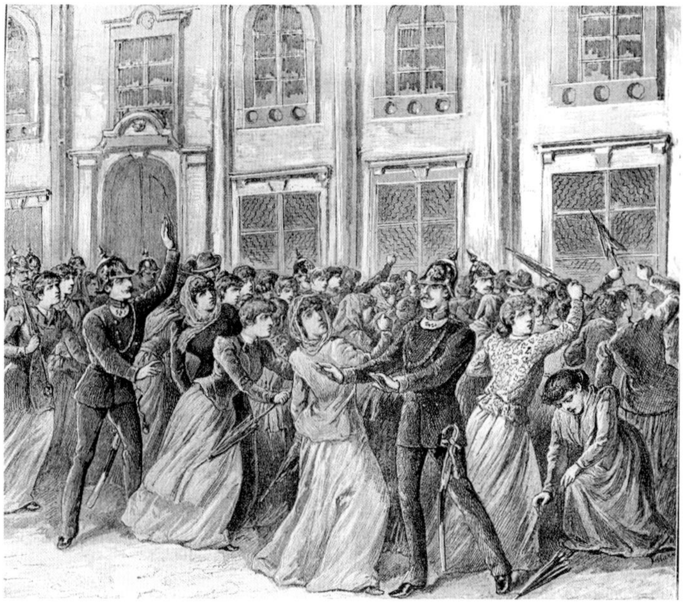

Fig. 3
Women's labor leader Adelheid Popp making a fighting speech to a gathering of unemployed women, 1892
Österreichische Nationalbibliothek, Bildarchiv und Grafiksammlung

Fig. 4
FRANZ KOLLARZ
Strike of women workers in a finishing and dyeing works for higher wages, in *Das interessante Blatt*, May 11, 1893
Österreichische Nationalbibliothek, Bildarchiv und Grafiksammlung

relative financial security, but this also resulted in the woman's absolute dependence on her husband. The objectives of the bourgeois and proletarian women's rights' movements diverged along these differences. The Wiener Frauen-Erwerbsverein [Viennese Women's Employment Association] was founded as early as 1866, to be followed by further middle-class associations representing professional, educational, and welfare interests, operating primarily on a practical-charitable level. Nonetheless, in 1870, Marianne Hainisch, pioneer of the bourgeois-liberal women's movement, already formulated the central demand that secondary school education should be accessible to "female intelligence from all [social] classes."[30] At this time, an equal education system was still a long way off, and women were effectively excluded from further education and university, as well as from most professions. The state-supported primary and secondary schools, with class sizes of up to eighty pupils, offered an elementary education characterized by drill and discipline.[31] Children from middle-class homes were sent to private educational institutions or received private tuition at home. In addition to the class-related educational inequality, at the end of the mandatory school age, there was the gender-based inequality. In so-called schools for young ladies, or finishing schools, girls from well-to-do families received piano and singing lessons, and were instructed in needlework and social etiquette; in conjunction with the supervised reading of books on manners and social graces, this type of education was entirely aimed at internalizing the socially legitimized gender roles, supposedly based on a natural dichotomy of genders, and preparing the young women just sufficiently so they "wouldn't bore their future husbands through a complete lack of education."[32] Young men, on the other hand, had access to—in some cases even publicly funded—training and further education; after all, they had to prepare for the role of patriarch and breadwinner.

Marianne Hainisch's call for the establishment of high schools for girls, and for making universities accessible to women, met with strong and unyielding resistance from a public concerned about morals and the mother's role. The first girls' high school, set up by the Association for Extended Women's Education, opened in Vienna in 1892—twenty-two years later—but public funding was still denied in 1897 and justified by a decree for the systematic prevention of equal educational opportunities for women, based on fears of competition in the labor market: "The educational administration does not fail to recognize the sign of the times, of providing young women with an education that is equivalent to that of young men, thereby providing them with greater employability, and does not wish to stand in the way of the same, provided it is grounded in female nature and in a genuine need. However, granting unlimited access for girls to the secondary schools and colleges established for the needs of young men, and, furthermore, opening to them all professions that are at present sufficiently and excessively filled by men, is not in their best interests. This would pose a serious risk to the mental condition and natural occupation of woman and, moreover, could not occur without serious disadvantages for men, whose employability in the face of the competition might drop to a degree that would make it difficult or impossible to form and maintain a family."[33]

Secondary schools and high schools for girls were not publicly acknowledged, thus receiving financial support, until 1919. Before that, higher education for women was dependent on high tuition fees and thereby on social status. In addition, Austria, along with Prussia, was the last European country to admit women to universities. From 1897, women were allowed to study humanities and natural sciences, from 1900 medicine, and from 1919 the legal faculty was open to female students. The Protestant-theological faculty was open to them from 1923, and the Catholic-theological not until 1946.[34] Although Hainisch had called for "female intelligence from all social classes," the long debate about the admission of women to higher education was, primarily, a bourgeois phenomenon. Demographic, social, and economic developments, meanwhile, had added vehemence to the education question. From the 1860s onward, women were demographically in the majority, which necessitated alternatives to the traditional bourgeois concept of ensuring a woman's financial security through marriage. Beyond a job as governess, there were not many opportunities for unmarried middle-class women to earn a living, while for married women there were none. In times of economic crisis, which also led to impoverishment among the middle-classes, this problem became more acute, and was dramatically intensified in cases when the husband fell ill or died. Such was the fate that befell a friend of Marianne Hainisch, which, as she describes in her memoirs, was the original cause for her enduring and persistent battle.[35]

Around 1890, against the backdrop of developments in society as a whole, the early forms of organization of the women's movement were followed by a true surge in the increasingly differentiated and politicized movement. At the political turning point of the formation of the main modern parties, the women's movement entered its "ideological" phase. Women became politically active and demanded broad-based equality and participation.[36] Thus, in 1890, the Social Democratic party founded the Working Women's Educational Association as a contact point and political forum for working women. There were also a number of Christian social groups and, from 1893, the General Austrian Women's Association, which built on the activities of the Association of Female Teachers and Educators, and was run largely by Auguste Fickert, Rosa Mayreder, and Marie Lang. Along with agitation for women's suffrage, which had already been at the center of the teachers' association's agenda, as well as for equal educational and professional rights, the General Austrian Women's Association set explicit social objectives, such as campaigning for disenfranchised servants, the extension of maternity protection, and the eight-hour day, i.e. objectives they clearly shared with their social-democratic colleagues. In her keynote speech at the association's founding meeting, Auguste Fickert defined the "social question" as the "most burning issue," and also the "most intimately entwined with the woman question."[37]

Also at issue was the creation of a critical discourse, for example, on topics such as prostitution or regarding the battle of the sexes, primarily discussed in the journal *Dokumente der Frauen*, which first appeared in 1899. Defining itself as a multi-partisan organization, the General Austrian Women's Association constantly sought to create an alliance with the Working Women's Educational Association, which was, however, fundamentally opposed. As the social democrat Adelheid Popp wrote in retrospect, she and her comrades found it "necessary, right from the start, to undertake a division between the proletarian and bourgeois women's movements." In keeping with the party line of the Social Democrats, the class question took priority over the woman question, which meant that the battle lines were drawn between proletariat and bourgeoisie, which included bourgeois women despite their clearly shared interests. Käthe Leichter's ironic assessment is an apt

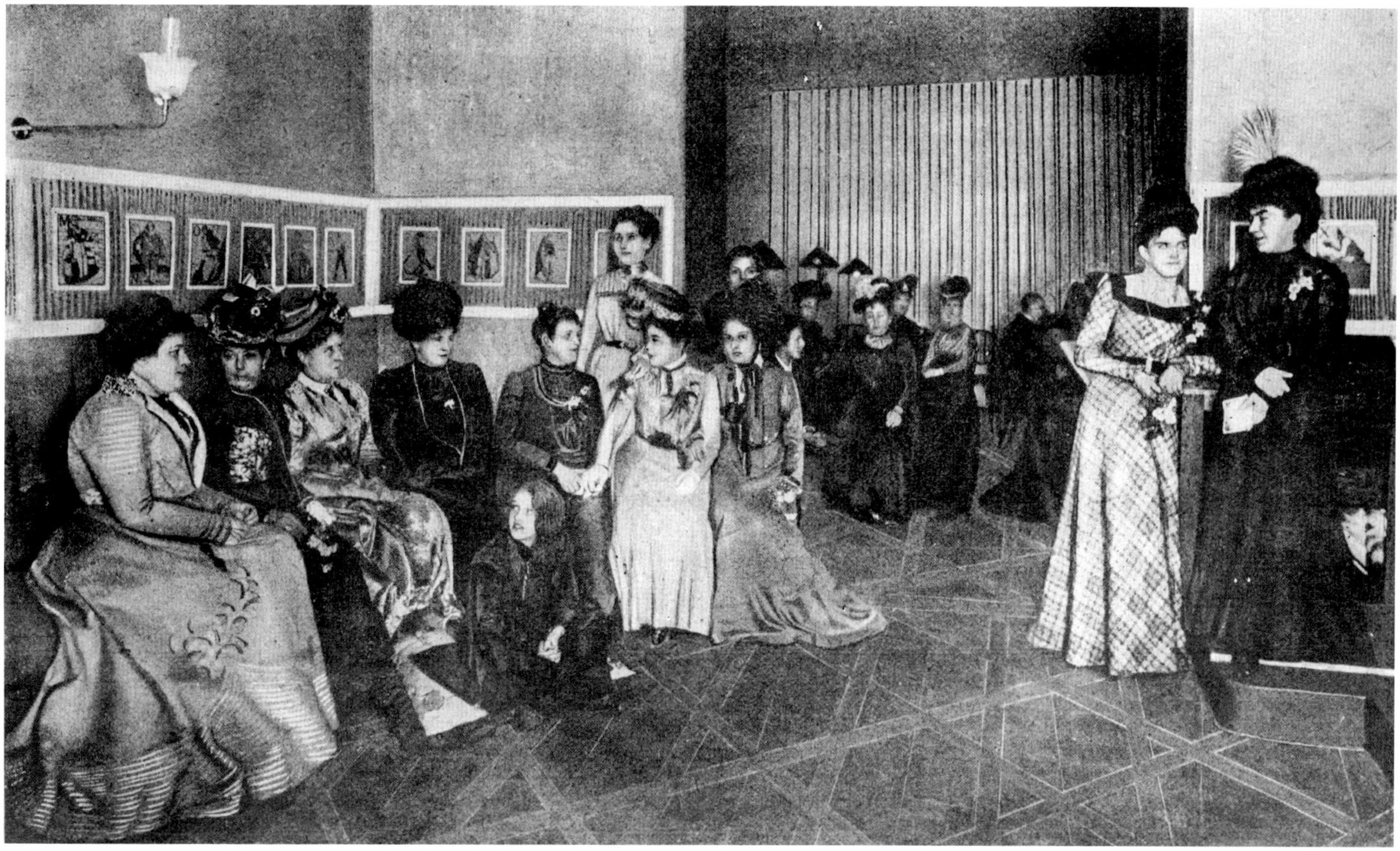

Fig. 5
Wiener Frauenclub in its new home: the executive board and committee members in the billiard room on the opening day, in *Das interessante Blatt,* November 22, 1900
Österreichische Nationalbibliothek, Bildarchiv und Grafiksammlung

summary of the social-democratic women's position "The struggle of the bourgeois women comprises mainly wearing reform clothing, smiling pityingly at any mention of the word 'man', sending petitions to parliament, organizing women's club evenings..., but otherwise constantly assuring that they absolutely not revolutionary and aim to achieve their rights peacefully, without upsetting the existing order. They raise a loud cheer when somewhere in the world a woman is made professor or assistant undersecretary or accomplishes some other achievement."[38]

Contrasting that, the activities of the Working Women's Educational Association were characterized by agitation at gatherings and in public places, demonstrations, and strikes, which brought constant conflict with officials and authorities, and at times even prison sentences. For example, on December 9, 1892, Adelheid Dworschak (whose married name became Popp), organized a lecture at "Zu den drei Engeln" in Vienna's fourth district, where she spoke to a gathering of 500 unemployed women on the subject of "women's unemployment, its causes and effects." In this, she addressed key issues affecting working-class women—starvation wages, which drove women to prostitution, the outdated nature of traditional gender roles and the institution of marriage—with the aim of creating an awareness of their social situation among the working women, who had been raised with a sense of absolute indifference to their own needs, and thereby empowering them to act.[39]

The first organized women's strike in May 1893 has become legendary. Led by women textile workers employed in three finishing factories in the suburb of Gumpendorf, their demands for a ten-hour day, a minimum wage of four guldens per week, and a holiday on May 1, were met after a fourteen-day strike by 700 women.[40] Like many social-democratic functionaries, Adelheid Dworschak knew the miserable working and living conditions from her own experience. The daughter of a Bohemian weaver, she had left school after just three years of education to begin paid work. She worked twelve hours a day in numerous workshops and factories until, in her early twenties, she took the position of editor at the newly founded women workers' magazine and became involved in politics for the rest of her life.[41]

Like the bourgeois women's movement, the social democrat women, too, demanded women's suffrage from the outset. One of the first meetings on this topic took place on the Penzinger Au in 1893. However, this demand was constantly subordinated to party interests and deferred in order not to jeopardize, for example, amendments regarding the voting rights of male workers. When equal, direct, and secret proportional representation for all citizens regardless of sex was finally introduced in November 1918, the following election in 1919 resulted in a total of eight women representatives entering the National Assembly—including seven Social Democrats, among them Adelheid Popp.[42]

3. The discursive "battle of the sexes"

Accompanying the rise of the organized women's movement around 1890 was an anti-feminism that, while not new, had intensified significantly. As Harriet Anderson explains, these confrontations were part of the core of feminist experience. As an example, she presents the Christian-socialist politicians' hurling of foul insults at bourgeois women, calling them prostitutes and sluts, for participating in Victor Adler's 1901 election campaign.[43] The most important weapon in this widespread phenomenon, which conservative politicians in particular liked to use, was the repressive sexual morality, against which they vilified women's rights activists as obviously oversexed. Their insatiable and unnatural hunger for sex and power were a threat to men and morals, they argued. The self-proclaimed "men's right's activist" Lanz von Liebenfels, former fraternity neophyte and mentor of Adolf Hitler, argued against women's rights activists as "poor child bearers and bad mothers" and defined the desire for women's social, economic, and political independence as "hostile to culture—yes, even more than that… hostile to life."[44]

In contrast to such misogynous reactionaries, many protagonists from Viennese Modernism were concerned with overcoming the patriarchal, bourgeois sexual morals, yet at the same time clung to the suppression of women.[45] Dominant here was not the image of the oversexed woman, but that of the frustrated woman, who had been alienated from her natural femininity. The assumption that women and men could carry out the same cultural duties was opposed by the cultural critic Karl Hauer, who argued that, clearly, culture was exclusively the work of men, and that women had a positive role in culture, "only as material for men's desire to create, as living artwork, or as an effective tonic, a multiplier of male energies."[46] Certainly the most well-known example of this wave of anti-feminist writing which used pseudo-scientific methods in an attempt to prove women's inferiority, is the bestseller *Sex and Character* by Otto Weininger, published in German in 1903, which denies woman any ability to emancipate and which climaxes in the oft-cited statement, "woman is nothing, she is only matter."[47]

In the end, these new myths of femininity are the expression of male feelings of extreme impotence and fear of failure in a society that has been shaken to the very core. If we understand the efforts at emancipation and the fundamental critique of patriarchy as essential motors of the social upheavals of the *fin de siècle*, then at issue is none other than escape from the male order of things and the creation of a "new woman," a "new world," and a "new social order," as Rosa Mayreder wrote: "And this is the will and the aim of the progressive movement among women, elevating woman from this secondary position, to place her as an equal being at the side of man. But what can be the ultimate, most profound sense of this endeavor! Her opponents have always misunderstood her, as though she wanted to turn woman into a man. And indeed, this could be the risk, if the women's movement is not accompanied by an essential transformation of the existing order; at the least, the female gender would have to let itself be pressed into the ways of life and demands that were created by men for men. Therefore, in the sense of the woman's life, transformation of the existing order is an indispensable requirement of the women's movement."[48]

1 Lily Braun, *Die Frauenfrage: Ihre geschichtliche Entwicklung und wirtschaftliche Seite*, Leipzig 1901. On its contemporary reception, see, for example, the comprehensive review in the context of international discourse by Mabel Atkinson in the influential *American Journal of Sociology*: Mabel Atkinson, "Review: *Die Frauenfrage: ihre geschichtliche Entwicklung und wirtschaftliche Seite* by Lily Braun," *American Journal of Sociology*, vol. 8, no. 5, March 1903, pp. 699–707.
2 Ibid.
3 On this, see Gisela Bock, "Begriffsgeschichten: 'Frauenemanzipation im Kontext der Emanzipationsbewegungen des 19. Jahrhunderts,'" in: ibid., *Geschlechtergeschichten der Neuzeit: Ideen, Politik, Praxis*, Göttingen 2014, pp. 100–152, especially pp. 117–128. The influence of August Bebel's 1879 publication *Die Frau und der Sozialismus* is evident—like him, Braun understood the repression of women as a class issue.
4 See Antje Trosien, "Claudia Walther, Lily Braun – Kämpferische und bekämpfte Sozialistin," in: *Zeitschrift für Sozialistische Politik und Wirtschaft*, no. 93, January/February 1997, p. 53.
5 Braun 1901 (see note 1), chapter 5, "Die Statistik der proletarischen Frauenarbeit nach den letzten Zählungen," p. 220.
6 Ibid., chapter 2, "Die treibenden Kräfte der bürgerlichen Frauenbewegung," p. 153.
7 "There is no newspaper, no organization, no gathering, that doesn't discuss this issue," said Louise Otto on founding the *Allgemeinen deutschen Frauenverein* in 1865, quoted by Bock 2014 (see note 3), p. 117.
8 See Hermann Glaser, *Sigmund Freuds Zwanzigstes Jahrhundert. Seelenbilder einer Epoche. Materialien und Analysen*, Munich 1976.
9 At least since the exhibition *Traum und Wirklichkeit. Wien 1870–1930*, shown at the Künstlerhaus in 1985, the *fin-de-siècle* has become a defining factor in Austria's image and self-perception. See Heidemarie Uhl, "'Wien um 1900' – das making of eines Gedächtnisortes," in: Monika Sommer, Marcus Gräser, Ursula Prutsch (eds.), *Imaging Vienna. Innensichten, Außensichten, Stadterzählungen*, Vienna 2006, pp. 47–70 and Monika Sommer-Sieghart, Luisa Ziaja, "Kulturhistorische Großausstellungen der 1980er Jahre im Künstlerhaus. Anmerkungen zu kuratorischen Kontinuitäten und Brüchen," in: Peter Bogner, Richard Kurdiovsky, Johannes Stoll (eds.), *Festschrift 150 Jahre Künstlerhaus*, Vienna 2015, pp. 358–365.
10 Hermann Broch, *Hugo von Hofmannsthal and his Time. The European Imagination, 1860–1920*, (translated and edited by Michael P. Steinberg), Chicago/London 1984, p. 65.
11 The Parisian adoption of the exhibition *Traum und Wirklichkeit* at the Centre Pompidou in 1986 occurred under the title *Vienne 1880–1938. L'Apocalypse Joyeuse* thus significantly extending the time focus to the year 1938; see Sommer-Sieghart, Ziaja, 2015 (see note 9), p. 364.
12 See, Carl E. Schorske, *Fin-de-siècle Vienna: Politics and Culture*, Cambridge 1981.
13 Only a small selection is listed here: Emil Brix, Patrick Werkner (eds.), *Die Wiener Moderne*, Vienna/Munich 1990; Jacques Le Rider, *Modernity and Crises of Identity: Culture and Society in Fin-de-Siècle Vienna*, New York 1993; Jürgen Nautz, Richard Vahrenkamp (eds.), *Die Wiener Jahrhundertwende*, Vienna/Cologne/Graz 1993; Steven Beller (ed.), *Rethinking Vienna 1900*, New York/Oxford 2001.
14 Le Rider 1993 (see note 13), p. 21.
15 See Heidemarie Uhl, "Wien um 1900 – ein ambivalenter Ort der Moderne," in: Tobias G. Natter, Gerbert Frodl (eds.), *Klimt's Women*, Berlin 2000, pp. 14–17, here 14.
16 See Frauke Severit, "Wien um 1900 – eine Stadt im Widerstreit von Tradition und Moderne," in: ibid. (ed.), *Das alles war ich: Politikerinnen, Künstlerinnen, Exzentrikerinnen der Wiener Moderne*, Vienna/Cologne/Weimar 1998, pp. 9–24, here 11.
17 Michael John, Albert Lichtblau, *Schmelztiegel Wien – einst und jetzt. Zur Geschichte und Gegenwart von Zuwanderung und Minderheiten*, Vienna/Cologne 1990, p. 12, quoted by Uhl, 2000, p. 15. This meant an increase of almost 80 percent for the inner districts, and more than 253 percent for the suburbs; see Peter Feldbauer, *Stadtwachstum und Wohnungsnot*, Vienna 1977, p. 39.
18 See Reinhard Sieder, "'Vata, derf i aufstehn?' Kindheitserfahrungen in Wiener Arbeiterfamilien um 1900," in Hubert Ch. Ehalt, Gernot Heiß, Hannes Stekl (eds.), *Glücklich ist, wer vergisst...? Das andere Wien um 1900*, Vienna/Cologne/Graz 1986, pp. 39–89, here 47.
19 See Feldbauer, 1977, p. 161; as well as Wolfgang Maderthaner, Lutz Musner, *Die Anarchie in der Vorstadt. Das andere Wien um 1900*, Frankfurt/M./New York 1999.
20 See Alfons Petzold, *Raw Life*, London 1926. – Max Winter, *Das schwarze Wienerherz. Sozialreportagen aus dem frühen 20. Jahrhundert*, Helmut Strutzmann (ed.), Vienna 1982. – Emil Kläger, *Durch die Wiener Quartiere des Elends und Verbrechens. Ein Wanderbuch aus dem Jenseits*, Vienna 1908.
21 See Uhl, 2000, p. 16.
22 Jacques Le Rider, *Mitteleuropa. Auf den Spuren eines Begriffs*, Vienna 1994, p. 78, quoted by Uhl, 2000, p. 16.
23 See Severit, 1998, p. 13.
24 Ibid.
25 Le Rider, 1990.
26 Schorske, 1994, p. XVIII.
27 See Allan Janik, "Vienna 1900: Reflections on Problems and Methods," in Emil Brix, Patrick Werkner (eds.) *Die Wiener Moderne*, 1990, p. 156.
28 See Wolfgang Mantl, "Modernisierung und Dekadenz," in: Nautz, Vahrenkamp (eds.) 1993 (see note 13), pp. 80–100, here 87 and 94.
29 On the theme of women's work, see Susan Zimmermann, "Frauenarbeit, soziale Politiken und die Umgestaltung von Geschlechterverhältnissen im Wien der Habsburgermonarchie," in: Lisa Fischer, Emil Brix (eds.), *Die Frauen der Wiener Moderne*, Vienna 1997, pp. 34–52; and on the theme of women's education: Waltraud Heindl, "Frauenbild und Frauenbildung in der Moderne," in: Fischer, Brix (ed.), 1997, pp. 21–33.
30 See Reingart Witzmann, "Frauenbewegung und Gesellschaft in Wien zur Jahrhundertwende," in: ibid. (ed.), *Aufbruch in das Jahrhundert der Frau? Rosa Mayreder und der Feminismus in Wien um 1900*, Vienna 1990, pp. 10–18.
31 Marina Fischer-Kowalski, Peter Seidl, *Von den Tugenden der Weiblichkeit. Mädchen und Frauen im österreichischen Bildungssystem*, Vienna 1986, p. 19.
32 See, Severit, 1998, p. 16.
33 Decree by the Austrian Ministry for Culture and Education in 1897, quoted from Fischer-Kowalski, Seidl 1986 (see note 31), p. 24.
34 See Heindl 1997 (see note 29), p. 24.
35 See Marianne Hainisch, *Zur Geschichte der österreichischen Frauenbewegung. Aus meinen Erinnerungen*, Vienna 1930, quoted in Heindl 1997 (see note 29), p. 23.
36 See Witzmann 1990 (see note 30), p. 12.
37 Ibid., p. 14.
38 Käthe Leichter (ed.), *Handbuch der Frauenarbeit in Österreich*, Vienna 1930, p. 505.
39 See Reingard Witzmann, "Zwischen Anpassung und Fortschritt – Der Berufsalltag der Frau," in: *Die Frau im Korsett. Wiener Frauenalltag zwischen Klischee und Wirklichkeit 1848–1920*, 88. Special exhibition at the Historisches Museum der Stadt Wien, Vienna 1985, pp. 11–20.
40 Ibid., pp. 11–20
41 See Elisabeth Freismuth, "Adelheid Popp – ihr Weg zur Höhe," in: Witzmann 1990 (see note 30), pp. 36–43.
42 See Elisabeth Freismuth, "Der Weg zum Frauenstimmrecht," in: Witzmann 1990 (see note 30), pp. 27–36.
43 See Harriet Anderson, *Vision und Leidenschaft. Die Frauenbewegung im Fin de Siècle Wiens*, Vienna 1994, pp. 9–10.
44 Ibid., p. 12.
45 Ibid.
46 See Karl Hauer, "Weib und Kultur," in: *Die Fackel*, no. 213, 1906, pp. 5–10, here 6, quoted from Anderson 1994 (see note 44), p. 1
47 Otto Weininger, *Sex and Character*, New York/Chicago 1906.
48 Rosa Mayreder, "Die Frau und der Krieg," in: ibid., *Zur Kritik der Weiblichkeit*, Munich 1981, p. 72.

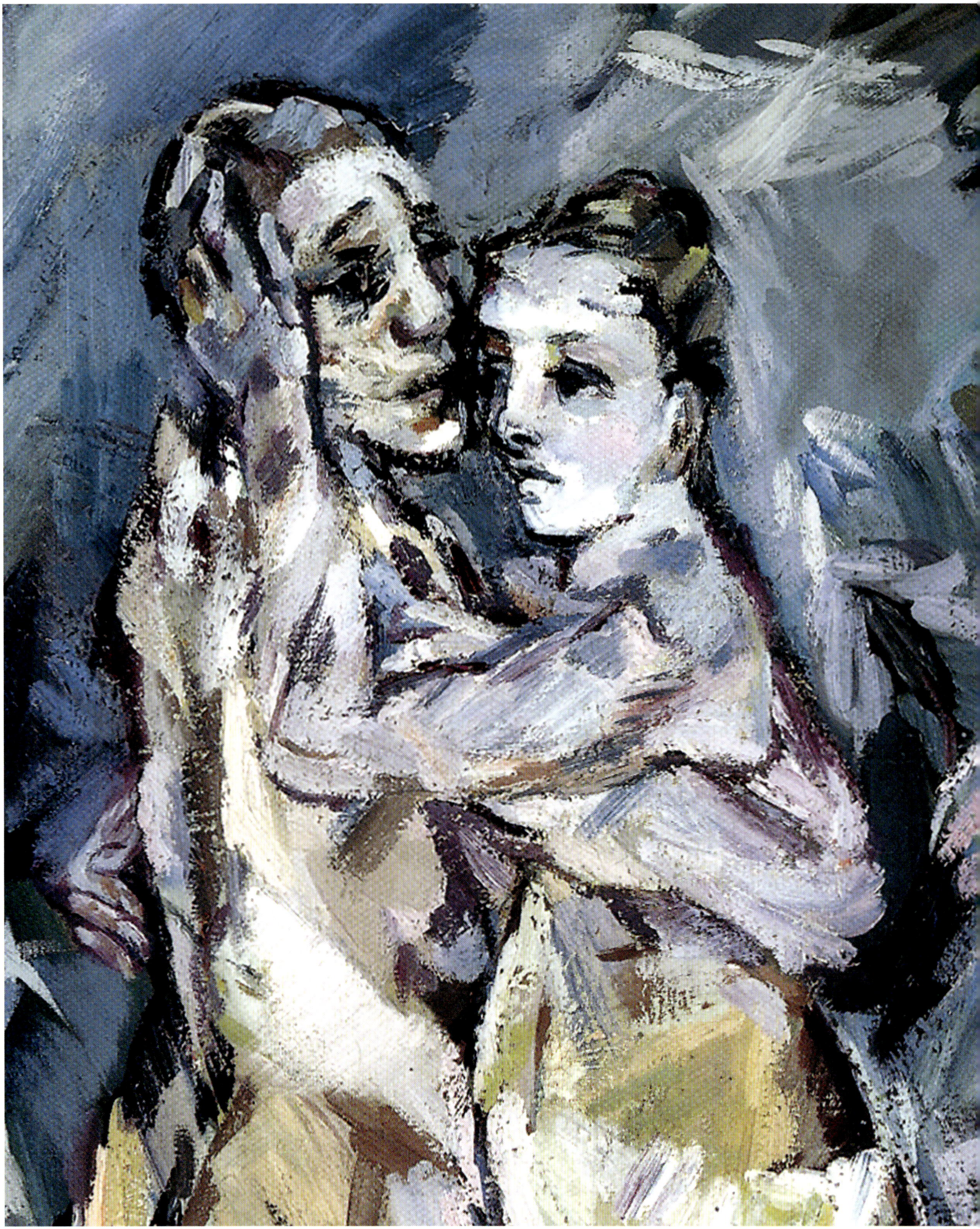

Competing Influences That Gave Rise to the Modern Representation of Women

Eric Kandel

Fig. 1
OSKAR KOKOSCHKA
Two Nudes (Lovers), 1913
(detail)
Museum of Fine Arts, Boston

Modernist thought—the thought that led to the world we live in today—emerged in good part in Vienna 1900, a time and place in which Freud, Schnitzler, Mahler, Schoenberg, Klimt, Kokoschka, Schiele, and many other notable artists and intellectuals lived and worked. It originated in part as a reaction to the restrictions and hypocrisies of everyday life in the mid-nineteenth century, but even more as a response to the Enlightenment of the eighteenth century, with its excessive emphasis on the rationality of human behavior.

Modernism represented a search for a new worldview, and it found one in the work of Charles Darwin. Darwin argued that we are not uniquely created individuals, but rather biological creatures that have evolved from simpler animal ancestors. Biological evolution, Darwin continued, is driven by sexual selection. Thus, from an evolutionary perspective, the primary function of a biological organism is to reproduce itself. Moreover, since sexual attraction and mate selection are central to all animal behavior, they must be central to human behavior as well. A key to sexual attraction and mate selection, which leads to all social interaction, is facial and bodily expression and the emotions they reveal.

Darwin's ideas greatly influenced Sigmund Freud, who pioneered the study of the unconscious mind. Freud argued that human beings are not rational creatures—we are driven by irrational, unconscious mental processes. Moreover, adult characteristics, including adult sexuality and aggression, can be traced to the mind of the child. Finally, Freud thought that there is no noise in the machine; that is, no mental event occurs by chance. Mental events adhere to scientific laws and follow the principles of psychic determinism. These ideas gave rise to our modern propensity for seeking meaning beneath the surface of behavior.

One of the defining characteristics of Viennese life in 1900 was the free and easy interaction of artists, writers, and scientists. Directly or indirectly, the ideas of Darwin and of Freud came to the attention of the three great Viennese modernist artists—Gustav Klimt, Oskar Kokoschka, and Egon Schiele—whose depictions of women are the focus of this exhibition. All three artists were very much taken with Darwin's emphasis on the role of facial expression and bodily movements in conveying emotion, and with Freud's view of the mind and its unconscious processes.

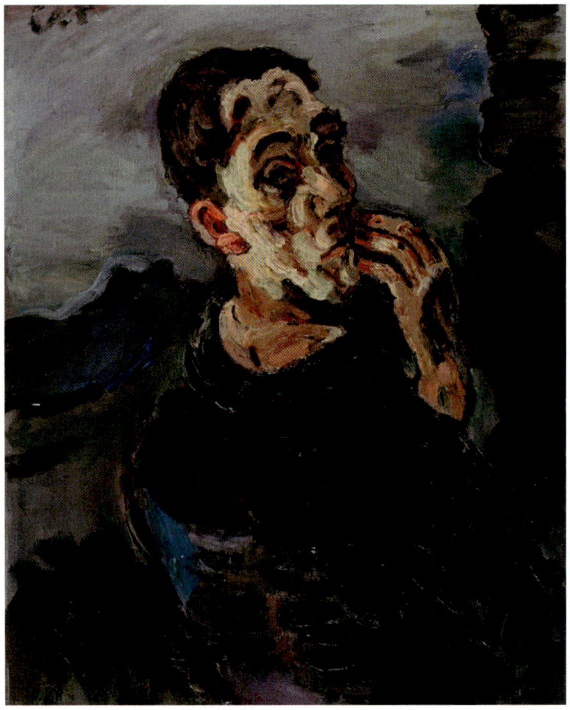

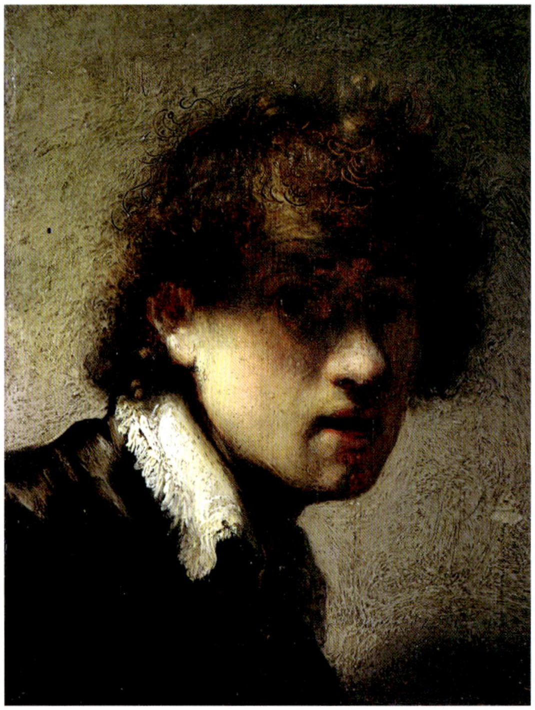

Fig. 2
OSKAR KOKOSCHKA
Self-Portrait, One Hand Touching the Face, 1918–19
Leopold Museum, Vienna

Fig. 3
REMBRANDT HARMENSZ VAN RIJN
Self-Portrait, 1629
Bayerische Staatsgemäldesammlungen – Alte Pinakothek, Munich

Oskar Kokoschka

The artist who appears to have been most aware of his unconscious mental processes and most profoundly influenced by them is Kokoschka. In fact, Kokoschka claimed to have discovered the existence of unconscious mental processes on his own, independently of Freud. Like Freud, Kokoschka believed that the study of the unconscious of others must begin with a study of one's self, and he developed an abiding interest in exploring his own emotional life as well as that of his subjects. Also like Freud, Kokoschka was fascinated with child and adolescent sexuality.

Whereas Klimt never painted himself, his disciple Kokoschka created numerous self-portraits. In keeping with his own zeitgeist and that of Vienna 1900, Kokoschka presented an unflinchingly honest, even merciless, analysis of his psyche (fig. 2). Consequently, his self-portraits are more penetrating and psychologically revealing than even those painted by great earlier artists when they were the same age, including Rembrandt (fig. 3) and Dürer. Perhaps the most interesting self-portraits were those done during his love affair with Alma Mahler, one of the most beautiful women in Vienna and the widow of composer Gustav Mahler. At age 33 Alma Mahler was much more mature and experienced than Kokoschka, who was only 26 years old. In April 1912, soon after they met, Kokoschka proposed to Alma in a passionate letter. The letter initiated a stormy erotic relationship in which Kokoschka never felt secure.

Throughout their affair, Kokoschka created several double portraits (fig. 1). In these portraits Alma is typically calm, whereas Kokoschka looks either passive or very anxious, almost terrified—on the verge of a nervous breakdown (fig. 4). In the most important of these, *The Tempest* (fig. 5), Kokoschka and Alma lie shipwrecked in a small boat in the midst of a raging storm, buffeted by the waves of their tempestuous relationship. She is sleeping calmly, while Kokoschka, as usual, is anxious, lying rigidly beside her, his emotional state heightened by the background colors.

In these double portraits, Kokoschka conveys a view of woman as being at once seductive and unobtainable. Although his affair with Alma lasted only three years, it dominated the artist's life for years afterward. The affair ended with Alma (who had earli-

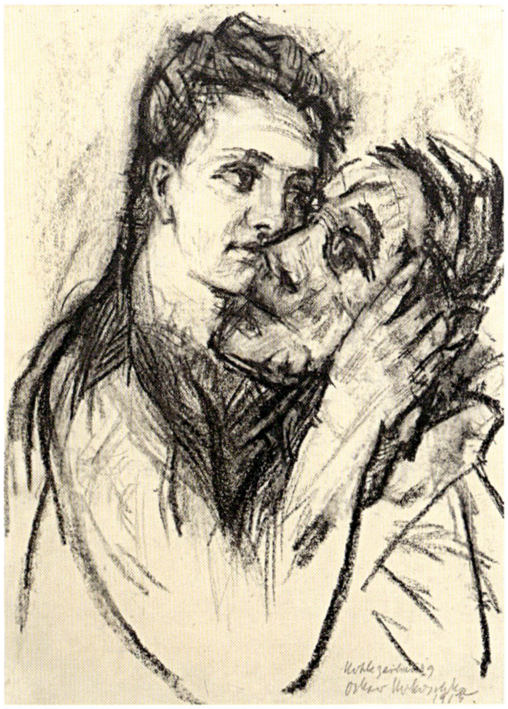

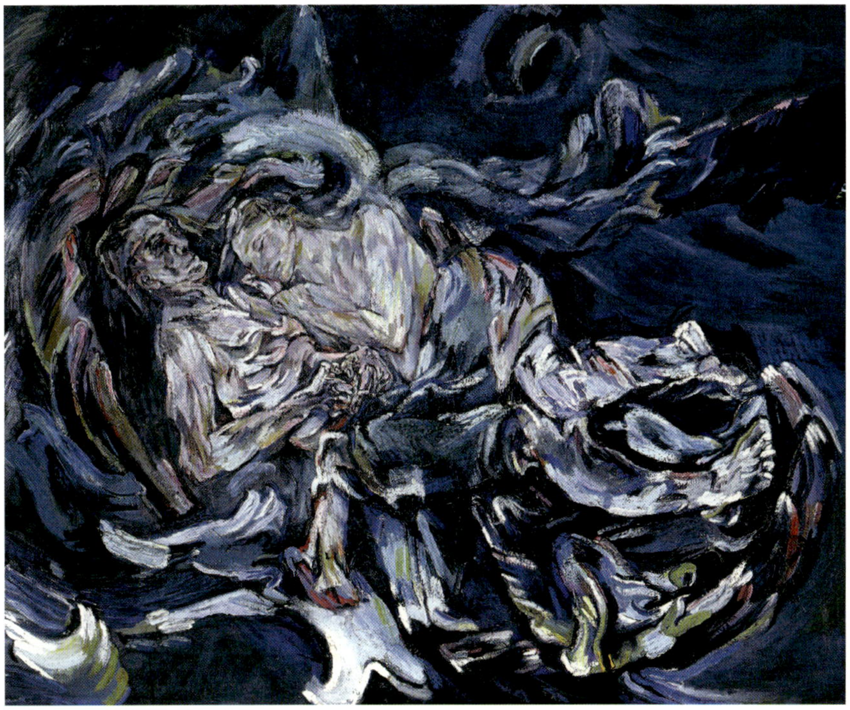

Fig. 4
OSKAR KOKOSCHKA
Self-Portrait with Lover (Alma Mahler), 1913
Leopold Museum, Vienna

Fig. 5
OSKAR KOKOSCHKA
The Tempest, 1914
Kunstmuseum, Basel

er aborted their unborn child) leaving Kokoschka for the architect Walter Gropius. Kokoschka expressed his depression in a series of self-portraits (fig. 2) and in the commissioning of a life-sized doll made in Alma's image, which he painted (cat. 143) and drew repeatedly, until he had exorcised her spirit.

Like Freud, the young Kokoschka was interested in the sexuality of children and adolescents, and in his early years he did many drawings of prepubescent youths. This is evident in his 1907 drawing, *Studies for the nude, Lilith Lang* (fig. 7). Kokoschka was attracted to Lilith, but their relationship was never consummated. Dürer had painted himself in the nude as an adolescent, but Kokoschka is one of the first artists to have drawn nude adolescent girls.

Kokoschka appreciated that, even early in their lives, children can have feelings driven by sexuality and aggression. In 1909, he painted 5-year-old Lotte and 8-year-old Walter, the children of Richard Stein, playing (cat. 71). Kokoschka suggests through their body language that their interaction is not completely innocent, that they struggle with their attraction to one another.

The art critic Ernst Gombrich, who considered Kokoschka the best portrait painter of his time, describes the painting of the Stein children in the following terms:

In the past, a child in a painting had to look pretty and contented. Grown-ups did not want to know about the sorrows and agonies of childhood, and they resented it if this aspect of it was brought home to them. But Kokoschka would not fall in with these demands of convention. We feel that he has looked at these children with a deep sympathy and compassion. He has caught their wistfulness and dreaminess, the awkwardness of their movements and the disharmonies of their growing bodies [...]. His work is all the more true to life for what it lacks in conventional accuracy.[1]

Thus, very much like Freud, Kokoschka grasped the importance of eroticism in children and adolescents as well as in adults.

Egon Schiele

Schiele, the Kafka of Viennese art, infused everything, including sexuality, with the existential anxiety of modern life. Since the women he depicted were complete equals with him in their sex-

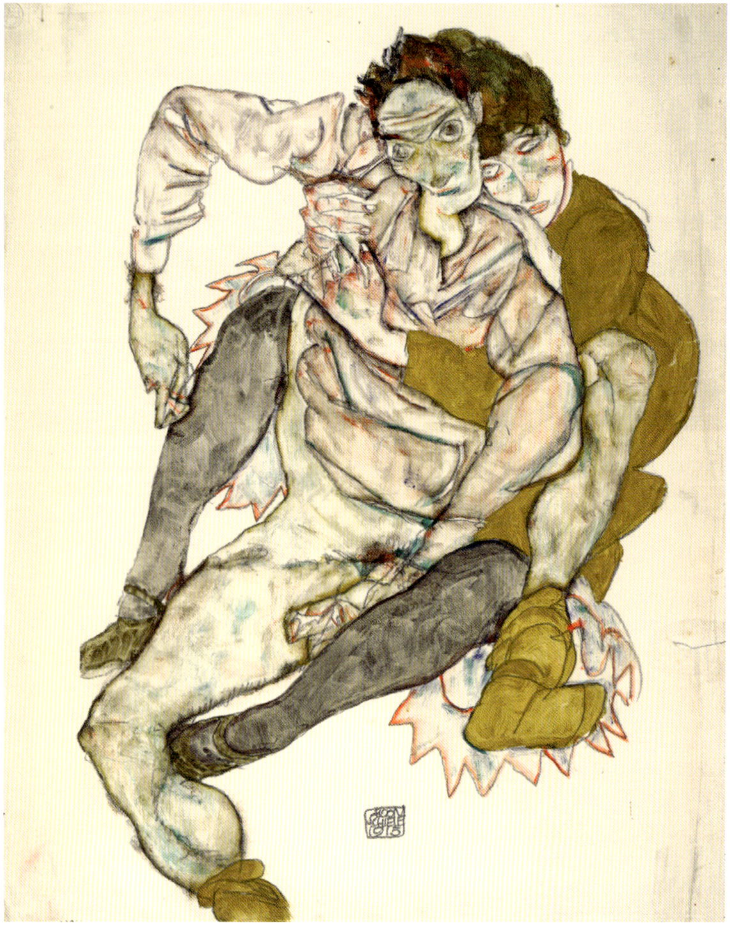

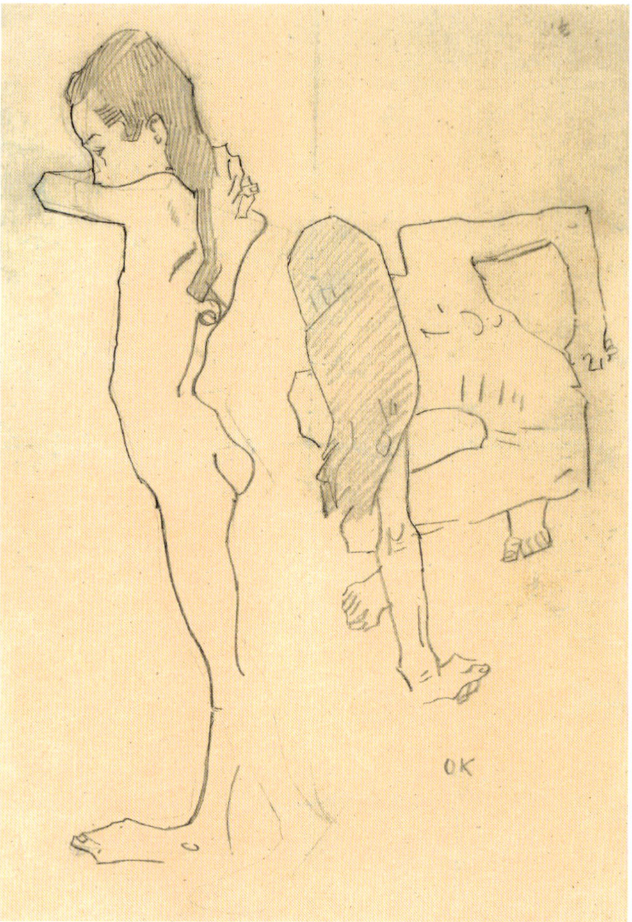

Fig. 6
EGON SCHIELE
Seated Couple, 1915
Albertina, Vienna

Fig. 7
OSKAR KOKOSCHKA
Studies for the nude, Lilith Lang, 1907
Private collection

ual relationship, they share his anxiety, unlike Alma Mahler, who remained emotionally aloof from Kokoschka's suffering. We see an expression of Schiele's eroticism and anxiety in the 1915 watercolors *Love Making* (Kd 1786) and *Seated Couple* (fig. 6), where he fuses sexuality, eroticism, world-weariness, exhaustion, and fear.

In 1911, Schiele met Valerie Neuzil, a 17-year-old redhead who called herself Wally. Schiele himself was 21 at the time. A former model and perhaps a mistress of Klimt's, Wally became Schiele's model and his lover. Thanks to Wally, Schiele developed a sense of the range of female eroticism. Like Kokoschka, he was fascinated by adolescent sexuality, and he posed the pubescent girls who modeled for him in sexually explicit positions. But Schiele went beyond Kokoschka: he depicted disturbing explorations of sexuality. Some of his images focus explicitly on genitalia (see cat. 123, 124, 131), while others focus on sexual acts (see. cat. 3–5, 9, 10, 96, 97).

In *Crouching Female Nude with Bent Head* of 1918 (fig. 8), Schiele conveys a girl's feelings by depicting her with her head deeply bowed and an expression of wistful melancholy on her face. Long, loose strands of hair frame her face, as if she were searching for protection and security.

In 1915, Schiele abandoned Wally to marry Edith Harms, a socially acceptable, middle-class young woman. In response to Edith's ultimatum that he break up with Wally, Schiele painted the double portrait *Death and the Maiden* (cat. 102). The painting, which is a view from above, shows Schiele and Wally lying on a mattress covered with a white sheet. Wally embraces Schiele with her head resting on his chest. Although the two lie in a position suggesting they had just made love, they are now staring past each other, as if they are thinking about something or someone else.

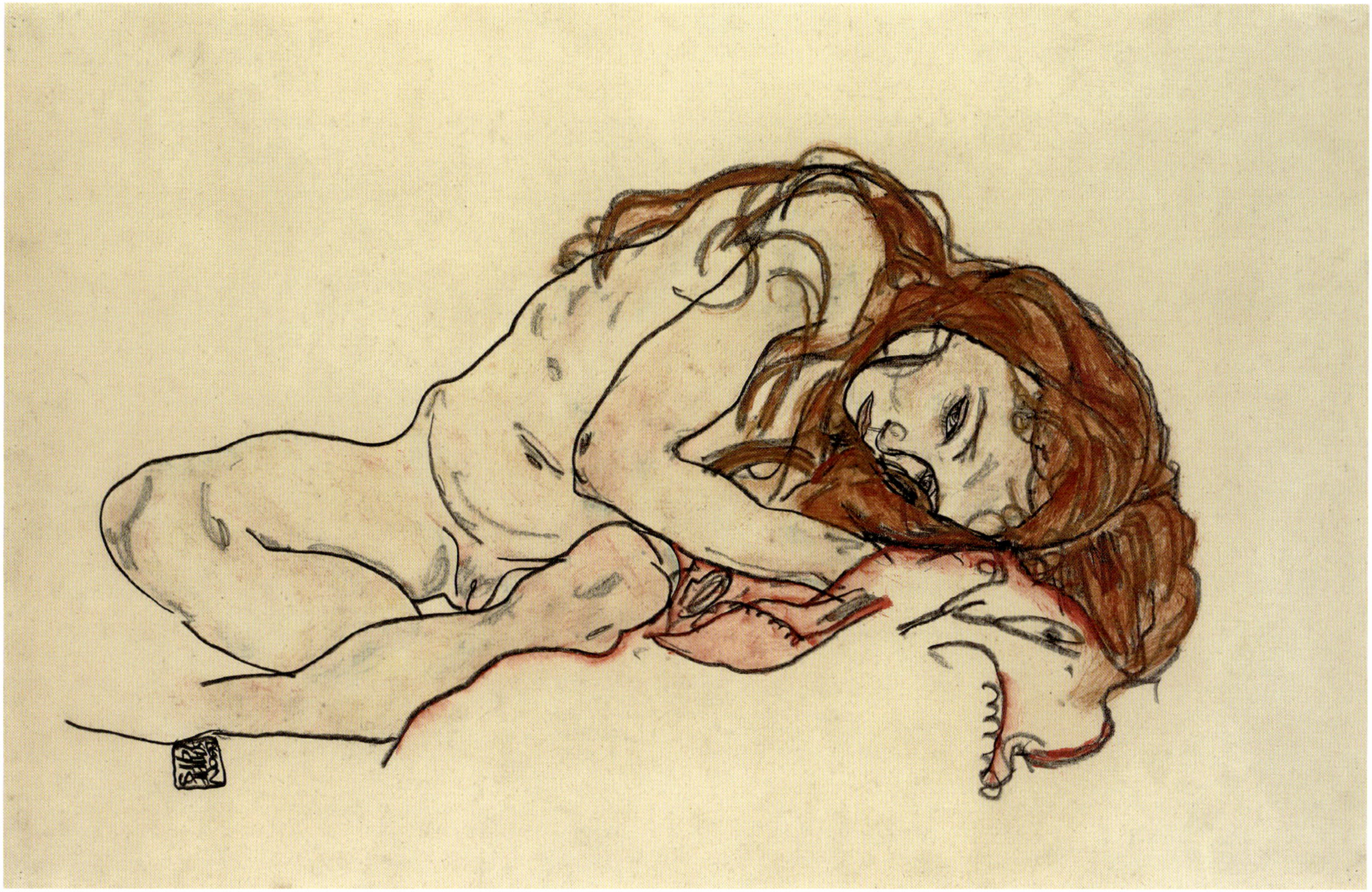

Fig. 8
EGON SCHIELE
Crouching Female Nude with Bent Head, 1918
Leopold Museum, Vienna

Death and the Maiden is often compared to Kokoschka's *The Tempest* (fig. 5), but here the situation is reversed: Whereas Alma rejected Kokoschka, Schiele has rejected Wally. Wally is experiencing a sense of isolation and desperation at the death of their relationship that is comparable to Schiele's own deep anxiety. In Schiele's world, no one is safe.

The brain's response to exaggerated facial expressions

One characteristic of the expressionist portraits of both Kokoschka and Schiele is their dramatic and exaggerated presentation of facial expressions. We are now beginning to understand how our brain processes faces and how it responds to exaggeration.
Charles Gross at Princeton and, later, Margaret Livingstone, Doris Tsao, and Winrich Freiwald at Harvard have made several important discoveries about how our brain analyzes faces. Using a combination of brain imaging and electrical recordings of signals from individual cells, they found six small structures in the temporal lobe of macaque monkeys that light up in response to a face. Each of these structures, or *face patches,* responds to a different aspect of the face: head-on view, side view, and so on. They found a similar, although smaller, set of face patches in the human brain. Studies by Tsao and a colleague[2] have shown that the monkey's face patches contain a high proportion of cells that respond only to faces. These cells are sensitive to changes in position, size, and direction of the gaze of the face, as well as to the shape of various parts of the face.
We can see in fig. 9 how a cell in a monkey's face patch responds to various images. Not surprisingly, the cell fires very nicely when the monkey is shown a picture of another monkey (a). The cell fires even

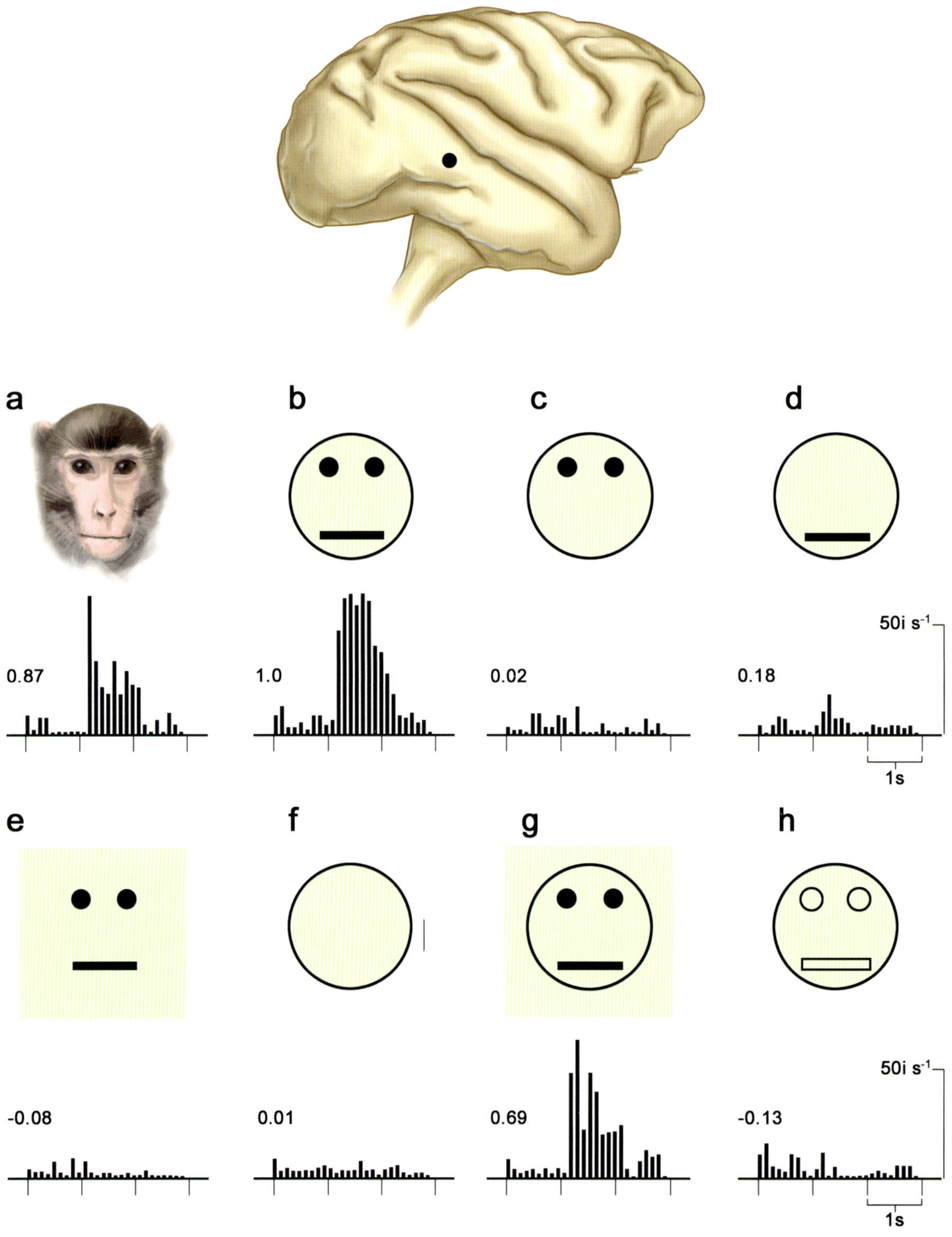

Fig. 9
Using a visual stimulus to excite a single cell in a macaque monkey's face patch.

Fig. 10
TITIAN
Venus of Urbino, before 1538
Galleria degli Uffizi, Florence

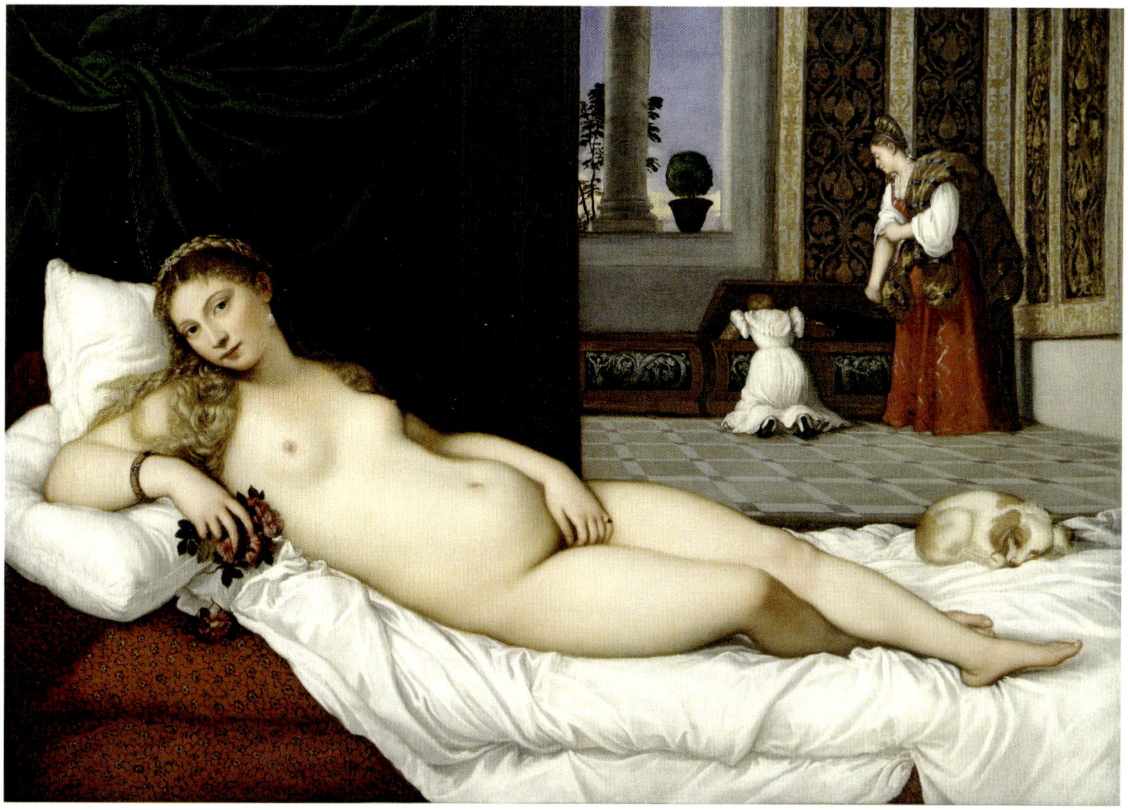

Fig. 11
EDOUARD MANET
Olympia, 1863
Musée d'Orsay, Paris

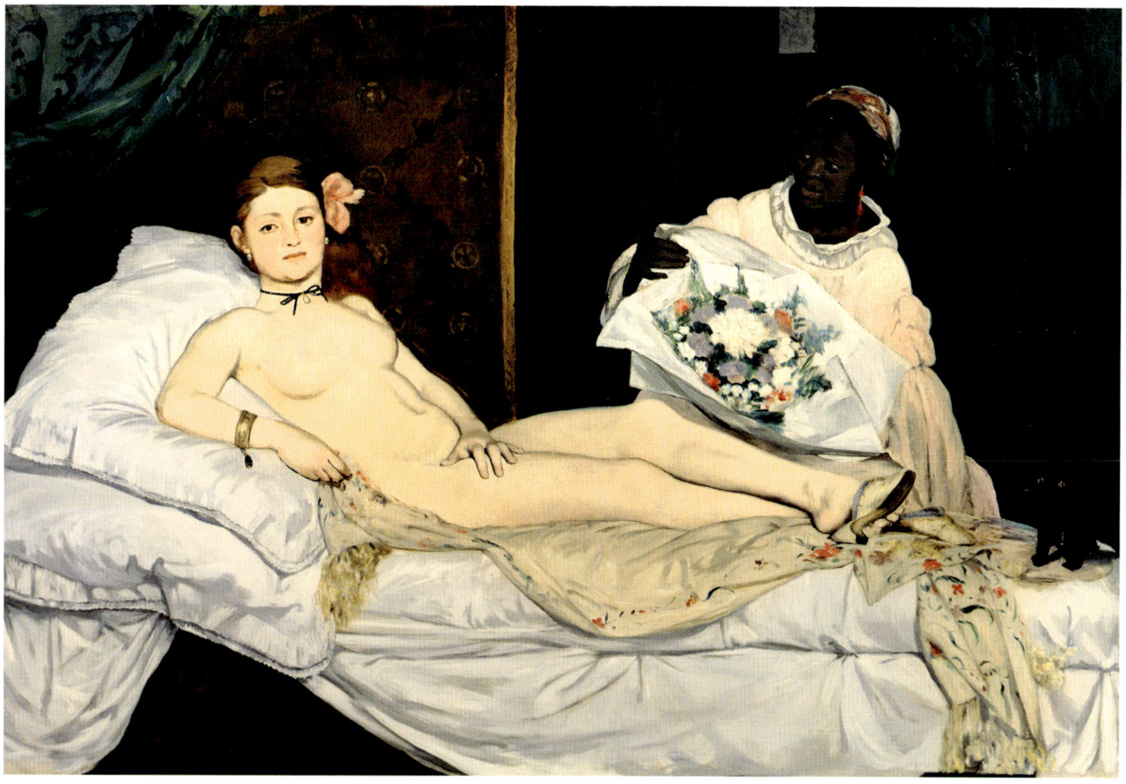

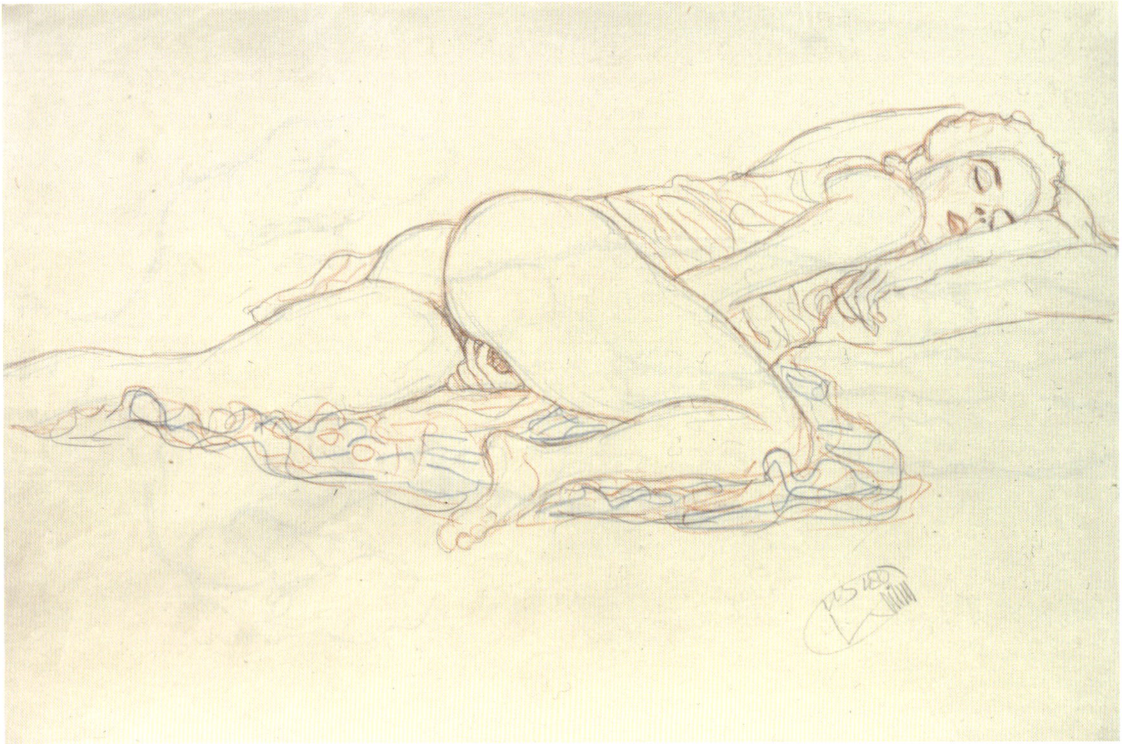

Fig. 12
GUSTAV KLIMT
Reclining Nude Facing Right, 1913
Private collection, courtesy of Neue Galerie, New York

more dramatically in response to a cartoon face (b). Monkeys, like people, respond more powerfully to cartoons than to real objects because the features in a cartoon are exaggerated. If the eyes are pushed farther apart or closer together, the cells fire more rapidly. But the cell in the monkey's face patch follows Gestalt principles: That is, a face has to be complete in order to elicit a response. Thus, when the monkey is shown two eyes in a circle (c), a mouth and no eyes (d), two eyes and a mouth inside a square (e), or simply a circle (f), it does not respond. The cell responds only to two eyes and a mouth inside a circle (g). If the circles and the mouth are only outlined, there is no longer a response (h). In addition, if the monkey is shown an inverted face, it does not respond.

These studies have shed new light on the nature of the templates our brain uses to detect faces. Behavioral studies suggest further that there is a powerful link between the brain's face detection machinery and the areas that control attention, which may explain why faces and portraits grab our attention so powerfully.

Gustav Klimt

Gustav Klimt was in many ways a role model for Kokoschka and Schiele. Although he never moved toward expressionism, as they did, he had great insight into the psychology of his subjects, almost all of whom were women. Despite Freud's many insights into the human psyche, he failed to understand certain aspects of human nature, particularly female sexuality. In his early thinking, Freud simply extended his view of male sexuality to women, seeing women as men without a penis. Because women don't have a penis, he pronounced, they experience penis envy. This, he argued, is the jealousy little girls feel toward boys and the resentment they feel toward their mothers, whom they blame for having deprived them of a penis. Freud also thought that women do not enjoy sex; they engage in sex only passively and primarily to have children, preferably boys.

Freud spells out these ideas in a 1925 paper entitled *Psychical Consequences of the Anatomical Distinction between the Sexes*: "Women oppose change, receive passively and add nothing of their own."[3]

Klimt, in contrast, had considerable insight into female sexuality. In a sense, he achieved a post-Darwinian breakthrough in the depiction of female sexuality. Influenced by Rodin, Klimt had his models move about the studio, until they assumed a pose that pleased him. This atmosphere of freedom encouraged these naked or semi-naked women to explore themselves and others sexually: to masturbate or couple, with one another or with male models (cat. 89–92, 94-97).

Moreover, since Klimt had extensive sexual experience himself, he knew that women have a rich, independent sexual life that in every way parallels the sexual life of men.

One can readily see the difference between Klimt's view of female sexuality and the conventional nude in Western art, as depicted by Giorgione (p. 36, fig. 36), Titian (fig. 10), and Manet (fig. 11). In the three latter paintings, the woman is a mythological character (Venus, or Olympia) who looks out at the presumably male beholder as if her only pleasure were to satisfy his erotic curiosity. Finally, each woman's left hand is covering her pubic area, either because of modesty or because she is masturbating—her intentions are ambiguous. In Klimt's drawing (fig. 12), the woman is focused solely on herself and her own erotic pleasure, and there is no ambiguity about her intentions.

What is particularly interesting about Klimt—and what separated him further from Freud—is that Klimt not only appreciated that women have erotic instincts equal to those of men, but that they, like men, can fuse eroticism with aggression. Klimt depicts this in his 1901 painting *Judith* (fig. 13).

Judith was a heroine of the Jewish people. In 500 BCE, the Assyrian general Holofernes led his troops in a siege of Bethulia, a small town near Jerusalem. After a week or two, the siege had become so severe that Judith, a modest young widow of about 24 years of age, decided to try to save her people. She managed to sneak past the troops and found Holofernes drinking at a banquet. She encouraged him to drink more, then went with him to his tent, where they made love. After Holofernes feel asleep, satiated with sex and wine, Judith took his sword and cut off his head.

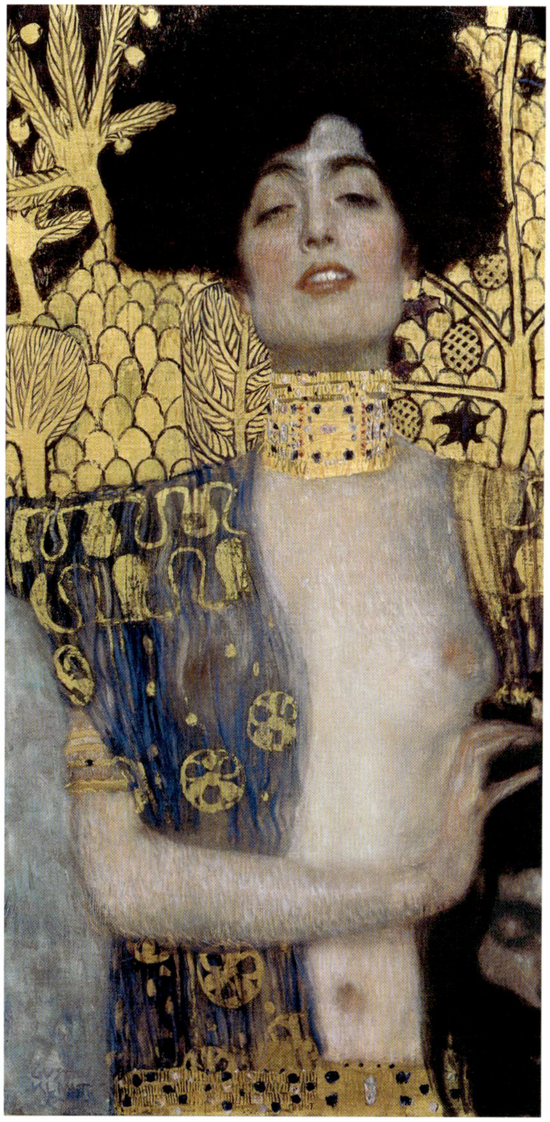

Fig. 13
GUSTAV KLIMT
Judith, 1901
Belvedere, Vienna

The image of Judith beheading Holofernes has been repeatedly depicted in Western art as the chaste widow sacrificing herself for her people. But in Klimt's painting Judith is no poor widow sacrificing herself. She is a femme fatale in a post-coital trance, wearing elegantly patterned clothing that leaves her left breast exposed and absentmindedly fondling Holofernes' severed head.

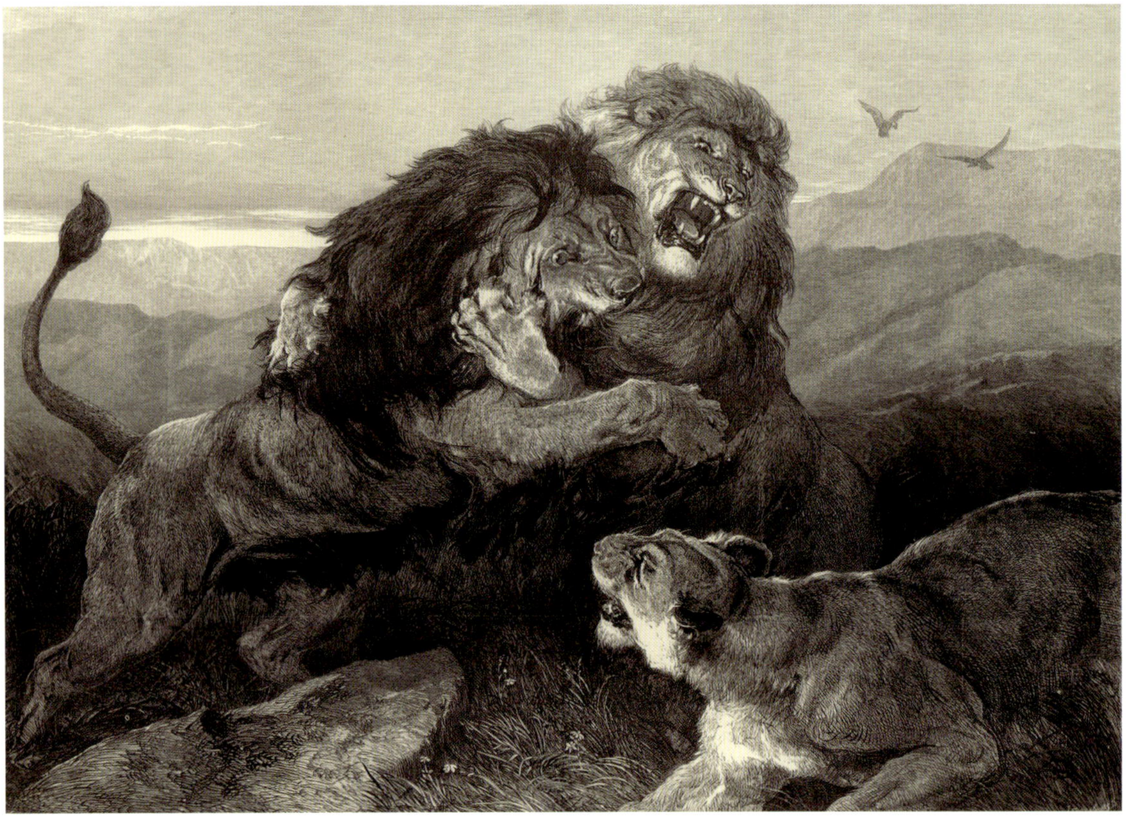

Fig. 14
HEYWOOD HARDY
Three Lions Fighting, 1873
Private collection

The interaction of eroticism and aggression in the brain

Today, brain scientists are examining the fusion of aggression and sex that Freud observed in men and that Klimt depicted in *Judith*. In his studies of the neurobiology of emotional behavior, David Anderson at the California Institute of Technology has found some of the biological underpinnings of this fusion of eroticism with aggression (fig. 14).[4]

We have known for some time that the region of our brain known as the amygdala orchestrates emotion and that it communicates with the hypothalamus, the region that houses the brain cells, or neurons, that control instinctive behavior such as parenting, feeding, mating, fear, and fighting (fig. 15). Anderson has found a nucleus, or cluster of neurons, within the hypothalamus that contains two distinct populations of neurons: one that regulates aggression and one that regulates mating. About 20 percent of the neurons located on the border between the two populations can be active during either mating or aggression. This suggests that the brain circuits regulating these two behaviors are intimately linked.

How can two mutually exclusive behaviors—mating and fighting—be mediated by the same population of neurons? Anderson found that the difference hinges on the intensity of the stimulus applied to the neurons. Weak sensory stimulation, such as foreplay, activates mating, whereas stronger stimulation, such as danger, activates fighting (fig. 16).

An expanded view of human sexuality: a search for self-knowledge through erotic love

We see in the women of Kokoschka, Schiele, and Klimt a view of the liberated woman who enjoys her sexuality as much as a man and who suffers as much as a man when rejected in love. Moreover, we see in Klimt's *Judith* the fusion of eroticism with aggression, and we see in Schiele's women the fusion of eroticism with anxiety.

The view that emerges from these three artists is that women are men's equals. As a result, sexuality

Fig. 15
The hypothalamus has two groups of neurons, one that regulates fighting and one that regulates mating. Some neurons are activated by either behavior.

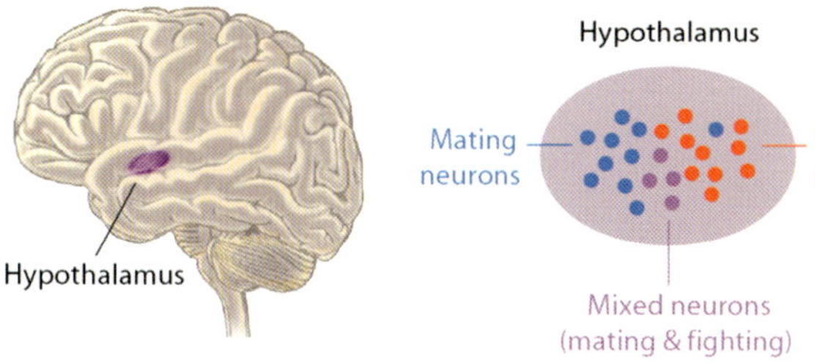

Fig. 16
The intensity of a stimulus determines which neurons are activated.

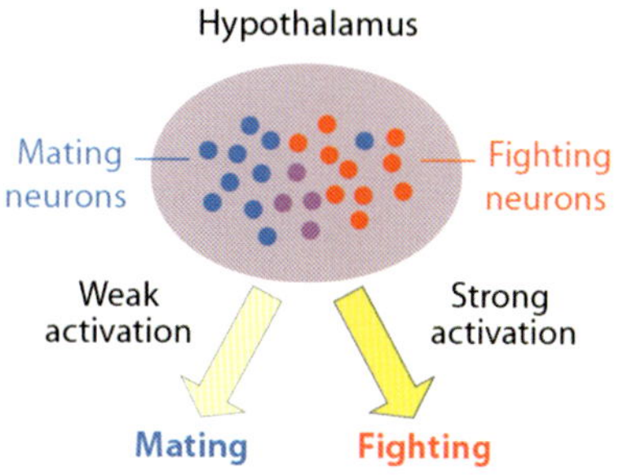

is not one-sided, it is a dialogue—a meta-psychological search for new experiences and new knowledge, especially new knowledge about oneself.

The power of women celebrated in these artists' portraits hearkens back to the ideal of "the eternal feminine," an ideal deeply rooted in German culture. Goethe invokes the eternal feminine to save Faust's soul from eternal damnation. Thus Mephistopheles is disarmed by the redemptive power of love. This concept is expressed in the well-known concluding lines of *Faust, Part II*:

Das Ewig-Weibliche
Zieht uns hinan[5]
(The eternal feminine draws us upward.)

But the concept of the eternal feminine goes beyond redemption. It also celebrates Faust's unremitting pursuit of knowledge and improvement. The angels carrying his soul to safety intone: "Wer immer strebend sich bemüht, den können wir erlösen"[6] (Whoever exerts himself in constant striving, him we can save).

The idea of the eternal feminine as inspiring the search for knowledge can be traced to Plato. In *The Republic*, Plato has Socrates say that falling in love involves not only physical desire, but also a striving for wisdom, the most significant of the urges. This theme, which was known to almost every literate Viennese, was emphasized anew in Vienna 1900 by Gustav Mahler (Alma Mahler's late husband), whose Eighth Symphony, composed in 1906, concludes with the last scene of *Faust II*.

According to Goethe—and, I would argue, according to Kokoschka, Schiele, and Klimt—one inspiration for this striving is the presence of the eternal feminine in men's lives and the knowledge men gain about themselves in the context of love. We can see this in the artists' depictions of women. In Kokoschka's depictions, we sense that his striving for Alma Mahler derives from his belief that he depends on her love for his creativity. He did his best early work in the context of that love relationship. In turn, Schiele's affair with Wally heightened his anxiety and allowed him to produce the angst-riddled art that defines his greatness. Schiele's marriage to Edith reduced the tormenting anxiety and allowed him to push his creativity into a different, more bourgeois, direction. Klimt's drawings and paintings of women are suffused with a remarkable sensitivity to the full range of women's sexuality, an understanding that stems from his own experience with women.

Thus, the modernist thought that emerged in Vienna 1900 not only emphasizes the equality of women and men in the striving for self-knowledge in the context of expressing their sexual urges, but implies that a higher wisdom can emerge from the redemptive power of love. These hallmarks of modernist thought are evident in Klimt, Kokoschka, and Schiele's depictions of women.

1 Ernst Gombrich, *The Story of Art*, London 1995, pp. 568–69.
2 Winrich Freiwald/Doris Tsao, "A face feature space in the macaque temporal lobe," in: *Nature Neuroscience*, no. 12, 2009, pp. 1187–1196. – Doris Tsao et al., "Comparing face patch systems in macaques and humans," in: *PNAS, Advance online publication*, 2008.
3 Sigmund Freud, "Some Psychical Consequences of the Anatomical Distinction between the Sexes," in: *Internationale Zeitschrift für Psychoanalyse*, no. 19, 1925, pp. 248–258.
4 David J. Anderson, "Optogenetics, Sex and Violence in the Brain: Implications for Psychiatry," in: *Biological Psychiatry*, vol. 71, issue 12, 2012, pp. 1081–1089.
5 Johann Wolfgang von Goethe, *Faust*, in: Ernst Merian-Genast (ed.), *Goethes Werke*, vol. 3, Basel 1944, p. 368.
6 Goethe 1944 (see note 5), p. 363.

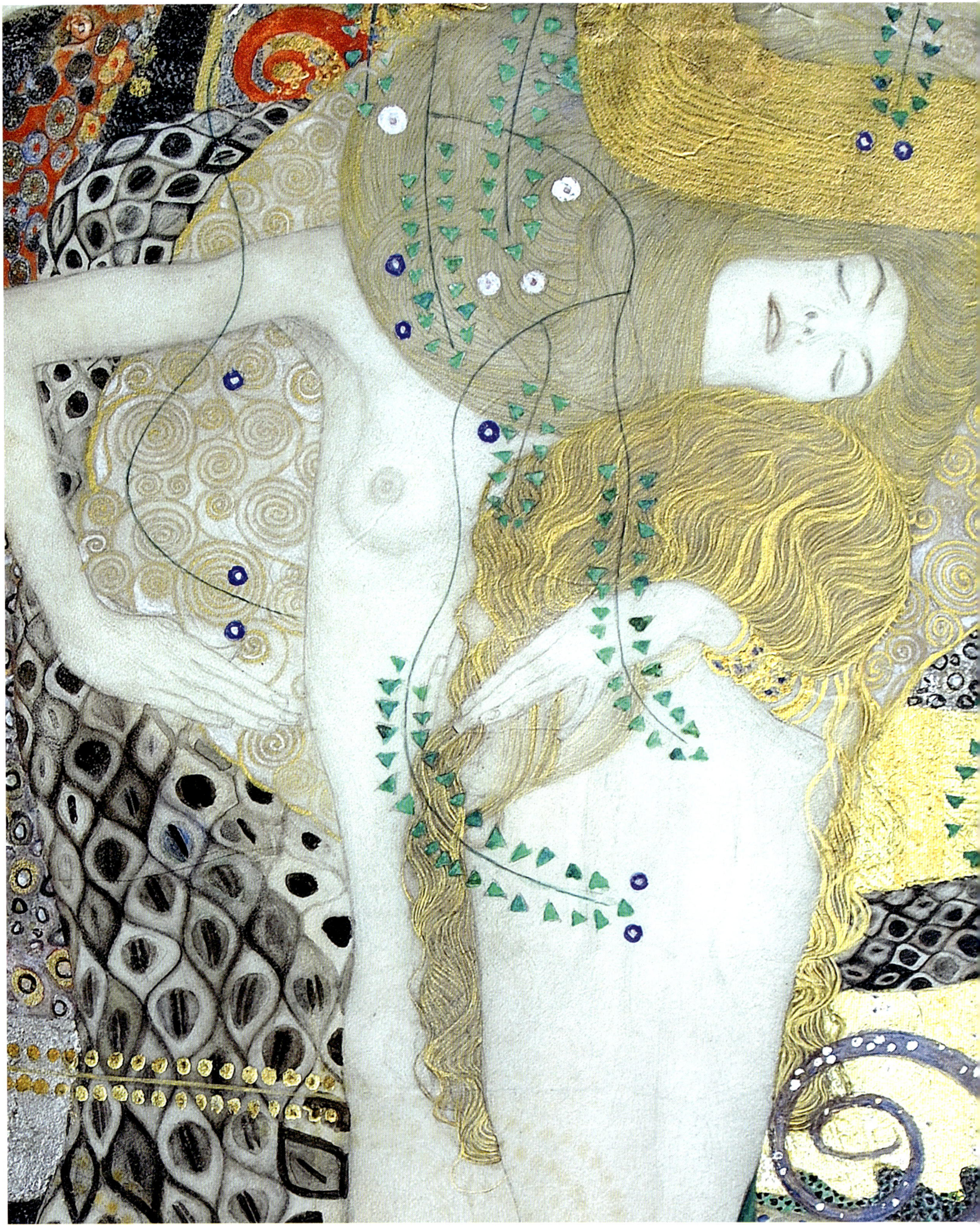

The *Primal Addiction* or the Pleasure in One's Own Body Feminine Sexuality in the Work of Gustav Klimt

Alfred Weidinger

Fig. 1
GUSTAV KLIMT
Girlfriends, 1904
Belvedere, Vienna

Gustav Klimt was not the first artist to depict a masturbating woman, but he was the first artist to treat female self-gratification as a separate genre. The revolutionary aspect of this emancipatory achievement cannot be overestimated, especially when we consider that society around 1900 was still decidedly patriarchal.[1] Klimt's focus on women's desire and his treatment of female intimacy are more than just unusual; after all, he was the first to depict them in his work as free of fear and shame. In order to give this achievement due weight, we need to shed light on the relationship of society toward masturbation and in particular toward female onanism, as well as address other artistic positions and consider how the artist Klimt handled this specific theme.

Masturbation up to Sigmund Freud

"The world seems to be interested in nothing else but onanism,"[2] Sigmund Freud asserted in 1912 in his concluding remarks to the "Discussion on Onanism" of the Viennese Psychoanalytical Society, thus clearly expressing that this subject, after centuries of medical demonization and moral contempt, had shifted to the center of serious, medical research.[3]

The rational and systematic study of sexual desire has a long history that reaches back to Antiquity. The lack of self-consciousness with which the Greeks in particular indulged in physical love and thus also onanism was matched by the force with which the freedom of human sex life was restricted by Christianity. Johannes Cassianus, the monk and writer born around 360 CE, was one of the first to

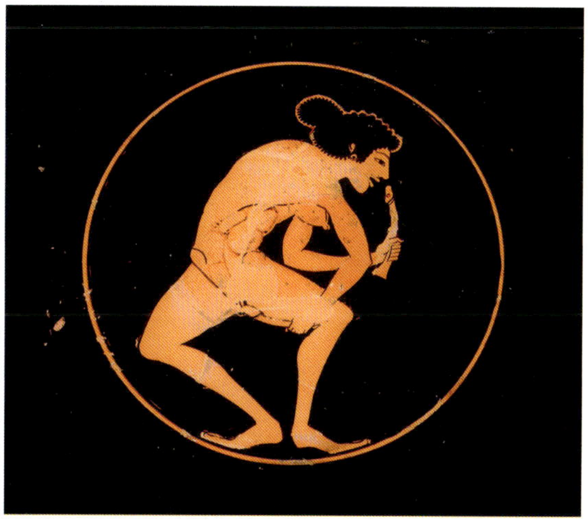

Fig. 2
NIKOSTHENES/
PAMPHAIOS
Greek woman masturbating with two olisboi,
520–500 BCE
British Museum, London

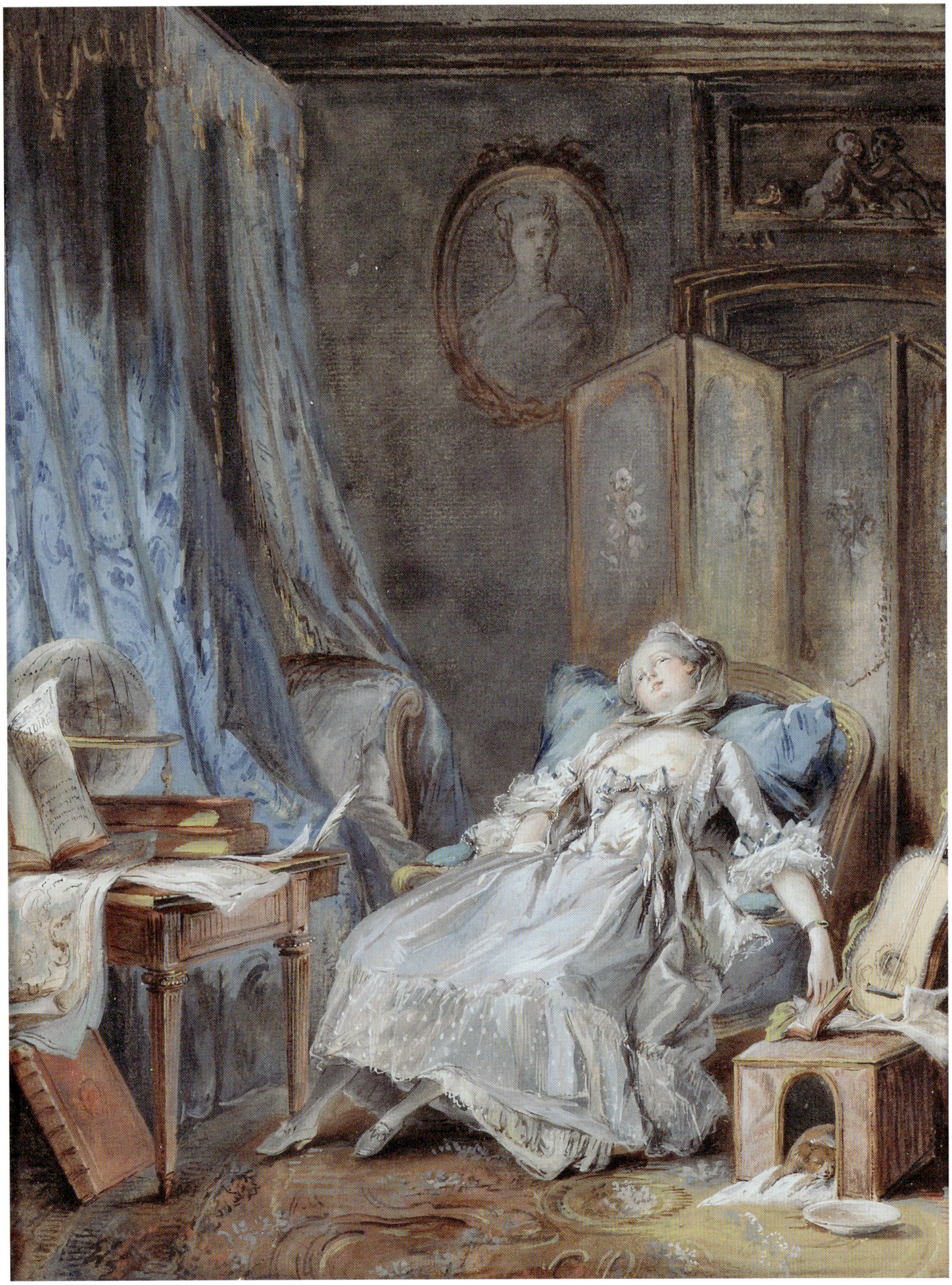

Fig. 3
PIERRE-ANTOINE BOUDOUIN
La Lecture I, c. 1760
Les Arts Décoratifs, Paris

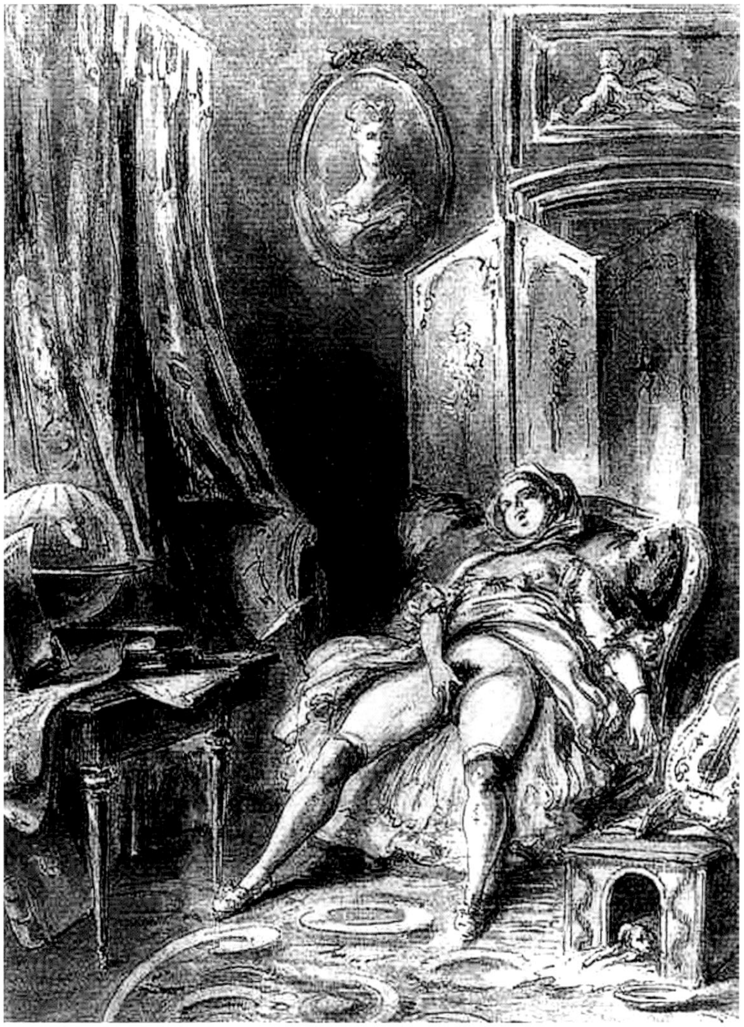

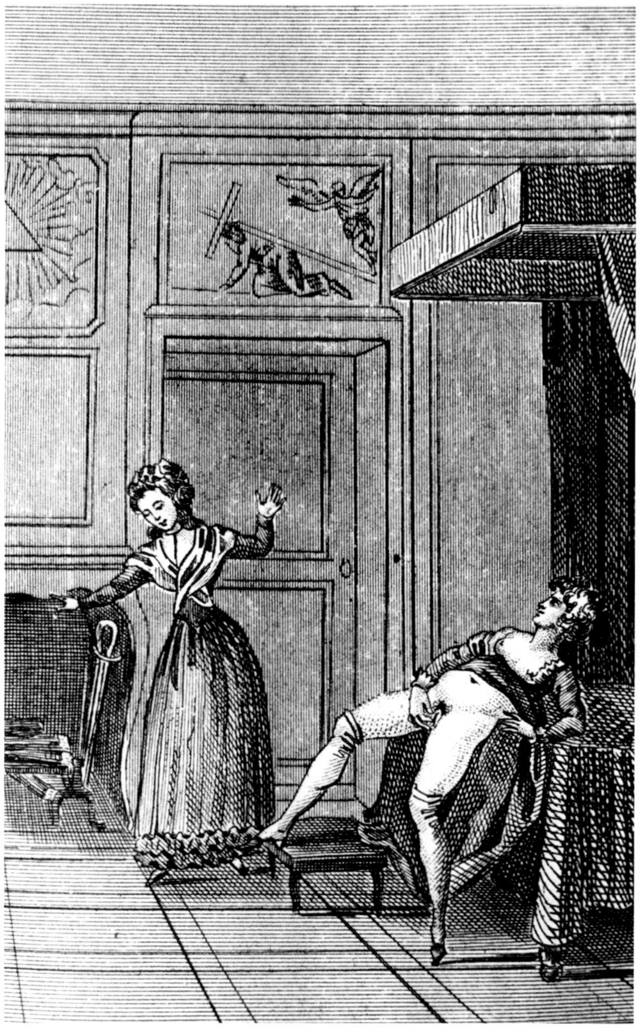

Fig. 4
PIERRE-ANTOINE BOUDOUIN
La Lecture II, c. 1760
Private collection

Fig. 5
ANONYMOUS
Masturbating woman from Marquis de Sade's novel *Justine*, 1797
Wienbibliothek im Rathaus, Druckschriftensammlung, Vienna

concern himself with masturbation in his texts, describing it as a vice that could be overcome.[4] In the numerous Christian prayer books of the Middle Ages too, masturbation—mention is also expressly made of female masturbators—was counted among the lighter offenses. Only with Pope Alexander VII was the pleasuring of one's own body condemned as a serious violation and so elevated to the status of a serious sin. What followed was theological damnation.

In contrast, medical research was long unable to reach an agreement on a unanimous doctrine. Not until 1720 did the book *Onania, or the Heinous Sin of Self-Pollution, And All Its Frightful Consequences*, written by an English doctor, set in chain a disastrous development. The consequences announced with such insistence in the title were depicted as wide-ranging for one's salvation and physical health. Within ten years, the book was republished annually in England alone, and by 1751 the title had already been published in German in its 15th edition.[5] Doctors such as Robert James, Samuel-Auguste Tissot, and John Harvey Kellogg wrote scientific treatises on onanism in the years to follow, describing it as a serious disease. Tissot[6] declared masturbation, in his monograph *Onanism, Or a Treatise on the Diseases That Originate from Self-Pollution,*[7] to be the evil of all evils, viewing it as the cause of all possible sufferings. His writings are the first to take female onanism as their theme in a special chapter. He describes the consequences for women as follows: "blue-tinged cheeks, brittleness

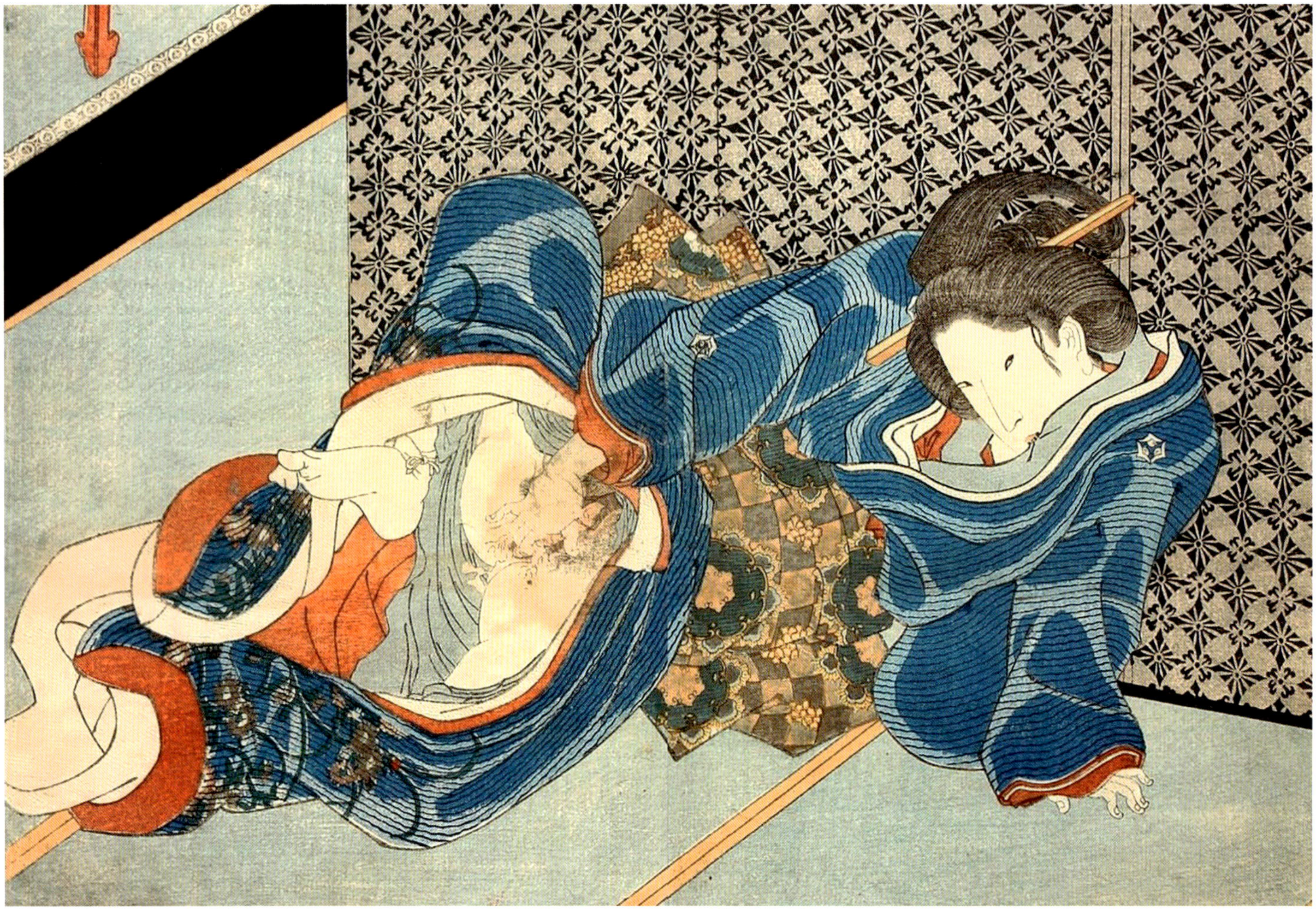

Fig. 6
UTAGAWA KUNISADA
Masturbating Woman, c. 1820
AK-Antiek, Coevorden

of skin; the eyes lose their glow, become dull, and announce the collapse of the whole machine through their faintness; the lips lose their agreeable rosiness, the teeth their whiteness, and not infrequently the whole shape of the body acquires a misshapen character."[8] In this way, the medical demonization of self-gratification was established for women, too.

Even philosophers such as Immanuel Kant[9] and Jean-Jacques Rousseau misconstrued masturbation as a grave social problem, and the latter saw in it the equivalent to mental rape. Rousseau's coming-of-age novel Émile,[10] first published in 1762, together with the opinion represented by Tissot, resulted ultimately in measures aimed at enlightenment and control. As a means of deterrence, people in the final stages of cancer and syphilis were brought before children in hospitals as victims of onanism.[11]

In the second half of the nineteenth century, in which Gustav Klimt was born and raised, radical surgical intervention was recommended for masturbating girls. One common method was to press the large labia together, drill through them and close them with a metal ring. Other surgeons cauterized, burned or removed the clitoris.[12] Only at the end of the nineteenth century did mainstream doctors gradually begin to question the theories of Tissot and his colleagues concerning the "numerous diseases from onanism."[13] As late as 1886, Richard von Krafft-Ebing blamed female onanism on the fear of unwanted pregnancy or disgust of the male sex, and presumed to see in it damage done to the mind and body, though he described the consequences as broadly insignificant.[14]

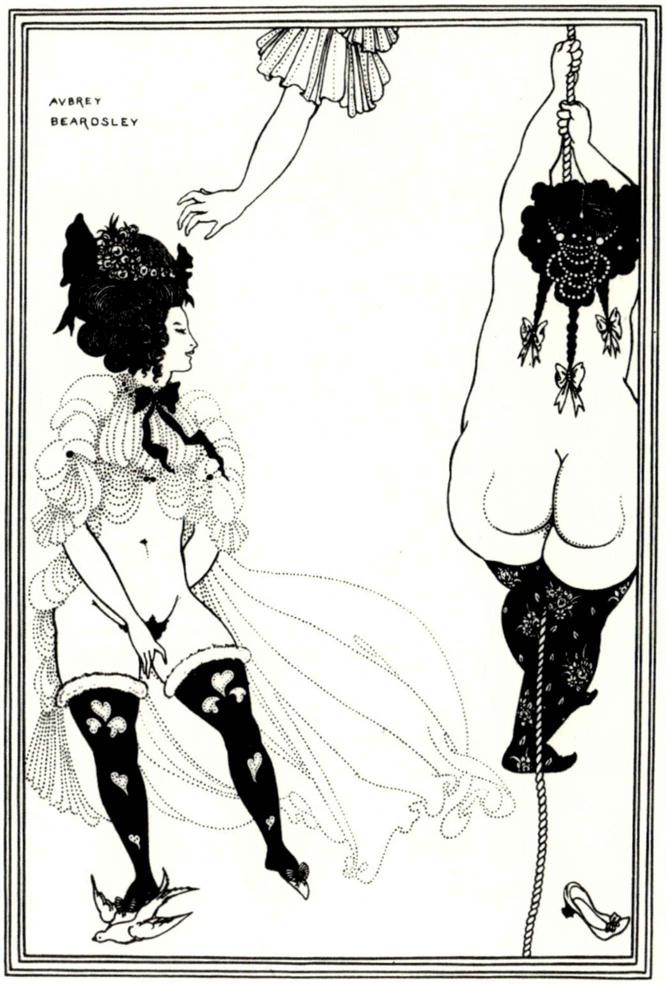

Fig. 7
AUBREY BEARDSLEY
Two Athenian Women
(illustration for Aristophanes'
Lysistrata), 1896
Private collection

In the years following 1900, sexual pathology spread from a sub-section of psychiatry to a general study of sexuality, not least due to the studies of Sigmund Freud, his scientific associates and fellow campaigners. From now on, sexual desire was seen as an anthropological key. Due to Sigmund Freud's *Three Essays on the Theory of Sexuality*, published in 1905, masturbation was placed on a level of science as befitted the time, and thus the foundations were laid for a new treatment of the theme. Yet views towards pleasure derived from one's own body were slow to change. As late as 1910, medical research was still far from seeing masturbation as free of any negative consequences. The sexual researcher Iwan Bloch was also unable to do much to counter this initially. In his work of enlightenment that appeared in 1906, *The Sexual Life of Our Time*, he categorized auto-eroticism as a disease only under certain conditions. He maintained that all experienced doctors who had concerned themselves with the study of onanism and its consequences were by now of the view that "moderate onanism has no grievous consequences for healthy persons with no genetic defects."[15] Yet, at around the same time, a symposium of the Viennese Psychoanalytical Society took place under Alfred Adler concerning the high suicide rate among young men, which was attributed to the processing of guilt feelings, especially those deriving from masturbation.[16] Scientists, such as the Swiss psychiatrist Auguste Forel, who was portrayed by Oskar Kokoschka (WE 40), saw a solution in sexual enlightenment;[17] others, by contrast, like the German philosopher and pedagogue Friedrich Wilhelm Foerster, in a heightened sense of shame.[18] Fo-

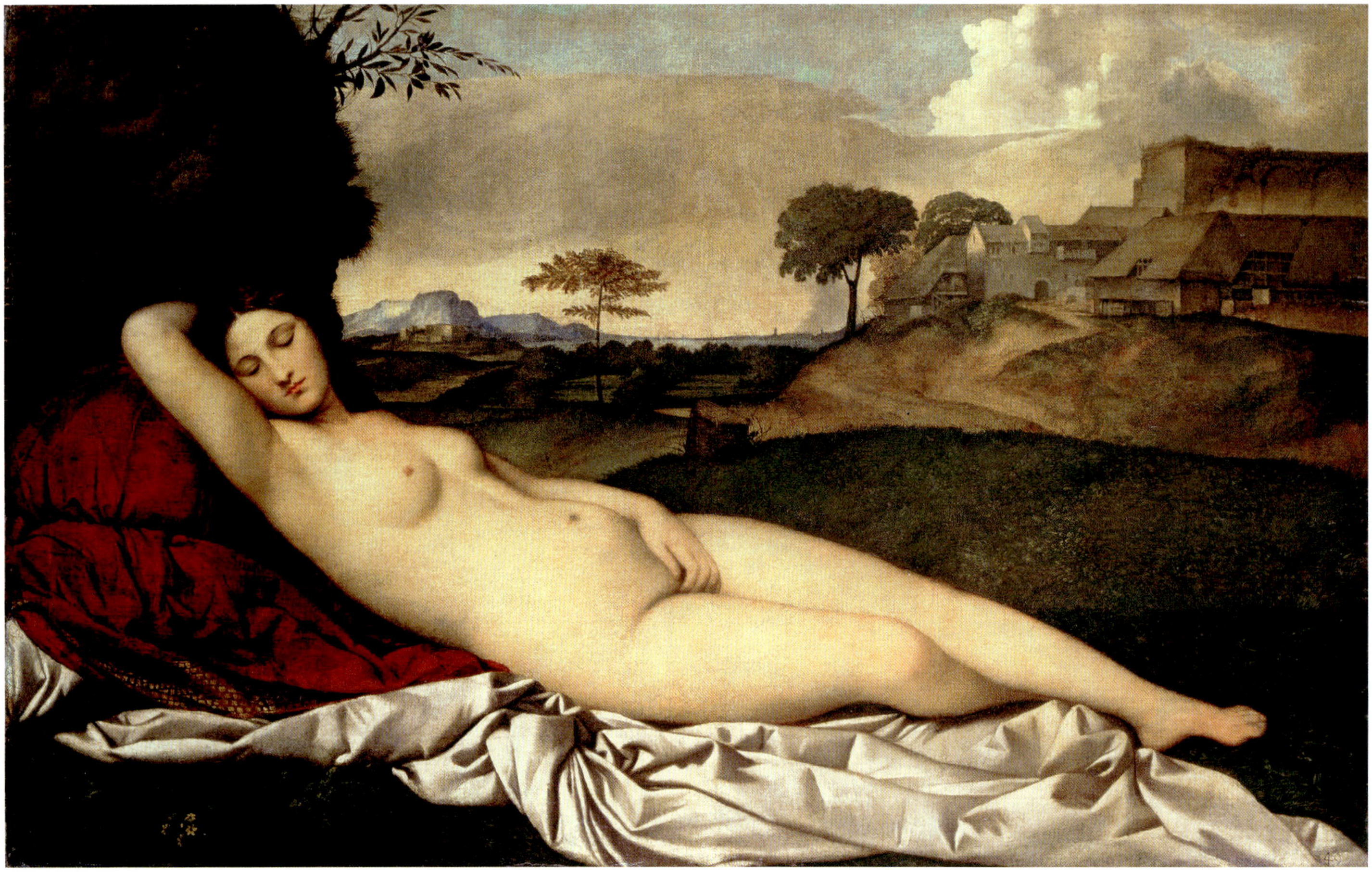

Fig. 8
GIORGIONE
The Sleeping Venus, 1508–10
Staatliche Kunstsammlungen Dresden, Old Masters' Picture Gallery, Dresden

erster expressed the belief in 1907 that he had discovered the means of eliminating "character-harming" onanism in exercises of willpower and abstinence.[19]
But where did Freud himself, whom we have so much to thank for regarding enlightenment, stand on masturbation, which he defined in a letter of 1897 to Wilhelm Fließ as the "primal addiction"?[20] Did he accept it as a natural sexual act? He did acknowledge it as "the single great habit" and a basic need, yet in three points he highlights possible damage and sums up as follows: "Let us keep in mind what significance masturbation acquires as an execution of fantasy, this intermediary kingdom that has interposed itself between life according to the principle of pleasure and that of reality, how onanism makes it possible to complete sexual developments and sublimations in our fantasy, which are not, after all, progress, rather just damaging compromises. The same compromise, however, renders grave tendencies to perversion harmless, according to Stekel,[21] and wards off the worst consequences of abstinence."[22]
Concerning women's masturbation, Freud regretted in his summary of 1912 that "onanism of woman" cannot be considered "to the same extent as that of man," and that "female masturbation" would merit special study.[23] In the mass of specific literature, only individual passages on women's masturbation can be found. The psychiatrist Krafft-Ebing revealed himself to be clueless concerning female sexuality, claiming in 1886 that, in contrast to the vivid sexual needs of man, women's sensual desire was just slight.[24] It thus comes as no surprise that not one single scientific essay or investigation was devoted specifically to this subject. Freud also noticed this state of affairs, yet despite his awareness of this deficit, he remained a child of his time after all.

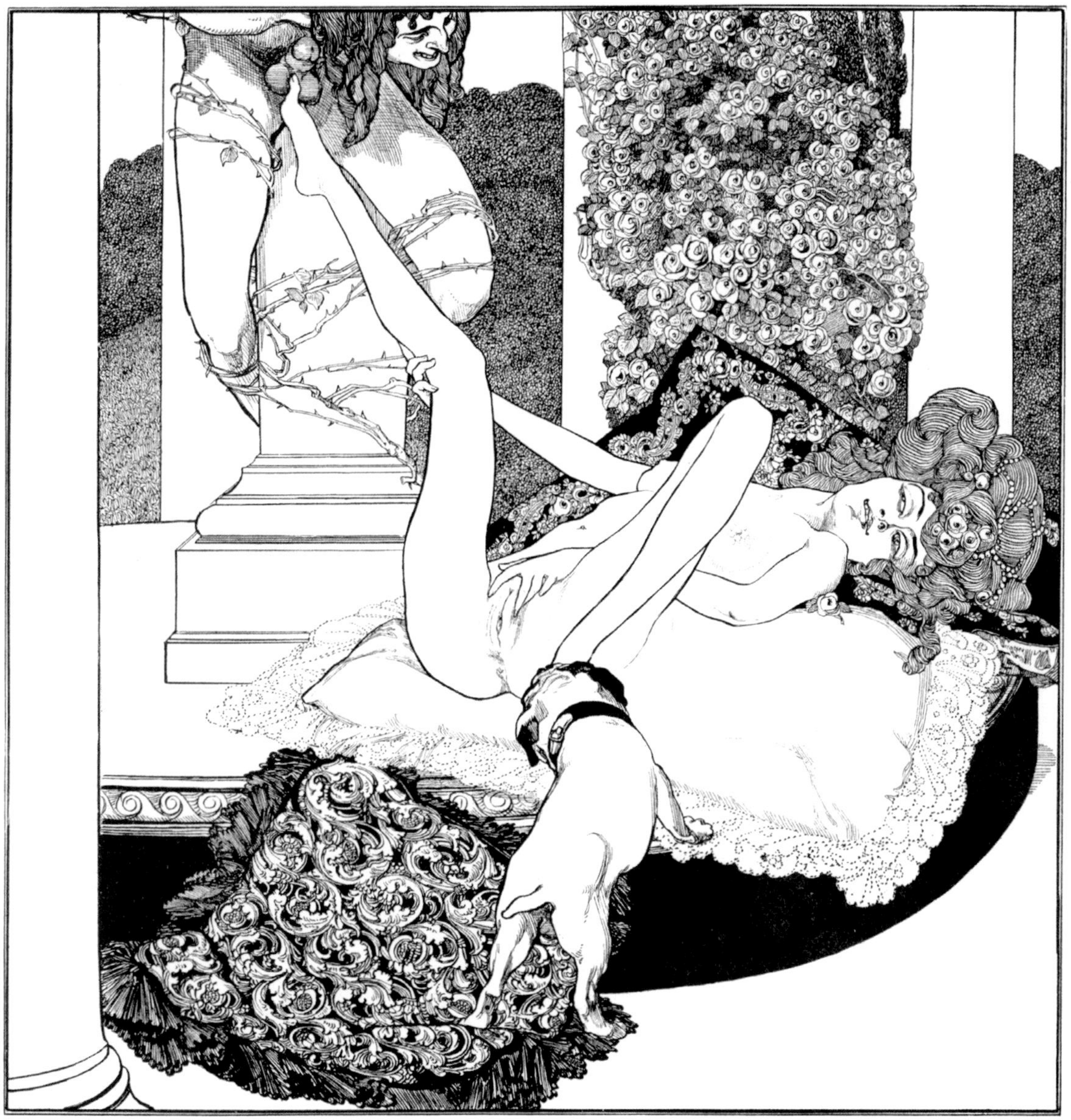

Fig. 9
FRANZ VON BAYROS
Illustration (cat. XIII) from the portfolio work *Tales from the Dressing Table*, 1908
Private collection

Female self-gratification in art

The rational and systematic study of sexual desire has a long history reaching back to Antiquity. The first known depictions of masturbating women in art are to be found on Attic bowls. Female onanism in Greek Antiquity was above all a means of sexual stimulus at symposia,[25] and was depicted primarily in a voyeuristic manner: frequently in the form of dancing hetaera, handling leather olisboi or masturbating (fig. 2).[26] That is no surprise when we consider that, unlike harlots, hetaera were seen in ancient Greece as cultivated companions, who were highly regarded by men not just as sexual playmates, but as independent-thinking, educated interlocutors. Autonomous pleasure in one's own body matched the elevated and emancipated lifestyle of the hetaera.

Following the demise of Antique culture, such explicit illustrations of desire and self-love became unthinkable for centuries. If we disregard the assumptions of individual authors that Giorgione depicted his sleeping Venus (fig. 8), and Titian his *Venus of Urbino* (p. 25, fig. 10), masturbating,[27] then masturbators do not play a role in art history until the emergence of the theme in medicine and,

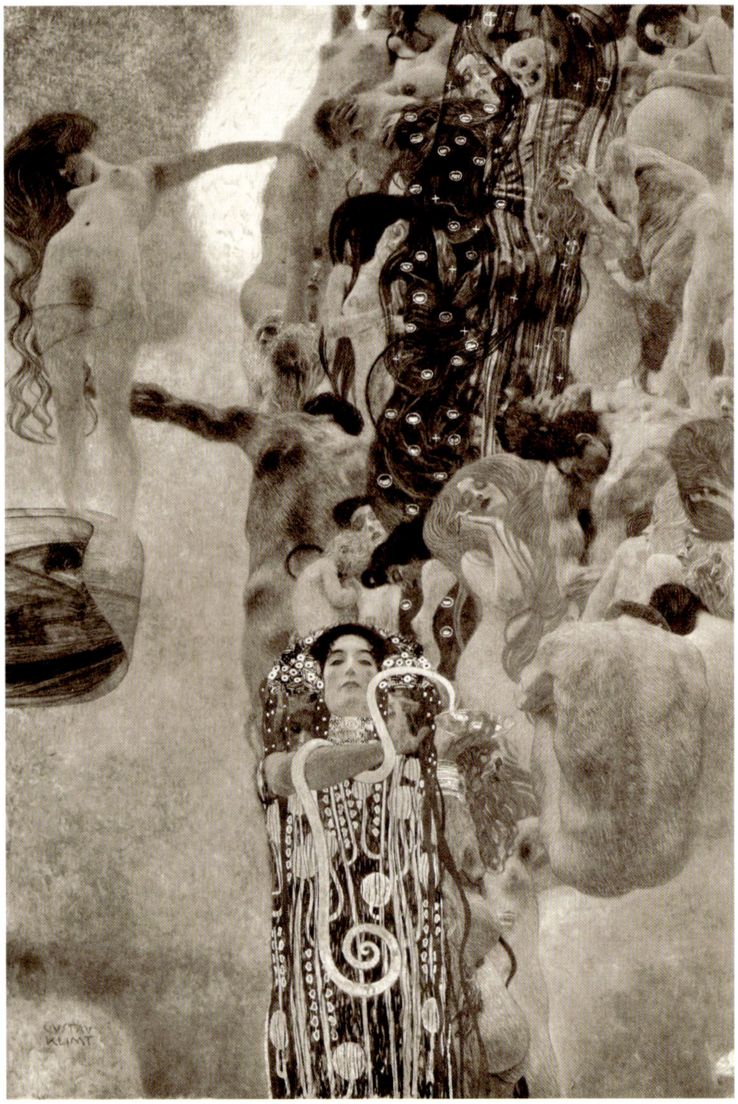

Fig. 10
GUSTAV KLIMT
Medicine, 1900
(destroyed in a fire in Schloss Immendorf in May 1945)

especially, in literature of the eighteenth century, although the sources of inspiration were quite different for each artist.

One of the earliest depictions of female onanism comes from Pierre-Antoine Baudouin (fig. 3). In the watercolor created around 1760, the French artist looks straight into the bedroom of a young woman. She lies sunken in the soft pillows of an expansive armchair. Her top has slipped down, revealing her breasts as far as the nipples. An obviously erotic book is falling to the side, while she uses her hand to masturbate under the dress. That this is in fact the case can be inferred from another watercolor by the artist, in which he repeats the same scene, this time with her private parts exposed and the woman's uncovered hand stroking her labia (fig. 4).[28]

Some forty years after the watercolor was created by Baudouin, the French nobleman Marquis de Sade commissioned an artist, who remained anonymous, to illustrate his two novels *Juliette* and *Justine* for a collected edition. Published in Holland in 1797, the work contains a total of 101 copper engravings on the predominately sadomasochistic fantasies of the Marquis de Sade.[29] The unknown artist clearly knew Baudouin's watercolor: on one of the first pages a woman lying on a bed can be seen in the act of masturbating (fig. 5). She seems to be stimulating her clitoris with her thumb, while she holds her index finger on the inner labia. De Sade's

Fig. 11
GUSTAV KLIMT
Medicine (detail), 1900
(destroyed in a fire in Schloss Immendorf in May 1945)

Fig. 12
GUSTAV KLIMT
Nuda Veritas, 1899
Österreichisches Theatermuseum, Vienna

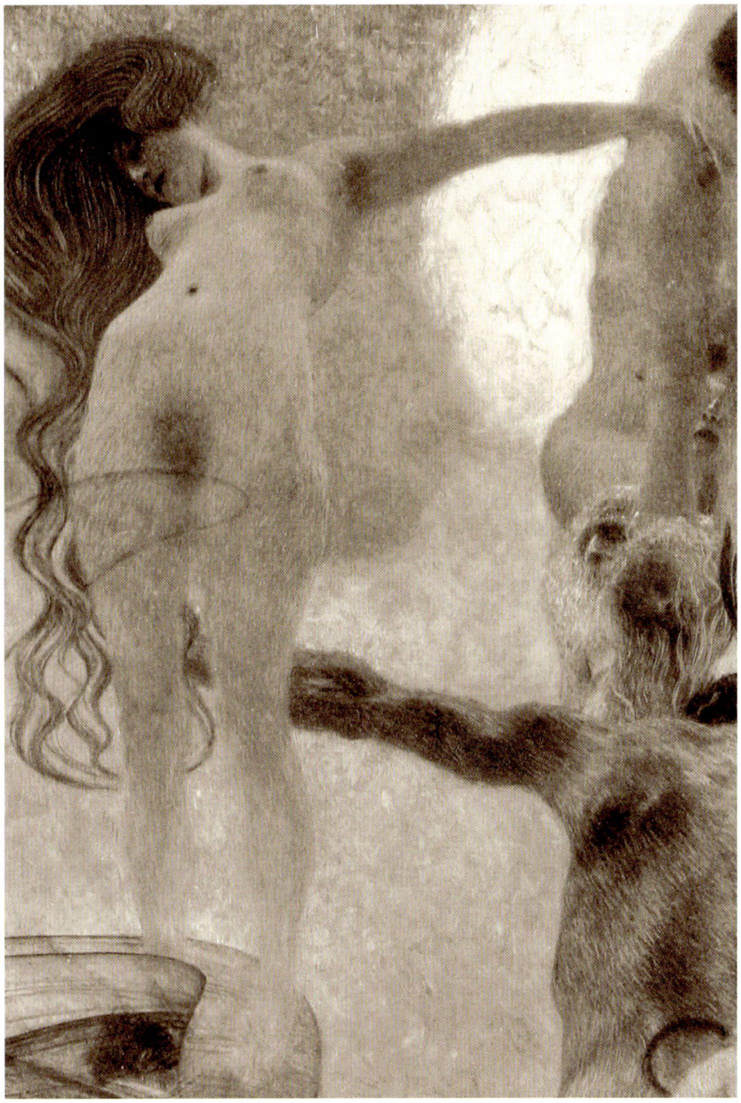

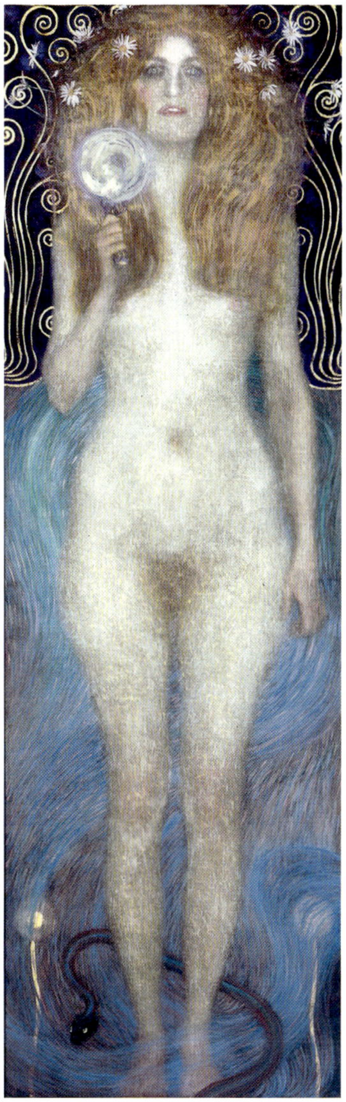

writings were widespread in artistic circles, and were illegally distributed and read in Vienna.[30] As a result, they were either copied or used by a limited number of artists as models for their own creations. With the invention of photography from 1850, nude photographs became increasingly important for artists as an erotic model for pictures. Daguerreotypes of masturbating women soon became popular collectors' items for connoisseurs.[31] But among artists, too, word quickly spread that it was considerably cheaper and more interesting to work from photographs rather than using professional models. With this, the so-called *academies* became obsolete, which up until then had been much appreciated and used as an alternative to living models. While showing female nudes in numerous positions, masturbation or sexual intercourse were out of the question, here.[32]

Most widespread among artists, however, had long been the resort to literary models and Japanese art. Yet in the context of female sexuality in Gustav Klimt's work, it must be emphasized that above all his drawings eschew any literary associations.[33] The literary model was of significance almost exclusively for his symbolist paintings. In developing his masturbating nudes, it was rather the Shunga, distributed illegally around 1900, that were important. The Shunga ("Spring Pictures") were multicolored woodblock prints of the highest artistic caliber, which first arrived in European artistic circles at the

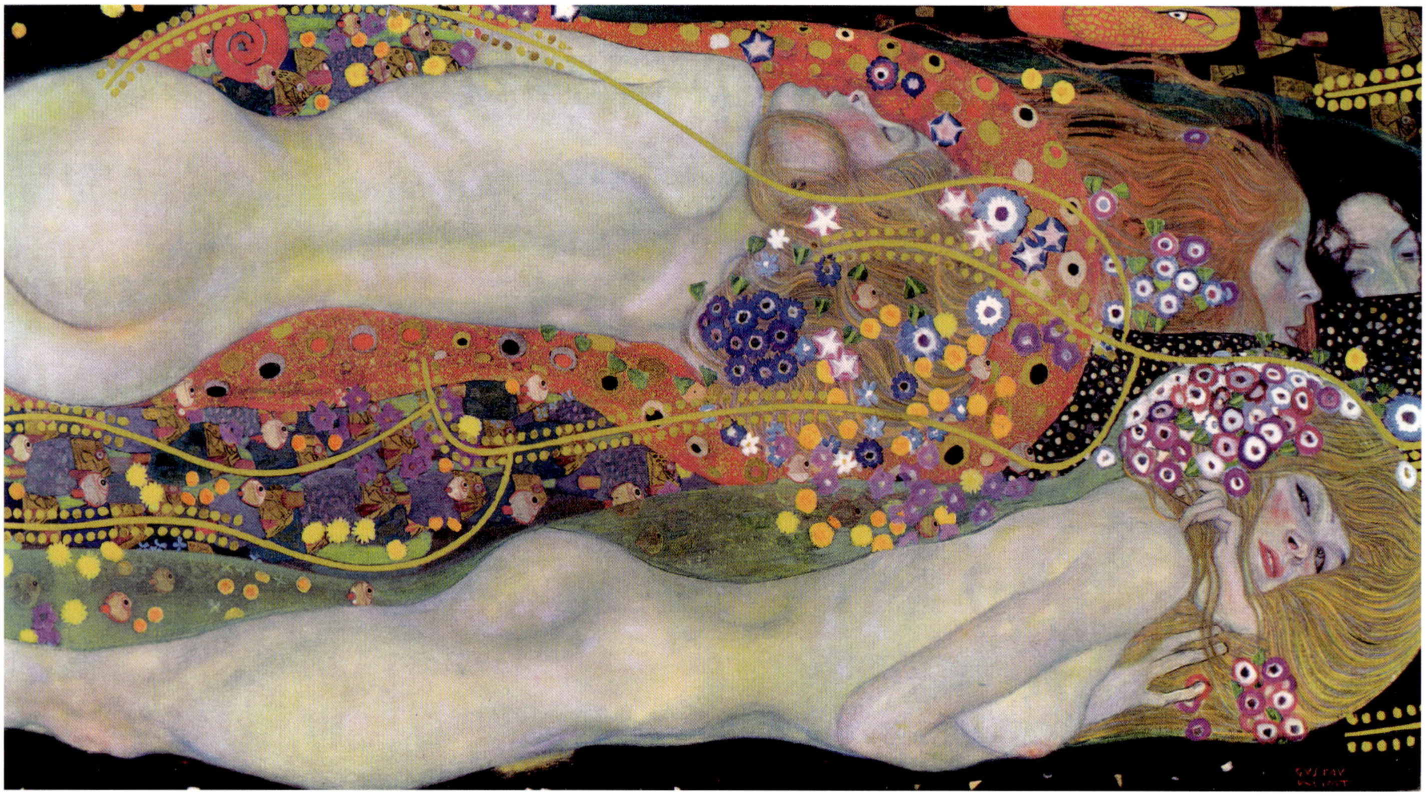

Fig. 13
GUSTAV KLIMT
Water Serpents, 1906-07
Private collection

Paris World Exhibitions of 1867, 1878, and 1889. Klimt was fascinated by their unabashed voyeurism and variation in the unchanging theme, which almost certainly inspired his serial work with nude models. Special about these depictions was less the nudity than the skilful focus on the greatly enlarged and closely illustrated female pudenda. One of the most important Shunga and a possible model for Klimt came from Utagawa Kunisada (fig. 6).

Unlike Klimt, one of the most important British illustrators of the previous turn of the century, Aubrey Beardsley, took bearings for his erotic drawings above all from literary models. In an illustration created in 1896 of Aristophanes' antique comedy *Lysistrata*, Beardsley visualized two Athenians during various acts of masturbation (fig. 7). Fritz Waerndorfer, co-founder and commercial director of the Wiener Werkstätte, owned an important collection of Beardsley's drawings. For this reason, the latter's works were well-known to Austrian artists, above all to Secessionists, offering them a welcome source of inspiration, both in terms of the strictly linear drawing style and the self-confident erotic depictions.[34]

An absolute admirer of Beardsley's illustrative art was Vienna-born Franz von Bayros. He made his living mainly through drawings of historically staged, frivolous costume parties. Bayros aestheticized the sadomasochistic fantasies of the Marquis de Sade, which he, like Beardsley too, circulated in the form of private prints. For sure not by chance, he later called himself Marquis de Bayros.[35] Among his most well-known illustrative works are *La Genouillière* (1907) and *Tales from the Dressing Table* (fig. 9).

Gustav Klimt's depictions of feminine sexuality

Alongside Egon Schiele and Oskar Kokoschka, Gustav Klimt unquestionably belongs to the most important erotic painters of his time,[36] a fact based mainly on his depictions of women in the symbolist paintings, but even more so when seen in connection with his nude drawings. The artist, who was regarded as a legitimate successor to the painter-prince Hans Makart on account of his decorative paint-

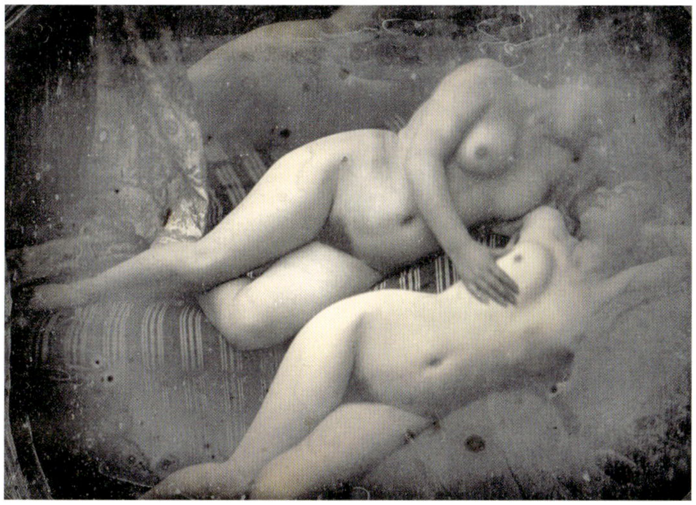

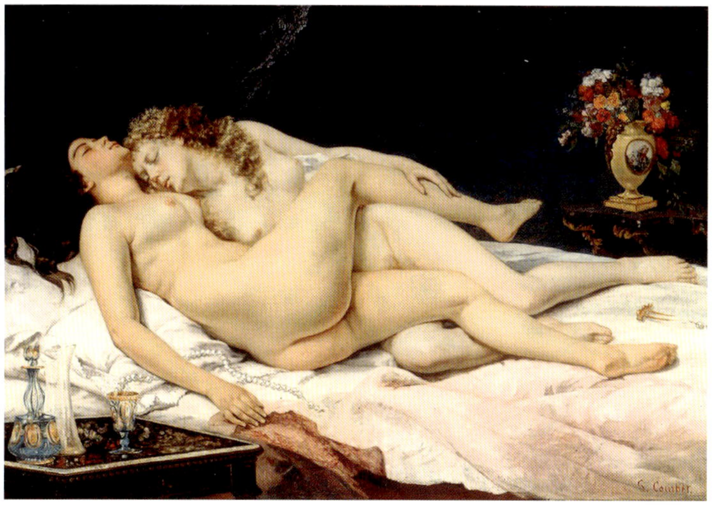

Fig. 14
ANONYMOUS DAGUERREOTYPIST
Girlfriends, c. 1850
J. Paul Getty Museum, Los Angeles

Fig. 15
GUSTAVE COURBET
The Sleepers, 1866
Musée des Beaux-Arts de la Ville de Paris

ings for numerous Ringstrasse palaces and magnificent buildings within the Austrian-Hungarian monarchy, rose above himself with the completion of his commission for the so-called "faculty pictures." In these works, he finally made woman the central theme of his art, using great physical and mental presence.

In the faculty pictures he decided in favor of his own interpretations, against the promoted guideline of personifying the faculties, which, in principle, justified the protest of the professors—not, however, their rejection. Klimt broke with all conventions with his visualization of *Medicine* especially (fig. 10). He painted the female nude, as he had already convincingly done with the depiction of the *Nuda Veritas* (fig. 12) of 1899, no longer in idealized or mythologized fashion, but rather as real and present, as the illustration of physical reality. Klimt painted forty figures in the *Medicine* faculty picture, of which thirty-three are women. It seems as though Klimt regarded *Medicine* as a purely female matter, with even the figuration of Death bearing feminine features. For this picture he painted the female nude in all conceivable variants and circumstances, with a pregnant young woman also to be found among them. Yet, while all these women are tied into the stream of humans, striving upward like one fused unit, the artist singles one of them out as a whole figure (fig. 11). Floating in mid-air, with her upper body arched far back, this one thrusts her pelvis forward for balance. Through the pronounced perspective from below and the forward-tilted hips, Klimt places particular emphasis on her private parts. She is one of the most exciting figures in all of art history, not only for compositional reasons. Gustave Courbet, with his 1866 small-format *L'Origine du Monde* (p. 174, fig. 3), had painted a female figure in similar fashion, although in this case it was a commission for a Turkish collector who wanted to enjoy the picture in his private chambers, not, as with Klimt's, a monumental work meant for public display.[37] Not even Auguste Rodin exposed his subjects in such sophisticated fashion. From now on, there were no more taboos for Klimt.

The next phase in his development was thus laid down. Once the public display of the female sex no longer represented a hurdle for Klimt, he could fully concentrate on the rendering of erotic and sexual inclinations among women. Early studies (e.g. AS 682[38]) for *Fish Blood* (cat. 111), for the hovering genii in the *Beethoven Frieze* (e.g. AS 746) and for *Will-O'-The Wisp* (e.g. AS 706) already announced the direction his artistic journey was to take. They show female nudes floating in a state of weightlessness, left to themselves. The genii or water creatures lie stretched out in various poses on low couches and cushions. Similar to how, in the *Medicine* faculty picture, the main female figure arches her back and so, in combination with the pronounced view

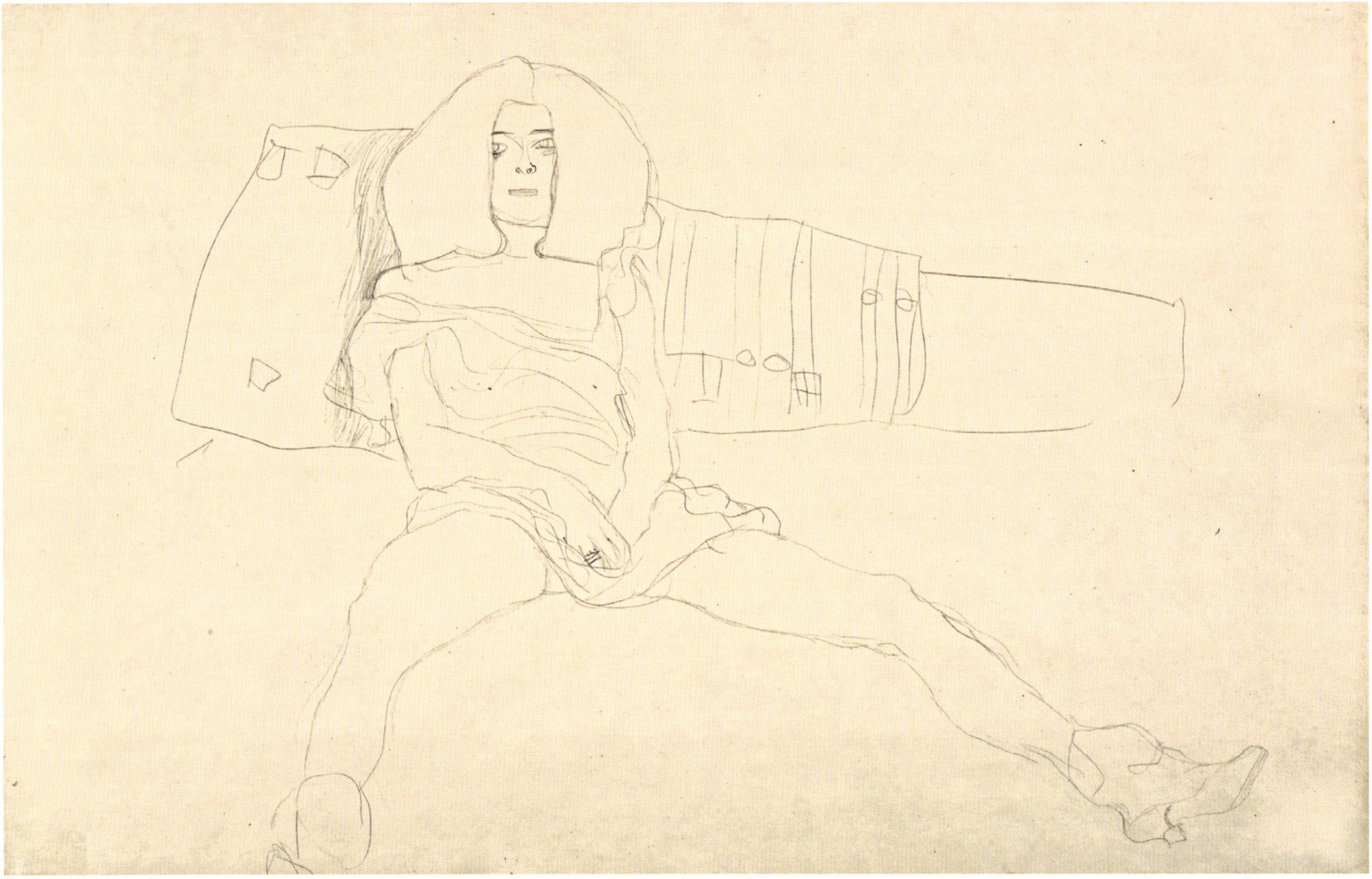

Fig. 16
GUSTAV KLIMT
Masturbating Young Woman, Sitting, 1904
Leopold Museum, Vienna

from below, projects her genitals in the direction of the near foreground, here too, the hairy mons veneris is especially emphasized. The dense brush strokes further define the pubic hair, adding to this effect. In contrast with the nude studies created a few years earlier, in the striving for eroticism the physiognomy of the breasts is also given significantly more attention. Up to this point, Klimt had represented women rather passively. His main focus had been on experimentation with the pose. Probably also on account of his individual experience and his personal confrontation with the subject of pregnancy[39]—Marie Zimmermann was pregnant with Klimt's son Otto from 1901–02—as well as the sensual relationship of women and their child-to-be, and his exploration of the no-less sensual theme of the Danae being sexually stimulated by the shower of gold (AW 187, first sketches around 1903), a completely new spectrum of observation and depiction opened up for Klimt, which ultimately exacted the painting *Hope* (p. 103, fig. 1) from the artist. He now regarded woman from a different perspective: from here on, her feelings and her sensual sensitivities assumed a leading role in his visualized ideas.

Similar to how Klimt removed the single naked female figure in the *Medicine* faculty picture from the flow of people and focused the gaze on her, so, in his 1904 parchment *Girlfriends* (fig. 1) did he concentrate on their loving-erotic embrace. The picture is one of the earliest icons of lesbian love, yet despite all his capacity for empathy and interest in female eroticism and sexuality, it was imperative for Klimt to integrate ornamental phalli into the dress of the figure in the foreground. The known drawings that depict lesbians, around eighty in number, created around the time of the *Girlfriends* parchment and the *Water Serpents* painting (fig. 13), op-

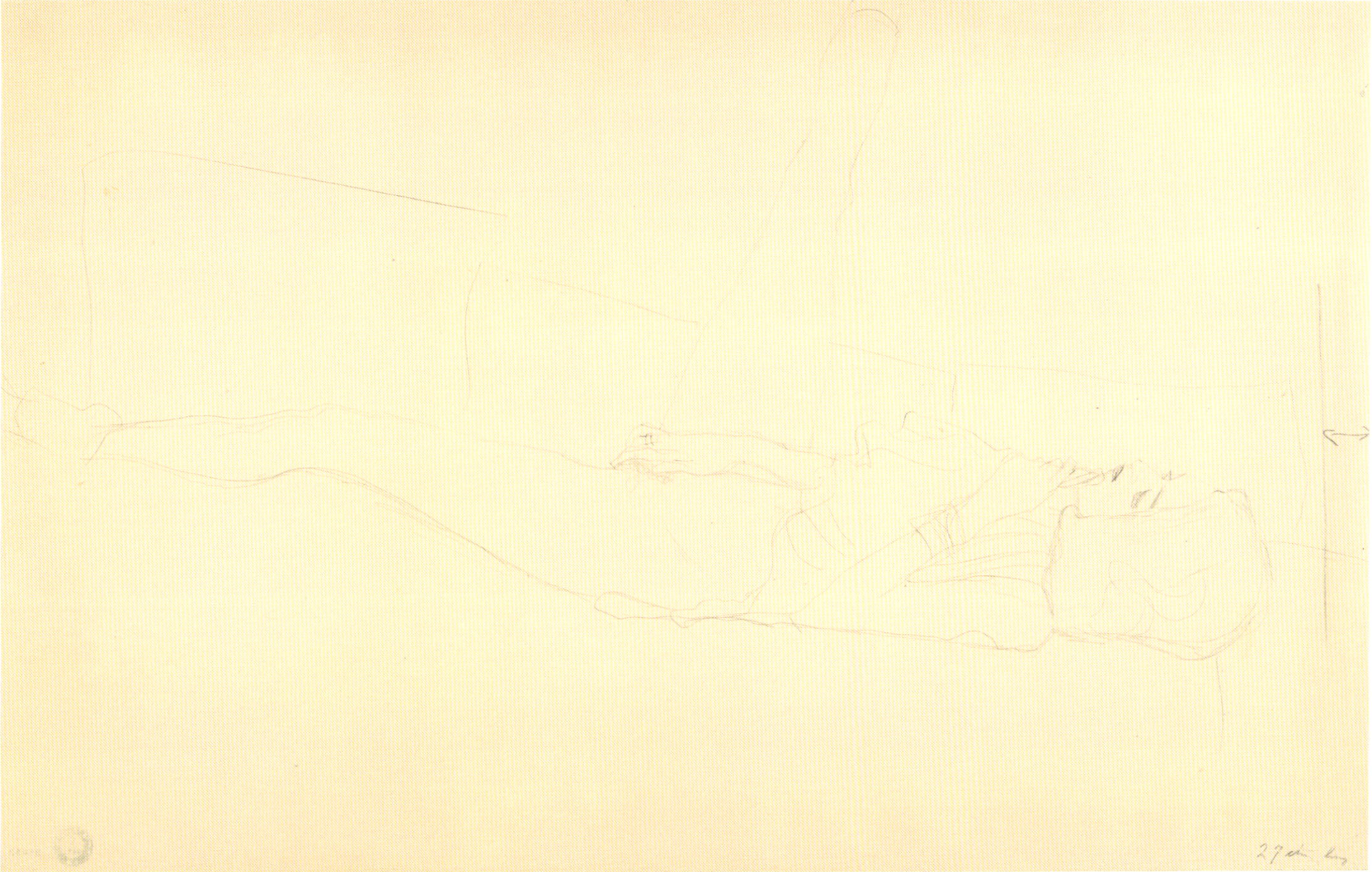

Fig. 17
GUSTAV KLIMT
Masturbating Young Woman with Raised Right Leg, Reclining, 1904
Albertina, Vienna

erate in a considerably more light-hearted manner.[40] Apart from seemingly near-ecstatic embraces, some studies show intimately kissing women (unquoted AS 1346–1348) as well as female oral sex (cat. 90, AS 1380). It is probable that Gustave Courbet's depiction painted in 1866 of two lesbians (*Le Sommeil,* fig. 15) was a possible model for Klimt's tackling of this subject. But one should also point out daguerreotypes (fig. 14) that certainly can be considered as sources of inspiration. Courbet in turn had responded in his work to Charles Baudelaire's volume of poetry *Les Fleurs du Mal,* first published in 1857, which was originally to be entitled *Les Lesbiennes.*[41]

In this context, mention should also be made, above all, of Félicien Rops. The Belgian graphic artist created numerous depictions of lesbians. After his death, a selection of nine printed graphics (cf. fig. 19) were bound into the book *Die Lesbierinnen* (text by Paul Marein), which was published privately in Leipzig in 1909.

In general, the illustration of masterpieces of erotic literature was a popular area of activity for artists around this time. In 1887, the French collector Paul Gallimard commissioned Auguste Rodin to illustrate Baudelaire's *Les Fleurs du Mal.* Although the book was not published until 1913, we may assume that Klimt had learned relatively early of the French master's project. He himself also undertook a commission of this kind: He provided fifteen nude drawings to illustrate the early editions of Lucian's work *Hetairikoi Dialogoi*, which started to be circulated in December 1905 as individual volumes.[42] The Austrian writer Franz Blei took care of the translation of the work, which was written around 160 CE. *Hetairikoi Dialogoi* concerns discussions between hetaerae, including Charmides' avowal of love for the courtesan Philemation. The

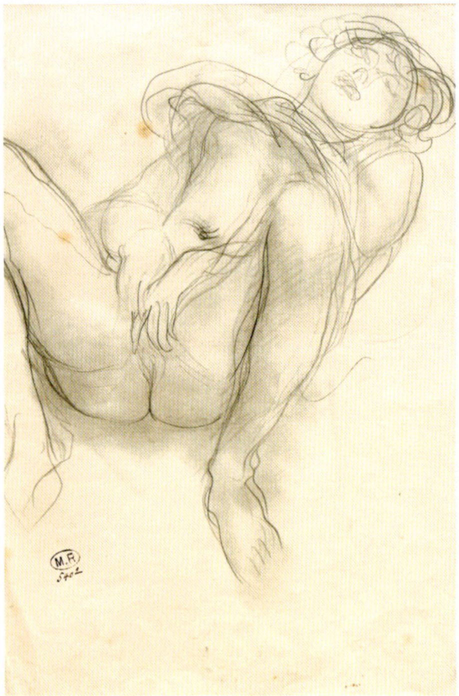

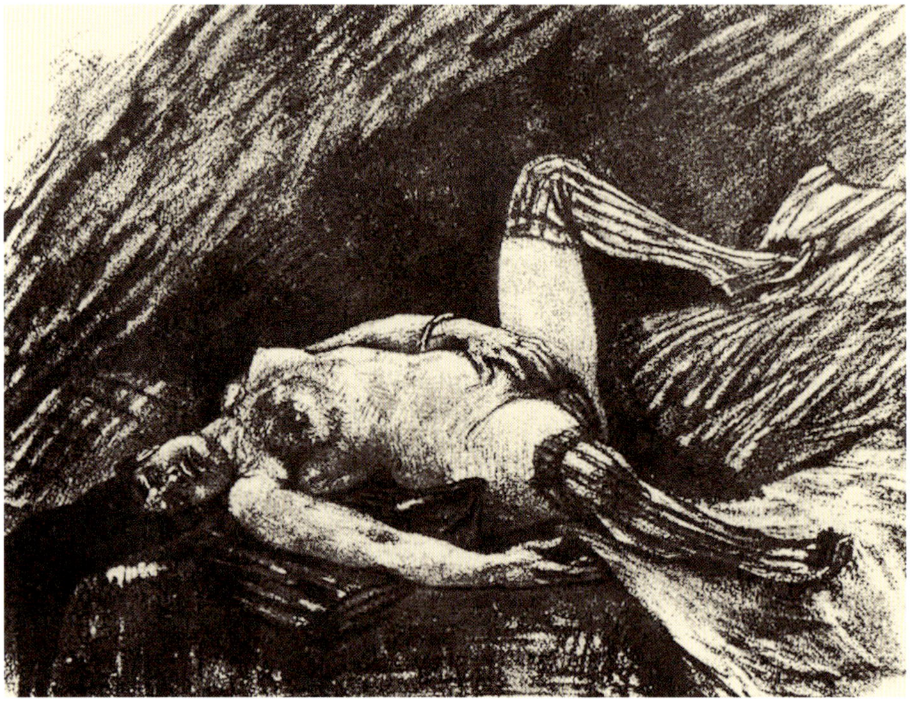

title already reveals what this is about, and what illustrations were expected of Klimt. The figure of the hetaera, in which high eroticism was combined with prostitution, exerted great fascination on the artist. In line with the number of chapters, he chose fifteen nude drawings, which were transferred to collotype technology and bound into the core of the book. The selection undertaken reflects Klimt's atmospheric notion of the carefree hetaerae, left to do as they please.[43] Besides individual portraits of the courtesans in lacy flounces, semi-nudes relaxing stretched out on a couch as well as a pair engaged in intercourse,[44] three drawings show Phrynes desiring one another. Three other depictions, created around 1904 (figs. 16, 17, 20), illustrate young women who are satisfying themselves clitorally and vaginally with the middle finger of their right hand. Klimt may well have known individual sketches of female masturbators by Auguste Rodin (fig. 8), which emboldened him to tackle this subject. Yet, notwithstanding all the similarities in themes, the formal differences could not be greater. The schematic sketches of the French grand master look like playful, deeply passionate finger exercises. Only a few curvilinear strokes hint at the female genitalia; the fingers on the labia and the right hand stimulating the clitoris remain sketchy. Unlike the sculptor Rodin, Klimt was primarily a painter, thus he regarded the medium of drawing as its own art form in line with the concept of the *Gesamtkunstwerk* (total work of art), assigning it complete autonomy. This is expressed in a significantly more intense treatment of the body in all its details, which he reproduced on the brown paper with great sensitivity and mastery. This comes to the fore most clearly in virtuosic drawings with a plot motif, such as that of masturbation. In these nude drawings, Klimt worked through not just one moment, but all of his impressions. Thus he created extensive series of sheets with depictions of masturbating women. One of the earliest was created around 1904 (cf. cat. 1, 2), and he drew more series from 1913 onwards (cat. 6, 7, 8). To date, around fifty drawings by Klimt depicting women pleasuring themselves are known.[45] The number of works created around this theme is much greater, however. It is thus imperative to consider each single drawing in the context of its respective series.
Apart from the depiction of a young woman stim-

Fig. 18
AUGUSTE RODIN
Masturbating Woman, c. 1900
Musée Rodin, Paris

Fig. 19
FÉLICIEN ROPS
Masturbating Woman, c. 1875
Private collection

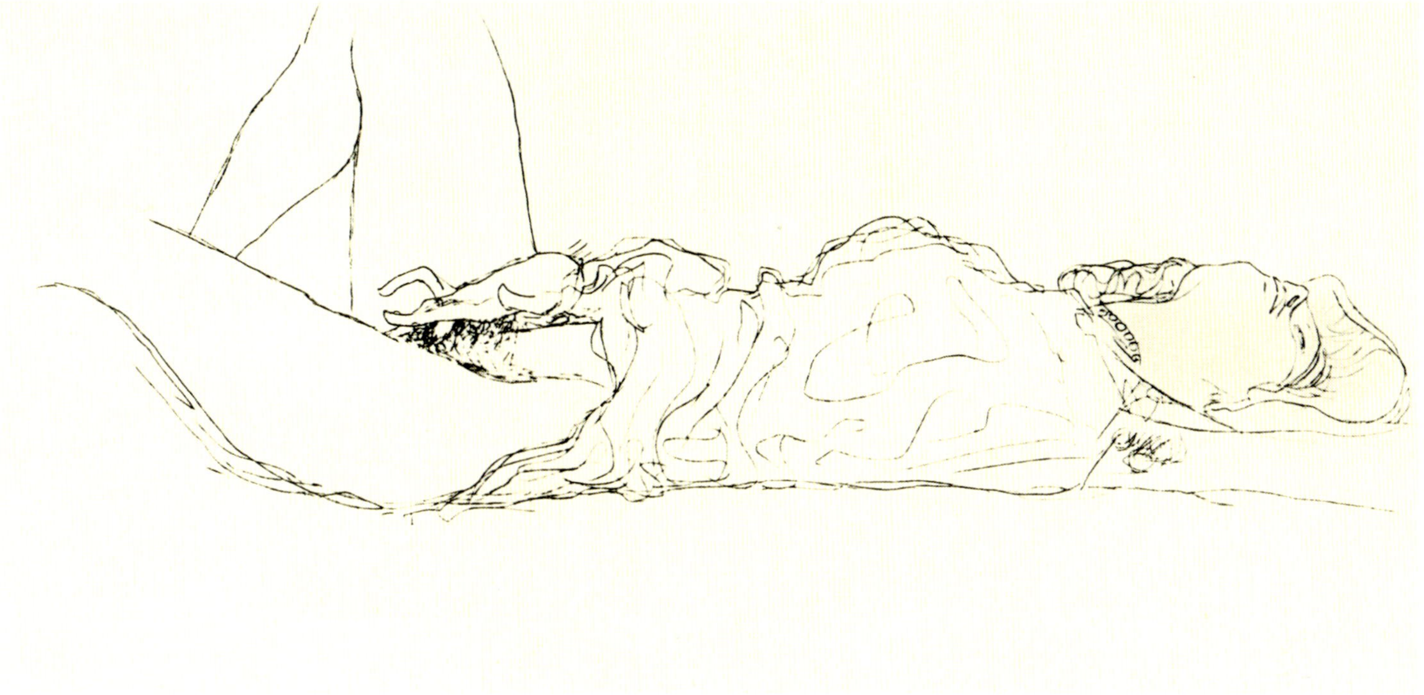

Fig. 20
GUSTAV KLIMT
Masturbating Young Woman with Necklace, Reclining, 1904
Private collection

ulating herself with a long knitting needle in her vagina (AS 2304), the image of a woman handling a dildo (AS 2340), and a drawing in which the man is possibly stimulating the clitoris of the woman lying beside him (AS 2451), Klimt was especially interested in clitoral and vaginal masturbation carried out with fingers. For the sheets concerned, we are dealing in essence with scenes from series of up to more than fifteen studies, which he created during one continuous session using a model. Very precisely and attentively, the artist observed and drew all the phases of masturbation: the stimulation of the clitoris and vagina, the sexual arousal, the resulting physical tension, and the phase of relaxation that follows, when the young women either rest in a state of complete relaxation or pass into a sleep-like state. It cannot be read from the drawings we know, whether Klimt preferred his models to adopt a particular position. He drew them lying on their stomach, sideways, or lying on their back. With their legs drawn up, with one arm wrapped around their thigh, or in a crouched position. There are no distractions in his drawings, no interference from the immediate surroundings. Klimt shows these women lost in themselves, following their own personal rhythm alone, focused on the rising stages of their sexual stimulation as these flow into each other, until, after climaxing, they float over into the relaxation phase. "Self-satisfied and self-contained, they evoke the image of a carefree paradise, far from anxiety, power, and change,"[46] as Anselm Wagner stated in his essay on the hermetic eroticism of Gustav Klimt. To capture the state of almost complete spiritual rapture, as well as the slipping—probably nourished by theosophical thoughts—into a weightless, cosmic parallel world, were two of the higher and most essential goals that Klimt pursued from 1908 onwards.

In view of the prejudices towards masturbation that still prevailed at the time the *Hetairikoi Dialogoi* were published, Klimt's liberal and uninhibited drawings of masturbating women resemble a silent scream. Like Baudouin before him, he also liberated women from being forced to experience sexual stimulation exclusively through men or female playmates. Yet no other artist has depicted this theme so clearly and unmistakably. On account of the forthrightness of his drawings, Klimt was berated by some as a pornographer,[47] which did not, however, hold him back from continuing to work on his erotic themes, and exhibiting those works in public.

In view of the subject matter, it is worth reminding ourselves that Gustav Klimt spent most of his life among women. Although he never married nor resided under one roof with a partner, he nevertheless lived together with his two sisters Klara and Hermine in their mother Anna's flat.[48] Klimt's family was thus the central point of his life, his personal "hortus conclusus" and absolutely taboo to the outside world. Living so closely with these three women also explains his familiarity with the emotional world and phases of women. Klimt was thus in a position to understand the intimate themes of a woman's life, and respond to them in his own way. During the day he stayed in his studio, where he was likewise almost constantly surrounded by women.[49] Besides the models for his sought-after portraits, there were frequently young women present, whose nudes he studied and drew. The atmosphere in his studio then probably resembled that depicted in Lucian's work, and Klimt himself was a part of the world of the hetaerae. Thus he could observe them without himself being perceived as a foreign body, he could listen to their conversations and draw them. In view of this permissiveness, it may then surprise us that none of the models in the drawings devote themselves to masturbation in a state of complete undress. They always wear light scarves, either pulled across their belly or covering their breasts, but also draped lasciviously over their midriff, creating the effect of a delicately placed frame motif to focus our attention on their vulva. Despite his explicit depictions of masturbators, and the highly erotic theme, Klimt never became pornographic nor perverse, but rather always remained true to his sensual aesthetic.

1 Cf. my contribution on Gustav Klimt's image of women on pp. 211–221.
2 Sigmund Freud, "Zur Onanie-Diskussion. Schlusswort", in: *Die Onanie: Vierzehn Beiträge zu einer Diskussion der Wiener Psychoanalytischen Vereinigung*, Wiesbaden 1912, p. 336.
3 The publication is the result of several debates on onanism, which took place in Vienna on January 24, February 28, March 13 and 20, and April 24, 1912. The last debate was led by Sigmund Freud.
4 "Vierundzwanzig Unterredungen mit den Vätern (Collationes patrum): Sämtliche Schriften des ehrwürdigen Johannes Cassianus," in: *Bibliothek der Kirchenväter*, 1st series, vol. 59, Kempten 1879.
5 Erhard Köllner, *Homosexualität als anthropologische Herausforderung: Konzeption einer homosexuellen Anthropologie*, Bad Heilbrunn 2001, p. 29.
6 Tissot celebrated his first great success with the medical paper *L'Onanisme* (1785, Latin 1758, French 1760), a controversial attempt to consider the theme from a medical perspective. The paper went through 67 editions in French up to the end of the nineteenth century and was translated into five languages.
7 Samuel Auguste Tissot, *Die Onanie, oder Abhandlung über die Krankheiten die von der Selbstbefleckung herrühren: Nach der vierten beträchtlich vermehrten Ausgabe aus dem Französischen übersetzt*, Eisenach 1776, 1774 (first edition 1758).
8 Tissot 1776, quoted in Sabine Todt, "'Seine erstorbenen Augen verkannten alle Gegenstände, die um ihn waren.' Das Tabu der Onanie und die Bedeutung von Wissen im 18. und 19. Jahrhundert," in: Ute Frietzsch/Konstanze Hanitzsch/Jennifer John/Beatrice Michaelis (ed.), *Geschlecht als Tabu: Orte, Dynamiken und Funktionen der De/Thematisierung von Geschlecht*, Bielefeld 2008, pp. 217–230, here p. 226.
9 Immanuel Kant, *Die Metaphysik der Sitten*, part 2 I, section 7, Königsberg 1797.
10 Jean-Jacques Rousseau, *Émile ou De l'éducation*, Amsterdam 1762.
11 Köllner 2001 (see note 5), pp. 34–35.
12 Caroline Erb/Deborah Klingler, *Mysterium Masturbation: Wenn sich Frauen selber lieben*, Frankfurt/M. 2004, p. 17. (Referring to Jos van Ussel, *Sexualunterdrückung: Geschichte der Sexualfeindschaft*, Gießen 1977.)
13 Köllner 2001(see note 5), p. 34.
14 Richard von Krafft-Ebing: *Psychopathia sexualis*, 14th edition, 1912, new edition, Berlin 1997, p. 227.
15 Iwan Bloch, *Das Sexualleben unserer Zeit in seinen Beziehungen zur modernen Kultur*, Berlin 1909 (first edition 1906), p. 471.
16 William M. Johnston, *The Austrian Mind: an Intellectual and Social History, 1848–1938*, Berkeley 1972, p. 187.
17 August Forel, *Die sexuelle Frage. Eine naturwissenschaftliche, psychologische, hygienische und soziologische Studie für Gebildete*, Munich 1905.
18 Hermann Rohleder makes a similar argument in his work *Die Masturbation*, published in Berlin in 1899.
19 Friedrich Wilhelm Foerster, *Sexualethik und Sexualpädagogik: Eine Auseinandersetzung mit den Modernen*, Kempten/Munich 1907, pp. 75–76.
20 "The insight occurred to me that masturbation is the single great habit, the 'primal addiction,' [and] only the other addictions to alcohol, morphine, tobacco etc. come into being as its substitution and replacement." Letter from Sigmund Freud to Wilhelm Fließ of December 22, 1897, in: Sigmund Freud, *Briefe an Wilhelm Fließ, 1887–1904*, Frankfurt 1986, p. 312–313.
21 Wilhelm Stekel was a Jewish-Austrian doctor and psychoanalyst. His most well-known work is a ten-volume series of books published between 1912 and 1928 entitled *Störungen des Trieb- und Affektlebens (die parapathischen Erkrankungen)*, Berlin/Vienna 1912–1928. In this context, we refer to volume 2, published in 1923 (*Onanie und Homosexualität. Die homosexuelle Parapathie*).
22 The extent to which this conclusion was the general doctrine of the age is illustrated by the title alone: "Discussion of the Harm Done by Onanism," which was held by the Vienna Group of the Vienna Psychoanalytical Society on June 1, 1910.
23 Freud 1912 (see note 2), p 336.

24 Richard von Krafft-Ebing, *Psychopathia sexualis. Eine klinisch-forensische Studie*, Stuttgart 1886, pp. 9–10.
25 For this, see Jonathan Margolis, *O., The Intimate History of the Orgasm*, New York 2004. Further examples can be found on a bowl in the Hermitage in Moscow, on a vase in the Museo Archeologico Regionale in Syracuse, Sicily, and on a bowl in the Louvre, Paris.
26 Hans Licht, a scholar of sexuality in ancient Greece, described the Greek women of Antiquity as enthusiastic masturbators. Cf. Hans Licht, *Liebe und Ehe in Griechenland*, (first edition 1925), Hamburg 2013, pp. 14–16.
27 For this, see: Rona Goffen, *Titian's Women*, New Haven 1997, p. 167–169.
28 Thomas W. Laqueur, *Solitary Sex: A Cultural History of Masturbation*, New York 2004, fig. 5.8b, p. 348. None less than Francisco de Goya convincingly developed this concept of revelation, with his two portraits of the young Maja.
29 Marquis de Sade, *La Nouvelle Justine ou les Malheurs de la vertu, suivie de l'histoire de Juliette, sa sœur*, Holland 1797.
30 For example, the Imperial and Royal Regional Court as Press Court in Vienna ruled, "In the Name of His Majesty the Emperor" in its decision of August 28, 1878, that various passages in the printed work *Die Schule der Wonne. Aus dem Französischen des Werkes: La philosophie dans le boudoir von Marquis de Sade, Verfasser von Justine und Juliette,* are classed a "crime" and pronounced it forbidden to further distribute this title. *Wiener Zeitung*, no. 204, September 1, 1878, "Amtsblatt zur *Wiener Zeitung*".
31 This applies especially to daguerreotypes of the French photographer Auguste Belloc.
32 Cf. J. A. Schmoll gen. Eisenwerth, "Akademien. Fotografische Studien des nackten Körpers von Künstlern für Künstler: Von Delacroix bis Loth," in: Gisela Barche/Michael Koehler (eds.) *Das Aktfoto: Ansichten vom Körper im fotografischen Zeitalter:* Ästhetik – Geschichte – Ideologie, Munich 1985, pp. 62–119.
33 Gert Mattenklott, "Figurenwerfen – Versuch über Klimts Zeichnungen," in: *Gustav Klimt – Zeichnungen 1880–1917*, Hannover 1984, pp. 27–35, esp. p. 34.
34 Beardsley was highly regarded among the Viennese Secessionists. To mark his early death, the Austrian art magazine *Ver Sacrum* dedicated a full page to an obituary written by Arthur Symons.
35 On Bayros, see Ludwig vom Brunn (ed.), *Franz von Bayros: Das galante Werk*, 2 vols., Hamburg 1966–67.
36 Nike Wagner, *Geist und Geschlecht: Karl Kraus und die Erotik der Wiener Moderne*, Frankfurt 1987 (first edition 1982), p. 41.
37 In connection with this work, mention should also be made of Alfred Kubin's drawing *Der Todessprung*, created around 1900.
38 Alice Strobl, *Gustav Klimt. Die Zeichnungen 1878–1903*, Salzburg 1980; Alice Strobl, *Gustav Klimt: Die Zeichnungen 1904–1912*, Salzburg 1982; Alice Strobl, *Gustav Klimt: Die Zeichnungen 1912–1918*, Salzburg 1984; Alice Strobl, *Gustav Klimt: Die Zeichnungen. Nachtrag 1878–1918*, Salzburg 1989. Catalogue of works of the drawings; the corresponding catalogue numbers are abbreviated with AS.
39 Cf. my contribution on Gustav Klimt's image of women on pp. 211–221.
40 For this, cf. Alice Strobl nos. 1346, 1354, 1372, 1380, 1397, 1452, 1512, 1516 etc.
41 In 1857, a court convicted the poet on charges of offending public morals and he had to remove six incriminated poems—*Lesbos, Femmes damnées, Le Lèthe, À celle qui est trop gaie, Les Bijoux, Les Métamorphoses du vampire*—from *Fleurs du Mal.*
42 Note to Dr. Julius Zeitler on a postcard of December 31, 1905. Tobias G. Natter, "Gustav Klimt and The Dialogues of the Heterae: Erotic Boundaries in Vienna Around 1900," in: Renée Price (ed.), *Gustav Klimt: The Ronald S. Lauder and Serge Sabarsky Collections* (exh. cat. Neue Galerie, New York), Munich/London/New York 2007, pp. 130–143, fig. 3 (p. 131). The book was officially published in 1907 in Leipzig.
43 Hermann Bahr wrote three letters to the translator on account of an example passed on to him by Blei, remarking about Klimt, in particularly chauvinistic fashion, "Here is the only one whose blossoming nature is not darkened by bourgeois shame. The only one who sees in a pagan way again. The only one to whom woman is woman everywhere—you cover up the few places that you find exciting about women, yet he knows that everything about woman is lust, that everything about woman is 'sex', that God gave us woman so as to fling up our depths through arousal, from which alone the meaning and will of all life steams." "Three letters to the editor from Hermann Bahr," in: Franz Blei (ed.), *Die Opale: Blätter für Kunst & Literatur*, 3rd and 4th parts, Leipzig 1907, p. 127.
44 Most likely inspired by a Shunga woodblock print created around 1800–05 by Kitagawa Utamaro.
45 AS 1393–1395, 1398, 1401, 1409, 2261–2263, 2277, 2300, 2301, 2303–2309, 2311, 2315, 2319, 2324, 2338–2340, 2351, 2385, 2400, 2402, 2404, 2405, 2441, 2450, 2963, 2964, 2966, 2967, 2970–2972, 3627, 3661, 3664, 3665.
46 Anselm Wagner, "Ich schließe mich selbst ein: Zur hermetischen Erotik Gustav Klimts", in: Alfred Weidinger (ed.) *Inselräume: Teschner, Klimt & Flöge am Attersee*, pp. 79–83, Seewalchen 1989 (first edition 1988), pp. 79–83, citation p. 79.
47 A. F. Seligmann characterized Klimt's drawings exhibited in 1913 as works of "pornography." (F. A. Seligmann, "Schwarz-Weiß," in: *Neue Freie Presse*, Vienna, December 17, 1913, p. 3.
48 The Klimt family lived on Westbahnstraße no. 36 in Vienna from 1894 onwards.
49 Cf. my contribution on Gustav Klimt's image of women on pp. 211–221.

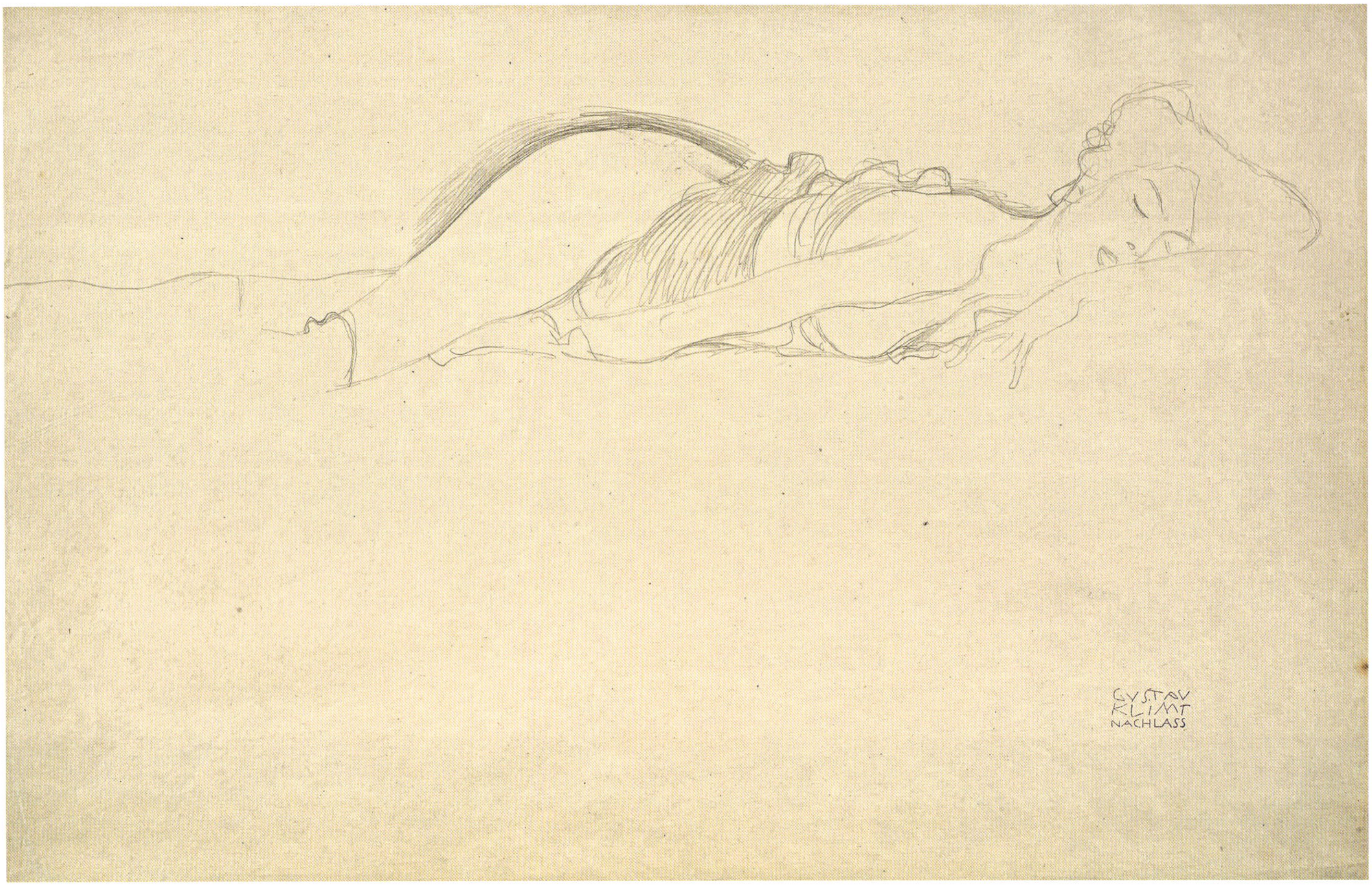

Cat. 1
GUSTAV KLIMT
Reclining Nude Lying on Her Stomach, Facing Right, 1904
Pencil on Japanese paper, 34.9 x 55 cm
Leopold Museum, Vienna

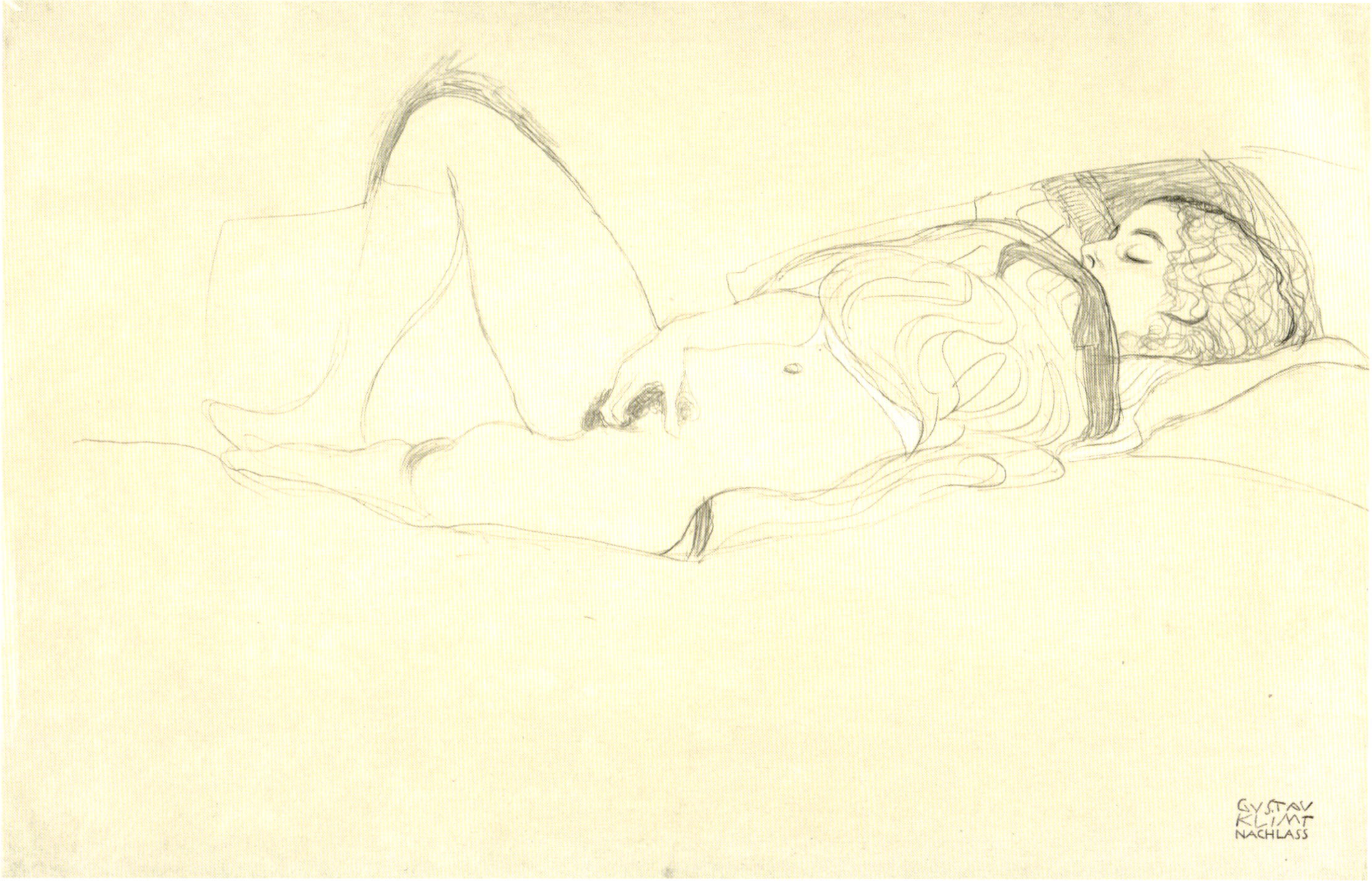

Cat. 2
GUSTAV KLIMT
Reclining Masturbating Half-Nude (Seen from the Right) with Right Leg Drawn Up, 1904
Pencil and white crayon on paper, 37.2 x 56.5 cm
Collection Dr. Eberhard W. Kornfeld, Bern

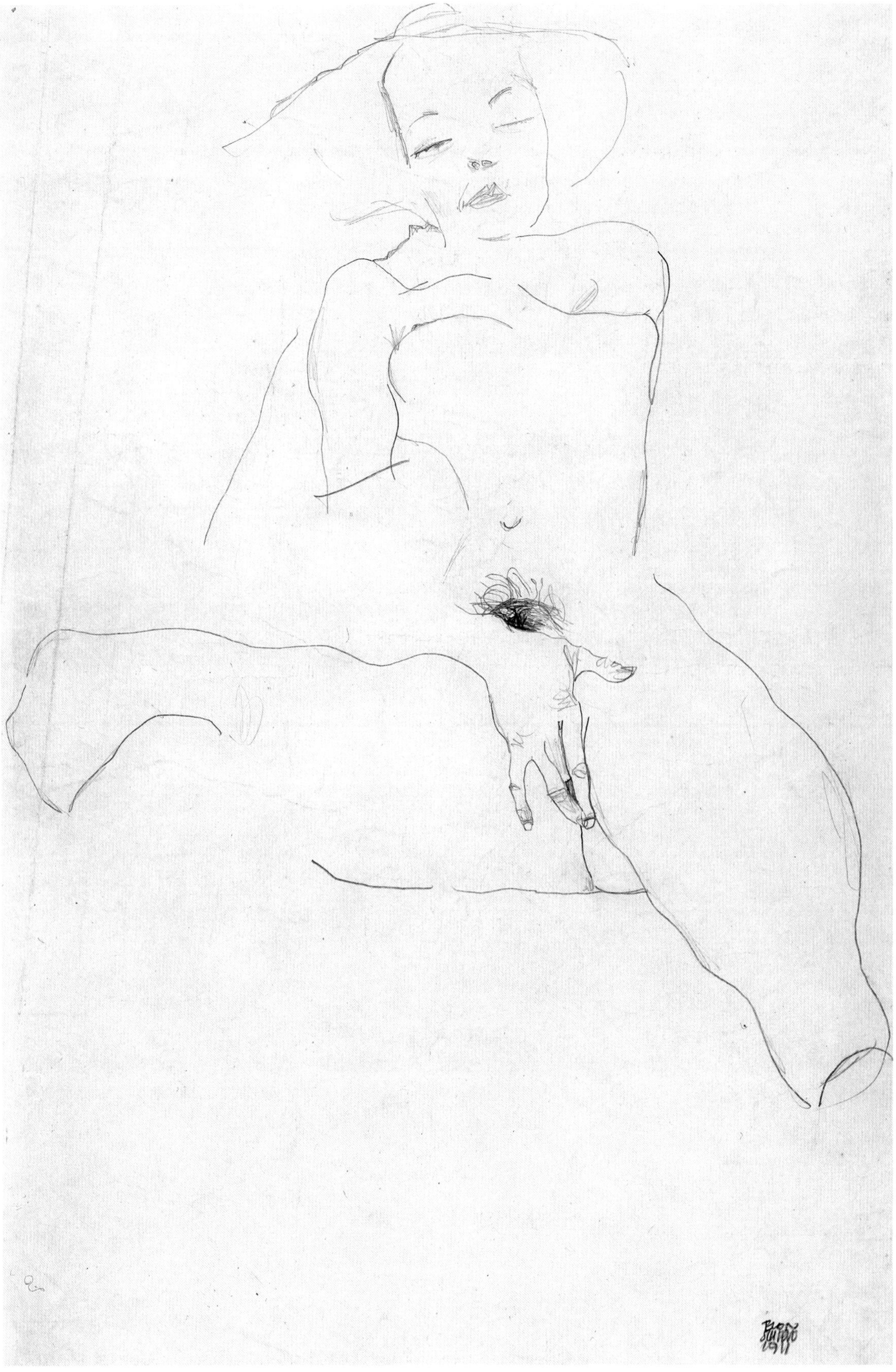

Cat. 3
EGON SCHIELE
Seated Female Nude,
Masturbating, 1911
Pencil on paper, 56 x 37.1 cm
Private collection

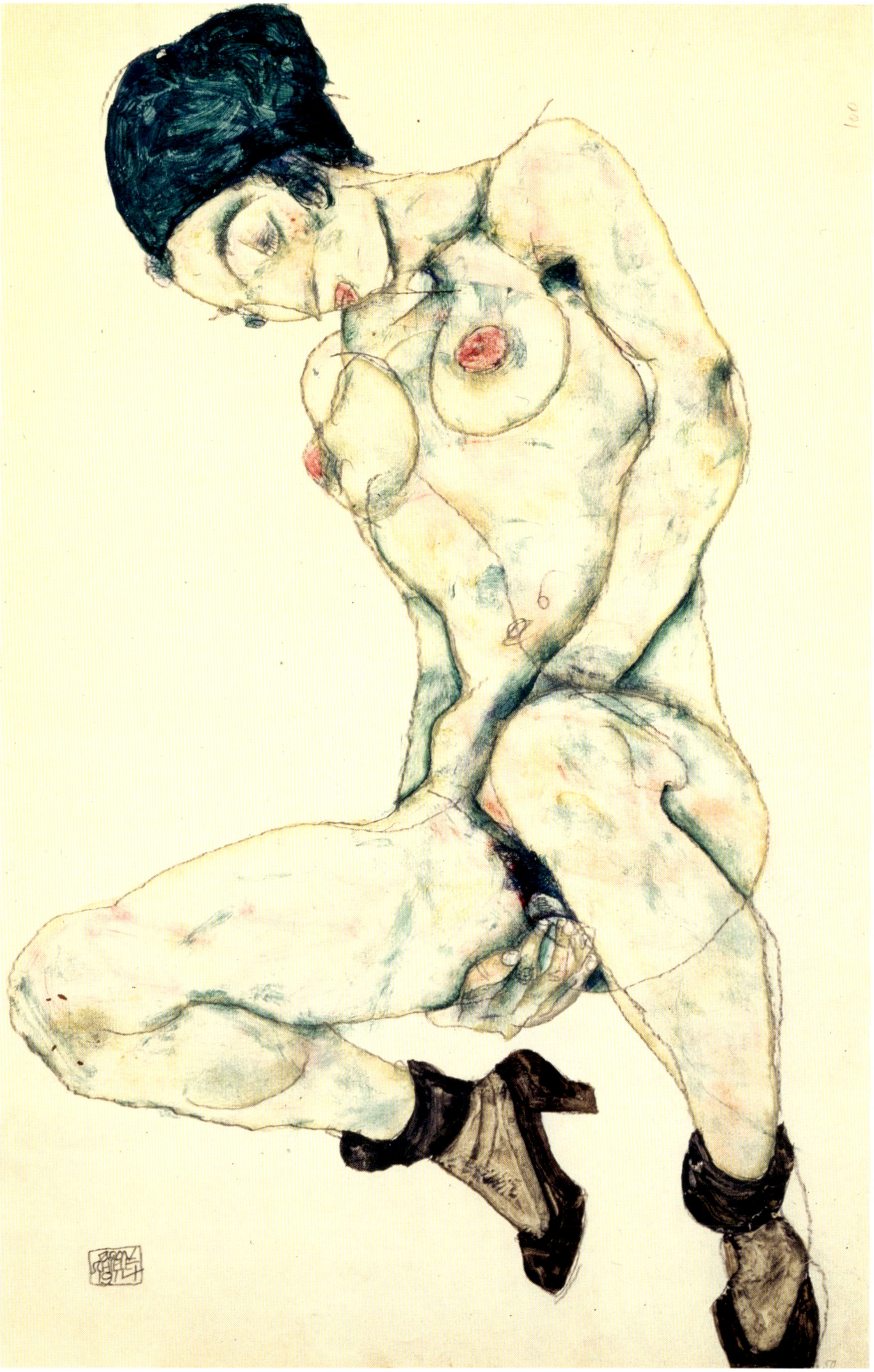

Cat. 4
EGON SCHIELE
Masturbating Nude with Green Turban, 1914
Gouache and pencil on paper,
32 x 48 cm
Private collection

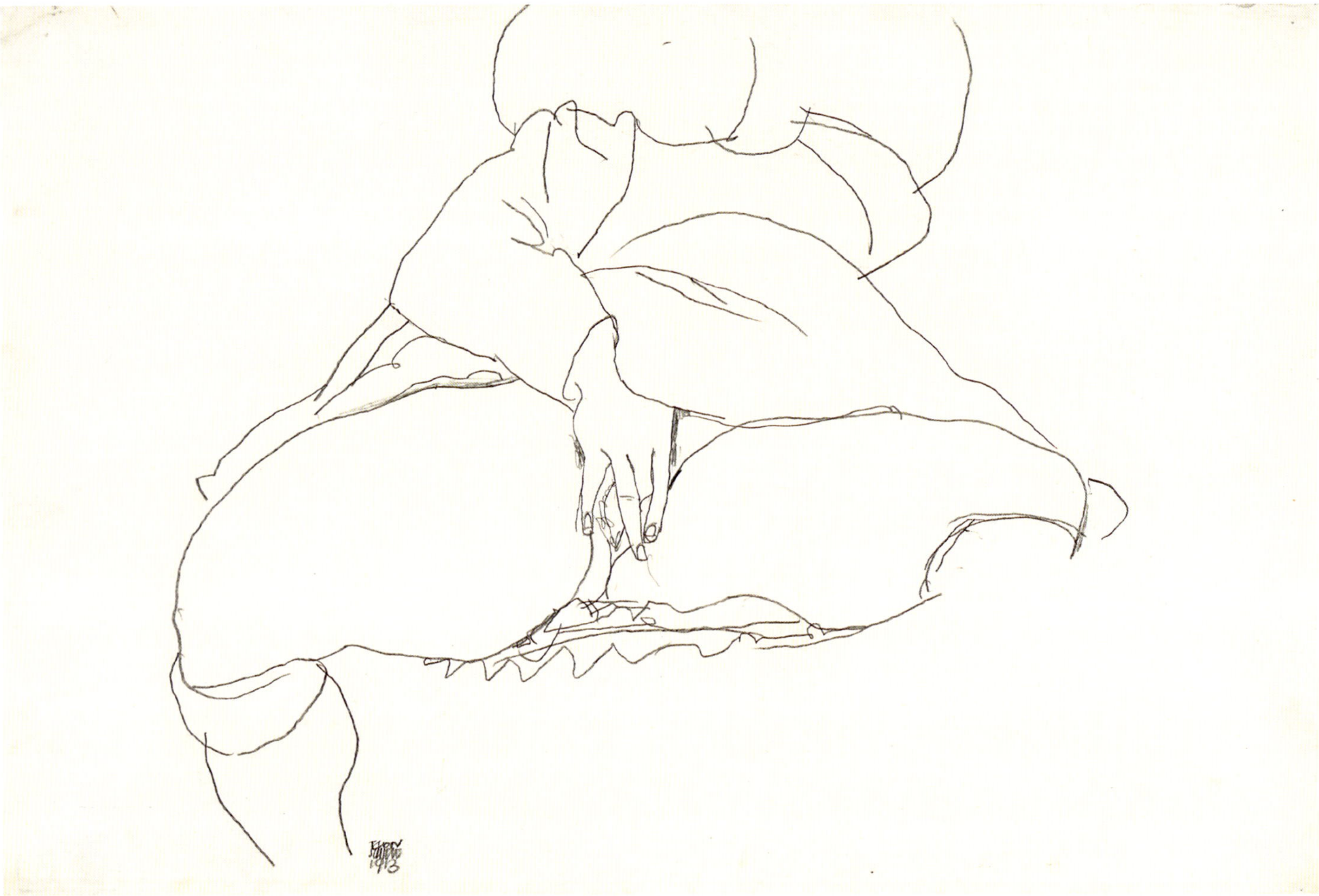

Cat. 5
EGON SCHIELE
Masturbating Woman with Spread Thighs, 1913
Pencil on paper, 32.2 x 48 cm
Leopold Museum, Vienna

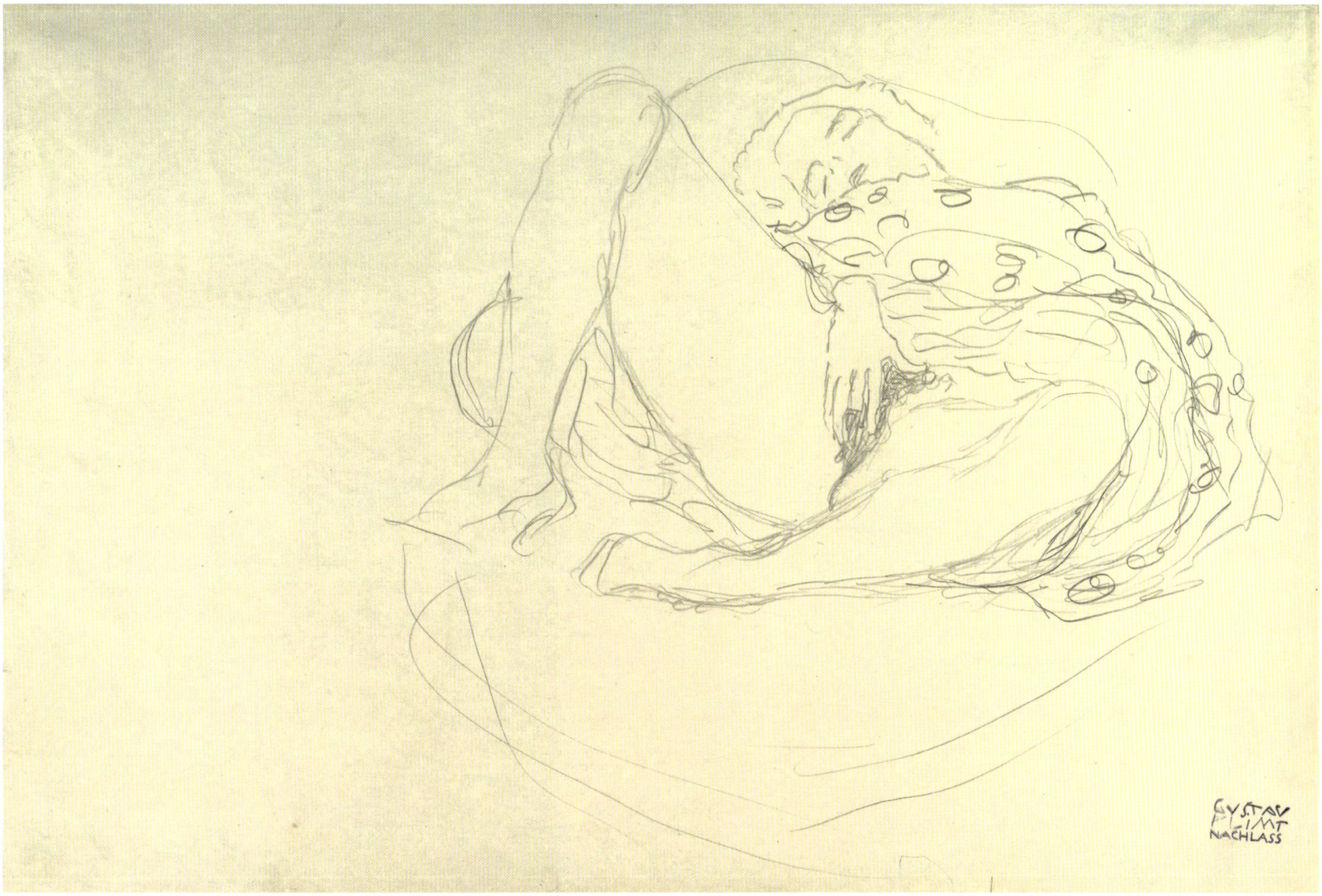

Cat. 6
GUSTAV KLIMT
Reclining Masturbating Nude with Drapery, 1913
Pencil on paper, 37.1 x 55.9 cm
The Metropolitan Museum of Art, New York, bequest of Scofield Thayer, 1982

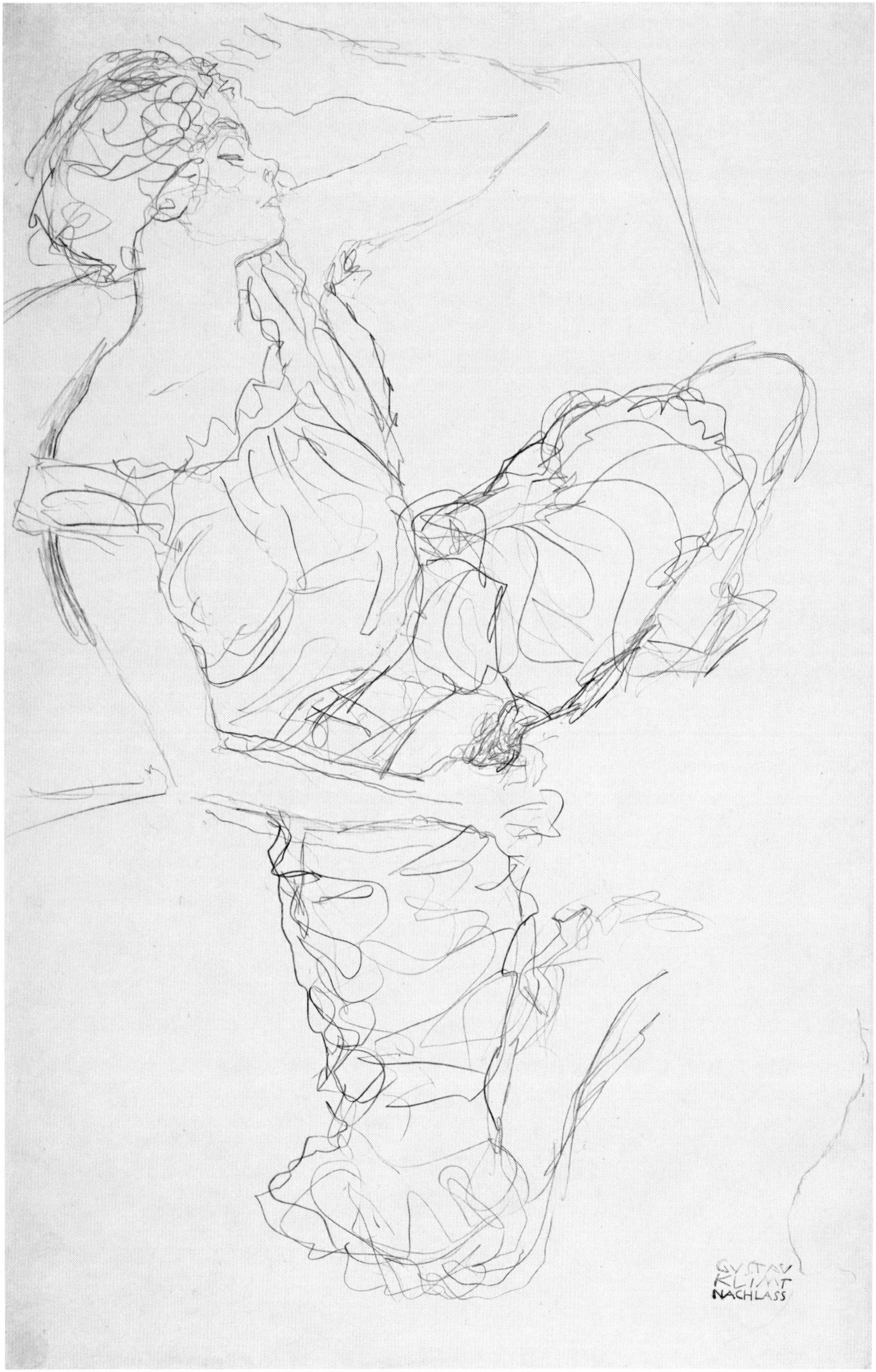

Cat. 7
GUSTAV KLIMT
Reclining Woman in Underwear with Spread Thighs (Masturbating), 1916–17
Pencil on Japanese paper,
56.9 x 36.5 cm
Leopold Museum, Vienna

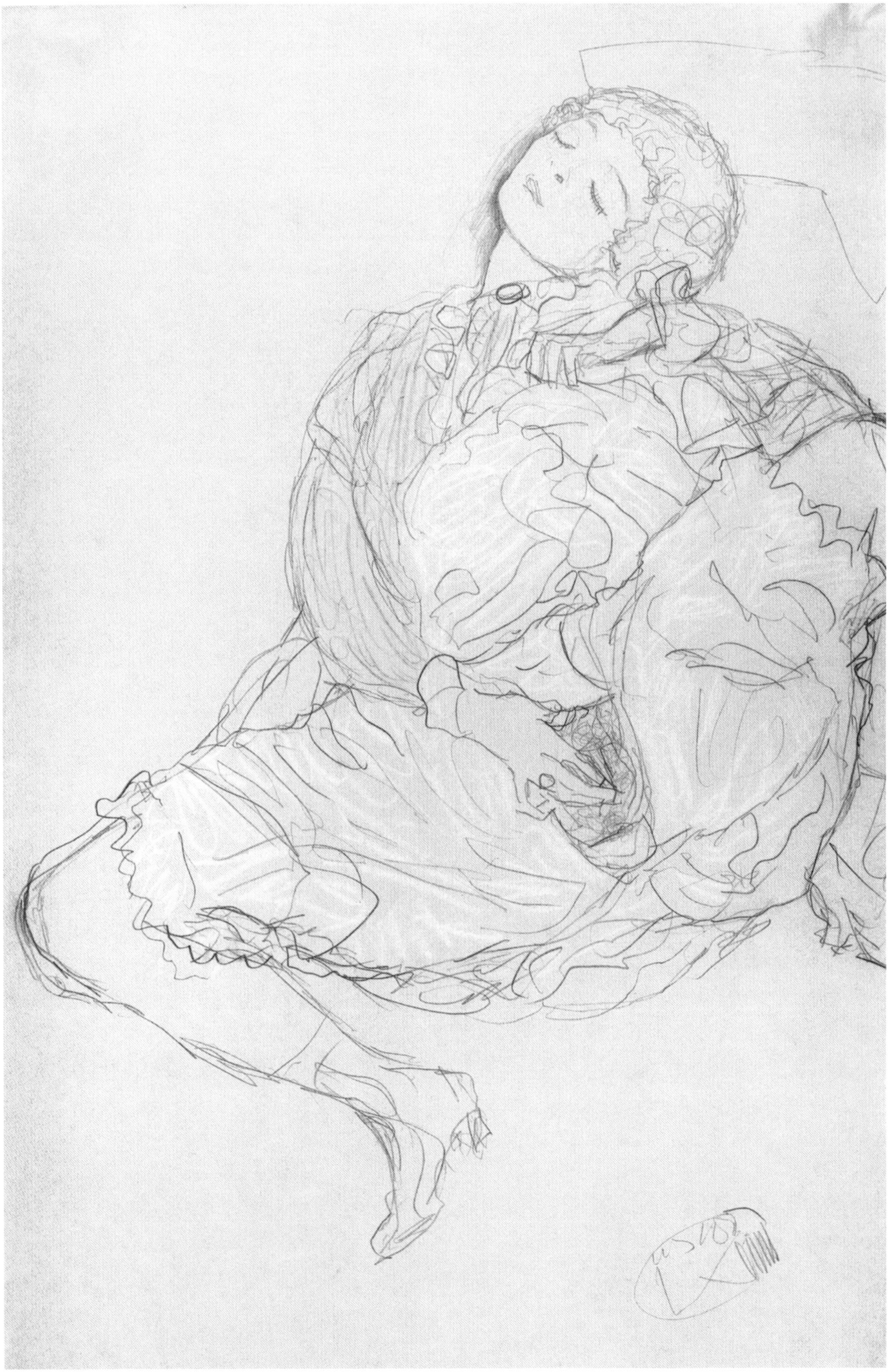

Cat. 8
GUSTAV KLIMT
Reclining Masturbating Woman with Spread Thighs, 1916–17
Pencil, red pencil and white crayon on paper, 57 x 37.5 cm
Private collection, courtesy of Neue Galerie, New York

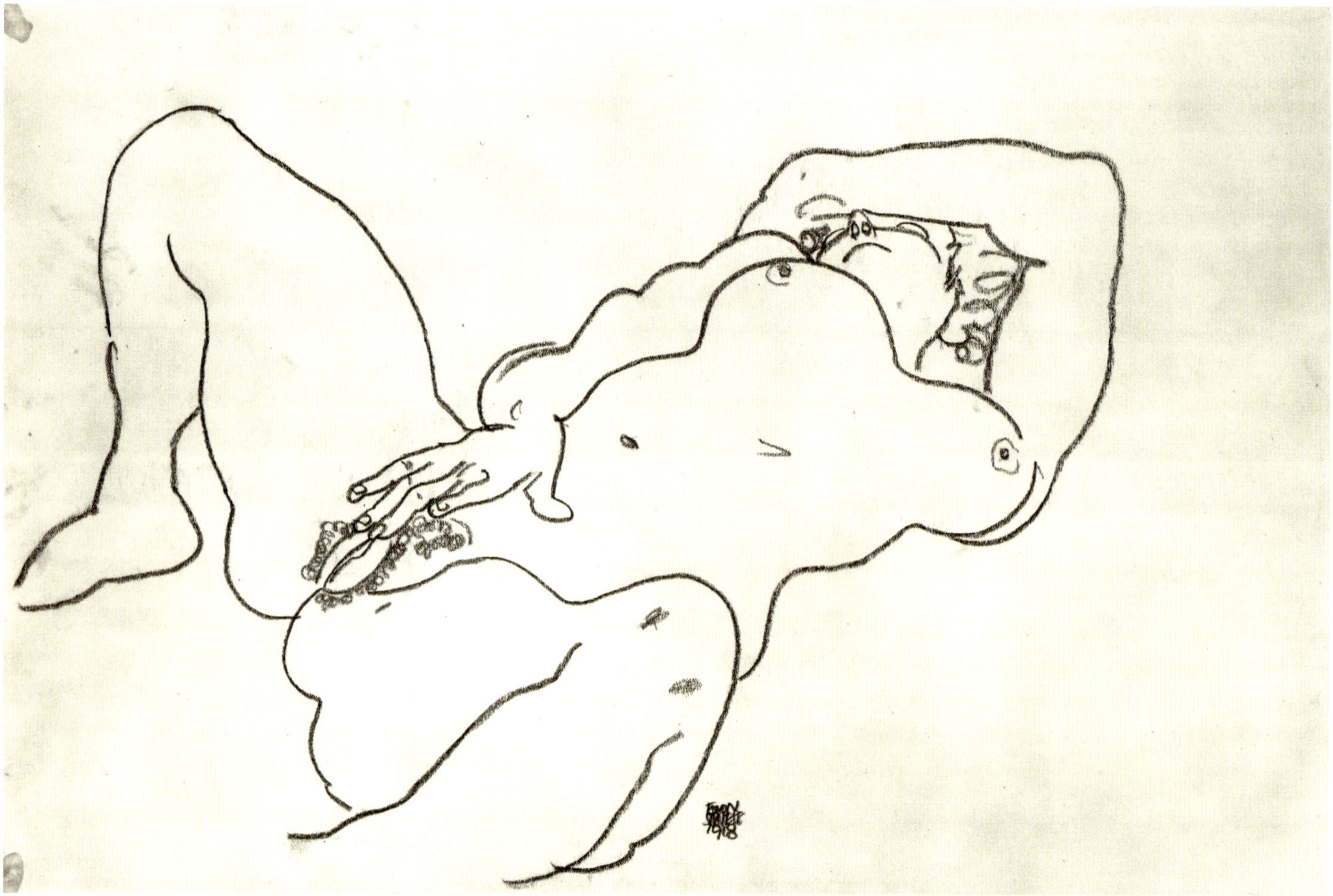

Cat. 9
EGON SCHIELE
Reclining Masturbating Nude, 1918
Black crayon on paper, 29.8 x 46.4 cm
The Metropolitan Museum of Art, New York, bequest of Scofield Thayer, 1982

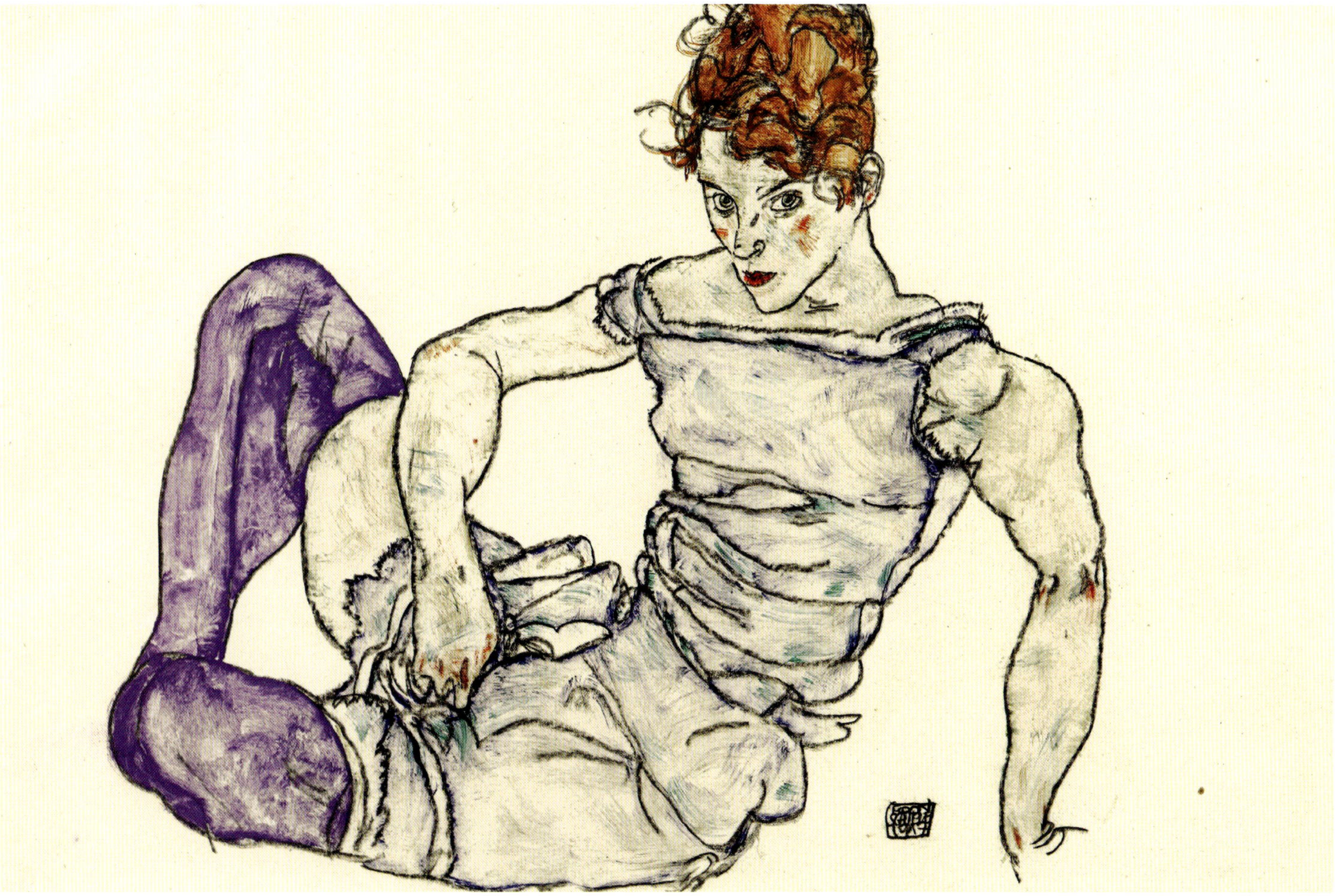

Cat. 10
EGON SCHIELE
Seated Woman in Violet Stockings, 1917
Gouache and black crayon, 29.6 x 44.2 cm
Private collection, courtesy of Richard Nagy Ltd., London

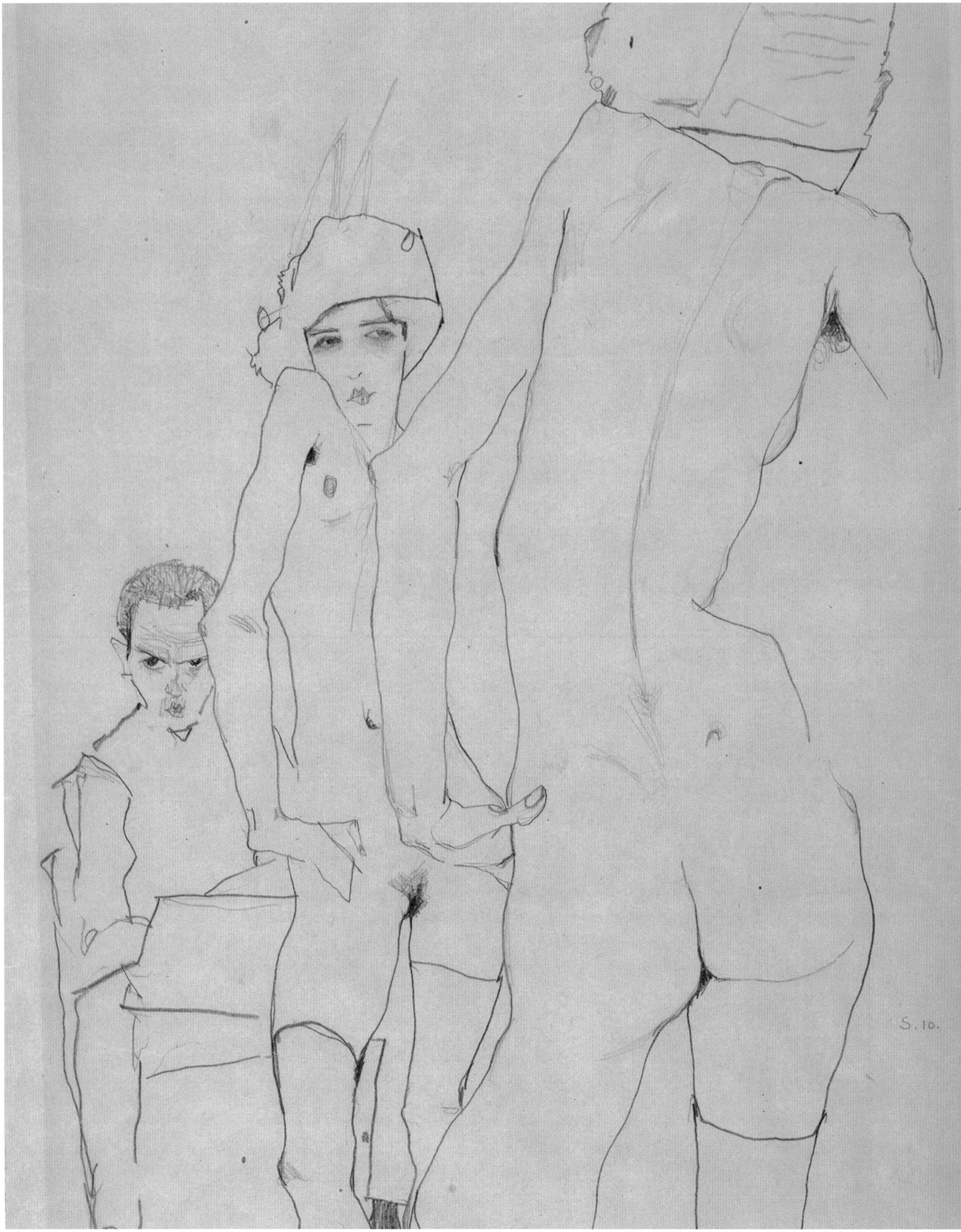
S. 10.

Gustav Klimt, Egon Schiele, Oskar Kokoschka Men Looking at Women Looking at Men

Jane Kallir

Fig. 1
EGON SCHIELE
Schiele Drawing a Nude Model before a Mirror, 1910
Albertina, Vienna

Prior to the twentieth century, most Western artists were male, but females were a primary artistic subject. Women appeared frequently in portraits, and the nude was so predominantly female that gender is implicit in the term itself. The Madonna was an overarching emblem of motherhood that also influenced secular iterations of the theme. Depictions of (mostly heterosexual) couples ranged from idealizations of romantic love to parables of sexual aggression. Overtly erotic subjects were usually given a narrative overlay taken from classical mythology, literature, history, or the Bible. Thus was the prurient transformed into the paradigmatic. In all cases, the point of view was that of the male; the female was the passive object of his gaze and judgment.

The advent of industrial capitalism in the nineteenth century brought sweeping changes to European society and to the position of women therein. As men ventured forth to earn their living through entrepreneurship and the capital markets (if they were lucky) or in factories (if they were not), the premise that "a woman's place is in the home" became increasingly untenable. Women who lacked male providers were often compelled to seek outside employment, but their options were pitifully curtailed by low pay, inferior education and overt gender discrimination. Bourgeois wives, on the other hand, chafed at the confines of their enforced domesticity. They began demanding expanded professional and educational opportunities, both for themselves and on behalf of their poorer sisters.

By the turn of the twentieth century, these incipient moves toward feminine equality had sparked a significant backlash within the male population. Men used the latest scientific discoveries to support the contention that, not only were they the superior sex, but the entire future of civilization depended on their remaining so. Evolution, it was said, had given women smaller bones and brains than men, making them inherently weaker and stupider.[1] Just as hermaphroditic life forms had gradually evolved into creatures with two distinct genders, theorists suggested that the human sexes had become more sharply differentiated over time. Gender parity came to be associated with the threat of devolution or degeneration, and male dominance with human progress.

Fin-de-siècle Vienna was awash with such hypotheses, which ranged from the scientific investigations of Sigmund Freud to the crackpot formulations of Otto Weininger. In his hugely popular tract, *Sex and Character*, Weininger proclaimed that "in [...] the absolute female, there are no logical and ethical phenomena, and therefore the ground for the assumption of a soul is absent."[2] "The woman is devoted totally to sexual matters," he explained, "that is to say, to the spheres of begetting and reproduction." Whereas "man possesses sexual organs, her sexual organs possess woman."[3] Freud, to the contrary, believed that "exaggerated sexual cravings" in a woman are not normal. "Libido," he averred, "is invariably and necessarily of a masculine nature."[4]

Inevitably, this stew of ideas came to inform contemporary representations of women. Weininger's and Freud's contradictory views of female sexuality were reconciled in the common Madonna/whore dichotomy. *Fin-de-siècle* art abounds with images of chaste mothers and lascivious female sexual predators. Gustav Klimt's vaunted society portraits might be said to epitomize Weininger's soulless females: woman reduced to the totality of her glittery raiment. If these proper ladies have the sexless allure of Byzantine Madonnas, the wanton "whore" is amply represented in other facets of the artist's oeuvre: his treacherous *Judith* (p. 27, fig. 13); his slithery *Waterserpents* (p. 40, fig. 13). Klimt even embodied the double standard in his personal life, fathering an unknown number of illegitimate children with lower-class models, while maintaining a lifelong platonic relationship with the bourgeois Emilie Flöge.[5]

The double standard was a way for *fin-de-siècle* man to compartmentalize his libido, to exert rational control over instinctual urges that were as frightening in himself as they were in his female partners. Nonetheless, by the early twentieth century, the bourgeois conventions that enforced this compartmentalization had come to seem patently hypocritical if not downright pernicious. It is no coincidence that Klimt and his younger colleagues Egon Schiele and Oskar Kokoschka turned repeatedly to classical female artistic subjects—the portrait, the mother and child, the couple and the nude—in seeking to resolve the urgent mysteries of gender. By exploring such subjects, the three artists simultaneously exhumed their own sexuality: their fears, sorrows, hopes, and ecstasies. Schiele and Kokoschka picked up where Klimt left off, testing and revisiting established gender norms as their life experiences and perspectives changed.

By the end of 1918, Klimt and Schiele were dead. Only Kokoschka would live on, into the 1920s and beyond. The Habsburg monarchy had collapsed, and with it the Austro-Hungarian Empire. In 1919, the new Austrian republic established female suffrage as well as universal secondary education for girls. Increasingly, women were permitted to attend university and pursue serious professional careers. This so-called "new woman" had been anticipated in the work of Schiele and Kokoschka. During the waning years of Habsburg rule, they had transformed the female image, refashioning traditional tropes for the modern era. Their women do not necessarily submit passively to the male artistic gaze. They look back and demand to be understood on their own terms.

1 See, for example, Emile Durkheim, *The Divisions of Labor in Society*, 1893, and Arabella Kenealy, *Feminism and Sex-Extinction*, London 1920. The German psychiatrist Paul Julius Möbius encapsulated this concept in the title of his 1900 treatise, *Über den physiologischen Schwachsinn des Weibe*s (On the Physiological Feeble-Mindedness of Women).
2 Cited in Bram Dijkstra, *Idols of Perversity: Fantasies of Feminine Evil in Fin-de-Siècle Culture*, New York 1986, p. 219.
3 Ibid.
4 Sigmund Freud, "The Sexual Instinct in Neurotics," in *Three Essays on the Theory of Sexuality*, 1905, reprinted in Peter Gay (ed.), *The Freud Reader*, New York 1989, p. 255.
5 Hedwig Langer, who lived near the house on the Attersee where Klimt and Flöge summered, insisted: "They were never real lovers, they had no relationship! Never!" (cited in Alfred Weidinger [ed.], *Gustav Klimt*, New York/Munich 2007, p. 209).

Portraiture

Throughout much of Europe, the importance of portraiture declined after the invention of photography, and the painted likeness was of comparatively little interest to most avant-garde artists. However, the genre enjoyed a lingering vogue in *fin-de-siècle* Austria. Unlike their colleagues in other European cities, Vienna's Modernists did not have a robust network of commercial galleries to support them. Artist-run initiatives such as the Vienna Secession (founded in 1897), the Wiener Werkstätte (1903–1932), the 1908 *Kunstschau* and the 1909 *Internationale Kunstschau,* were the avant-garde's principal marketing tools. Direct contact between artist and patron thus remained the norm in Austria far longer than was the case elsewhere in Europe, and this, in turn, established the basis for a flourishing portrait market. Even as industrial capitalism was transforming social and aesthetic values across the continent, newly wealthy Austrians sought immortality by commissioning portraits, much as their aristocratic predecessors had done.

Klimt was, without question, the preeminent portraitist of his era, and after 1900 all his portrait subjects were female. Frequently married off to wealthy older men for business reasons, prevented from pursuing any sort of professional ambition, these women expressed their intellectual and artistic proclivities as hostesses and collectors. The Klimt *Dame*, cloaked in the latest fashions and up to her neck in ruffles or jewels, represented an extreme of luxury that was simultaneously seductive and imprisoning. The artist's canvases were prized for their rich surfaces. The pseudo-pointillist brushwork in his Portrait of *Marie Henneberg* (cat. 13) gave way to the ornament-studded geometry of the gold period (cat. 15), and then to the bright, painterly patterns seen in the portrait of Eugenie Primavasi (cat. 30). Foreground melted into background. Often all that remained of the sitter was her pale face and hands, the sole three-dimensional elements in an essentially abstract scheme.

One is hard-pressed to discern the personalities of Klimt's women. The contemporary critic Bertha Zuckerkandl noted approvingly that the artist did away with "any individual characteristics, so that only the typical, a sublime extract of the female type, is captured in pure style."[1] When the famous Portrait *of Adele Bloch-Bauer I* (fig. 2) was first exhibited in Vienna, one wag remarked that it was, "more *Blech* (tin) than Bloch." There is no way of guessing from the painting that its subject was a frustrated intellectual, headachy, frail, and stuck in

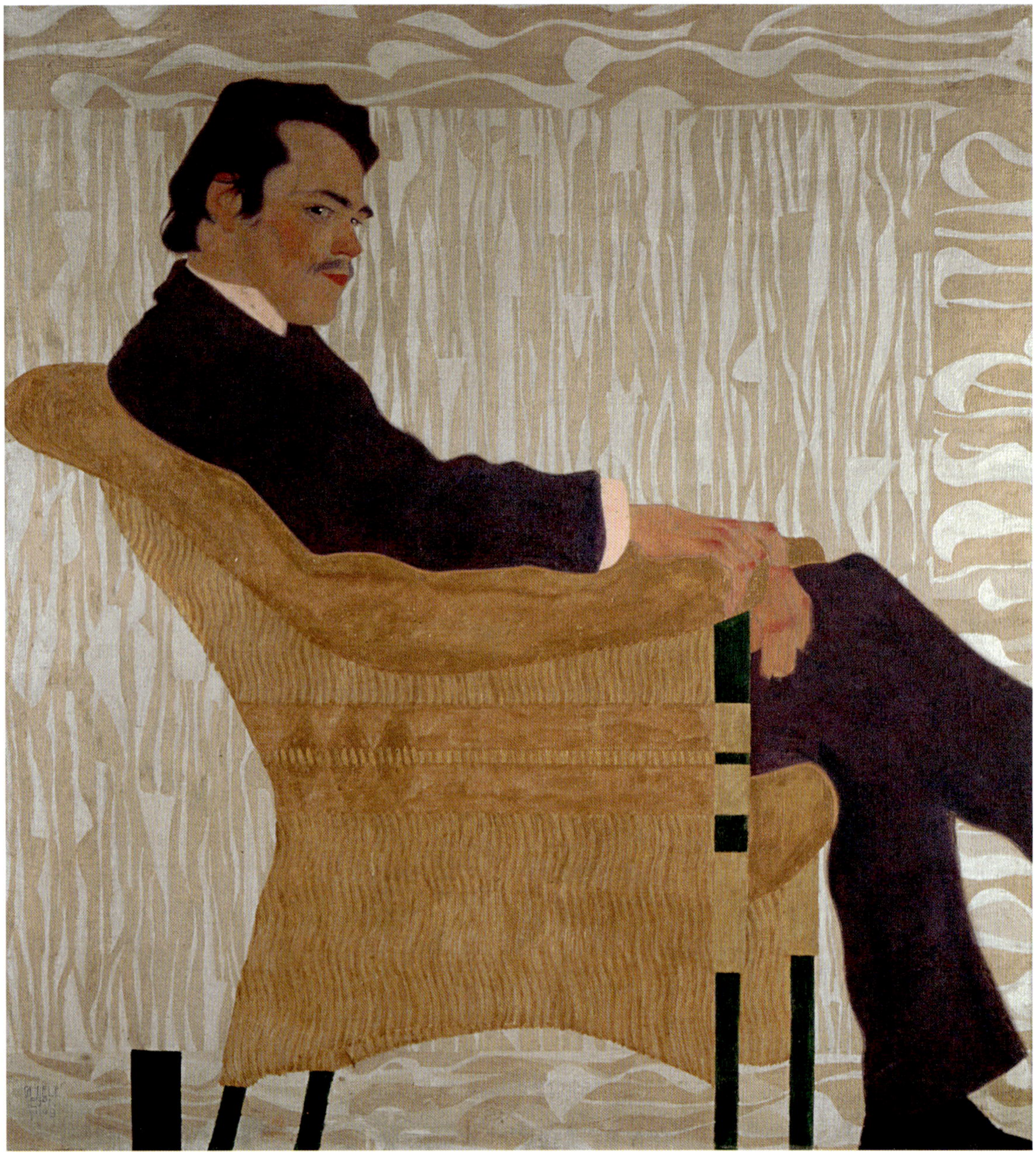

Fig. 1
EGON SCHIELE
The Painter Hans Massmann, 1909
Kunsthaus Zug, Stiftung Sammlung Kamm, Zug

a loveless marriage. Klimt did more than 130 studies for this portrait (cat. 11, 12), exploring the contours of Adele's face and the folds of her dress in obsessive detail, but never touching her soul. What went on under that golden shell was a mystery. Although Klimt, elsewhere in his work, was a connoisseur of female sexuality, his portraits are surprisingly sexless. Except for the occasional hint of demure décolleté, the sitters' bodies are completely concealed. Each woman is encased in a flat decorative surround, much like a figure in a Russian icon. However, embedded in this surround are emblems that allude to her underlying sexual identity. Several art historians have identified symbols said to represent sperm and ova in the gold-period paintings.[2] Klimt inserted motifs lifted from East Asian art in later portraits, establishing a connection between the sitter and what would then have been considered "primitive" cultures. For better or for worse, woman at this time was seen as the antithesis of

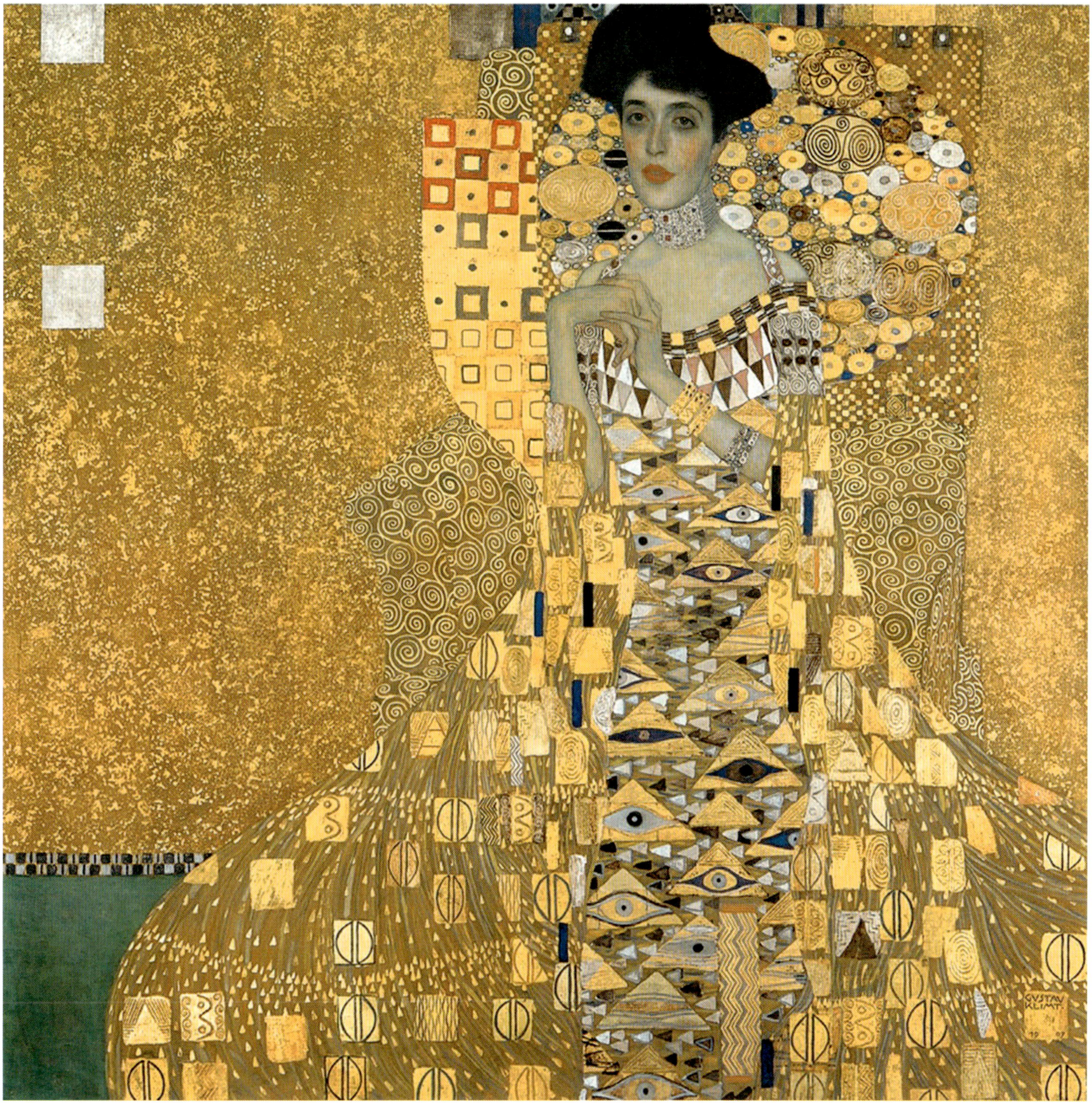

Fig. 2
GUSTAV KLIMT
Adele Bloch-Bauer I, 1907
Neue Galerie, New York

Western rationalism. No matter how heavily cloaked by the mantel of bourgeois propriety, she could not escape her fundamental nature.

The 1908 *Kunstschau* and the 1909 *Internationale Kunstschau* are generally recognized as marking the transition from Klimt's heyday to the Expressionist era. Kokoschka, then twenty-two, made his public debut in 1908, and Schiele, then nineteen, made his in 1909. Both were still strongly influenced by the decorative figuration of the Viennese *Jugendstil*.

Kokoschka in 1908 was studying to be an art teacher at the Kunstgewerbeschule [School of Applied Arts] and doing decorative illustrations for the Wiener Werkstätte. Schiele was so bowled over by Klimt's contributions to the 1908 *Kunstschau* that he spent the ensuing year paraphrasing them (fig. 1). The portraits Schiele exhibited at the 1909 *Internationale Kunstschau* shamelessly emulated the master's use of triangulated, off-center poses, geometric patterning and metallic pigment (fig. 2, cat. 15). The breakthrough contribution to the *Kunstschau* was Kokoschka's portrait of the actor Ernst Reinhold (WE 11). Unlike Schiele, Kokoschka had not been academically educated, and he drew his influences as much from ethnographic as from fine arts sources. Applying paint with his fingertips, scoring the surface with the pointed tip of his brush, he created some of Austria's first Expressionist paintings.[3] The architect Adolf Loos, who despised the Wiener Werkstätte, decided that Kokoschka was a potential ally. Loos persuaded the fledgling painter to leave the Werkstätte by offering to set him up as a portraitist.

Even as the tide began to turn in favor of the younger Expressionists, portraiture remained *the* way to establish an artistic reputation.[4] By early 1910, Kokoschka had completed thirty-one paintings of Loos's friends and acquaintances.[5] At around the same time, Schiele met the art critic Arthur Roessler, who likewise endeavored to secure portrait commissions for his protégé. Schiele had at this point abandoned the decorative approach of his *Kunstschau* portraits, though a Klimtian residue survives in his elegant use of line and sensitive deployment of negative space. While the scraped surfaces and muted tonalities of Schiele's 1910 portraits echo Kokoschka's work, the more direct influence was probably Max Oppenheimer, a painter whose style was very similar.[6]

Of thirty-seven portraits painted by Kokoschka in 1909 and 1910, only eleven depict women (WE 23, 32, 33, 34, 36, 38, 39, 42, 47, 54, 58). Schiele executed only three commissioned paintings of women over the course of his entire brief career (Kp 201, 223, 276). The contemporary critic Wilhelm Michel, channeling Otto Weininger, averred that women were inherently ill-suited to the new "psychological" type of portraiture practiced by the Expressionists. "As a rule, lovers of the mysterious and interpreters of the soul will not find [in the female portrait] any treasures to tempt them," he wrote.[7] However, there is no indication that either Kokoschka or Schiele thought this way. The paucity of female sitters in their work was caused by an aversion on the part of the subjects themselves.

Because Loos had to inveigle sitters by promising to buy the results if they were dissatisfied, he ended up with some thirty of Kokoschka's early oils, including the portraits of Martha Hirsch (cat. 21), Elizabeth Reitler (cat. 16) and Emma Veronika Sanders (cat. 19).[8] Karen Michaelis's reaction to her Kokoschka portrait (WS 343) is typical, if perhaps somewhat extreme: "What a picture! A three-month prison term would not have been punishment enough for the 'damage to my name and reputation' which he caused me."[9] Trying to convince Lotte Franzos (WE 34) to accept her portrait, the artist explained that facial resemblance was not the point. "Do you really think the way a person affects me is cut off at the neck?" he asked. "Hair, hands, dress and movement are just as important to me. [...] I do not paint anatomical specimens."[10] Kokoschka claimed to be blessed with "second sight." Speaking about the portrait of Emma Veronika Sanders, he explained that the subject "had seemed so distant and absent-minded that her 'inner face' revealed itself."[11] Reality evidently caught up with the portrait when, a few years later, Sanders suffered a mental breakdown. Kokoschka's ability to foreshadow such events, to see below a carefully constructed façade, accounts for the discomfort experienced by male and female subjects alike.

Schiele, like Kokoschka, had difficulty getting his early sitters to accept or pay for their portraits.[12] His first commissioned painting of a woman was done in 1911 at the behest of the dentist Hermann Engel, probably in exchange for professional services (cat. 26). It is not known what exactly transpired between Schiele and Engel's daughter Trude, but it may be inferred that the two had a sexual dalliance. Enraged, Hermann ended up over-painting a portion of the canvas he found "too intimate."[13] Schiele's next female portrait, of Arthur Roessler's wife Ida (cat. 25), suggests that no love

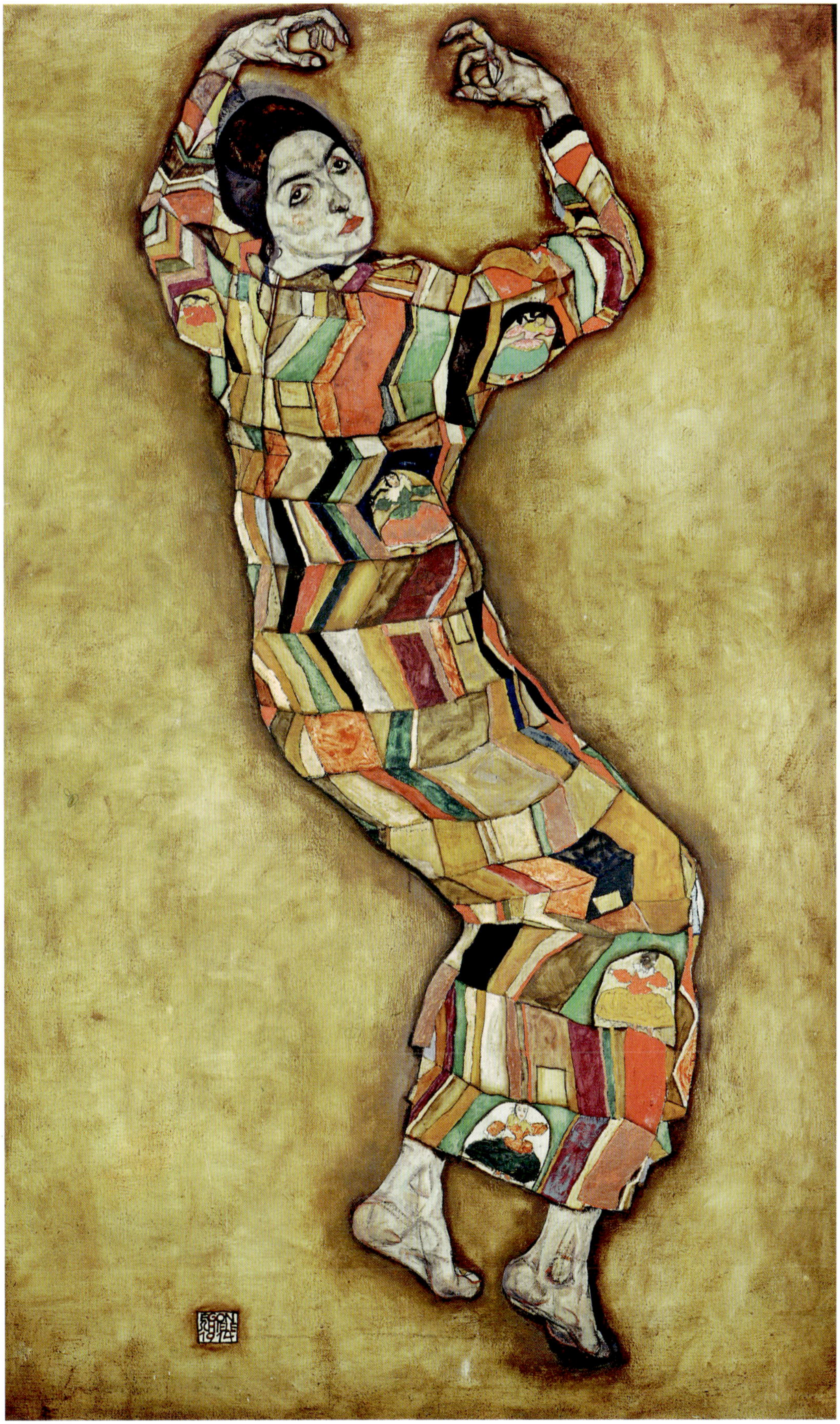

Fig. 3
EGON SCHIELE
Friederike Maria Beer, 1914
Private collection

was lost between these two. Ida Roessler probably disapproved of the artist's more erotic works, which were a powerful attraction for many male collectors.[14] Schiele's final commissioned female portrait, of Friederike Maria Beer (fig. 3, cat. 32), was his most ambitious, but it, too, was not entirely well received. "My mistress [...] looks as though she lies in the tomb!" the sitter's maid exclaimed.[15]

Many of Schiele's paintings of women, starting with his 1909 depiction of his sister Gerti (cat. 17), can be described as inside-out Klimts. Although the women are colorfully dressed, the patterning does not extend into the background. Kokoschka's portrait backgrounds are similarly vacant, but he lacked Schiele's sensitivity to negative space. By focusing on the tension between his subject and the surrounding void, Schiele created a profound sense of existential anxiety. The woman is pinioned like a butterfly in a specimen box or, as Beer's maid put it, like a corpse in a coffin. Schiele's first full-length portrait of his wife Edith (cat. 37) seems almost to caricature the doll-like beauties that populate Klimt's paintings. Edith's sister Adele is said to have been infuriated. "Why did he have to show her so dumb-looking?" she complained.[16]

Schiele's marriage was not especially happy, but over the course of time his interactions with Edith sensitized him to the workings of the female psyche. A second large portrait of Edith (cat. 41), completed in 1918, reveals a far more fully developed personality than does the first. While the artist never completed another female portrait oil, he did do many drawings of women in 1917–18. Always a demon draftsman, he was able to capture their moods with photographic precision. These late portraits have the spontaneity of snapshots: fleeting images that nonetheless provide glimpses into the soul (cat. 39, 40, 42, 43). The women are real human beings, not Klimtian emblems of femininity.

Like Schiele, Kokoschka adjusted his approach to female portraiture as he gained greater familiarity with the opposite sex. But unlike Schiele, he never succeeded in penetrating the female personality. Nor, perhaps, did he want to. Kokoschka's portraits of Alma Mahler, his lover from 1912 to 1915, are remarkably opaque (cat. 24). The most important of these (fig. 4) was in fact intended as a "new Gioconda": a replacement for Leonardo Da Vinci's renowned woman of mystery, which had recently been stolen from the Louvre.[17] Oskar was attracted to Alma's iconic remoteness. It is no coincidence that both she and his subsequent lover, the soprano Anna Kallin (cat. 45, 46), belonged to the world of music, a realm of largely wordless communication. Each of the women listening to *The Concert* (WW 140–144) in Kokoschka's 1920 series of that name is lost in a transportive reverie. In these and other female portraits from the period, the artist tried to capture a spiritual commonality beyond individual identity.

Kokoschka eventually became a successful painter of both men and women. From the outset, he had treated the two genders identically in his portraits. It is not so much "second sight" as a singular vision that characterizes these works. Kokoschka placed his personal stylistic imprint on each sitter, and in the process elevated him or her to the status of art object. The nature of portraiture had changed. People were now aware of the aesthetic and interpretive nuances that distinguish a painting from a photograph. Although the practical function of the painted portrait had diminished, its artistic possibilities had multiplied.

1 Bertha Zuckerkandl, "Gustav Klimt: Zur Eröffnung seiner Ausstellung," *Wiener Allgemeine Zeitung*, Nov. 14, 1903 (translated by Emily Braun).

2 See Emily Braun, "Ornament as Evolution: Gustav Klimt and Berta Zuckerkandl," in: Renée Price (ed.), *Gustav Klimt: The Ronald S. Lauder and Serge Sabarsky Collections* (exh. cat. Neue Galerie, New York), New York 2007, pp. 162–63. – Eric R. Kandel, *The Age of Insight*, New York 2012, pp. 115–118. – Alessandra Comini, *Gustav Klimt*, New York 1975, p. 15.

3 The painter Richard Gerstl, who committed suicide in 1908, was probably Austria's first Expressionist. Max Oppenheimer, a colleague of Kokoschka's, developed a very similar painting style around the same time.

4 The architect Otto Wagner is said to have advised the young Schiele as follows: "Paint a series of portraits of famous Viennese personalities—painters, sculptors, architects, graphic artists, musicians, poets, critics, prominent collectors, intellectuals, maybe even politicians. At least one dozen, preferably two. As soon as you have them together, you can become famous in a single stroke," cited in Arthur Roessler, *Erinnerungen an Egon Schiele*, Vienna 1948, pp. 19–20 (translated by Jane Kallir).

5 Alfred Weidinger and Alice Strobl, *Oskar Kokoschka: Die Zeichnungen und Aquarelle 1897–1916*, Salzburg 2008, pp. 209–210.

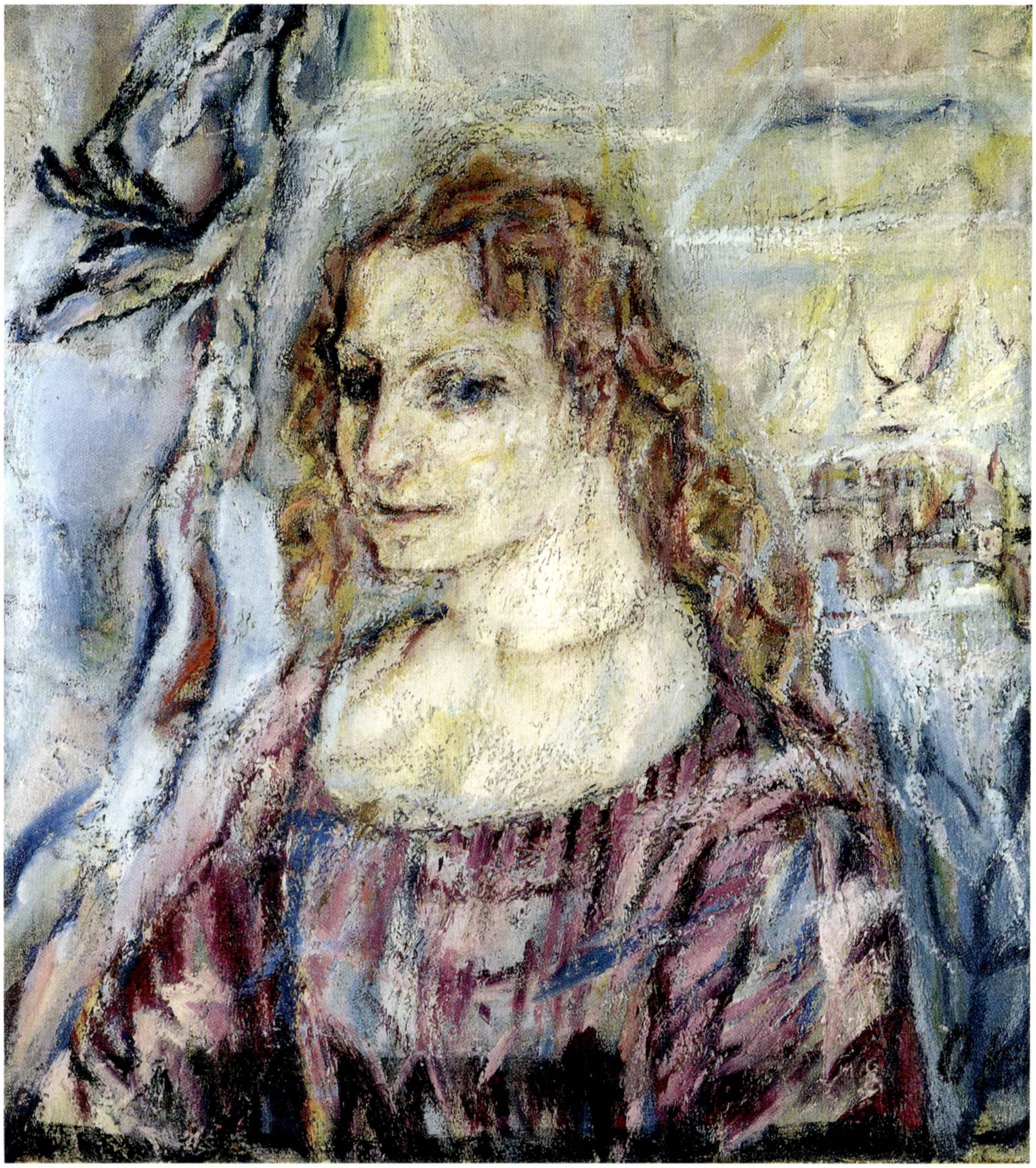

Fig. 4
OSKAR KOKOSCHKA
Alma Mahler, 1912
National Museum of Modern Art, Tokyo

6 Jane Kallir, *Egon Schiele: The Complete Works*, New York 1990, p. 62.
7 William Michel, *Max Oppenheimer*, Munich 1911, pp. 32–33 (translated by Michael Foster).
8 Werner J. Schweiger, "'Your Love Affair with my Paintings': Oskar Kokoschka and his Early Viennese Collectors," in: Tobias Natter (ed.), *Oskar Kokoschka: Early Portraits from Vienna and Berlin 1909–1914* (exh. cat. Neue Galerie, New York), New York 2002, p. 61.
9 Karin Michaelis, "Der tolle Kokoschka," in: *Das Kunstblatt*, vol. 2, no. 12, 1918, p. 361 (translated by Louise Schaefer).
10 Oskar Kokoschka, letter to Lotte Franzos, January 28, 1910, in: Olda Kokoschka and Heinz Spielmann (eds.), *Oskar Kokoschka Briefe I, 1905–1919*, Düsseldorf 1984, p. 11 (translated by Mary Whitall).
11 Michaelis 1918 (see note 9).
12 Otto Wagner (Kp 164) never completed his portrait sittings; Eduard Kosmak (Kp 165) evidently kept his portrait but refused to pay for it; Oskar Reichel (Kp 166) initially rejected his portrait and then almost immediately resold it.
13 Kallir 1990 (see note 6), p. 302.
14 Heinrich Benesch's wife and Erich Lederer's mother were among the women who voiced objections to Schiele and/or his work on moral grounds (see Christian M. Nebehay, *Egon Schiele 1890–1918: Leben, Briefe, Gedichte,* Salzburg/Vienna 1979, no. 190. – Christian M. Nebehay, *Gustav Klimt, Egon Schiele und die Familie Lederer*, Bern 1987, pp. 33, 94).
15 Alessandra Comini, *Egon Schiele's Portraits*, Berkeley 1974, p. 129.
16 Alessandra Comini, *Egon Schiele: Portraits* (exh. cat. Neue Galerie, New York), New York 2014, p. 38, note 25.
17 Weidinger and Strobl 2008 (see note 5), p. 292.

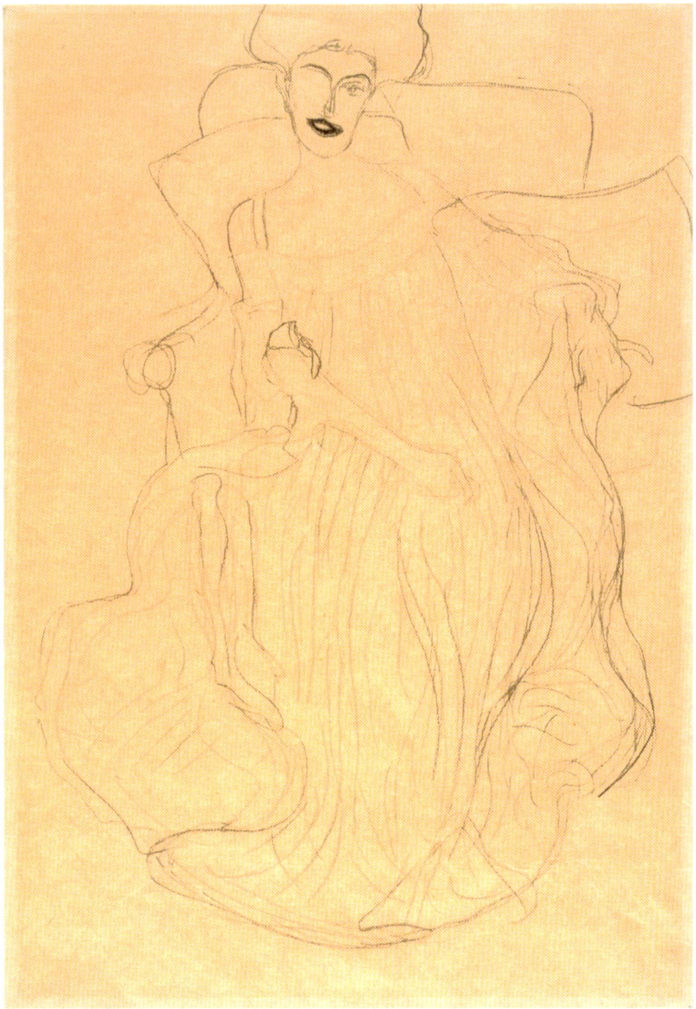

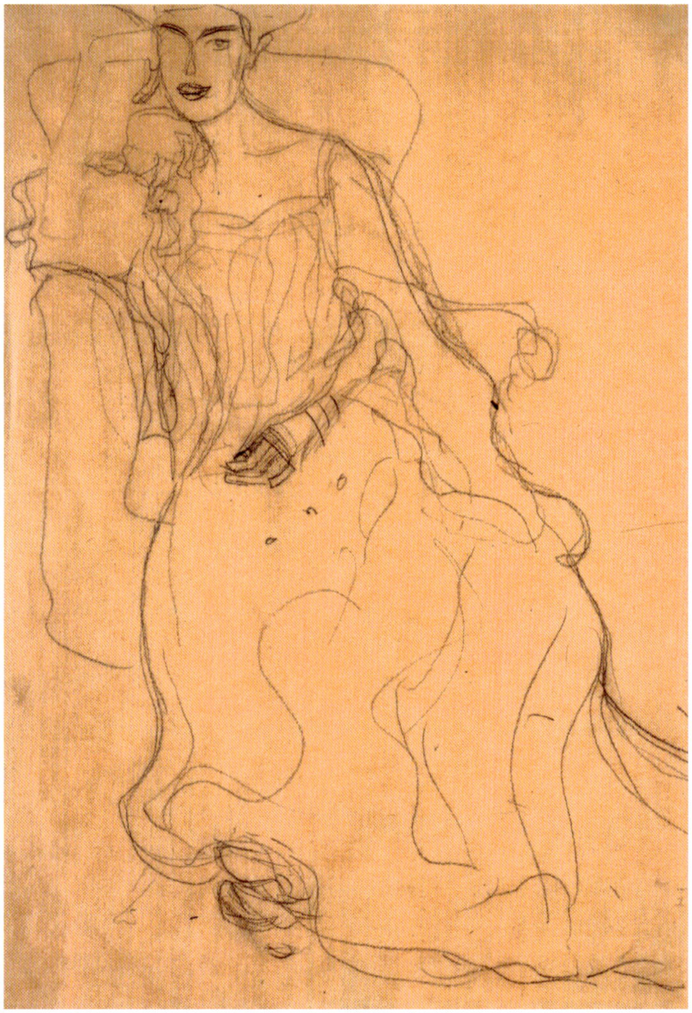

Cat. 11
GUSTAV KLIMT
Adele Bloch-Bauer Seated, Left Arm on Armrest, 1903
Black crayon on paper
45 x 31.5 cm
Private collection

Cat. 12
GUSTAV KLIMT
Adele Bloch-Bauer Seated in Armchair Facing Forward, Resting Her Temple on Her Right Hand, 1903
Black crayon on paper, 45.3 x 31.7 cm
Neue Galerie, New York

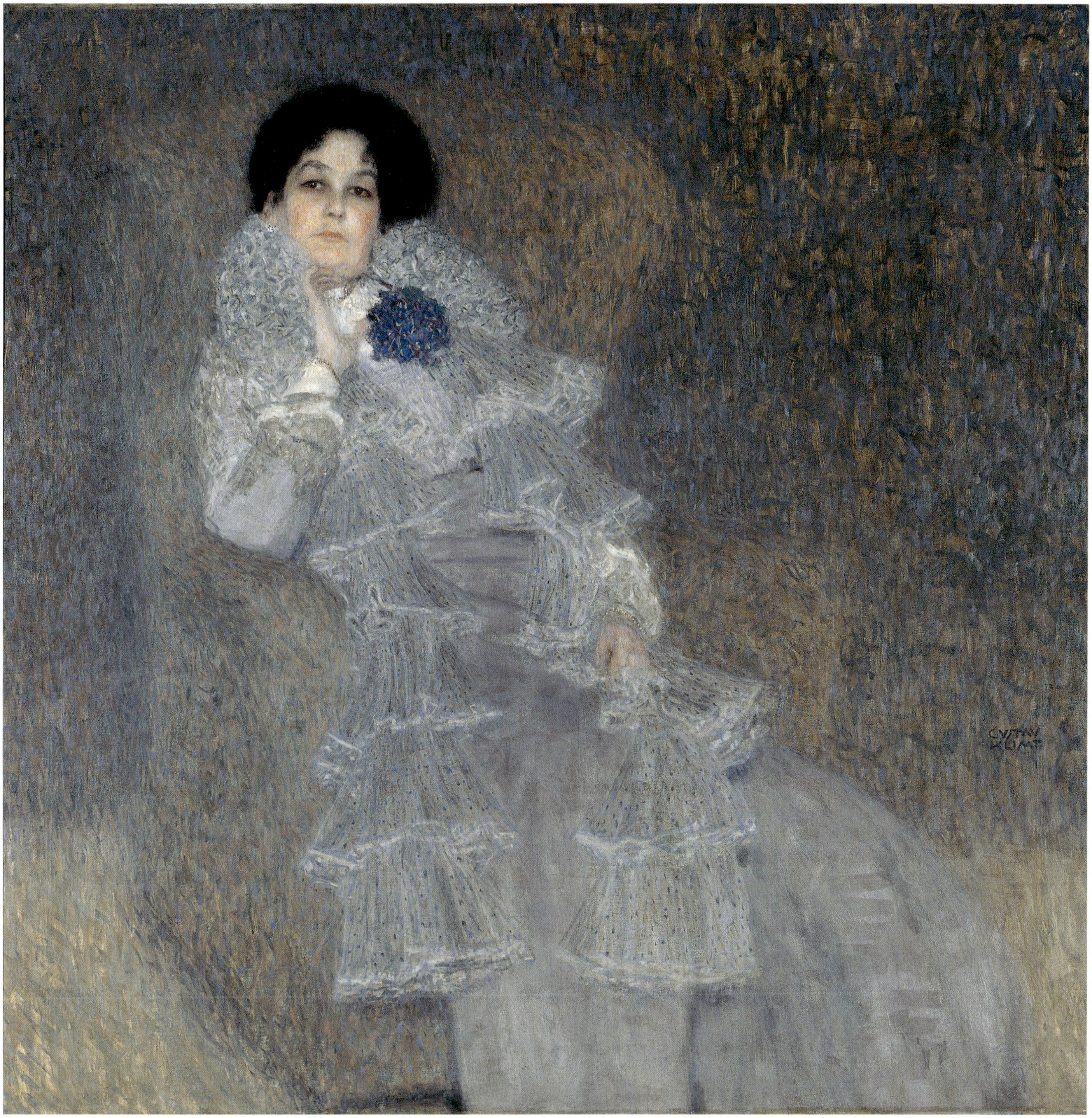

Cat.13
GUSTAV KLIMT
Marie Henneberg, 1901–02
Oil on canvas, 140 x 140 cm
Kunstmuseum Moritzburg, Halle (Saale)

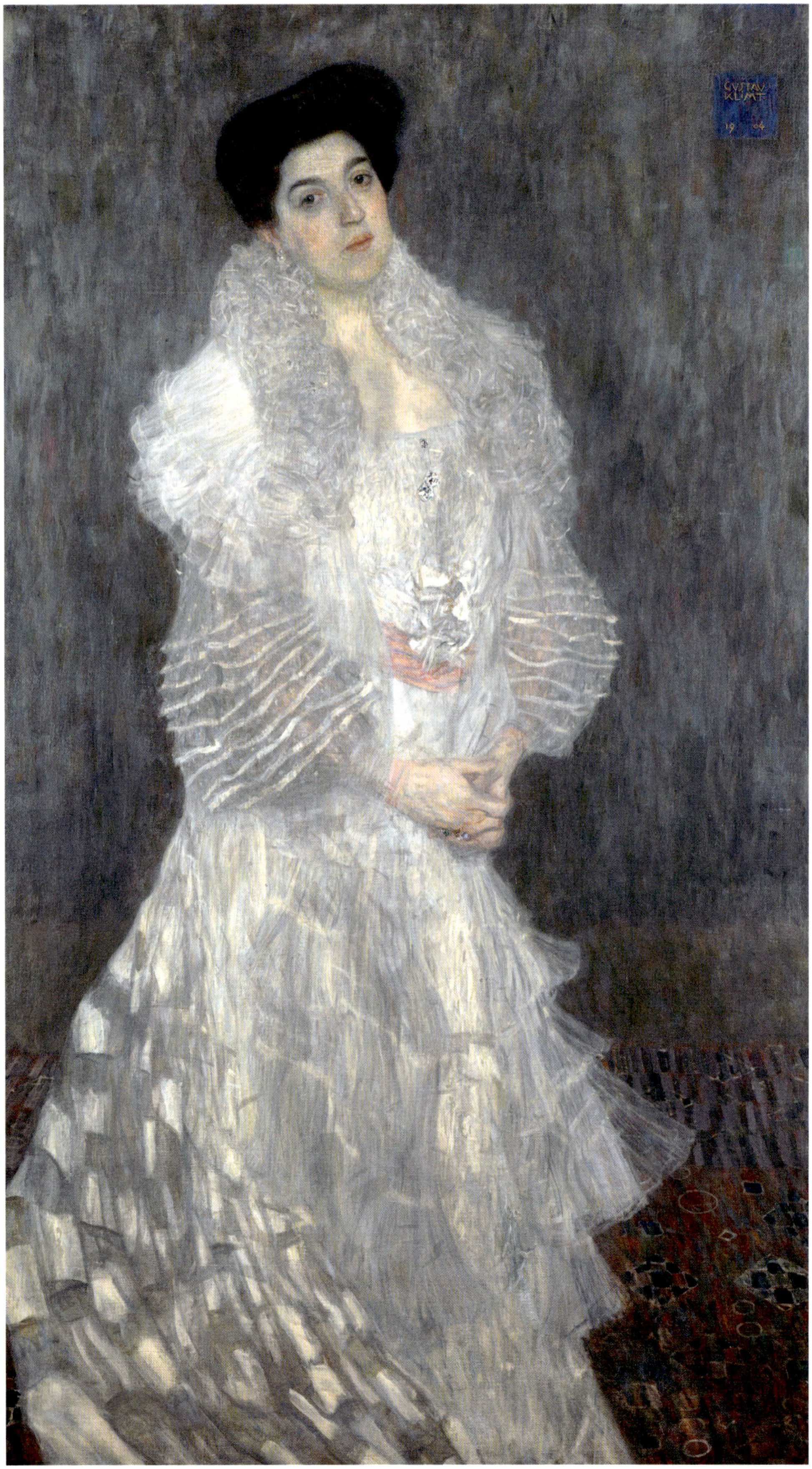

Cat. 14
GUSTAV KLIMT
Hermine Gallia, 1903–04
Oil on canvas, 170.5 x 96.5 cm
The National Gallery, London

Cat. 15
GUSTAV KLIMT
Fritza Riedler, 1906
Oil on canvas, 153 x 133 cm
Belvedere, Vienna

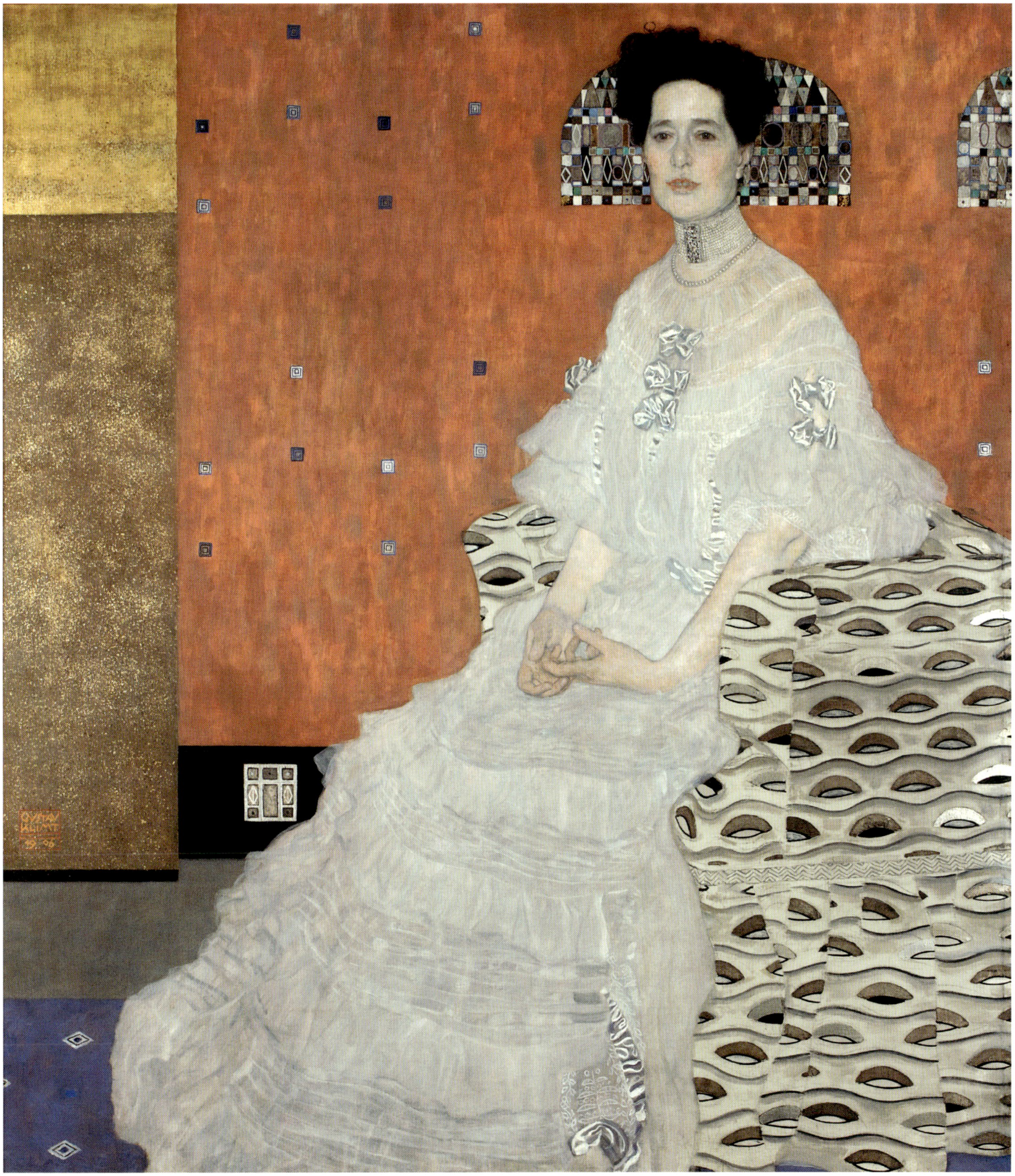

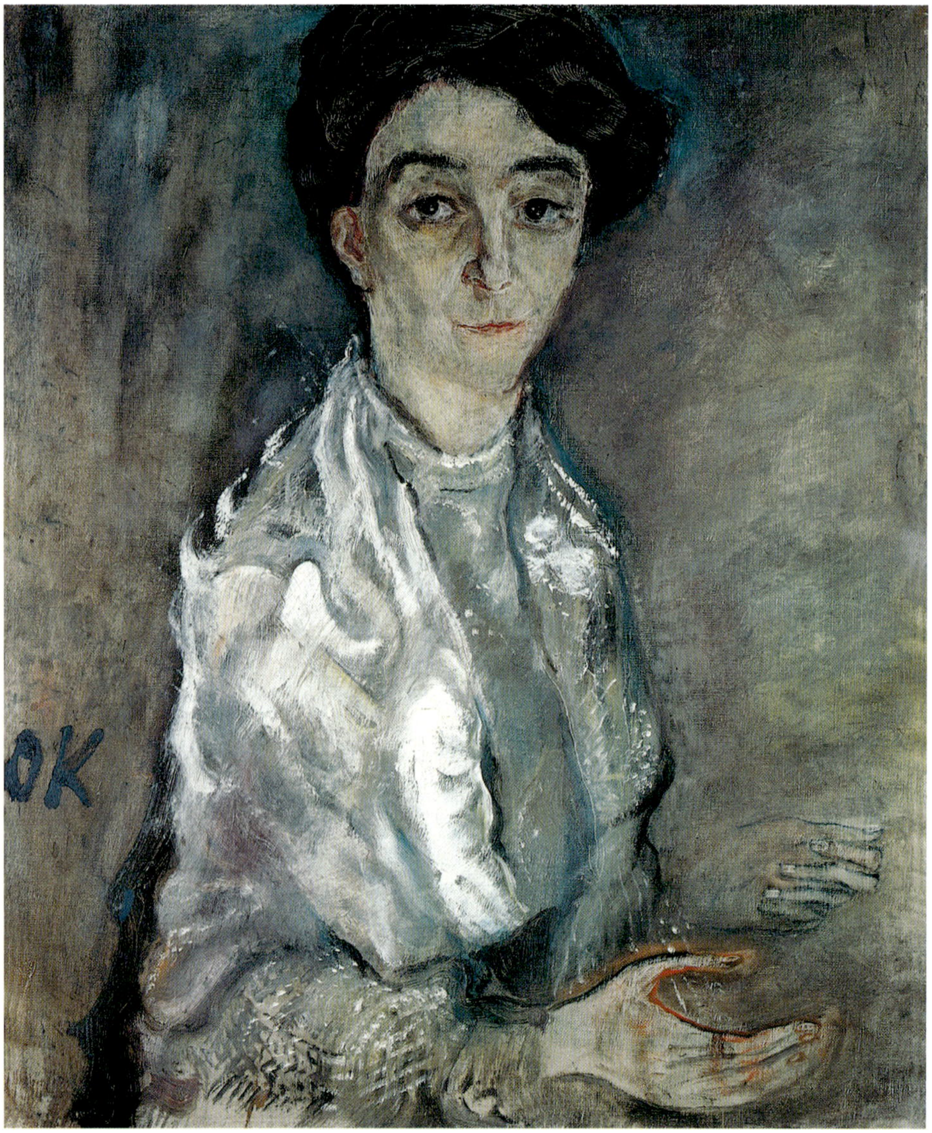

Cat. 16
OSKAR KOKOSCHKA
Elisabeth Reitler, 1909
Oil on canvas, 65 x 54 cm
Von der Heydt-Museum, Wuppertal

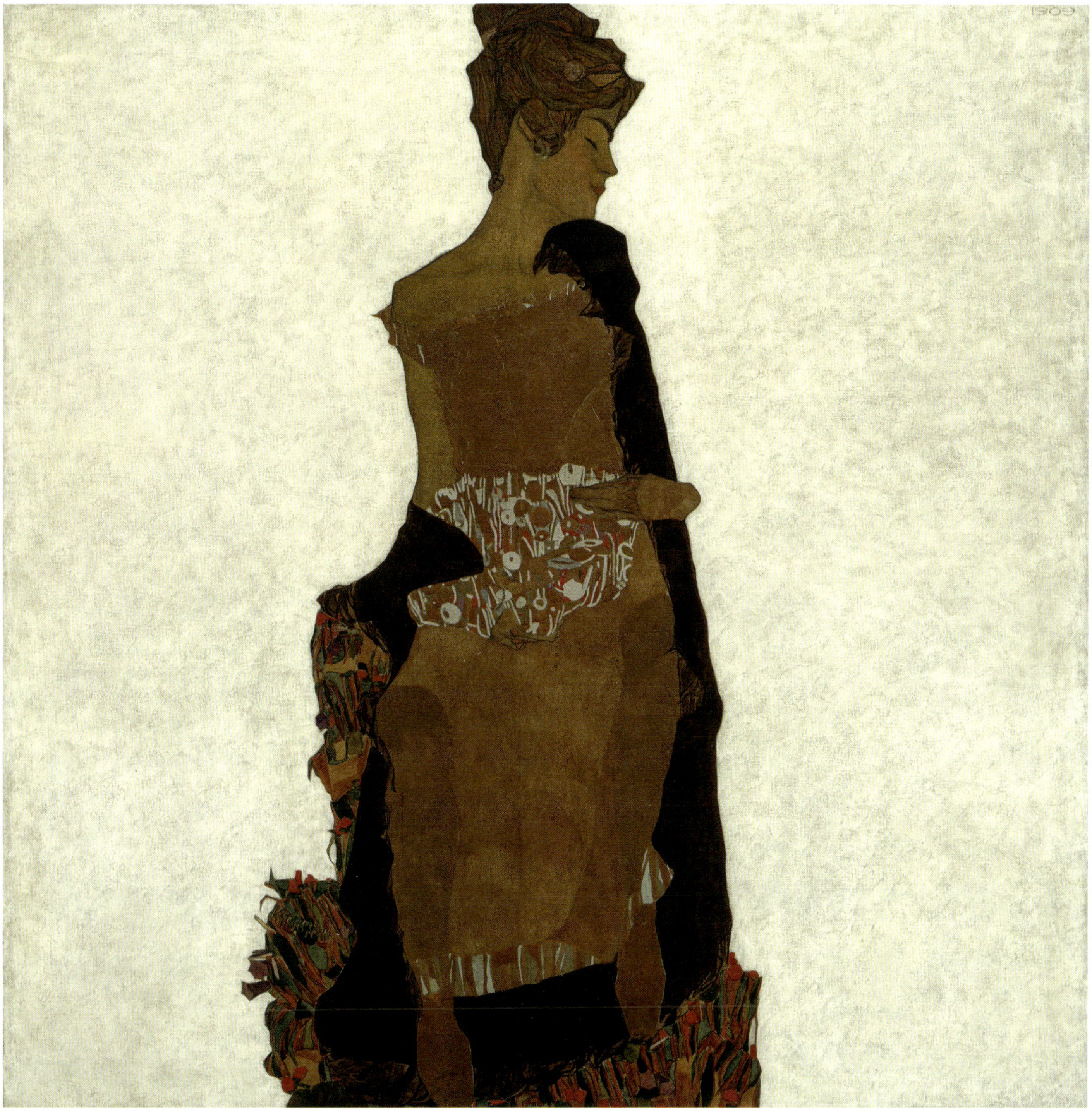

Cat. 17
EGON SCHIELE
Gerti Schiele, 1909
Oil and metallic paint on canvas, 139.5 x 140.5 cm
The Museum of Modern Art, New York, Purchase and partial gift of the Lauder family, 1982, and private collection, 1982

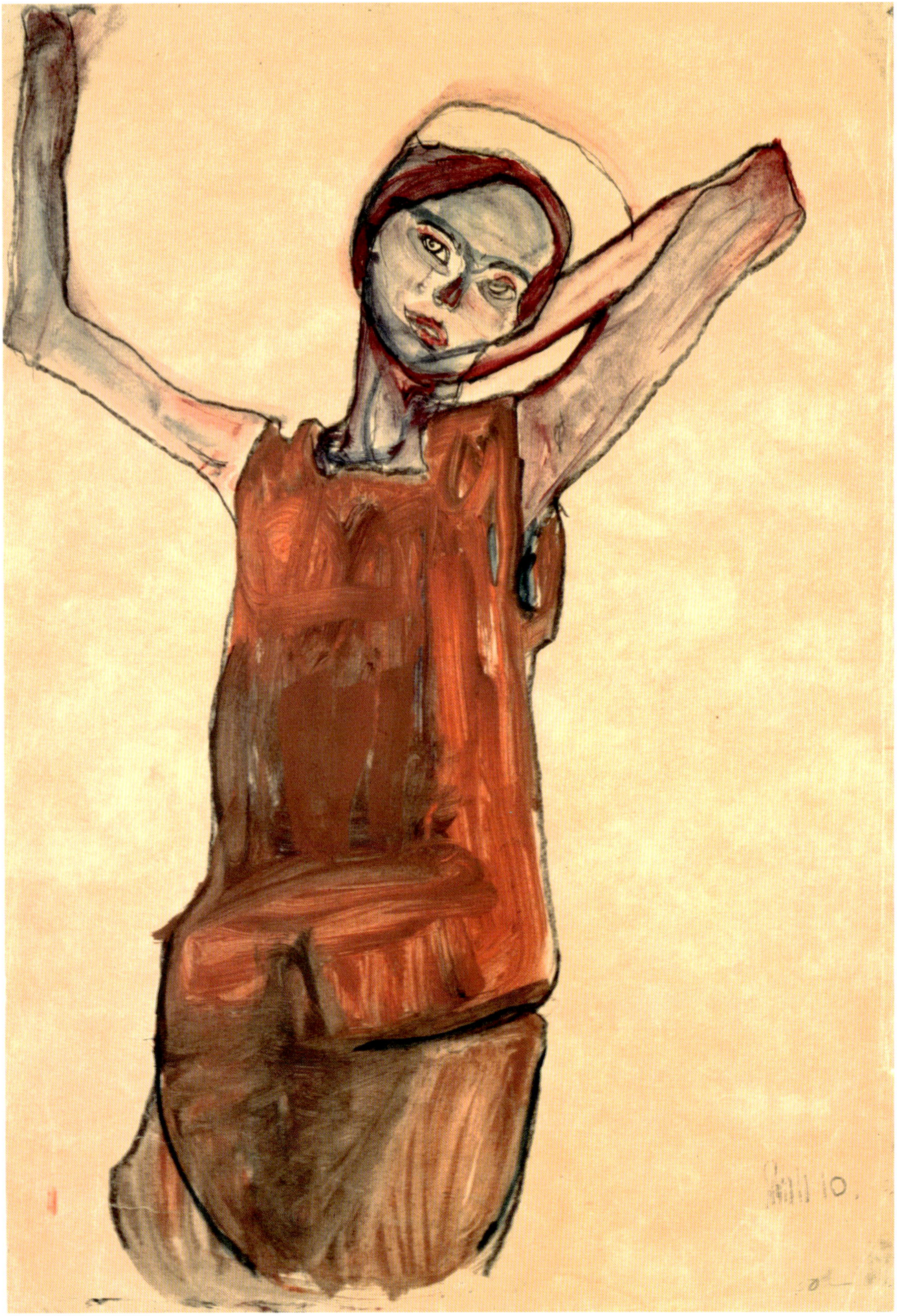

Cat. 18
EGON SCHIELE
Girl with Raised Arms, 1910
Gouache, watercolor, and charcoal on paper, 43.8 x 29.8 cm
Private collection

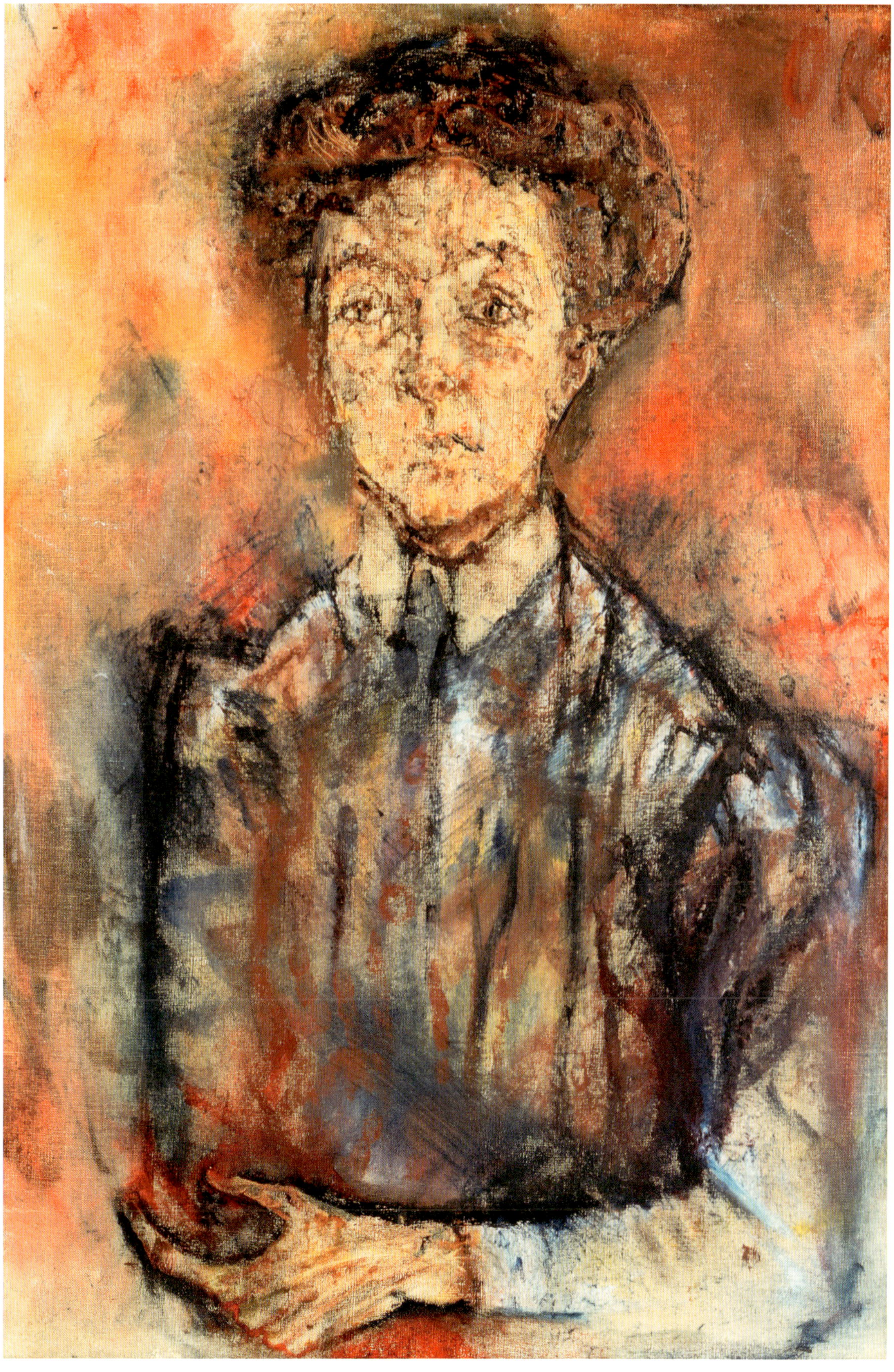

Cat. 19
OSKAR KOKOSCHKA
Emma Veronika Sanders, 1910
Oil on canvas, 82.7 x 56.7 cm
The Museum of Modern Art, New York, Gift of Mr. and Mrs. William Mazer, 1967

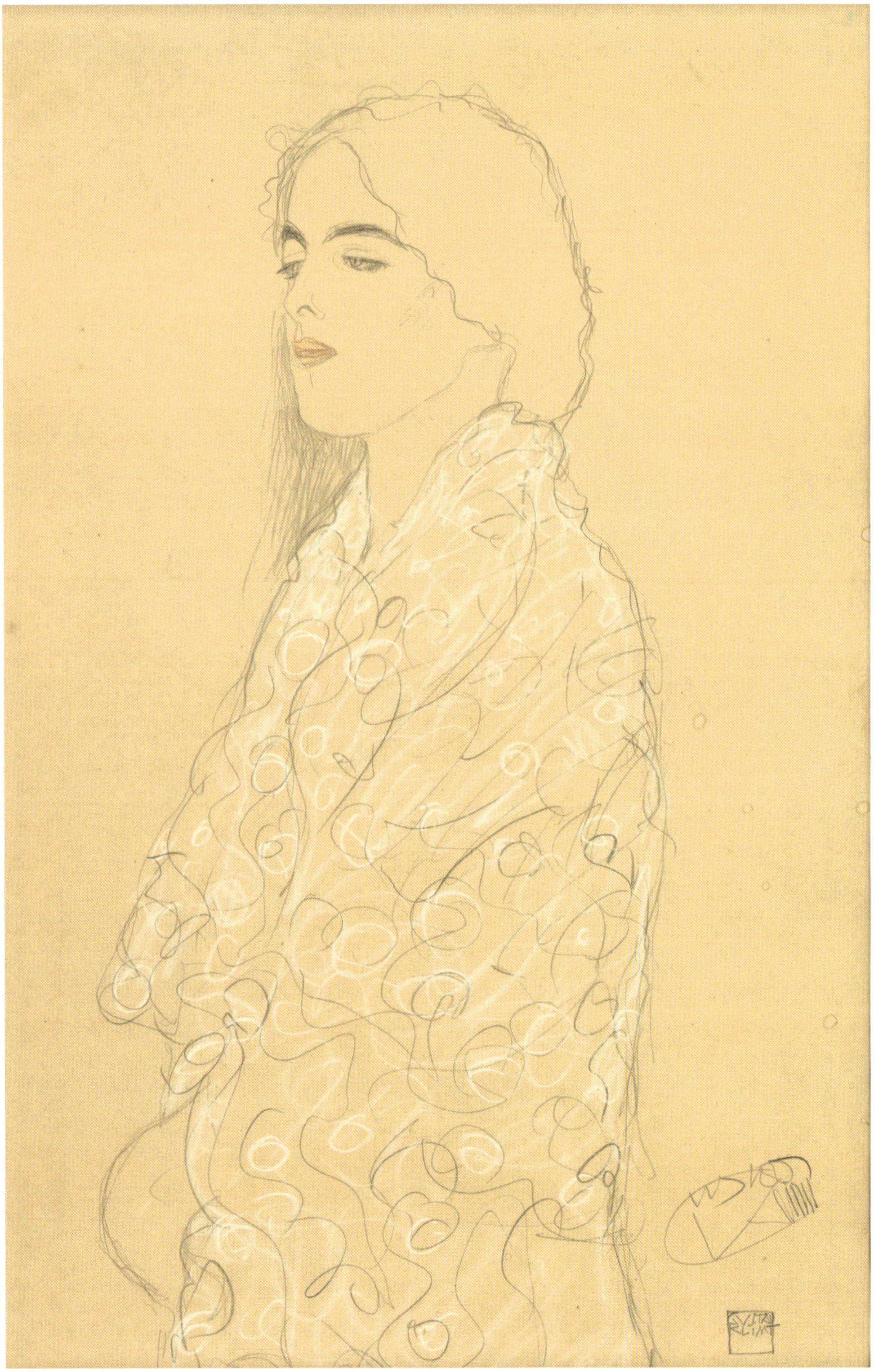

Cat. 20
GUSTAV KLIMT
Woman in Kimono Facing Left, 1910
Pencil, red pencil on paper, heightened, 54.8 x 36.9 cm
Private collection, courtesy of Neue Galerie, New York

Cat. 21
OSKAR KOKOSCHKA
Martha Hirsch, 1909
Oil on canvas, 88 x 70 cm
Private collection

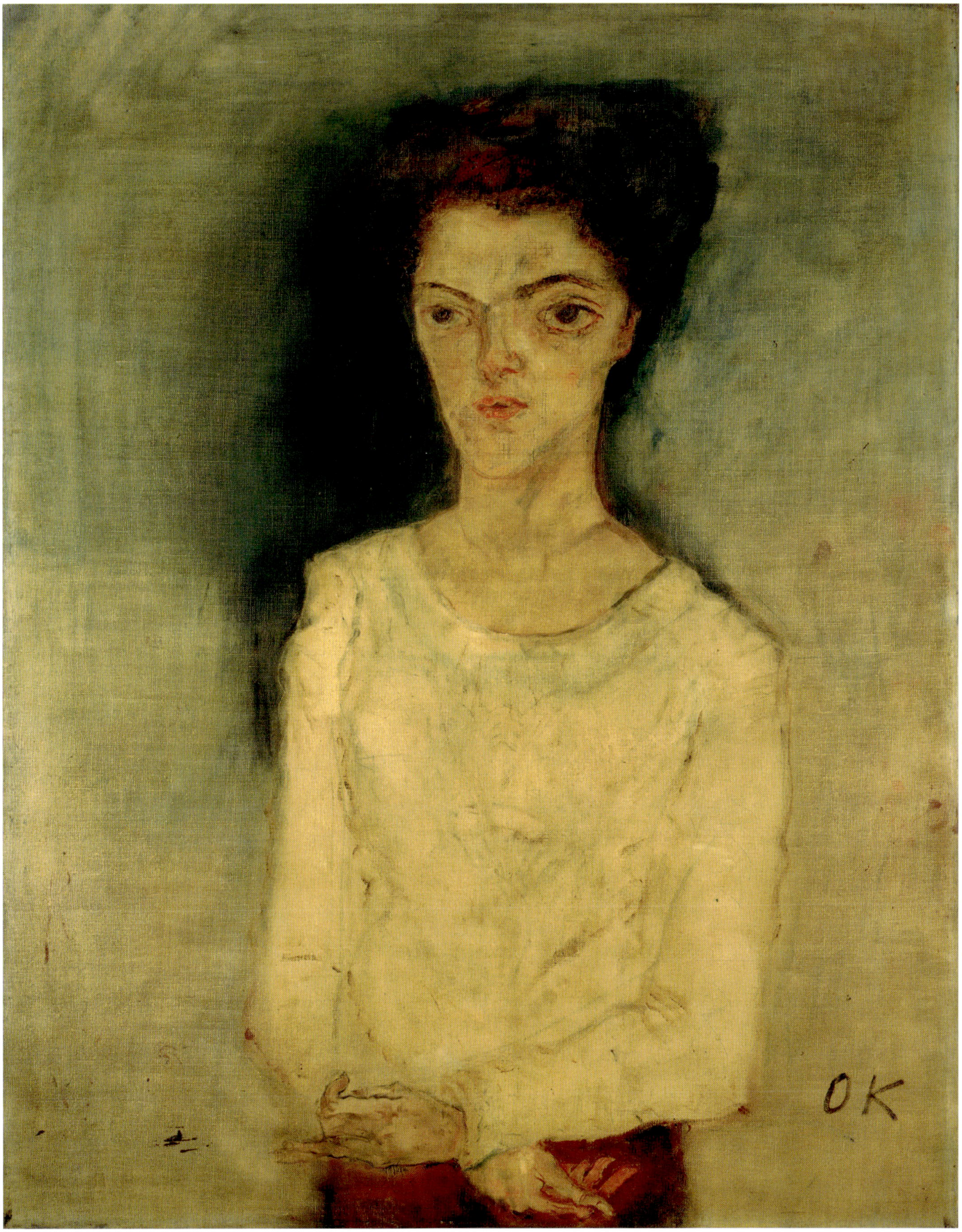
OK

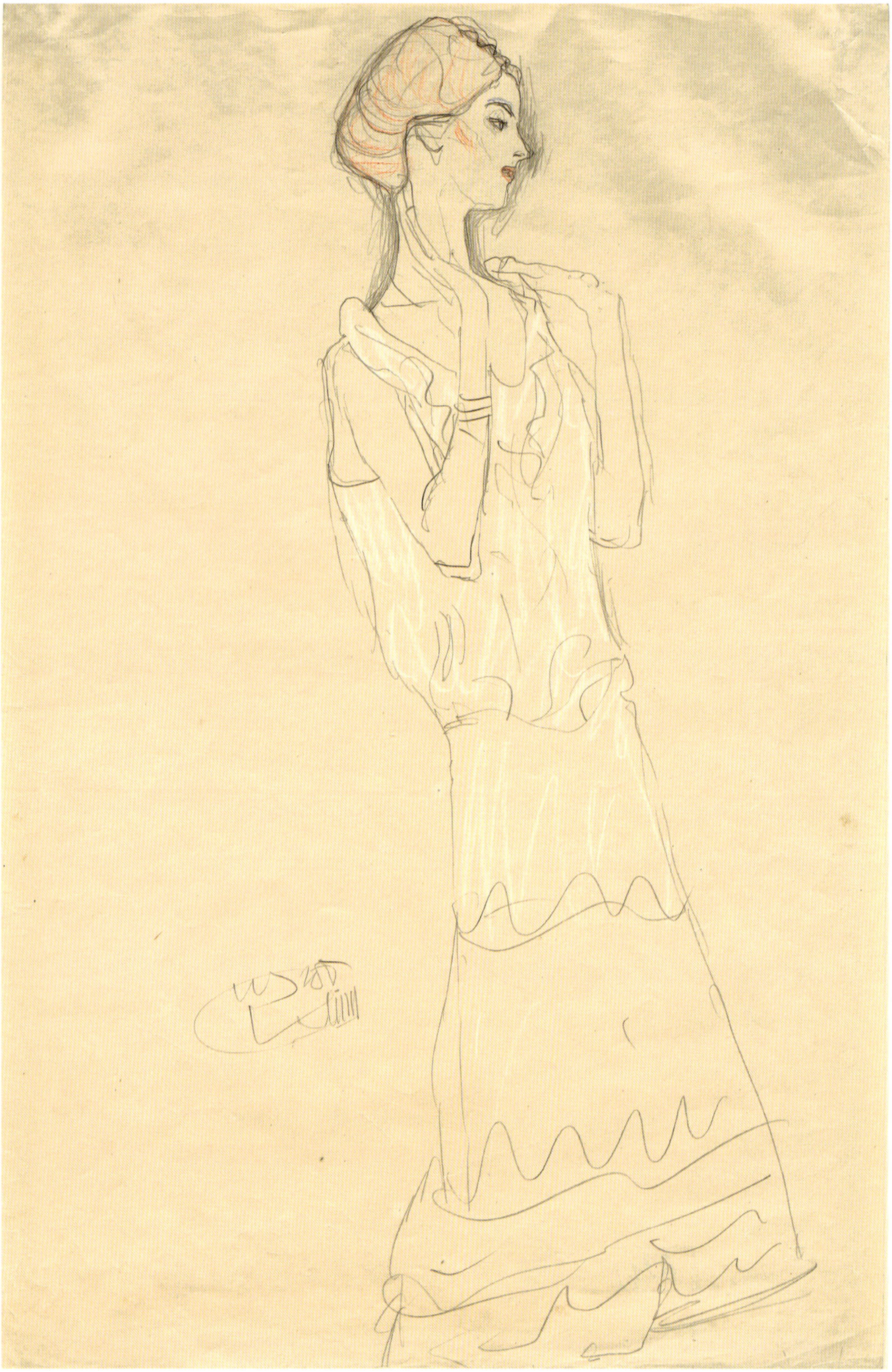

Cat. 22
GUSTAV KLIMT
Woman, Raised Lower Arms, Hands Bent Backwards, 1905–11
Pencil, red pencil and white crayon on paper, 55.9 x 36.8 cm
Private collection, courtesy of Neue Galerie, New York

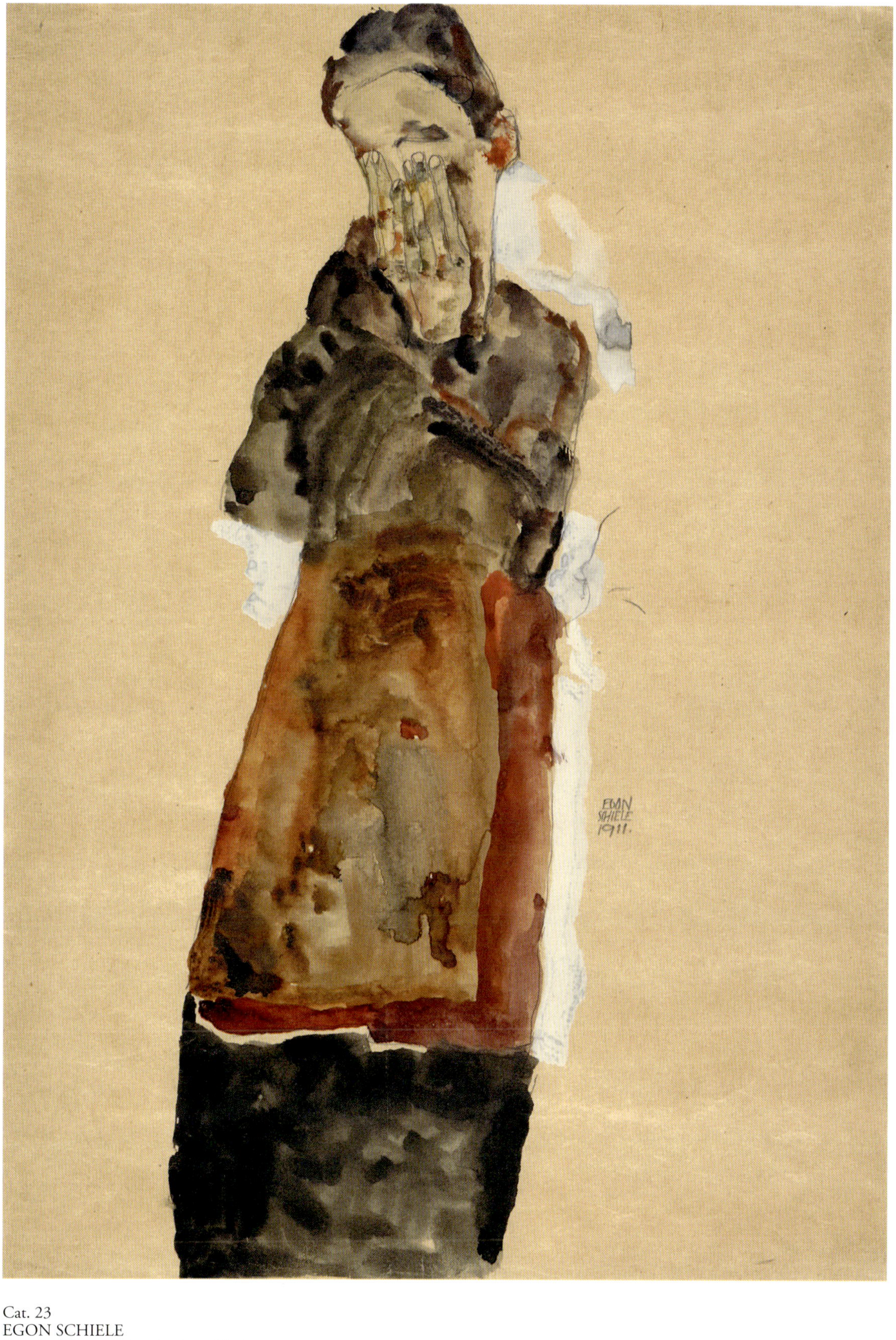

Cat. 23
EGON SCHIELE
Standing Woman, Covering Face, 1911
Gouache, watercolor, and pencil on paper, 44.8 x 31.4 cm
Private collection, London

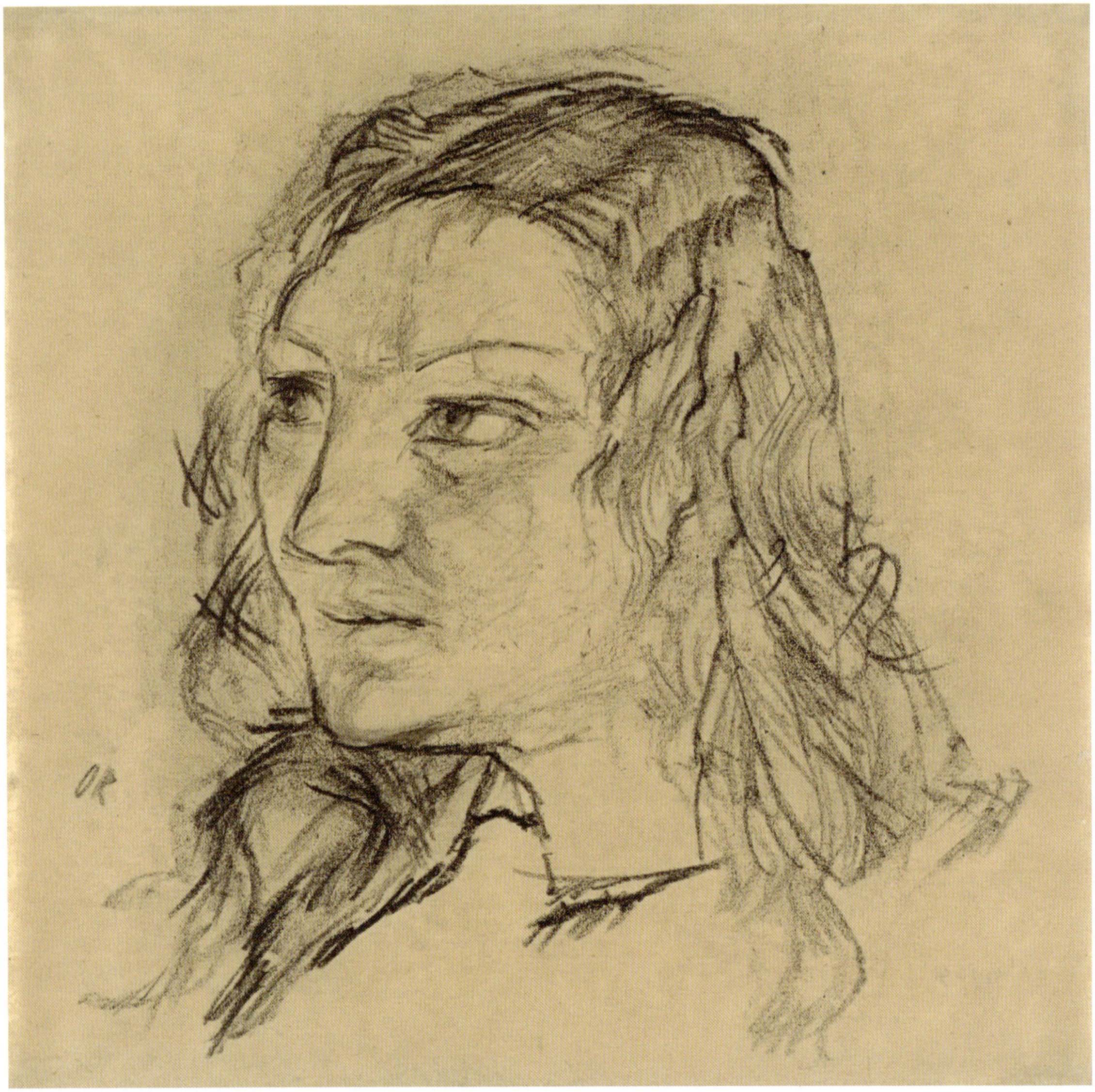

Cat. 24
OSKAR KOKOSCHKA
Alma Mahler, 1912
Black crayon on paper, 33.3 x 33.7 cm
Staatliche Kunstsammlungen Dresden, Collection of Prints, Drawings and Photographs, Dresden

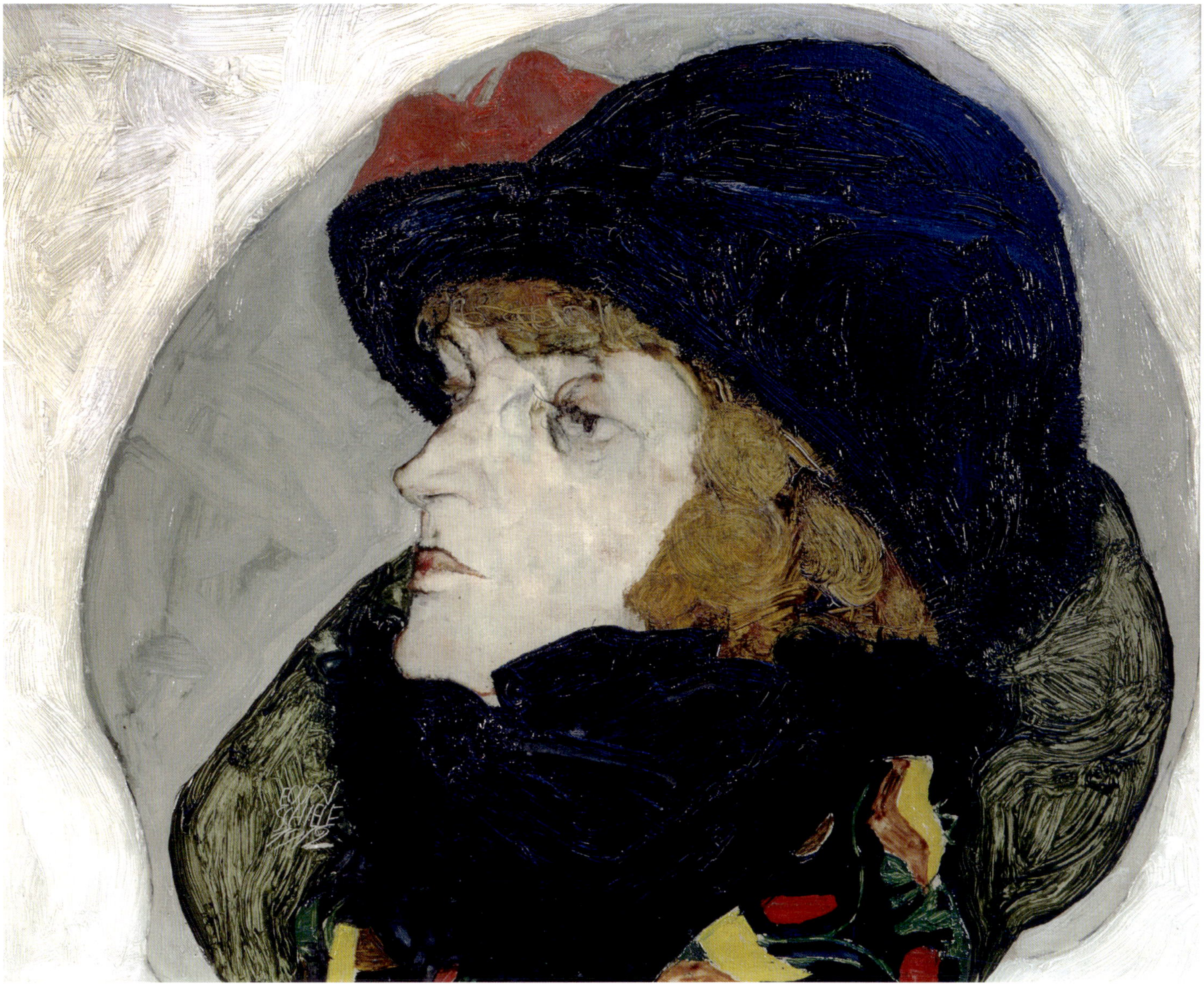

Cat. 25
EGON SCHIELE
Ida Roessler, 1912
Oil on wood, 31.6 x 39.4 cm
Wien Museum, Vienna

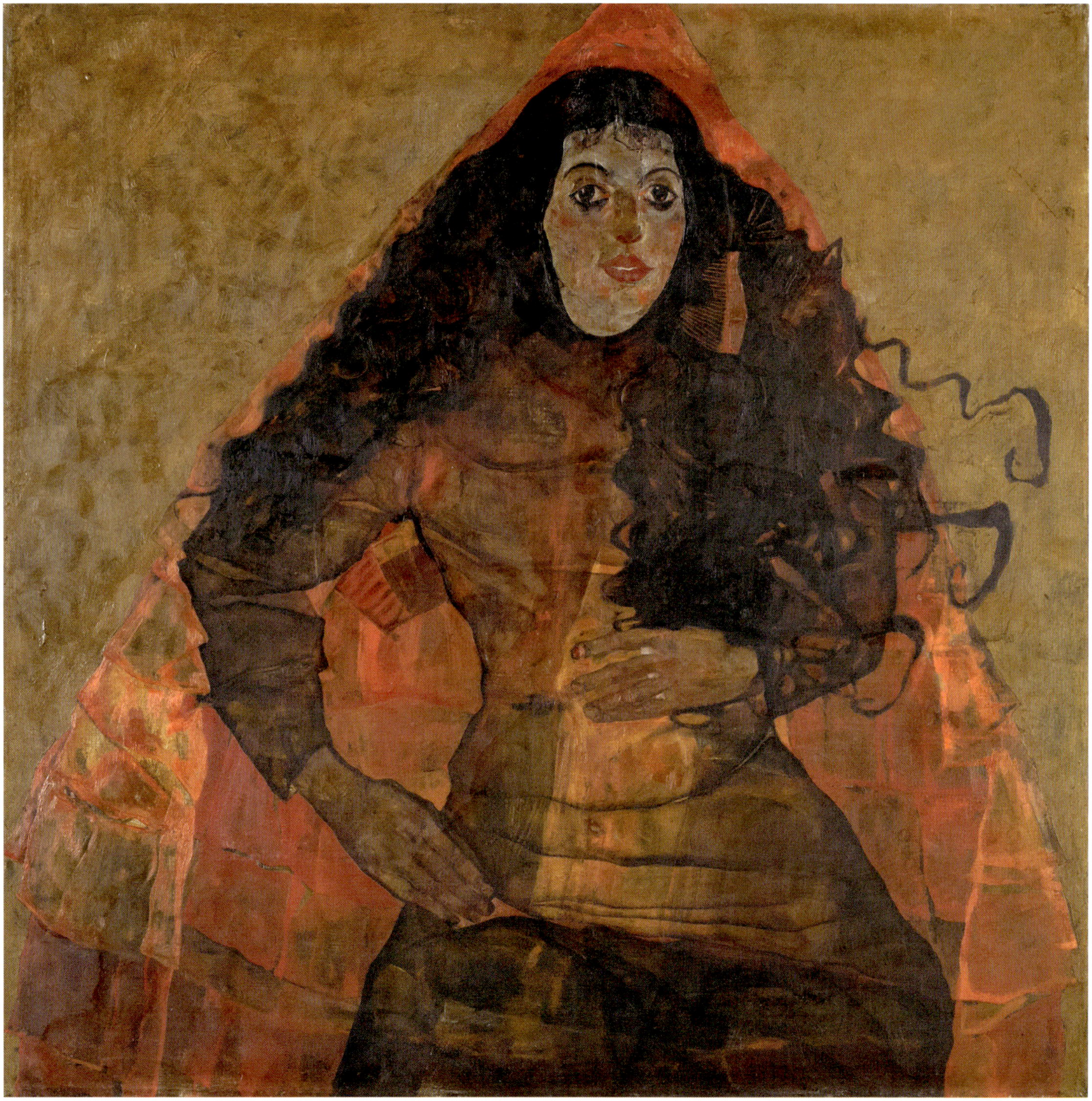

Cat. 26
EGON SCHIELE
Trude Engel, 1915
Oil on canvas, 100 x 100 cm
LENTOS Kunstmuseum, Linz

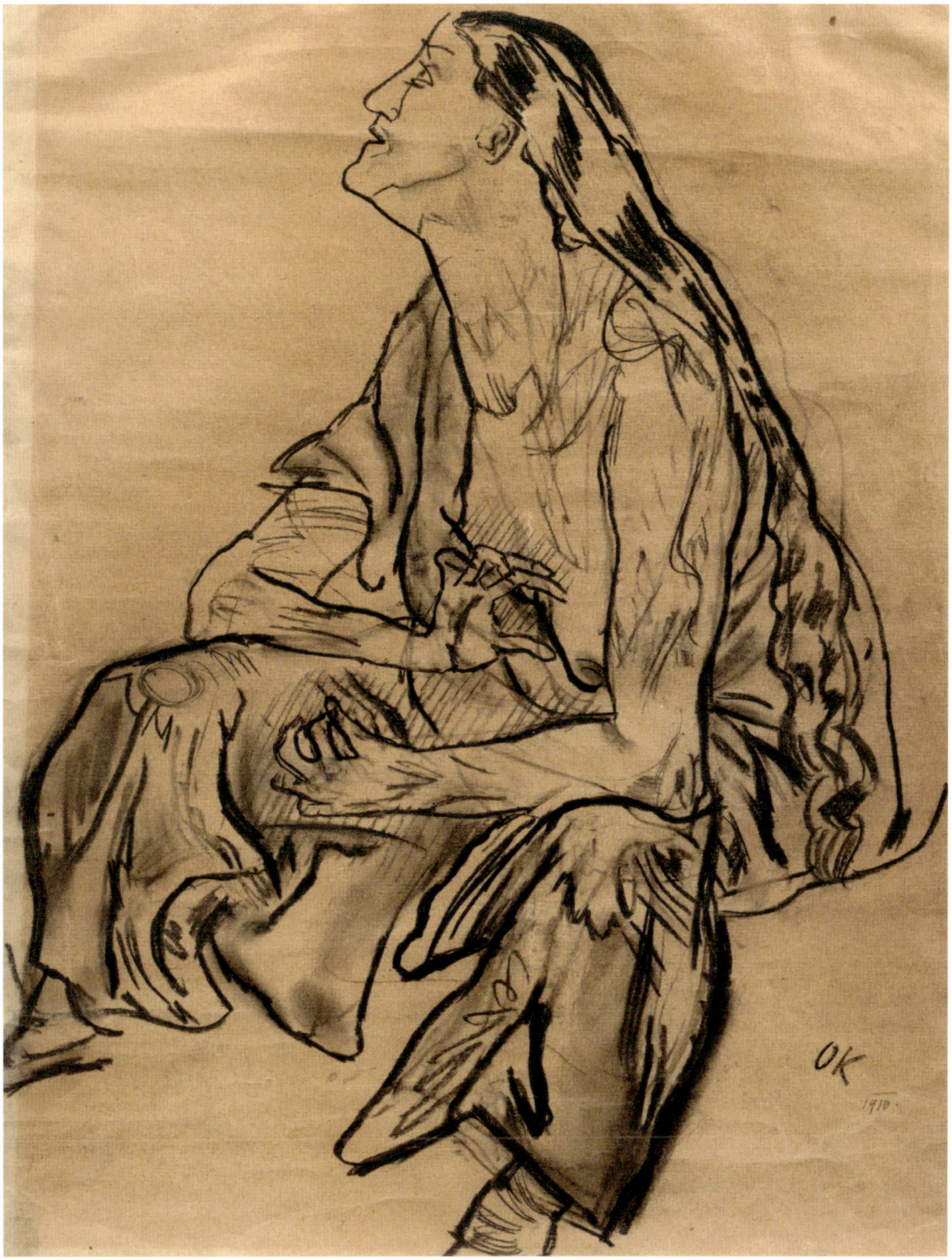

Cat. 27
OSKAR KOKOSCHKA
Mania, 1913–14
Charcoal on paper, 44.5 x 33.5 cm
Private collection, USA, courtesy of Wienerroither & Kohlbacher. Vienna

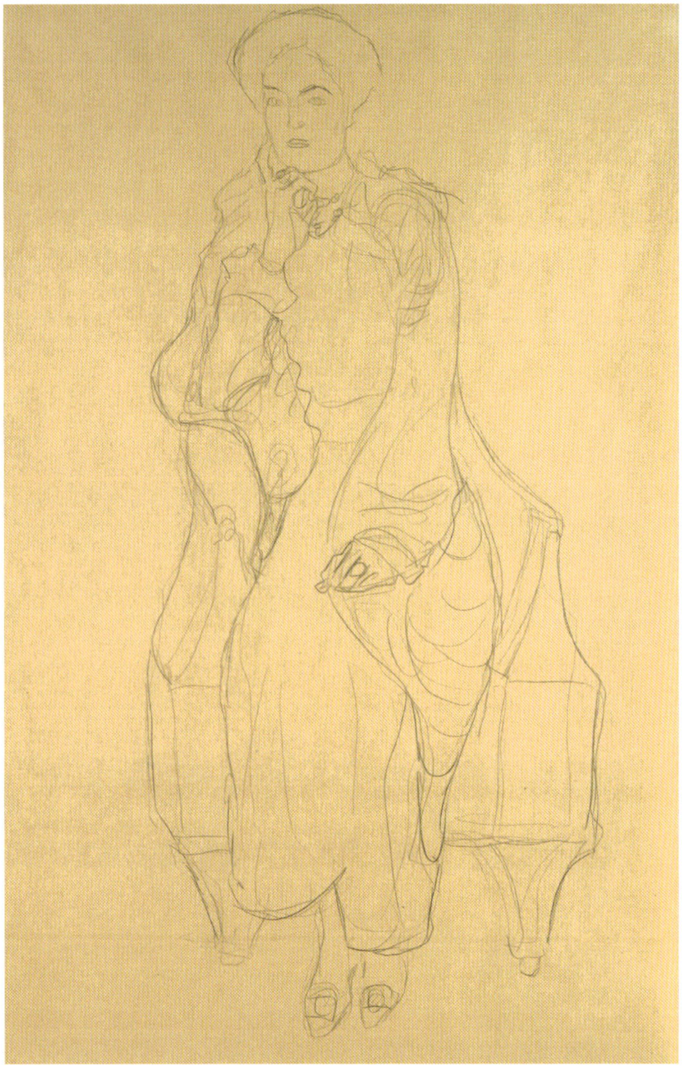

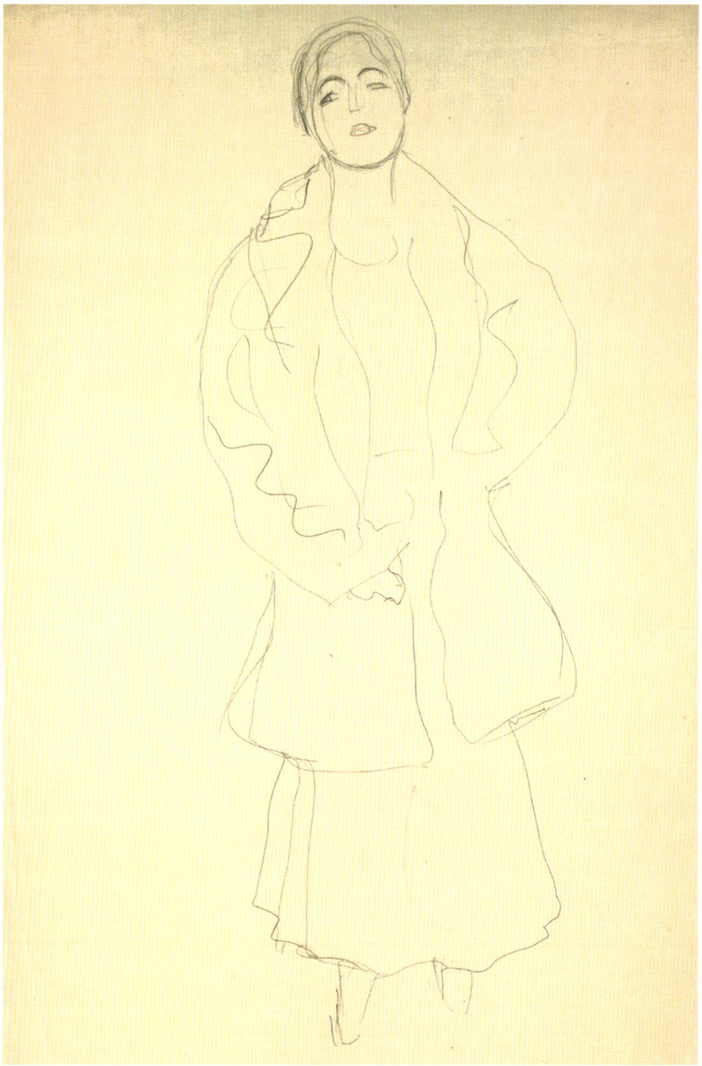

Cat. 28
GUSTAV KLIMT
Paula Zuckerkandl, 1911
Pencil on paper, 57 × 37.5 cm
Private collection, Vienna

Cat. 29
GUSTAV KLIMT
Standing Woman in Short Jacket, 1915–16
Pencil, red and blue pencil on paper, 57 x 37.2 cm
Albertina, Vienna, on permanent loan, Collection Hans Robert Pippal and Eugenie Pippal-Kottnig

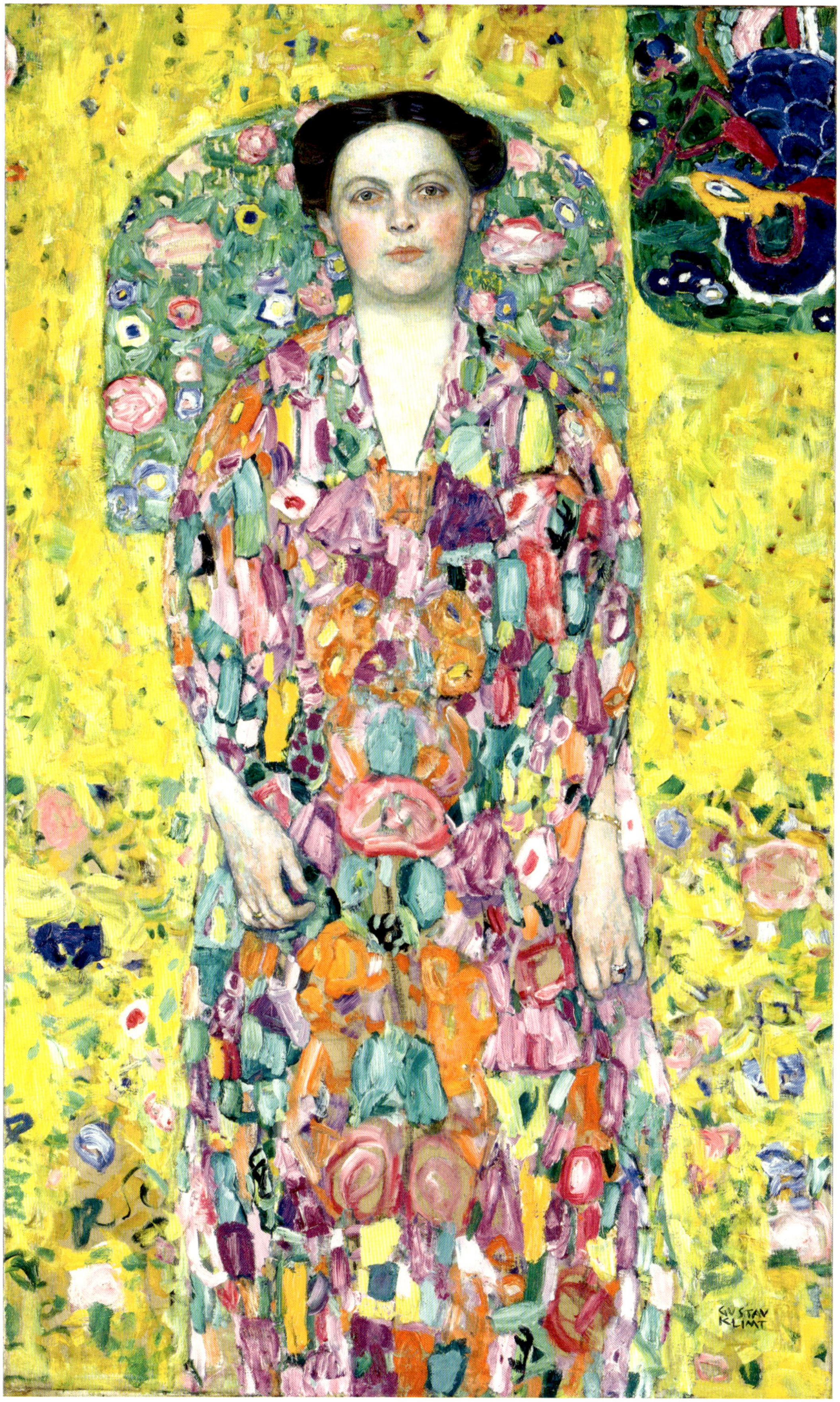

Cat. 30
GUSTAV KLIMT
Eugenia Primavesi, 1913–14
Oil on canvas, 140 x 85 cm
Toyota Municipal Museum of Art,
Toyota

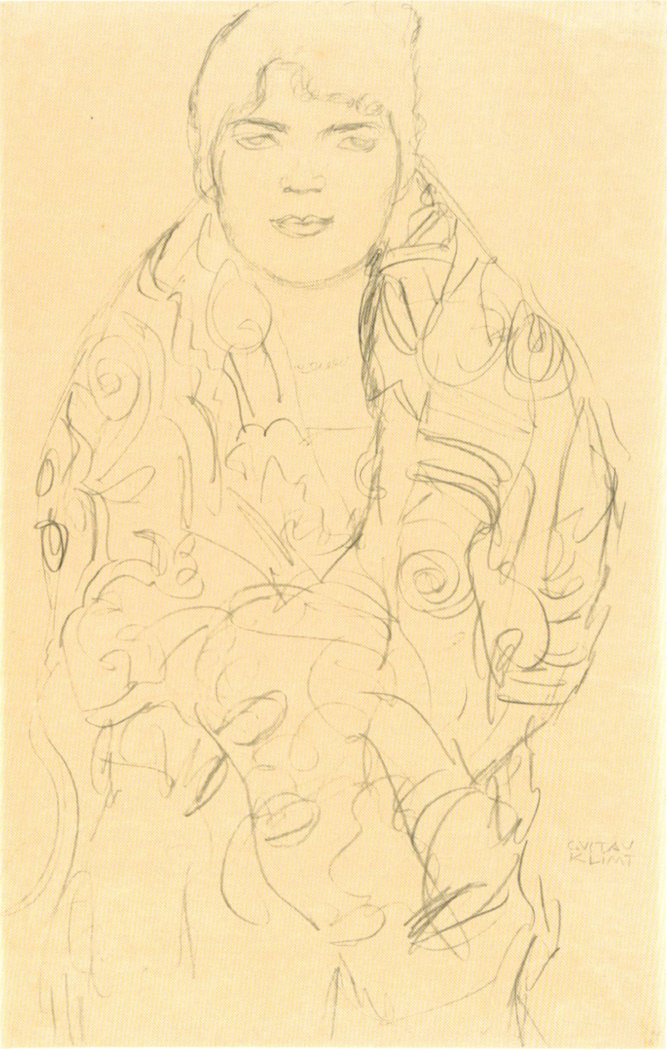

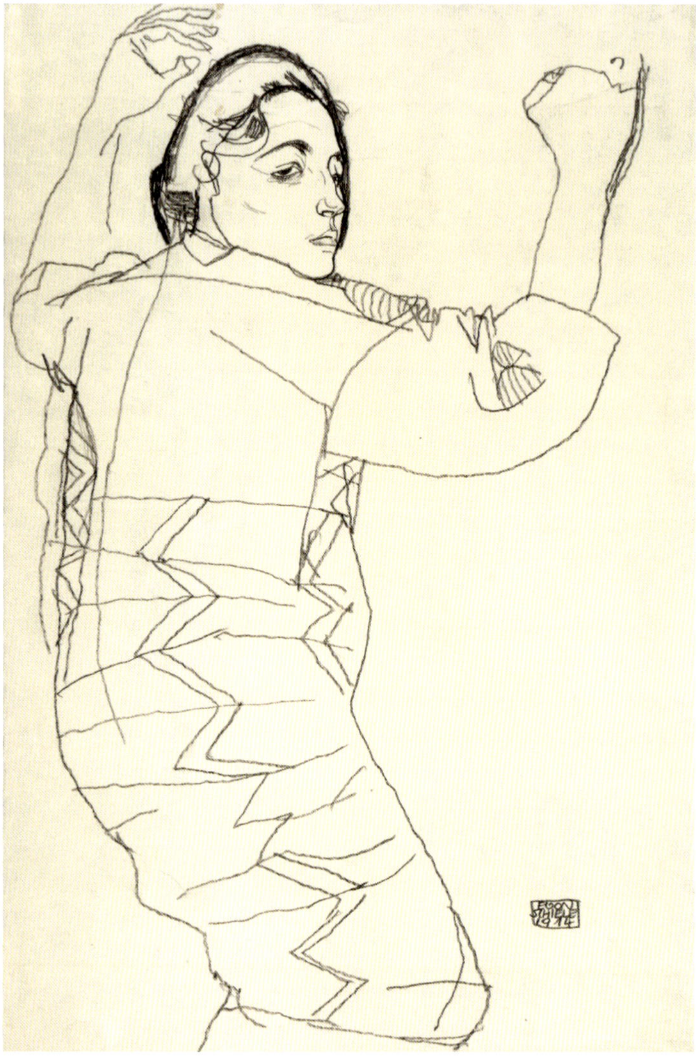

Cat. 31
GUSTAV KLIMT
Friederike Maria Beer, Knee-length Portrait, Facing Front, 1916
Pencil on paper, 49.5 x 32 cm
Private collection, courtesy of Galerie St. Etienne, New York

Cat. 32
EGON SCHIELE
Back View of Girl with Raised Hands (Friederike Maria Beer), 1914
Pencil on paper, 48.3 x 42.2 cm
Coninx-Stiftung, Zurich

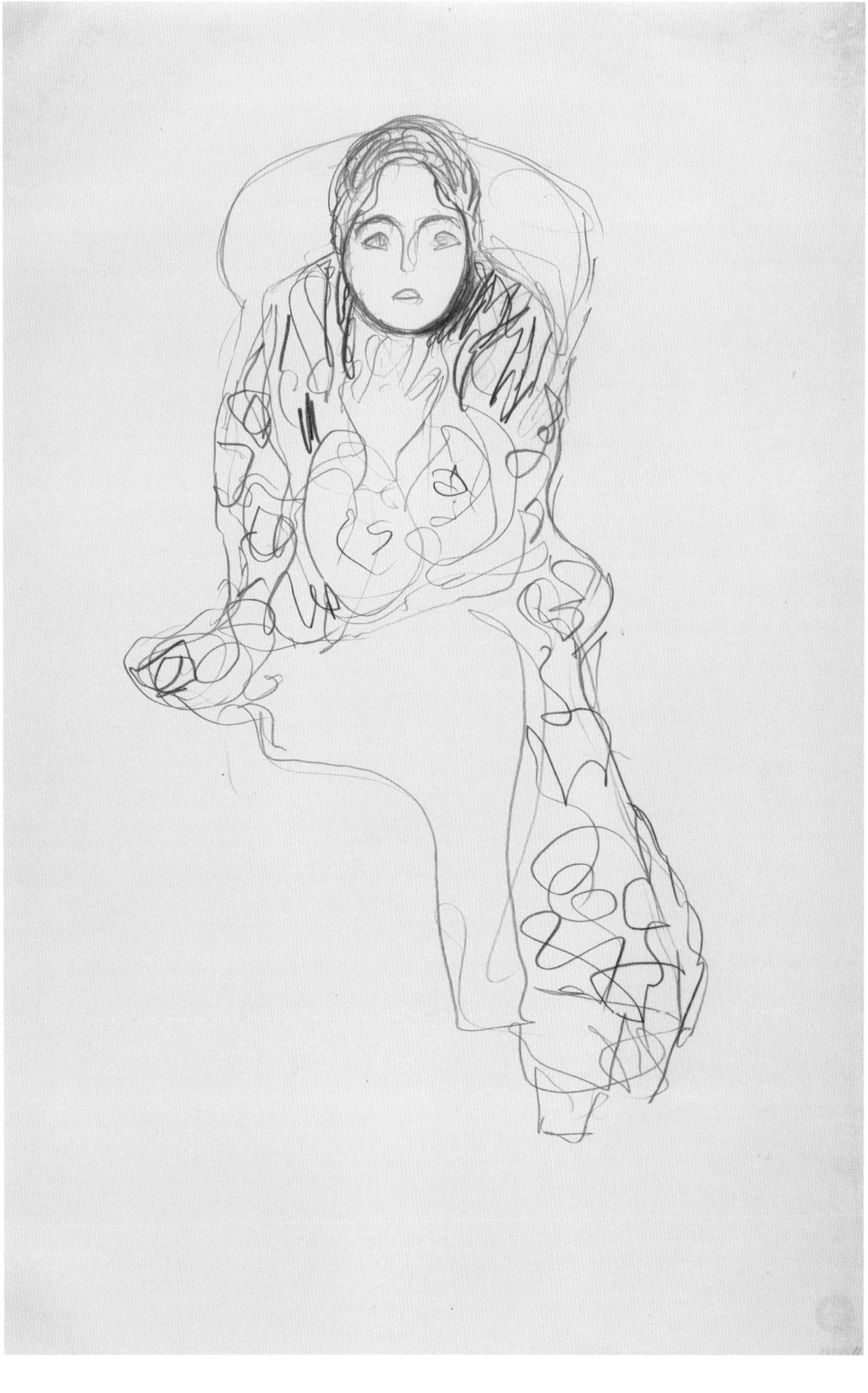

Cat. 33
GUSTAV KLIMT
Friederike Maria Beer Seated, Facing Front, Resting Her Chin on Her Hands, 1916
Pencil on paper, 57 x 37.4 cm
Albertina, Vienna

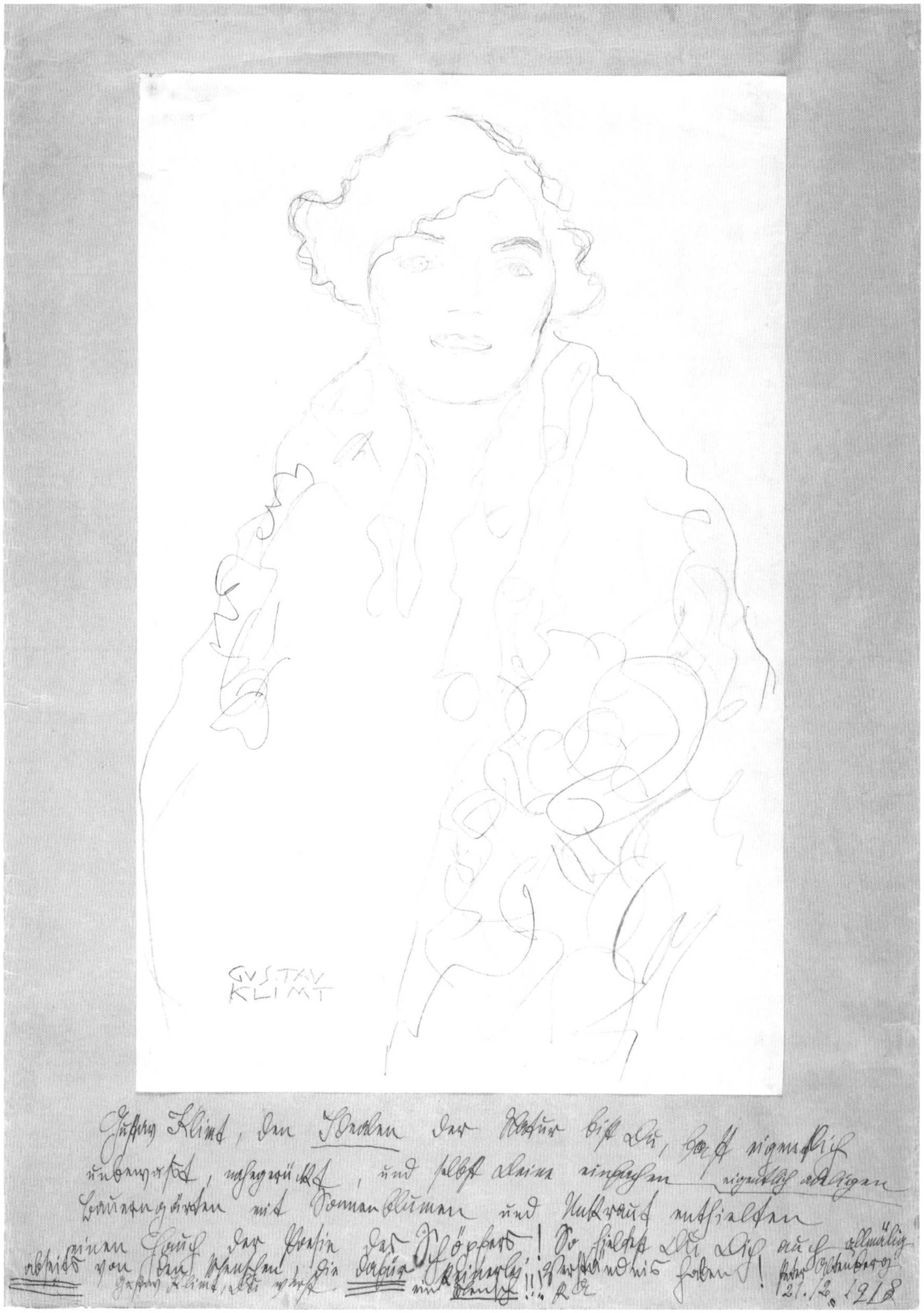

Cat. 34
GUSTAV KLIMT
Johanna Staude Facing Front, 1917
Pencil on paper, 50.1 x 32.5 cm
Private collection

Cat. 35
GUSTAV KLIMT
Johanna Staude, 1917
Oil on canvas, 70 x 50 cm
Belvedere, Vienna

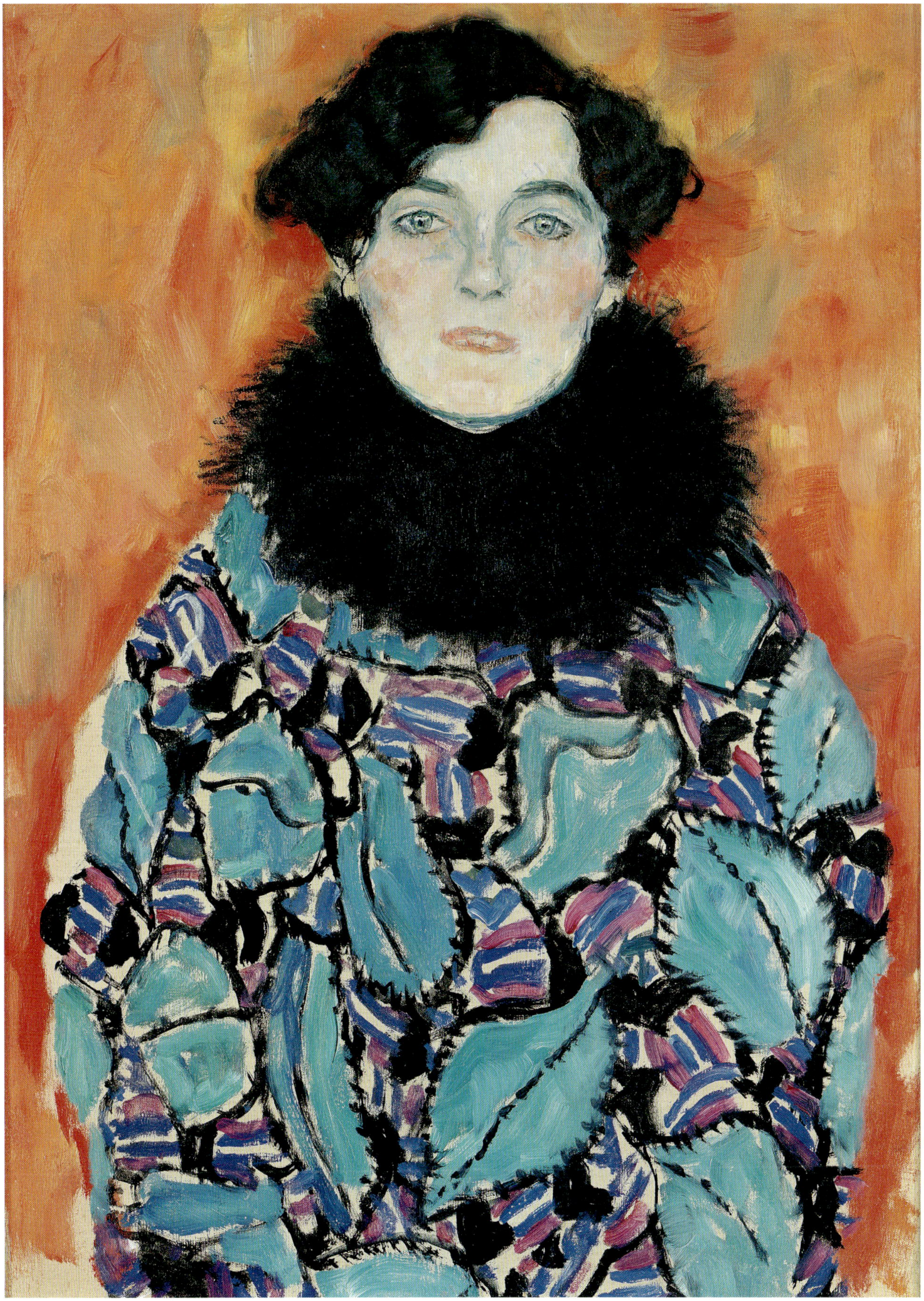

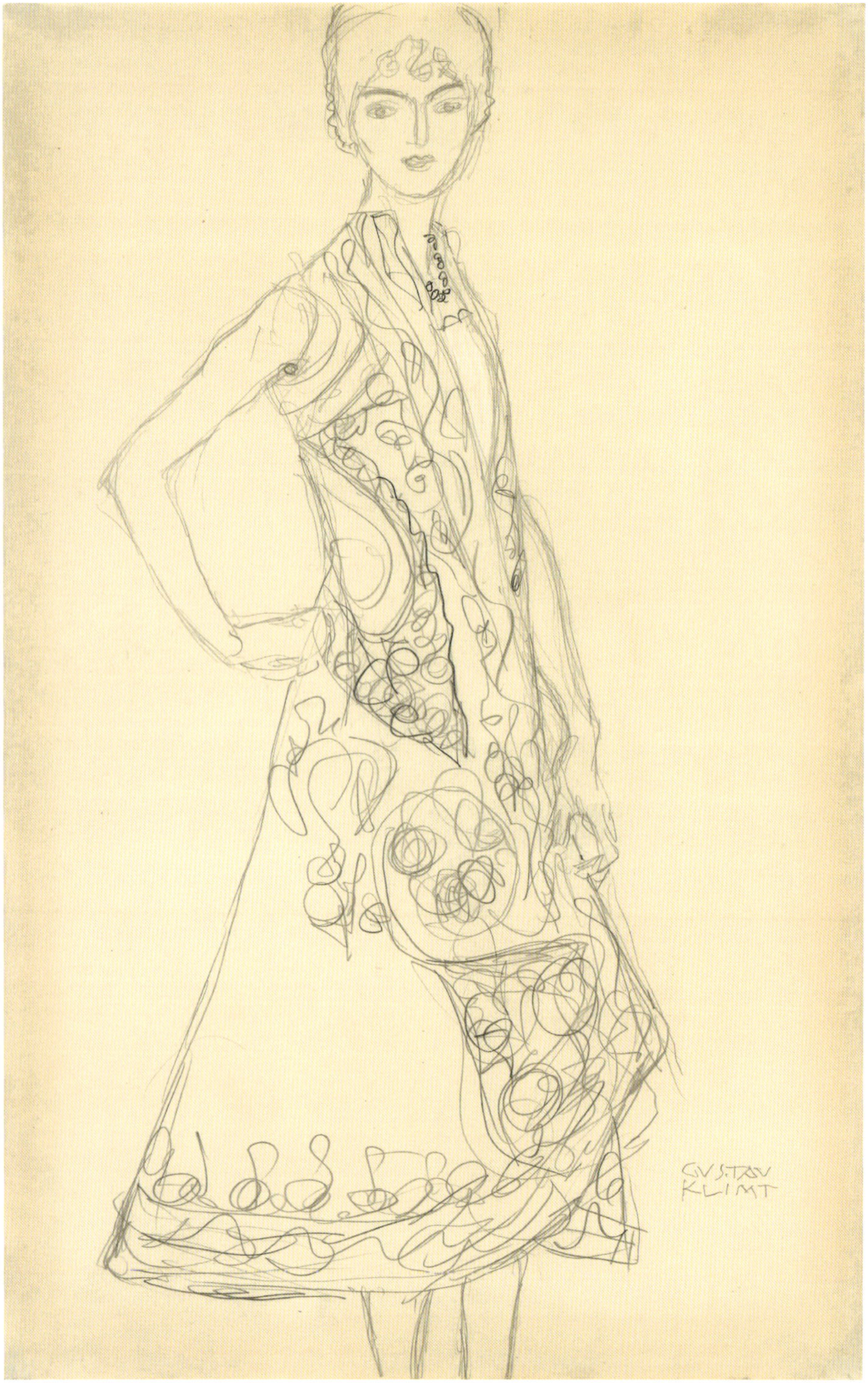

Cat. 36
GUSTAV KLIMT
Woman in Richly Patterned Dress, Right Hand Resting on Hip, 1916–17
Pencil and white crayon on paper, 50 x 32.5 cm
Private collection, courtesy of Neue Galerie, New York

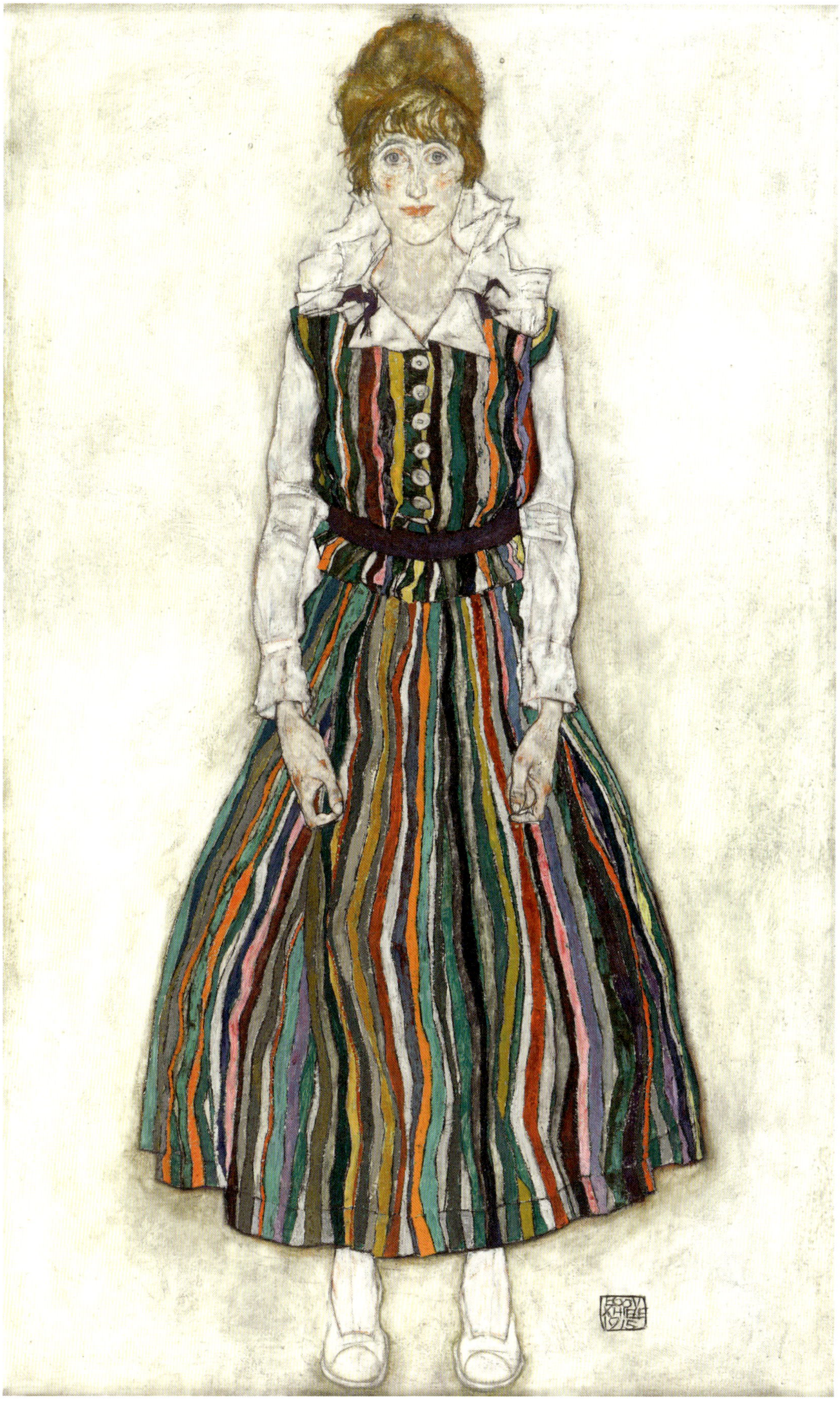

Cat. 37
EGON SCHIELE
Edith Schiele in Striped Dress,
1915
Oil on canvas, 180 x 110 cm
Collection of the Gemeentemuseum
Den Haag

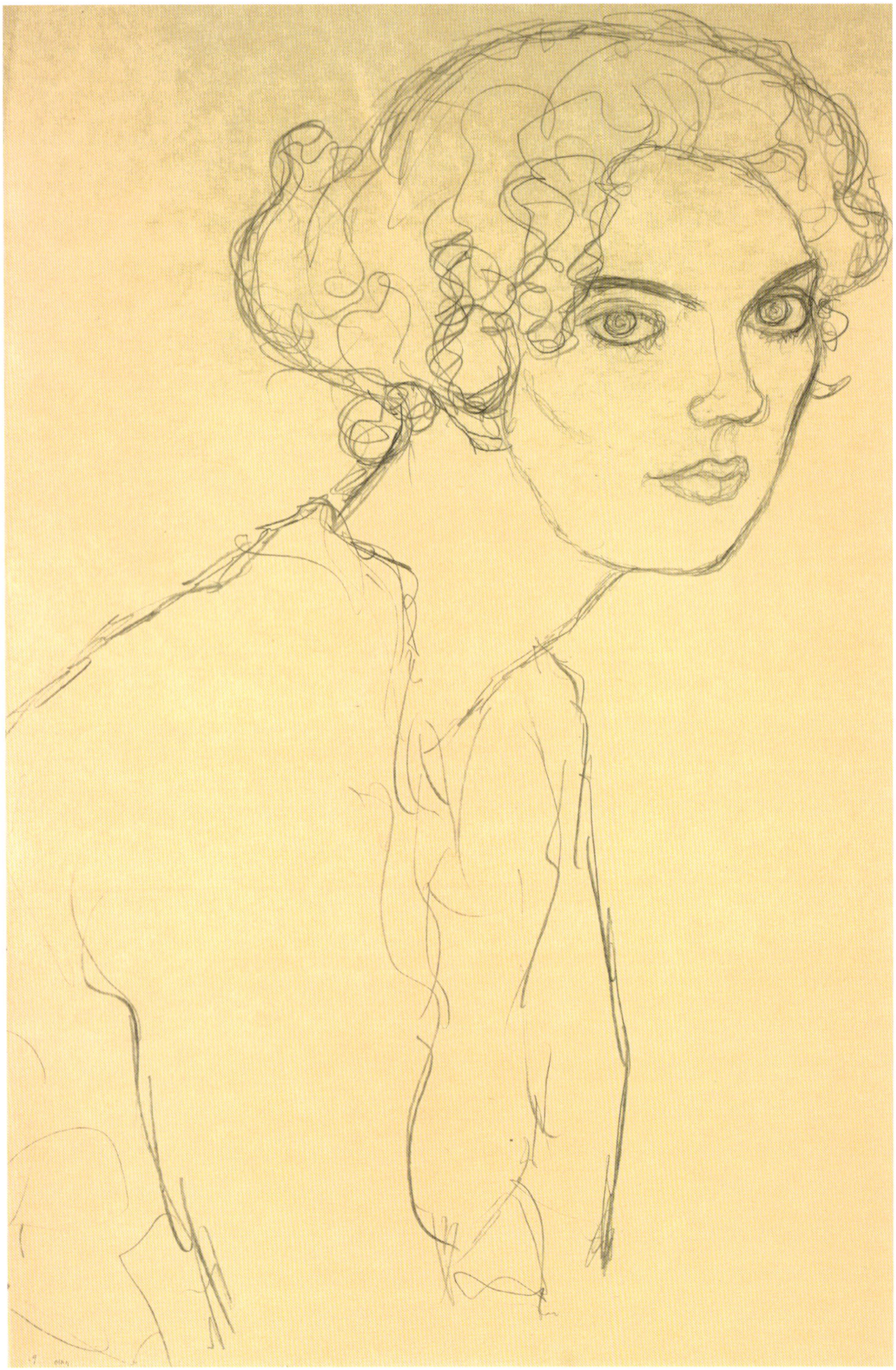

Cat. 38
GUSTAV KLIMT
Portrait of a Woman Facing Right, c. 1916
Pencil on paper, 56 x 36.5 cm
Albertina, Vienna, on permanent loan from a private collection

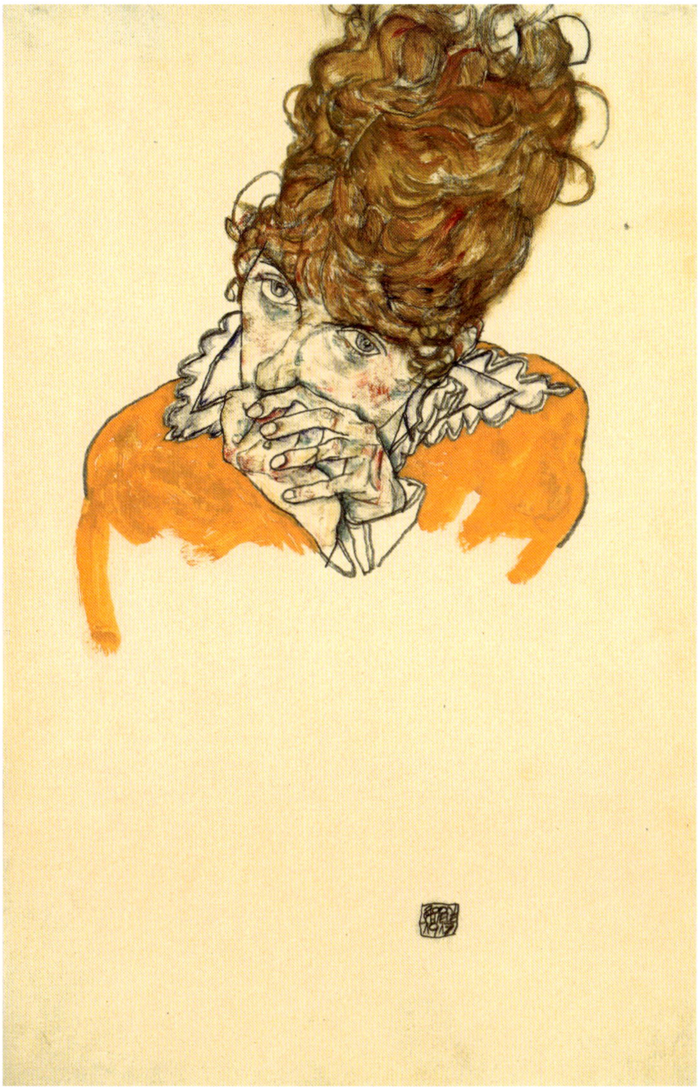

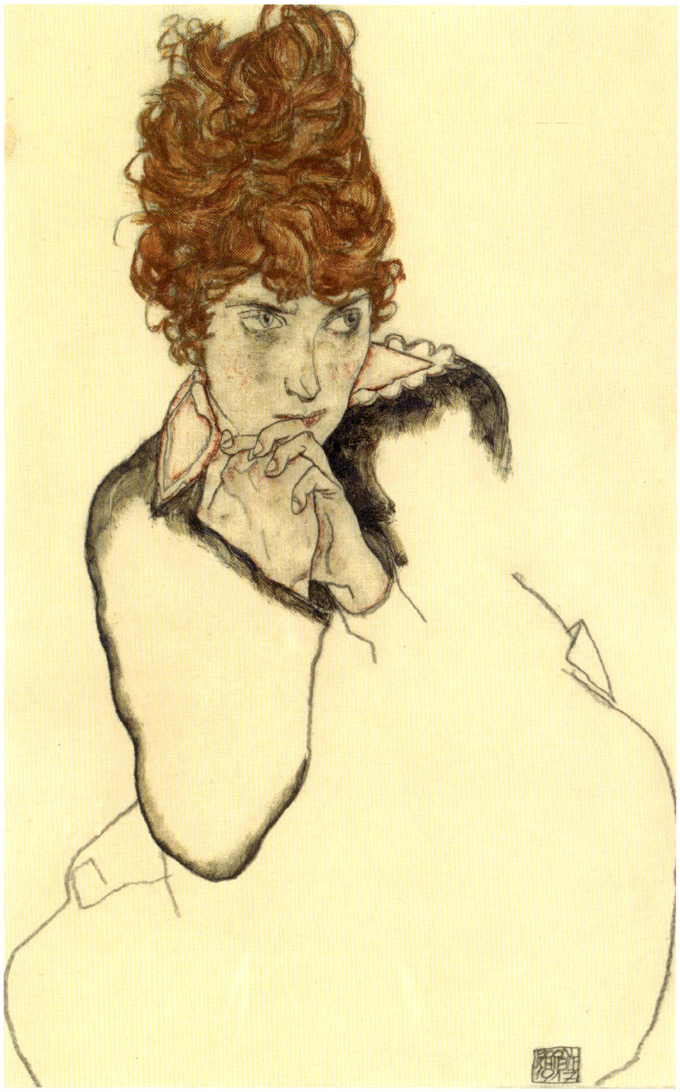

Cat. 39
EGON SCHIELE
The Artist's Sister-in-Law, Covering Mouth with Hands, 1917
Gouache and black crayon on paper, 43 x 28 cm
Private collection

Cat. 40
EGON SCHIELE
The Artist's Sister-in-Law with Clasped Hands, 1917
Gouache and charcoal on paper, 45.3 x 28.5 cm
Private collection

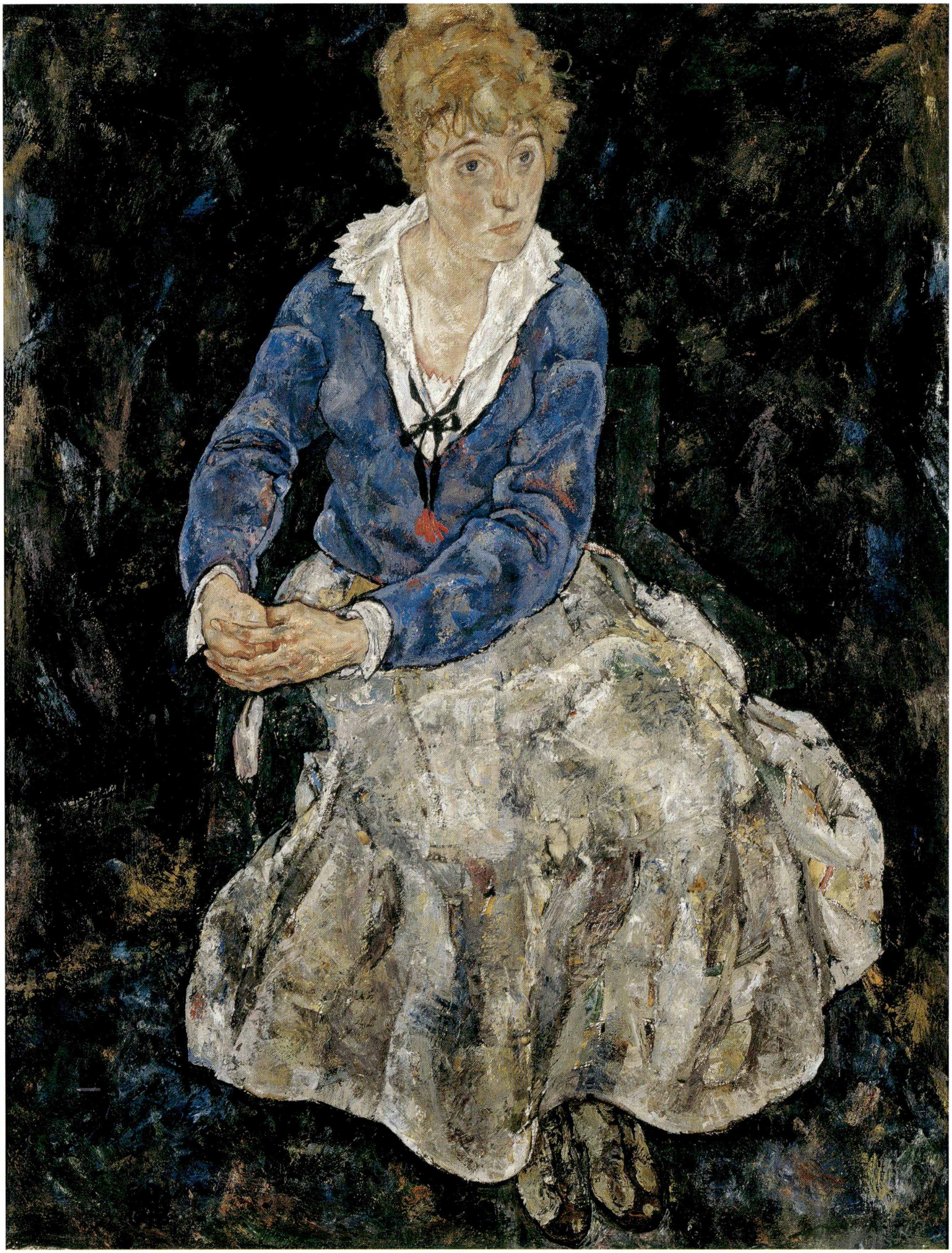

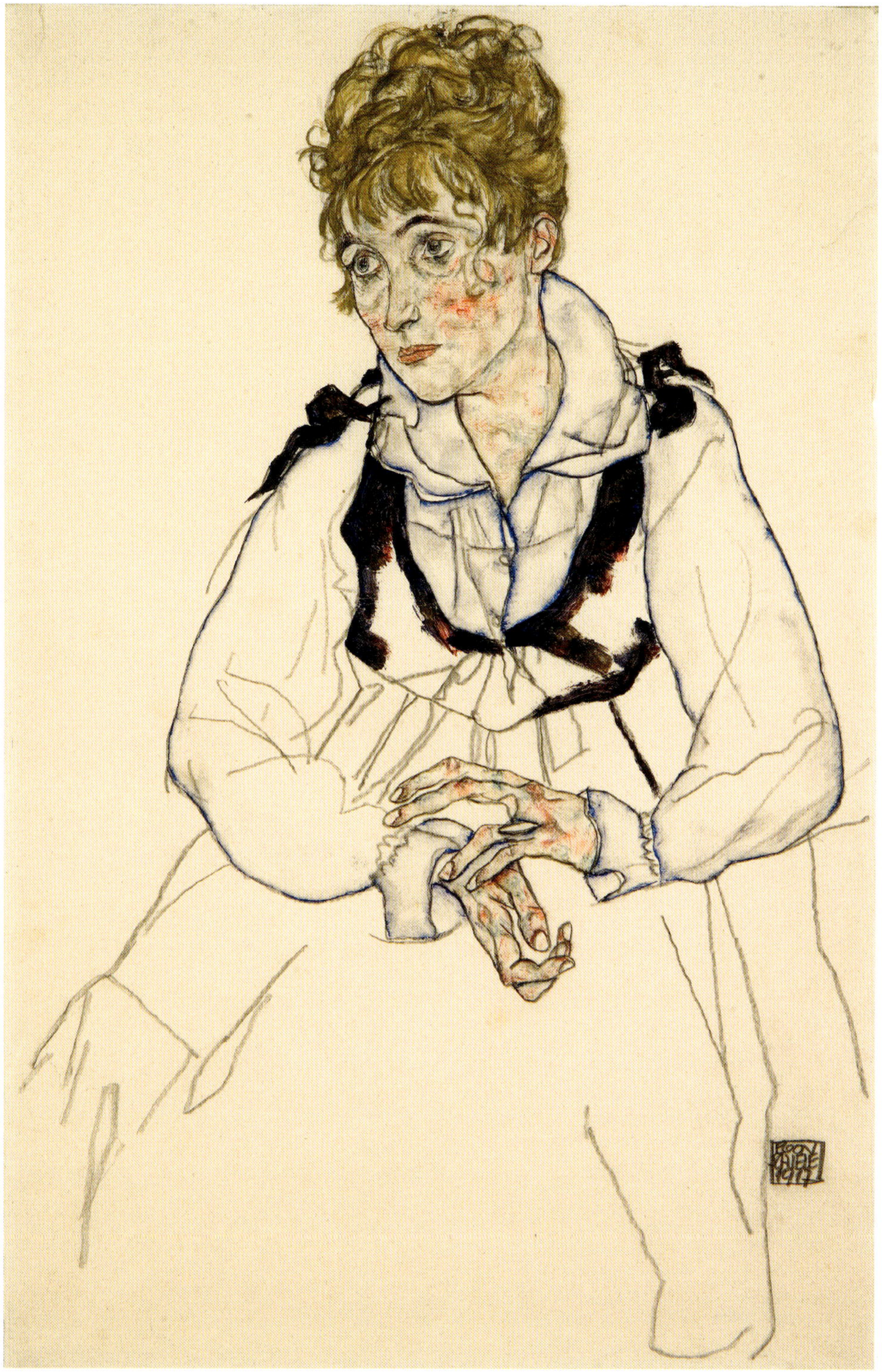

Cat. 41
EGON SCHIELE
Edith Schiele, 1918
Oil on canvas, 139.5 x 109.2 cm
Belvedere, Vienna

Cat. 42
EGON SCHIELE
Edith Schiele, 1917
Gouache and black crayon on paper, 46.1 x 29.7 cm
Belvedere, Vienna

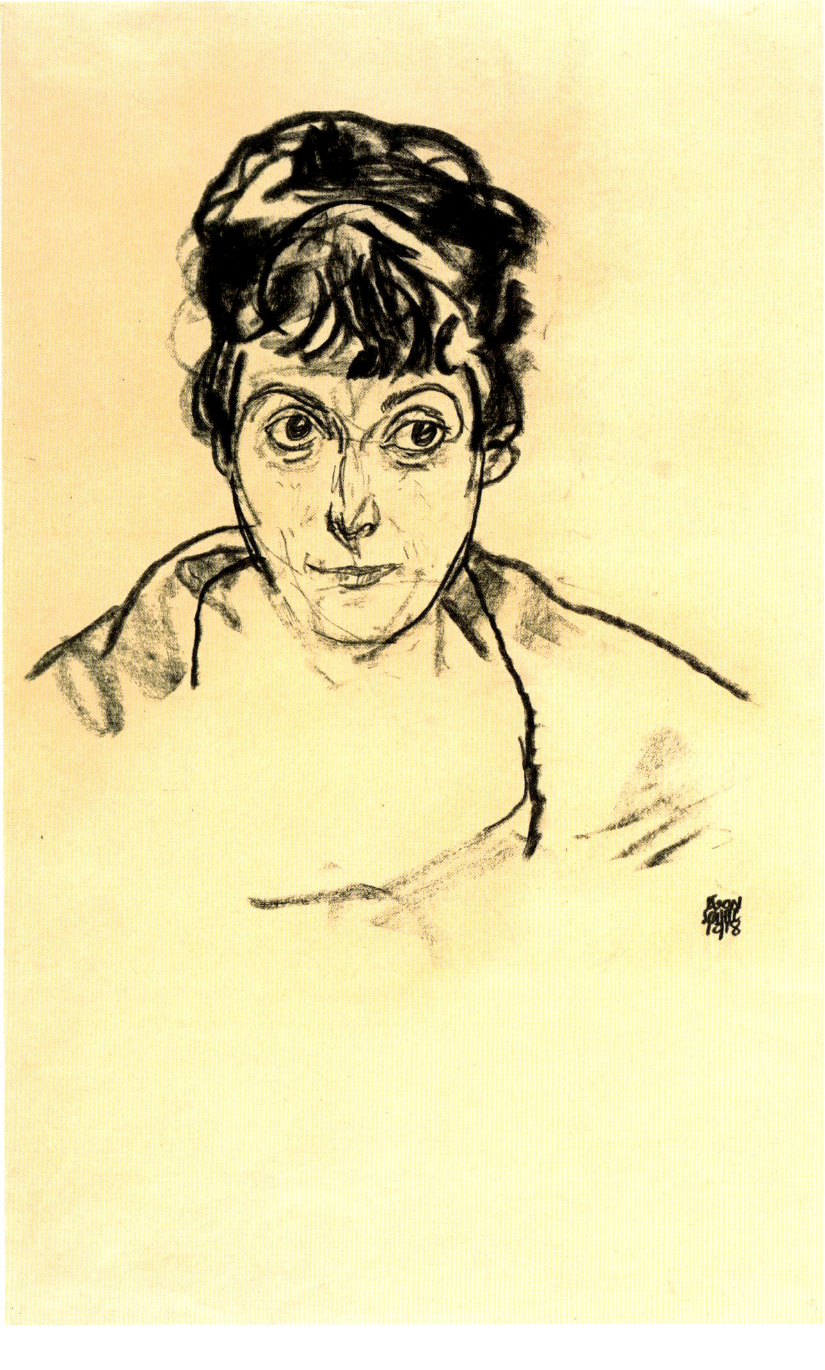

Cat. 43
EGON SCHIELE
Black-haired Woman, 1918
Black crayon on paper, 46.7 x 29.5 cm
Private collection, London

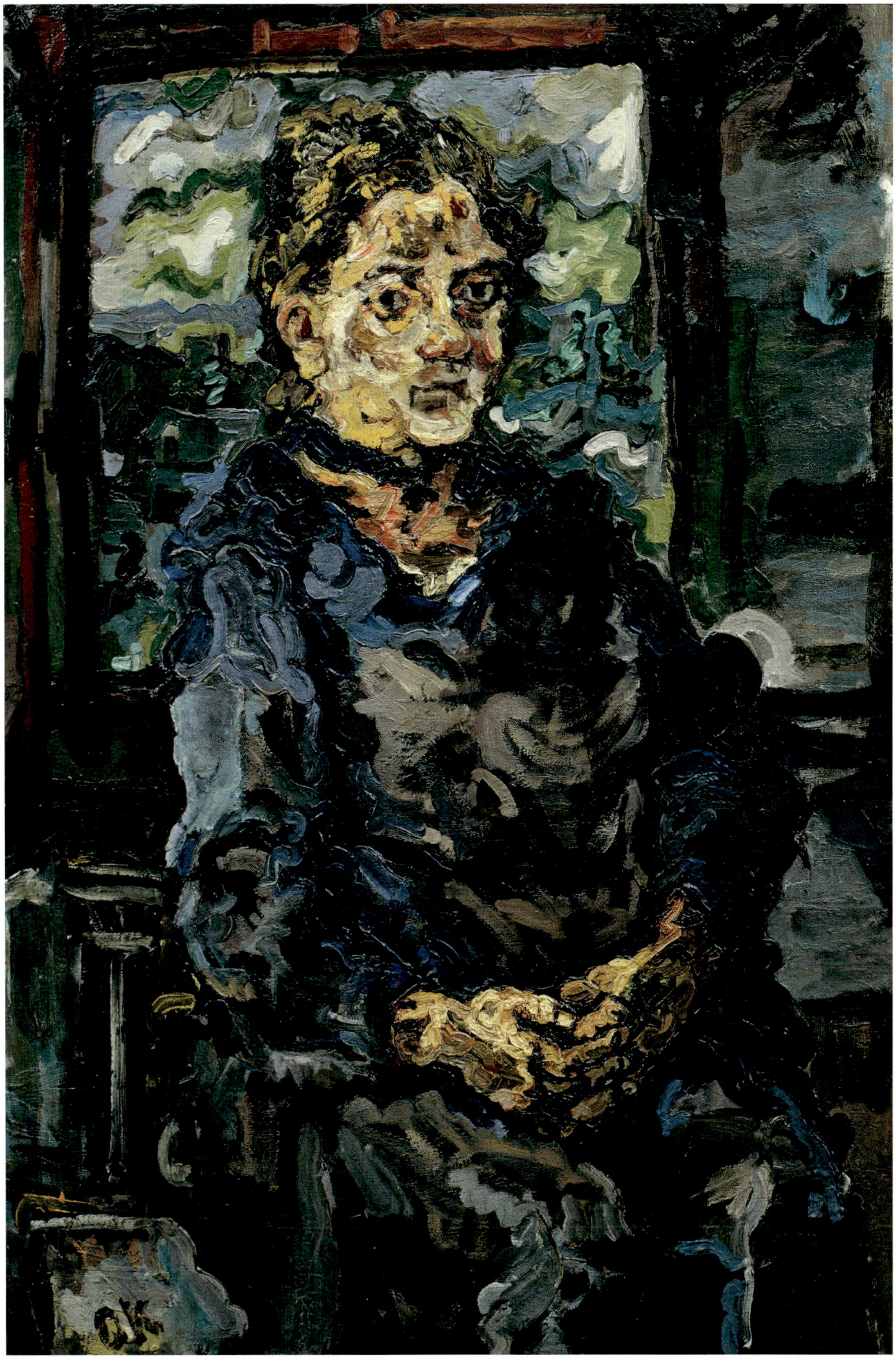

Cat. 44
OSKAR KOKOSCHKA
Romana Kokoschka, 1917
Oil on canvas, 112 x 75 cm
Belvedere, Vienna

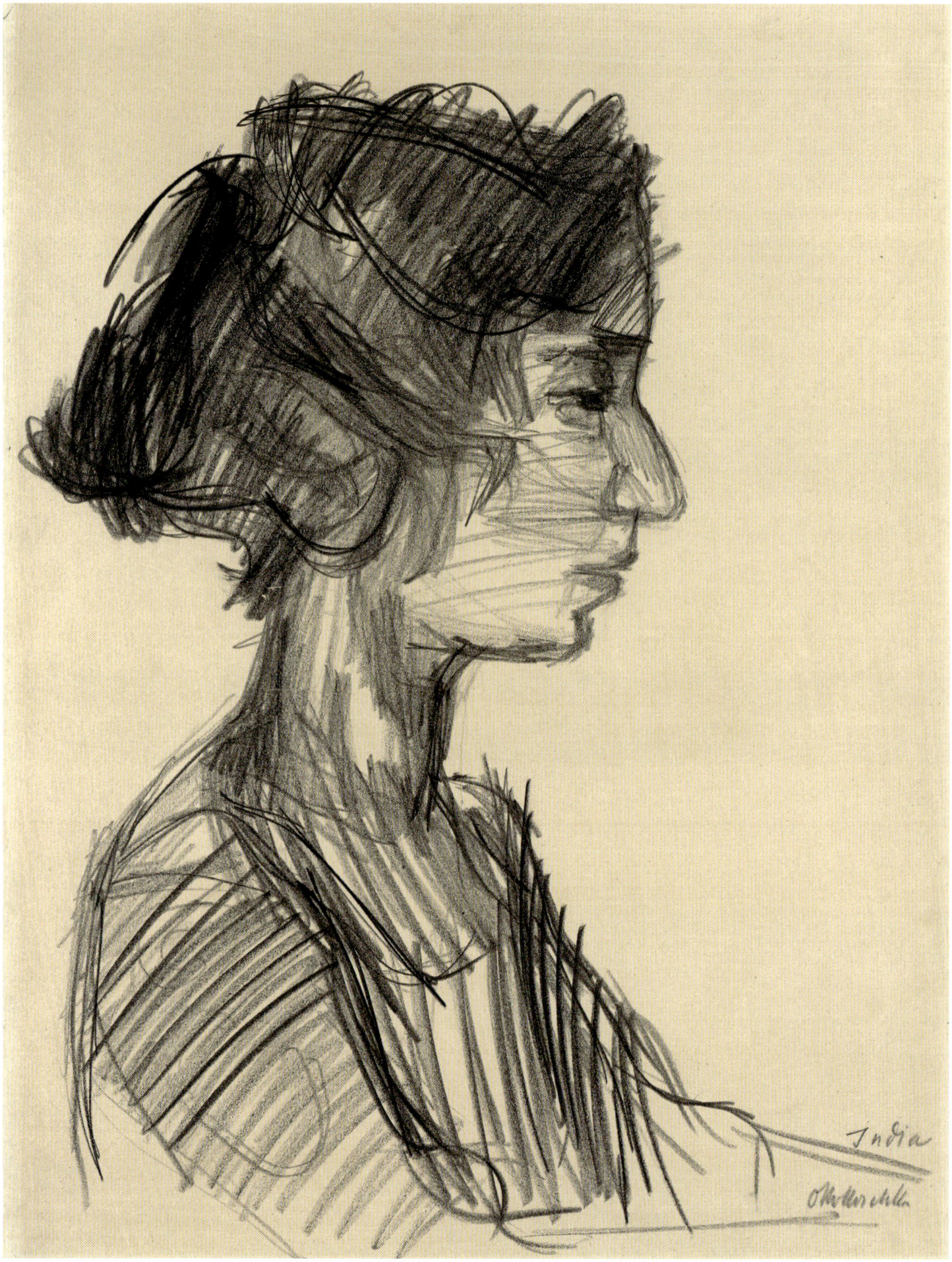

Cat. 45
OSKAR KOKOSCHKA
Indra I (Anna Kallin), 1921
Lithographic chalk on paper, mounted on cardboard, 66.1 x 49.5 cm
Staatliche Kunstsammlungen Dresden, Collection of Prints, Drawings and Photographs, Dresden

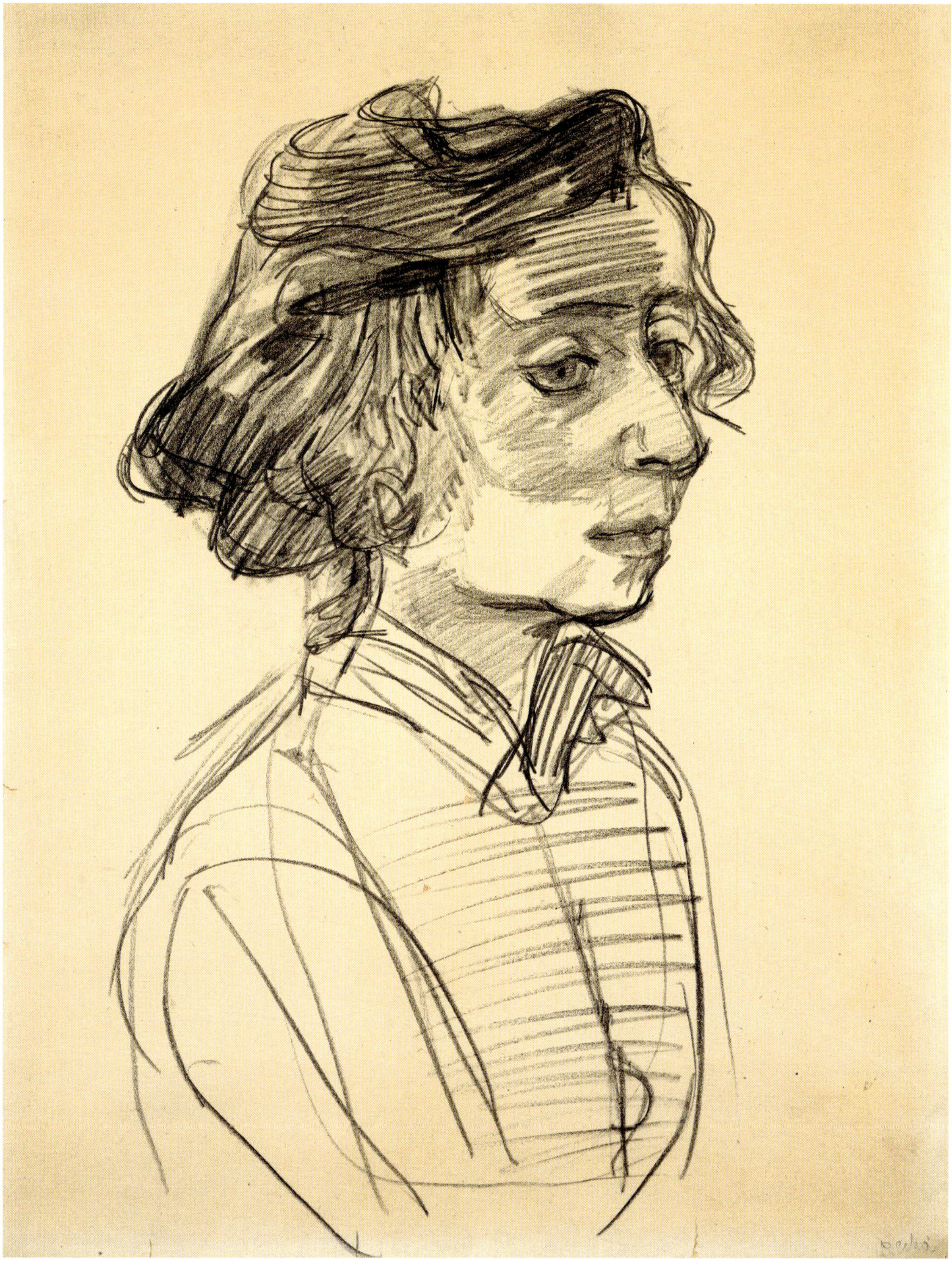

Cat. 46
OSKAR KOKOSCHKA
Anna Kallin, 1921
Black crayon on paper, 65 x 48.5 cm
Fondation Oskar Kokoschka, Vevey

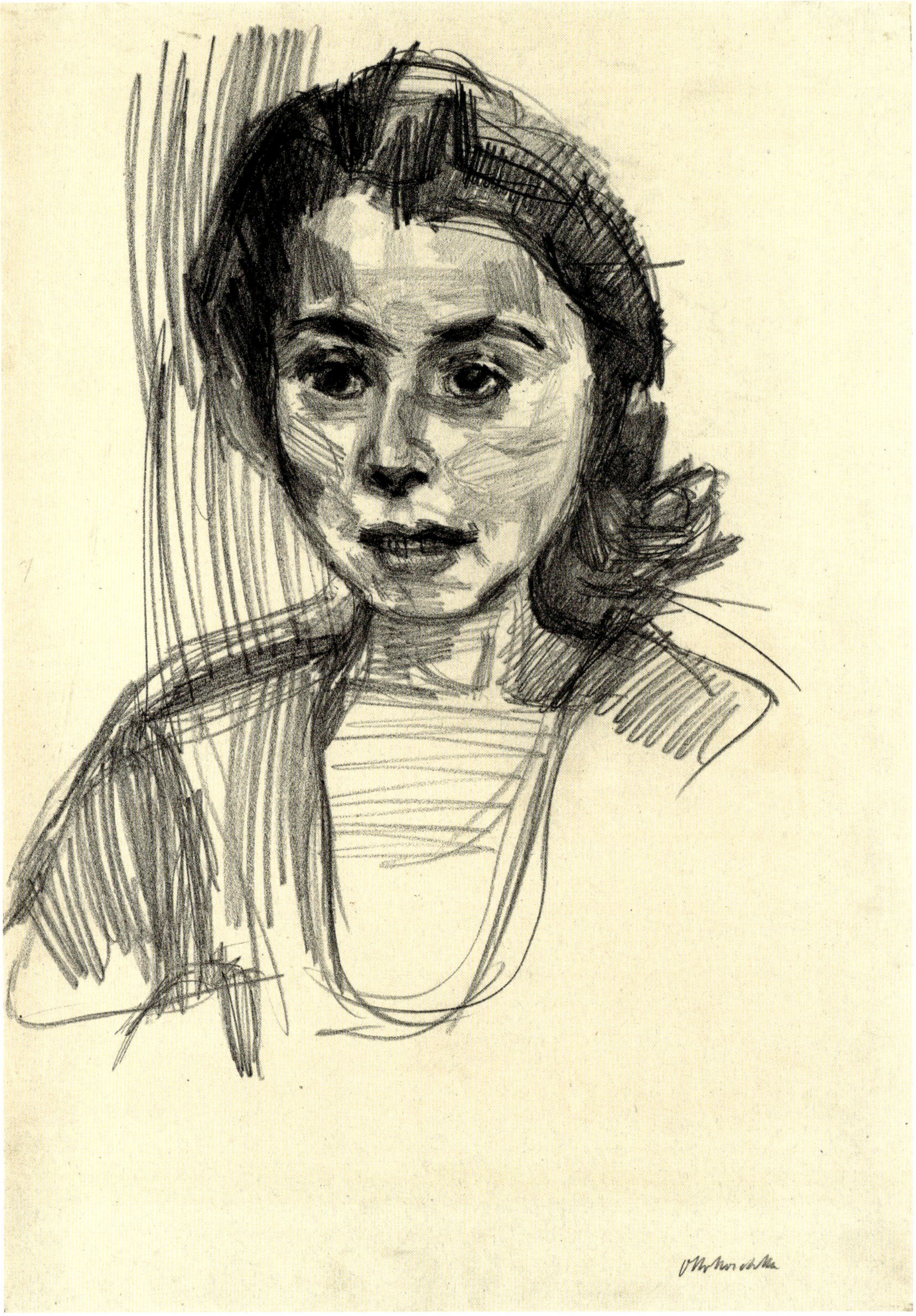

Cat. 47
OSKAR KOKOSCHKA
Head of a Woman, 1921–22
Black crayon on paper, 70.1 x 49.6 cm
Staatliche Kunstsammlungen Dresden, Collection of Prints, Drawings and Photographs, Dresden

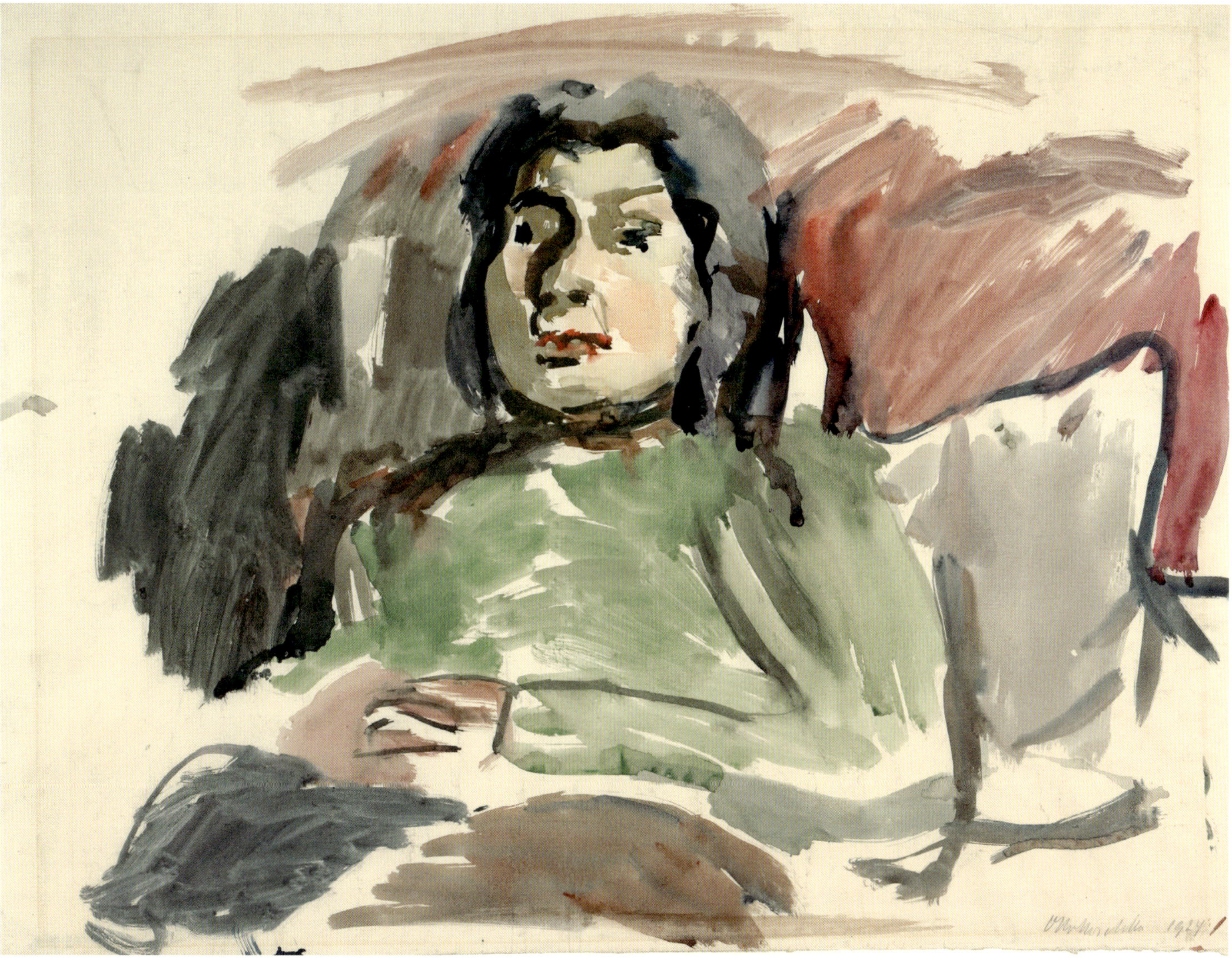

Cat. 48
OSKAR KOKOSCHKA
Reclining Woman, 1924
Watercolor on paper, 51.2 x 66.9 cm
Albertina, Vienna

Mothers and Children

Portraits, even if not commissioned, entail an implicit compact between the subject and the artist. Such paintings are judged, to some extent, in accordance with the expectations of the sitter and of society at large. Klimt's, Schiele's and Kokoschka's depictions of motherhood, on the other hand, were not commissioned or assigned and had only to meet the idiosyncratic needs of the artist himself. Accordingly, each painter approached the theme in terms of his specific experiences.

In the early twentieth century, heterosexual intercourse entailed an uncontrollable risk of pregnancy, and this in turn endangered the lives of mother and child alike. Mothers not infrequently died in childbirth; many children did not survive infancy. Venereal disease, too, was a mortal threat. Klimt is believed to have suffered from syphilis, and Schiele's father died of the illness. It has been suggested that Klimt never married his companion Emilie Flöge because he feared infecting her.[1] He had no such scruples, evidently, with regard to the lower-class women whom he repeatedly impregnated.

Klimt fathered at least six illegitimate children.[2] The names of the mothers and the identities of the offspring, however, are only partially known. In the summer of 1899, the artist begat two little Gustavs: sons of a model, Marie Zimmerman, and of his cleaning woman, Marie Ucicka. Zimmerman subsequently gave birth to a second son, Otto, who died at the age of just three months in September 1902.[3]

Although Klimt had incorporated the theme of pregnancy tangentially in his allegory *Medicine* (p. 38, fig. 10), Otto seems to have inspired his first in-depth exploration of the subject, *Hope I* (fig. 1). After losing the child, the artist decided to substitute a parade of ghouls for the original landscape background.[4] He created many studies for *Hope I*, using several different pregnant models, sometimes paired with a solicitous male partner (cat. 50, 52). The role of caring father was one that Klimt himself evidently abandoned in the wake of Otto's death.[5]

Hope I was to have been included in Klimt's 1903 retrospective at the Vienna Secession, but it was removed at the instigation of the Minister of Education, who feared a public outcry. The painting's first owner, Wiener Werkstätte financier Fritz Waerndorfer, kept it concealed in a special cabinet to avoid offending visitors. The aura of scandal surrounding *Hope I*, hard to comprehend today,

Fig. 1
GUSTAV KLIMT
Hope I, 1903–04
National Gallery of Canada, Ottawa

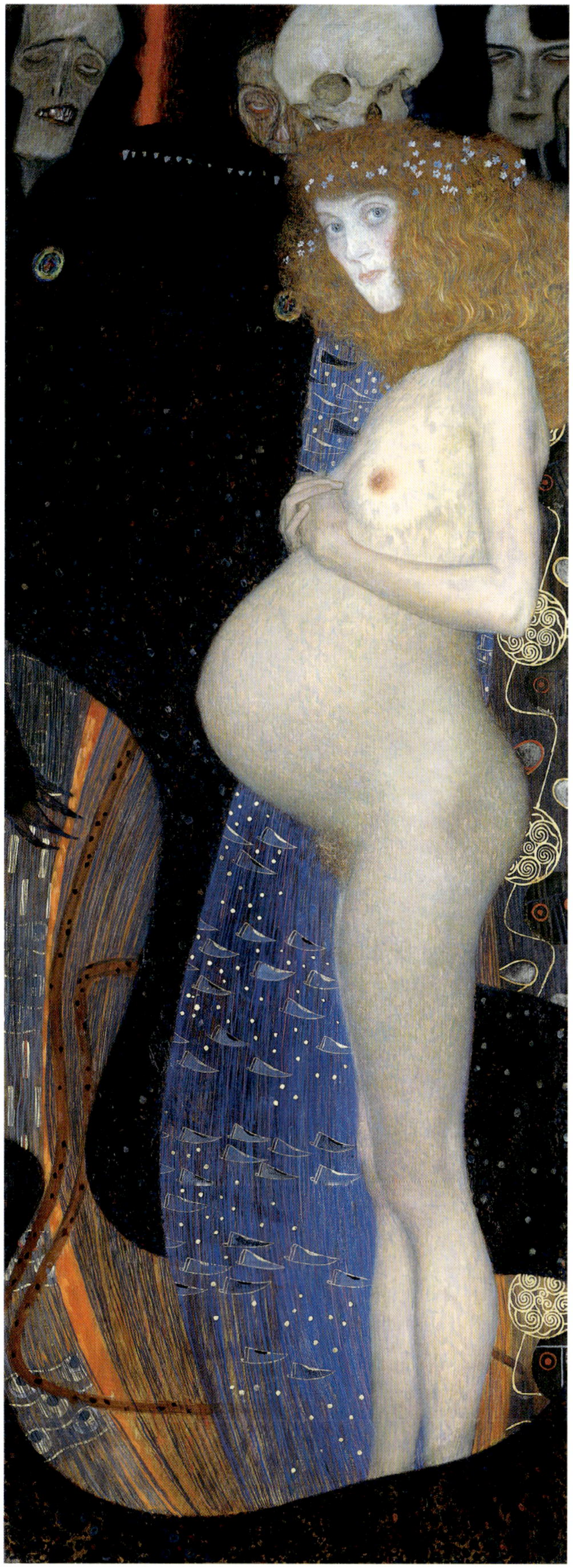

derived from the painting's overt pairing of sex and maternity. Clearly this is no chaste Madonna. The expectant mother's promiscuity is underscored by her full-figure nudity, seductive gaze and the swirl of suggestive ornamentation that surrounds her.

Not long after completing *Hope I*, Klimt painted his masterpiece on the theme of motherhood, *The Three Stages of Life* (cat. 51). This was a common allegorical subject, painted by Titian and Caspar David Friedrich, among others. For most artists, the "life" in question was a man's life. While Edvard Munch did a number of works depicting the *Three Stages of Woman*, the viewpoint was still resoundingly male: the women were given the stock roles of virgin, whore and nun (fig. 2). In Klimt's painting, one sees a woman passing through stages of life common to *both* genders, from infancy to adulthood to old age. Nevertheless, Klimt's woman is defined by her reproductive capacity. Eyes closed to the outer world, she occupies a separate realm shot through with symbols of ova, phalluses, sperm, pollen and amniotic fluid.[6] Once she has lost her childbearing potential, she is finished; a shriveled hag whose protruding belly mocks her former fecundity.

Schiele was similarly drawn to traditional allegorical representations of motherhood. His closest affinity was to the "dead mother," another of Munch's recurrent themes (fig. 3), and one also depicted in a well-known etching by Max Klinger (fig. 4). The surviving progeny in Schiele's *Dead Mother* paintings (Kp 177, 195) resemble more closely the indifferent incubus who sits atop the mother's bier in Klinger's etching than the bereft child in Munch's work. At the time he executed those paintings (1910–11), Schiele did not have a particularly good relationship with his own mother, a widow torn between a desire to support her son's vocation and the criticisms of her bourgeois relatives, who considered the young artist a disgrace. Perhaps as a result, he found it relatively easy to dispatch the mother in his work. What interested him was the child. Eyes wide open, the infant bursts with curiosity and creative potential. Schiele in fact titled his second version of the subject *The Birth of Genius* (fig. 5).

Schiele saw procreation and art as kindred forces, the only two ways to conquer death. In his view, the mother was just an expedient, a means to this end. The wide-eyed baby "genius" recurs in many of the artist's later depictions of mothers with children. And the mother, if no longer dead, often averts or shuts her eyes (cat. 58, 60, 62). The composition of Schiele's 1915–17 painting *Mother with Two Children* (cat. 62) is similar to Klimt's 1909–10 canvas *The Family* (cat. 61). However, whereas the eyes of all three figures are closed in the Klimt (suggesting the same self-contained feminine reverie alluded to in *The Three Ages of Life*), Schiele's figures engage the world, each in an emblematic manner. The infants represent two possible responses to life: the one passive and sleepy, the other alert and forward-looking. The mother, in her dun-colored shawl, recedes. Schiele assigns responsibility to the children, in effect balancing nature with nurture as the factors critical to an individual's fate.

Like Klimt, Schiele did numerous drawings of pregnant nudes, who were put at his disposal by their gynecologist, Erwin von Graff. [7] One can well imagine that these women, presumably charity cases or prostitutes, felt deeply humiliated. Sometimes their faces are blanked out, but in other instances the models stare at the artist with undisguised disdain (cat. 54). Schiele's own fear and horror literally color the women's swollen bellies: orange, yellow and poison green. Masterful evocations of mutual unease, these nudes are a far cry from Klimt's fertility goddesses.

Schiele had a further reason to call upon Dr. von Graff in the spring of 1910, when a girlfriend, known only by the initials L.A., apparently became pregnant. [8] It is not clear what happened to the child, who may have died, been aborted, adopted out or raised by L.A. Coincidentally (or not), toward the end of 1910 Schiele began a relationship with two models (probably prostitutes), one of whom had a baby (cat. 56). Schiele's drawings of this infant are in most cases very different from the vital allegorical babies in his paintings. Often faceless, the child is presented as a sucking homunculus, a lumpy appendage grasping blindly at its mother. Childbirth appealed to Schiele more as metaphor than as a reality. After his wife Edith conceived in early 1918, he never once drew or painted her in a state of noticeable pregnancy. His late masterpiece, *The Family* (Kp 326), was not an autobiographical statement,[9] but rather an allegorical representation of an ideal that Schiele, in life, was never to achieve.

Kokoschka, too, never had an identifiable child, though he yearned for one when he was in his late twenties. Unlike Klimt and Schiele, who had repeated liaisons with members of the *demi-monde*, Kokoschka had fallen in love with a proper lady, the beautiful widow Alma Schindler Mahler. As a widow, Alma enjoyed a special status: she was an available woman who was neither virgin nor whore. This was a powerful attraction, and yet also deeply troubling to Oskar. He wanted Alma to bear his child, to bind her to him and neutralize her appeal to others. Twice he impregnated her. The first time she aborted the fetus.[10] The second time she either miscarried or had another abortion.[11] Visiting his lover in the sanitarium after she had terminated the first pregnancy, Oskar took away the cotton pad that had been used to stanch her bleeding. "That is, and will always be, my only child," he told her. Thereafter, Alma recalled, "He always had with him that dried-out cotton pad."[12]

Kokoschka brooded inconsolably about Alma's abortion(s), working through the trauma in numerous drawings and prints.[13] With a curious sort of wishful thinking, he repeatedly allegorized Alma as the Virgin Mary: as if, by bearing his child, she might have been returned to a state of purity. His lover receives the news of her second pregnancy in the form of a divine Annunciation (WW 56); she holds their dead child like a Pietà (cat. 98). Oskar identified so closely with the unborn child (who, he was convinced, had been a boy) that he consistently gave him his own face (cat. 68) and often depicted him as a full-grown man. In effect, it was not a fetus, but Oskar whom Alma had killed. One wonders whether the artist truly wanted to be a father, or merely to himself benefit from Alma's maternal love. Like Klimt, Kokoschka saw the mother and child as a self-contained unit (cat. 67, 81),[14] and he perhaps hoped to return to that protective cocoon.

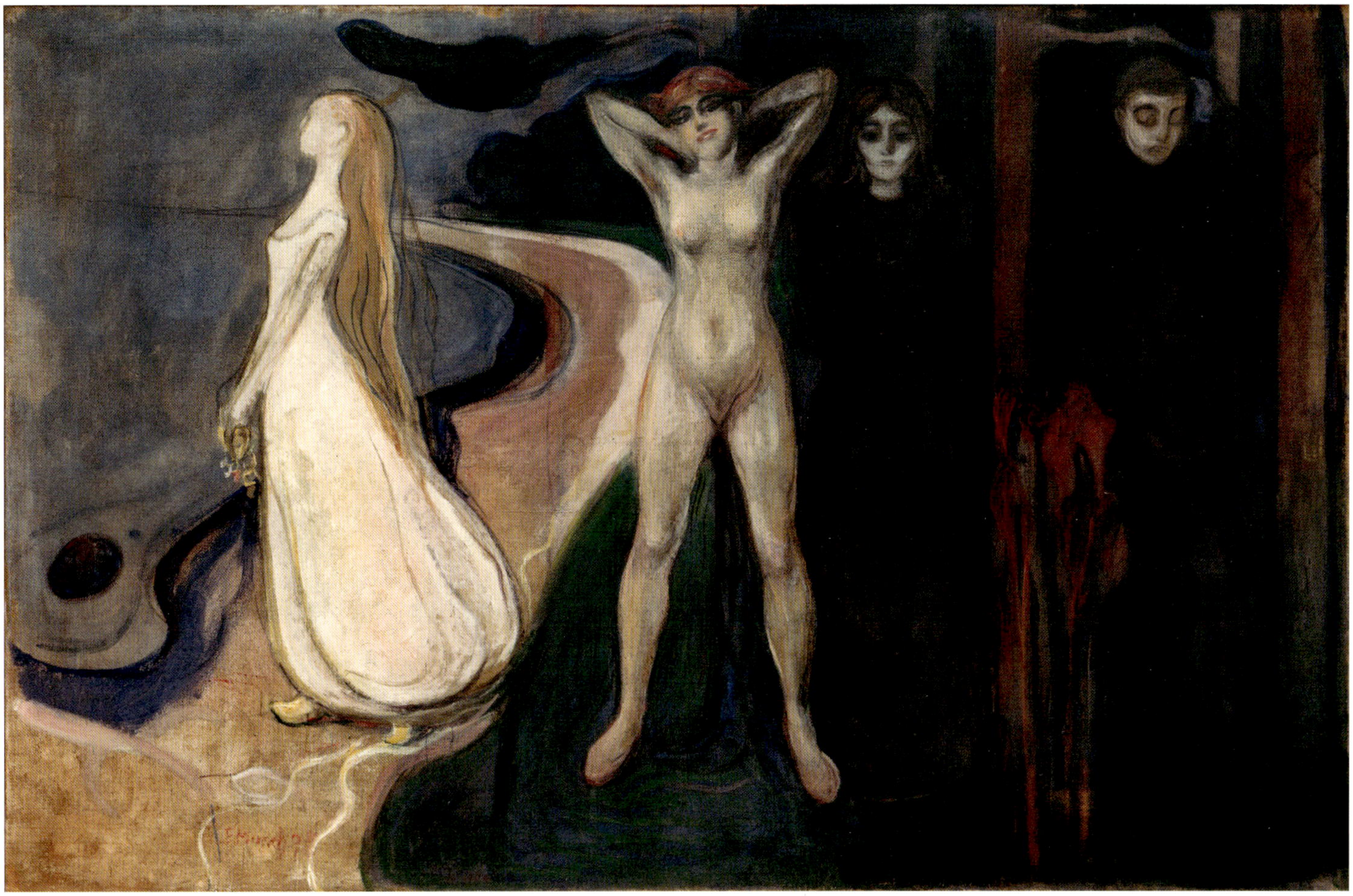

Fig. 2
EDVARD MUNCH
The Three Stages of Woman, 1894
KODE – Art museums of Bergen, Rasmus Meyers Collection

The desire for a female love object devoid of carnal knowledge was in no way unique to Kokoschka. His older cronies Adolf Loos and Peter Altenberg idealized the so-called *Kind-Mädchen* (child-girl). Altenberg once said that he preferred girls "when they are about five or six years old and no longer wet their pants."[15] Loos would marry—and divorce—three much younger wives.[16] He was convicted of molesting a minor in 1928, when he was fifty-eight. Karl Kraus, also a member of this clique, defended a mutual friend, Theodor Beer, who was accused of pedophilia.[17]

But unlike Loos, Kraus and Altenberg, Kokoschka was a *Kind-Mann*, twenty-one years old, when he created his paean to adolescent love, *Die träumenden Knaben* (The Dreaming Youths). The subject of Kokoschka's "dream" was a sixteen-year-old Kunstgewerbeschule classmate, Lilith Lang. Not only was the artist's infatuation age appropriate, but it was never consummated. Despite Kokoschka's fierce text, his illustrations for *Die träumenden Knaben* are surprisingly innocent. Androgyny blunts Lilith's sexuality. In the final plate (p. 232, fig. 4), the only one that shows her with Oskar, it is hard to tell which figure is the boy and which the girl, harder still to imagine that the two, each isolated in a white surround, could ever mate. Contemporaneous drawings of Lilith and other adolescent nudes similarly elide all secondary sexual characteristics, making the girls look younger than they probably were (fig. 6, cat. 69, 70, 72).

Even as Sigmund Freud was promulgating his theories about infant sexuality,[18] Kokoschka saw childhood as an Edenic state of innocence. Speaking of his double portrait, *Children Playing* (cat. 71), he noted that he had been careful to avoid "treading on the snake that already caused Adam and Eve to fall."[19] Like Adam and Eve, the naked

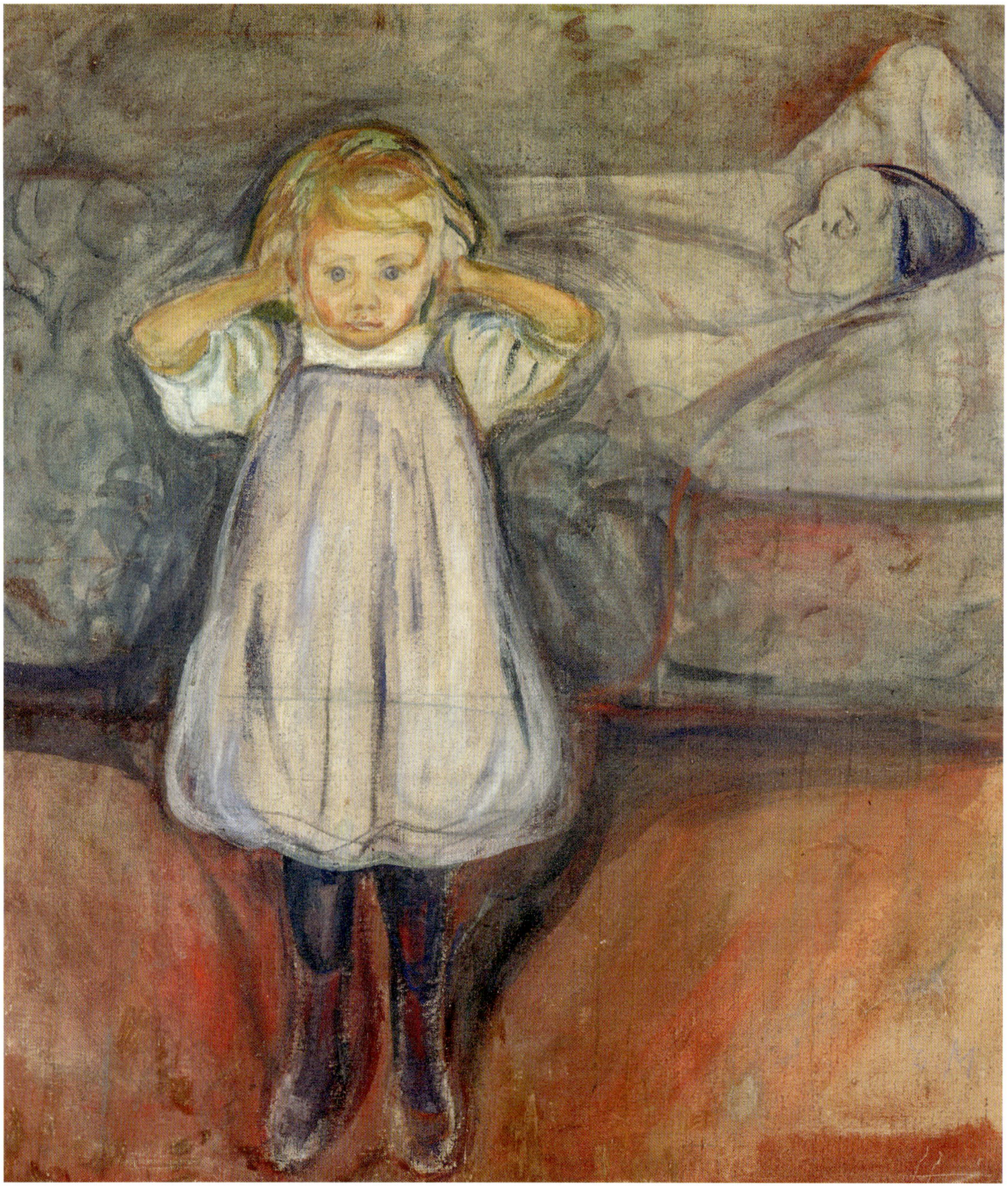

Fig. 3
EDVARD MUNCH
The Child and Death, 1899
Kunsthalle Bremen – Der Kunstverein in Bremen

children in Kokoschka's drawings and watercolors never seem aware of their nudity (cat. 73, 74). The artist believed that children occupy a "dream-realm (*Traumreich*), much of which is lost to adults, even if they try to be childish."[20] Knowing that he could not return to this *Traumreich*, Kokoschka nonetheless tried to capture that sense of separateness in his many portraits of children (cat. 75, 76, 78, 79).

Schiele's view of childhood was more jaded. "There are many children who are corrupted," he wrote. "But then what does it actually mean: corrupted? Have adults forgotten how corrupted, that is, incited and aroused by the sex impulse, they themselves were as children?"[21] Schiele's arrest on morals charges in 1912 is often interpreted as a case of pedophilia. However, there is no evidence that the artist was guilty of such an offense.

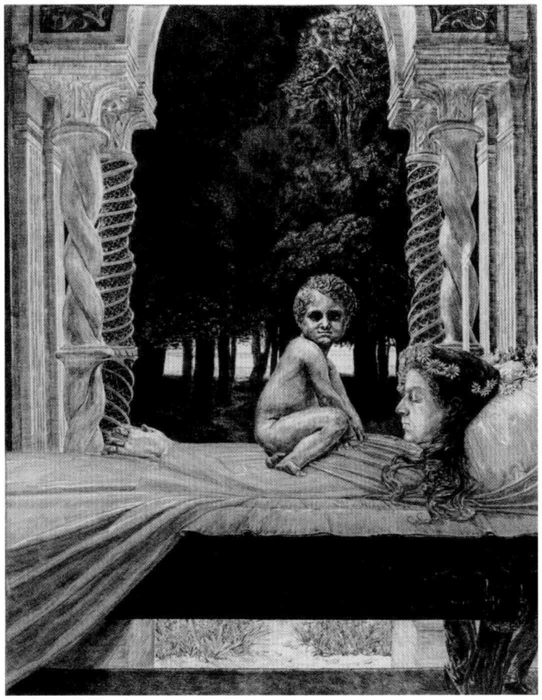

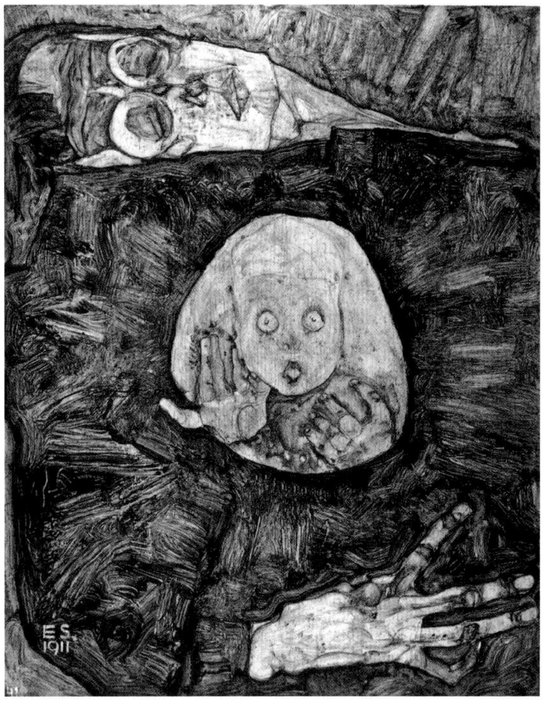

Fig. 4
MAX KLINGER
The Dead Mother,
c. 1898–1910
Museum der bildenden Künste, Leipzig

Fig. 5
EGON SCHIELE
The Birth of a Genius (Dead Mother II), 1911
Presumed destroyed

Schiele, who viewed himself as an "eternal child,"[22] felt at ease with children, and they with him. Neighborhood kids liked hanging out at his studios, first in Vienna and then in the more buttoned-down village of Neulengbach. Of course, bourgeois parents, fantasizing that the studio was a den of iniquity, did not consider it an appropriate hangout. Schiele in the end was convicted of "offenses against public morality" for exposing minors to erotic artworks.[23]

Schiele's explorations of adolescent sexuality were undertaken with prostitutes who were in all likelihood above the legal age of consent (cat. 123).[24] Very few of the artist's drawings depict underage children in the nude. The subjects of these nudes include (mostly male) street urchins and the daughter of one of his professional models (cat. 65). Naked or clothed, however, Schiele's children almost never appear innocent. Perhaps because they were for the most part members of the underclass, they exude a worldliness well beyond their years (cat. 55, 66).

Klimt was less interested in childhood *per se* than were Kokoschka and Schiele. Nevertheless, Klimt's one commissioned painting of a child, Mäda Primavesi (fig. 8, cat. 63, 64), is surprisingly insightful. In fact, this spunky, self-aware little girl evinces considerably more character than is revealed in the artist's painting of her mother (cat. 30) or indeed most of his portraits of grown women. Klimt had a close relationship with Emilie Flöge's little niece, Gertrude Flöge (fig. 7), and his affinity to children is demonstrated in numerous drawings. Although the three artists differed in their approaches, each felt a freedom with child subjects that was sometimes absent in their more tendentious treatment of adult themes.

1 Alfred Weidinger [ed.], *Gustav Klimt*, New York/Munich 2007, p. 210.
2 Christian Nebehay (*Gustav Klimt: Von der Skizze zum Bild*, Vienna 1992, p. 264) makes mention of fourteen children, but Hansjörg Krug, the current proprietor of the Nebehay Gallery, says that the existence of only six children (two of whom died in infancy) can be proven. Three mothers (Marie Ucicka, Marie Zimmerman and an unnamed woman) received payments from the artist's estate.
3 Marian Bisanz-Prakken, *Gustav Klimt: The Magic of Line* (exh. cat. J. Paul Getty Museum, Los Angeles), Los Angeles 2012, p. 156.
4 Hans Koppel, "Wiener Neuigkeiten bei Gustav Klimt," in: *Die Zeit*, Nov. 15, 1903, p. 4.
5 Weidinger 2007 (see note 1), pp. 274–75.

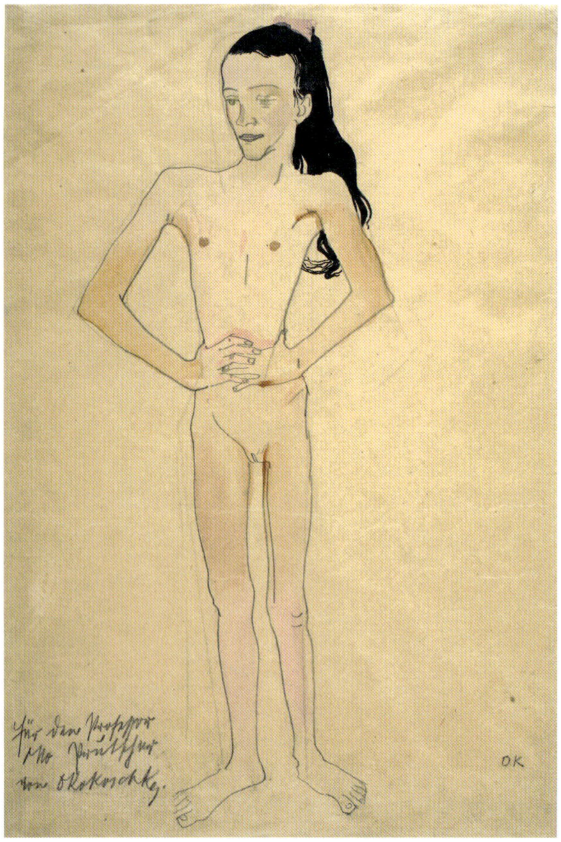

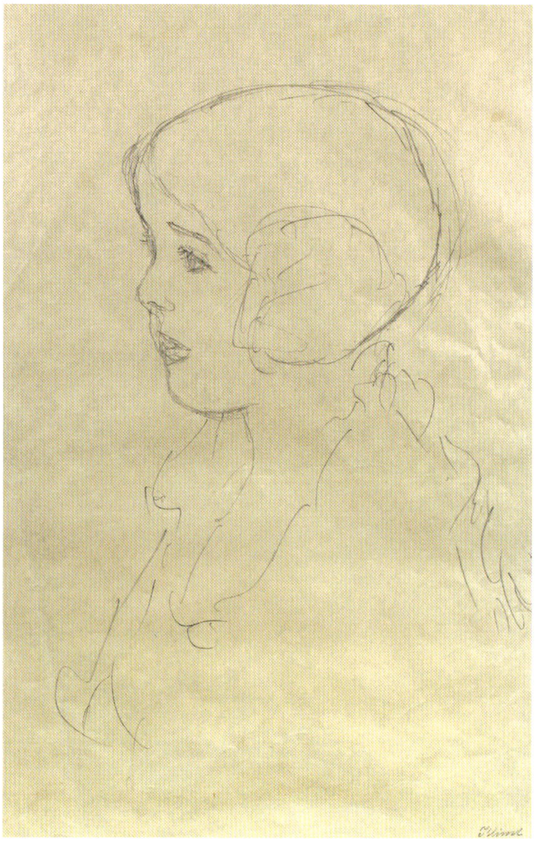

Fig. 6
OSKAR KOKOSCHKA
Girl Nude, Hands on her Waist, 1907
Private collection

Fig. 7
GUSTAV KLIMT
Gertrude Flöge, 1912
Private collection

6 Emily Braun, "Ornament as Evolution: Gustav Klimt and Berta Zuckerkandl," in: Renée Price (ed.), *Gustav Klimt: The Ronald S. Lauder and Serge Sabarsky Collections* (exh. cat. Neue Galerie, New York), New York 2007, pp. 153–54.
7 Jane Kallir, *Egon Schiele: The Complete Works*, New York 1990, p. 75.
8 Christian M. Nebehay, *Egon Schiele 1890–1918: Leben, Briefe, Gedichte,* Salzburg/Vienna 1979, no. 102.
9 *Squatting Couple*, Schiele's title for *The Family*, places the painting within a contemporaneous allegorical cycle on the stages of human existence. The woman is not the artist's wife, but a professional model.
10 Alfred Weidinger, *Kokoschka and Alma Mahler*, New York/ Munich 1996, p. 22.
11 Alfred Weidinger and Alice Strobl, *Oskar Kokoschka: Die Zeichnungen und Aquarelle 1897–1916*, Salzburg 2008, pp. 360–61, 407.
12 Weidinger 1996 (see note 10), p. 22.
13 Of four print cycles depicting Kokoschka's relationship with Alma Mahler (*Columbus in Chains*, *The Chinese Wall*, *The Bach Cantata* and *Allos Makar*), the first two deal most directly with the abortion.
14 Weidinger and Strobl 2008 (see note 11), p. 72.
15 "So von dem Alter an, in dem sie sich nicht mehr anwischerln, so zwischen fünf und sechs!" (cited in Alexander Sixtus von Reden and Josef Schweikhardt, *Eros unterm Doppeladler: Eine Sittengeschichte Altösterreichs,* Vienna 1993*,* p. 168 [translated by Jane Kallir]).
16 Loos separated from his first wife, Lina Obertimpfler, in 1905, after three years of marriage. Loos's second marriage, in 1919, to Elsie Grünfeld-Altmann, also ended in divorce (in 1926), as did his 1929 marriage to Claire Beck (the couple divorced in 1932).
17 Burkhard Rukschio and Roland Schachel, *Adolf Loos: Leben und Werk*, Salzburg 1982, p. 95.
18 Sigmund Freud, "The Sexual Instinct in Neurotics," in *Three Essays on the Theory of Sexuality*, 1905, reprinted in Peter Gay (ed.), *The Freud Reader*, New York 1989.
19 Oskar Kokoschka, *Mein Leben*, Munich 1969, p. 86 (translated by Jane Kallir).
20 Ibid.
21 Alessandra Comini, *Schiele in Prison*, New York 1973, p. 59.
22 Nebehay 1979 (see note 8), no. 171.
23 Kallir 1990 (see note 7), pp. 136–37.
24 In the late nineteenth century, the age of consent in Austria was fourteen, and the majority of prostitutes were adolescents. (See Sander L. Gilman, *Difference and Pathology: Stereotypes of Sexuality, Race and Madness*, Ithaca, NY 1985, p. 41).

Fig. 8
GUSTAV KLIMT
Mäda Primavesi, 1913
Metropolitan Museum of Art, New York

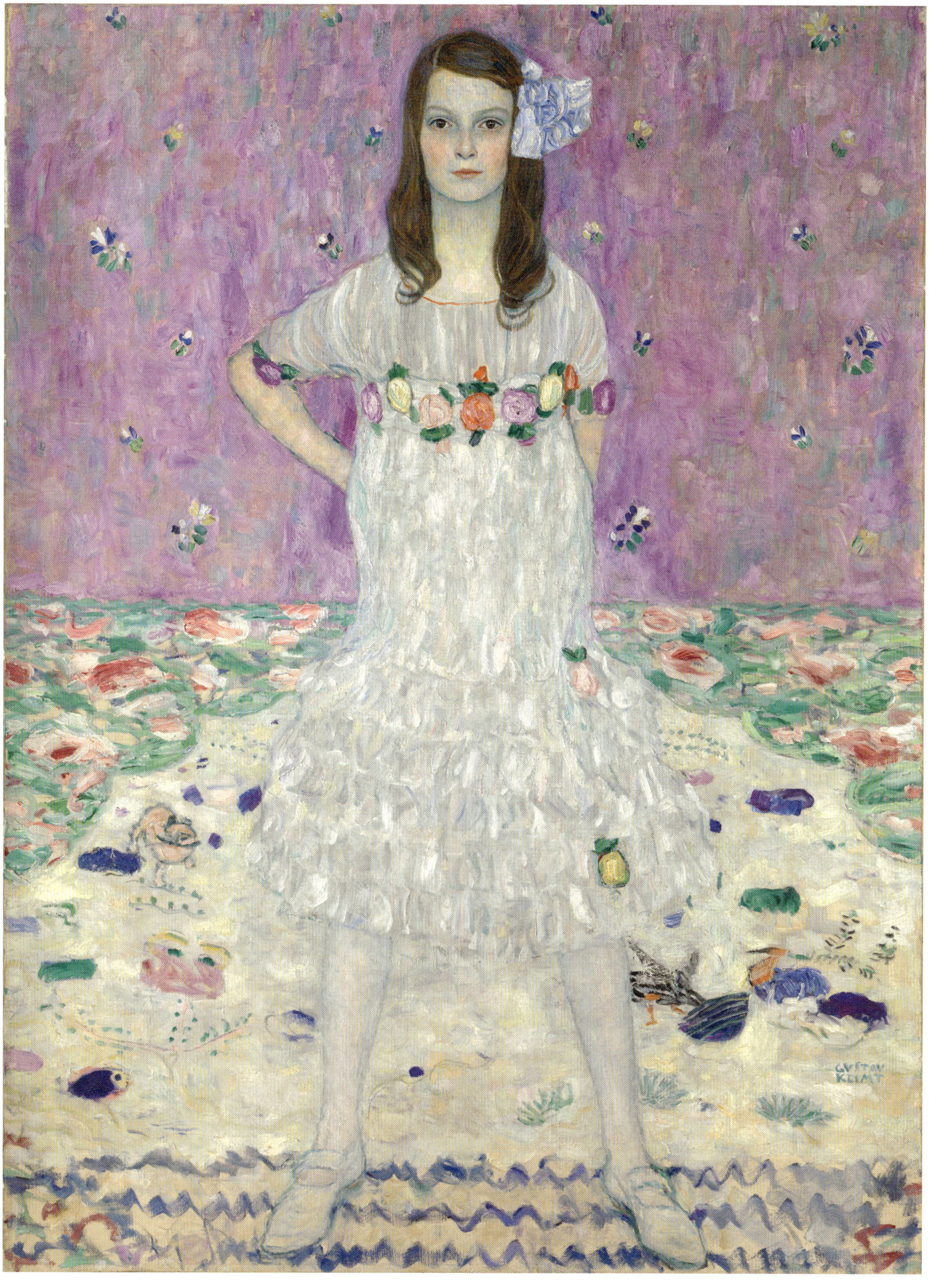
GUSTAV
KLIMT

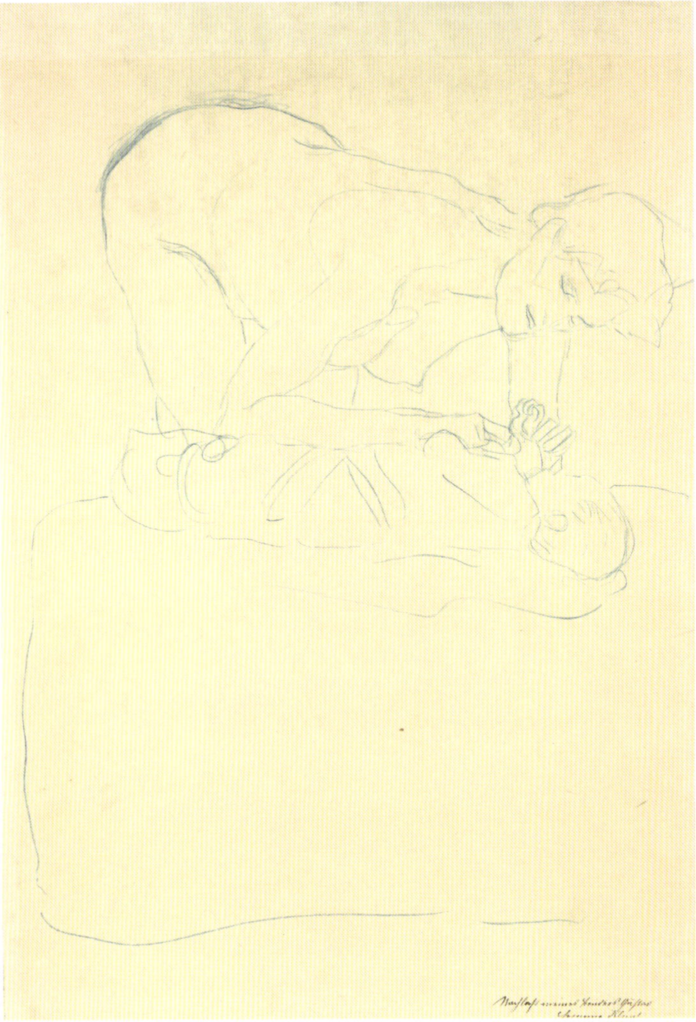

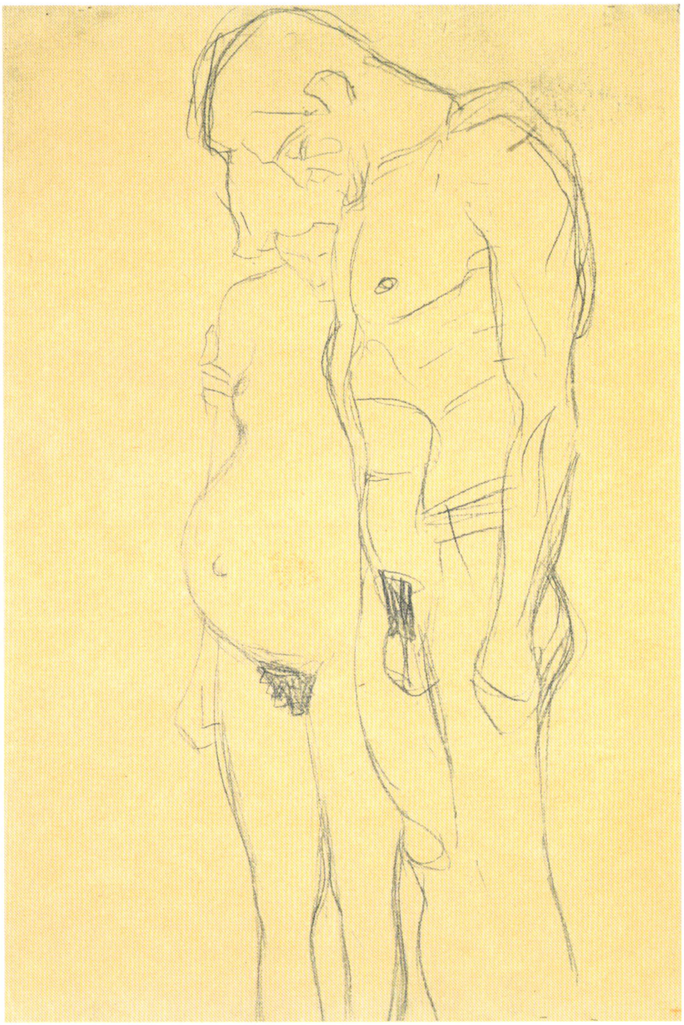

Cat. 49
GUSTAV KLIMT
Mother and Child, 1906–07
Blue pencil on paper, 53 x 37 cm
Albertina, Vienna

Cat. 50
GUSTAV KLIMT
Pregnant Woman and Man, 1903–04
Blue crayon on paper, 44.8 x 30.8 cm
Private collection

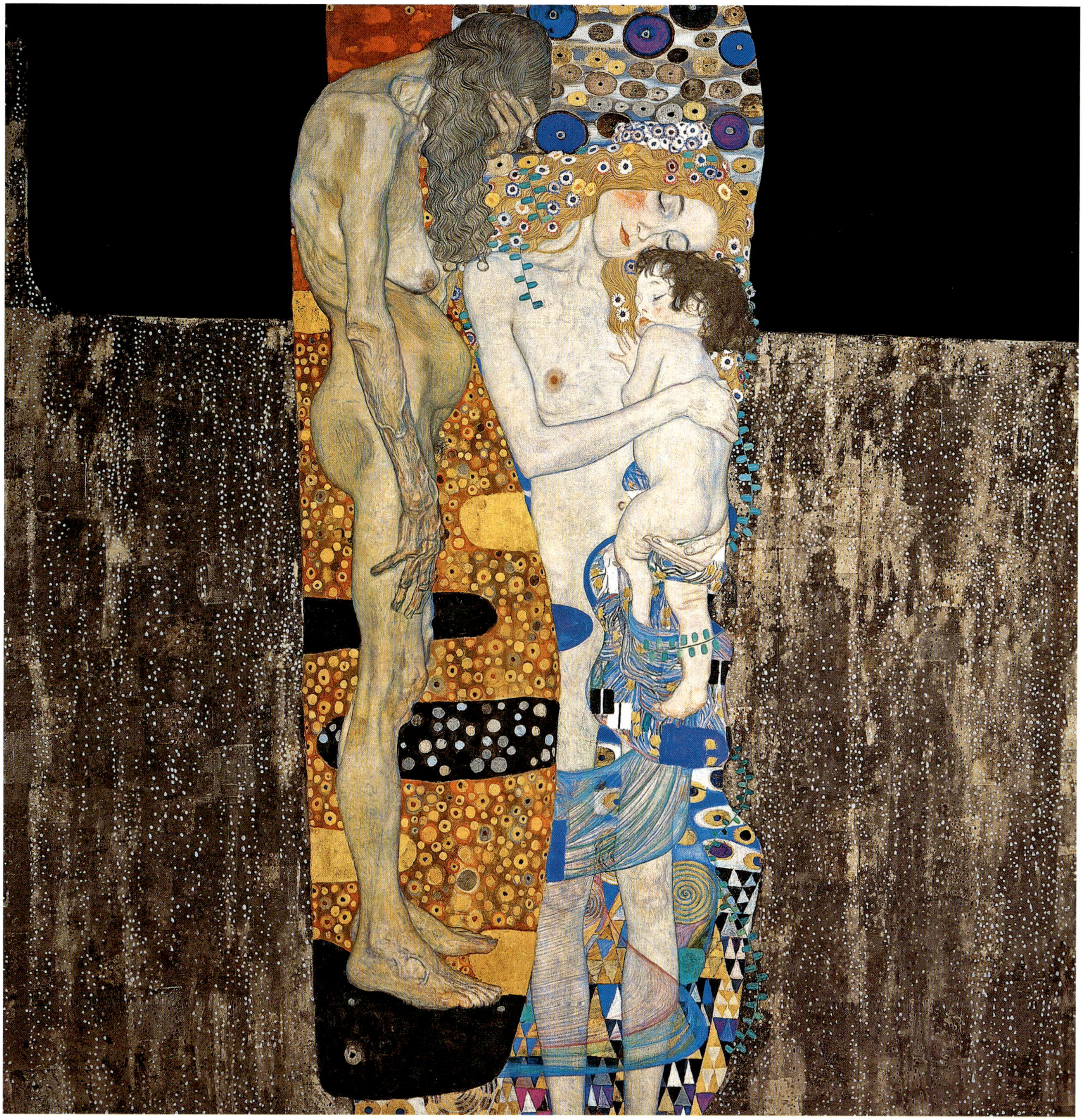

Cat. 51
GUSTAV KLIMT
The Three Ages of Woman, 1905
Oil on canvas, 180 x 180 cm
Galleria Nazionale d'Arte Moderna, Rome

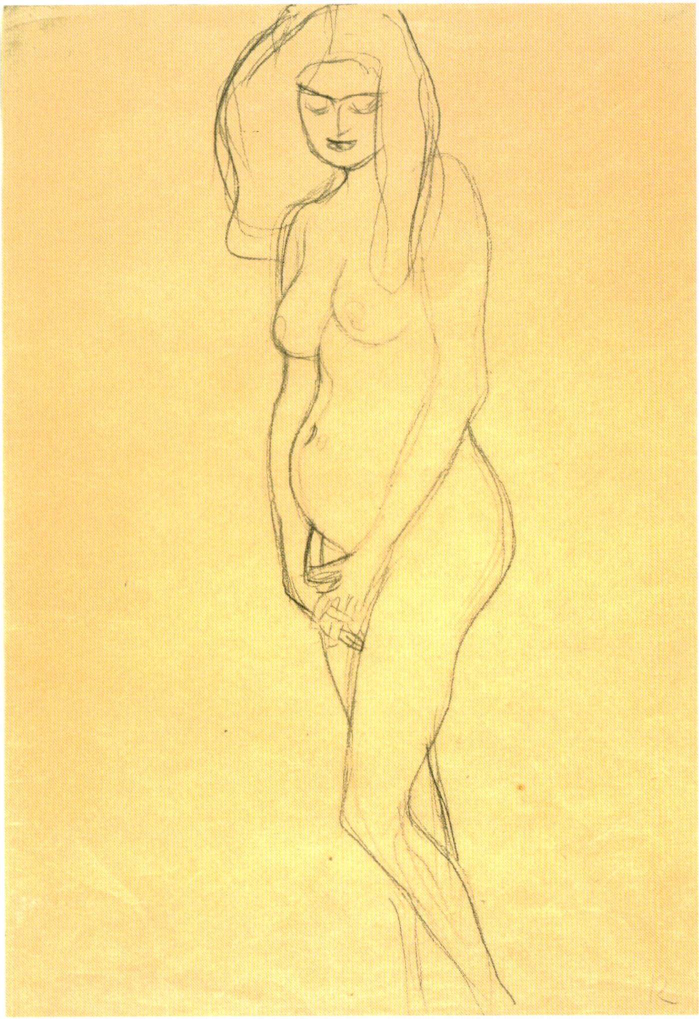

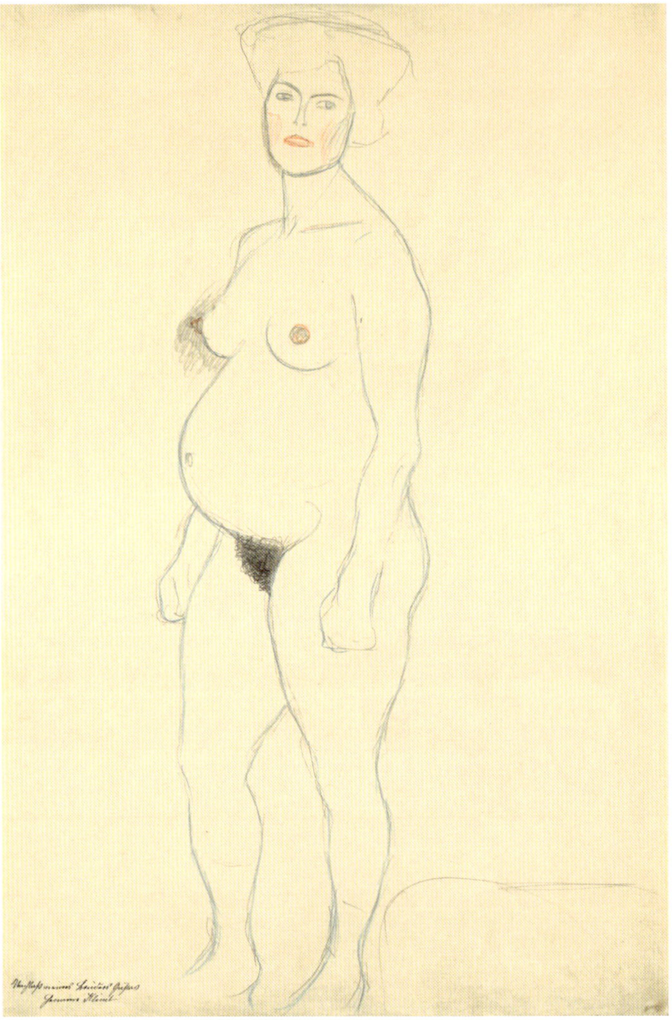

Cat. 52
GUSTAV KLIMT
Standing Pregnant Woman, Facing Left, 1903–04
Black crayon, 44.8 x 31.4 cm
Private collection

Cat. 53
GUSTAV KLIMT
Pregnant Nude, Standing (Study for Hope II), 1907–08
Pencil, red and blue pencil on paper, 55.8 × 37.1 cm
Wien Museum, Vienna

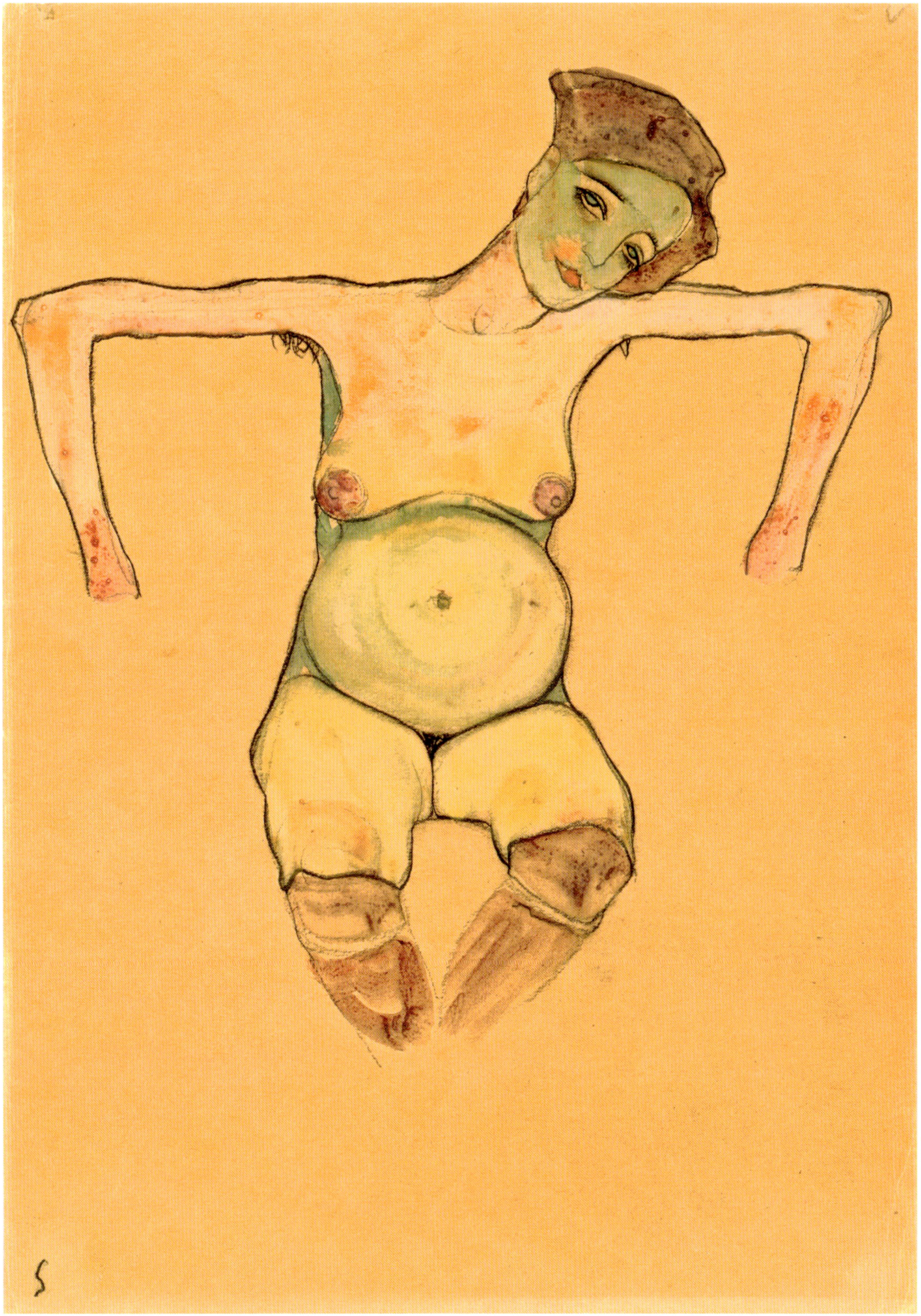

Cat. 54
EGON SCHIELE
Pregnant Woman, 1910
Watercolor and charcoal on paper,
45.1 x 31.1 cm
Private collection

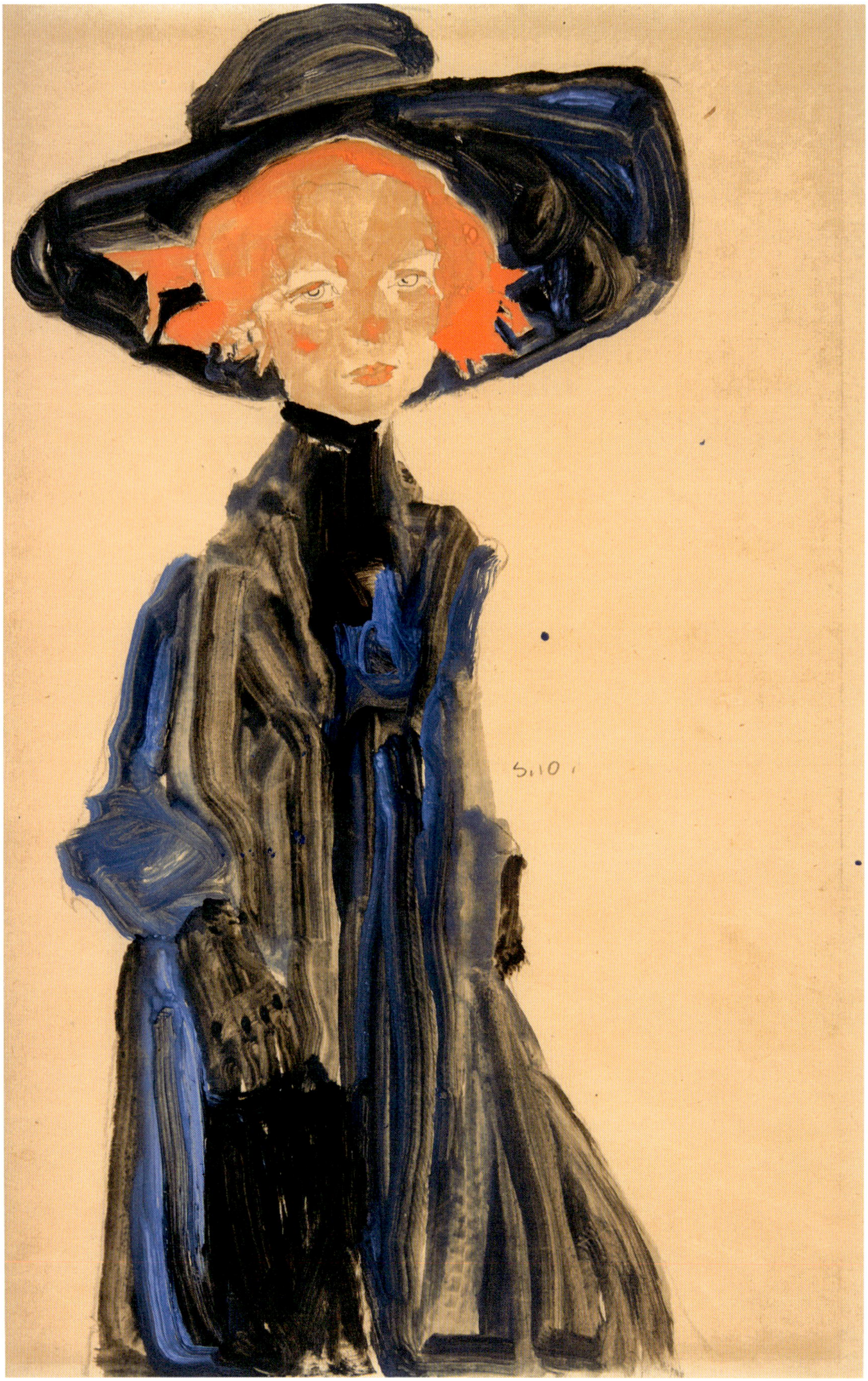

Cat. 55
EGON SCHIELE
Girl in Blue, 1910
Watercolor on paper, 43.5 x 27.5 cm
NordseeMuseum. Nissenhaus Husum

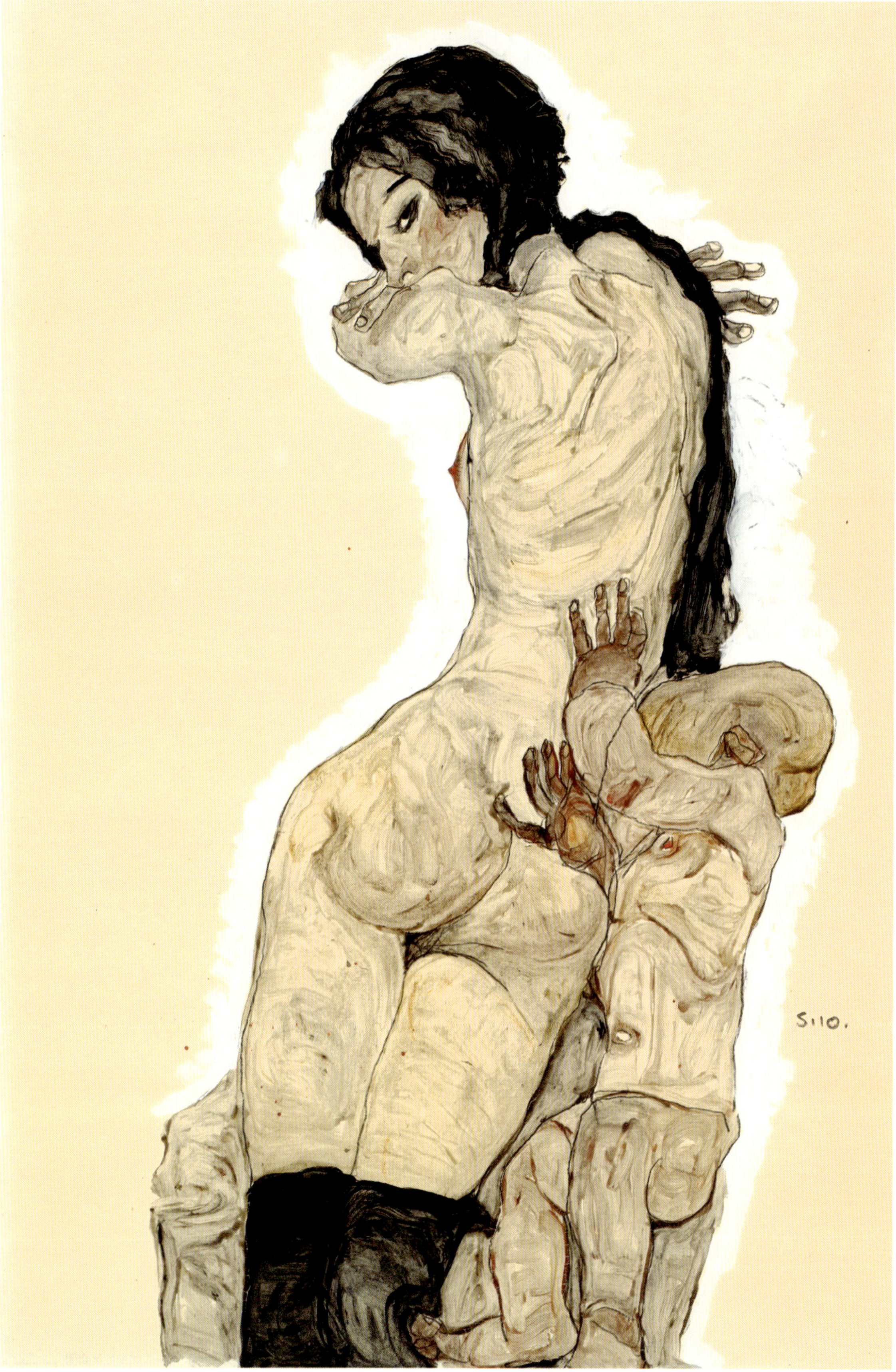

Cat. 56
EGON SCHIELE
Mother and Child, 1910
Gouache, watercolor, and pencil on paper, 55.6 x 36.5 cm
Private collection, courtesy of Richard Nagy Ltd., London

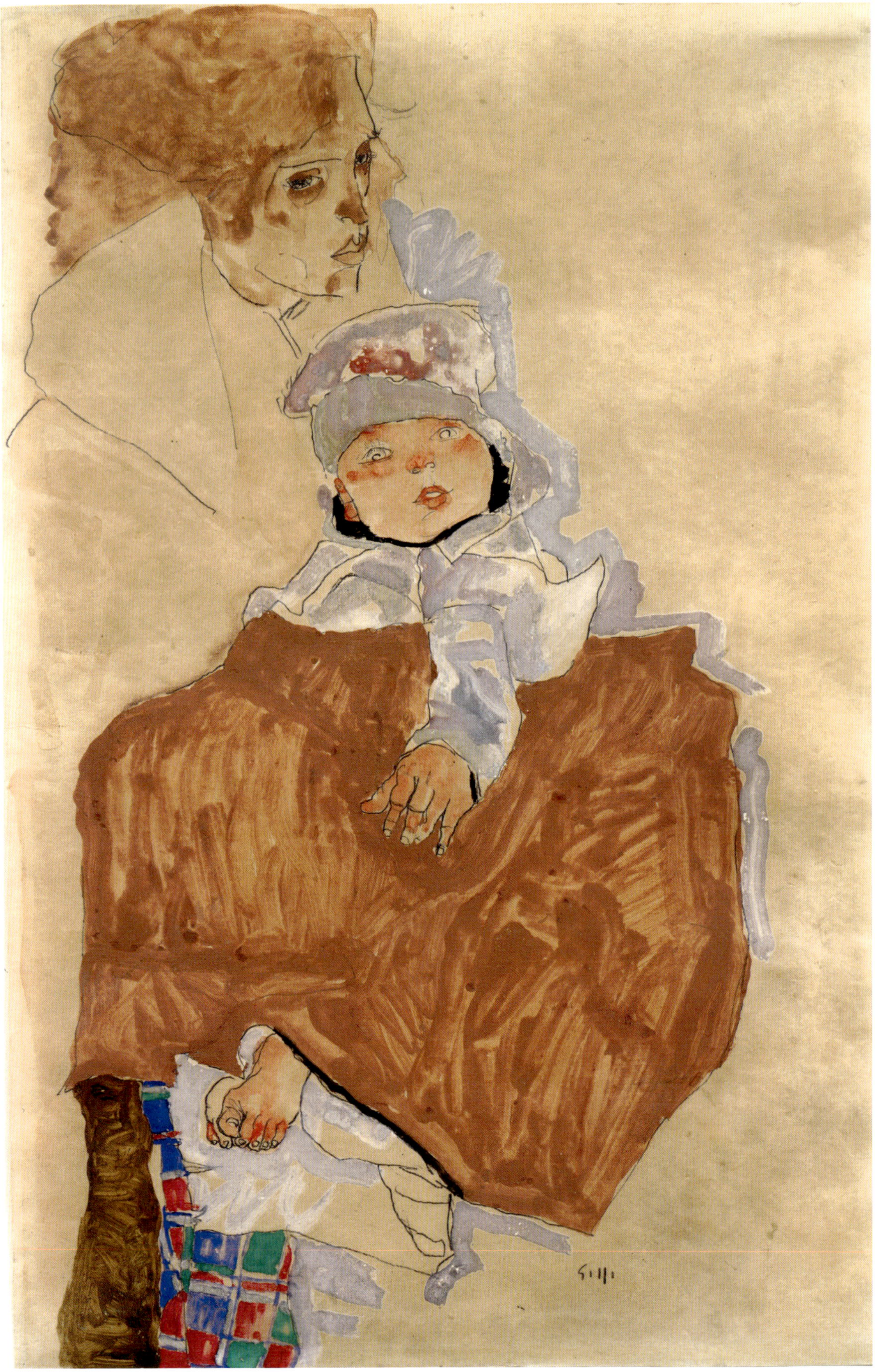

Cat. 57
EGON SCHIELE
Mother and Child, 1911
Gouache and pencil on paper,
54 x 35 cm
Private collection,
courtesy of Galerie St. Etienne,
New York

Cat. 58
EGON SCHIELE
Mother and Child II, 1912
Oil on wood, 36.5 x 29.2 cm
Leopold Museum, Vienna

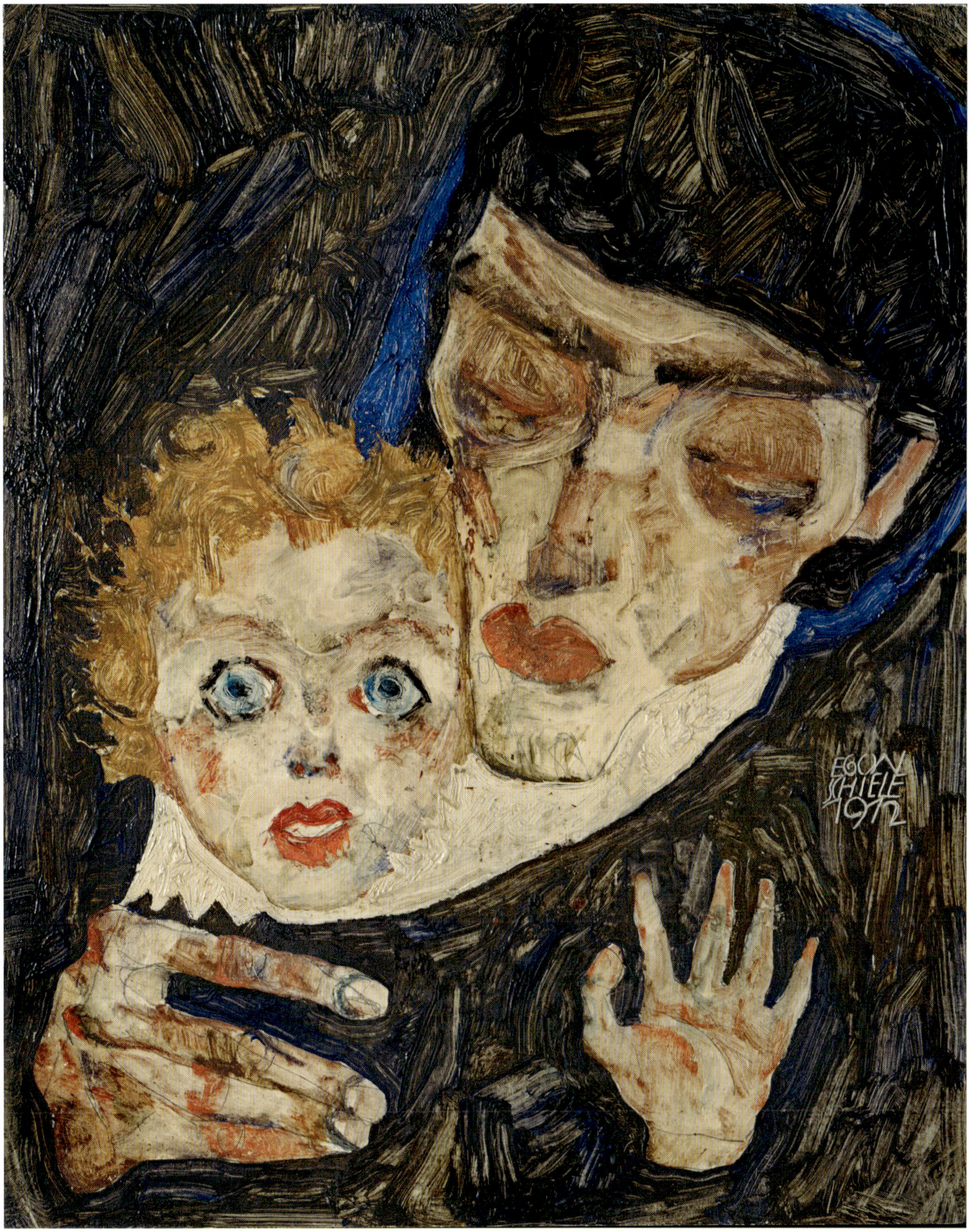
EGON
SCHIELE
1912

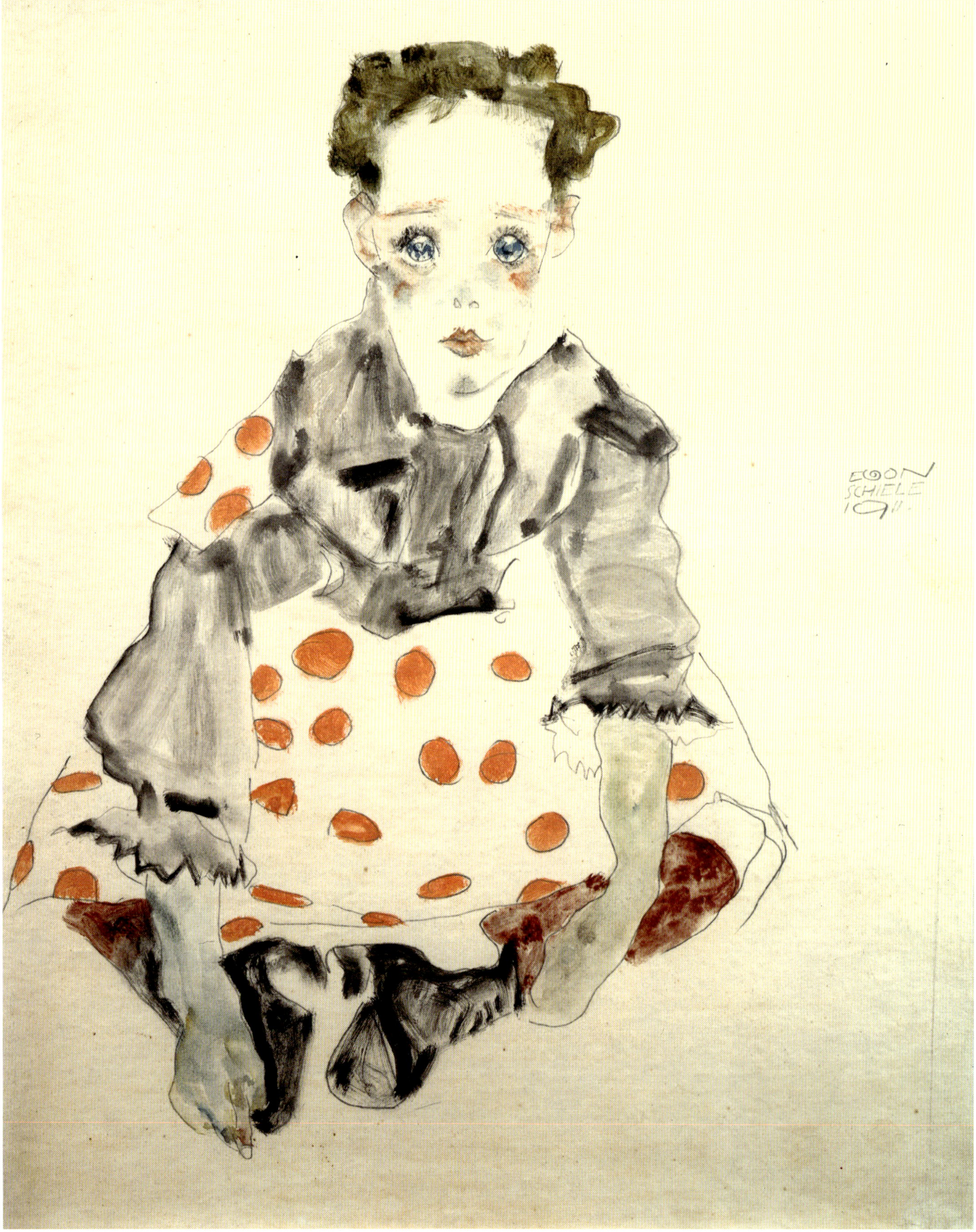
EGON
SCHIELE
1911

Cat. 59
EGON SCHIELE
Girl in Polka-Dot Dress, 1911
Watercolor and pencil on paper,
43.3 x 30.3 cm
Private collection, courtesy of
Galerie St. Etienne, New York

Cat. 60
EGON SCHIELE
Mother and Child, 1914
Gouache and pencil on paper,
48.2 x 31.9 cm
Leopold Museum, Vienna

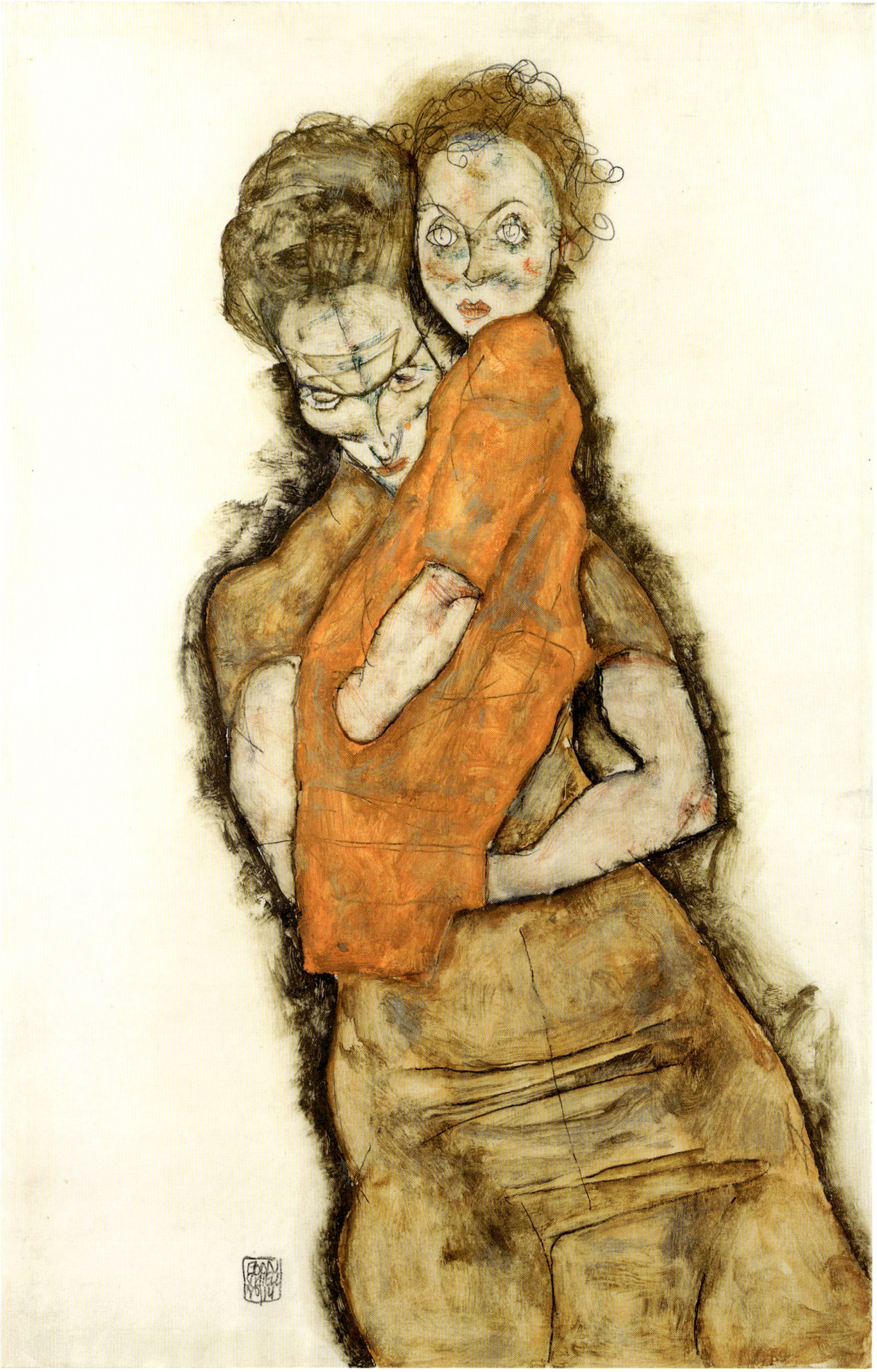

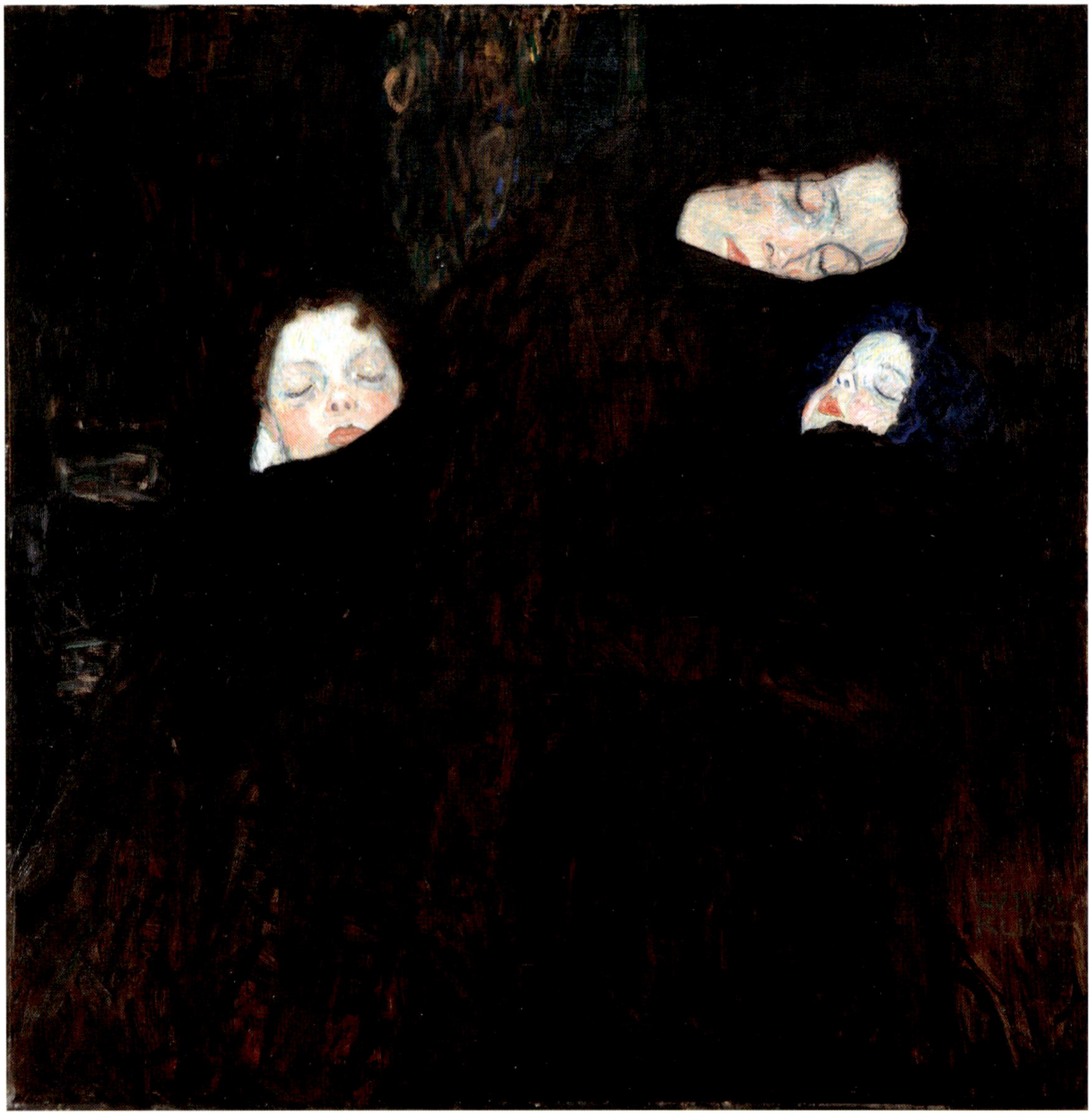

Cat. 61
GUSTAV KLIMT
Family, 1909–10
Oil on canvas, 90 x 90 cm
Belvedere, Vienna

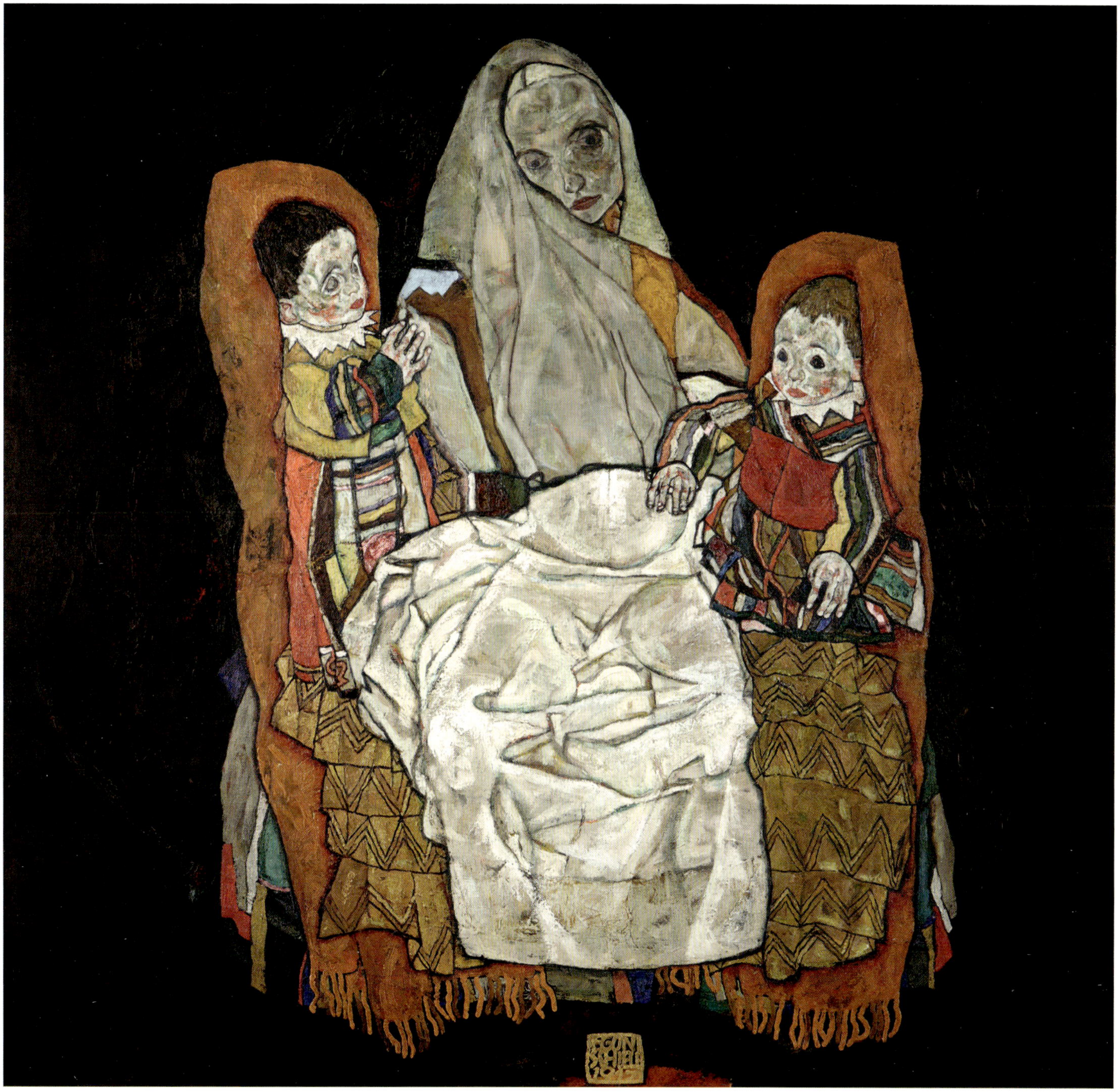

Cat. 62
EGON SCHIELE
Mother with Two Children III, 1917
Oil on canvas, 150 x 158.7 cm
Belvedere, Vienna

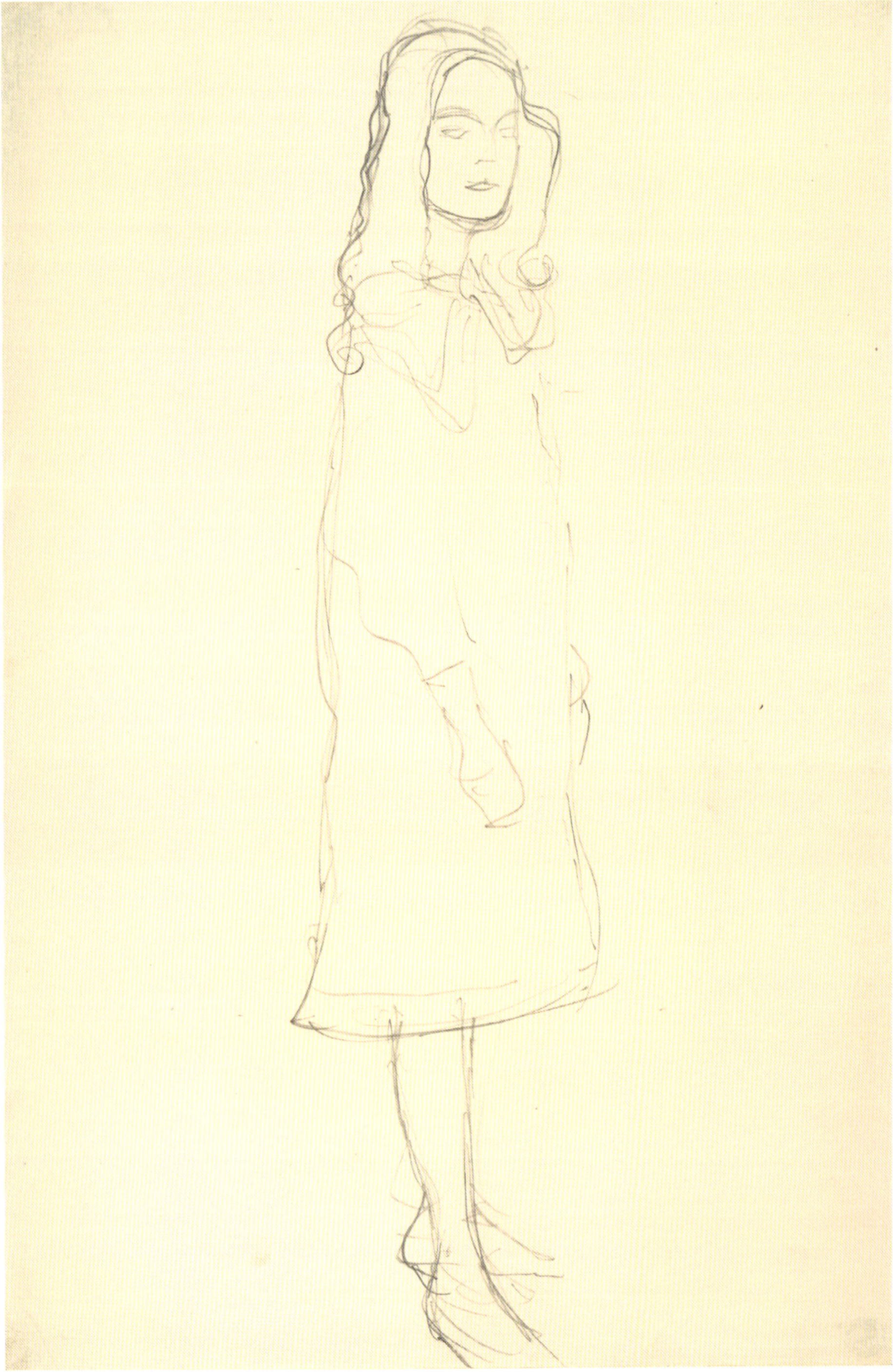

Cat. 63
GUSTAV KLIMT
Standing Girl with Coat, Facing Right (study for Mäda Primavesi), 1912–13
Pencil on paper, 55.9 x 36.7 cm
Albertina, Vienna

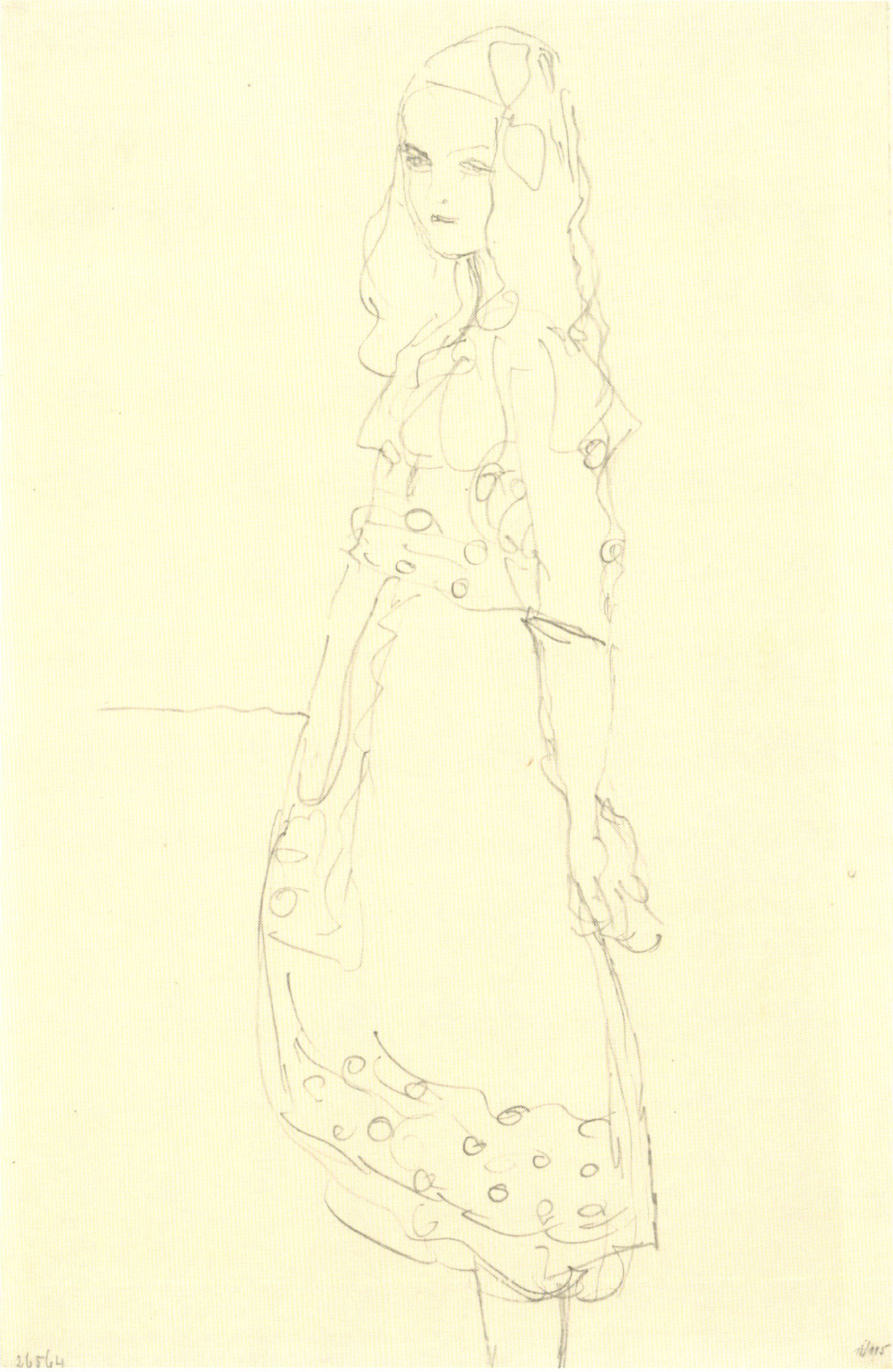

Cat. 64
GUSTAV KLIMT
Mäda Primavesi, Standing, Facing Left, 1912–13
Pencil on paper, 56 x 36.7 cm
Academy of Fine Arts, Vienna, Graphic Collection

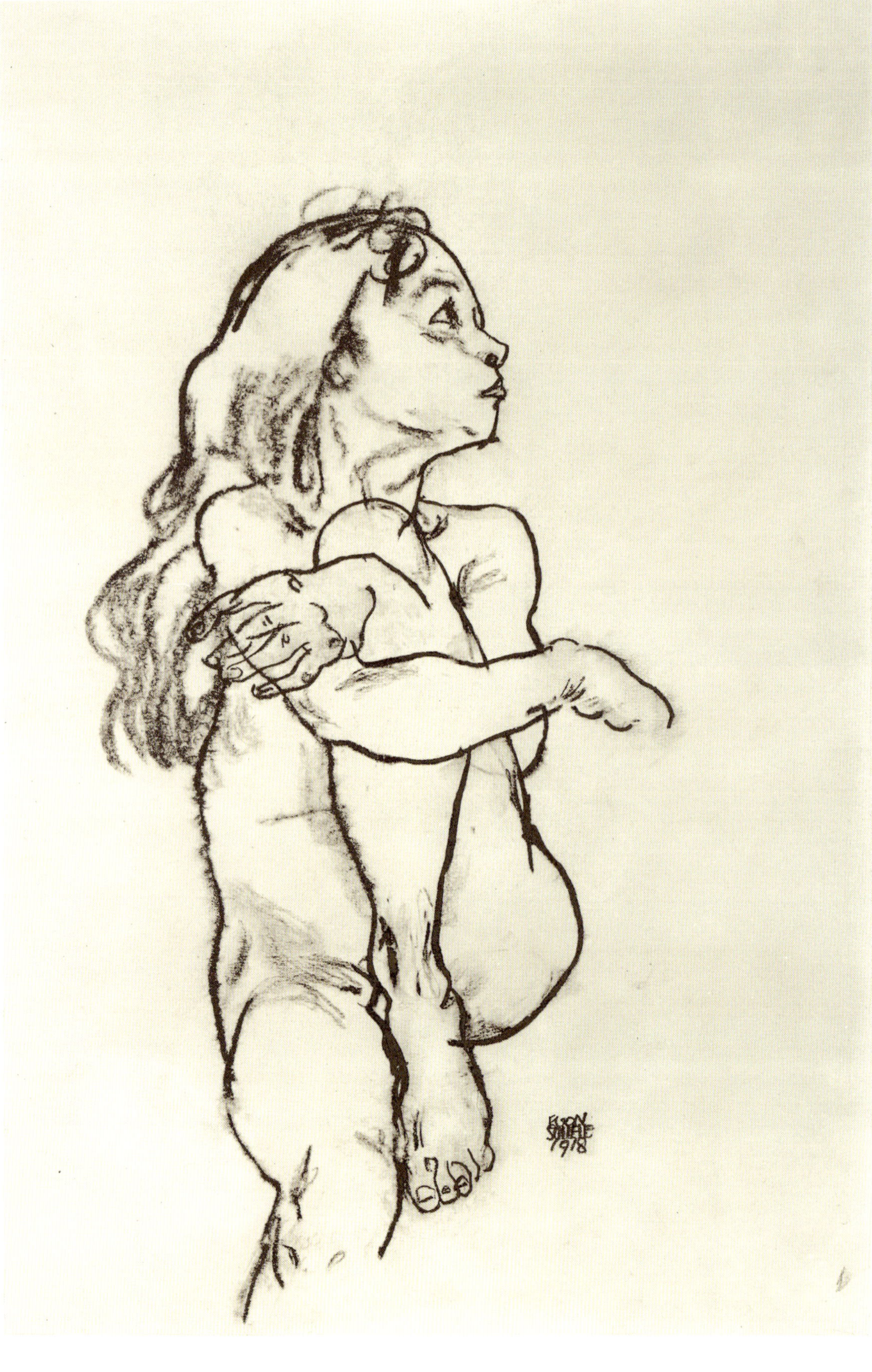

Cat. 65
EGON SCHIELE
Seated Nude Girl Clasping Her Knee, 1918
Charcoal on paper, 46.4 x 26.4 cm
The Metropolitan Museum of Art, New York, bequest of Scofield Thayer, 1982

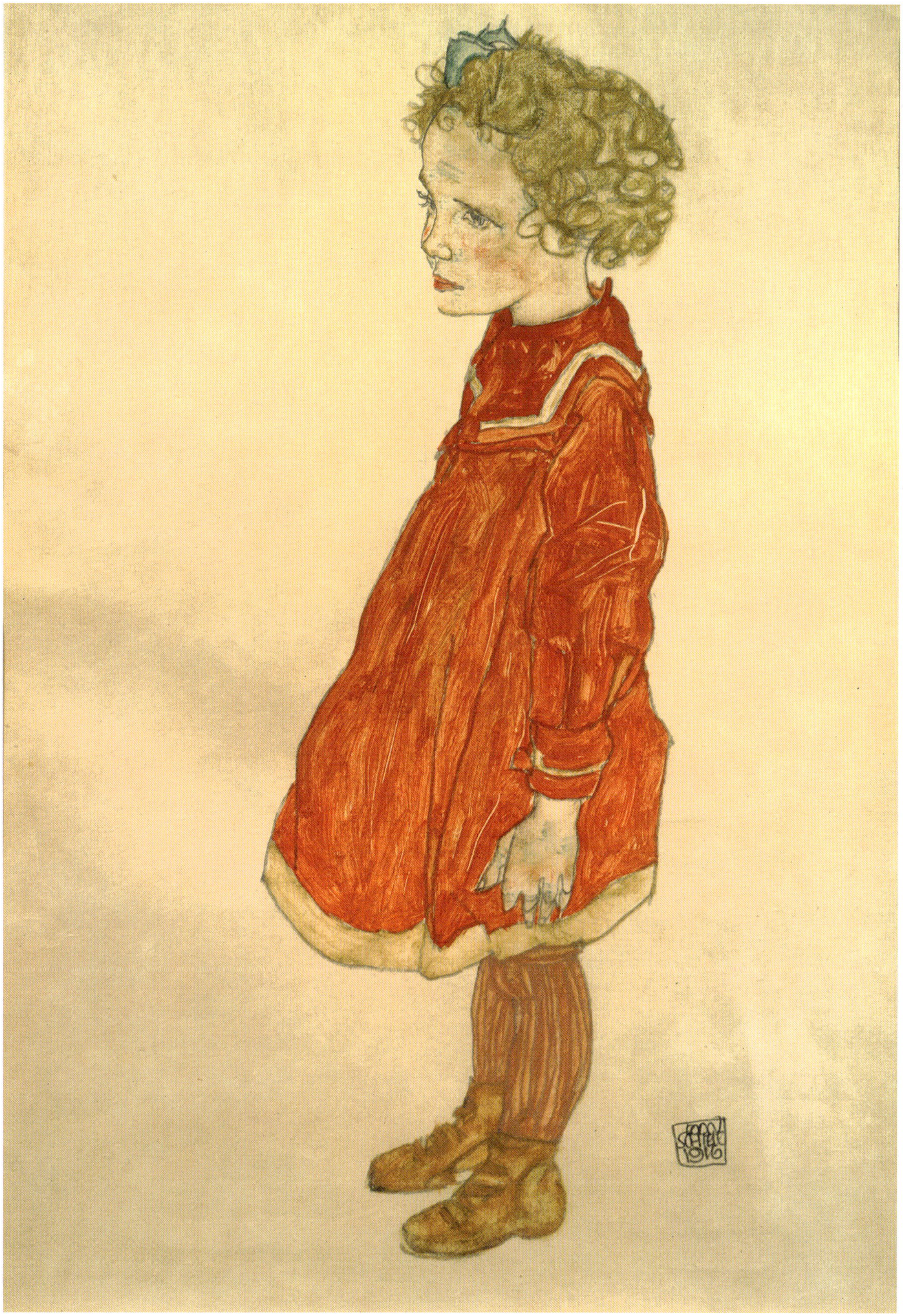

Cat. 66
EGON SCHIELE
Little Girl with Blonde Hair in Red Dress, 1916
Gouache and pencil on paper, 46 x 30.8 cm
Private collection

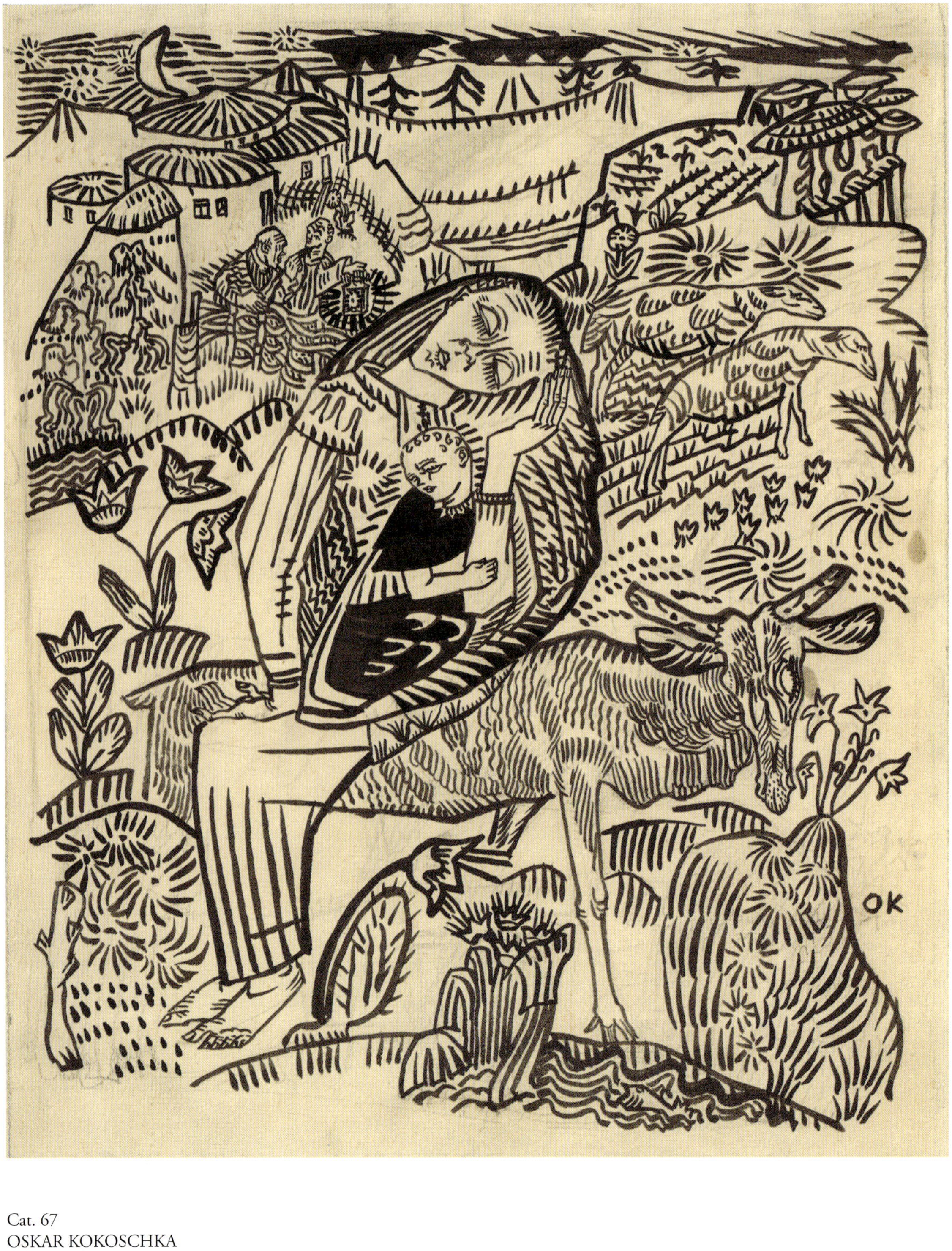

Cat. 67
OSKAR KOKOSCHKA
Mother and Child, Riding on a Doe, 1908
Watercolor and pencil on paper, mounted on cardboard, 24.5 x 21 cm
Albertina, Vienna

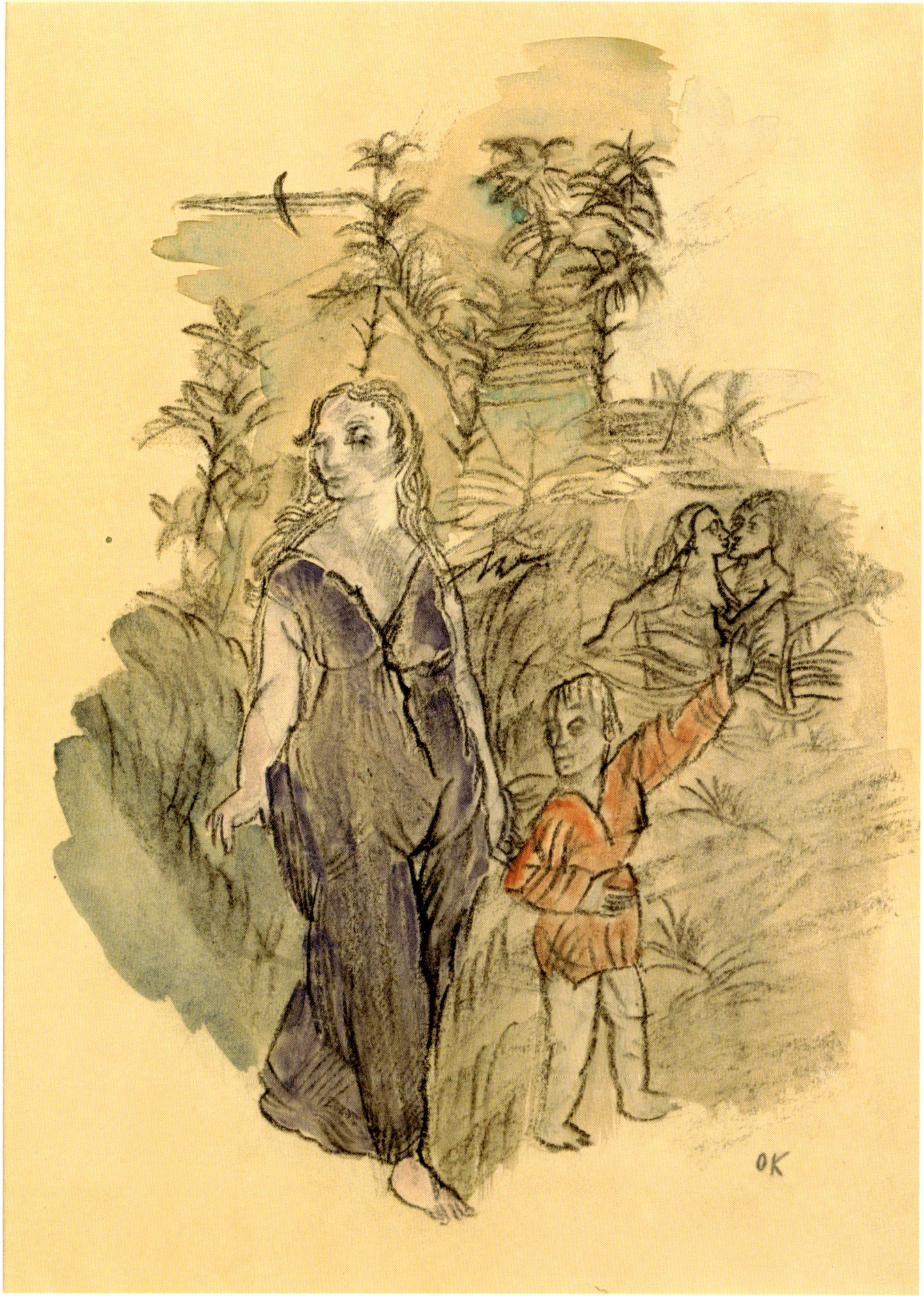

Cat. 68
OSKAR KOKOSCHKA
Alma Mahler with Kokoschka's longed-for child (Christian Love), 1913
Black crayon and watercolor on paper, 43.9 x 29.6 cm
Private collection

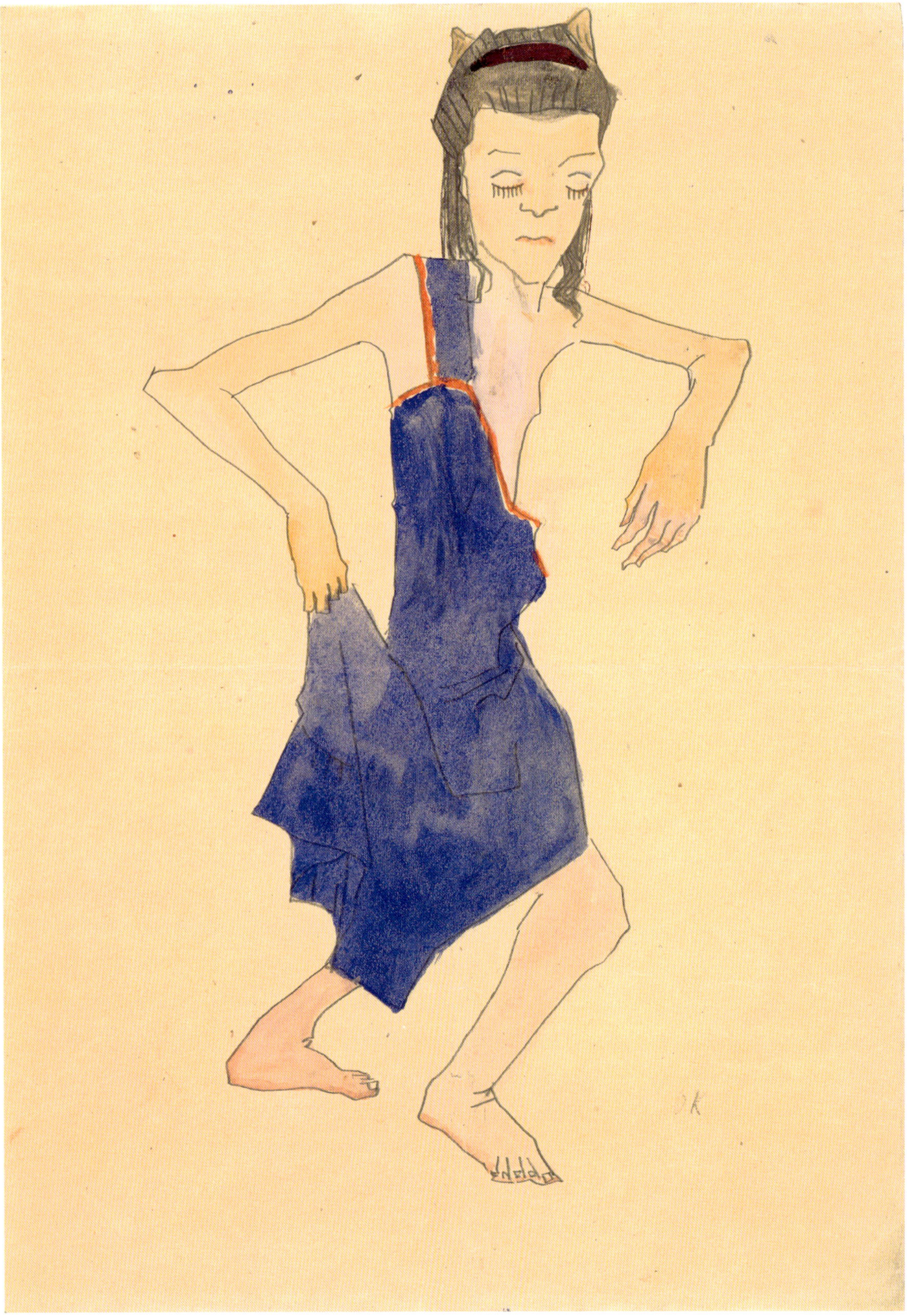

Cat. 69
OSKAR KOKOSCHKA
Dancing Young Girl in a Blue Dress, 1908
Watercolor, tempera and pencil on paper, 45 x 31.6 cm
Private collection

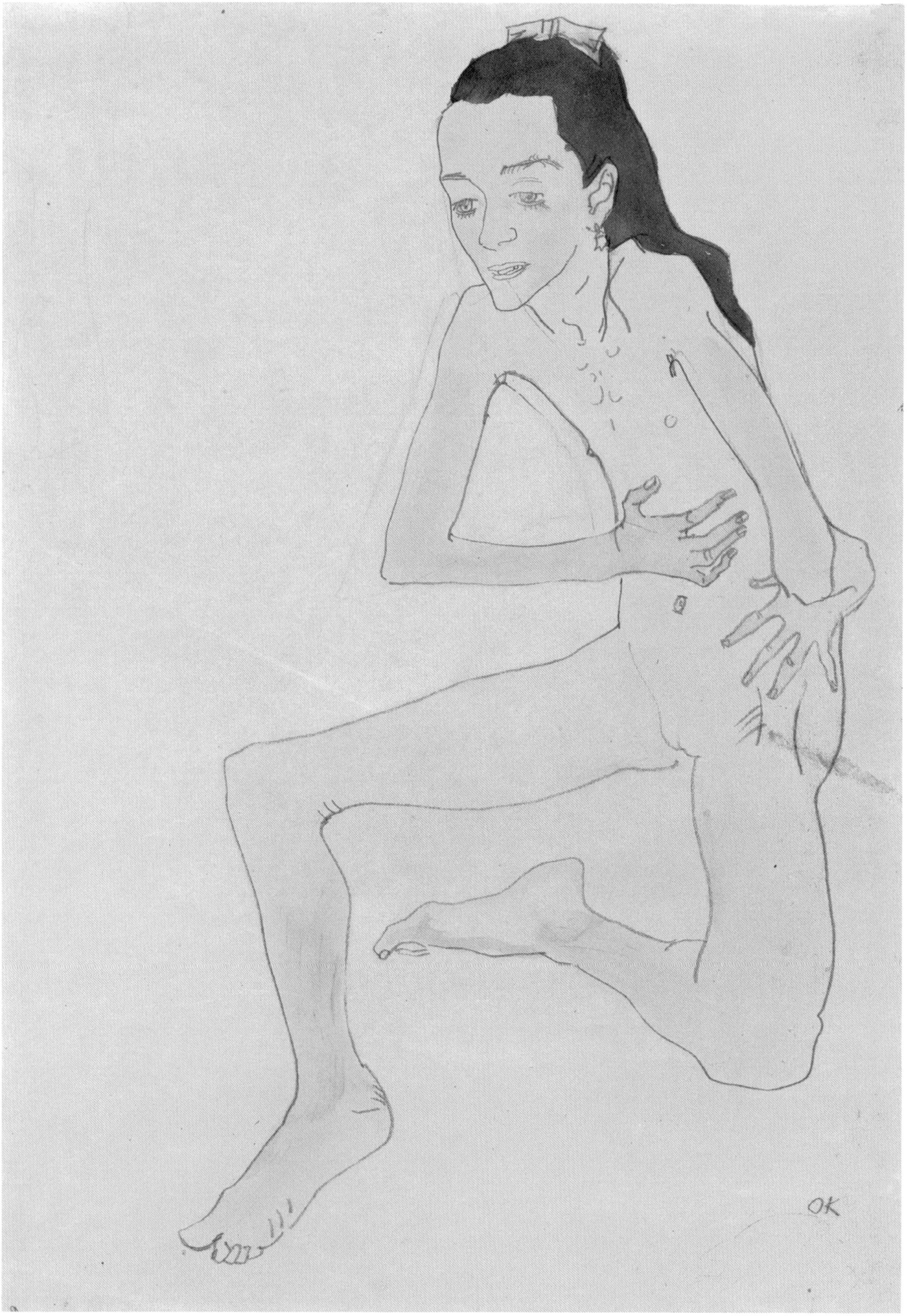

Cat. 70
OSKAR KOKOSCHKA
Seated Nude Girl, 1908
Pencil, watercolor and Indian ink on paper, 43.7 x 30.5 cm
Private collection

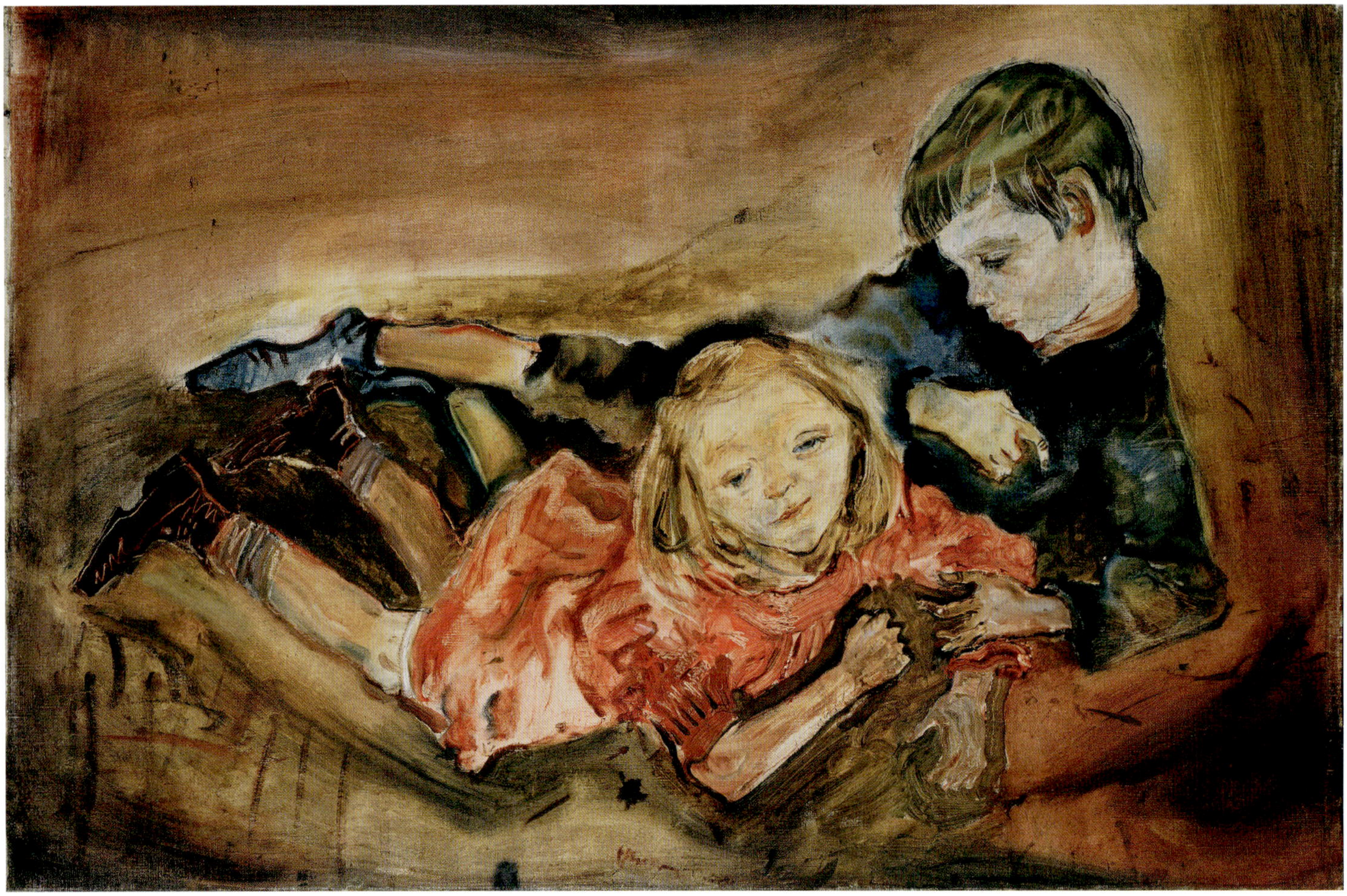

Cat. 71
OSKAR KOKOSCHKA
Children Playing, 1909
Oil on canvas, 72 x 108 cm
Lehmbruck Museum, Duisburg

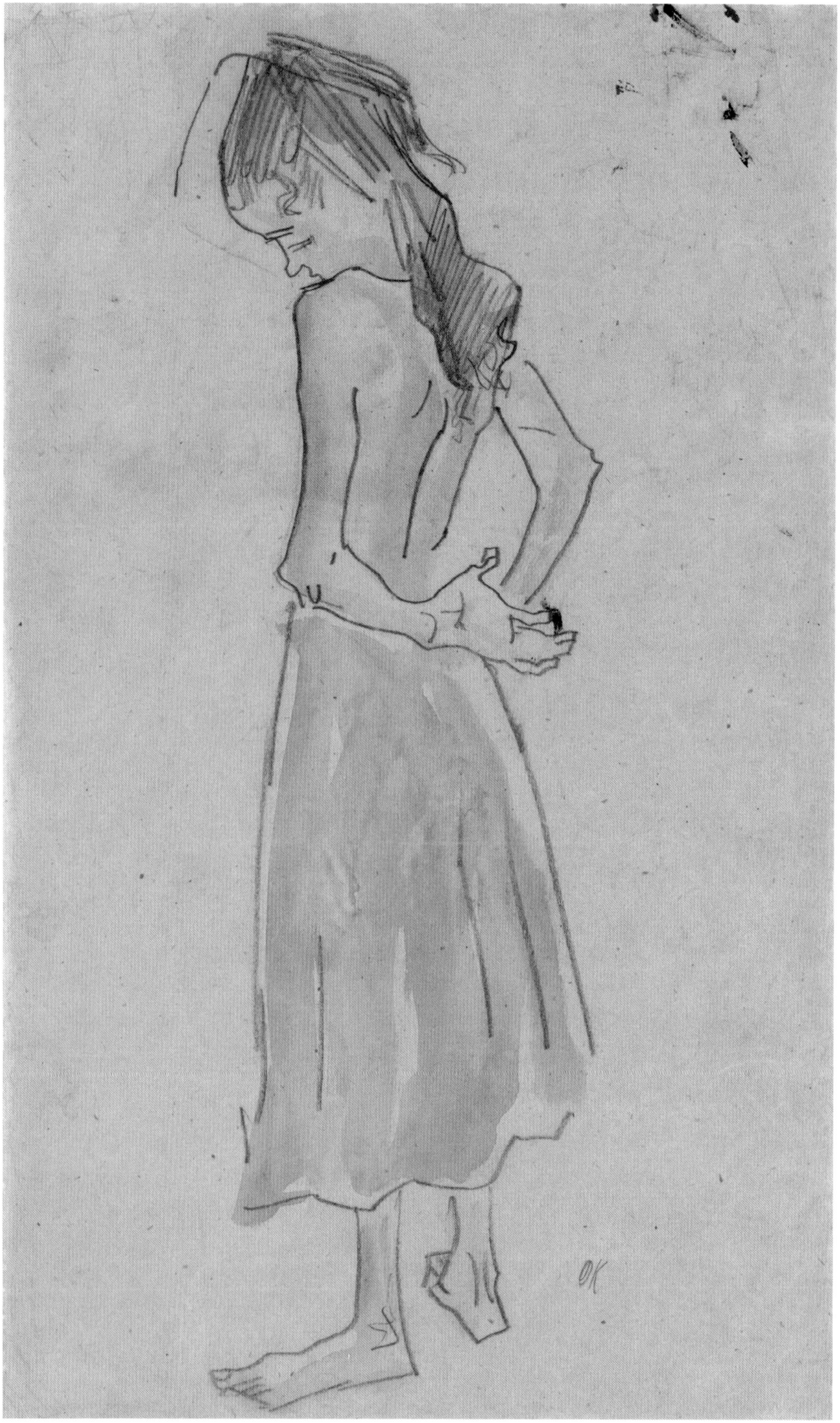

Cat. 72
OSKAR KOKOSCHKA
Standing Young Girl in a Blue Dress, 1908
Pencil, watercolor and gouache on paper, 43 x 25.5 cm
Staatliche Kunstsammlungen Dresden, Collection of Prints, Drawings and Photographs, Dresden

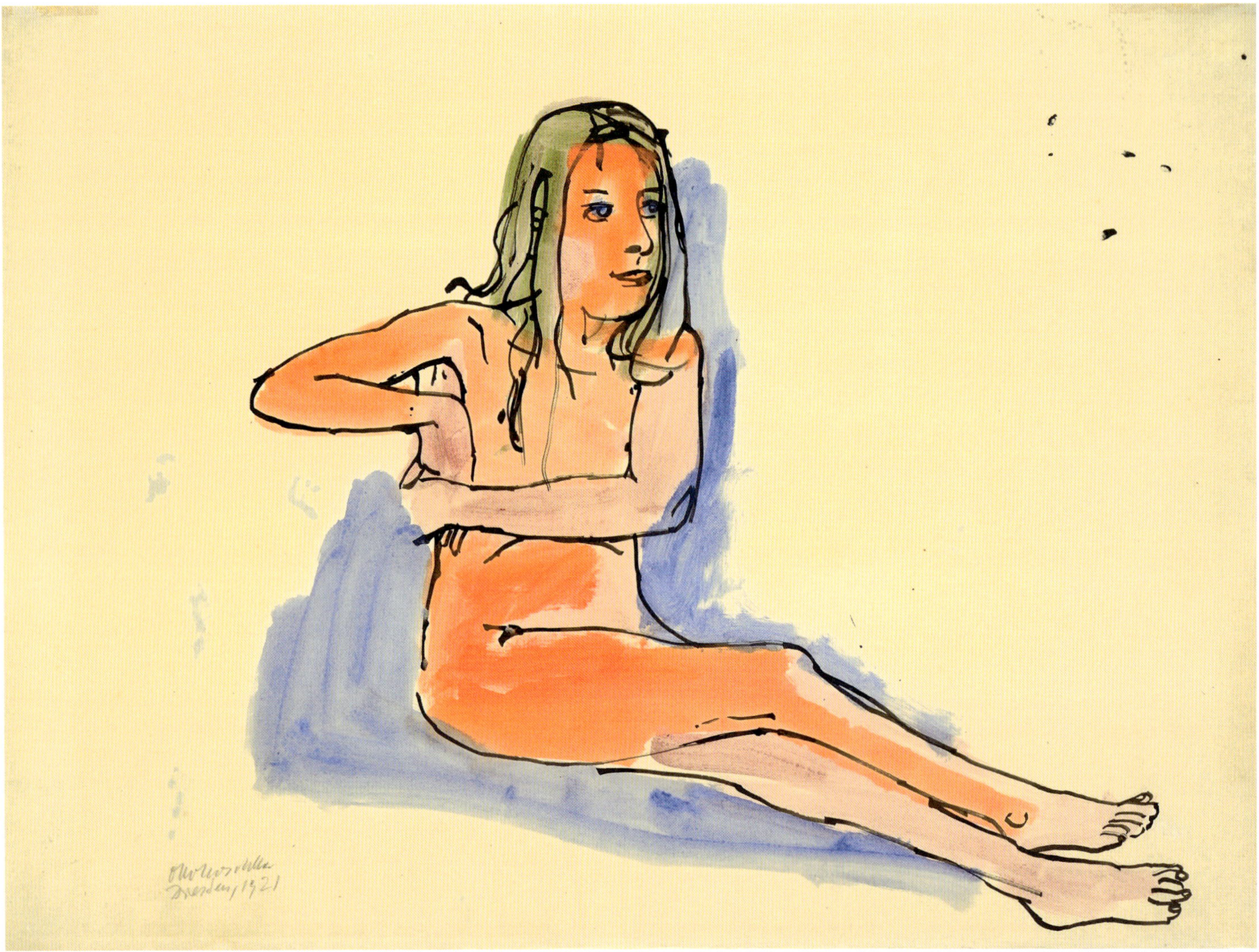

Cat. 73
OSKAR KOKOSCHKA
Seated Nude Girl, 1921
Black Indian ink and watercolor on paper, 52 x 71 cm
Staatliche Kunstsammlungen Dresden, Collection of Prints, Drawings and Photographs, Dresden

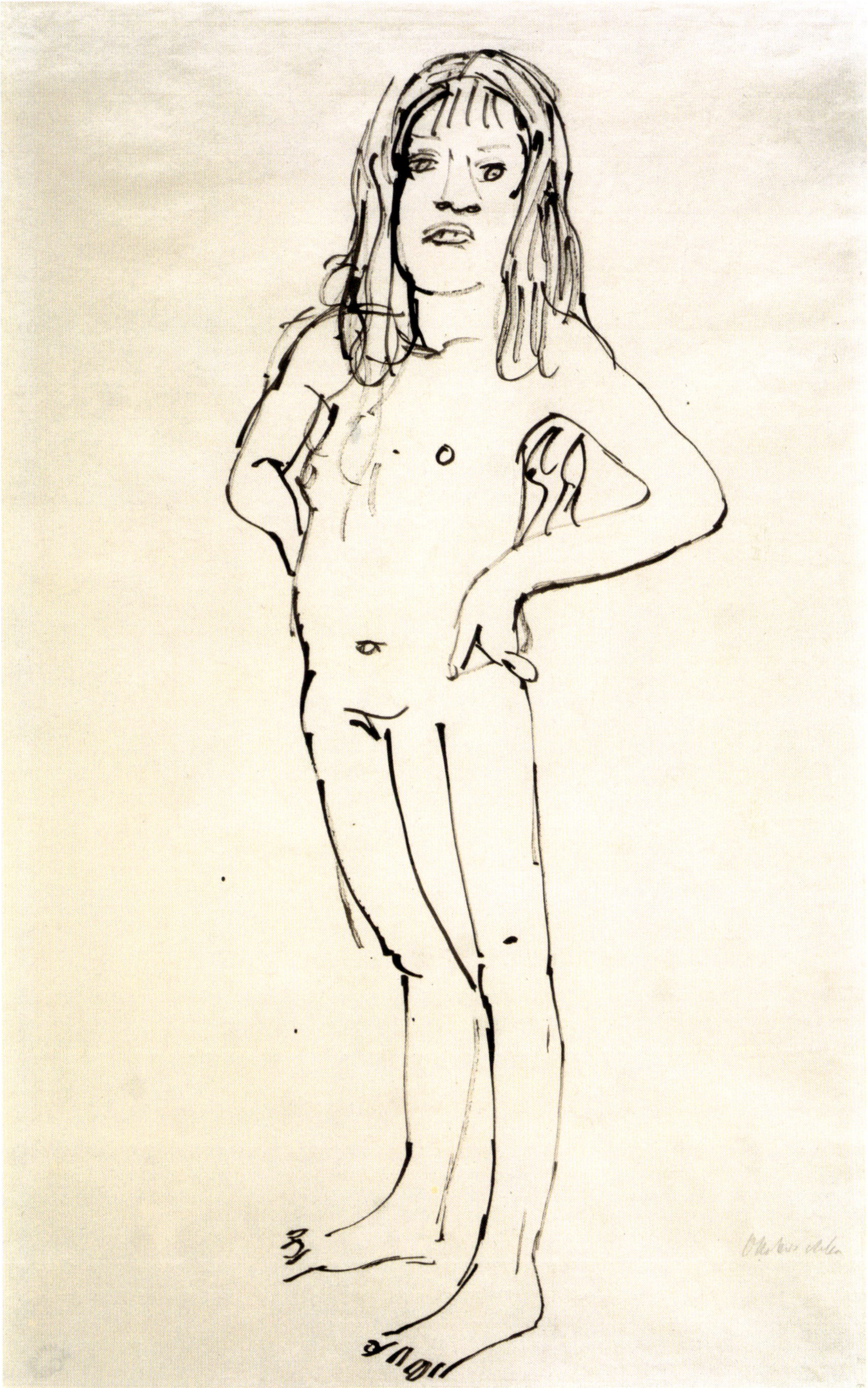

Cat. 74
OSKAR KOKOSCHKA
Standing Nude Girl, 1919
Indian ink on paper, 67 x 41.9 cm
Private collection

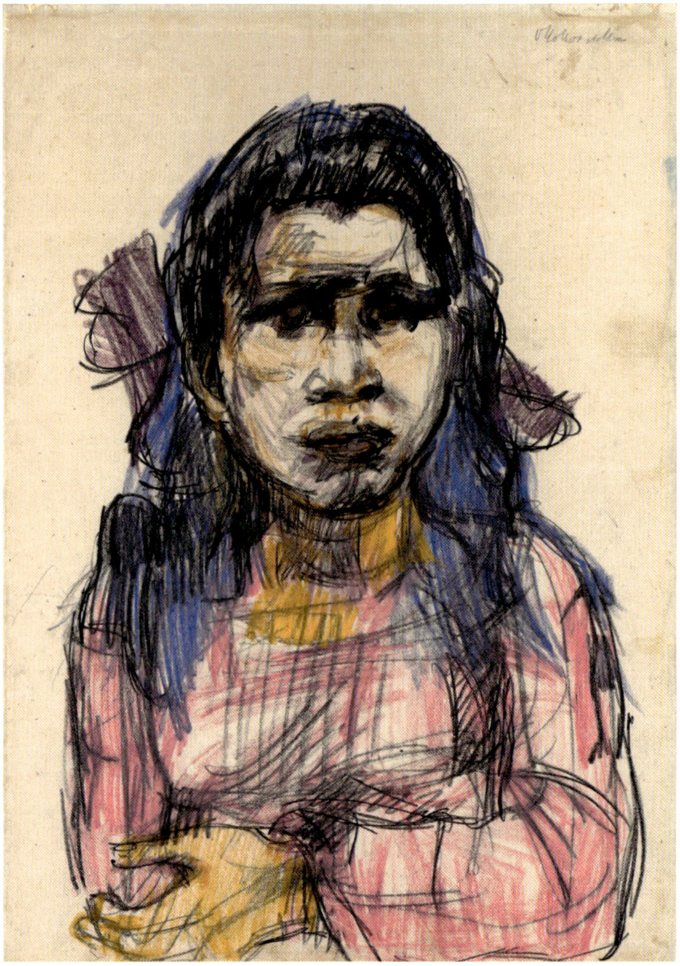

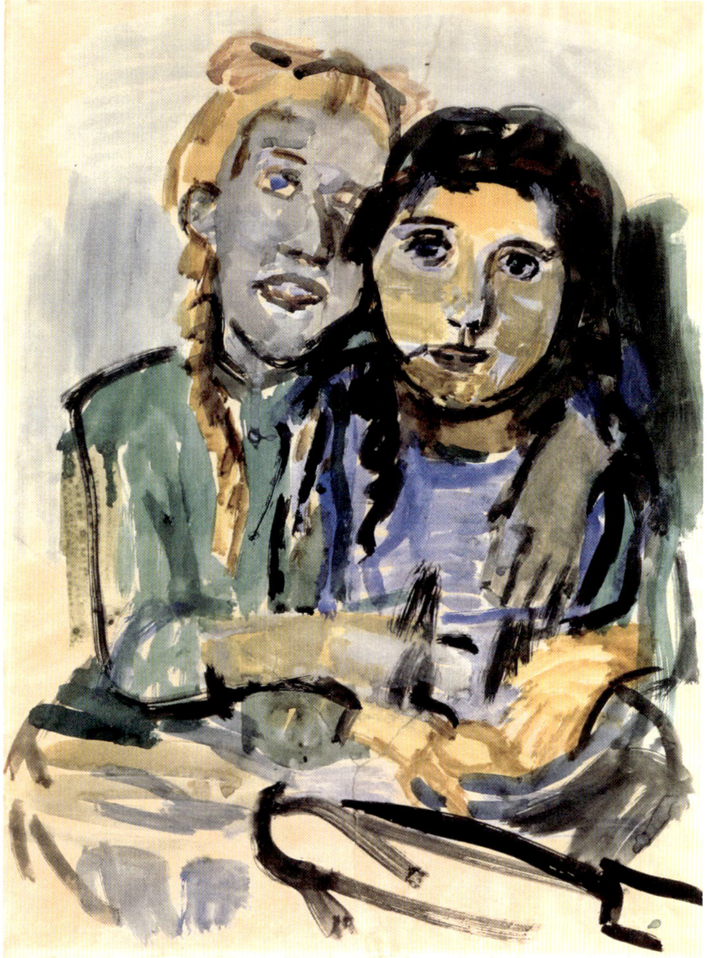

Cat. 75
OSKAR KOKOSCHKA
Portrait of Girl, 1921
Pencil, black crayon and colored crayon on paper, mounted on cardboard, 70.2 x 50 cm
Staatliche Kunstsammlungen Dresden, Collection of Prints, Drawings and Photographs, Dresden

Cat. 76
OSKAR KOKOSCHKA
Two Sisters, 1922
Watercolor on paper, 69.5 x 51.5 cm
Fondation Oskar Kokoschka, Vevey

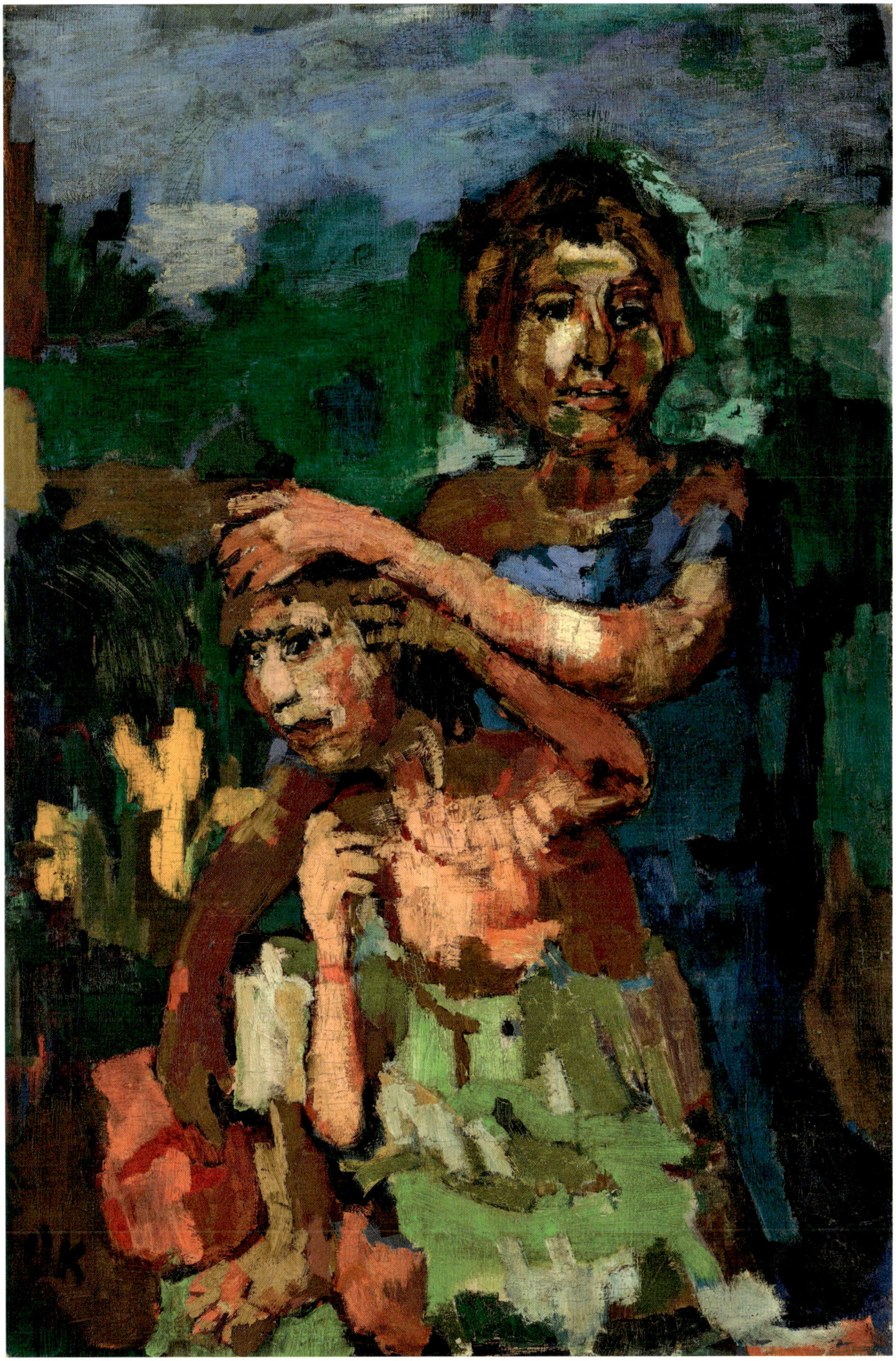

Cat. 77
OSKAR KOKOSCHKA
Two Girls, 1921–22
Oil on canvas, 120 x 81 cm
Private collection,
courtesy of Sotheby's, London

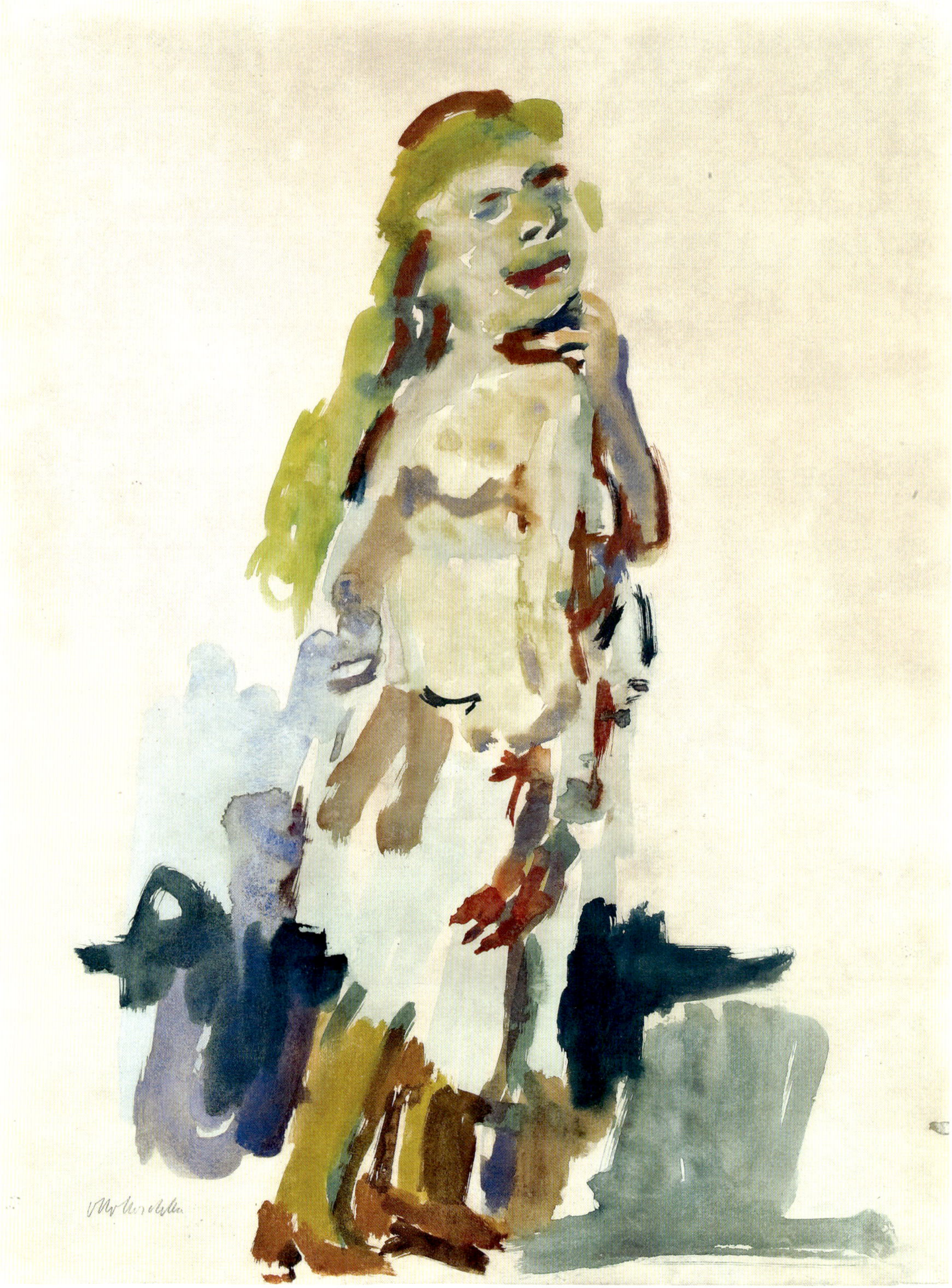

Cat. 78
OSKAR KOKOSCHKA
Standing Girl with a Doll,
c. 1921–22
Watercolor on paper, 66.5 x 50 cm
Private collection, Vienna, courtesy of Kunsthandel Giese & Schweiger, Vienna

Cat. 79
OSKAR KOKOSCHKA
Girl with Doll, 1921–22
Oil on canvas, 92 x 81.2 cm
Detroit Institute of Arts, bequest of Dr. William R. Valentiner

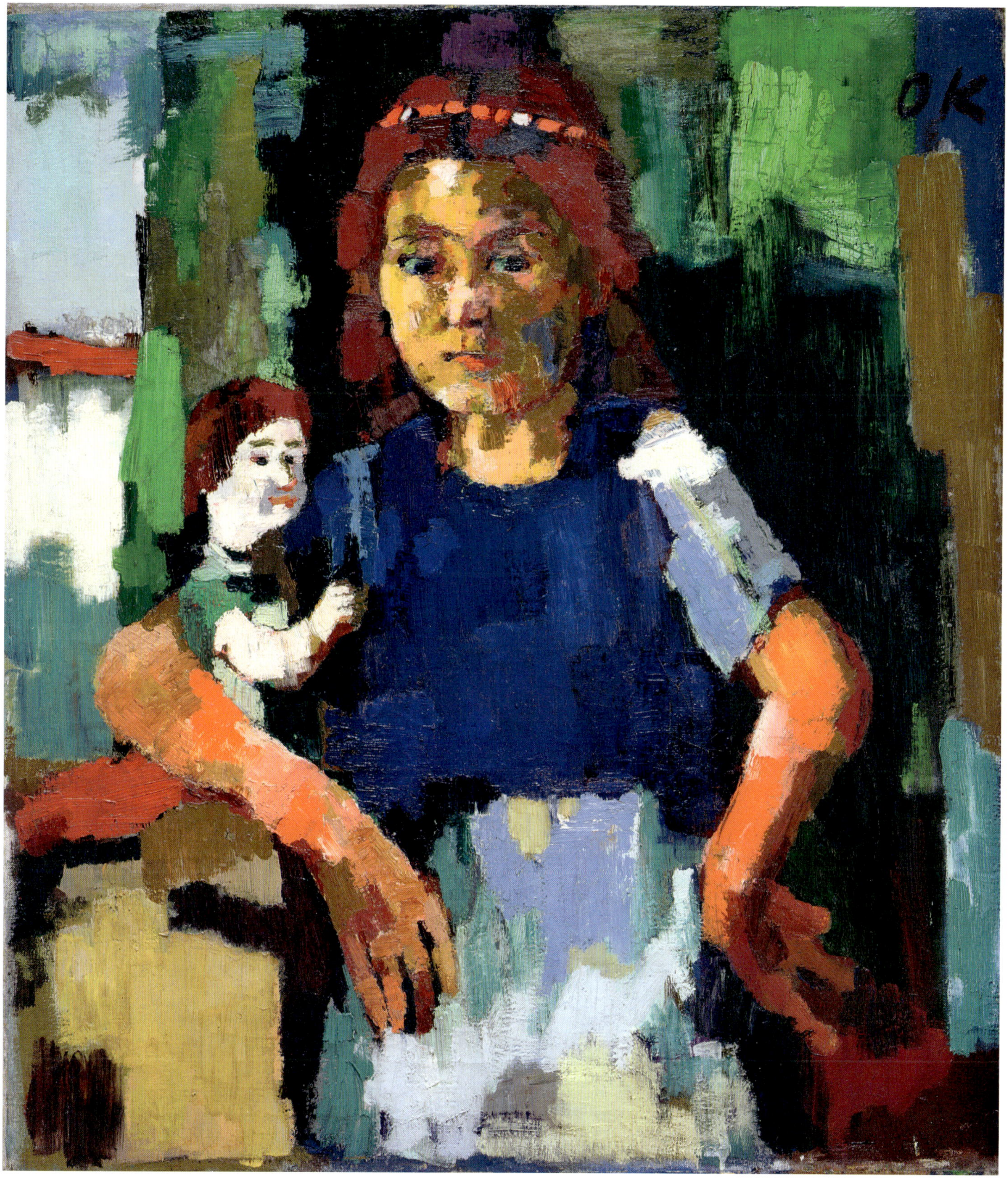
OK

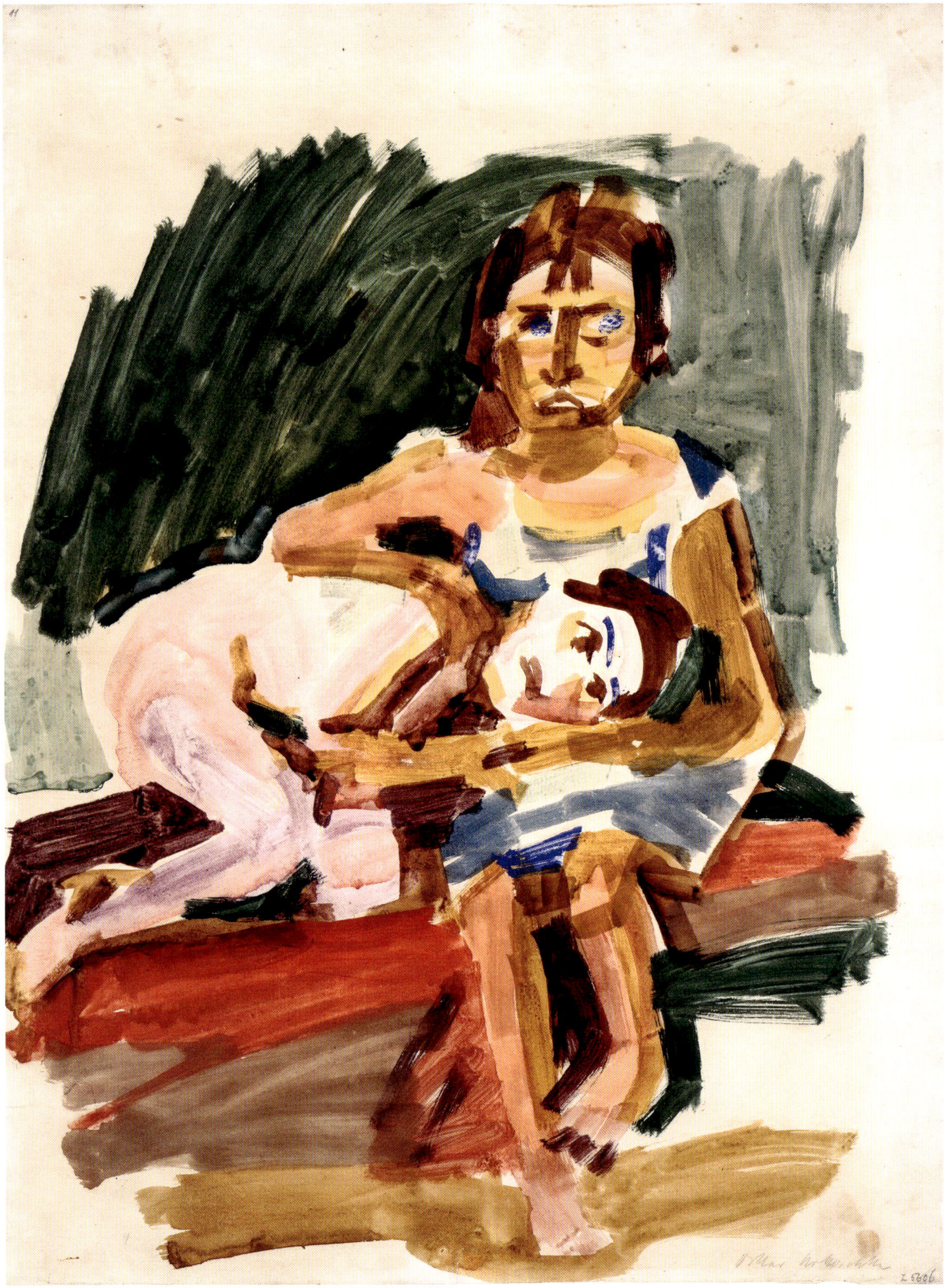

Cat. 80
OSKAR KOKOSCHKA
Two Girls, 1922–23
Watercolor on paper, 65 x 47 cm
Fondation Oskar Kokoschka, Vevey

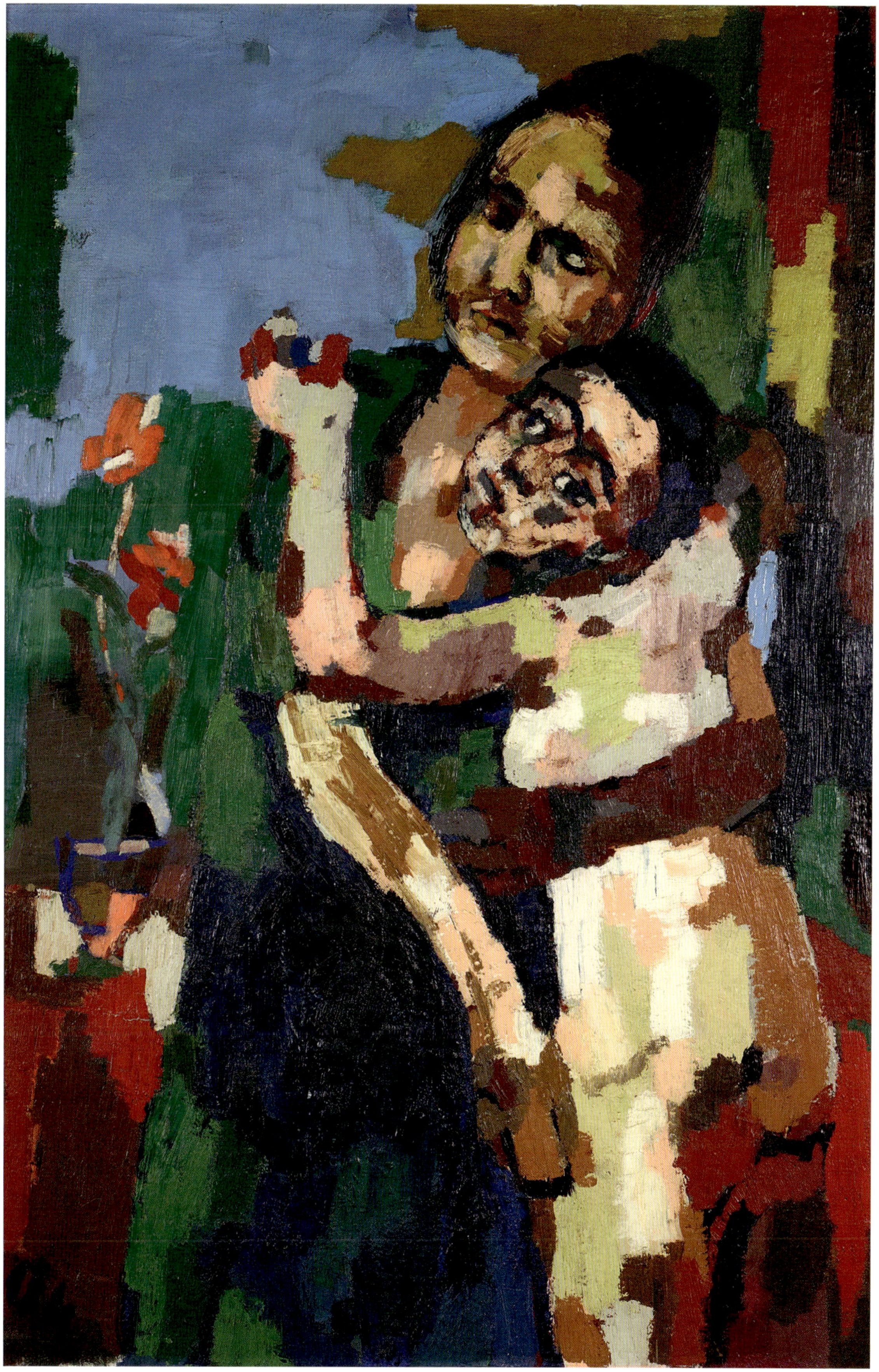

Cat. 81
OSKAR KOKOSCHKA
Mother and Child, Embracing,
1922
Oil on canvas, 121 x 81 cm
Belvedere, Vienna

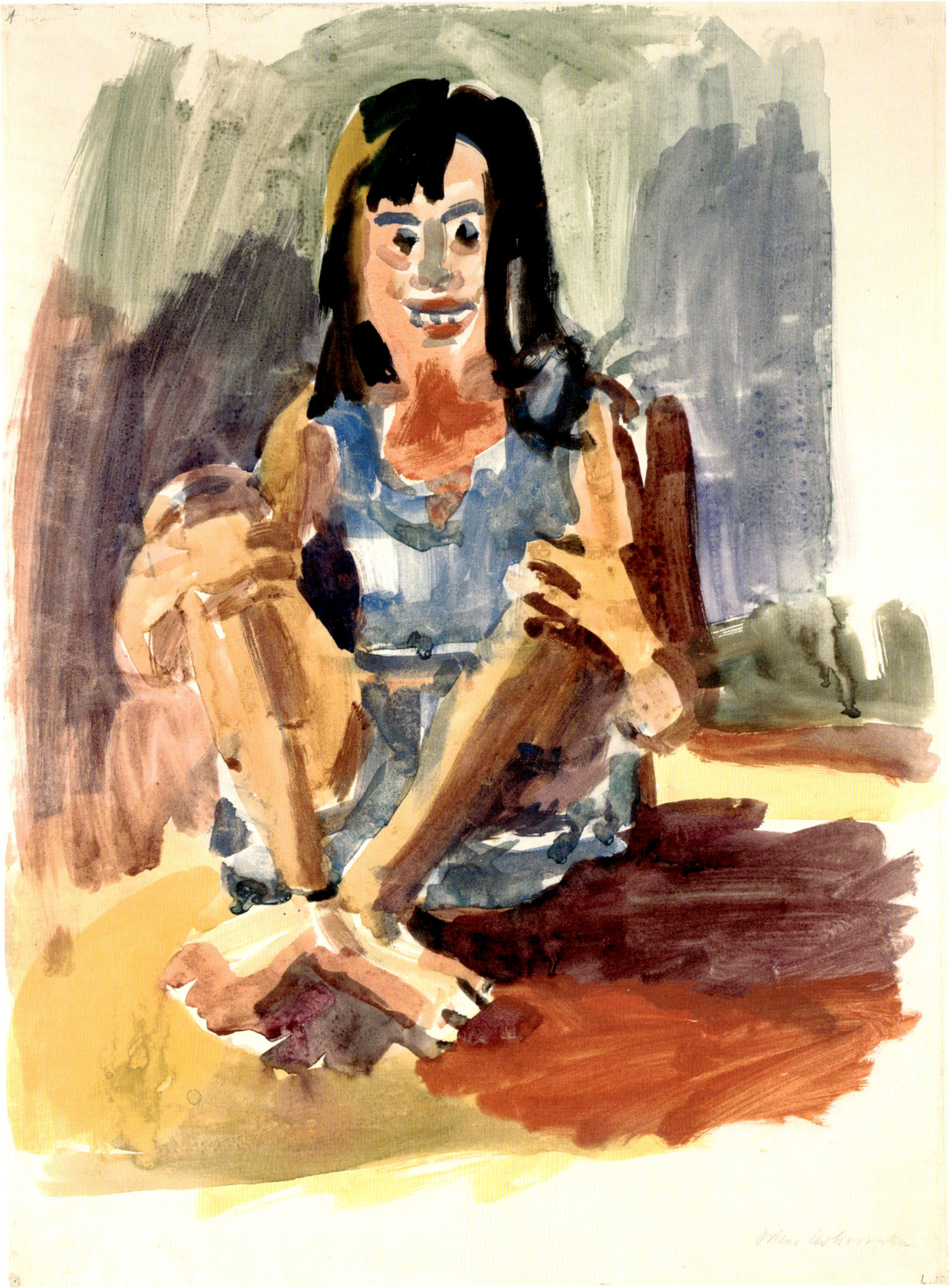

Cat. 82
OSKAR KOKOSCHKA
Seated Girl, 1922–23
Watercolor on paper, 69.5 x 52.5 cm
Fondation Oskar Kokoschka, Vevey

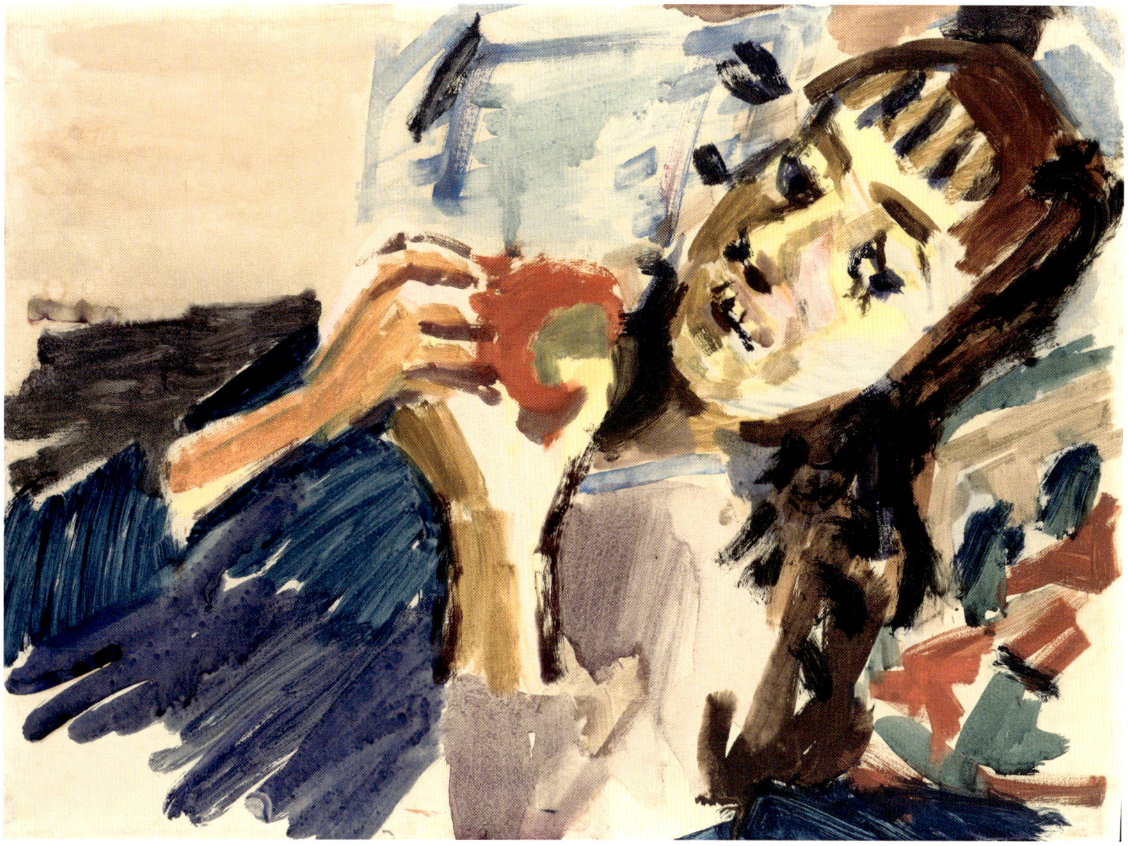

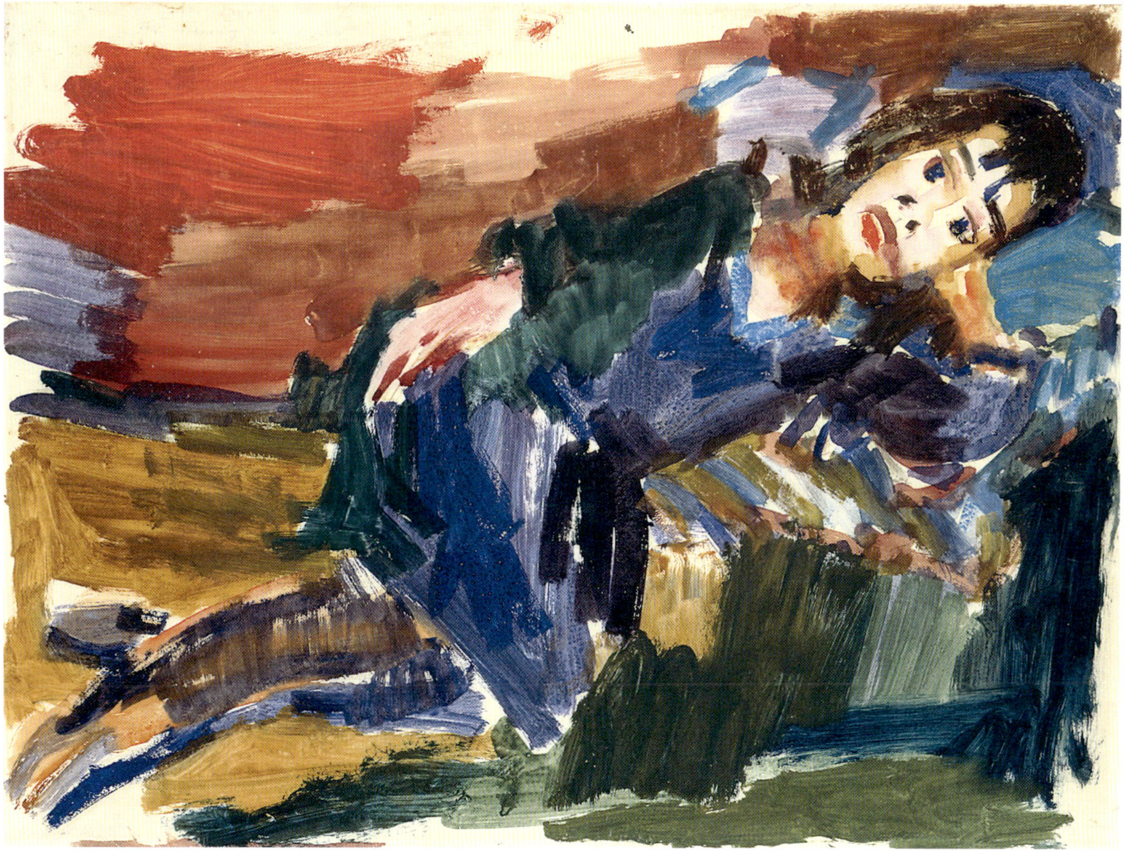

Cat. 83
OSKAR KOKOSCHKA
Girl with Apple, 1922–23
Watercolor on paper, 49.5 x 67 cm
Fondation Oskar Kokoschka, Vevey

Cat. 84
OSKAR KOKOSCHKA
Girl in a Blue and Green Dress, c. 1920
Tempera and watercolor on paper, 52.5 x 70 cm
Museum der Moderne, Salzburg

Couples

Judging from their work, Klimt, Schiele, and Kokoschka shared a belief in romantic love: a union of soul mates sealed by erotic passion. However, at a time when bourgeois propriety demanded the sequestration of sexual impulses, such a union was difficult to sustain. So long as males and females were deemed opposites, the former rational/spiritual and the latter irrational/carnal, the two could never be fully joined.

Klimt saw love as part of the cycle of life: a link in an organic chain of becoming, being, and passing. The specters of birth and death hover over the couple in his 1898 painting *Love* (cat. 86), but for the moment the two are oblivious, lost to their mutual rapture. Klimt followed *Love* with what may well be the world's most famous representation of the subject, *Lovers* (*The Kiss)* (AW 189, cat. 85). Like other canvases from the gold period, the surface of *The Kiss* is encrusted with sexual symbols (phallic rectangles on the man, ovular or vaginal circles on the woman). Nevertheless, by concealing the bodies of both figures, Klimt shifts the focus from the physical to the spiritual.

Klimt was more explicit in his drawings. Although some of these depict heterosexual intercourse (cat. 95), a surprising number of the artist's erotic drawings feature lesbian couples (cat. 89, 90, 92). A common pornographic subject (fig. 1), lesbianism fascinated male voyeurs, despite (or because of) the fact that homosexuality was at the time strictly taboo. Lesbianism affirmed prevalent ideas of feminine erotic self-sufficiency. Woman was so purely sexual that she did not require a male partner. Sexual self-sufficiency also evoked contemporary notions of hermaphroditism and the reversion to primitive life forms associated with devolution (p. 30, fig. 1; cat. 111, 112, 114).

Despite the tangles of nudes, male and female, that recur in Klimt's allegories, his late canvas *Adam and Eve* (cat. 106) is his only painting depicting a single naked couple. The scene is set before the Fall, possibly at the moment of Eve's creation. Not yet tarnished by original sin, Eve is at this moment humankind's sole truly chaste woman. Blond and buxom, she differs noticeably from Klimt's dark, skinny *femmes fatales* (see p. 27, fig. 13) Unaware of her nakedness, she nonetheless flaunts it. Klimt here plays with the notion of Christian shame, celebrating Eve's purity while slyly provoking an audience fully susceptible to sexual temptation. Only in a state of prelapsarian grace can man lust without guilt.

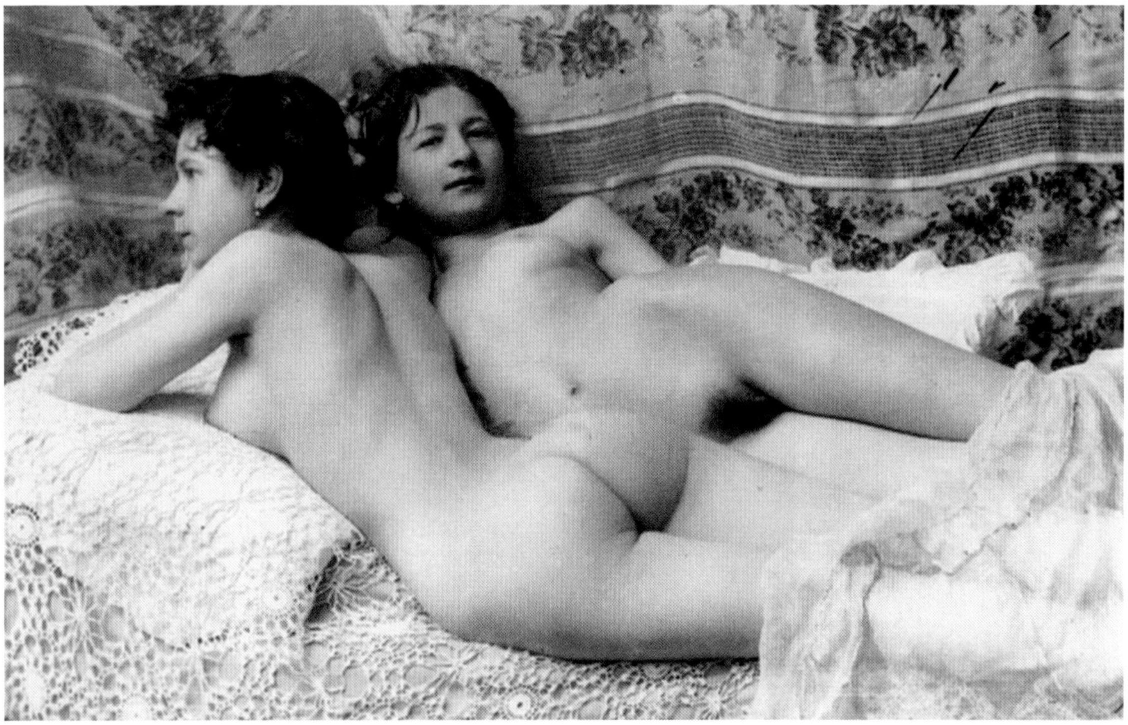

Fig. 1
UNKNOWN PHOTOGRAPHER
Two Reclining Female Nudes, c. 1900
Private collection

Kokoschka was obsessed with the fall from grace, for which he (like the Bible) blamed woman. His romantic narratives often begin with an "Adam and Eve" scene (WW 51). But then that pesky snake intervenes (fig. 2) and sets off a deadly battle between the sexes. As suggested by the famous first lines of *Die träumenden Knaben*, Kokoschka was driven into a violent frenzy by his unrequited passion for Lilith Lang:

little red fish
little fish red
with my triple edged knife I stab you dead
with my fingers asunder rend
to bring your mute circling to an end[1]

From lightly veiled fantasies of penetrating the red "fish" with his "knife," Kokoschka soon advanced to the blunt symbolism of *Mörder, Hoffnung der Frauen* (Murderer, Hope of Women). It has been suggested that the plot of this drama, first performed at the 1909 *Kunstschau*, was influenced by Franz Wedekind's play *Pandora's Box*, which culminates with the murder of its prostitute-heroine, Lulu, by Jack the Ripper.[2] More gruesome even than Kokoschka's text are the illustrations for *Mörder, Hoffnung der Frauen* (fig. 3). The man, drained by the woman's lust, regains his strength by killing her. "Sexual union" as Otto Weininger put it, "is akin to murder."[3] One or the other partner, or both, must die.

In the beginning it was not clear who would triumph in Kokoschka's protracted struggle to possess Alma Mahler. Exhibiting the crazed tenacity of a stalker, he lurked outside her house looking for signs of infidelity and barraged her with over 400 love letters during a two-and-a-half-year period.[4] "I will not tolerate any other gods before me," he commanded. "I won't be diverted, you are of one mind with me and will live with me until I have pulled out by the roots everything in you that bewilders me, chills me and makes me unhappy [...] I will perfect you when once you find your support, your only repose, your bodily peace in my being. If you withdraw, my dear good woman [...] a time of torment will ensue for you that I would not wish or want."[5] At one point, Oskar had marriage banns issued without Alma's consent or knowledge, compelling her to go into hiding until the announced wedding date had passed.[6]

Alma evidently reciprocated Oskar's feelings, but she resisted his repeated marriage proposals and aborted their child. The artist likened their turbulent relationship to the doomed love/hate of Tristan and Isolde, the original title of his masterful double portrait *The Tempest* (see p.21, fig. 5). Probably inspired by a rain shower that had deluged the couple along the coast of Naples,[7] the painting shows Alma nestled in Oskar's arms. "He painted me lying trustingly against him in the midst of a storm and huge waves," she recalled, "relying utterly on him for help, while he, tyrannical in his expression and radiating energy, calms the waves."[8]

In other allegorical representations of the Mahler affair, it is Alma who has the upper hand. Though created during a relatively happy interlude, the 1912–13 picture cycle *Columbus in Chains* ends with Kokoschka's death (WW 53). A later series, *The Bach Cantata*, captures the poignant interplay of fear and hope that accompanies the demise of a profound love affair. In the second plate, Alma, like Dante's Beatrice, leads a passive Oskar past a grave marker (cat. 101). By the eighth plate, he is in his tomb, inscribed with the warning that in the *Divine Comedy* appears above the gates to hell: "Abandon hope, all ye who enter here" (cat. 100). The story concludes with a reprise of the Pietà theme, the corpse alluding simultaneously to Oskar and to his dead son (cat. 98). In 1915 Kokoschka went off to war, where he indeed did almost die, while Mahler immediately turned around and married the architect Walter Gropius. In a farewell painting, *The Knight Errant* (WE 115), Oskar depicts Alma as a sphinx, "who can neither live nor die, but slays the man who loves her."[9] For Klimt, the sphinx was the key to the riddle of human existence, but for Kokoschka she was a killer.[10] In keeping with the more misogynistic thinkers of his time, the younger artist believed that sexual desire makes men vulnerable, and he felt threatened by women's incipient quest for autonomy. He took his cue from people like Karl Kraus, who complained that he was living in a "vaginal epoch."[11] "The male imagination," Kokoschka wrote in his drama *Sphinx and Strawman*, "has become completely tied down by gynolatry."[12] "Woman sucks us dry, spiritually," their friend Peter Altenberg agreed.[13]

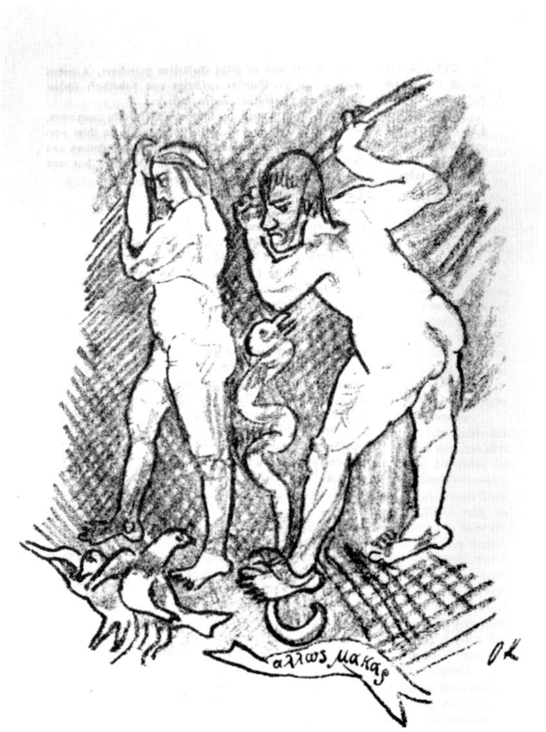

Fig. 2
OSKAR KOKOSCHKA
Allos Makar **–** *Man and Woman with Snake*, 1914
Private collection

Yet paradoxically, Altenberg also believed that "the 'beautiful' woman is placed on earth by the creator to awaken the world power of man."[14] And Kraus saw woman as "the primal spring at which the intellectuality of man finds renewal."[15] For Kokoschka, Alma Mahler was a muse as well as a murderess. He allegorized her as *Mania*: divine madness, inspiration (cat. 27). He called her his "maternal genius"[16] and commanded her "to give me new life like a magic potion."[17] Constantly, Oskar entreated Alma to devote herself exclusively to abetting his talent. "Where is my dear wife?" he asked sardonically. "Is she doing something for 'her happiness'? [...] Or is she at the side of him who cannot have enough help, support, and assistance?" [18] The relationship failed, finally, because Alma was not able, or willing, to live up to the artist's expectations.

Schiele also had a favorite muse: Wally (or Wallpurga) Neuzil, his lover and principal model from

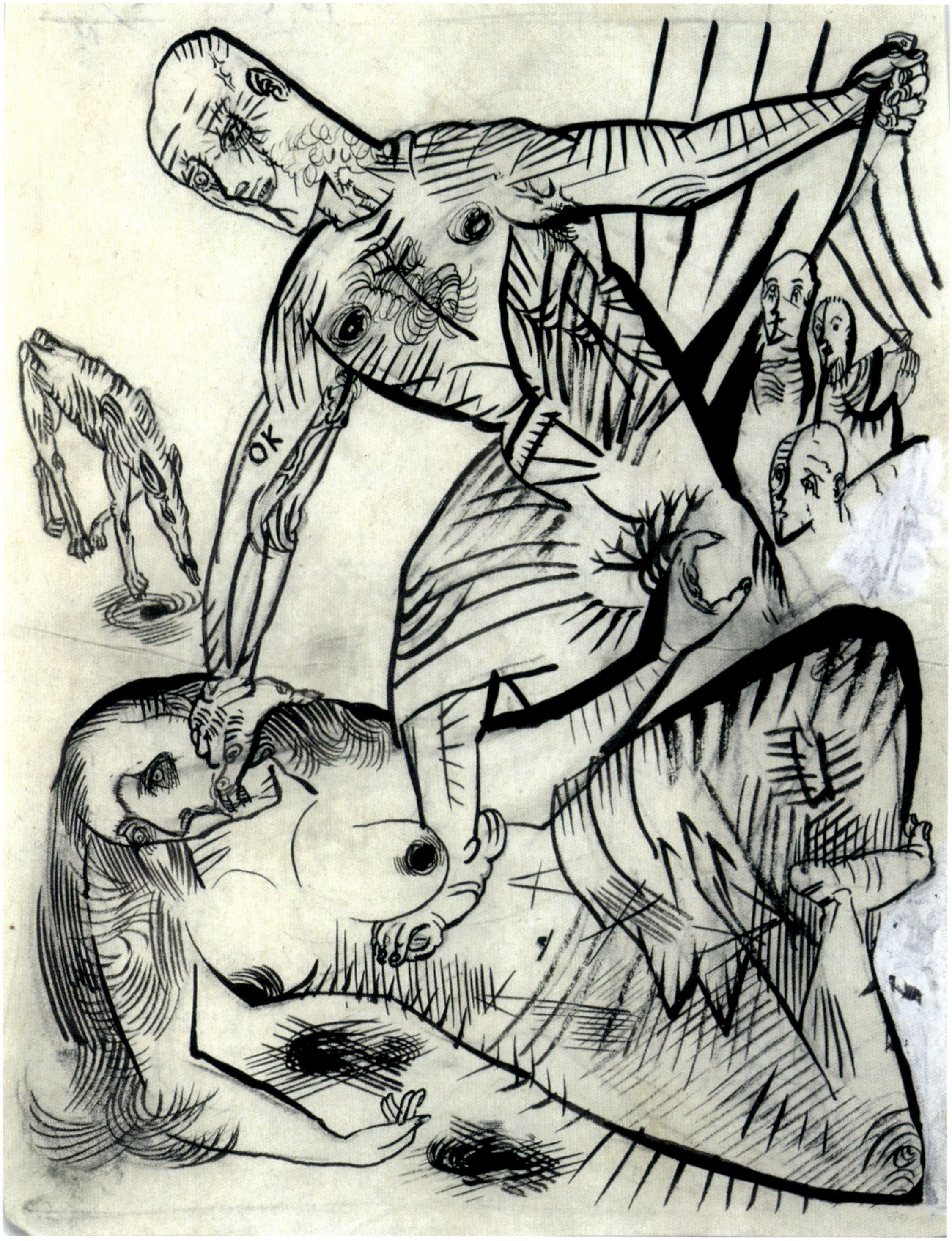

Fig. 3
OSKAR KOKOSCHKA
Murderer, Hope of Women III, 1910
Staatsgalerie Stuttgart

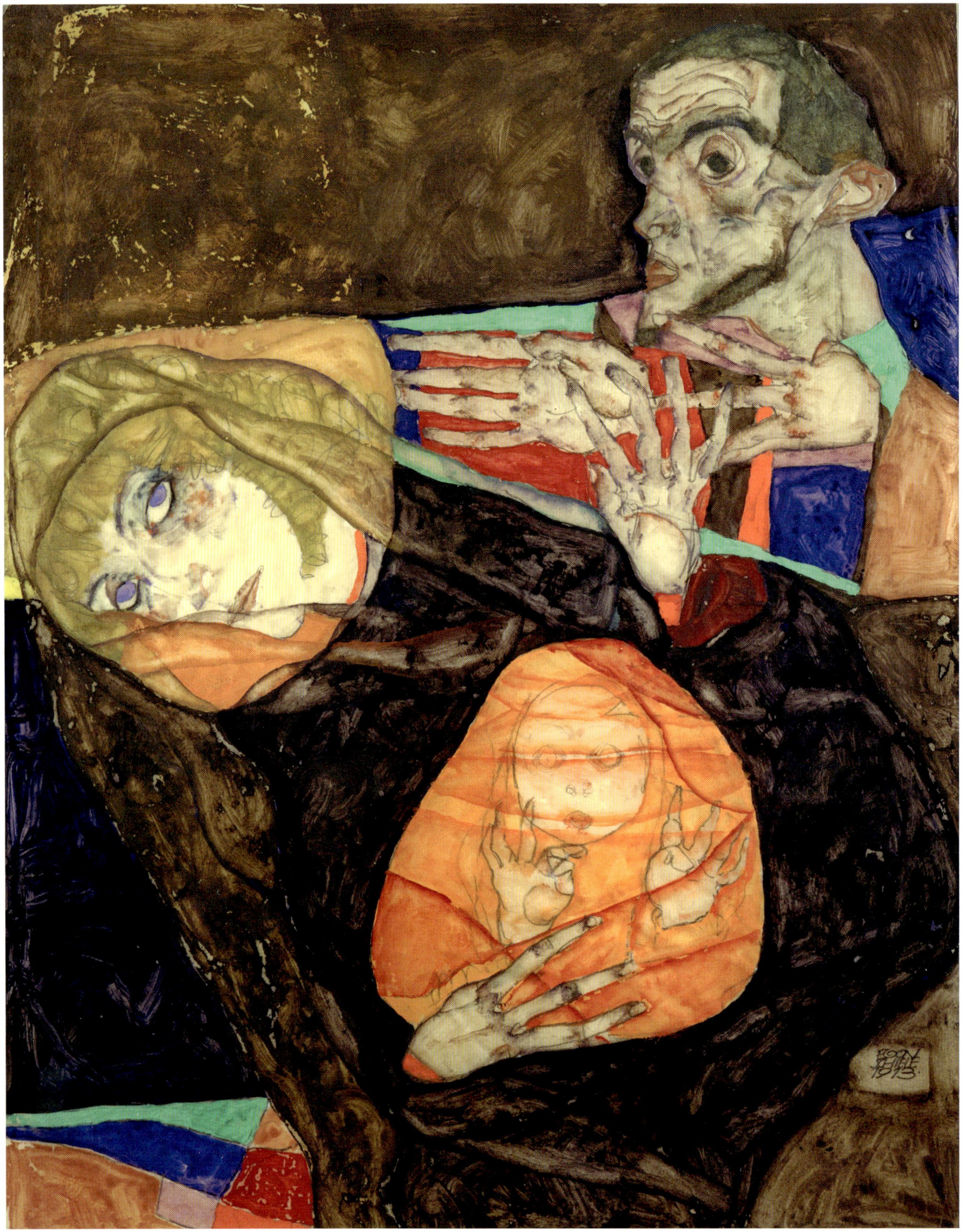

early 1911 until his marriage in the spring of 1915. But the relationship between Egon and Wally was very different from that between Oskar and Alma. On the one hand, it was always clear that Wally was Egon's social inferior; he even made her sign a statement affirming that she was not in love with him. On the other hand, Wally, like all the artist's best models, was a valued collaborator. She skillfully followed his direction, working with him in much the way that fashion models today work with photographers. In Schiele's view, they shared a spiritual mission. If he was the priest, Wally was his nun (cat. 99). If he was Joseph, she was Mary, and their sacred spawn was art (fig. 4).

Schiele did the unthinkable: he turned his "whore," Wally, into a Madonna. In a 1911 watercolor, *The Red Host* (cat. 97), he went further, equating fellatio with the Eucharist: the Catholic ritual whereby the repentant believer is united with Christ in Holy Communion. More directly than Klimt, Schiele attacked the Christian concept of shame, which results from an inability to reconcile the life of the spirit with that of the flesh. *The Red Host* bluntly acknowledges that this dichotomy is no longer credible. From a variety of perspectives, thinkers like Darwin, Freud, Schopenhauer and Ernst Mach had recently challenged the distinction between the mental and the corporal.[19] Taking these ideas to a logical conclusion, Schiele was positing a new religious truth for the modern age, wherein the spiritual and the physical might finally be joined.

Radical though Schiele's beliefs were for their time, he was a bourgeois at heart. He would not marry Wally, who as a professional model was socially little better than a prostitute. His chosen wife, Edith Harms, was far more conventional, and it appears that Egon never enjoyed with her the melding of body and soul that he championed in his art.[20] A series of drawings done around the time of their marriage demonstrates a painful inability to communicate (see p. 22, fig. 6). The figures' button eyes connote blindness, a lack of mutual understanding. Equally chilling is Egon's farewell to Wally, the monumental canvas *Death and Maiden* (cat. 102). Like Kokoschka's final self-portraits with Alma Mahler, Schiele's painting exudes the melancholy of hopeless love. But the culprit here is not an unwinnable battle between the sexes. Schiele's message is rather one of essential alienation and aloneness.

Fig. 4
EGON SCHIELE
Holy Family, 1913
Private collection

1 Michael Mitchell (trans.), *Oskar Kokoschka: Plays and Poems*, Riverside, CA 2001, p. 1. Frank Whitford (*Oskar Kokoschka: A Life* [New York, 1986], p. 37) notes that red was Lilith Lang's favorite color.
2 Alfred Weidinger and Alice Strobl, *Oskar Kokoschka: Die Zeichnungen und Aquarelle 1897–1916*, Salzburg 2008, V12.
3 Cited in Bram Dijkstra, *Evil Sisters: The Threat of Female Sexuality and the Cult of Manhood* (New York: Alfred A. Knopf, 1996), 87.
4 Alfred Weidinger, *Kokoschka and Alma Mahler*, New York/Munich 1996, p. 8.
5 Oskar Kokoschka, letter to Alma Mahler, May 1912, cited in Kokoschka and Spielmann 1984 (see note 16), pp. 41–42.
6 Weidinger 1996 (see note 4), p. 53.
7 Weidinger and Strobl 2008 (see note 2), p. 355.
8 Weidinger 1996 (see note 4), p. 37.
9 Letter from Oskar Kokoschka to Alma Mahler, May 10, 1914, cited in Kokoschka and Spielmann 1984 (see note 16), p. 160.
10 According to Greek myth, the sphinx guarded the entrance to the city of Thebes and killed any traveler who could not answer her riddle: "What creature speaks with a single voice, yet walks with four-feet, two-feet and then three-feet?" Oedipus solved the riddle by answering: "Man—who crawls on all fours as a baby, stands on two feet as an adult, and uses a cane in old age." Klimt depicted the sphinx as guardian of life's mysteries in his painting *Philosophy* (AW 138) and allegorized the solution to her riddle in *The Three Ages of Life*.
11 Cited in Chandak Sengoopta, *Otto Weininger: Sex, Science, and Self in Imperial Vienna*, Chicago/London 2000, p. 142.
12 Mitchell 2001 (see note 1), p. 46.
13 "Das Weib saugt uns geistig aus," cited in Werner J. Schweiger (ed.), *Peter Altenberg, Expedition in den Alltag: Gesammelte Skizzen, 1895–1989*, Vienna/Frankfurt 1987, p. 325 (translated by Jane Kallir).
14 "Die 'schöne' Frau ist die vom Schopfer in die Welt gesetzte Weckerin der Welt-Kräfte des Mannes," undated letter from Peter Altenberg to the actress Annie Kalmar, Wiener Stadt-Bibliothek (translated by Andrew Barker).
15 Cited in Sengoopta 2000 (see note 11), p. 141.
16 Oskar Kokoschka, letter to Alma Mahler, May 10, 1914, cited in Olda Kokoschka and Heinz Spielmann (eds.), *Oskar Kokoschka Briefe I, 1905–1919*, Düsseldorf 1984, p. 159.
17 Weidinger 1996 (see note 4), p. 60.
18 Kokoschka and Spielmann 1984 (see note 16), p. 159.
19 Several recent Schiele studies have explored the impact that *fin de siècle* scientific and philosophical revelations had on the notion of a stable, fixed self and the concomitant blurring of the distinction between body and mind. See Kimberly A. Smith, *Between Ruin and Renewal: Egon Schiele's Landscapes*, New Haven/London 2004. – *Egon Schiele: "Das Unrettbare Ich,"* (exh. cat.) Cologne 2011.
20 Jane Kallir, *Egon Schiele's Women*, Munich/London/New York 2012, pp. 214–24.

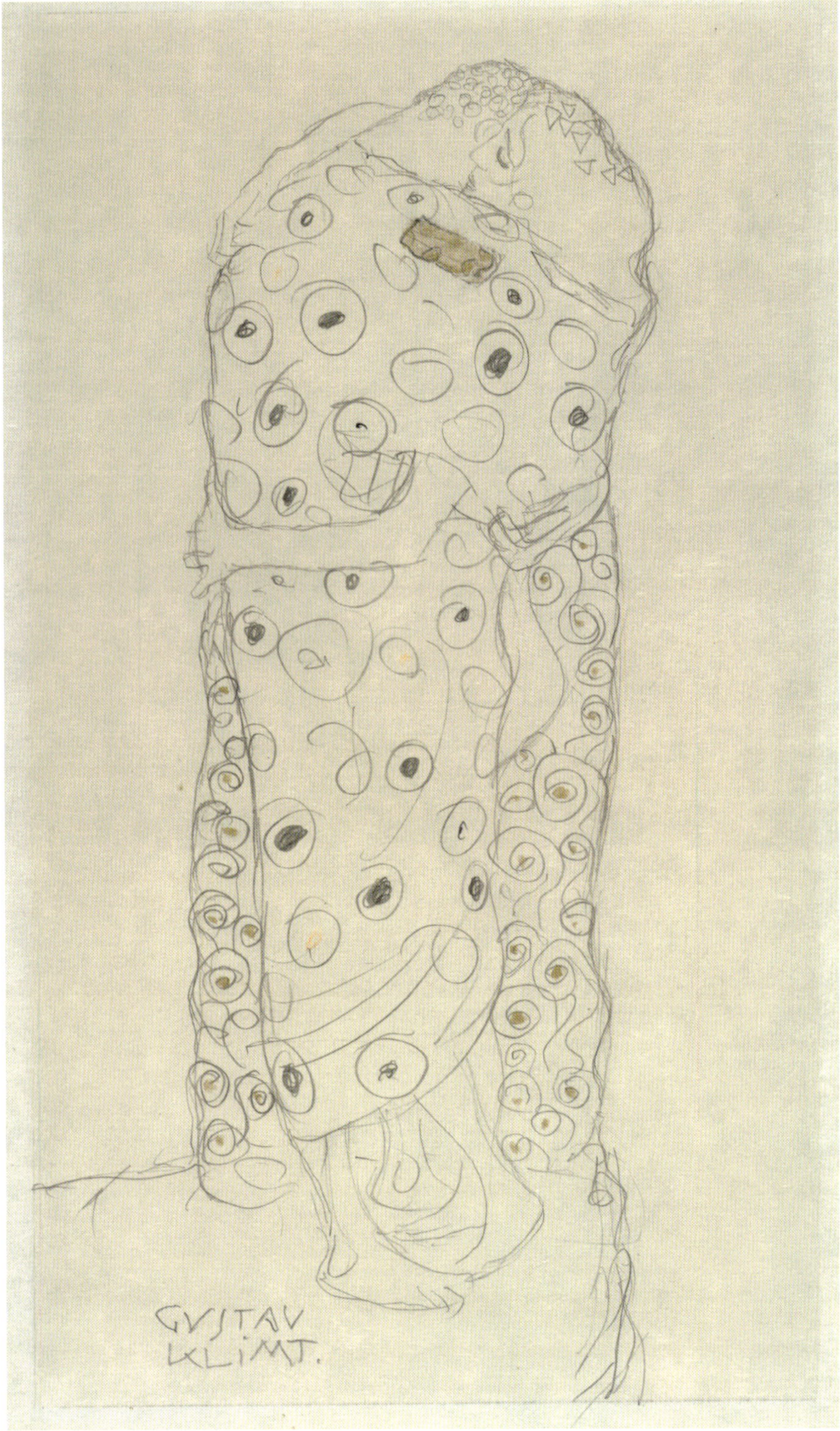

Cat. 85
GUSTAV KLIMT
Standing Couple, 1907–08
Pencil, colored pencil, gold paint on paper, 29.6 x 28.2 cm
Albertina, Vienna, Collection Batliner

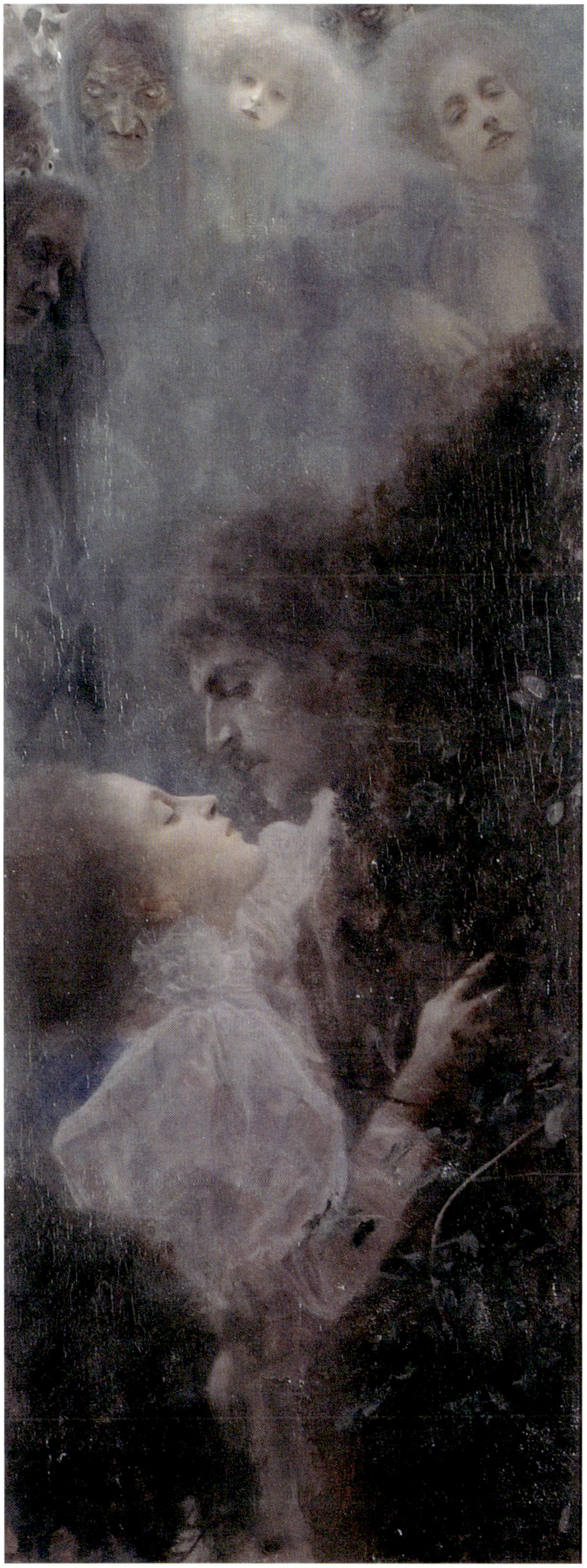

Cat. 86
GUSTAV KLIMT
Love, 1895
Oil on canvas, 60 x 44 cm
Wien Museum, Vienna

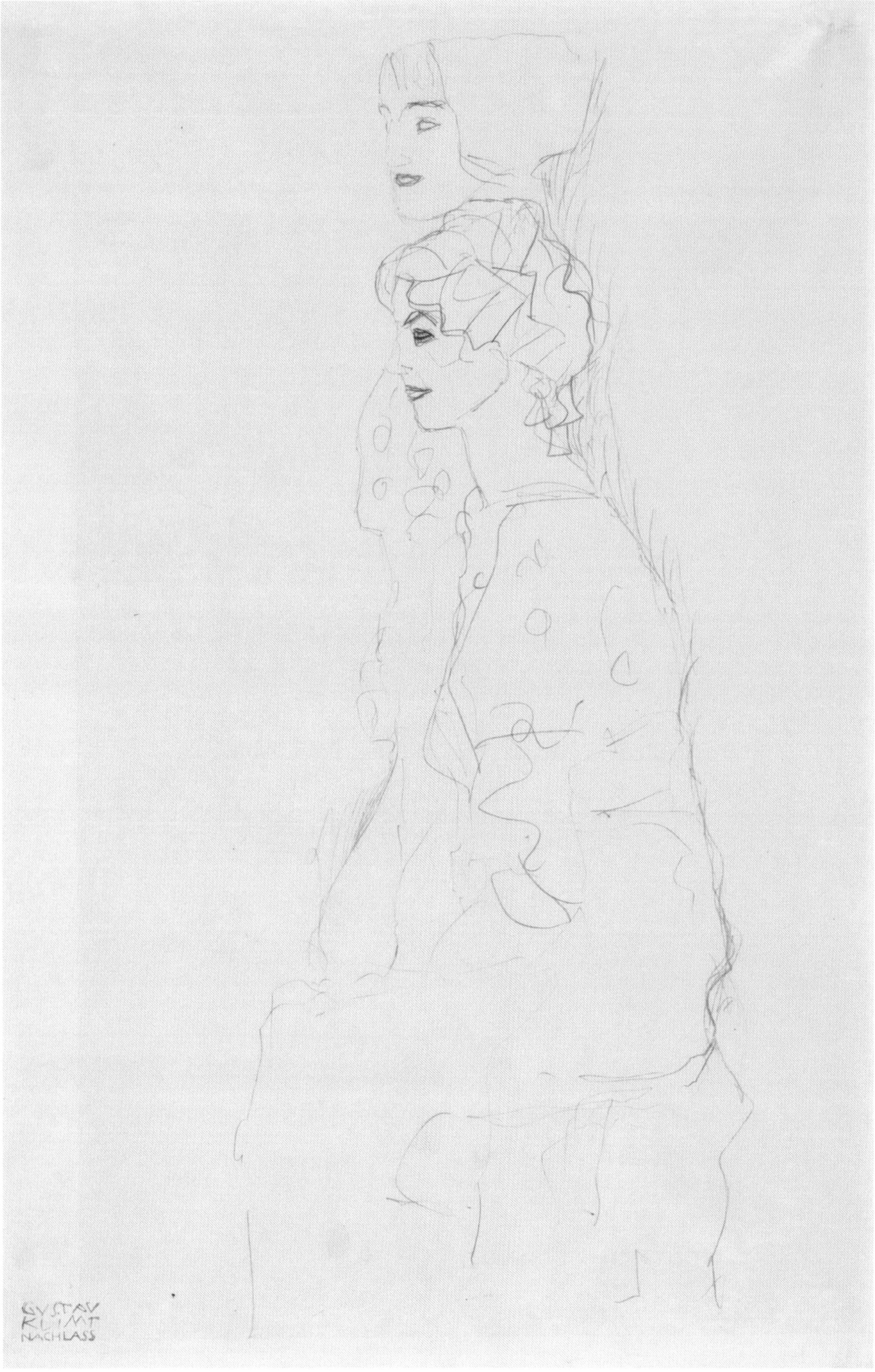

Cat. 87
GUSTAV KLIMT
Girlfriends, 1916–17
Pencil on paper, 55.9 x 37.2 cm
Private collection

Cat. 88
GUSTAV KLIMT
The Sisters, 1907
Oil on canvas, 125 x 42 cm
Klimt-Foundation, Vienna

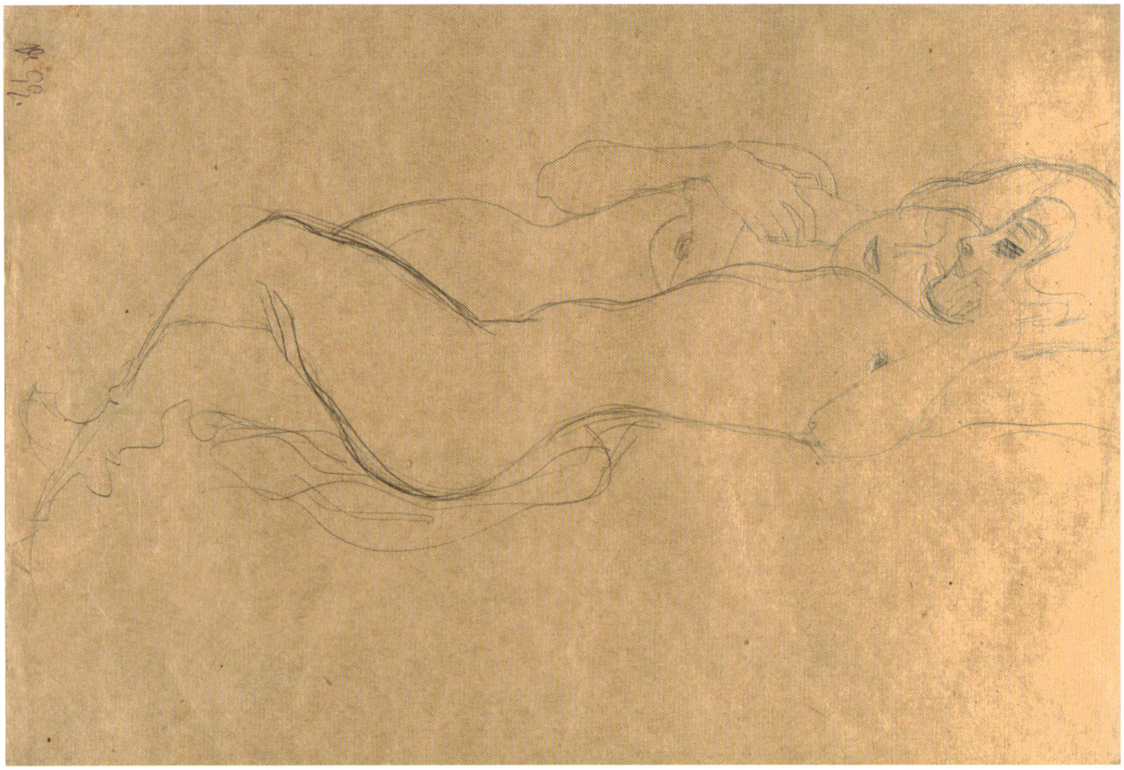

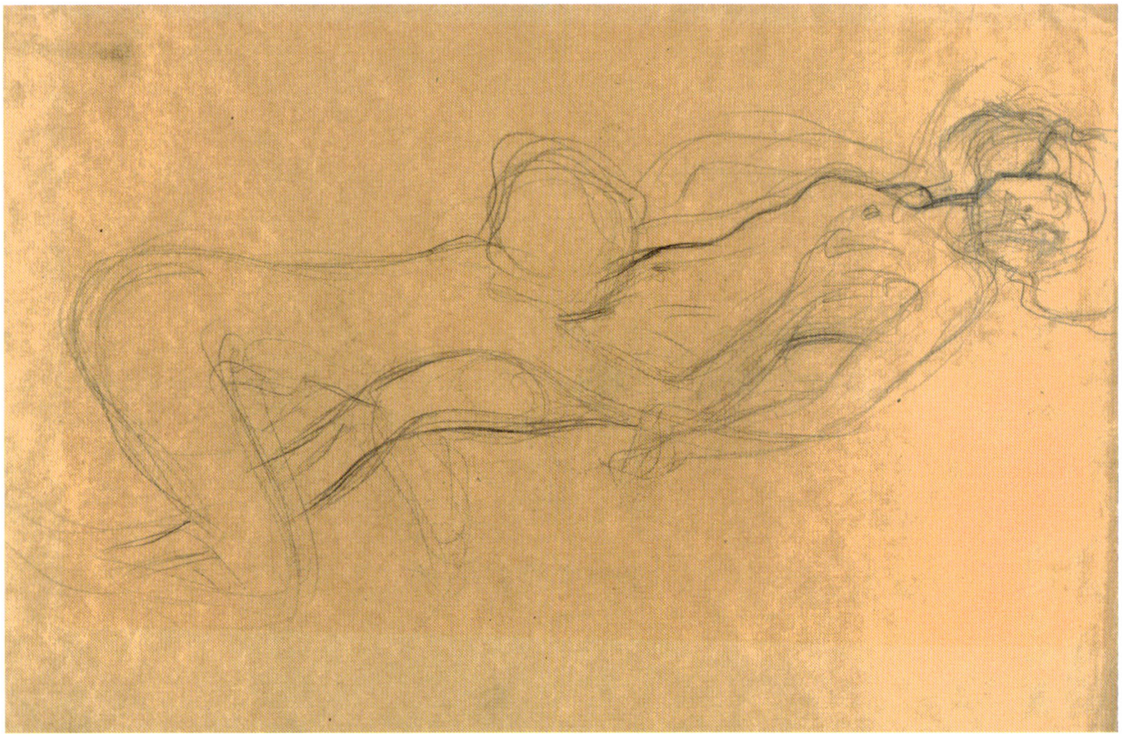

Cat. 89
GUSTAV KLIMT
Two Reclining Female Nudes,
1905–06
Pencil on paper, 31.1 x 45.6 cm
Wien Museum, Vienna

Cat. 90
GUSTAV KLIMT
Two Female Nudes, 1905–06
Pencil on paper, 30 x 45.8 cm
Wien Museum, Vienna

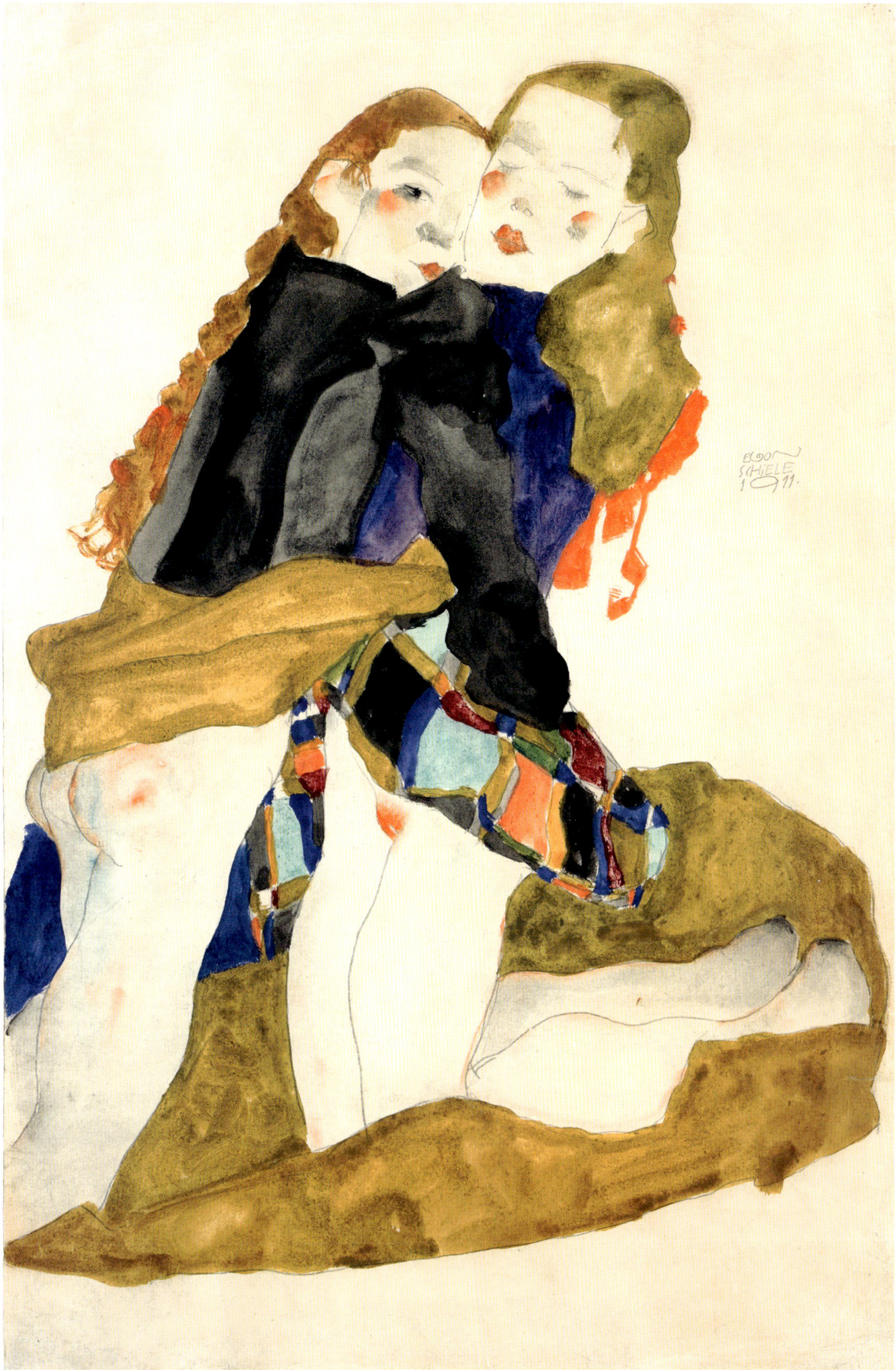

Cat. 91
EGON SCHIELE
Kneeling Girls, 1911
Gouache, watercolor and pencil,
47.2 x 31.5 cm
Private collection, courtesy of
Richard Nagy Ltd., London

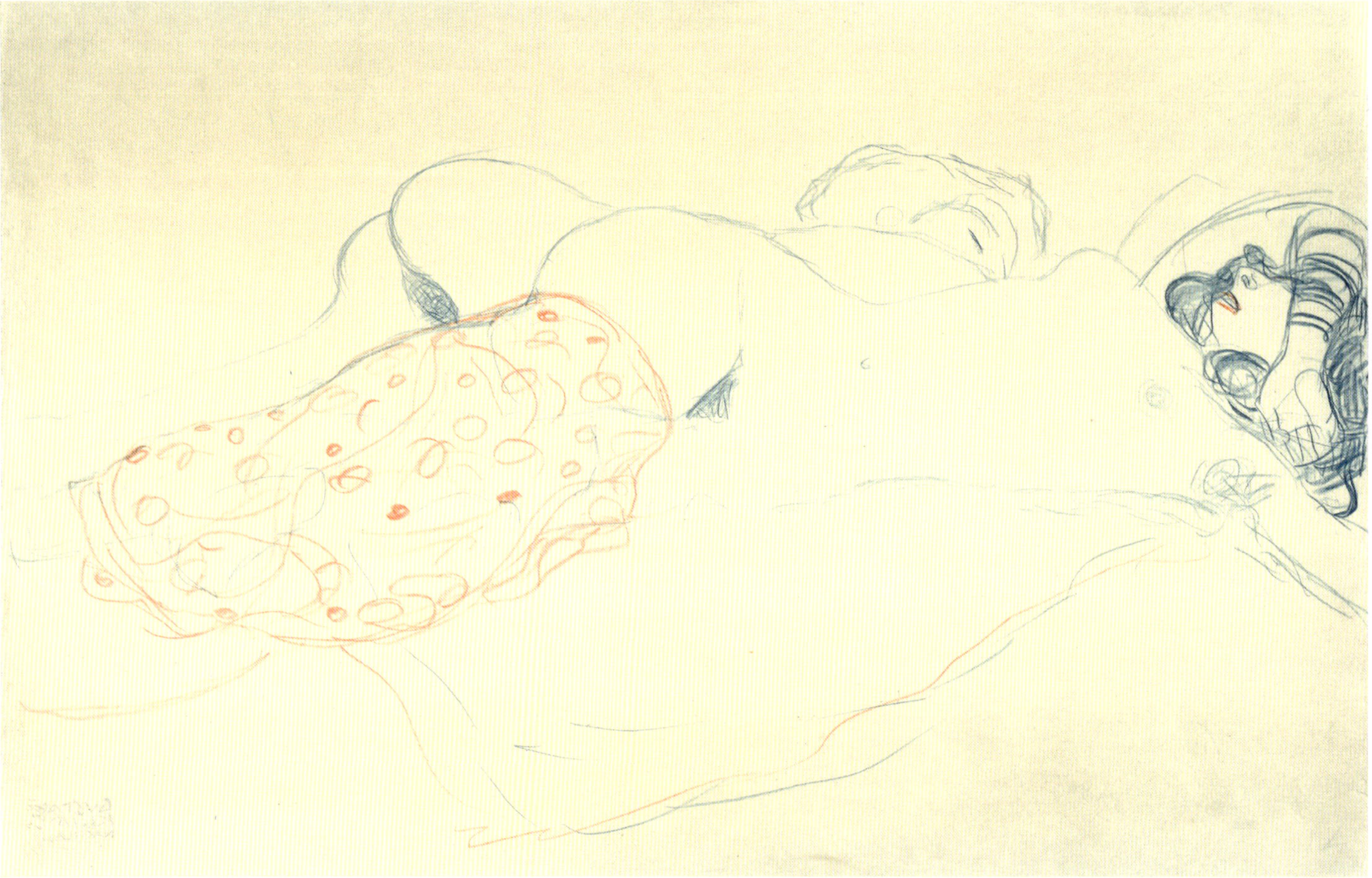

Cat. 92
GUSTAV KLIMT
Two Reclining Nudes Facing Right, 1913–14
Blue and red pencil on paper, 34.9 x 55.1 cm
Coninx-Stiftung, Zurich

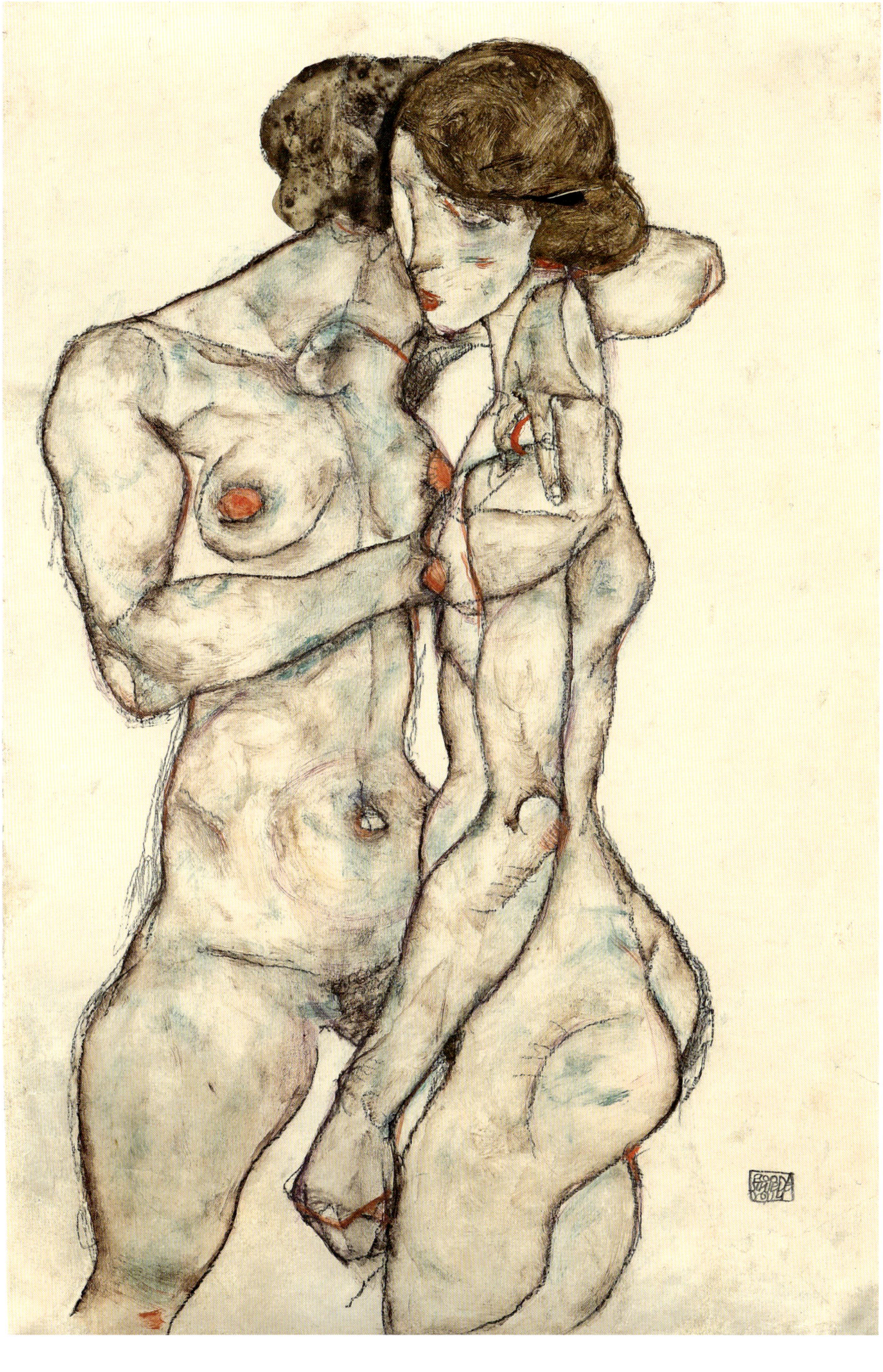

Cat. 93
EGON SCHIELE
Friends, 1914
Gouache and pencil on paper,
48.5 x 32.5 cm
Private collection, London

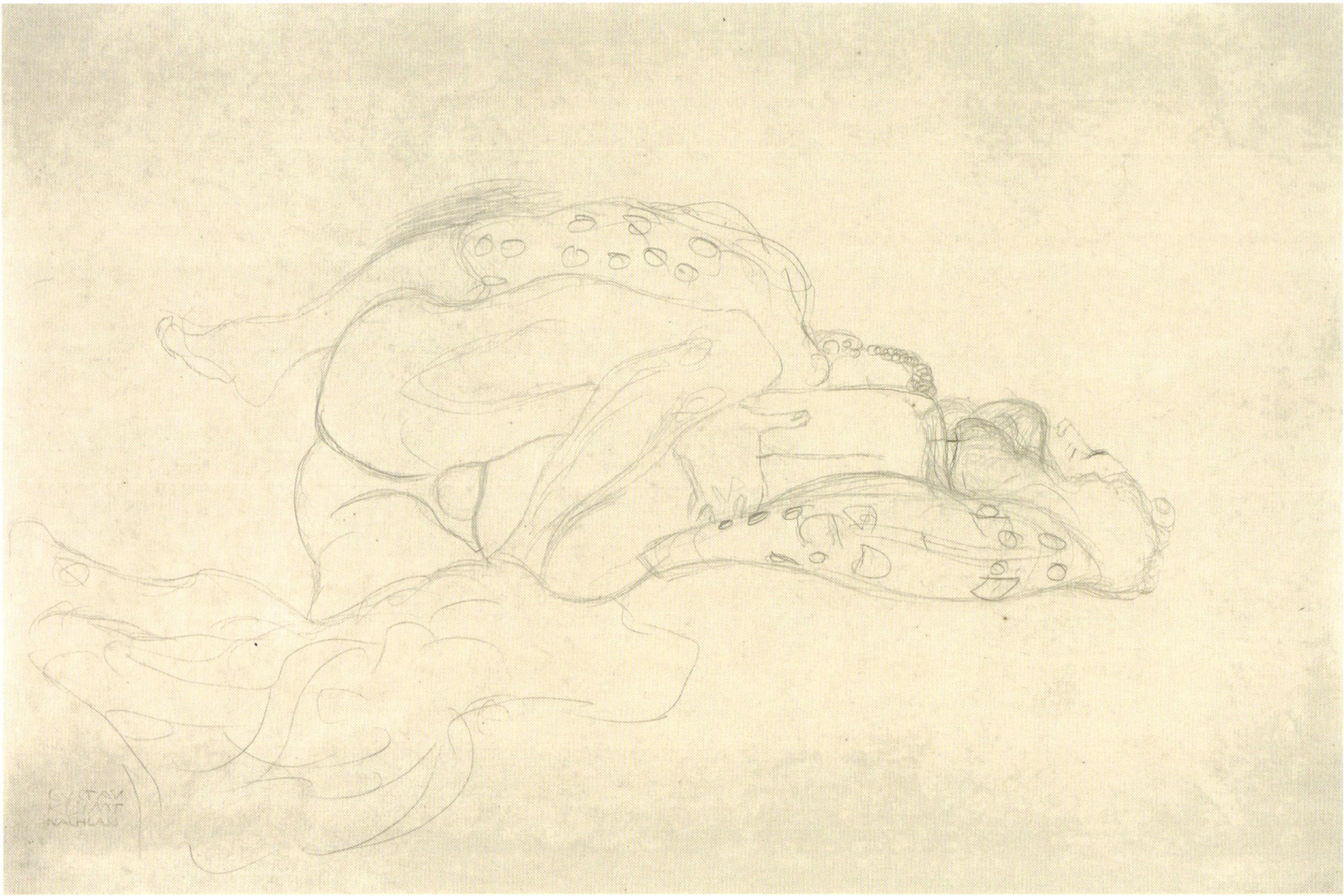

Cat. 94
GUSTAV KLIMT
Lovers, c. 1907
Pencil on paper, 37.1 x 56.5 cm
Adolf Loos Apartment and Gallery, Prague

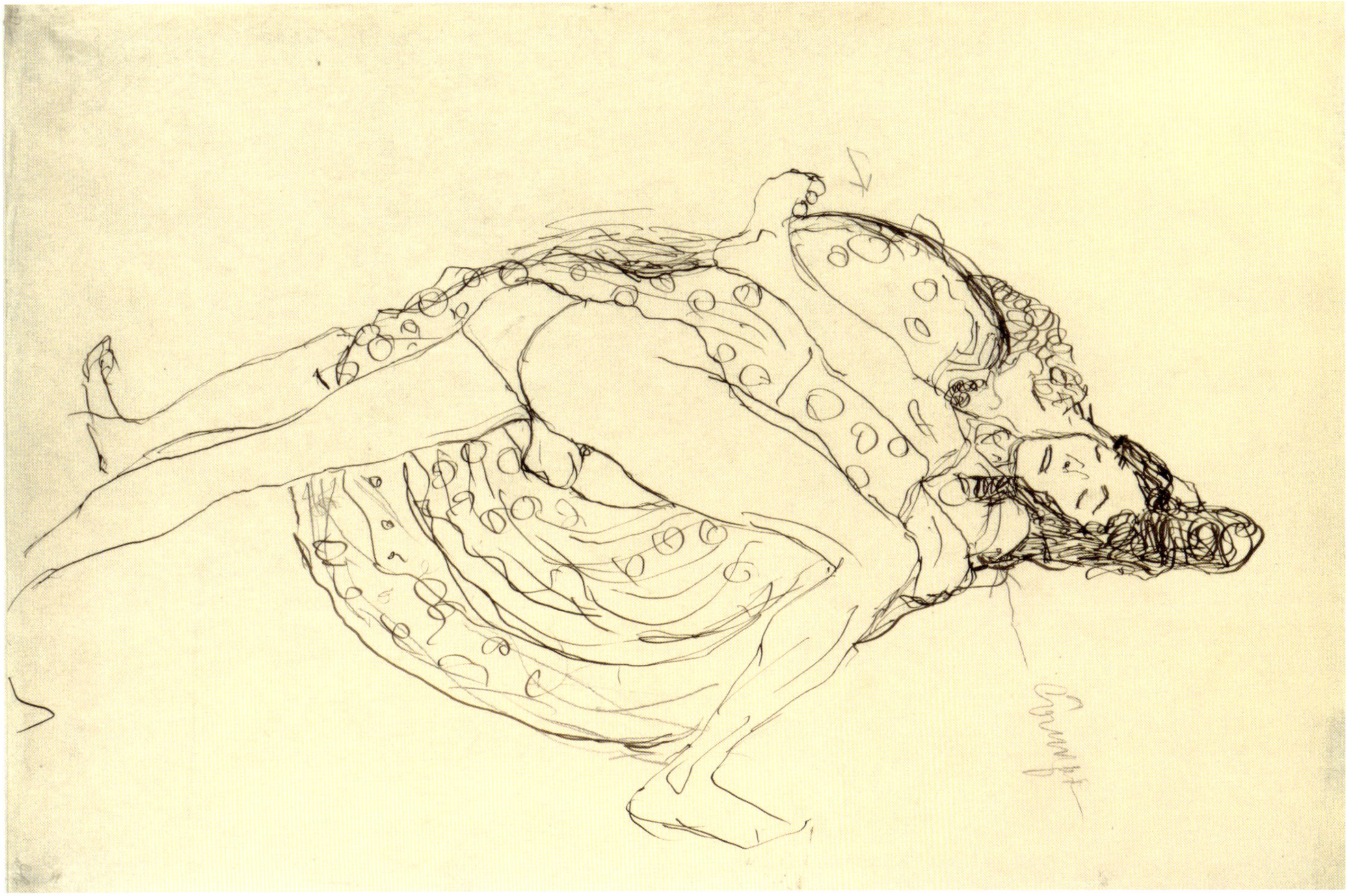

Cat. 95
GUSTAV KLIMT
Couple Facing Right, 1913
Ink on Japanese paper, 36.5 × 56.5 cm
Private collection, courtesy of Galerie St. Etienne, New York

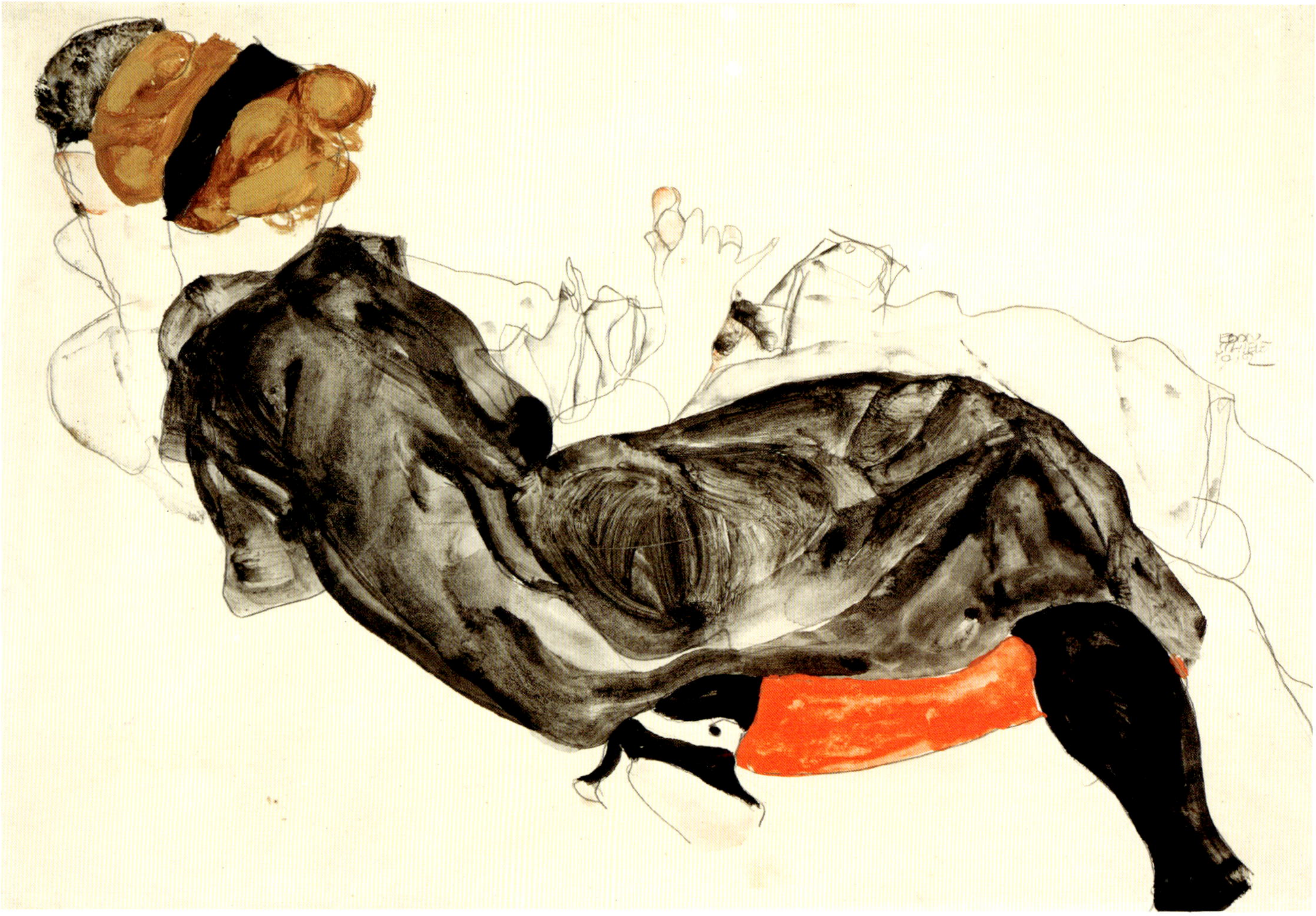

Cat. 96
EGON SCHIELE
Reclining Couple, 1912
Watercolor, gouache, and pencil on paper, 30.5 x 44.5 cm
Private collection, Vienna

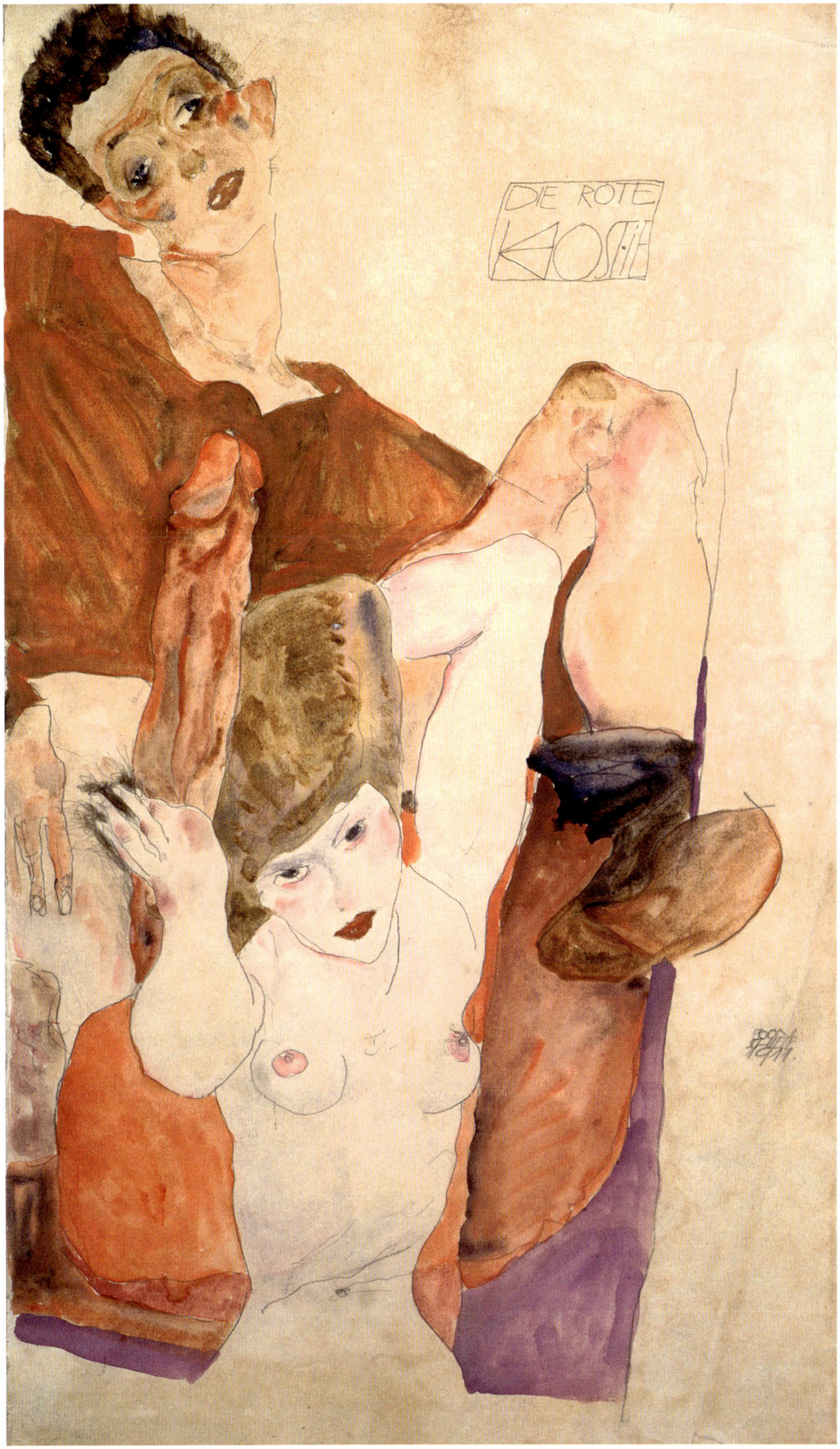

Cat. 97
EGON SCHIELE
The Red Host, 1911
Watercolor and pencil on paper,
48.2 x 28.2 cm
Private collection, courtesy of Galerie
St. Etienne, New York

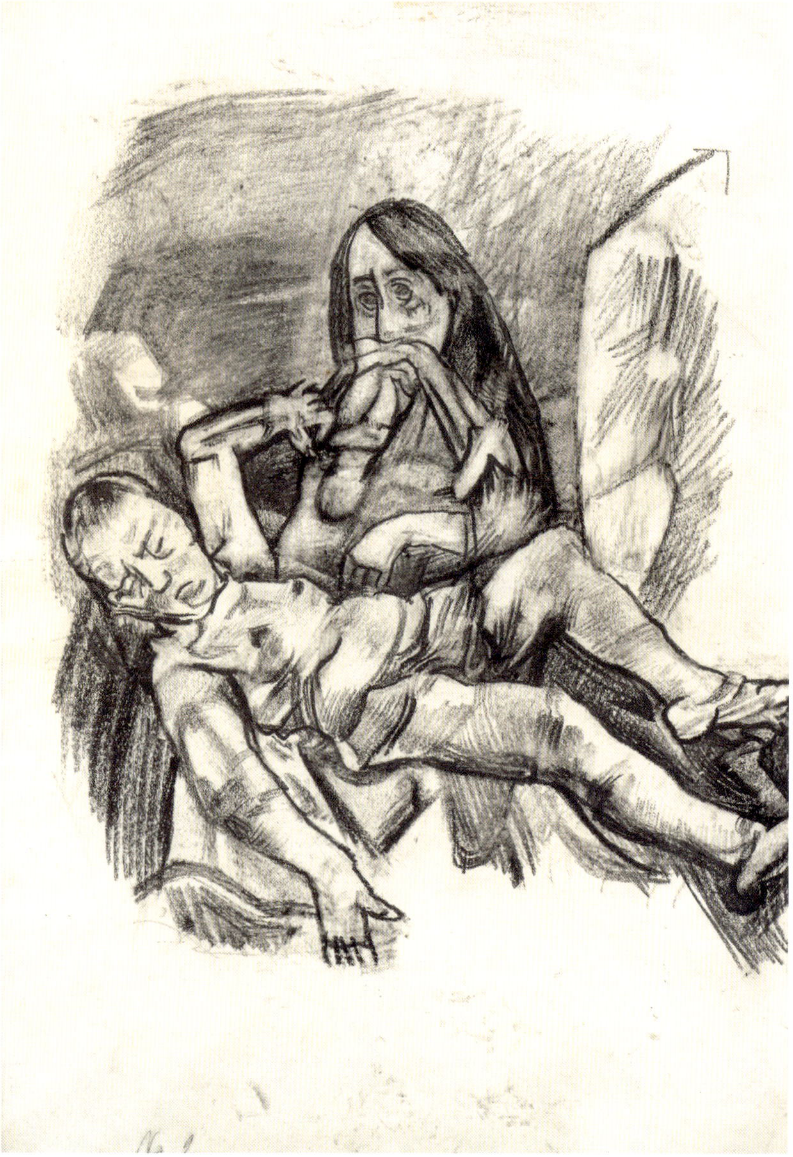

Cat. 98
OSKAR KOKOSCHKA
Pietà: "It is Enough" I, 1914
Black crayon on Japanese paper, 46.6 x 31.7 cm
Private collection

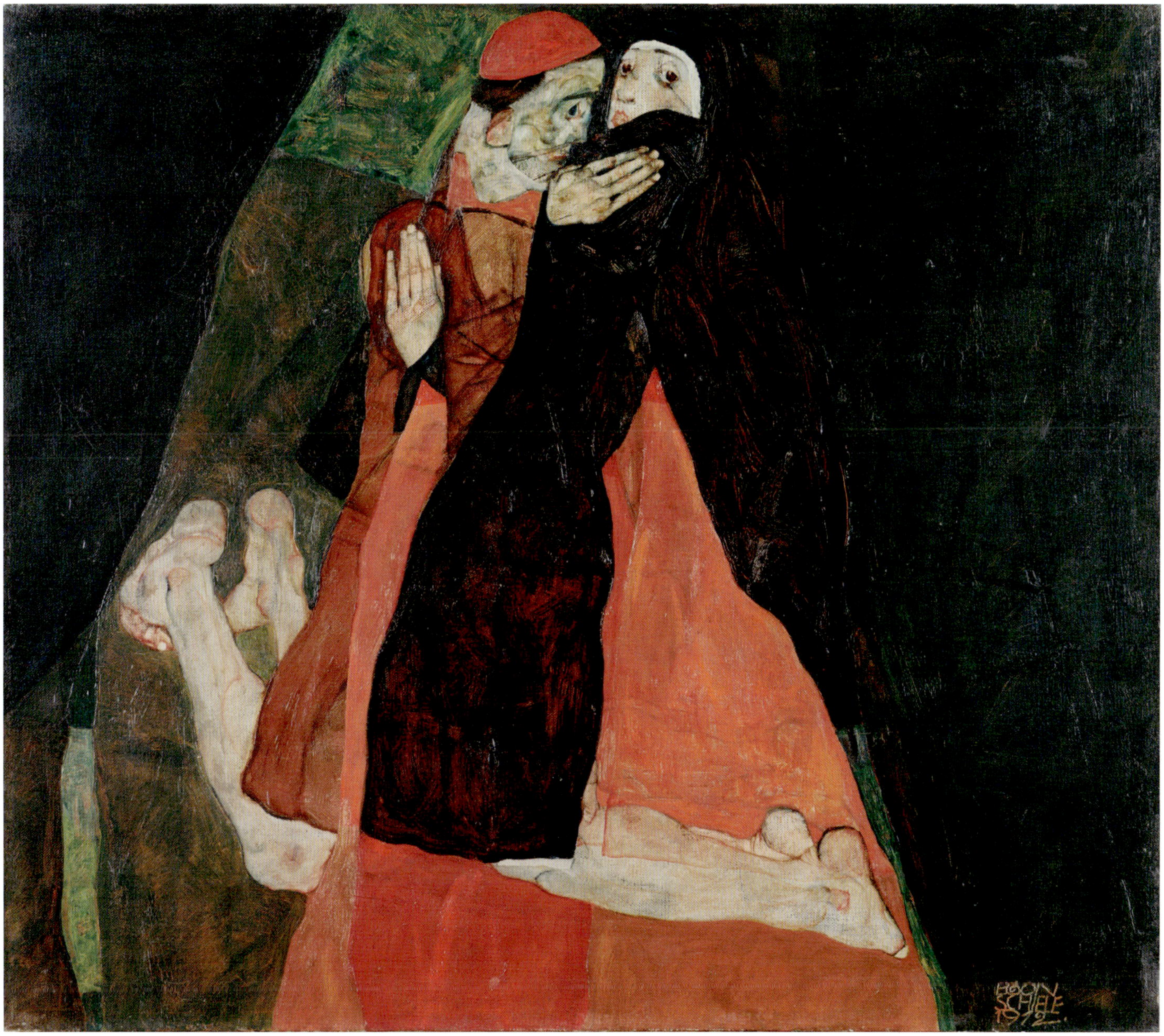

Cat. 99
EGON SCHIELE
Cardinal and Nun, 1912
Oil on canvas, 70 x 80.5 cm
Leopold Museum, Vienna

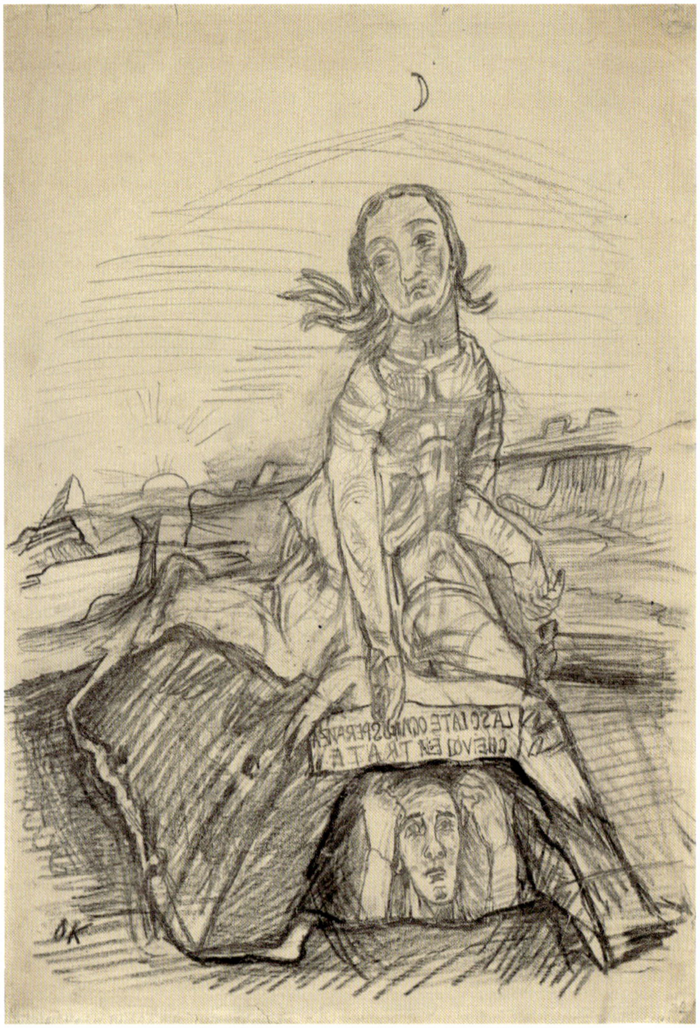

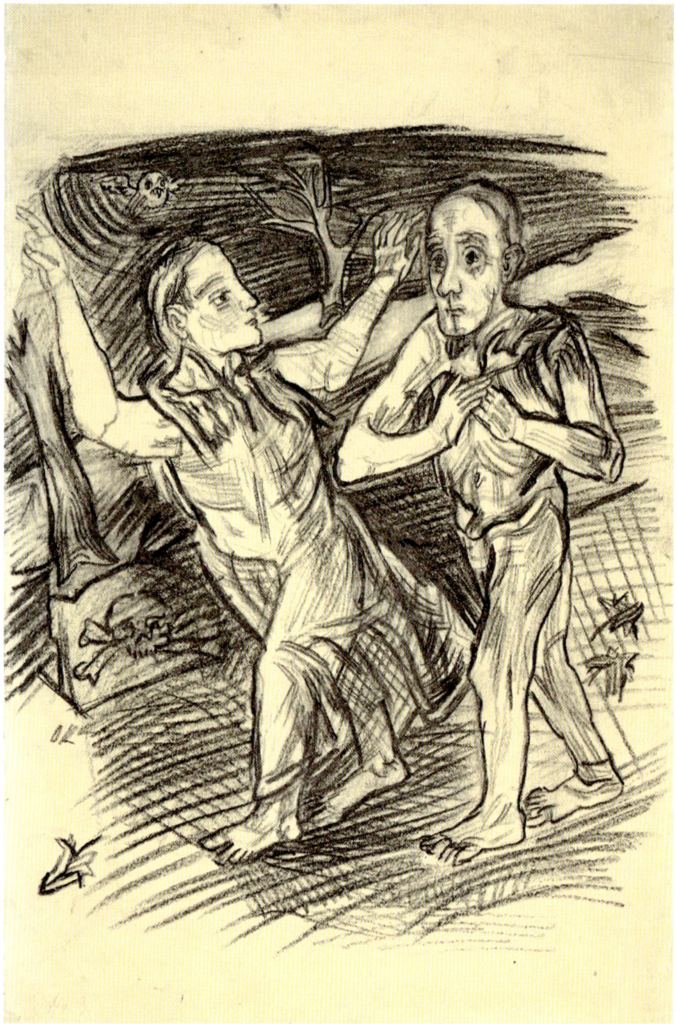

Cat. 100
OSKAR KOKOSCHKA
The Man Raises His Head from the Grave on Which the Woman Sits, 1914
Black crayon on paper, 49.5 x 35.2 cm
Staatliche Kunstsammlungen Dresden, Collection of Prints, Drawings and Photographs, Dresden

Cat. 101
OSKAR KOKOSCHKA
The Woman Leads the Man, 1914
Black crayon on paper, 48.1 x 31.3 cm
Staatliche Kunstsammlungen Dresden, Collection of Prints, Drawings and Photographs, Dresden

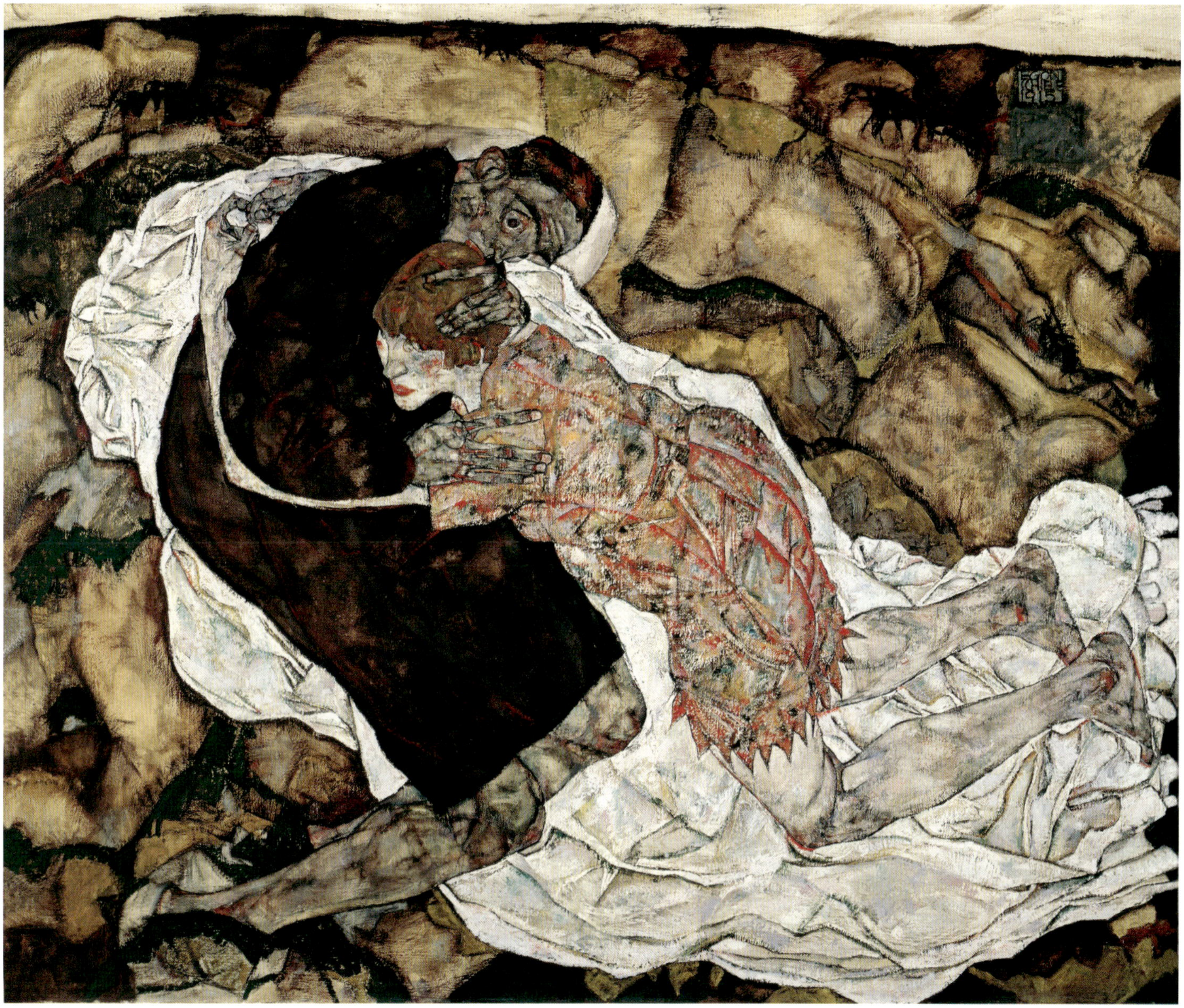

Cat. 102
EGON SCHIELE
Death and Maiden, 1915
Oil on canvas, 150 x 180 cm
Belvedere, Vienna

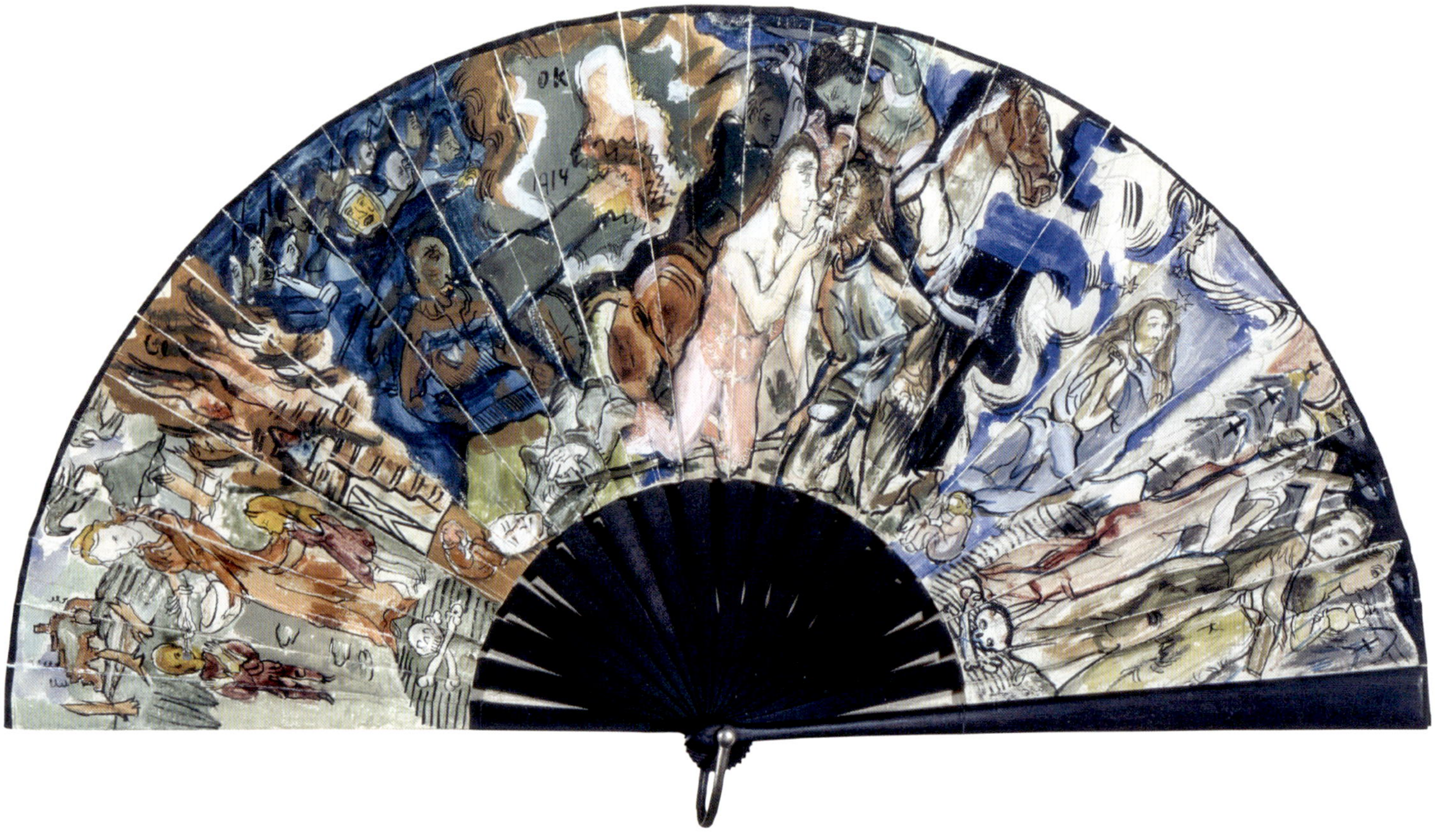

Cat. 103
OSKAR KOKOSCHKA
Sixth Fan for Alma Mahler, 1914
Watercolor, Black ink and pencil on goatskin parchment, mounted on ebony, 21.5 x 40 cm
Museum für Kunst und Gewerbe, Hamburg

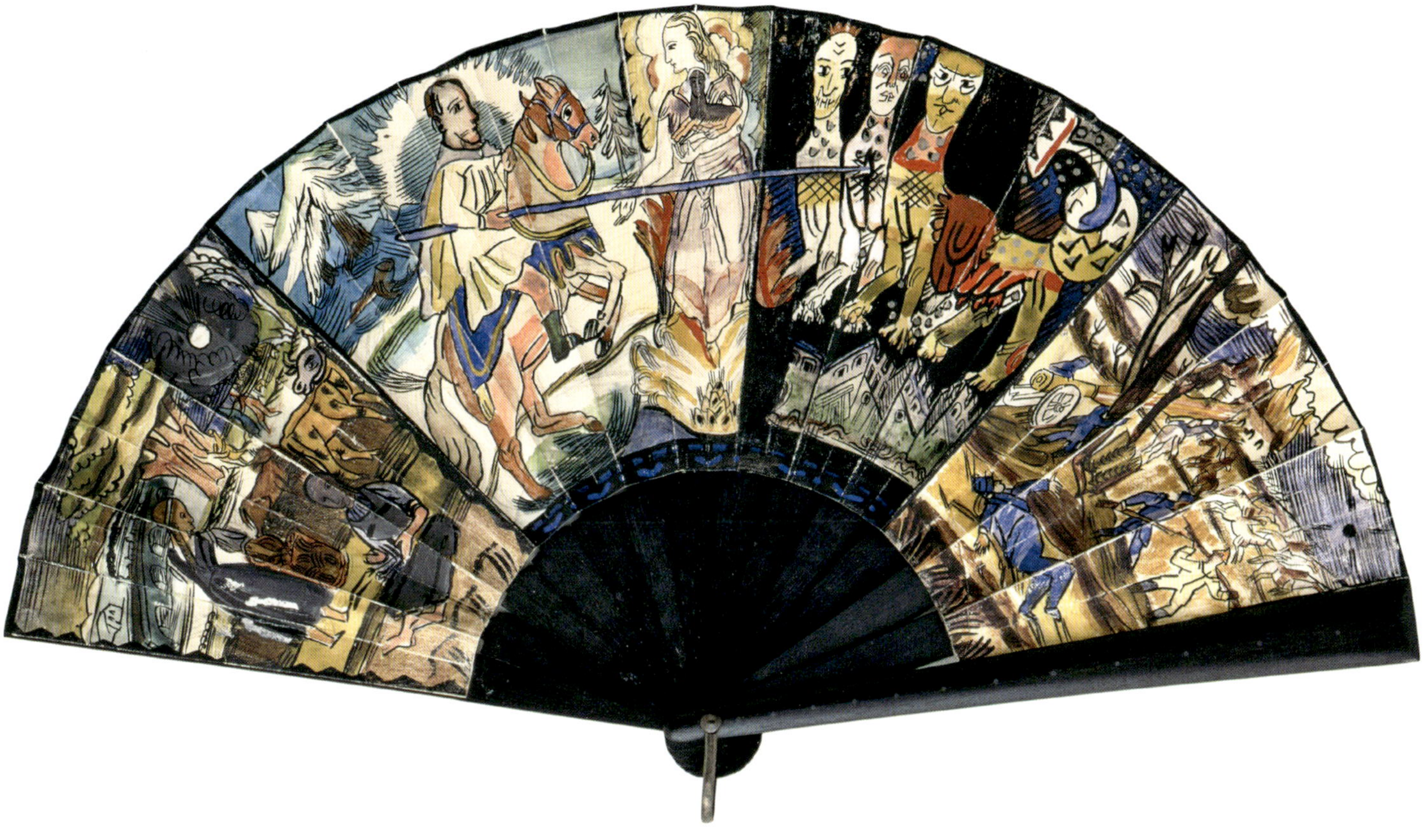

Cat. 104
OSKAR KOKOSCHKA
Seventh Fan for Alma Mahler, 1915
Watercolor, Black ink and pencil on goatskin parchment, mounted on ebony, 21.5 x 40 cm
Museum für Kunst und Gewerbe, Hamburg

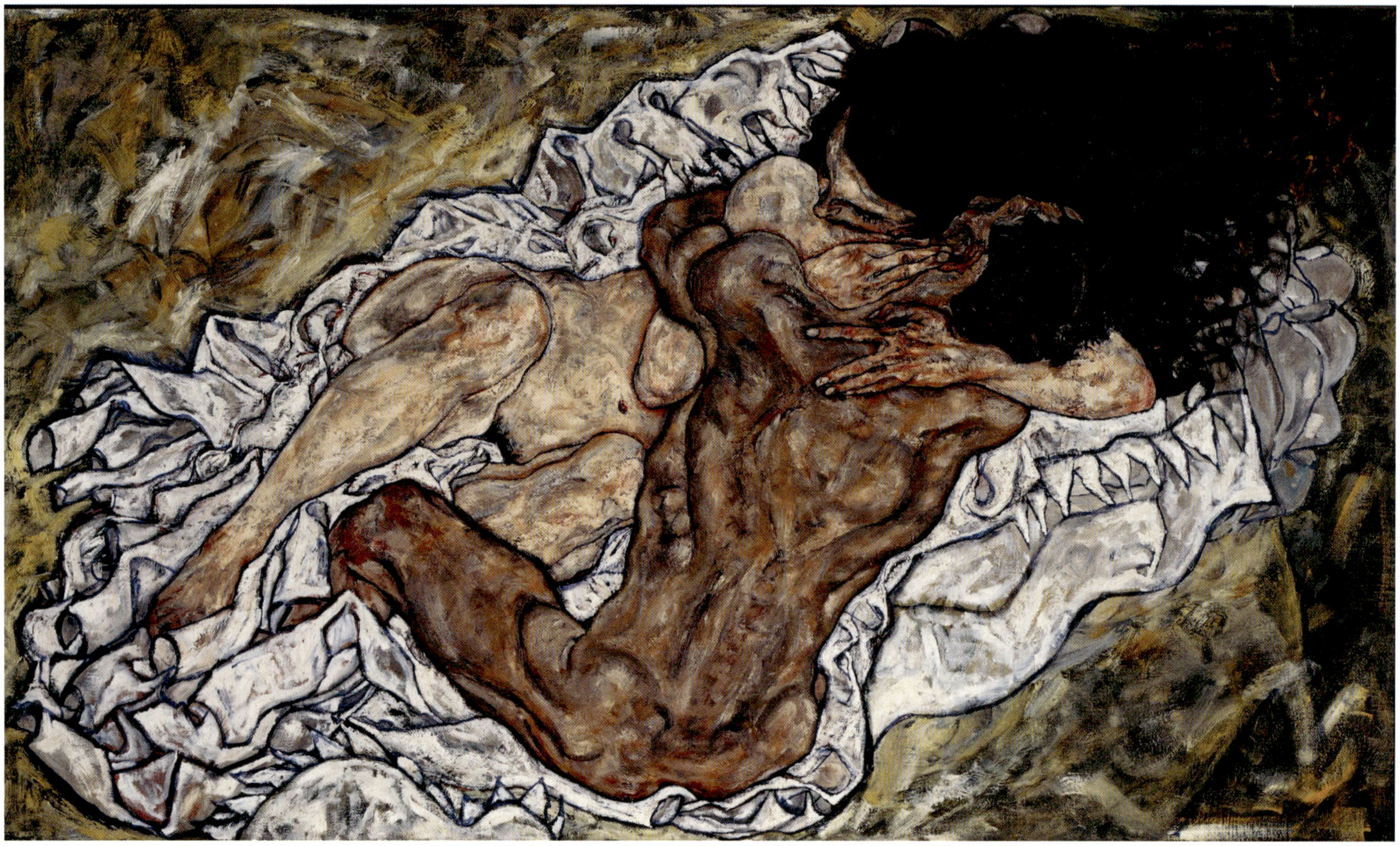

Cat. 105
EGON SCHIELE
Embrace, 1917
Oil on canvas, 100 x 170.2 cm
Belvedere, Vienna

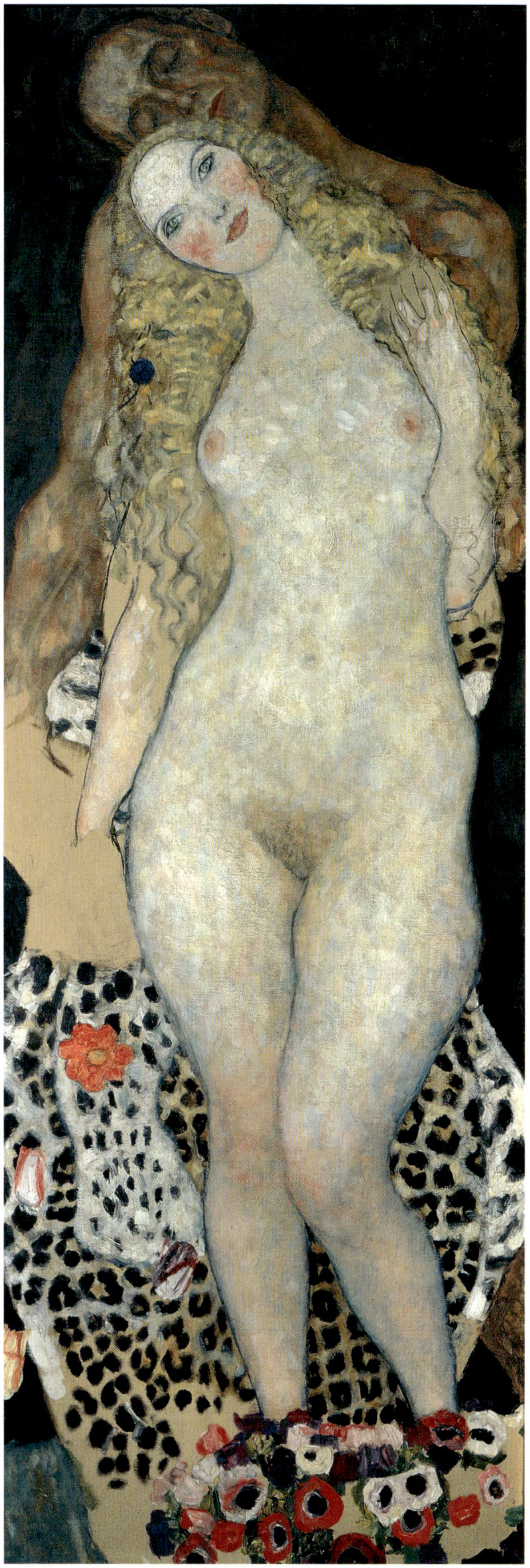

Cat. 106
GUSTAV KLIMT
Adam and Eve, 1917
Oil on canvas, 173 x 60 cm
Belvedere, Vienna

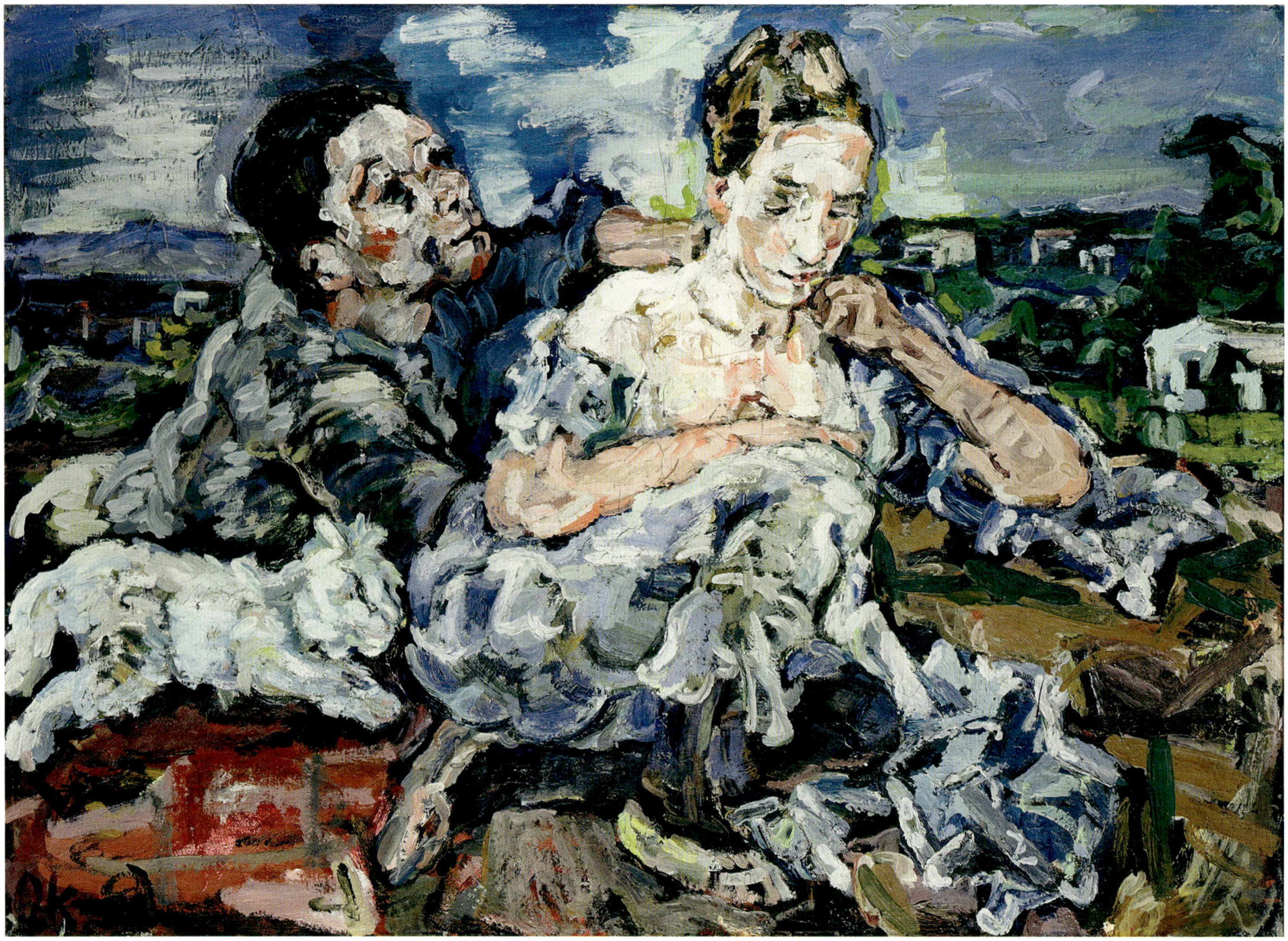

Cat. 107
OSKAR KOKOSCHKA
Lovers with Cat, 1917
Oil on canvas, 93.5 x 130.5 cm
Kunsthaus Zurich

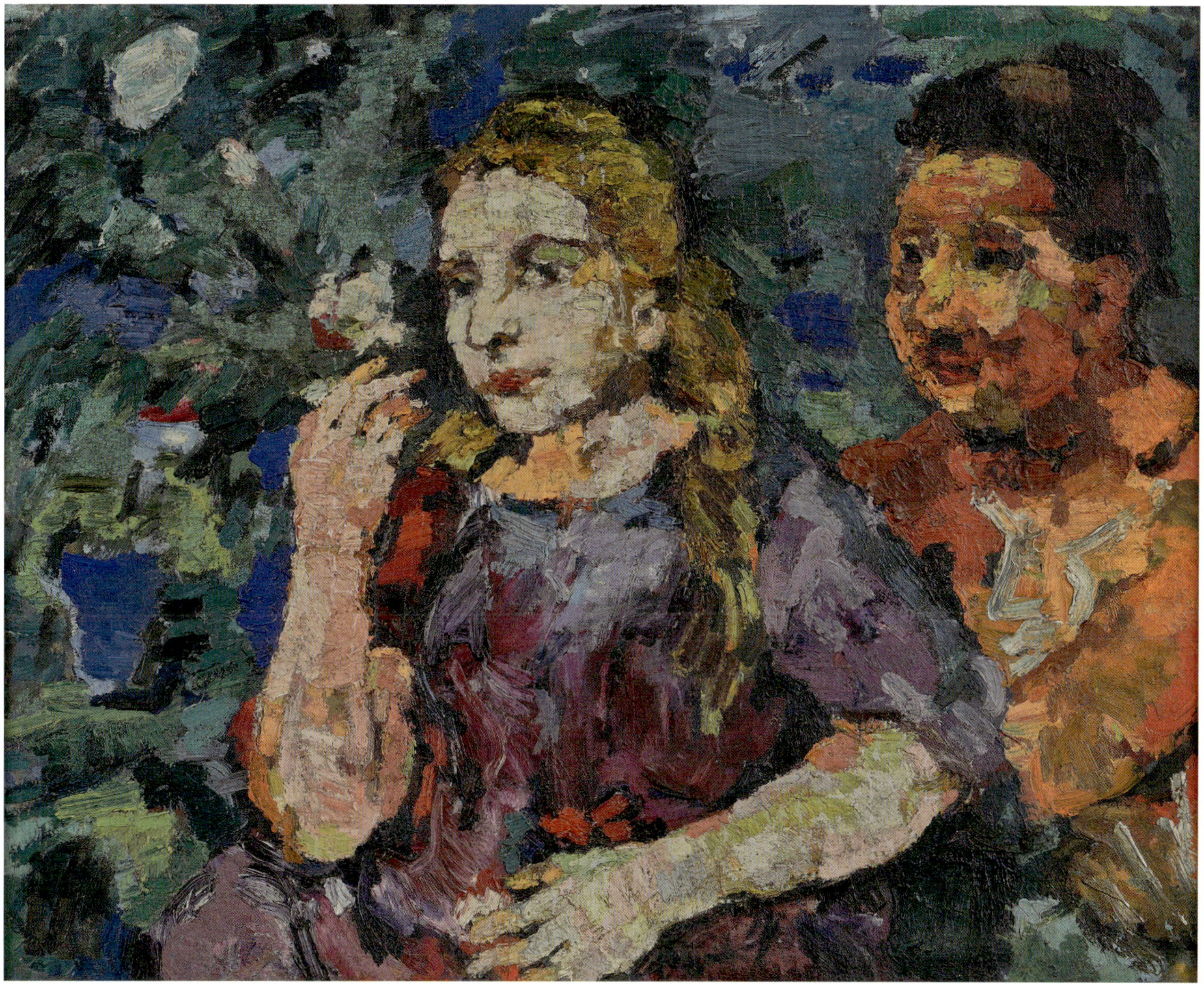

Cat. 108
OSKAR KOKOSCHKA
Woman with Slave, 1920
Oil on canvas, 92.5 x 109.5 cm
Galerie Zlatá husa, Prague

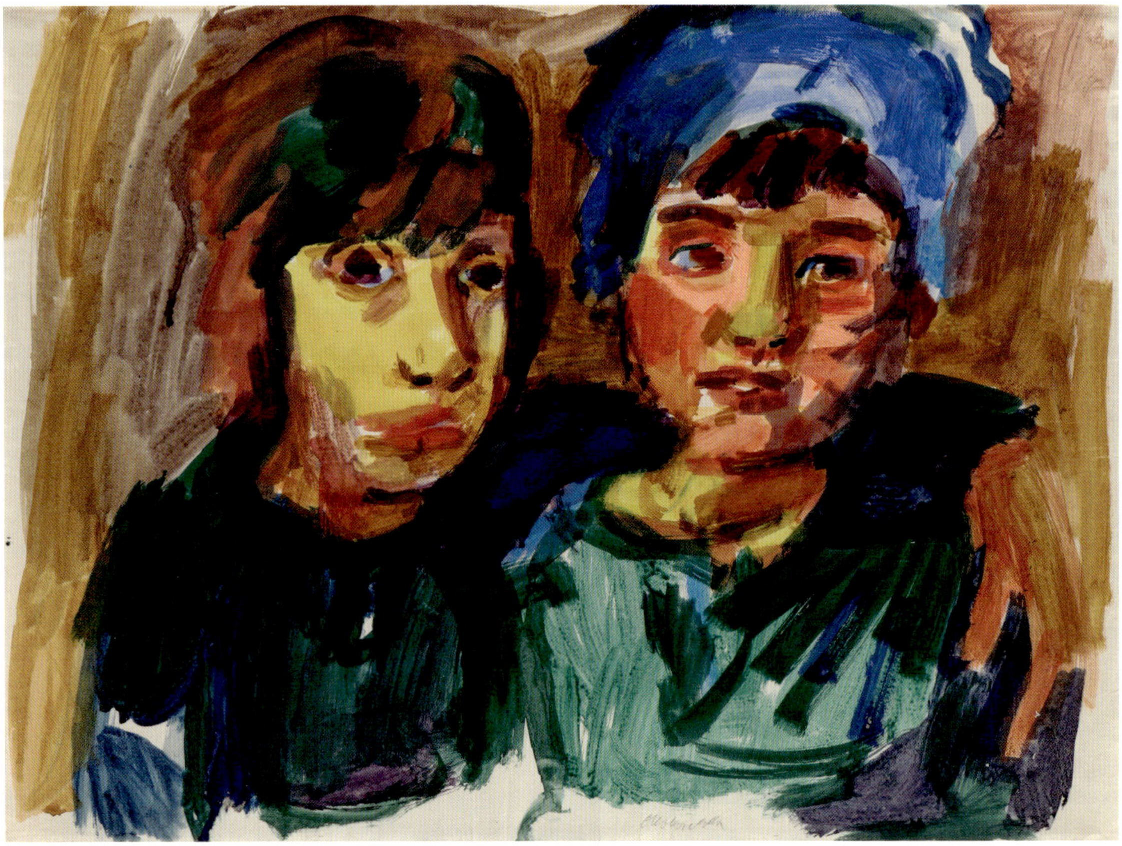

Cat. 109
OSKAR KOKOSCHKA
Girlfriends, 1921
Watercolor and gouache on paper, 50.6 x 96.2 cm
Staatliche Kunstsammlungen Dresden, Collection of Prints, Drawings and Photographs, Dresden

Cat. 110
OSKAR KOKOSCHKA
The Slave Girl, 1921
Oil on canvas, 110.5 x 80 cm
Saint Louis Art Museum,
bequest of Morton D. May

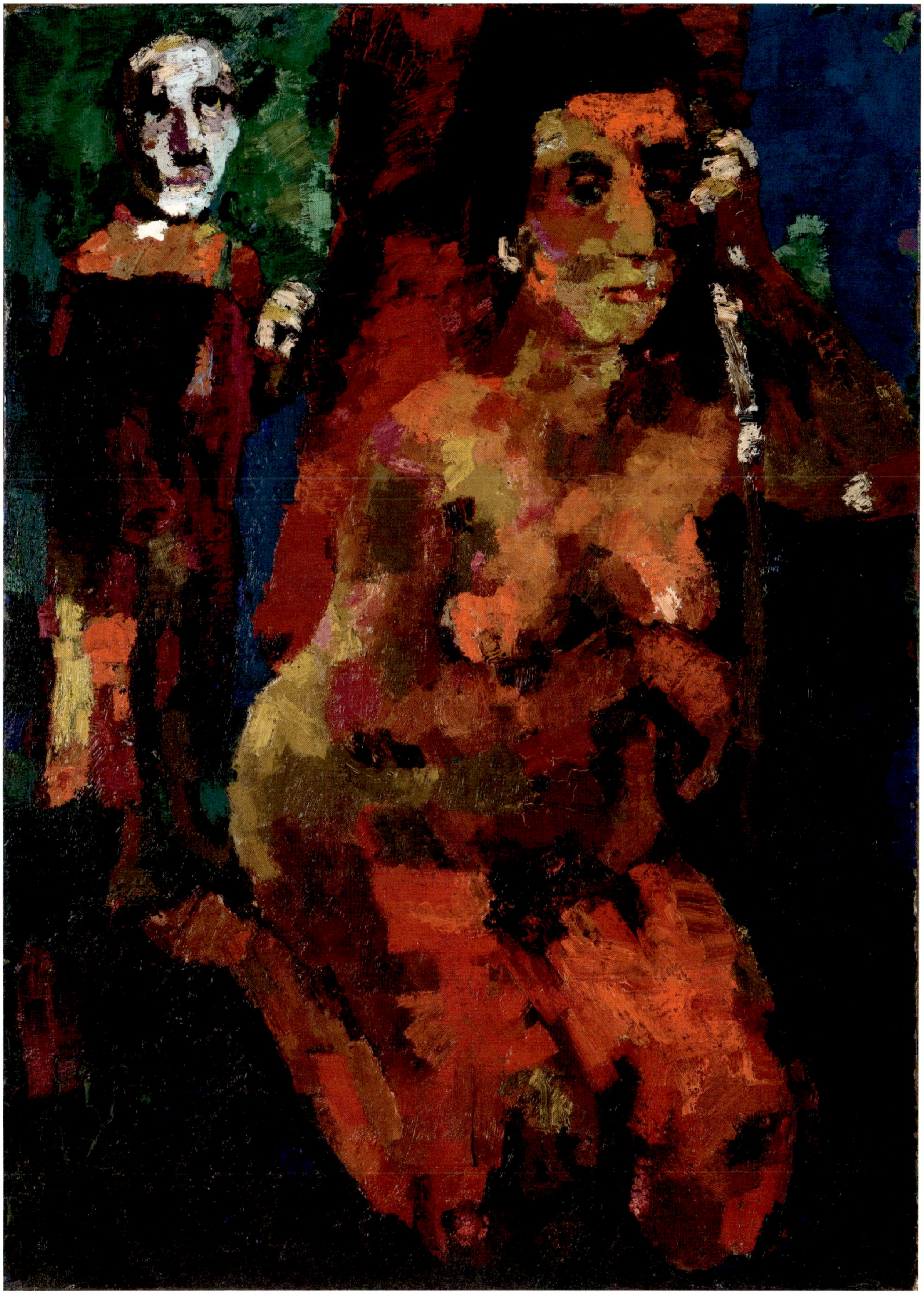

Nudes

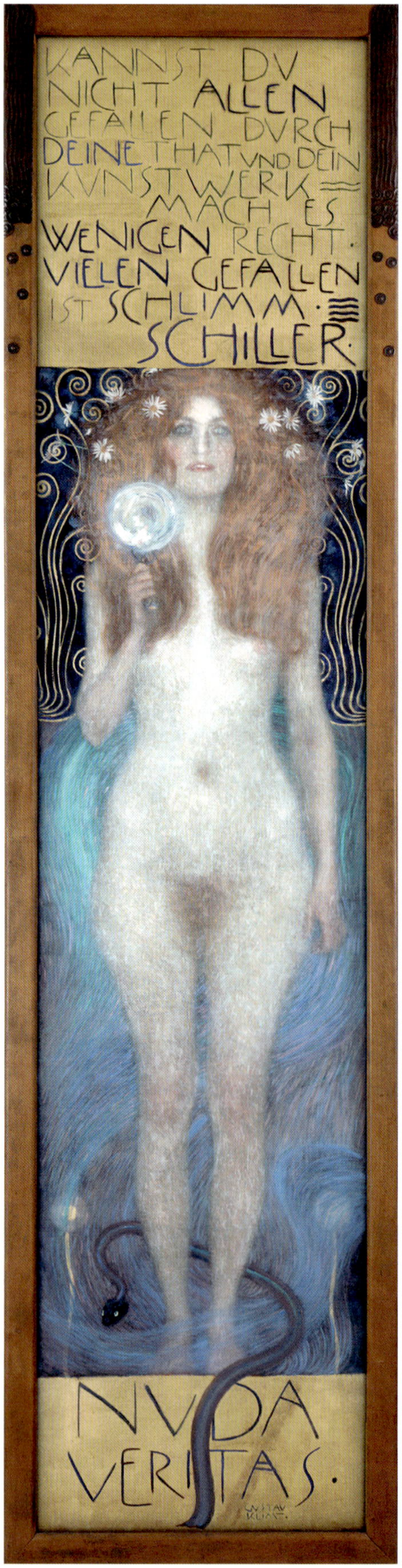

Fig. 1
GUSTAV KLIMT
Nuda Veritas, 1899
Österreichisches Theatermuseum, Vienna

Unlike the other pictorial genres featuring women, the nude represented an aspect of femininity that was largely repressed within polite society. "A young girl of good family was not allowed to have any idea of how a male body was formed, or to know how children came into the world," Stefan Zweig recalled. "The angel was to enter into matrimony not only physically untouched, but completely 'pure' spiritually as well."[1] Despite—or more probably because of—this emphasis on "purity," roughly 90 percent of adult Austrian males at the turn of the last century frequented prostitutes.[2] Since only prostitutes wantonly disrobed for men, the artist's studio was in effect an extension of the brothel: a private space in which an artist was free to project his sexual feelings on naked women.

Though the prurient appeal of the nude was undeniable, classical examples of the genre downplayed its eroticism. As the art historian Kenneth Clark noted in his famous treatise on the subject, the provocative naked body was transformed into a non-threatening artistic nude through a process of ordering and control.[3] The nude was, first and foremost, passive, and typically portrayed in a reclining pose. Single-point perspective firmly pinioned her within the picture frame and

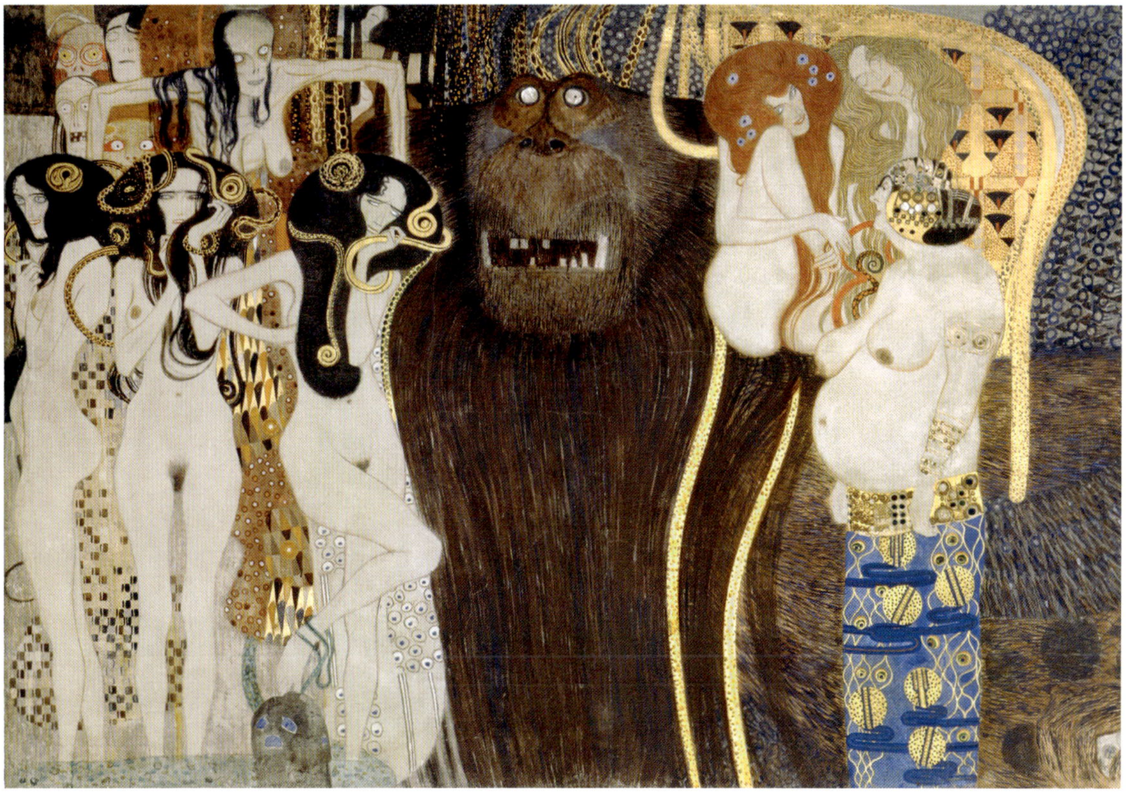

Fig. 2
GUSTAV KLIMT
Beethoven Frieze: The Hostile Forces, 1901
Belvedere, Vienna

distanced her from the male observer. Looking was the man's prerogative. The female nude did not usually respond to the artist's gaze or engage directly with the hypothetical viewer. Beauty further accentuated the nude's status as an idealized artistic object. She was unblemished, a perfect specimen of nubile flesh and soothing, voluptuous form. Usually her pubic area was discreetly masked. Beyond this, by placing the nude in a mythical, historical, or Biblical context, the artist could subordinate her eroticism to a higher purpose. Passivity reinforced the classical nude's submission to male authority, while beauty and metaphor imbued her with moral goodness.

The scandals surrounding Klimt in the early years of the twentieth century were occasioned by his violation of the foregoing standards. Male and female nudes cavort freely, without any mollifying narrative pretext, in the artist's three canvases for the University of Vienna (AW 138, 139, 166; see p. 38, fig. 10). Some of his nudes are conventionally beautiful, but others are wizened, haggard, obese or plain wicked. The naked woman in *Nuda Veritas* (fig. 1, cat. 113), shameless despite the evil snake at her feet, renounces all claims to moral superiority. The canvas is inscribed with a quote from Friedrich Schiller: "If you cannot please everyone with your deeds and your art, do right by the few; it is bad to please the masses." Klimt's intransigence in the face of scandal is reiterated in *Goldfish* (cat. 114), originally titled *To My Critics*. Three seductive nudes here taunt a prudish audience, one of the women mischievously thrusting her bare buttocks in the viewer's face.

Notwithstanding his offenses against bourgeois propriety, Klimt's work was largely in sync with the gender politics of his time. Writing enthusiastically about the artist's nudes, the critic Hermann Bahr might have been quoting Otto Weininger: "Everything about the woman belongs to lust," Bahr observed. "Every part of woman is 'sex.' "[4] And woman's unabated lust could feel as threatening to Klimt as it did to Weininger. *Judith*, was the ultimate femme fatale (p. 27, fig. 13): a dark-haired minx brazenly flaunting the severed head of Holofernes, or possibly that of John the Baptist as *Salomé* (AW 193). In the *Beethoven Frieze*, the "Hostile Forces" are represented by a cluster of witchy nudes (in contrast to the fully clothed angels who her-

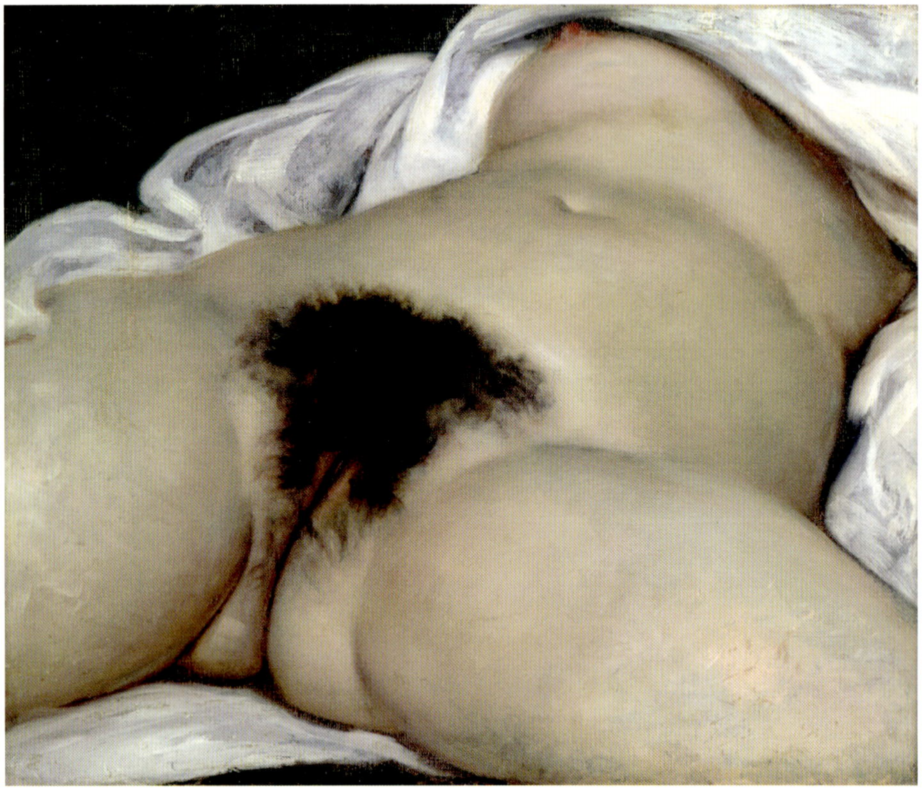

Fig. 3
GUSTAVE COURBET
The Origin of the World, 1866
Musée d'Orsay, Paris

ald man's redemption at the end). A massive gorilla, nestled amidst the nudes, alludes to contemporary notions of effeminate devolution (fig. 2).

Klimt's embrace of Darwinian theory melded proto-feminism with misogyny.[5] Like Gustav Courbet in his scandalous 1866 canvas *The Origin of the World* (fig. 3), created seven years after the publication of *On the Origin of Species*, Klimt saw the vagina and womb as central to the mystery of human existence.[6] The theory of evolution had transformed sexual intercourse from a sin into a neutral biological fact. Nature, not God, was the source of life, and woman was the ultimate force of nature. However, this was a double-edged sword. By representing nudes as amphibious creatures in such works as *Waterserpents* (p. 40, fig. 13), *Goldfish* (cat. 114), *Moving Water* (cat. 112), and *Fishblood* (cat. 111), Klimt tacitly affirmed the common stereotype of woman as primitive and irrational. Klimt trod a fine line between the acceptable and the unacceptable, the "pornographic" and the "artistic." Explaining the difference between pornography and art, Kenneth Clark wrote that "art exists in the realm of contemplation, and is bound by some sort of imaginative transposition. The moment art becomes an incentive to action, it loses its true character."[7] Put more bluntly, pornographic images are designed to elicit male arousal and accompany masturbation. However, the boundary separating pornography from art can be difficult to locate, and it shifts according to contemporary mores.

In *fin-de-siècle* Austria, "pornography" was often defined more by context than by content. Works selected for exhibition at the Vienna Secession qualified as art simply because they had been so chosen. An attempt to prosecute the Secession's journal, *Ver Sacrum,* for publishing a Klimt nude study was dismissed because *Ver Sacrum* was deemed a "specialist periodical" aimed at a limited audience of connoisseurs.[8] Postcards depicting nudes could be sold in museum shops, but not displayed in gallery windows. Provocative works that might be considered acceptable within an exhibition setting could not be reproduced on promotional posters.[9] In all instances, the authorities were most concerned with policing the public domain. Although scandal became an integral part of avant-garde mythology, outright censorship was relatively rare.[10]

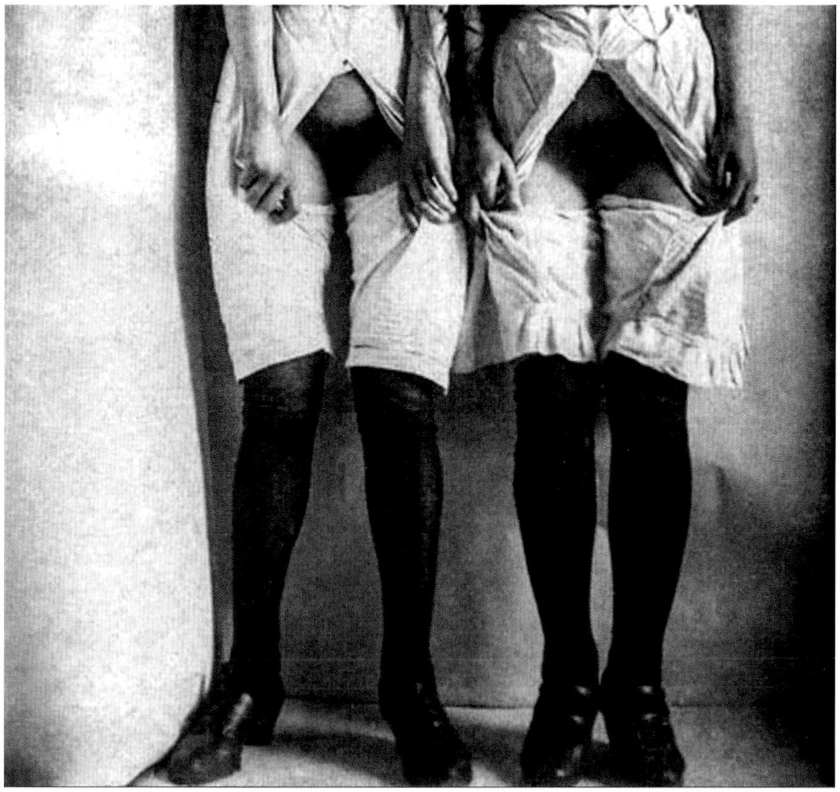

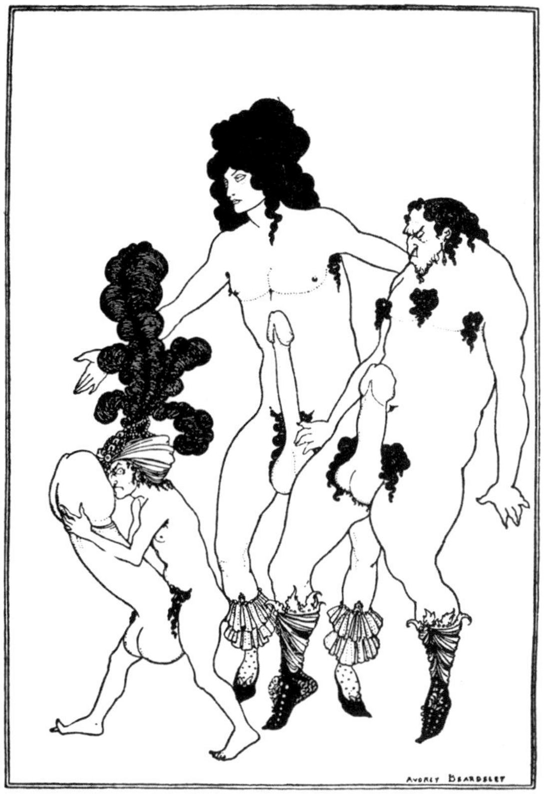

Fig. 4
OTTO SCHMIDT KUNSTVERLAG
Two Viennese Girls in Whites, c. 1900
Private collection

Fig. 5
AUBREY BEARDSLEY
The Lacedaemonian Ambassadors, illustration for *Lysistrata* by Aristophanes, 1896
Private collection

Behind closed doors, pornography flourished. The Biedermeier court painter Peter Fendi is believed to have produced erotic watercolors on the side.[11] The academically trained artist Franz von Bayros specialized in portfolios of lewd drawings (p. 37, fig. 9) bearing such titles as *Fleurettens Purpurschnecke* (Fleurette's Purple Snail), *Die Bonbonniere* (The Candy Dish), *Bilder aus dem Boudoir der Madame C. C.* (Pictures from the Boudoir of Madam C. C.), and *Der Gerupfte Amor* (Amor Unveiled). The work of the British erotic illustrator Aubrey Beardsley (fig. 5) was avidly collected by Fritz Waerndorfer, co-founder of the Wiener Werkstätte, and by the young Schiele aficionado Erich Lederer. Both pornographic "use" photographs and "artistic" photographs of nudes, ostensibly produced to save artists the expense of live models, were popular, [12] as were Japanese erotic woodcuts (Shunga) (see p. 34, fig. 6).

This vast pre-existing repertoire of erotic imagery informed the nudes created by Klimt and Schiele. Recognizing that a partially clad woman is often more enticing than a full nude, each artist relished details like upturned skirts, peak-a-boo bloomers, stockings and high-heeled shoes, accessories also favored by pornographic photographers (fig. 4). The taboo subject of masturbation had established precedents in pornography. The giant penis in Schiele's *Red Host* (cat. 97) was anticipated by Beardsley (fig. 5) and Japanese Shunga. But whereas earlier pornographic illustrators like Fendi, Bayros, and Beardsley constructed fanciful settings for their sexual escapades, Klimt and Schiele dispensed with such extraneous detail. Probably influenced by the more straightforward compositions found in nude photography, they focused exclusively on the woman.[13] Thus the emphasis in their work shifted from pornographic fantasy to reality.

Both Klimt and Schiele addressed female sexuality most directly in their drawings, which in the early twentieth-century still constituted a quasi-private realm. [14] Particularly in the last ten years of his life, Klimt drew a great many nudes. Though some of these studies are tangentially related to his allegories *The Virgin* (fig. 6) and *The Bride* (AW 252), all of them function as independent explorations of sexuality.[15] Klimt's late nudes are for the most part quite different from the femmes fatales who populate his earlier paintings. Seldom do they try to seduce or engage the viewer directly. Nor do they seem all that dangerous. The four emotional "types" depicted in *The Virgin*—lustful, mysterious, joyful and dreamy—recede into secure, autonomous worlds. The nudes in Klimt's contemporaneous drawings are even more remote. Eyes closed, these women often seem lost in an orgasmic trance (cat. 2, 6, 7, 8).

But, of course, Klimt's models knew he was watching them, even when they appear to be masturbating or climaxing. The scenarios were staged for the artist's benefit and at his direction.[16] Conventional framing devices neutralize the power of female lust, and the women's passivity is reinforced by their supine poses and near catatonic obliviousness. Nothing in these nudes upsets the primacy of the male gaze. Female sexuality has been transformed from a threat into an enticing mystery. The subject is male, not female, sexual response.

Schiele also used the nude to explore his own sexual responses. But he was far younger than Klimt, and his responses were tentative, unformed, and more openly fearful. Schiele's artistic and emotional development in 1910, when he turned twenty, was extremely rapid. At the beginning of the year, he was most comfortable using his sister Gerti as a model (cat. 134). Then he turned his attention to the male nude.[17] Finally, toward the end of the year, he developed a relationship with two young women, the so-called "black-haired girls" (cat. 56, 123).[18]

Whereas the gynecological nudes done in the spring of 1910 are relatively impersonal (cat. 54), the black-haired girls are Schiele's first regular female models (excluding family members), identifiable by face if not by name. It is probable that they were prostitutes, and evident that the artist had sex with at least one of them.[19] Like all models, they performed for the artist, but unlike classical nudes, the black-haired girls are not passive. Often they return the artist's gaze. They strike various attitudes: sullen, coy, brazen, and so on. It is impossible, however, to know if they are acting or sincere; impossible to know whether these images depict their reactions to Schiele, or his reactions to them. It is not clear who is subject and who is object.

The divide between subject and object is further obscured by Schiele's compositional strategy. He habitually asked the model to lie on a mattress placed on the floor, while he perched above her on a stool or ladder. The mattress, which along with any supporting paraphernalia would be omitted from the finished drawing, became analogous to the blank sheet of paper. Pictorial unity was achieved by consciously manipulating the figure within the surrounding negative space. A legacy of *Jugendstil* poster design, Schiele's approach created a tension between the figure and the edge of the picture plane that called into question the ability of the latter to contain the former. Far from receding into the distance, his nudes seem to jump out at the viewer. Most disturbing of all is the artist's habit of signing drawings of recumbent models as verticals (cat. 4). Although this was an organic outgrowth of his elevated perspective, the nude's verticality transforms her from a neutral object of contemplation into a sexual aggressor.

Herein lies the key to the transgressive nature of Schiele's erotic drawings. By tipping the reclining nude upright, by allowing her to return his gaze, by violating the boundaries between subject and object, he ratified the independent power of female sexuality. Erratic cropping, broken contours and contorted poses further undermined any illusion of harmony. The naked female came into her own, and with her twisted limbs and impenetrable stare, she was far more frightening than any of Klimt's femmes fatales. There was no longer a controlling male narrative holding the woman in check.

As Schiele grew up, he became acclimated to the privileges of patriarchy. He was less terrified, more dominant in his sexual relationships, first with his lover, Wally, and then with his wife, Edith. Though Wally had been both companion and model (cat. 127), Edith proved reluctant to pose naked (cat. 130). Egon's depictions of his wife masturbating, her face concealed or disguised, are almost painful to behold (cat. 129). It might be said that he had reverted to the bourgeois double standard. Edith ruled the domestic sphere, as wife and, in 1918, mother-to-be. Egon's models and lovers occupied a separate realm.

While Schiele's formal portraits of women became more insightful after his marriage, his late nudes are more in keeping with conventional examples of the genre. Both his drawing and painting styles had grown increasingly realistic. Greater verisimilitude reduced the erotic volatility of the nudes by giving them a self-contained three-dimensional presence that dis-

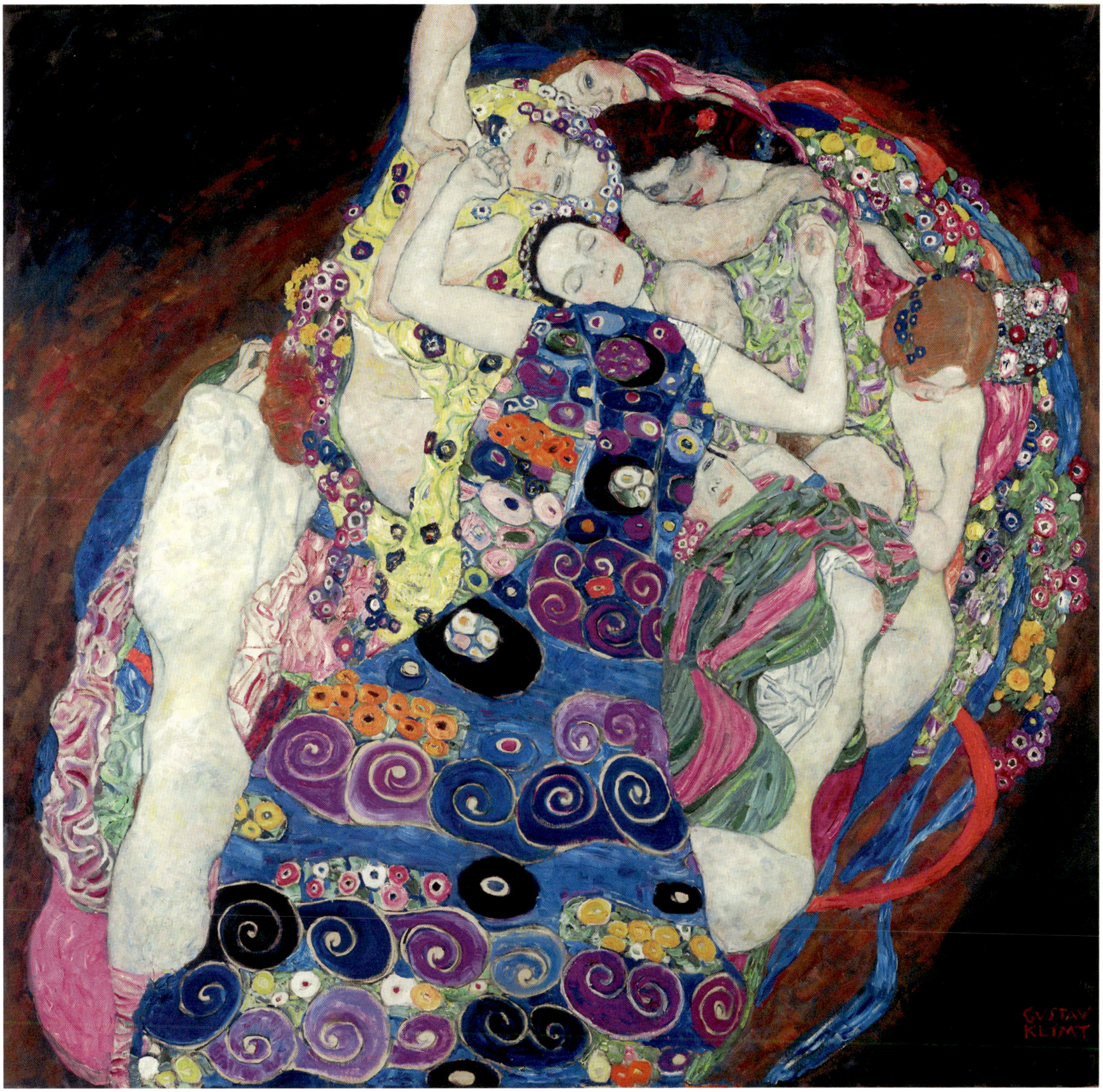

Fig. 6
GUSTAV KLIMT
The Virgin, 1913
Národni Galerie, Prague

tances them from the viewer's space (cat. 131). Though jarring elements such as truncated limbs and odd compositional angles remain, these are softened by the voluptuous contours of the subjects' bodies. Schiele's nudes are now less confrontational, more serenely objectified.

In other respects, however, Schiele strayed from the traditional paradigms. His late nudes are neither frightening nor passive. Often the models stare shamelessly at the viewer. They take pride in their seductive bodies and are empowered by their allure (cat. 10, 128, 132). In a sense they are the forerunners of every sexy female who would be used to sell products in late-twentieth-century advertising. And like all modern women, they are caught in a double bind, exploiting and being exploited for their sexuality.

For *fin-de-siècle* man, engagement with the opposite sex entailed a precarious balancing of fear and attraction that could only be achieved through an assertion of dominance. At least until the 1920s, this balance eluded Kokoschka.[20] Lilith Lang rejected him outright, and Alma Mahler was eventually repulsed by his attempts to control her. Although Kokoschka had an unpleasant tendency to denounce any artist he considered a professional competitor, starting with Max Oppenheimer and ending with Picasso, his jealousy of Schiele may also have had a sexual component. As late as 1962, Kokoschka remained bitter. "Schiele always had swarms of girls about him," he recalled. "Women, hangers-on, it began even when he was at the Academy. They were his undoing."[21]

For a number of reasons, the nude has a less significant place in Kokoschka's work than in the art of Klimt and Schiele. It was not so much that Kokoschka was less attractive to women than Schiele (though this may have been the case), but that for Schiele, as for Klimt, the roles of model and lover were interchangeable. Both had repeated sexual experiences with lower-class women, whereas Kokoschka's early love interests, Lilith and Alma, were above him in social station. Furthermore, both Klimt and Schiele had been trained in the classical manner, and life drawing was central to their studio practice. Kokoschka's education at the Kunstgewerbeschule was more progressive. He did book illustrations, poster designs, and decorative assignments for the Wiener Werkstätte. Life drawing was also part of the curriculum, but Kokoschka often managed to avoid these classes.[22] In the autumn of 1909, when he embarked on his career as a portrait painter, his production of drawings declined precipitously.[23] During this period the two branches of his oeuvre were not very closely connected.

Rejecting "boring academic instruction," Kokoschka preferred to make quick studies from moving models.[24] Though he took credit for "inventing" this method, it had in fact been introduced to the Kunstgewerbeschule by Alfred Roller in 1901.[25] Spontaneity and speed of execution were qualities prized by many of the era's foremost draughtsmen, including Auguste Rodin, Klimt and Schiele.[26] In keeping with the requirements of *Jugendstil* design, Kokoschka's early motion studies are flat, angular contour drawings with little interior detail (cat. 69, 70, 72, 133). After he started painting in 1909–10, the artist applied more painterly techniques to his drawings, dabbing on color with his fingertips and scarifying the contours (cat. 136, 137).[27] His nudes became more fulsome, more adult. Kokoschka's production of nudes increased further in 1912–13, when he was teaching the evening life class at the Kunstgewerbeschule (cat. 126, 138, 139). The post gave him regular access to models, on whom he projected his feelings for Alma Mahler.[28]

From the time of Kokoschka's meeting with Mahler in the spring of 1912, she became "everywoman" to him, and every woman became Alma. Whether she, a *Dame*, actually posed naked is uncertain, but Oskar put her imprint on almost all the nudes he created during the period of their affair. One of his first Alma nudes is a painting called *The Visitation* (cat. 140). The New Testament story—in which the pregnant Virgin Mary visits Elisabeth to bless the latter's unborn son, John the Baptist—is a curious way to celebrate a nascent love affair. Already Oskar was dreaming of Alma as a virgin and a mother. What she clearly is not, is a sex object. Indeed, Kokoschka's nudes are strikingly unattractive, devoid of the erotic frisson that animates the work of Klimt and Schiele.

The curious coda to the Mahler affair came in 1918, after Kokoschka had settled in Dresden to recover from his emotional wounds and from injuries sustained in battle during World War I. Still pining for his lost love, he commissioned a life-sized, anatomically correct doll in Alma's likeness. To assist the doll maker, Hermine Moos, he painted a large nude from memory (cat. 143). "The private parts must be fully and voluptuously detailed, and covered with hair," he instructed, "otherwise it will not be a woman, but a monster. And I can only be inspired to create art by a woman."[29] Perhaps inevitably, he was disappointed with the results, although the Alma effigy does appear in numerous drawings and at least two paintings (WE 136, 158).[30] Finally, however, the artist grew tired of his inanimate lover, and beheaded "her" at a drunken party.

In 1921, Kokoschka began a relationship with Anna Kallin (cat. 45, 46), a Russian émigré studying music in Dresden. Ten years younger than the artist, Kallin initially seemed to fulfill his need for a woman "pure, above all doubt."[31] He wanted a "helpmate, friend and child,"[32] as well as a caretaker willing "to adopt an orphan who sighs for a Mama."[33] These fantasies were expressed in *The Slave Girl* (cat. 110), which depicts Anna, naked, in the title role, with a diminutive Oskar in the background. "In years to come," the artist predicted, "when I am well established, [...] I shall probably be some woman's very devoted and grateful lover, in proportion to how far she has surrendered to my wishes."[34] That honor would not go to Kallin, who ended up moving to England and working for the BBC.

In 1941, at the age of fifty-five, Kokoschka married Olda Palkovská, the twenty-six-year-old daughter of a Czech attorney.

1 Stefan Zweig, *The World of Yesterday*, New York 1943, p. 78.
2 Alexander Sixtus von Reden and Josef Schweikhardt, *Eros unterm Doppeladler: Eine Sittengeschichte Altösterreichs,* Vienna 1993, p. 23.
3 Kenneth Clark, *The Nude: A Study of Ideal Art*, London 1956.
4 Hermann Bahr, letter to Franz Blei, cited in Franz Blei (ed.), *Die Opale: Blätter für Kunst und Literatur*, Leipzig 1907, pp. 127–28 (translated by Jane Kallir).
5 See Emily Braun, "Ornament as Evolution: Gustav Klimt and Berta Zuckerkandl," in: Renée Price (ed.), *Gustav Klimt: The Ronald S. Lauder and Serge Sabarsky Collections* (exh. cat. Neue Galerie, New York), New York 2007, pp. 145–69.
6 Marian Bisanz-Prakken, *Gustav Klimt: The Magic of Line* (exh. cat. J. Paul Getty Museum, Los Angeles), Los Angeles 2012, p. 242.
7 Lord Longford, *Pornography: The Longford Report*, London 1972, pp. 99–100.
8 Tobias G. Natter, "On the Limits of the Exhibitable," in: Tobias G. Natter and Max Hollein (eds.), *The Naked Truth: Klimt, Schiele, Kokoschka, and Other Scandals (*exh. cat. Schirn Kunsthalle, Frankfurt; Leopold Museum, Vienna) Frankfurt/Vienna 2005, p. 29.
9 Ibid., pp. 28–29. One of the most notorious incidents of this kind involved the censorship of Klimt's poster for the Vienna Secession's first exhibition in 1898, which depicted Theseus slaying the Minotaur. Klimt was persuaded to cover Theseus's originally exposed genitals with decorative weeds.
10 In 1910, the police removed fourteen Schiele drawings from a Prague exhibition. On the other hand, no attempt was made to censor *Die Hetärengespräche des Lukian*, a portfolio reproducing erotic Klimt drawings that was published by the Wiener Werkstätte in 1905.
11 In 1910, a portfolio reproducing erotic watercolors attributed to Peter Fendi (1796–1842) was published in Leipzig. However, the accuracy of this attribution has been questioned.
12 Von Reden and Schweikhardt 1993 (see note 2), pp. 213–14.
13 For an in-depth discussion of the influence of photography on Gustav Klimt, see Marian Bisanz-Prakken, "Gustav Klimt: The Late Work, New Light on *The Virgin* and *The Bride*," in: Renée Price (ed.), *Gustav Klimt: The Ronald S. Lauder and Serge Sabarsky Collections* (exh. cat. Neue Galerie, New York) New York 2007, pp. 105–29.
14 The scandals surrounding Klimt escalated when he began exhibiting his drawings more prominently, first at the Galerie Miethke in 1910, and then at the *Internationale Schwarz-Weiss Ausstellung* in 1913.
15 Bisanz-Prakken 2007 (see note 13), p. 105.
16 Ibid., p. 119.
17 See Jane Kallir, *Egon Schiele's Women*, Munich/London/New York 2012, pp. 68–70. It is likely that these nudes were not, as has been frequently asserted, self-portraits, but depictions of Schiele's friends Max Oppenheimer (who was gay) and Erwin Osen (who was bisexual).
18 Ibid., pp. 104–12.
19 See Kd 961–71.
20 I am grateful to Mateusz Mayer for pointing out that Kokoschka's sexual inexperience may have influenced his depictions of women in the years before World War I.
21 Ludwig Goldscheider, *Kokoschka*, London 1963, p. 9.
22 Frank Whitford, *Oskar Kokoschka: A Life*, New York 1986, pp. 50–51; Alfred Weidinger and Alice Strobl, *Oskar Kokoschka: Die Zeichnungen und Aquarelle 1897–1916*, Salzburg 2008, p. 170.
23 Weidinger and Strobl 2008 (see note 22), p. 210.
24 Whitford 1986 (see note 22), p. 51.
25 Stephen Steinlein, "Ludwig Heinrich Jungnickel, München," in: *Deutsche Kunst und Dekoration*, vol. XVII, November 1905, p. 118.
26 Contemporaries noted that both Klimt and Schiele worked from moving models, who wandered freely in their studios (see Franz Servaes, "Gustav Klimt," in: *Velhagen und Klasings Monatsheften*, vol. 1918/19, pp. 23–24. – Albert Paris von Gütersloh, "Über Egon Schiele," in: *Gustav Klimt—Egon Schiele: Zum Gedächtnis ihres Todes vor 50 Jahren* [exh. cat. Albertina, Vienna], Vienna 1968, p. 74).
27 Weidinger and Strobl 2008 (see note 22), p. 210.
28 Alfred Weidinger, *Kokoschka and Alma Mahler*, New York/Munich 1996, pp. 22–24.
29 Oskar Kokoschka, letter to Hermine Moos, January 23, 1919, cited in Olda Kokoschka and Heinz Spielmann (eds.), *Oskar Kokoschka Briefe I, 1905–1919*, Düsseldorf 1984, p. 306.
30 Smaller dolls appear in WE 157, 159, 160.
31 Oskar Kokoschka, letter to Anna Kallin, September 1921, cited in Olda Kokoschka and Heinz Spielmann (eds.), *Oskar Kokoschka Briefe II, 1919–1934*, Düsseldorf 1985, p. 25 (translated by Mary Whitall).
32 Oskar Kokoschka, letter to Anna Kallin, March 1923, cited in Kokoschka and Spielmann, 1985 (see note 31).
33 Oskar Kokoschka, letter to Alice Lahmann, May 1922, cited in Kokoschka and Spielmann, 1985 (see note 31), p. 43.
34 Oskar Kokoschka, letter to Anna Kallin, September 1921, cited in Kokoschka and Spielmann, 1985 (see note 31), p. 33.

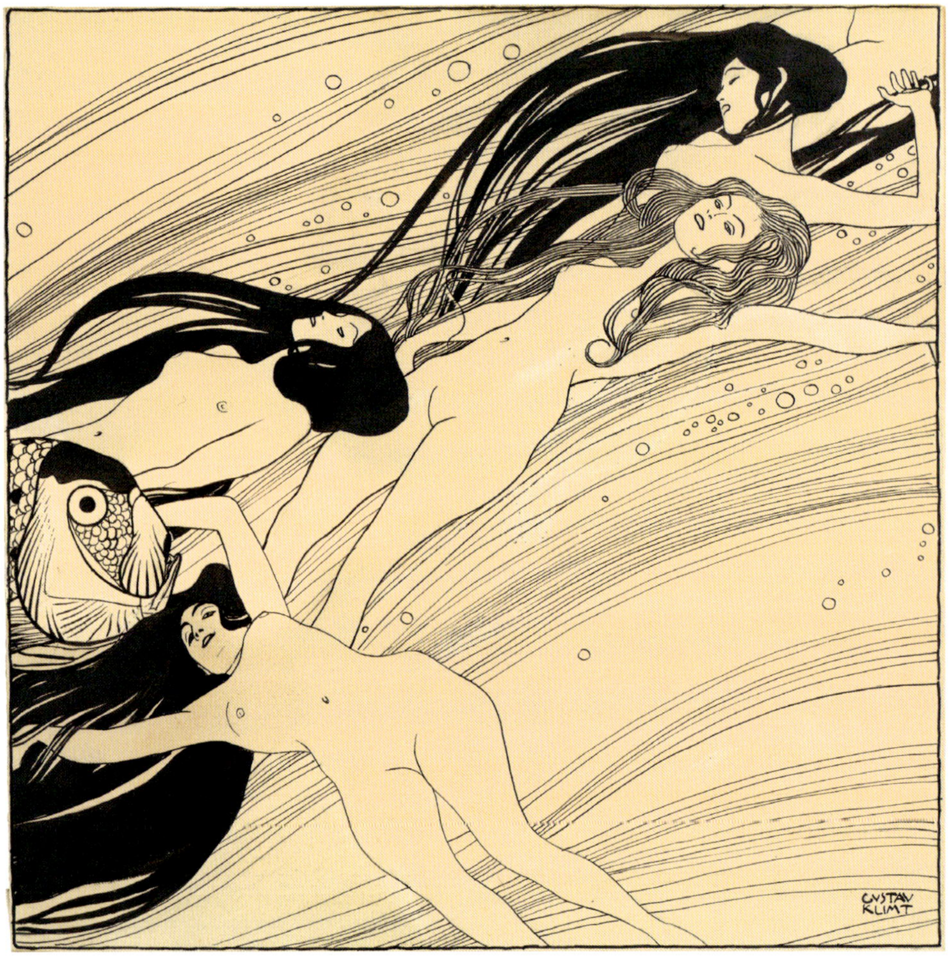

Cat. 111
GUSTAV KLIMT
Fishblood, 1898
Pencil and ink on paper, 40 x 40.3 cm
David Lachenmann Collection

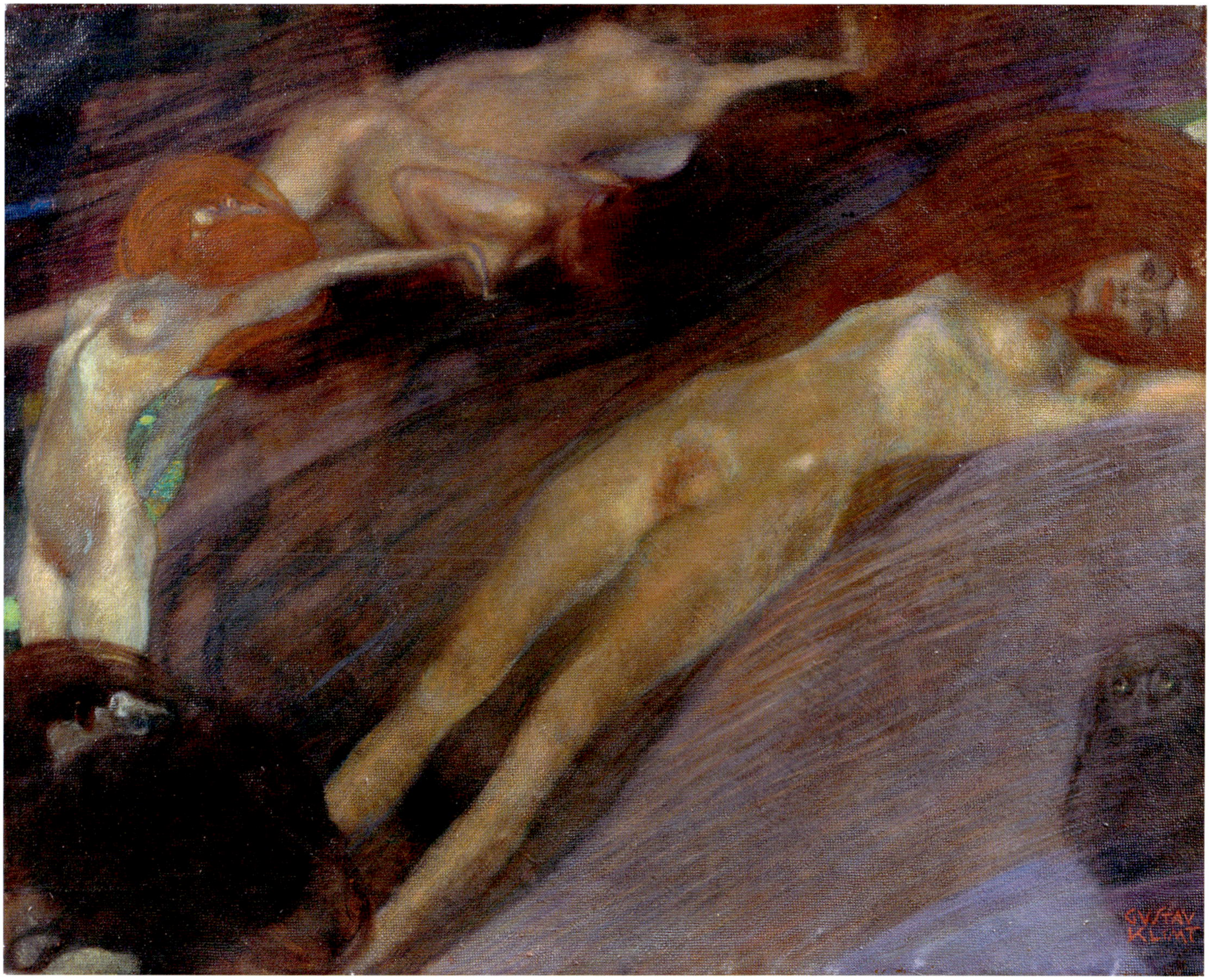

Cat. 112
GUSTAV KLIMT
Moving Water, 1898
Oil on canvas, 52 x 65 cm
Private collection, courtesy of Galerie St. Etienne, New York

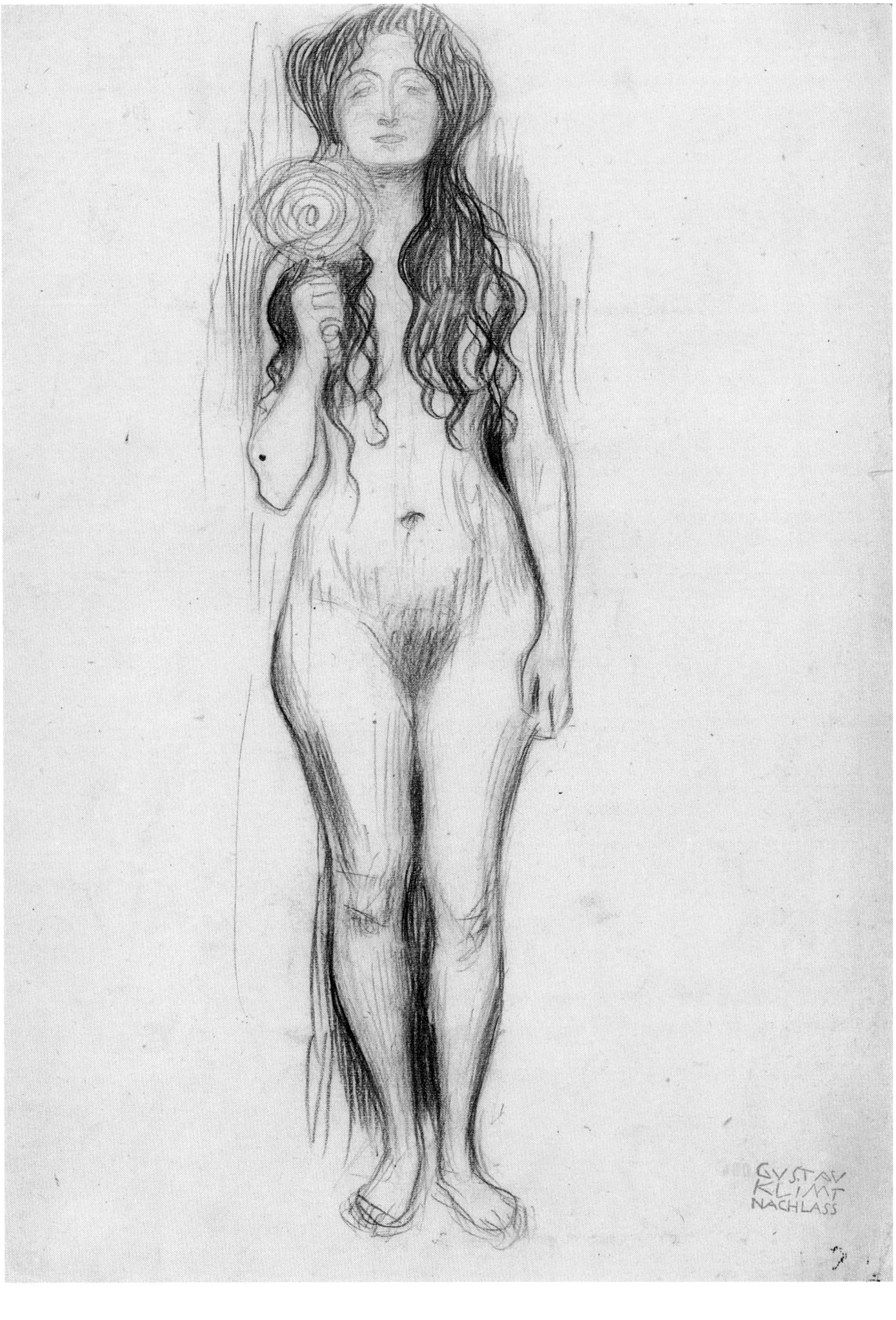

Cat. 113
GUSTAV KLIMT
Female Nude With Mirror in Right Hand, 1898
Charcoal on paper, 45 x 33 cm
Private collection, courtesy of Neue Galerie New York

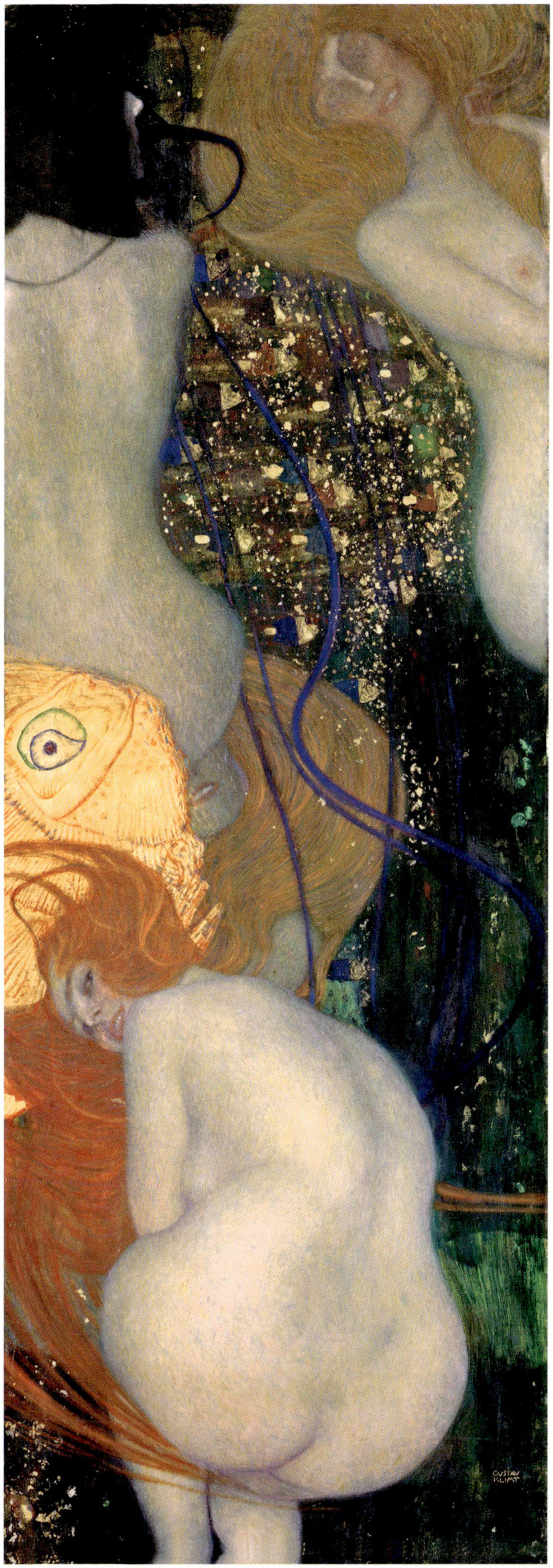

Cat. 114
GUSTAV KLIMT
Goldfish, 1901–02
Oil on canvas, 181 x 67 cm
Kunstmuseum Solothurn, Dübi-Müller-Stiftung, 1980

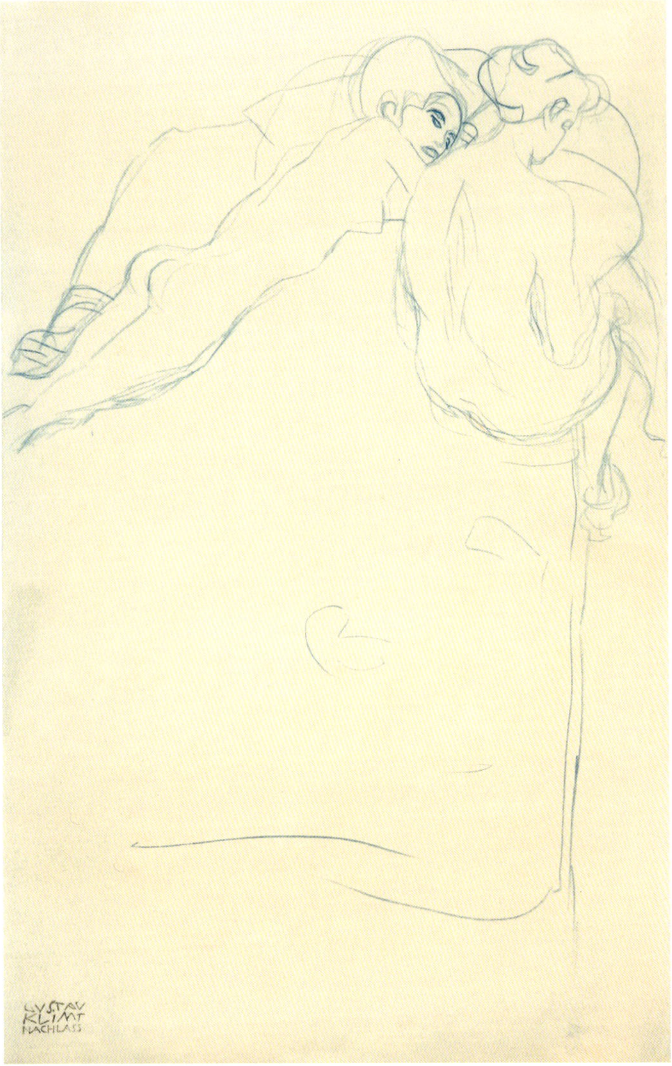

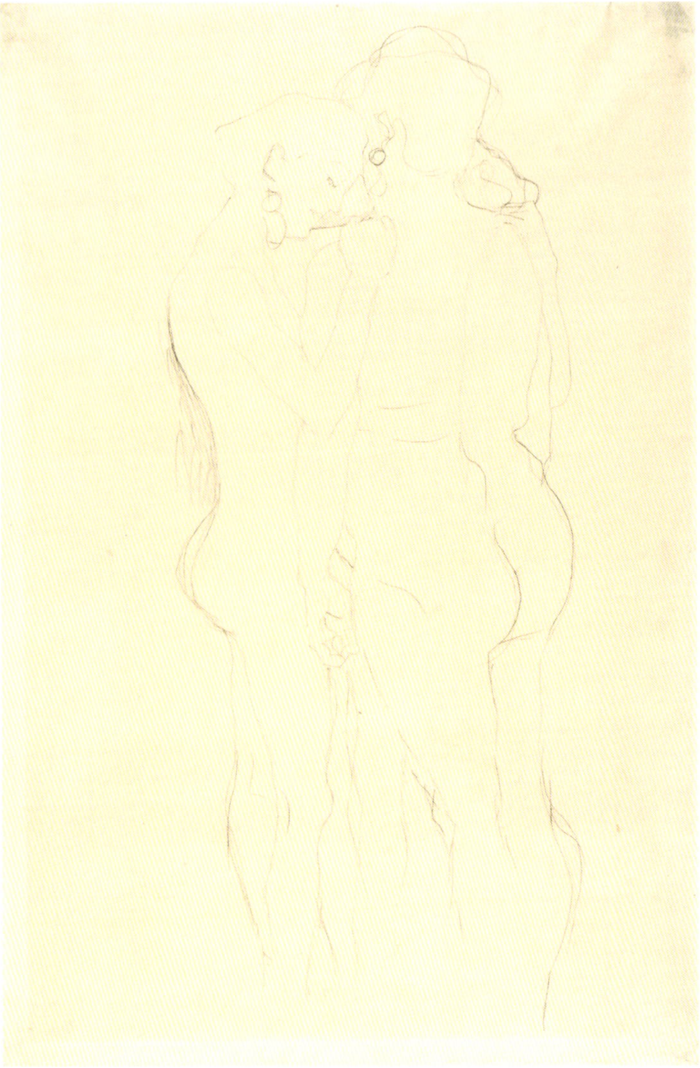

Cat. 115
GUSTAV KLIMT
Two Girlfriends, 1907
Blue pencil on paper, 55 x 35 cm
Wienerroither & Kohlbacher, Vienna

Cat. 116
GUSTAV KLIMT
Three Female Nudes, c. 1908
Pencil on paper, 56.5 x 37.2 cm
Private collection

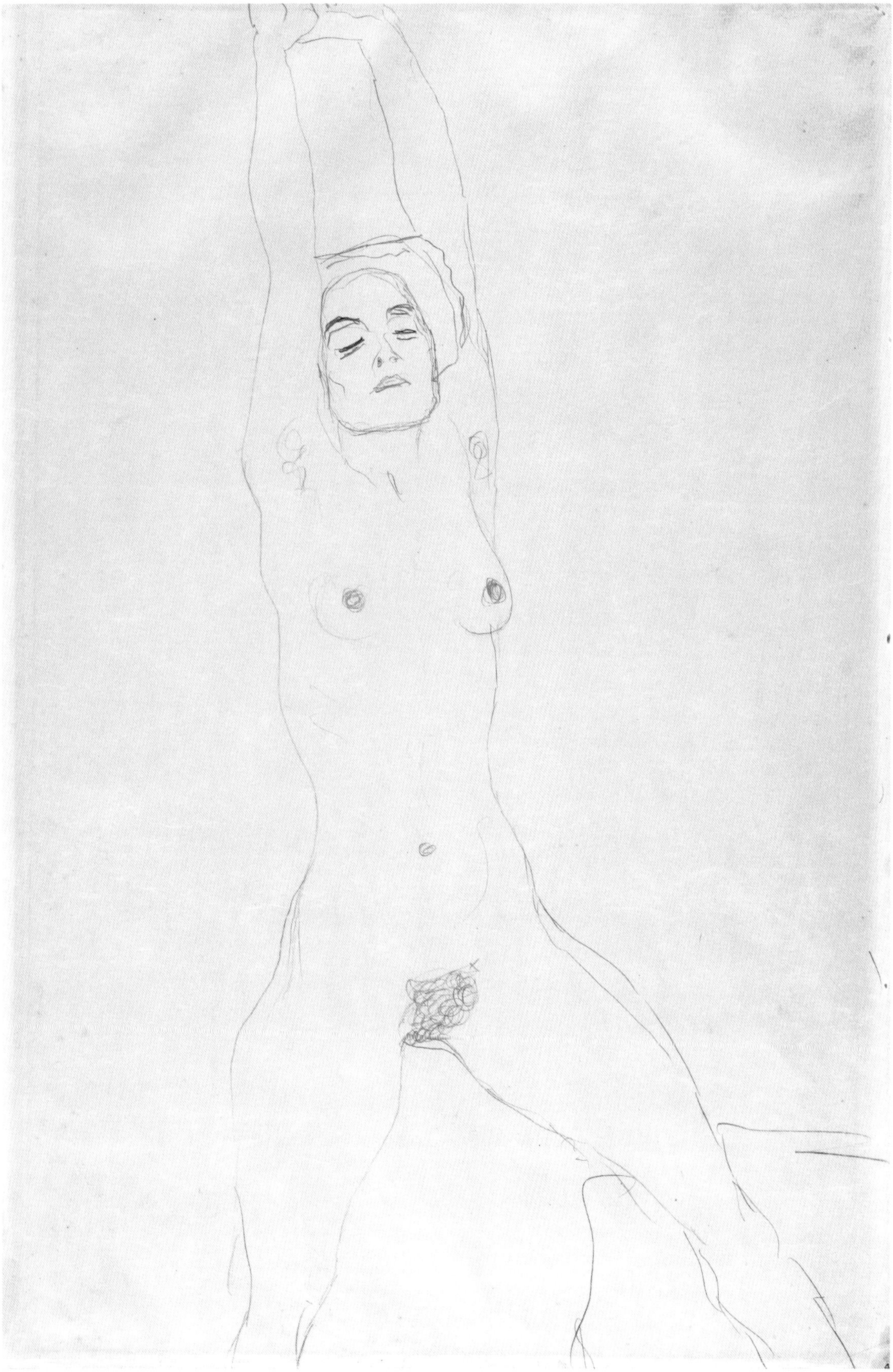

Cat. 117
GUSTAV KLIMT
Nude with Raised Arms,
1917–18
Pencil on paper, 55.6 x 36.8 cm
Private collection, courtesy of
Galerie St. Etienne, New York

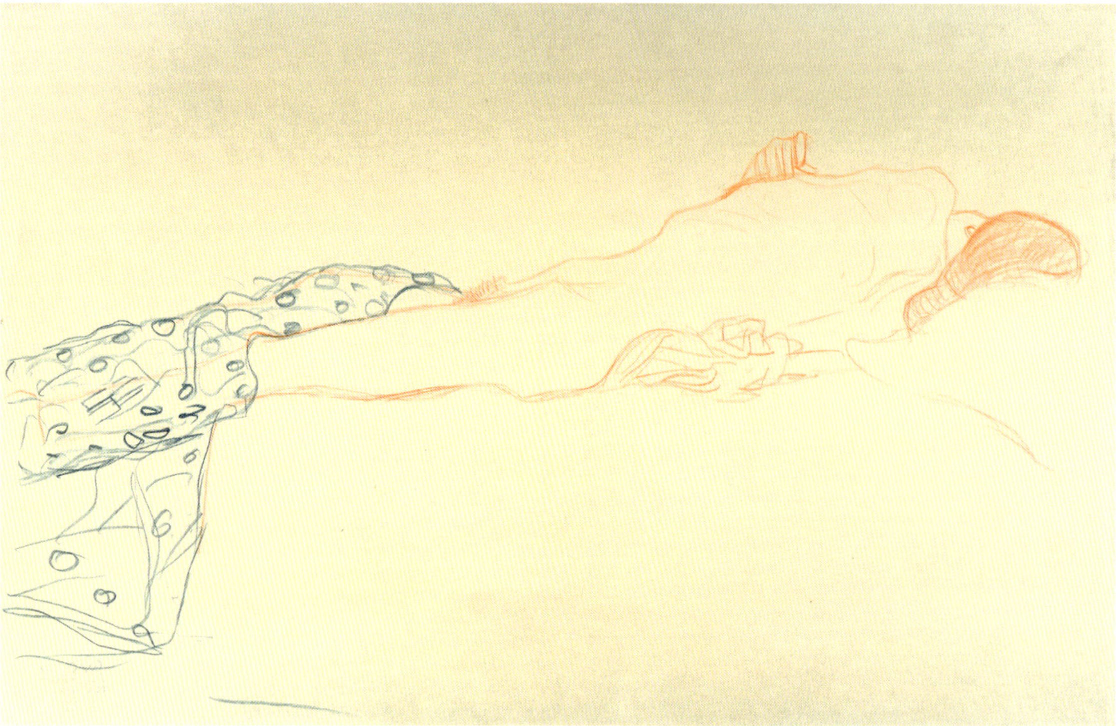

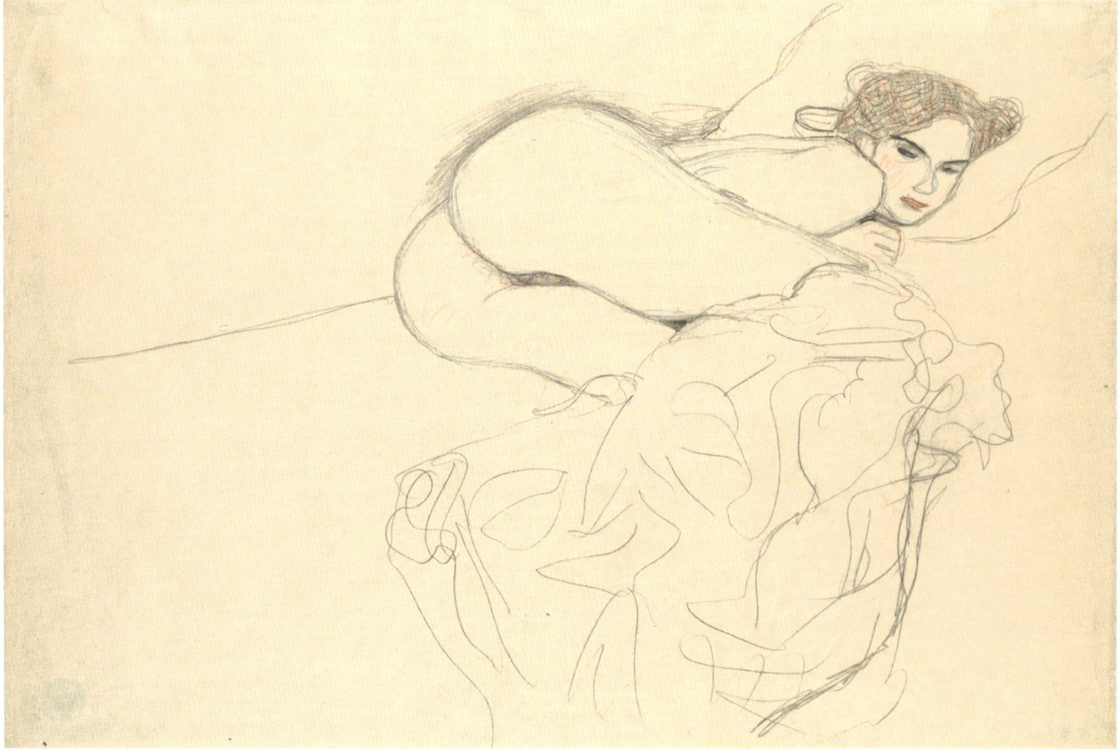

Cat. 118
GUSTAV KLIMT
Reclining Nude Facing Right, 1905–06
Red and blue pencil on paper, 35 x 55.3 cm
Coninx-Stiftung, Zurich

Cat. 119
GUSTAV KLIMT
Reclining Nude in a Crouched Position, 1912–13
Pencil, red and blue pencil on paper, 37 x 55.8 cm
Wien Museum, Vienna

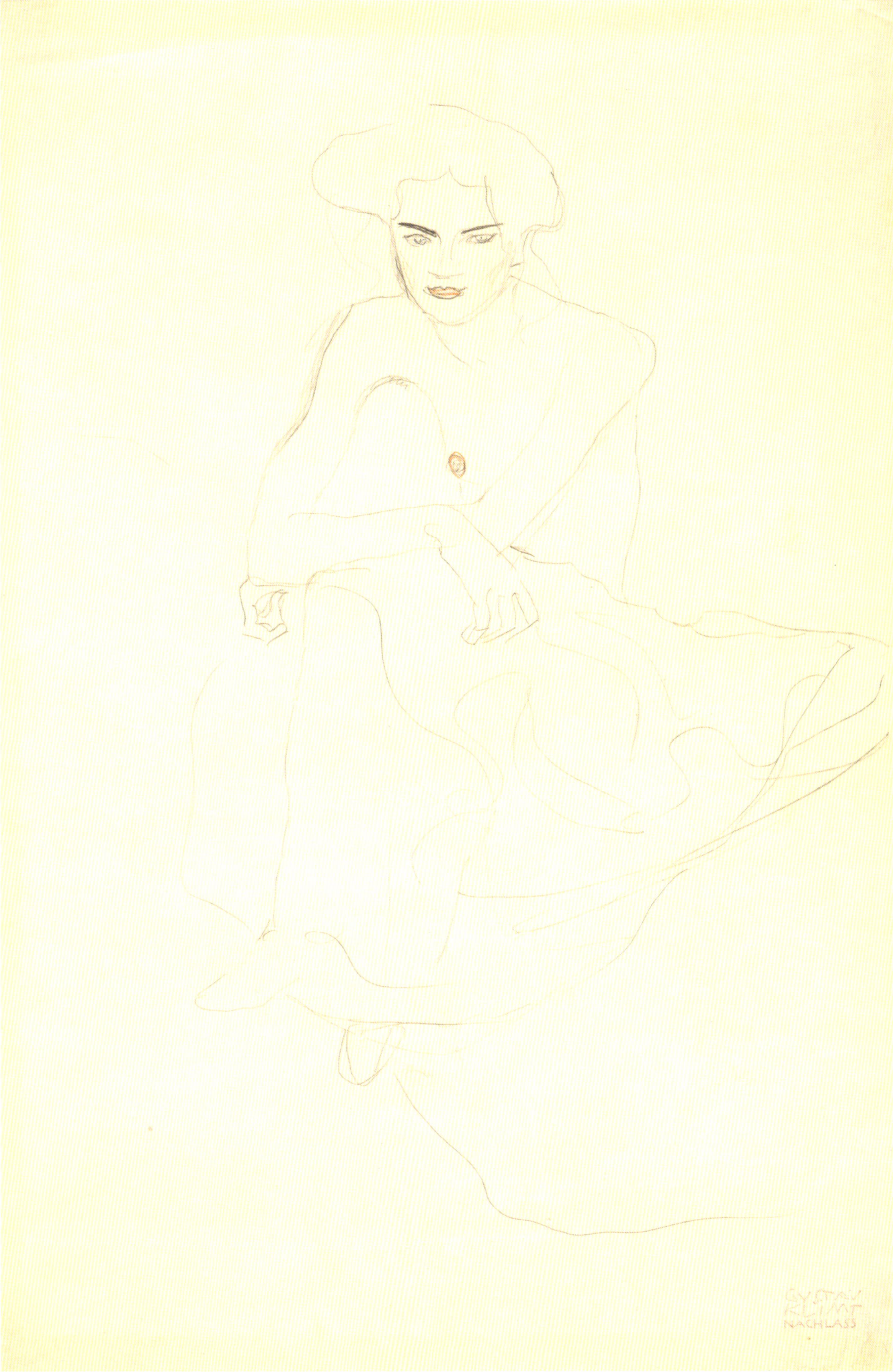

Cat. 120
GUSTAV KLIMT
Seated Female Nude, Facing Front, c. 1907
Pencil, red and blue pencil on paper, 55.9 x 37.1 cm
Private collection, London

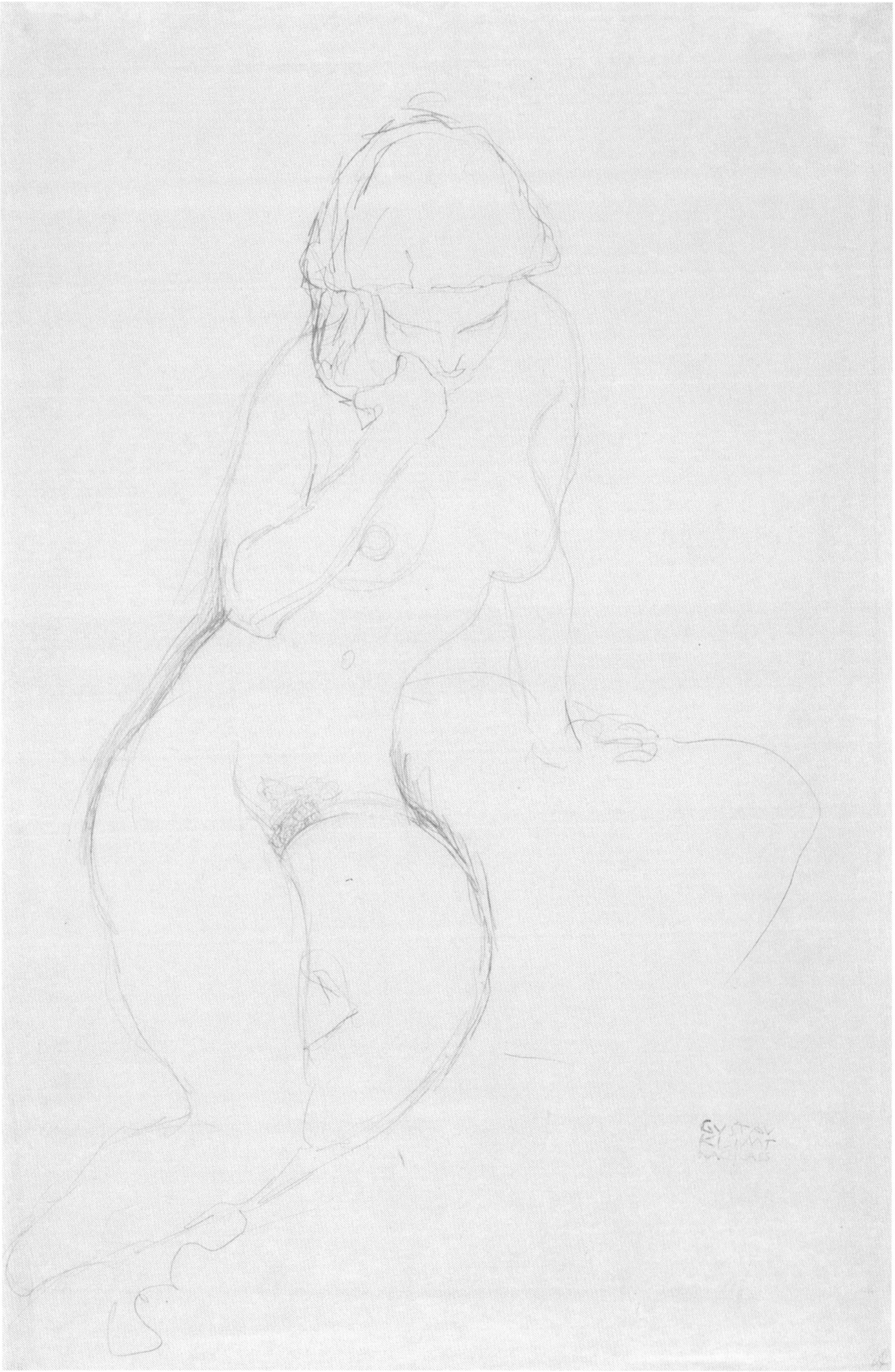

Cat. 121
GUSTAV KLIMT
Seated Nude with Hand to Chin,
1913
Pencil on paper, 57.2 x 37.5 cm
Private collection

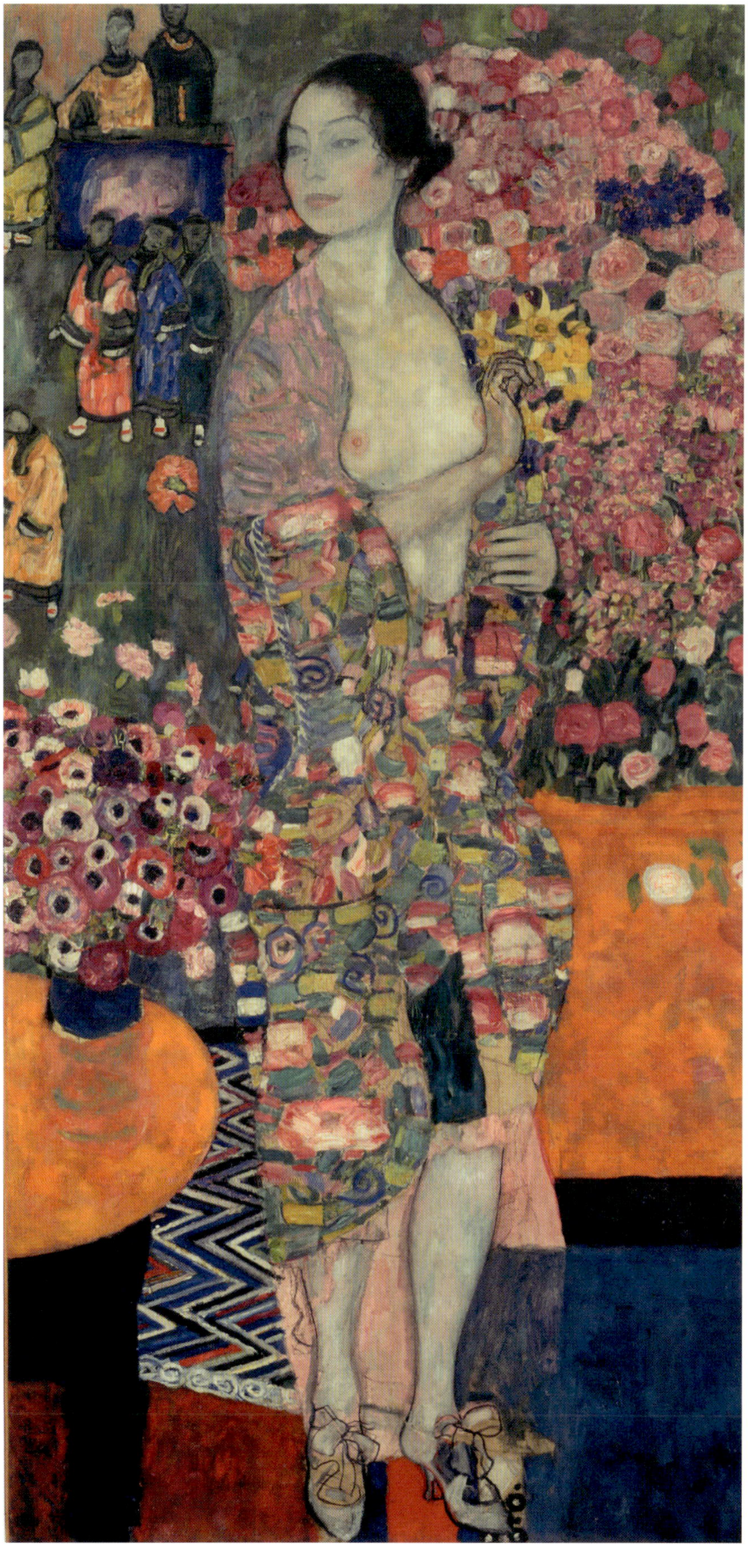

Cat. 122
GUSTAV KLIMT
The Dancer, 1916–17
Oil on canvas, 180 x 90 cm
Private collection, courtesy of Neue Galerie, New York

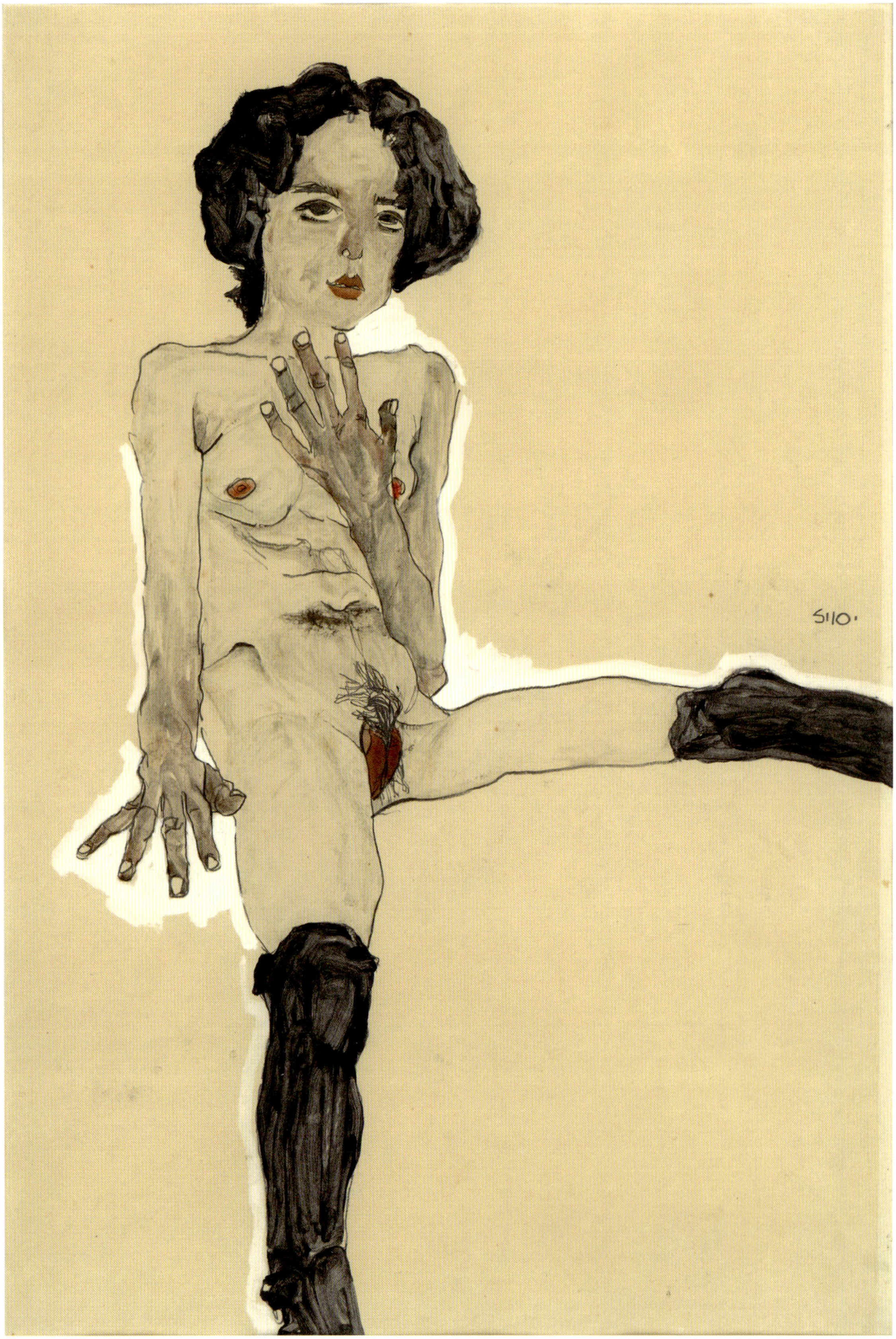

Cat. 123
EGON SCHIELE
Seated Female Nude with Black Stockings, 1910
Gouache, watercolor, and pencil with white heightening, on paper, 54 x 36.5 cm
Neue Galerie New York, donated by Ronald S. Lauder

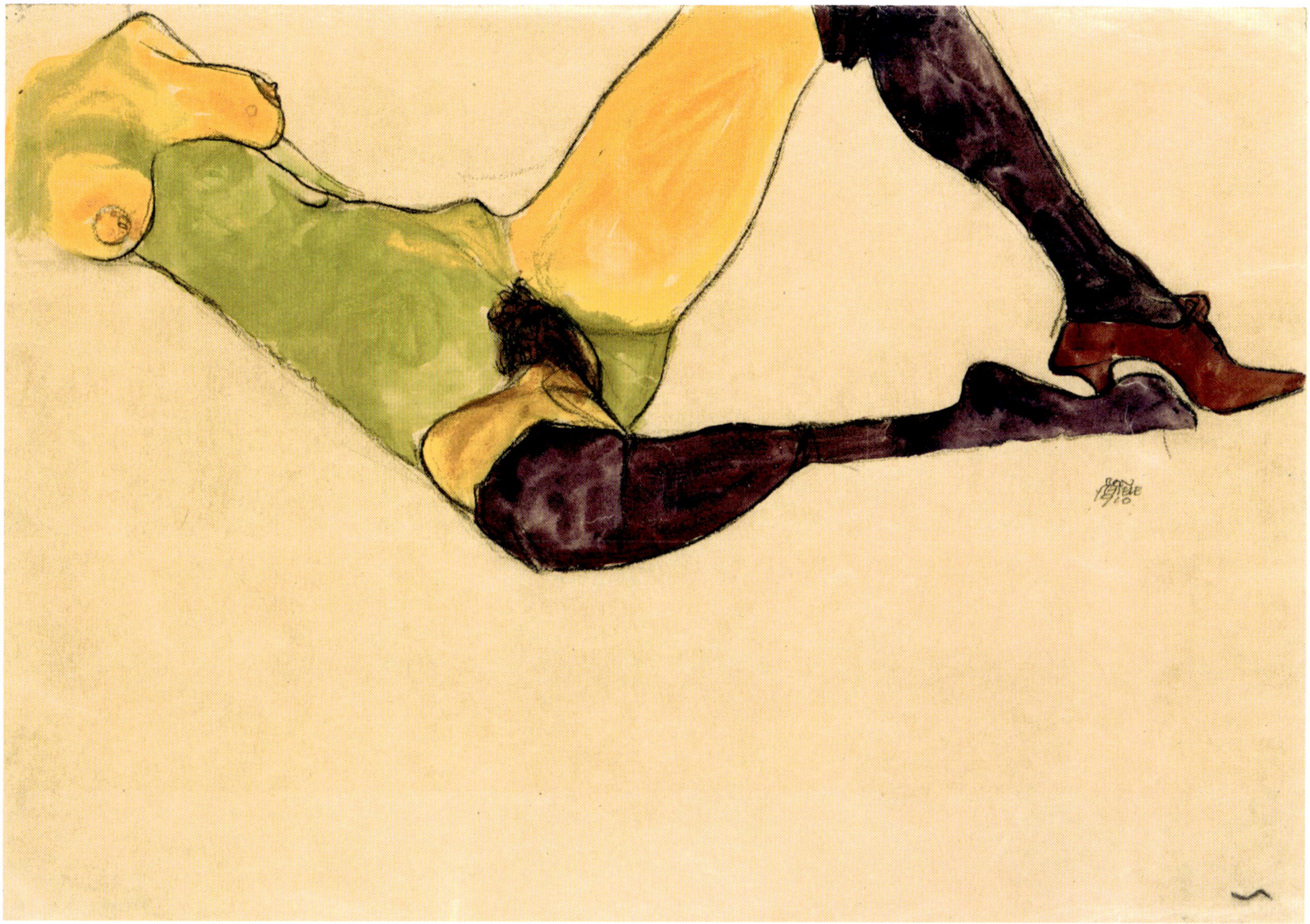

Cat. 124
EGON SCHIELE
Reclining Female Torso, Nude, 1910
Gouache, watercolor, and black crayon on paper, 31.6 x 44.9 cm
Private collection, courtesy of Richard Nagy Ltd., London

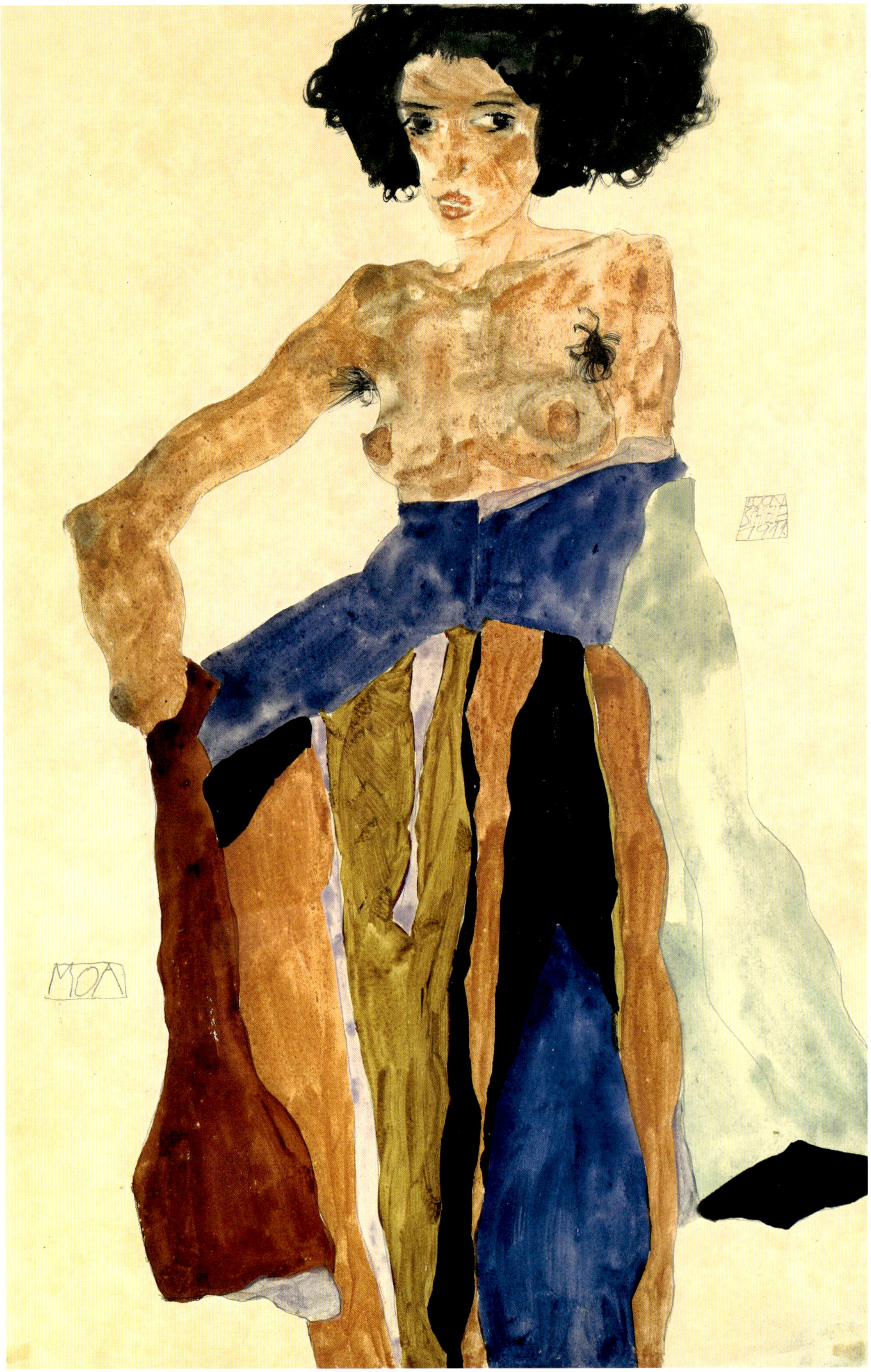

Cat. 125
EGON SCHIELE
Moa, 1911
Gouache, watercolor, and pencil on paper, 48 x 31 cm
Private collection, London

Cat. 126
OSKAR KOKOSCHKA
Seated Female Nude with Hands on Her Head 1912
Ink, watercolor, and pencil on brown paper, 45 x 30.8 cm
Sammlung Deutsche Bank, Frankfurt a. M.

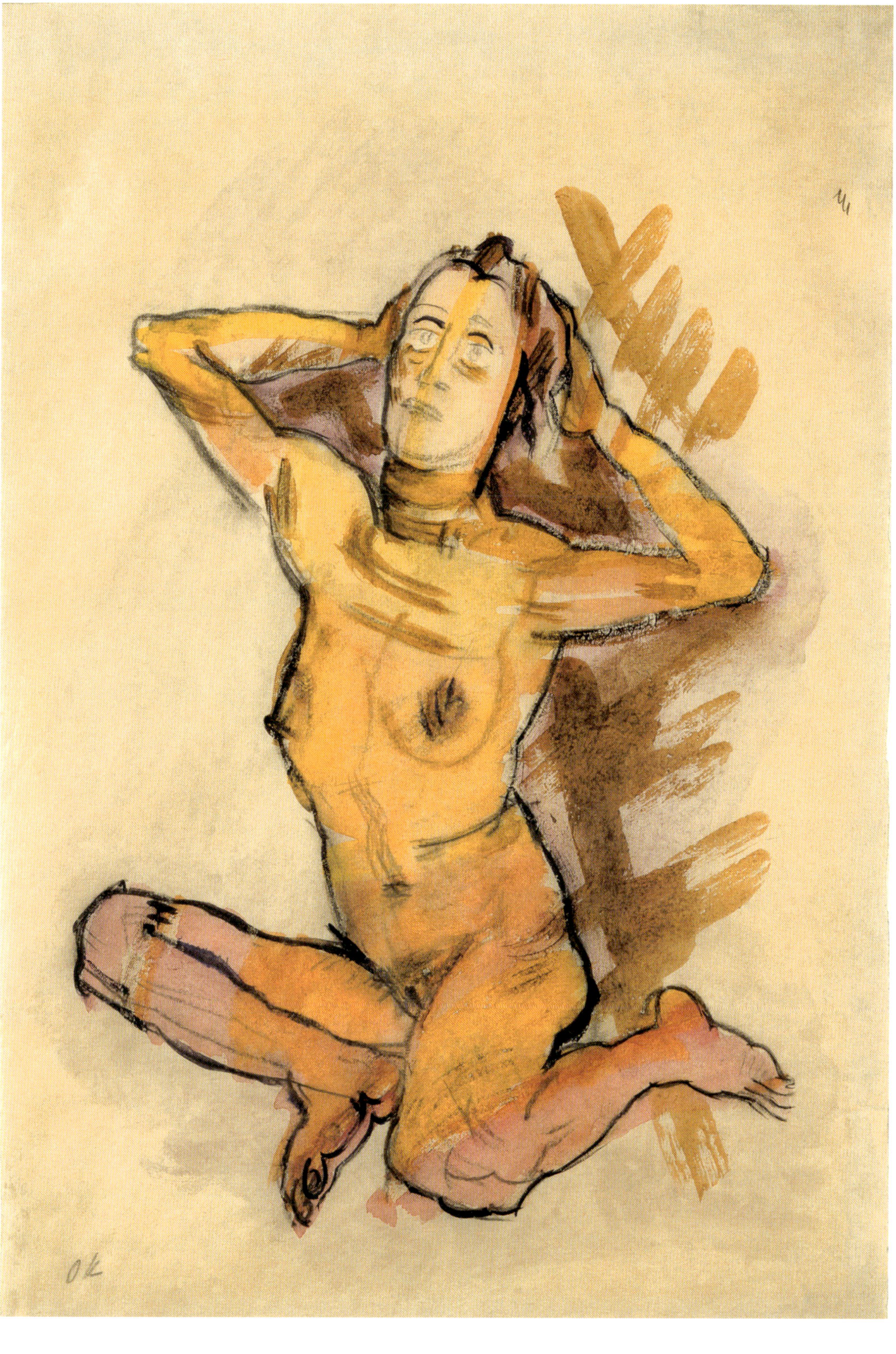

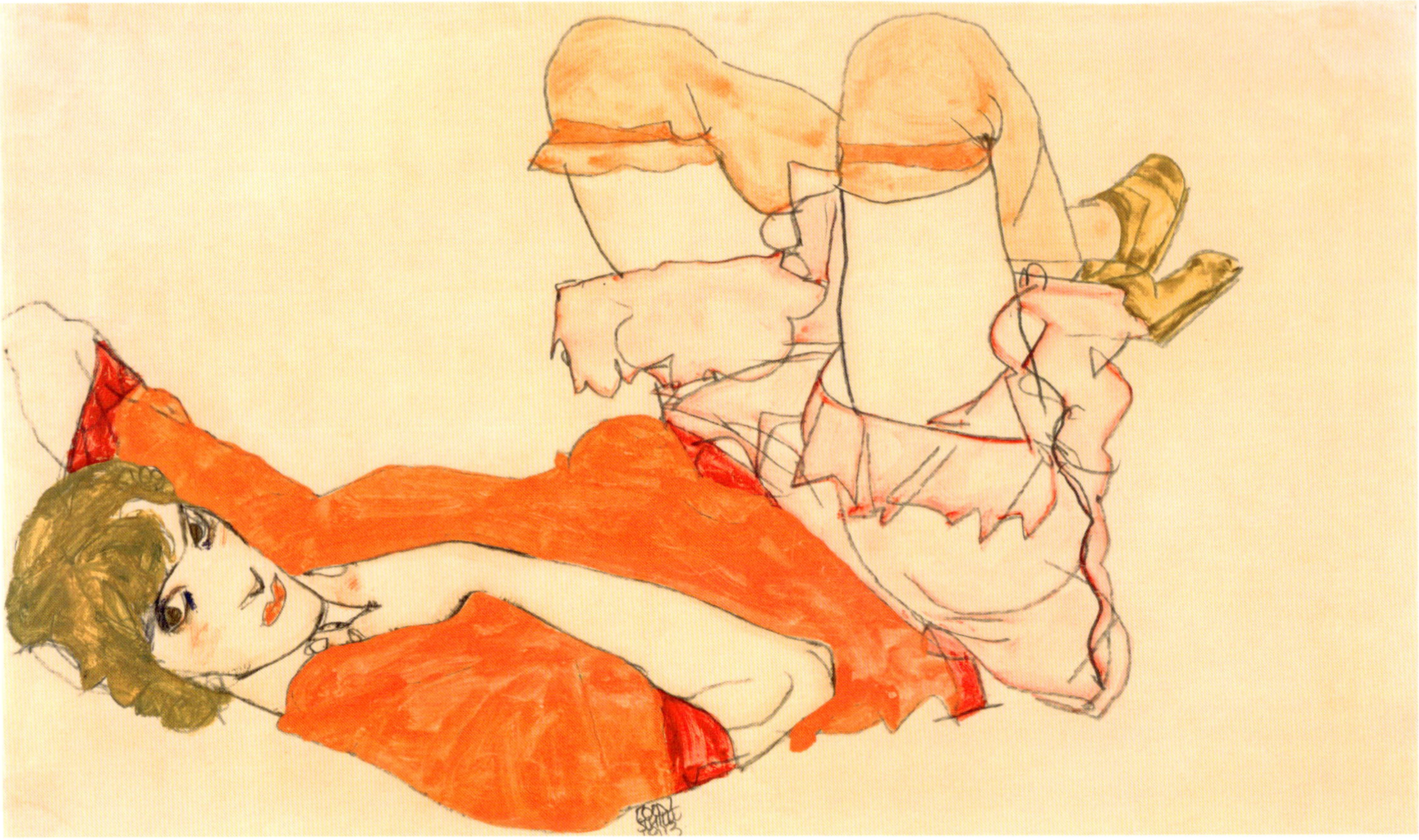

Cat. 127
EGON SCHIELE
Wally in Red Blouse with Raised Knees, 1913
Gouache, watercolor, and pencil on paper, 31.8 x 48 cm
Private collection

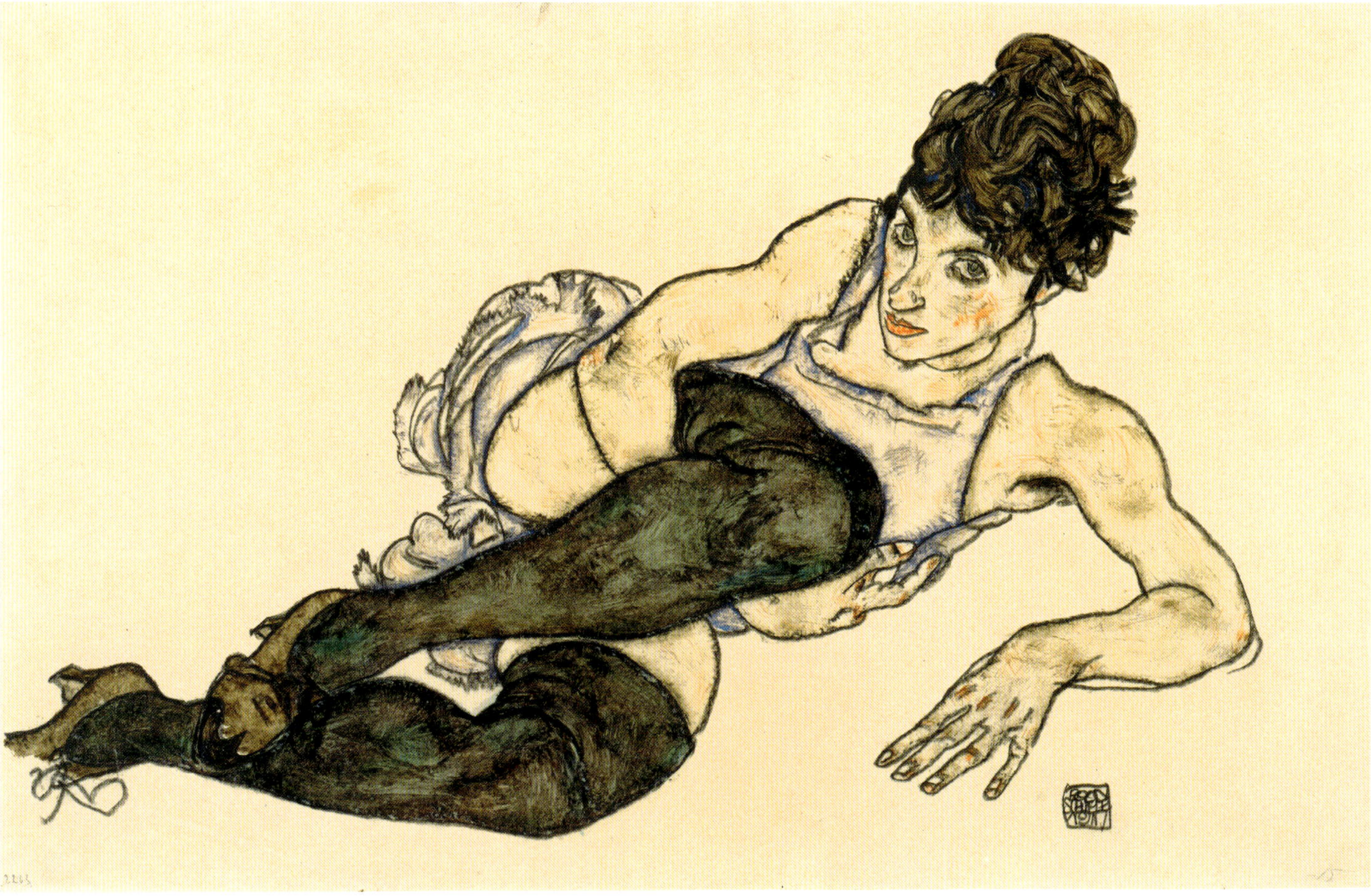

Cat. 128
EGON SCHIELE
Reclining Woman with Green Stockings, 1917
Gouache and black crayon on paper, 29.4 x 46 cm
Private collection, courtesy of Galerie St. Etienne, New York

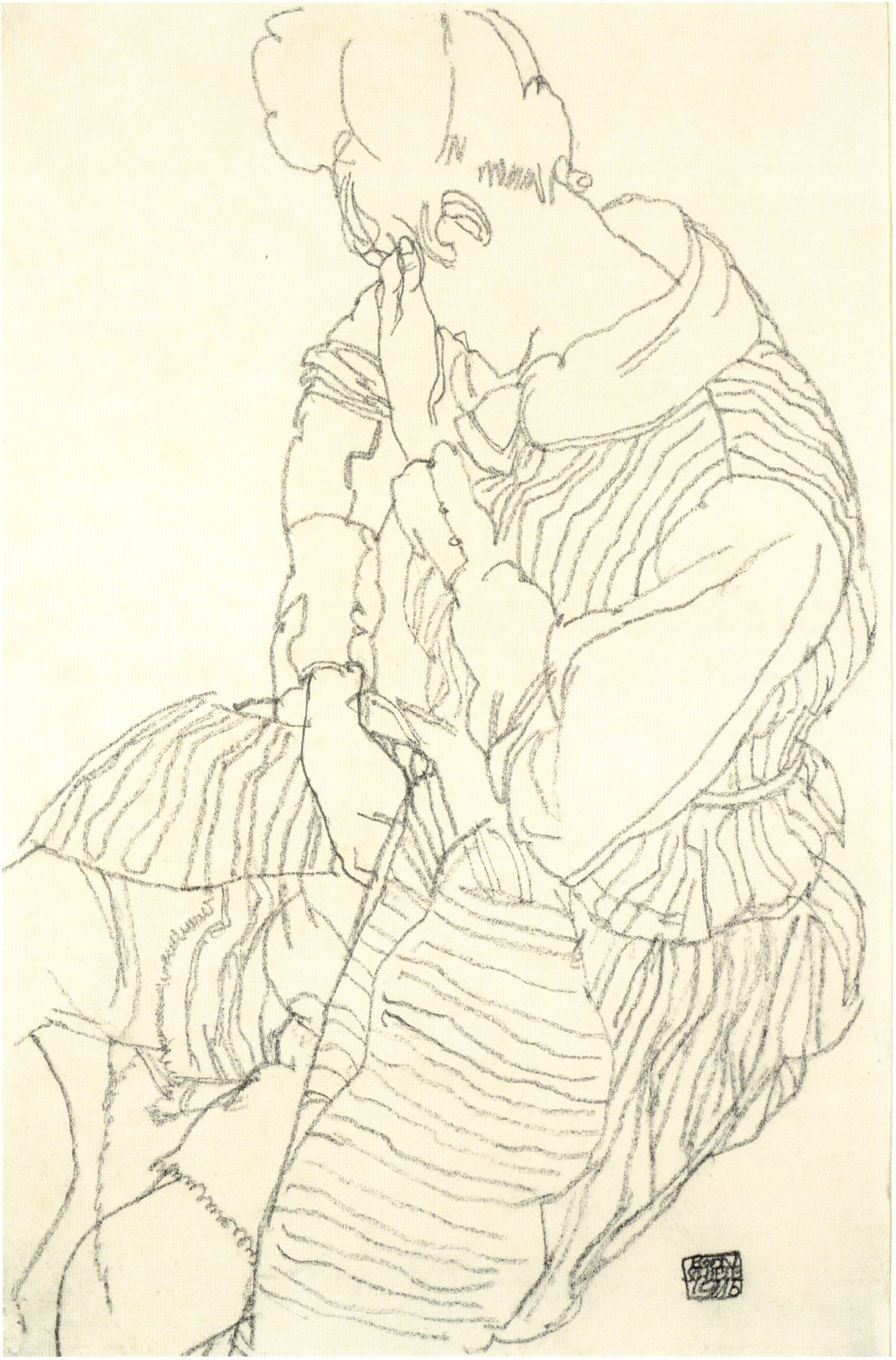

Cat. 129
EGON SCHIELE
Woman in Striped Dress, Masturbating (Edith Schiele), 1916
Black crayon on paper, 48 x 32 cm
Private collection, courtesy of Richard Nagy Ltd., London

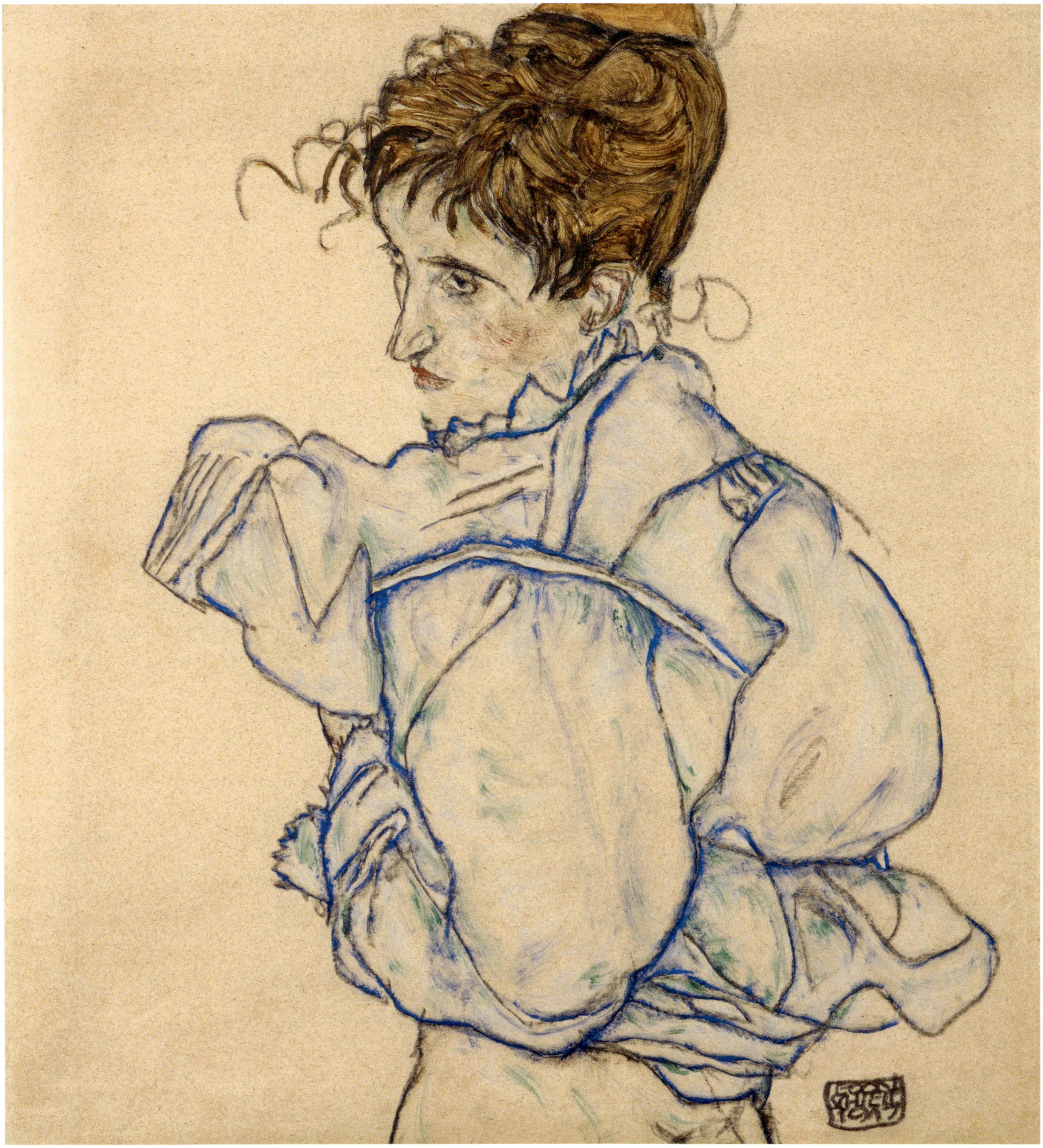

Cat. 130
EGON SCHIELE
Woman Disrobing (Edith Schiele), 1917
Gouache and pencil on paper, 32 x 29.5 cm
Private collection, courtesy of Richard Nagy Ltd., London

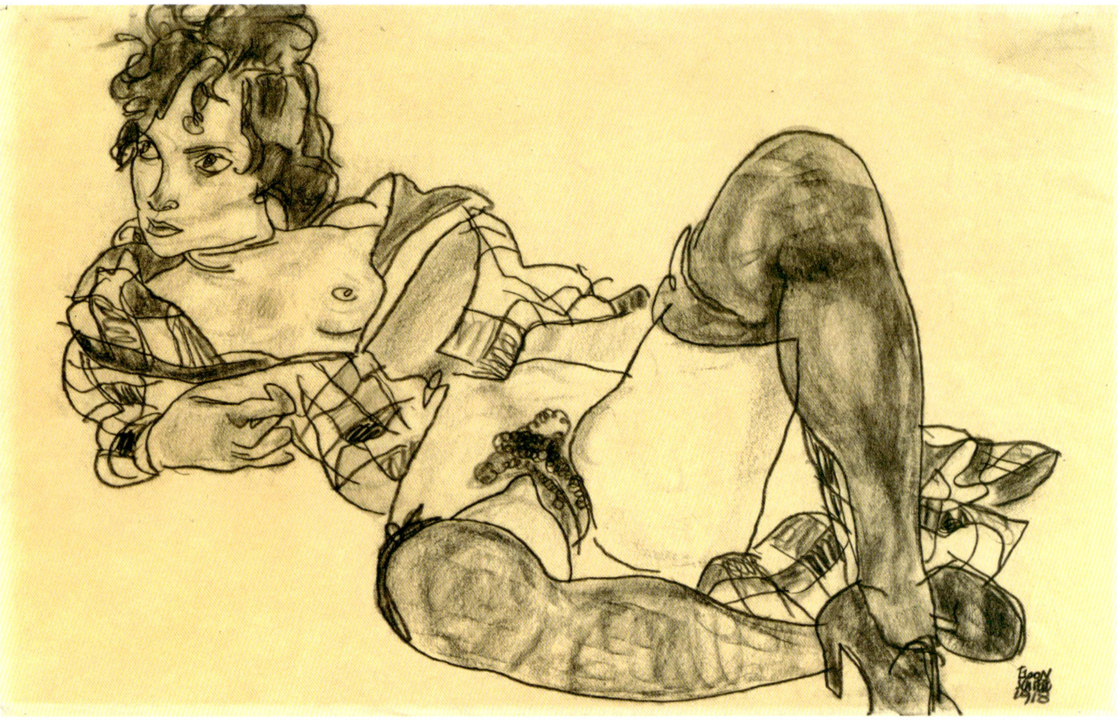

Cat. 131
EGON SCHIELE
Reclining Woman, 1918
Charcoal on paper, 29.5 x 46.4 cm
Private collection, courtesy of Galerie St. Etienne, New York

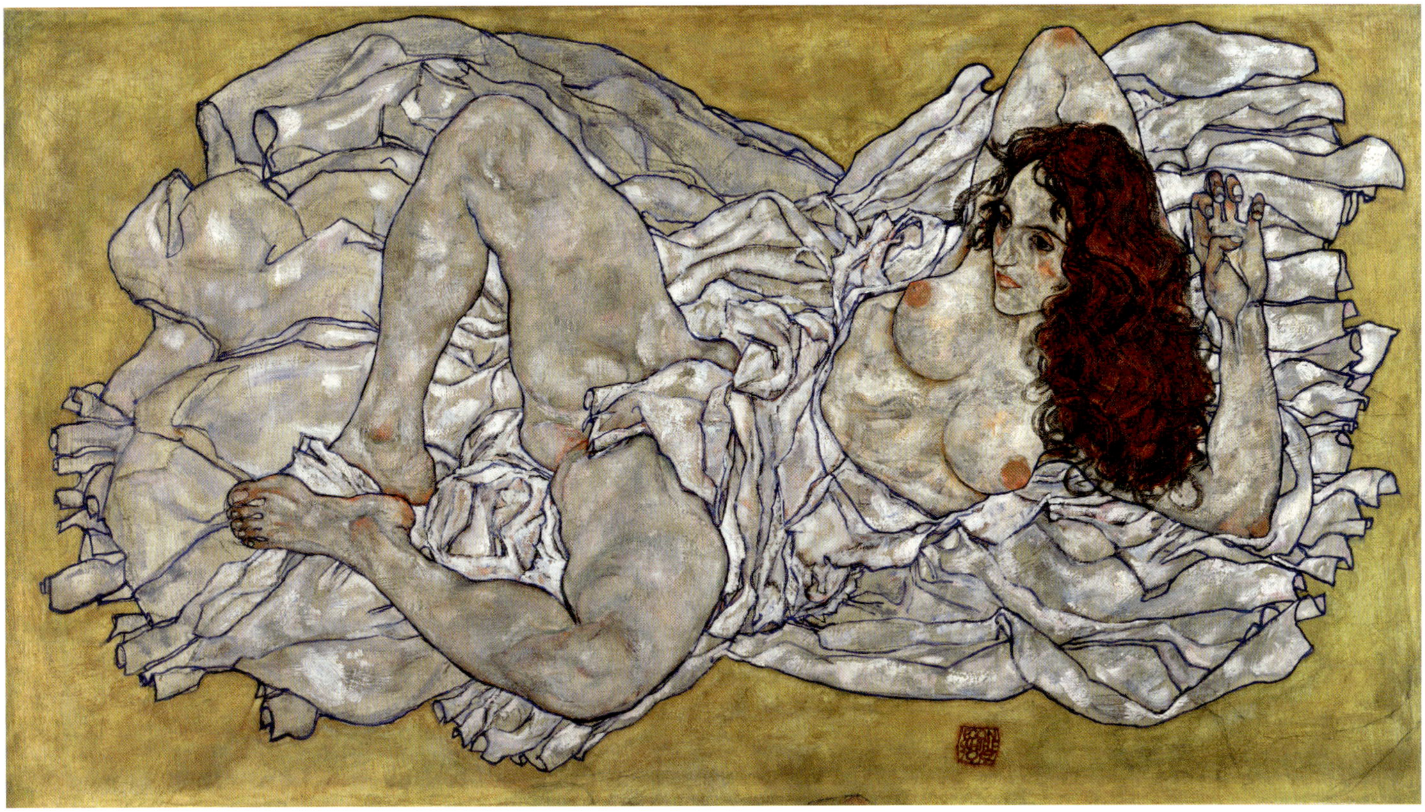

Cat. 132
EGON SCHIELE
Reclining Woman, 1917
Oil on canvas, 96 x 171 cm
Leopold Museum, Vienna

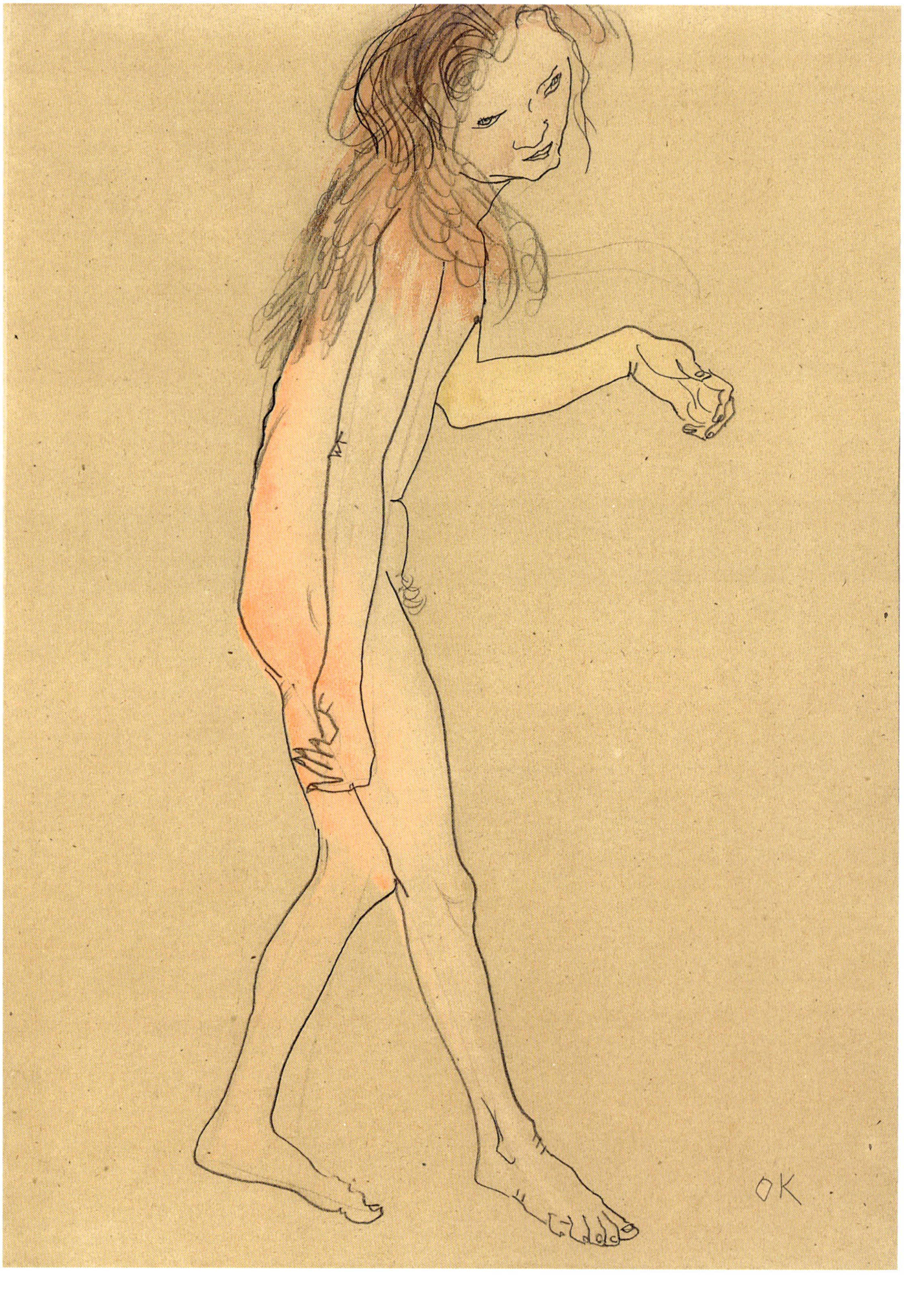

Cat. 133
OSKAR KOKOSCHKA
Standing Female Nude,
1907
Watercolor and pencil on paper,
45.1 x 31.7 cm
Private collection, courtesy of
Richard Nagy Ltd., London

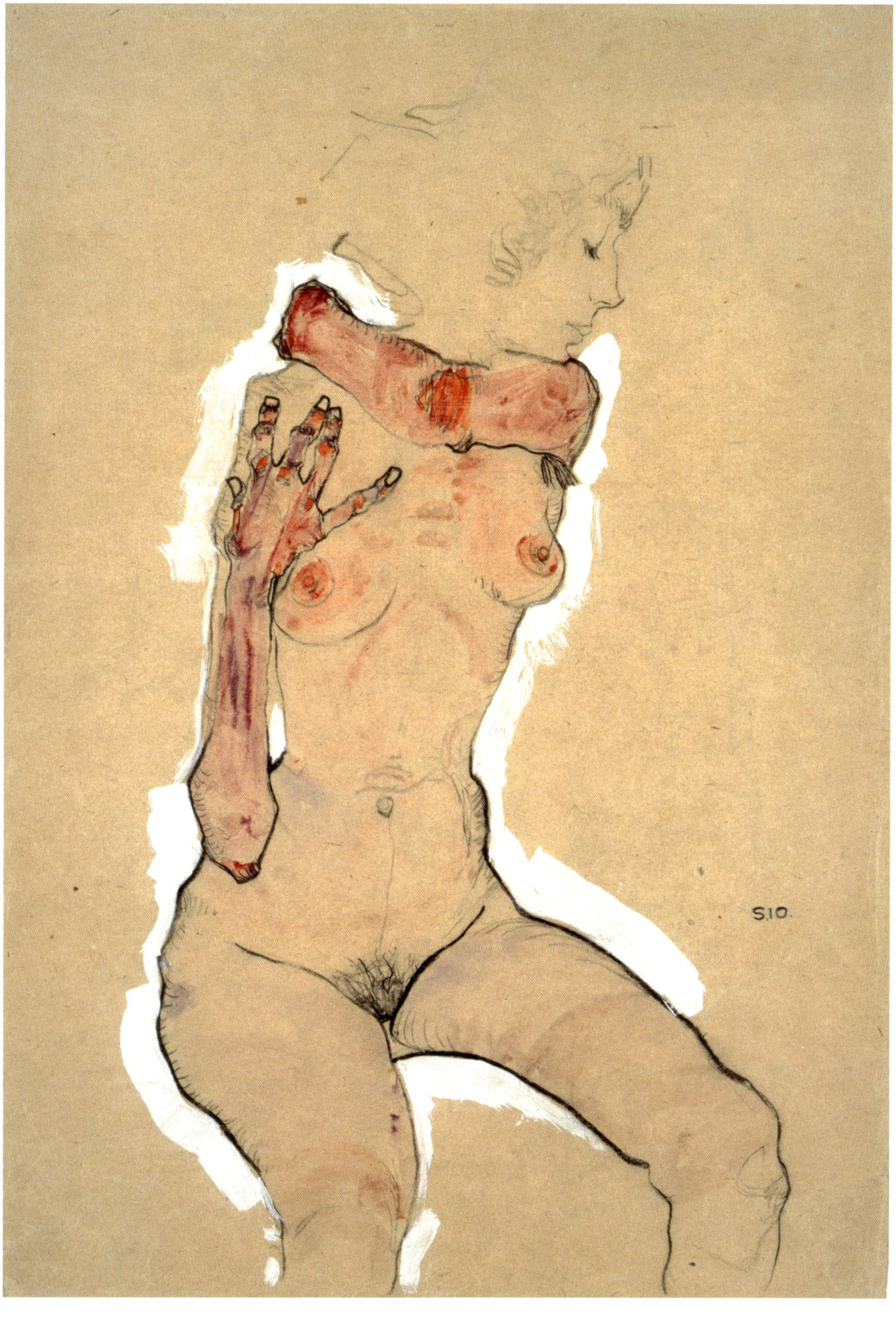

Cat. 134
EGON SCHIELE
Seated Nude (Gertrude Schiele),
1910
Gouache and black crayon on paper,
53 x 45 cm
Collection Fondation Pierre
Gianadda, Martigny, Suisse

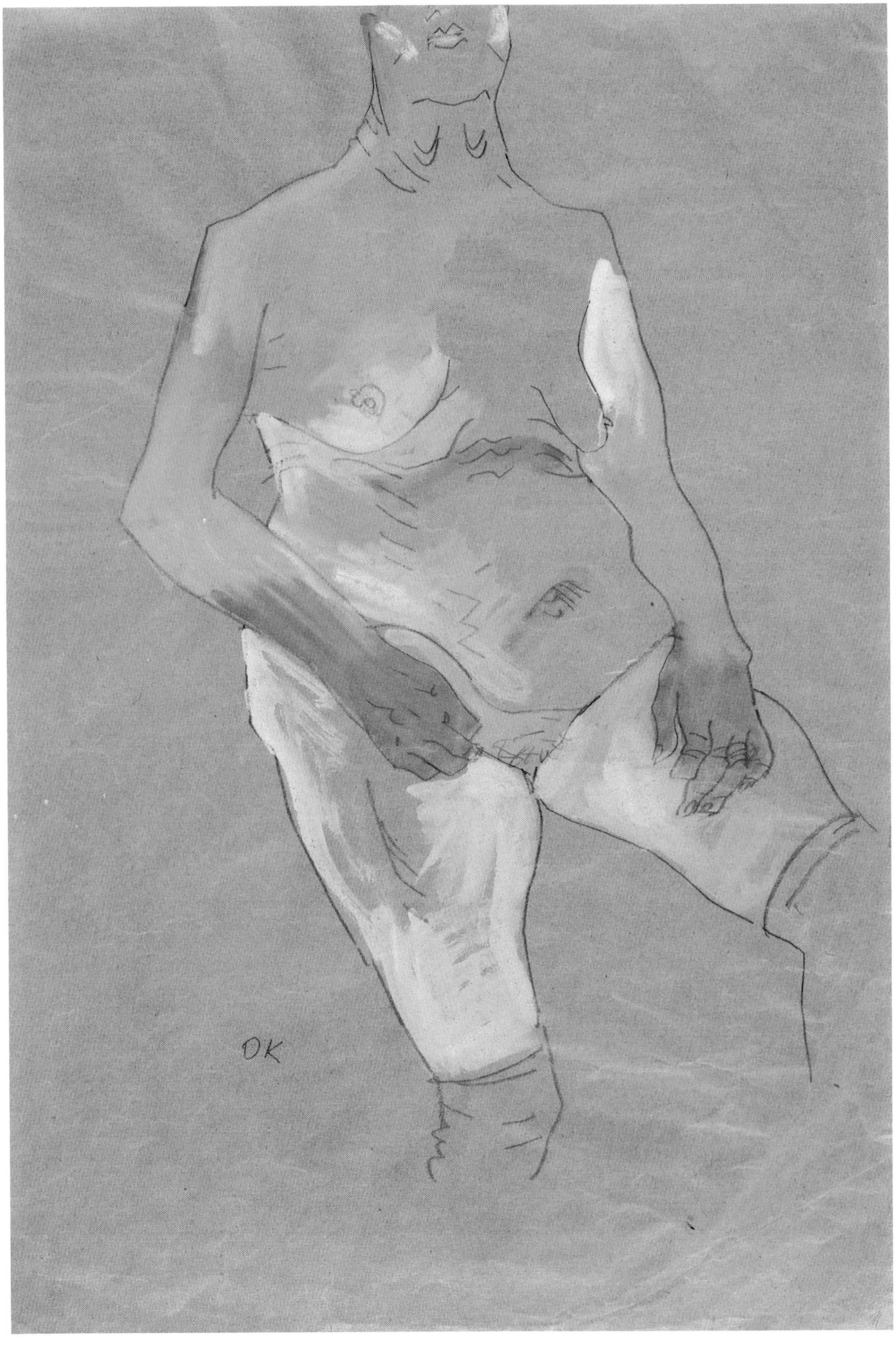

Cat. 135
OSKAR KOKOSCHKA
Seated Female Nude in Stockings, 1907
Pencil, watercolor, and opaque white on brown paper,
45.1 x 31.7 cm
Private collection

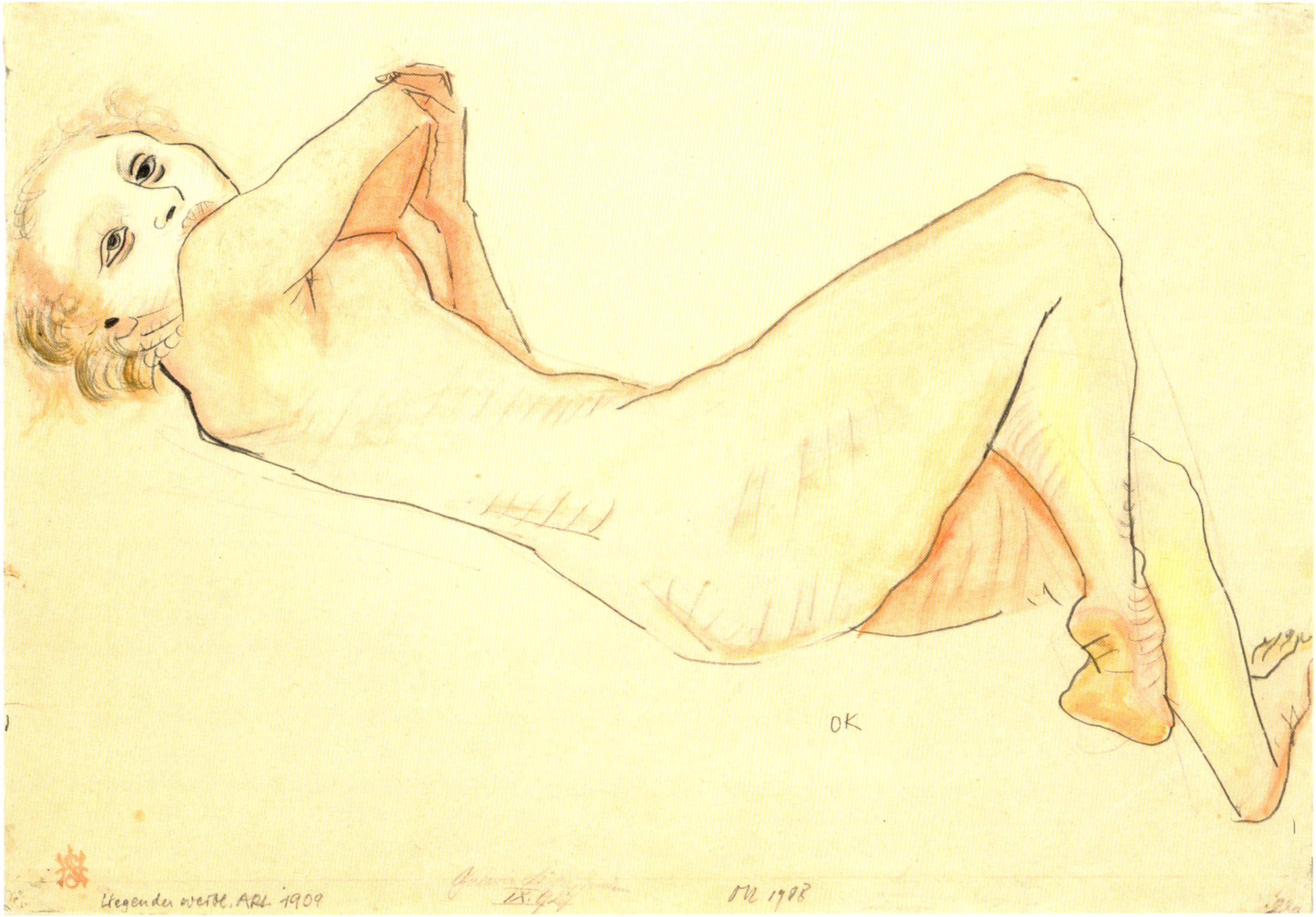

Cat. 136
OSKAR KOKOSCHKA
Reclining Female Nude, 1909
Pencil, watercolor, and opaque white on paper, 31.3 x 45 cm
Private collection

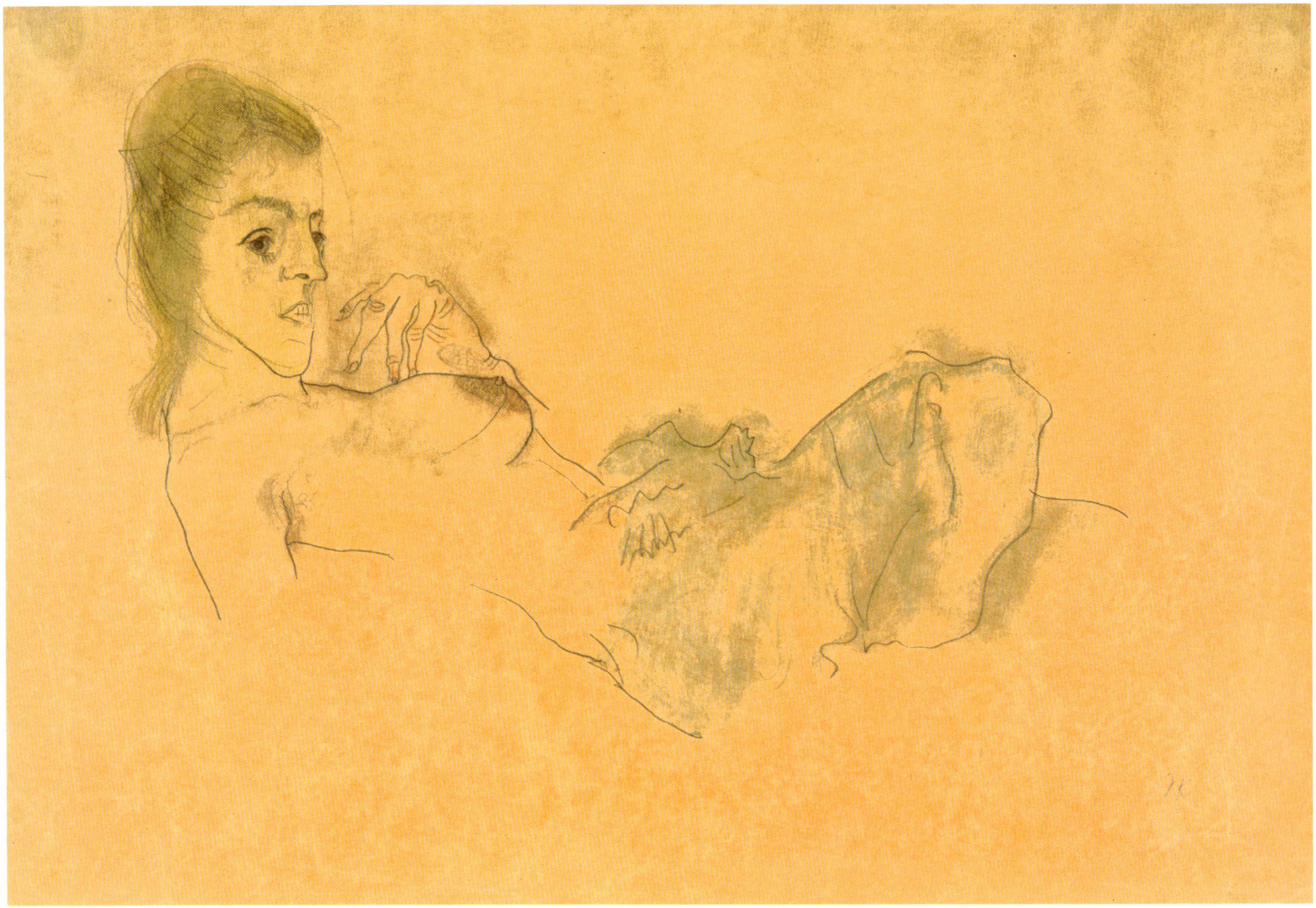

Cat. 137
OSKAR KOKOSCHKA
Reclining Female Semi-Nude (Bertha Eckstein-Diener), 1910
Watercolor, gouache, and pencil on paper, 30.8 x 45 cm
Private collection

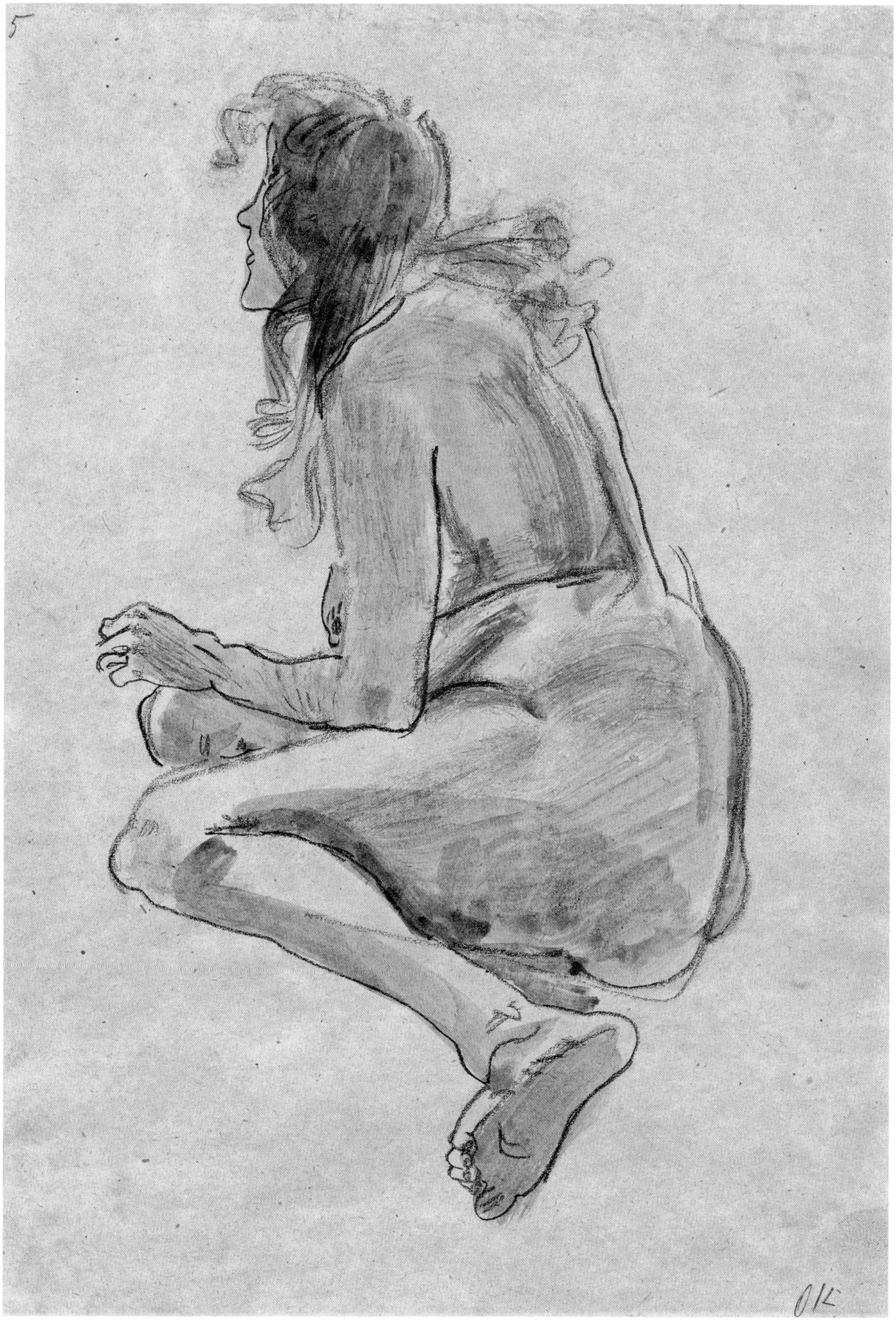

Cat. 138
OSKAR KOKOSCHKA
Seated Female Nude, Facing Left, 1913
Watercolor and black crayon on paper, 44.3 x 31.2 cm
Private collection, courtesy of Galerie St Etienne, New York, and Richard Nagy Ltd., London

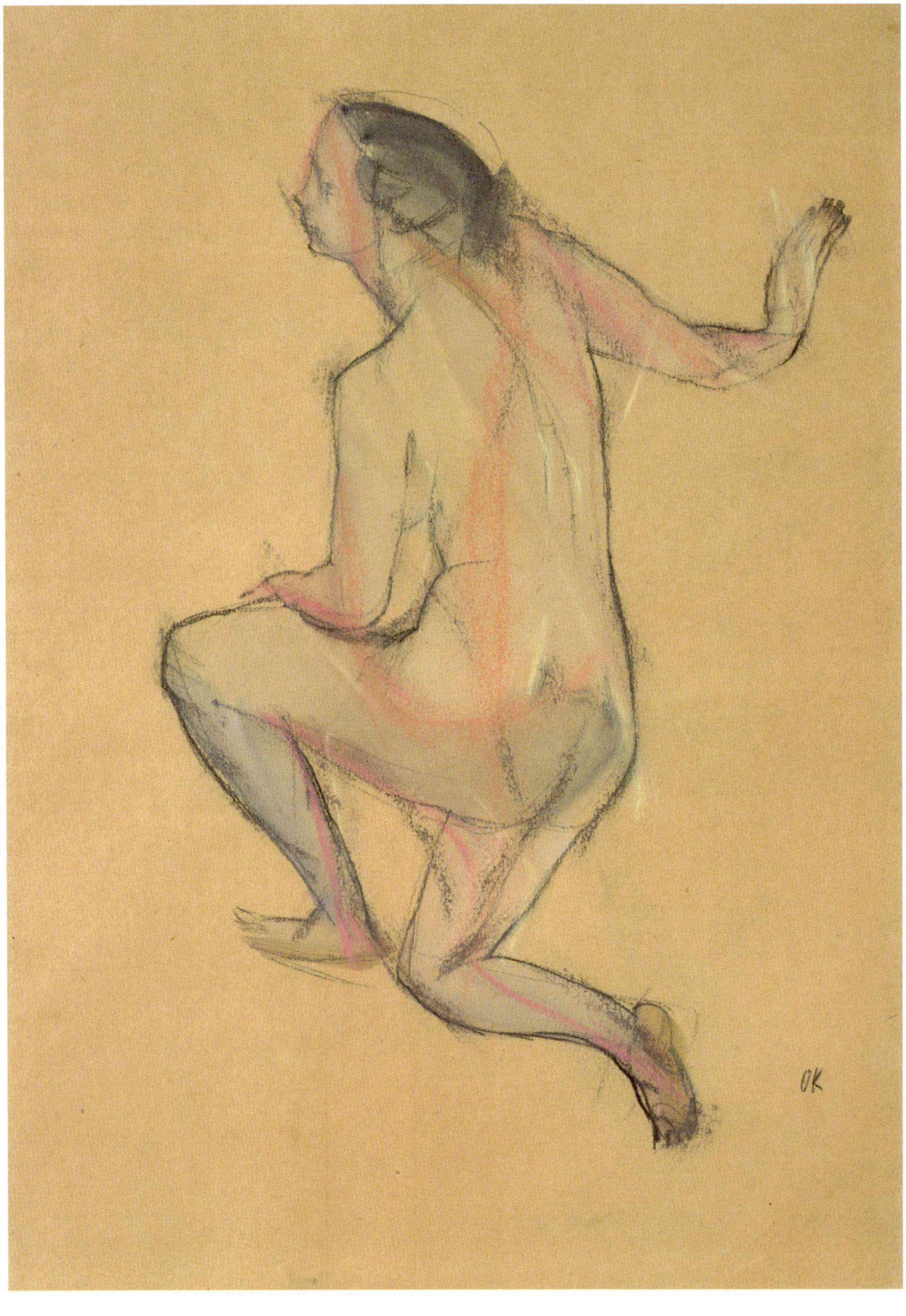

Cat. 139
OSKAR KOKOSCHKA
Kneeling Female Nude, Facing Left, 1912
Black crayon and watercolor on brown paper, 45.2 x 31.3 cm
Albertina, Vienna

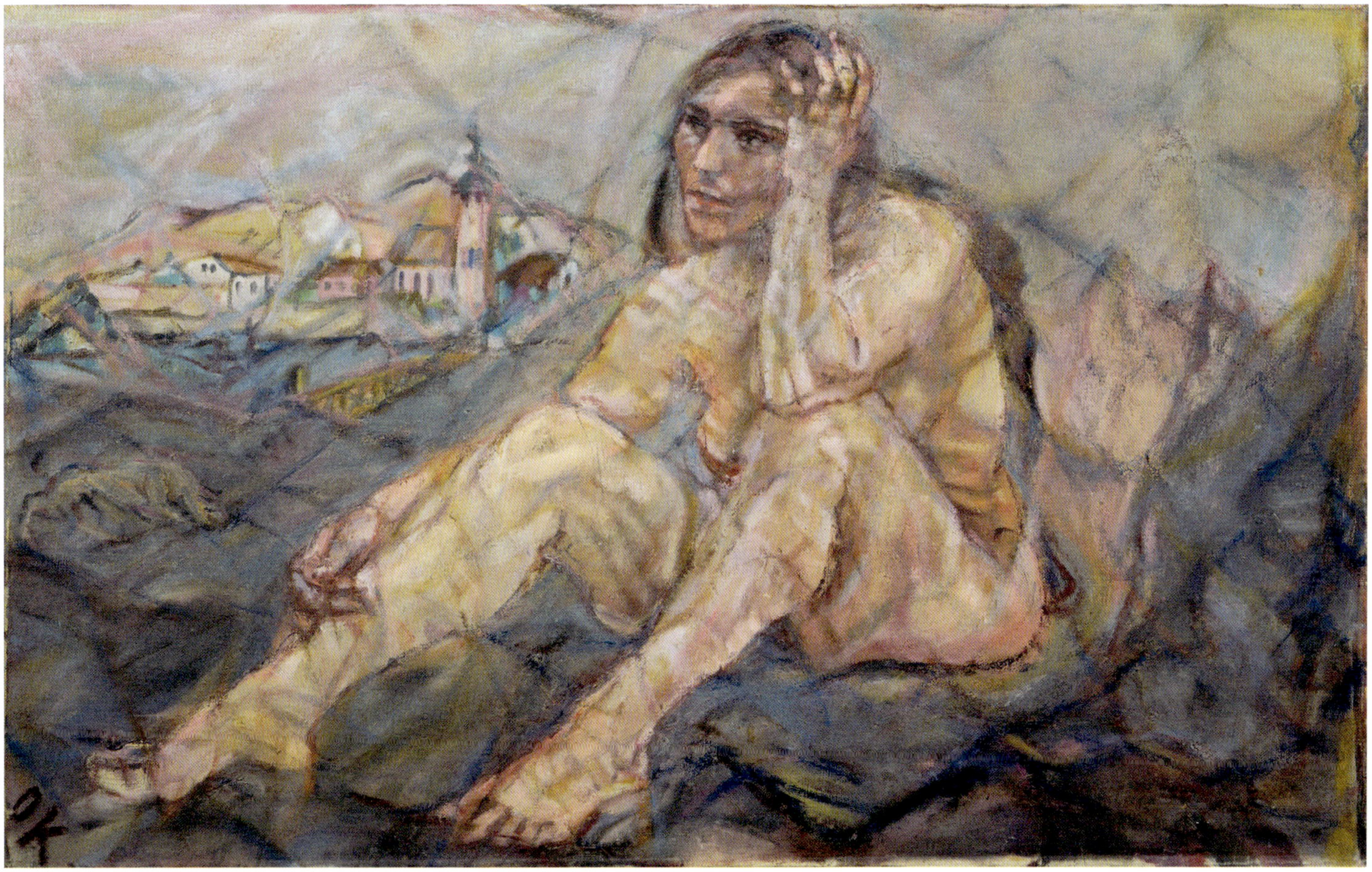

Cat. 140
OSKAR KOKOSCHKA
The Visitation, 1912
Oil on canvas, 80 x 127 cm
Belvedere, Vienna

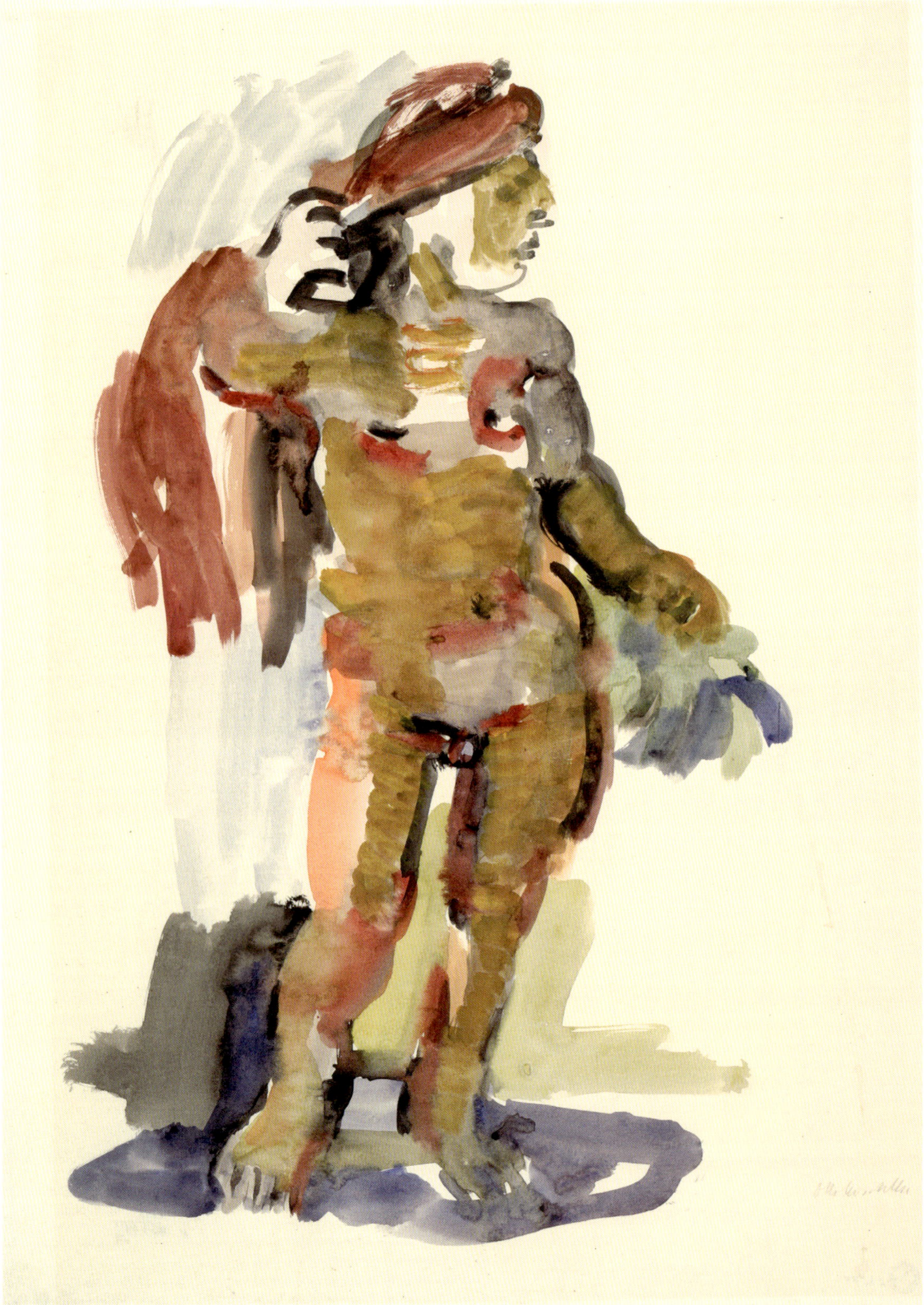

Cat. 141
OSKAR KOKOSCHKA
Standing Nude, 1922–23
Watercolor on paper, 66.3 x 48.1 cm
Albertina, Vienna

Cat. 142
EGON SCHIELE
Girl, 1917
Oil on canvas, 180.8 x 66.2 cm
Leopold Privatsammlung

Cat. 143
OSKAR KOKOSCHKA
Standing Female Nude (Alma Mahler), 1918
Oil on paper on canvas,
180 x 85 cm
Private collection, courtesy of
Caroline Schmidt Fine Art LLC

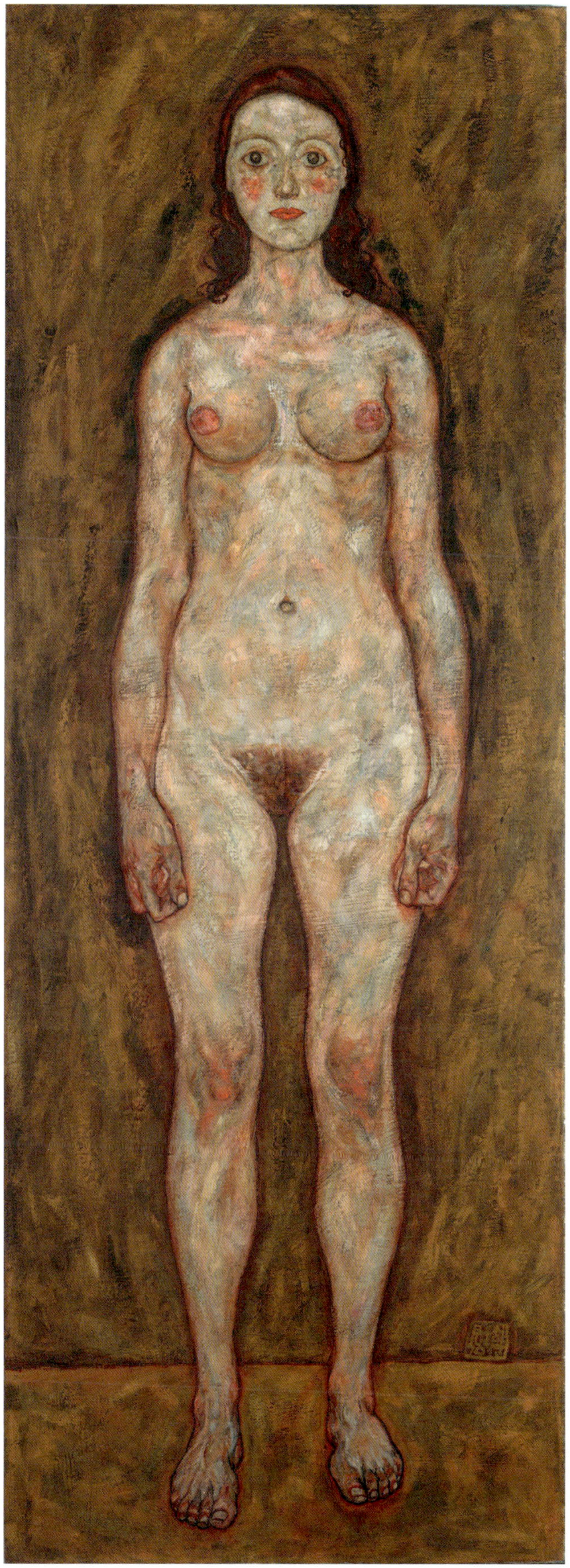

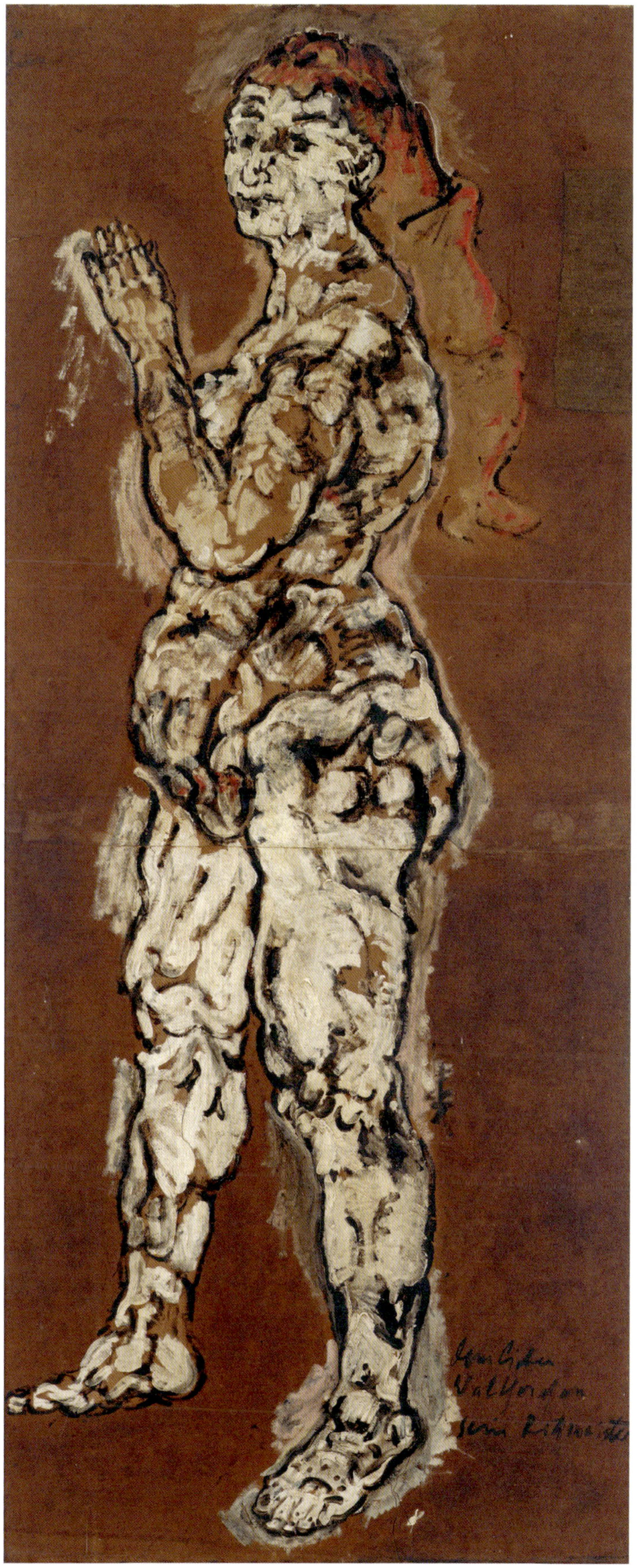

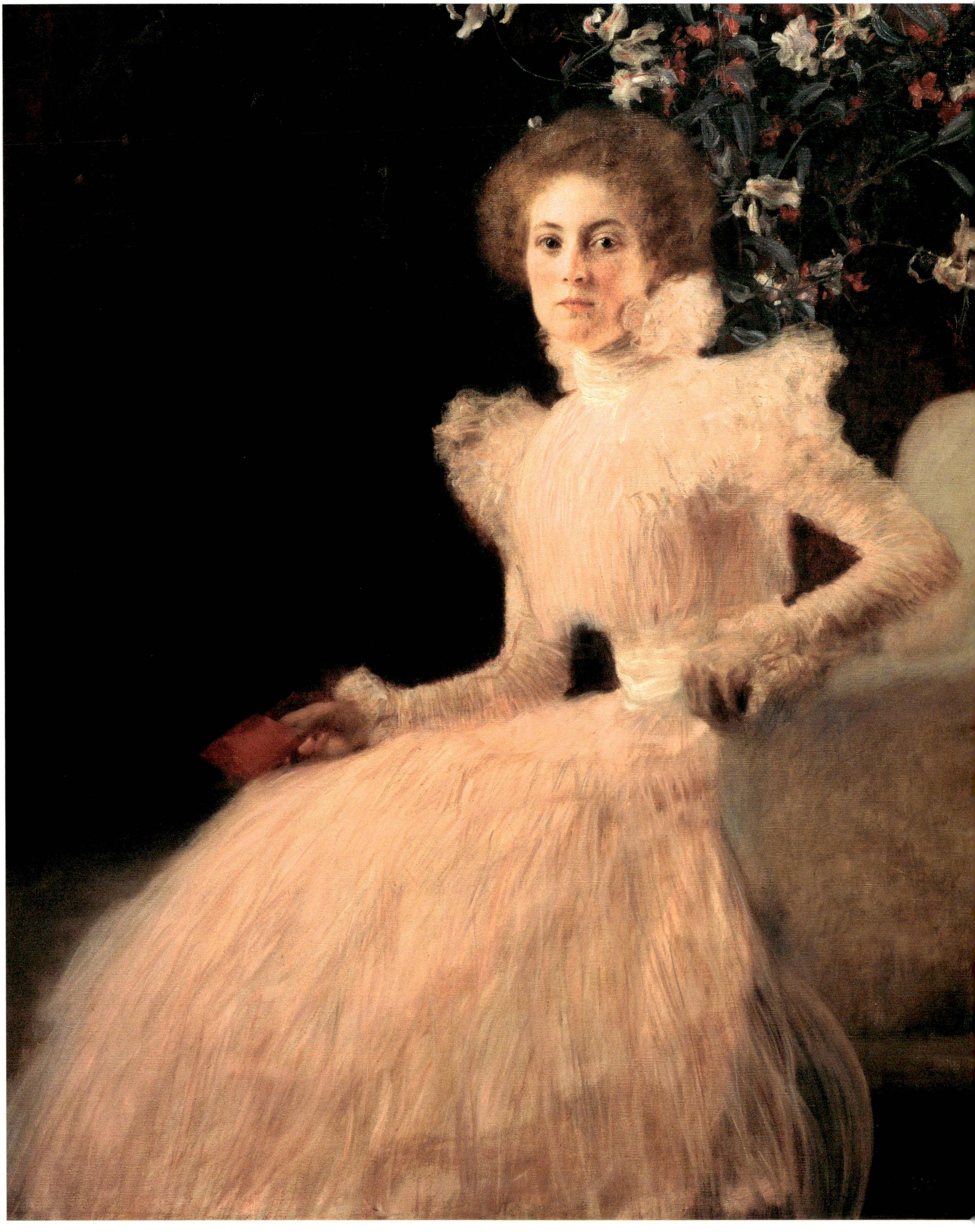

Gustav Klimt – Machismo and Nervous Heroines Thoughts on the Image of Women

Alfred Weidinger

Fig. 1
GUSTAV KLIMT
Sonja Knips, 1897/98
Belvedere, Vienna

"Klimt—the painter of women." Surrounding every one of his portraits of women is a web of rumors, suspicions, and also evidence of the artist's erotic escapades. "Without women, who offer themselves to his art as a morning gift, Klimt would be simply unimaginable. They are interwoven with his work like a wreath of flowers: Viennese, simple girls and genteel women, Jews and aristocrats. He knew them perfectly and lived, as it were, in the fragrance of their aura. And he became their champion—one of the very few that the modern European woman had," wrote the journalist Franz Servaes in 1918.[1] Women were the fertile ground that fed his creativity. They were everything for him: models, muses, and passion. When he observed and painted women in his studio, a physical closeness was created without any contact (not always), an ecstasy that he attempted to capture in the eroticizing lines of his drawings or the refined compositions on canvas. For Klimt, the numerous intimate relationships, and in some cases children, that resulted were inevitable, but not important enough for him to attach himself exclusively to a new family.[2] Klimt never married. A "tender bond of love"[3] developed between him and his sister-in-law Emilie Flöge from 1895 to 1899, but this did not prevent him from having sexual relations with his nude models, his clients, and his housekeepers. When, in 1983, Christian M. Nebehay spread the rumor about Klimt's fourteen illegitimate children, he fanned the flames of the widespread mythology surrounding Klimt's love life.[4]

In reality, Klimt was probably not a very complex person. He was direct in his thinking, consistent and single-minded in his actions, and extremely determined in his sensual needs. If modern historians are to be believed, he was very popular with women in spite of—or perhaps because of—this. Klimt's "lusty strength had a powerful effect on people, particularly women," recalled the art historian Hans Tietze in his 1919 obituary, stating that Klimt breathed a strong "earthy scent."[5] After visiting Klimt's studio in 1903, Hans Koppel described the artist as a "beautiful masculine apparition: medium height, of stocky and powerful regularity, but athletically supple and slim."[6]

Over the course of the last few decades, "Klimt—the painter of women" has become an effective publicity cliché. Since the 150th anniversary of Klimt's death in 2012,[7] the Vienna Tourist Board has been stylizing Klimt's portraits of women as symbols of the emergence of a self-assured middle class and presenting Klimt as the portrayer of the wealthy Viennese grande bourgeoisie. Klimt had a pragmatic attitude to his pictures of the ladies of the grande bourgeoisie. They were the basis for his reputation and made him wealthy enough to allow a degree of artistic and social freedom. Moreover, his success as a portrait painter was closely linked with the amendment to the constitution in Austria in 1849,[8] which for the first time allowed Jews to own property. As a result of this, rich Jewish families were able to build stately mansions in Vienna, which they furnished in grand bourgeois style. The portrait of the lady of the house was an absolute requirement, but posed a problem for the husband: only a few reputed Viennese painters had as liberal an attitude to Jews as Klimt.

There are several considerations to be taken into account when seeking to understand Klimt's society portraits. While bearing in mind the artist's biography, the artist and the person must be considered separately. "I firmly believe that I am not particularly interesting as a person. There is nothing unusual about me. I am an artist who paints every day from morning till evening. [...] Those who want to know anything about me—solely as an artist—should look carefully at my paintings and seek to find out from them what I am and what I want," said Klimt of himself.[9] When his attitude to the women within his own family, his relationships with the mothers of his children, his affairs, models, and clients are all taken into account, it is possible to obtain a clearer picture of Klimt's relationship to women. However, this attitude was multifaceted and contradictory, and to label him simply as a "lover of women," as "the most important eroticist in the history of art," or even as a "womanizer," does neither him nor the women full justice. Added to this is the fact that his life is only comprehensible in the context of the social developments of the time, which were not dictated by the grande bourgeoisie but by the efforts of women from socially disadvantaged classes and of wealthy Jewish citizens to emancipate themselves. Klimt and his women shine a light on both sides of Viennese society, beyond the salon culture of the grande bourgeoisie.

The woman in a doll's house

Klimt grew up and matured as an artist in a patriarchal society that gave women little scope for development. Even though the last two decades of the nineteenth century are seen as a time of change, during which the established categories of gender, education, family, and marriage were redefined, it was still the men who continued to confirm the prevailing cliché in Viennese bourgeois society by investing disproportionate amounts in the building and furnishing of their mansions and, where possible, in private art collections. Guests were received into residences with stately Gründerzeit façades. The woman of the house organized elaborate dinners, hosted a high-society salon, in that way furthering her husband's career. The function of a bourgeois woman was to serve as a wife to her husband as head of the family.

The scandal surrounding Henrik Ibsen's play *A Doll's House* (fig. 2), performed for the first time in Austria at the Stadttheater[10] in 1881, is symptomatic of the perceived status of women in Viennese society in the last two decades of the nineteenth century. In keeping with contemporary conventions, Ibsen's main character Nora is regarded by her husband as his possession. Although appreciated by her family, Nora is not allowed any independence by her husband, nor does he take her seriously as a partner. It is as if she lived in a doll's house. In the last act, Nora breaks out of this existence and leaves her husband and children. The Hofburgtheater had planned a performance of the play in 1880, but the plan was delayed because the director at the time asked Ibsen to change the provocative ending.[11] Evidently, a woman protagonist who rebelled against all of her domestic and maternal duties and demanded the right to an independent life was too scandalous and unacceptable for the Viennese theater. Ibsen complied with the theater director's wishes, and when the Stadttheater eventually managed, a year later, to show the original version, criticism of the ending was so harsh that the management felt obliged, "in view of the discomforting effect that the end of the third act of Ibsen's *Nora* had on the audience," to change the ending for the next performance.[12] Only a few people recognized the relevance of Ibsen's message in public and summarized it as well as Felix Salten did in his review of the play in 1894: "People continue to turn to the important questions that still remain unanswered. [...] This is why *Nora* is performed again from time to time. This play seems to be asking an immense question about humanity and is hugely symbolic. [...] There is a vague sensation that the play could

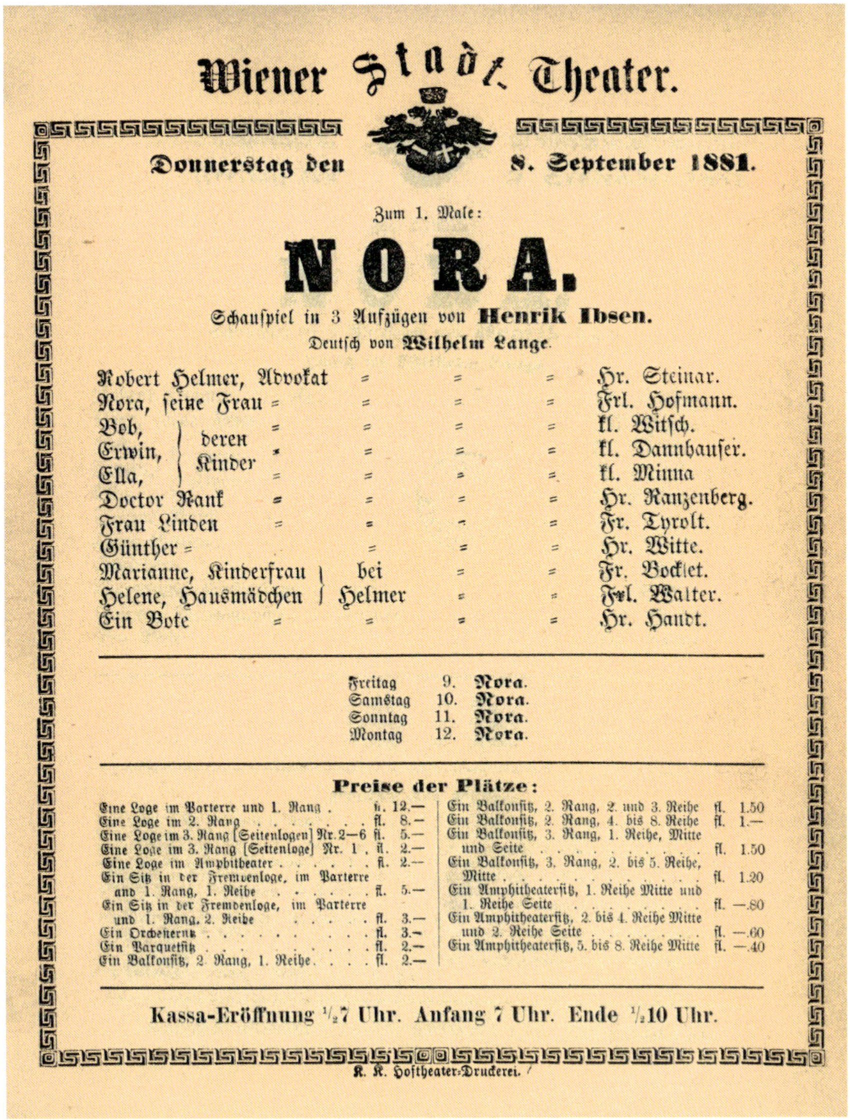

Fig. 2
Advertisement for the Austrian premiere of Ibsen's *Nora* at the Wiener Stadttheater, Wien Bibliothek im Rathaus, Druckschriftensammlung

well prove to be right after all and that we would then realize how much there is to make up and feel guilty about."[13]

However much the male-dominated society attempted to maintain its rules and laws, the subject of women's rights could no longer be ignored. More and more middle-class women protested and organized themselves in women's movements, but it was women workers who led the way. They were not only interested in a revision of the male-dominated education system, their purely representative status as wives, and the meaningless conventions, but also explicitly demanded their rights and insisted on a re-evaluation and reinterpretation of gender roles. Among the pioneers of the Austrian women's movement were Rosa Mayreder, Marie Lang, Auguste Fickert, and Marianne Hainisch. The last-named spoke in 1899 at the International Women's Congress in London about her sobering observation that most women, "partly through worldly innocence, partly because they didn't want to spoil their relationships with men, and partly because they realize that their emancipation would impose many obligations on them," were skeptical of the new women's movement.[14] The willingness of women to fight for their rights was by no means widespread in 1900, particularly among the middle classes. Social Democratic workers and Jewish women proved to be much more courageous and committed. They were involved in both the radical Allgemeiner Österreichischer Frauenverein [General Austrian Women's Association] founded in 1893 and the moderate Bund österreichischer Frauenvereine [Federation of Austrian Women's Associations] set up in 1902 by Marianne Hainisch. Both associations concentrated on the assertion of women's legal, intellectual, economic, and political rights.[15]

The emancipation efforts of Austrian women provoked a massive reaction from men, who feared a loss of power and were also experiencing an orientation and identity crisis. Above all, they suffered from a total lack of comprehension of women and a deep-seated insecurity vis-à-vis the female sex. The result was a certain demonization and mystification of women. It was practically impossible for members of society to ignore the topic, which became a key question in academic, medical, intellectual, and artistic discourse that was typically infused with misogyny and idolatry.[16]

Although Helene von Druskowitz's thesis, published in 1905, that men were a "logical and moral impossibility and a curse of the world"[17] was no less polemic and subjective than her opponents' assertions, we can see it today as an understandable retaliation in a heated atmosphere.

Psychologists, analysts, and philosophers now evolved an interpretation of women as a disruptive factor in the social order. They were perceived as a threat and analyzed in detail as such. Otto Weininger, one of the most vehement opponents of female emancipation, attempted in his major work

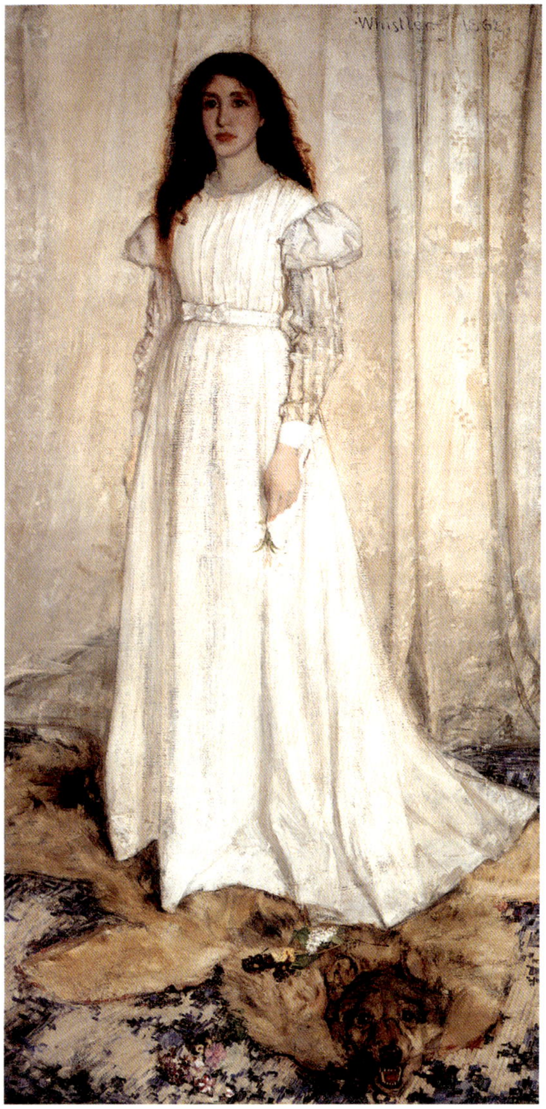

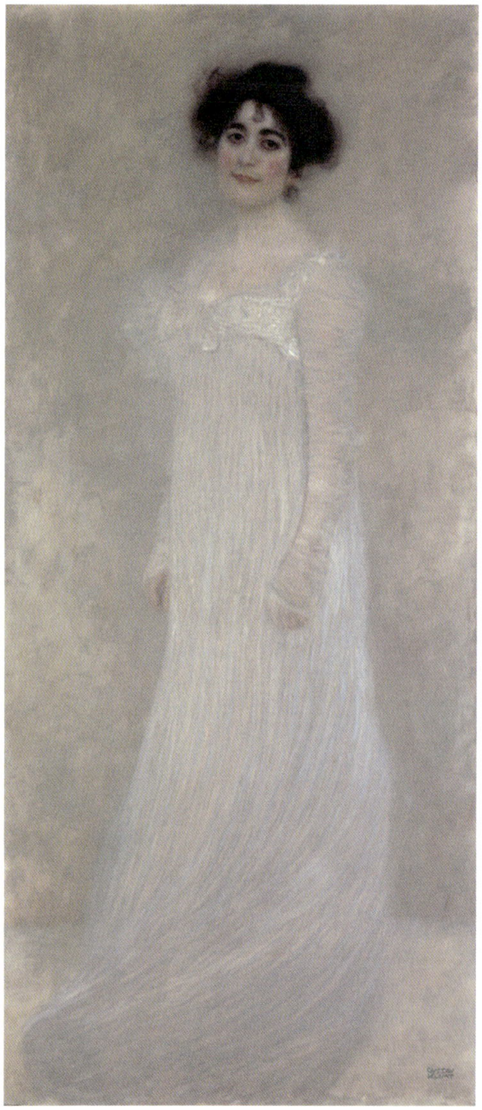

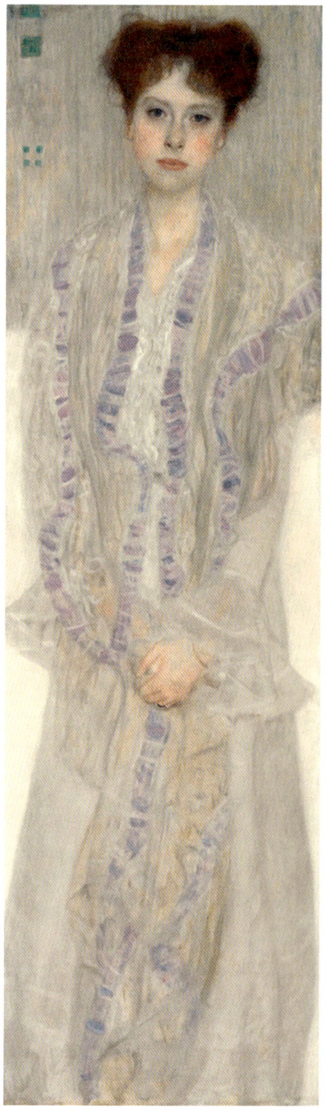

Geschlecht und Charakter[18], published in 1903, to prove the inferiority of women and obstinately denied the existence of a female soul. He believed that the desire by women for access to education was a threat to society. He also claimed that women were incapable of intellectual orientation and creative productivity. Weininger rejected the demand of women's rights proponents for active and passive suffrage by pointing out that "children, the feeble-minded, and criminals" did not have a political voice and that "women should be kept away from affairs in which there was a great danger that the female influence would do nothing but harm."[19]

The question of women in culture also played a role in the battle of the sexes.[20] Out of fear of the consequences of the progressive emancipation of women, artists and intellectuals created a myth of femininity. The Vienna Modernists deliberately chose the word "Weib" as an antagonistic term for "Frau," loading it with erotic and sensual connotations and "misusing" it for their "higher" purposes. In the late historicist period, artists were seeking new challenges, and, as the question of women gained prominence in social discourse, they finally found what they had been so desperately looking for. So as not to directly attack the socially legitimized and institutionalized woman as such, they chose the literary term "Weib" to appropriate women for their

Fig. 3
JAMES ABBOTT MCNEILL WHISTLER
Symphony in White, No. 1: The White Girl, 1861–62
National Gallery of Art, Washington D. C.

Fig. 4
GUSTAV KLIMT
Serena Lederer, 1899
Metropolitan Museum of Art, New York

Fig. 5
GUSTAV KLIMT
Gertrud Loew, 1902
Joe Lewis Collection, Bahamas

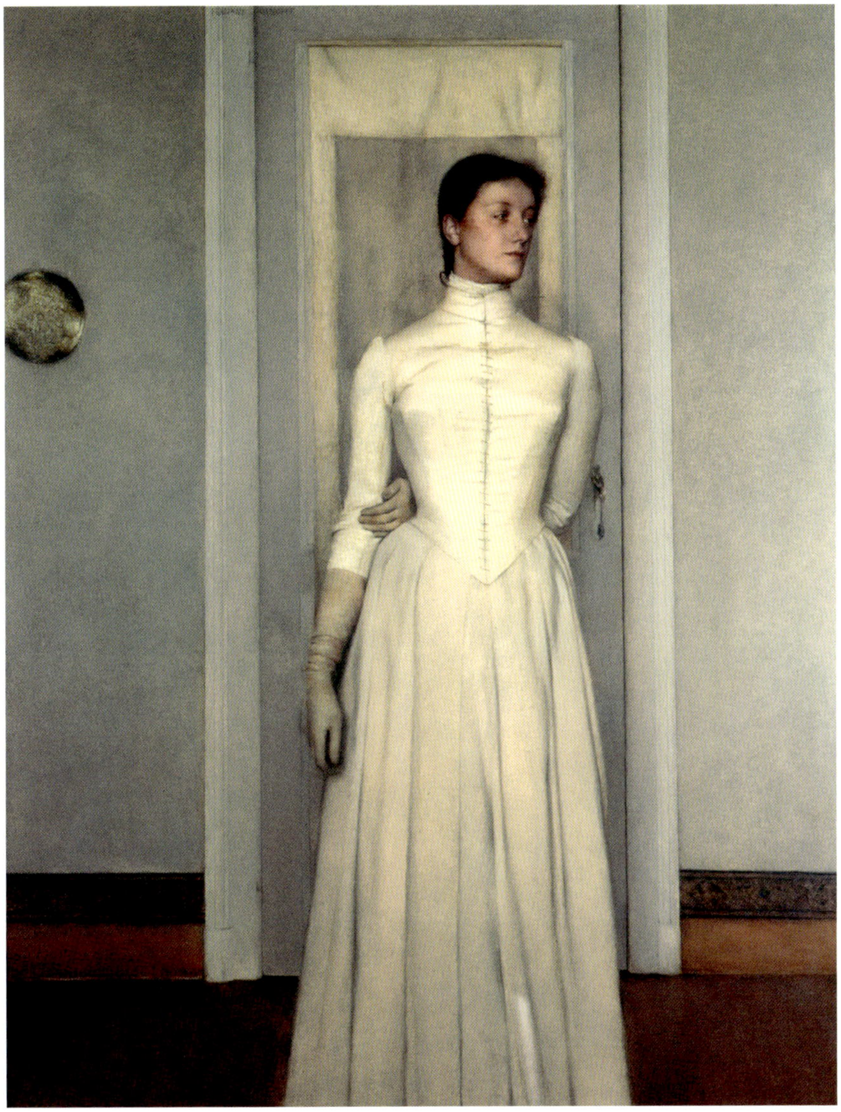

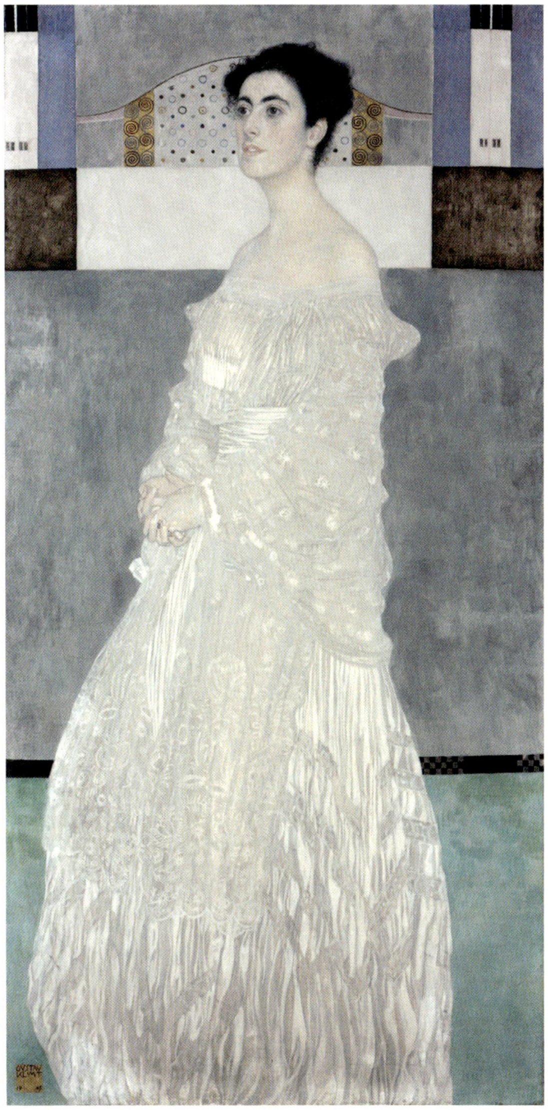

Fig. 6
FERNAND KHNOPFF
Marguerite Khnopff, 1887
Musées royaux des Beaux Arts de Belgique, Brussels

Fig. 7
GUSTAV KLIMT
Margarethe Stonborough-Wittgenstein, 1905
Bayerische Staatsgemälde-sammlungen – Neue Pinakothek, Munich

sacrosanct artistic world. The Vienna Modernists either idealized women as Madonnas, reduced them to malleable girls, functionalized them as disparaged muses, vilified them as whores, or relegated them to the status of sex objects.[21] Female independence was thus deliberately destroyed and, at the same time, appropriated for male artistic endeavors.

Gustav Klimt's character as a man and an artist is rooted in this spirit of the time. Thanks to his success, he ultimately became an essential component of the movement that Musil described with reference to intellectuals: "Nobody was able to say whether it was to be a new art, a New Man, a new morality or perhaps a reshuffling of society […] but people were standing up on all sides to fight against the old way of life."[22] Klimt moved in these circles and responded in his works above all to the omnipresent discussion about the "mystery of women," which became a focus of his creativity from around 1900. His art concentrated thereafter on the female sex, albeit in three very different ways.

Klimt's society portraits

In 1897, Klimt became president of the Secession in Vienna. Following its establishment in Vienna, the Vereinigung bildender Künstler Österreichs

[Union of Austrian Artists] staged the first "elite exhibition of forthright modern works of art" from other countries.[23] The artists in the Secession movement thus shared the hope of artistic innovation and internationalization of the Vienna art scene. This period also coincides with Klimt's artistic emancipation, marked by his first commission for a society portrait. Apart from the portrait of a young Viennese women four years earlier and the portrait of his mother Anna (1898, AW 108), which remains lost, *Sonja Knips*, using a square format for the first time, was Klimt's first "official" portrait of a woman (fig. 1). With its display at the second Secession exhibition in November 1898, Klimt, who had hitherto made his way above all as a decorative painter, progressed overnight to become a serious portrait painter.

This second exhibition continued to focus on recent works by international artists, particularly Belgian symbolism and Fernand Khnopff.[24] His pictures were not hung right next to Klimt's, "[...] but although Khnopff was banished to the opposite end of the exhibition, it was still not far enough away to characterize the distance between Klimt and the Belgian mystic, whose individuality epitomized all of the late and over-refined aspects of Anglo-French culture that have come into bloom as a perhaps sickly and not very painterly but intellectually infinitely proper and intense sensibility."[25]

Soon afterwards, Klimt painted the life-size portraits *Serena Lederer* (fig. 4) and *Gertrude Steiner* (1900, AW 137), in which, using pale colors, he applied a color and painting concept derived from Khnopff, albeit not very successfully, possibly taking inspiration for the composition from portraits by James McNeill Whistler (fig. 3). It was not until the portrait *Rosalie von Rosthorn-Friedmann* (1901, AW 145) that he found a functioning solution, particularly as regards the nervous style of the background. In doing so, his painterly experience with the university ceiling paintings (the so-called "faculty pictures") and some impressionistic landscapes from the same time proved to be of great assistance. In the portrait *Marie Henneberg* (cat. 13), wife of the renowned scientist and art photographer, Klimt's post-impressionist style reached its highpoint. Like the Pictorialists, including Hugo Henneberg, who blurred the contour definition to generate flowing transitions, Klimt's portrait is set in a dense mosaic of paint. Only the subject's face and the flouncing lace of her dress have any tangible presence.[26]

Soon after the completion of the *Beethoven Frieze* (1901), to mark the fifty-fifth birthday of the renowned doctor Anton Loew, Klimt was commissioned to paint a portrait of his 19 year old daughter Getrud (fig. 5).[27] Here, the nervous ductus, reminiscent of French Post-Impressionism, gradually gave way to more homogeneous surfaces. The portrait, conceived without any symbolic intent and designed to produce an undulating overall appearance, with the face as anchor point of the composition, along with its unusual coloring, make it one of the artist's most significant portraits. The radical ponderation of the balance between subject and background are in keeping with the style of the time. In *Envy*, an illustration drawn in 1899 for *Ver Sacrum*, for example, Klimt had already given an inkling of the modern approach to proportions. Koloman Moser's poster for *Jung-Wiener Theater zum lieben Augustin*, a literary cabaret which premiered on November 16, 1901 at Theater an der Wien, uses a similar approach.[28]

In the portrait *Gertrud Loew*, Klimt for the first time formally defined the concept used in his society paintings from 1898 onward: focus on the face and hands, pale complexion, flushed cheeks and flat chest, and—until 1912—no visible feet. The effect of these images of women differs markedly from all that had gone previously. In contrast to what was expected of an erotic painter of the time, Klimt's models are neither erotic nor formally complete. The angular, flat-chested bodies illustrate that Klimt apparently saw it as an artistic necessity, in contrast to his drawings and symbolic paintings, to portray his models without any erotic connotation. They arouse neither longing nor sexual desire. And, although the idea behind a portrait is to capture and convey the subject's personality, Klimt avoids precisely this. He progressively defeminizes and depersonalizes these women. The background and body merge, and the portraits do not place the woman in a pictorial setting, but present the individual body parts—head and hands—seemingly

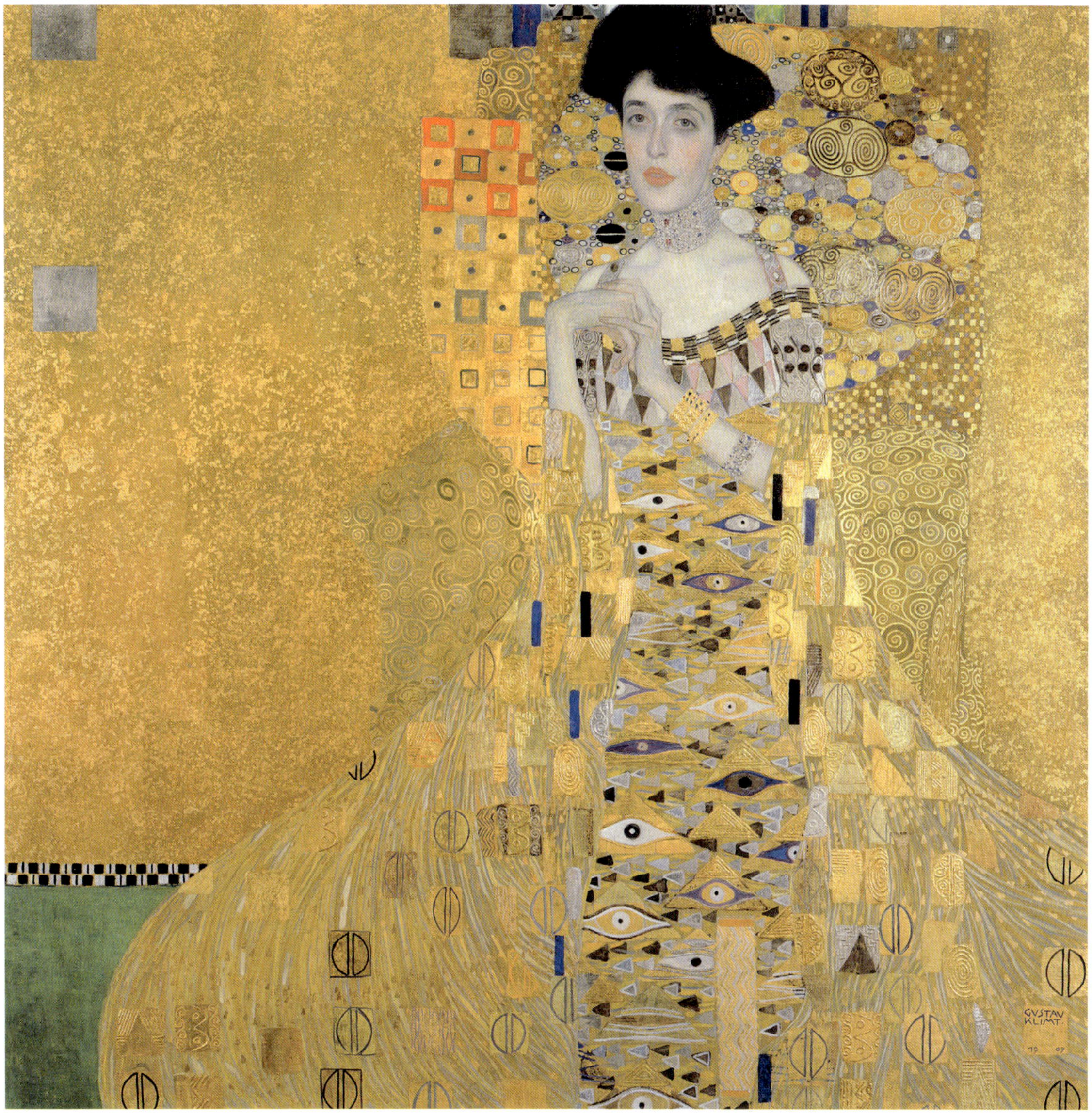

Fig. 8
GUSTAV KLIMT
Adele Bloch-Bauer I, 1907
Neue Galerie, New York

floating in space, detached from reality. The woman becomes an ornament, fulfilling her role as a decorative element in the domestic salon.

This portrait concept is followed up consistently in Klimt's work and reflects the image of women prevailing among the Viennese bourgeoisie. The wife was a showpiece for the husband and her function was that of a devoted adjutant. Physicality, not to mention any hint of sexuality, would have been out of place in these portraits. Only the reddened cheeks, a trademark of Klimt and appearing in all his portraits of women, were a deliberate characteristic running contrary to this demand. Superficially they bear the stigma of innocence and make the women appear weak, innocent, and coy. But blushing is above all a sign of excitement, and psychoanalysis interprets shy blushing as a psychological transfer of shame from the genitals to the face.

In the 1905 portrait *Margarethe Stonborough-Wittgenstein* (fig. 7), the pictorial ornamentation behind the subject's head is connected with the background. This formal stringency is found again in the 1906 portrait *Fritza Riedler* (cat. 15). As in *Lady in an Armchair* (1897–98, AW 105), *Lady by the Fireplace* (1897–98, AW 106), and *Sonja Knips*, the composition is borrowed in its entirety from

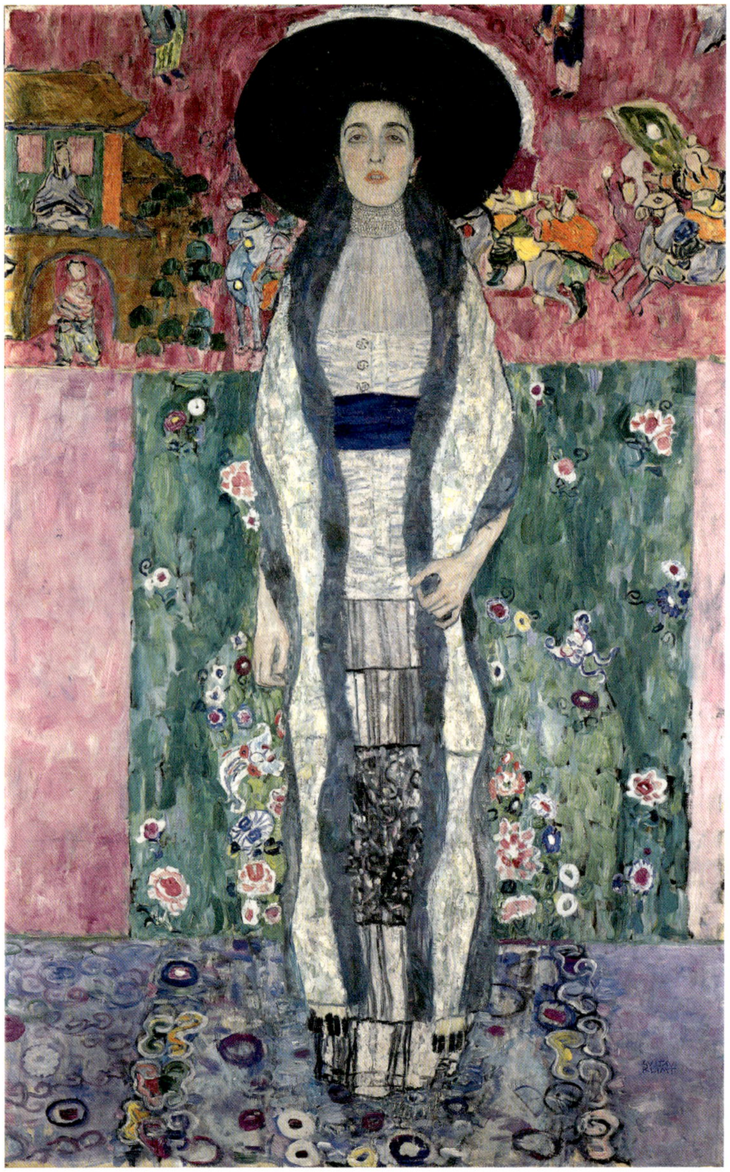

Fig. 9
GUSTAV KLIMT
Adele Bloch-Bauer II, 1912
Museum of Modern Art, New York,
Long-term loan from a private
collection

James Abbott McNeill Whistler's *Arrangement in Grey and Black* (1871). The background in the portrait *Margarethe Stonborough-Wittgenstein* seems like an integral component of an (imaginary) Wiener Werkstätte wall design.[29] It is the painting *Fritza Riedler*, however, that most epitomizes this decorative creative phase influenced by the stylistic stringency of the Wiener Werkstätte. The abstract door of the cabinet designed by Josef Hoffmann in Klimt's studio in Josefstädter Strasse and the reference to Velázquez behind the subject's head, showing a mosaic inspired by Leopold Forstner, place this portrait clearly in context.

With the founding of the Wiener Werkstätte in 1903, arts and crafts became part of the artistic program. Klimt had a particular sensitivity to this and subordinated everything from then on to his desire for ornamentation and stylization. The modern mosaic portrait, which Ludwig Hevesi claimed to have been Klimt's invention, was derived partly from Klimt's memory of the Byzantine mosaics in the Basilica di San Marco in Venice and the church of San Vitale in Ravenna. But Leopold Forstner, mentioned earlier, also played an important role. Like Klimt, he had attended the Kunstgewerbe-

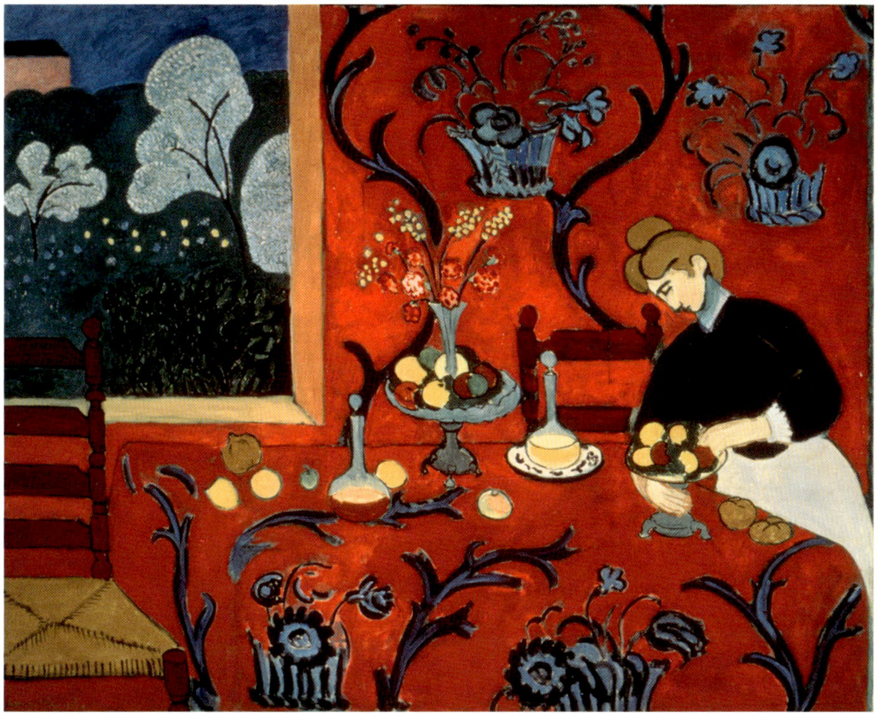

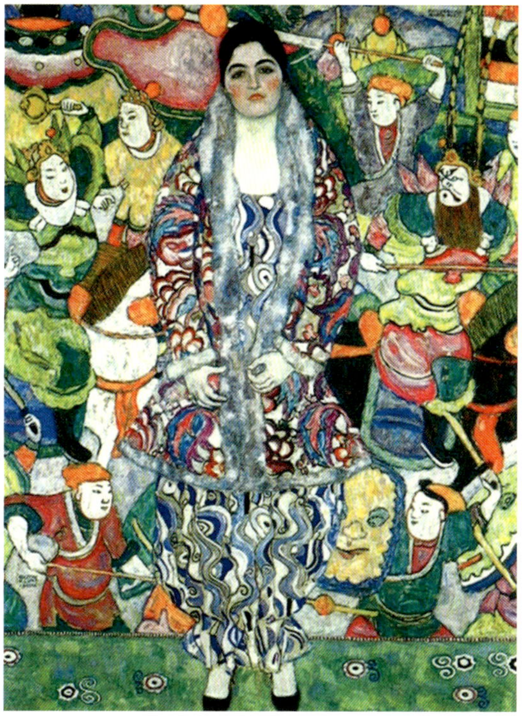

Fig. 10
HENRI MATISSE
Harmonie rouge, 1908
State Hermitage Museum, St. Petersburg

Fig. 11
GUSTAV KLIMT
Friederike Maria Beer, 1916
Tel Aviv Museum of Art, Mizne-Blumental Collection

schule [School of Applied Arts] and had studied with Koloman Moser. He had traveled to Italy on several occasions to see the early Christian mosaics in Ravenna and Rome and the later works in San Marco in Venice. On his return to Vienna, he attempted to inject a new spirit into the old mosaic art, founding the Wiener Mosaikwerkstätte in the same year that Klimt painted *Fritza Riedler*. This was instrumental in bringing about a genuine revival of mosaic art in Vienna, which also impacted on Klimt. It was at this time that he started developing initial ideas for a monumental mosaic frieze for the dining room of Palais Stoclet in Brussels, designed by Josef Hoffmann (1909–11). While the influence of Fernand Khnopff's deliberate rectangular architectural background is still evident in the 1905 portrait *Margarethe Stonborough-Wittgenstein* (fig. 7),[30] through his work on the Stoclet frieze, the background to his pictures assumed a new function for Klimt. The unlimited financing enabled him to complete the mosaic using precious materials, presenting him with an exciting decorative challenge. In his paintings he was unable to use this technique for economic reasons, and instead developed his painting style accordingly.

After 1905, the background took on a new significance in Klimt's portraits, so that, in the artist's final creative phase, almost as much attention was devoted to the background as to the female subject itself. This is especially noticeable in the portrait *Fritza Riedler*, in which he paid particular attention to the painted mosaic surfaces. He not only broke down the background into geometrical sections, but also wove the figure into a triangular composition, a theme taken up again soon afterwards in the portrait *Adele Bloch-Bauer I* (fig. 8). A common feature of all of these paintings is the tension between the highly realistic depiction of the face and hands and the contrasting painterly development of the background and clothing. Klimt used the potential of photography systematically as a style-defining factor.[31]

The unusual feature of *The Woman in Gold*, in which Klimt's approach to portraiture does not, in fact, differ significantly from the portrait *Fritza Riedler*, is the decorative application of gold. Based on his experience with gold backgrounds, he used the metal as a material but also as a figurative design element. The gold background, which came to Europe from Byzantium in the fourth century CE, was originally reserved for portrayals of saints and rulers. Gold was regarded as a symbol of the sun and represented the transcendental sphere of the divine. Klimt, however, used the precious metal solely for decorative purposes. Its cultural significance is nevertheless implicitly conveyed. It is perhaps for that reason that the *Wiener Allgemeine Zeitung* described the portrait as an "idol in a glittering temple shrine."[32]

Even in his early paintings of women, Klimt had already begun to merge the subject with the background. As an opaque material, gold was ideal for taking this desired effect even further, with the figure dissolving completely into the ornamental surroundings. The body is recognizable only in its contours created through the distinct ornamental sections of the clothing. In the portrait *Marie Henneberg* (cat. 13), Klimt had already tried merging the spiral ornamentation of the armchair with the background, using a shimmery pointillist technique. As in the portrait *Fritza Riedler* (cat. 15), the figure is part of a triangular composition, counterpointed by the geometric mosaic pieces behind her head. In the portrait *Adele Bloch-Bauer I*, only head and hands are realistically portrayed, indicating the use of portrait photographs as an aide-mémoire and prop. The mosaic intersects the hair, taking the emphasis away from the face and thus indeed lending the portrait the appearance an icon in a gilded shrine.

Following the phase of playful symbolic references with eroticizing and gender-related ornamentation and its suggestive interplay with the female subjects, Klimt started taking a more sober approach, in which ornamentation, explicitly depicted as such, became even more significant, but was no longer constructed, nor governed by an overriding design intention.

Together with Joseph Hofmann, Klimt was responsible for the selection of the artists and works to be shown at the *Internationale Kunstschau* in 1909, which included some of the latest creations by the Paris Modernists. The works by Matisse, Gauguin, van Gogh, and others, shown in rooms 13 and 14, inspired him to use color to a greater extent. The impact these Expressionist works had on him was so strong that, despite his general unwillingness to travel, he visited Paris in October 1909 for the first and only time in his life. This trip marked a turning point in his work. The gold phase was replaced by an orgiastic experiment in color. The stylization in gold and mosaic-like, geometric ornamentation became organic and reflected the influence of Japanese art, as used by the French Fauvists. The pathos of the idealized imagery disappeared, making way for a plethora of magnificent floral arrangements, animals, and Oriental figures.

This development can be seen particularly well in the portrait *Adele Bloch-Bauer II* (fig. 9) completed in 1912. As in the gold version, Adele's body disappears in a large dress. Only her hands and face are visible, and a large hat frames her head. The stiff posture and empty expression are referenced in the background—in a wall divided into five sections, evoking living-room wallpaper. The picture calls to mind Henri Matisse's 1908 painting *Harmonie Rouge* (fig. 10), in which the artist came close to achieving his aim of complete reduction and synthesis of line, color, and space. Like Klimt, Matisse organized the canvas by arranging it into large sections. In the portrait *Adele Bloch-Bauer II*, the colors practically stand alone as a result of their large-scale decorative and ornamental function and the absence of three-dimensional elements. Through his use of quasi-Fauvist techniques, Klimt created a pictorial world in which the subject was no longer more important than the space itself. The relationships between objects become secondary and are blurred, although not completely ignored. The pathos and the witty, chivalrous erotic allusions in the ornaments and image content disappear. The female subject becomes the backdrop for orgiastic experiments in color.

This arrangement is also to be found in the portraits *Mäda Primavesi* (1913, p. 109, fig. 8), *Elisabeth Lederer* (1914, AW 227), and *Friederike Maria Beer* (fig. 11). The portrait *Eugenia Primavesi* (cat. 30) is an exception. The floral decoration in the background at the top of the painting behind the subject's head recalls the ornaments in the portraits *Fritza Riedler* and *Margarethe Stonborough-Wittgenstein*. The dress is replaced by a veritable sea of flowers, and the deep yellow of the wall echoes the gold in the paintings of 1907–08.

On July 28, 1914, following the assassination of

Crown Prince Franz Ferdinand, Austria-Hungary declared war on Serbia, marking the start of World War I. Klimt received fewer and fewer commissions. The first portrait painted by him during the war was *Barbara Flöge* (1915, AW 222), Emilie's mother. Apart from commissions by August Lederer, the only portraits were *Friederike Maria Beer* and *Margarethe Constance Lieser* (1917, AW 245), the small-format *Johanna Staude* (cat. 35), and the portrait *Amalie Zuckerkandl* (1917, AW 250). Klimt soon began to paint portraits without commission. They were not portraits as such, but representations of women whom Klimt had invited to his studio as models. The art patrons August Lederer and the Jewish book and art dealer Richard Lányi were two of the few purchasers of these pictures. The latter purchased *The Fur Collar* (1916, AW 229), *The Dancer* (cat. 122), and *Lady with a Muff* (1917, AW 241).

On Friday, January 11, 1918, Klimt suffered a stroke that left him paralyzed on one side. He died on February 6, 1918, at the General Hospital in Vienna, leaving several unfinished portraits of women, including *Portrait of a Woman Facing Front* (1917, AW 249), the portrait *Johanna Staude*, and *Portrait of a Woman* (1917, AW 246).

1 Franz Servaes, "Gustav Klimt," in: *Velhagen & Klasings Monatshefte*, yr. 32, 1917/18, vol. III, pp. 21–32, here p. 24.
2 With reference to the probate proceedings, Christian M. Nebehay mentions fourteen illegitimate children, whose mothers made claims on Klimt's estate. Settlements were made in four cases, and the rest waived their claims. Christian M. Nebehay, *Die goldenen Sessel meines Vaters*, Vienna 1983, p. 114.
3 Agnes Husslein-Arco/Alfred Weidinger, "Dear Emilie! To my baby … (Love) letters from Gustav Klimt to Emilie Flöge, 1895–1899," in: ibid. (eds.), *150 Years Gustav Klimt* (exh. cat. Belvedere Vienna), Vienna 2012, pp. 281–91.
4 Nebehay 1983 (see note 2), p. 114.
5 Hans Tietze, "Gustav Klimts Persönlichkeit: Nach Mitteilungen seiner Freunde," in: *Die Bildenden Künste. Wiener Monatshefte*, yr. 2, bklt. 1/2, 1919, pp. 1–14.
6 Hans Koppel, "Bei Gustav Klimt," in: *Die Zeit*, no. 406, November 15, 1903, pp. 4–5, here p. 4.
7 The Belvedere organized an exhibition at the time entitled *150 Years Gustav Klimt*, and published a catalogue with the same title, edited by Agnes Husslein-Arco and Alfred Weidinger (see note 3).
8 March Constitution of March 29, 1849. The right of Jews to own property was abolished again in the "Silvesterpatent" of 1851 and only finally reinstated by the law of March 1860.
9 Christian M. Nebehay, *Gustav Klimt: Dokumentation*, Vienna 1969, p. 32.
10 Later Ronacher Theater.
11 See Kathrin Sonntag, "Die Rezeption von Henrik Ibsens Werk in der Wiener Moderne," diss., University of Vienna, 2010.
12 *Neue Freie Presse*, September 10, 1881, p. 6.
13 Felix Salten, "Deutsches Volkstheater, *Nora oder ein Puppenheim*, Schauspiel in drei Akten von Henrik Ibsen," in: *Wiener Allgemeine Zeitung*, no. 5033, December 18, 1894, supplement, p. 7.
14 Marianne Hainisch, "Bericht an den Internationalen Frauenkongress in London über weibliche Fachschulen in Österreich," in: *Dokumente der Frauen*, vol. 9, July 15, 1899, pp. 240–46, here pp. 243–44.
15 Elisabeth Malleier, "Jüdische Feministinnen in der Wiener bürgerlichen Frauenbewegung und in internationalen Frauenbewegungsorganisationen," in: Barbara Eichinger/Frank Stern (eds.), *Wien und die jüdische Erfahrung 1900–1938: Akkulturation – Antisemitismus – Zionismus*, Vienna 2009, pp. 277–98, here p. 279.
16 Nike Wagner, *Geist und Geschlecht: Karl Kraus und die Erotik der Wiener Moderne*, Frankfurt/M. 1987, p. 9.
17 Erna [Helene von Druskowitz], *Pessimistische Kardinalsätze: Ein Vademekum für die freiesten Geister*, Wittenberg 1905.
18 Otto Weininger, *Geschlecht und Charakter: Eine prinzipielle Untersuchung*, Vienna/Leipzig 1903.
19 Ibid., p. 450.
20 Wagner 1987 (see note 16), p. 8.
21 Lisa Fischer, "Geschlechterasymmetrien der Wiener Moderne," in: Tobias G. Natter (ed.), *Klimt und die Frauen* (exh. cat. Belvedere Vienna), Vienna 2000, pp. 32–37, here p. 33.
22 Robert Musil, *The Man Without Qualities*, vol. 1, (translated by Eithne Wilkins and Ernst Kaiser), London 1979, p. 59. Musil was referring to the situation in the last two decades of the nineteenth century.
23 Foreword to *Katalog der I. Kunst-Ausstellung der Vereinigung bildender Künstler Österreichs*, Vienna 1898, pp. 3–5, here p. 3. Apart from Gustav Klimt as president and Carl Moll as vice-president, the other members of the working committee were Rudolf Bacher, Wilhelm Bernatzik, Adolf Böhm, Josef Engelhart, J. Victor Krämer, Max Kurzweil, and Anton Nowak.
24 The exhibition took place from March 26 to June 15, 1898, in the Gartenbaugesellschaft pavilion at Parkring 12.
25 Franz Arnold, "Die Ausstellung der Secession," in: *Neue Freie Presse*, morning edition, no. 12305, November 24, 1898, pp. 1–3, here p. 3.
26 In 1904, Klimt attempted to use this painting style once again in the portrait *Hermine Gallia* (cat. 14) but was no longer able to achieve the same quality as he had with *Marie Henneberg*.
27 Anton Loew was born on October 20, 1847, in Pozsony (Bratislava).
28 The artistic director was Felix Salten.
29 See *Ver Sacrum*, vol. 4, 1901, title page. Moser's metal reliefs for a fitted wall designed in 1904 for the salon of the apartment of Hermann Wittgenstein, a cousin of Margarethe, is also interesting in this context. It shows dancers moving in auras with floating triangles or squares. It is possible that Klimt was inspired by this design.
30 See Alfred Weidinger, "Gustav Klimt: Frauenbildnis und Hintergrund," in: Barbara Steffen (ed.), *Wien 1900: Klimt, Schiele und ihre Zeit: Ein Gesamtkunstwerk* (exh. cat. Fondation Beyeler, Riehen/Basel), Ostfildern 2010, pp. 35–39.
31 See Alfred Weidinger, "Gustav Klimt und die Fotografie," in: ibid./Agnes Husslein-Arco (eds.), *Gustav Klimt und Emilie Flöge: Fotografien*, Munich 2012, pp. 11–17.
32 Berta Zuckerkandl, "Die Kunstschau 1908," in: *Wiener Allgemeine Zeitung*, June 6, 1908, p. 4.

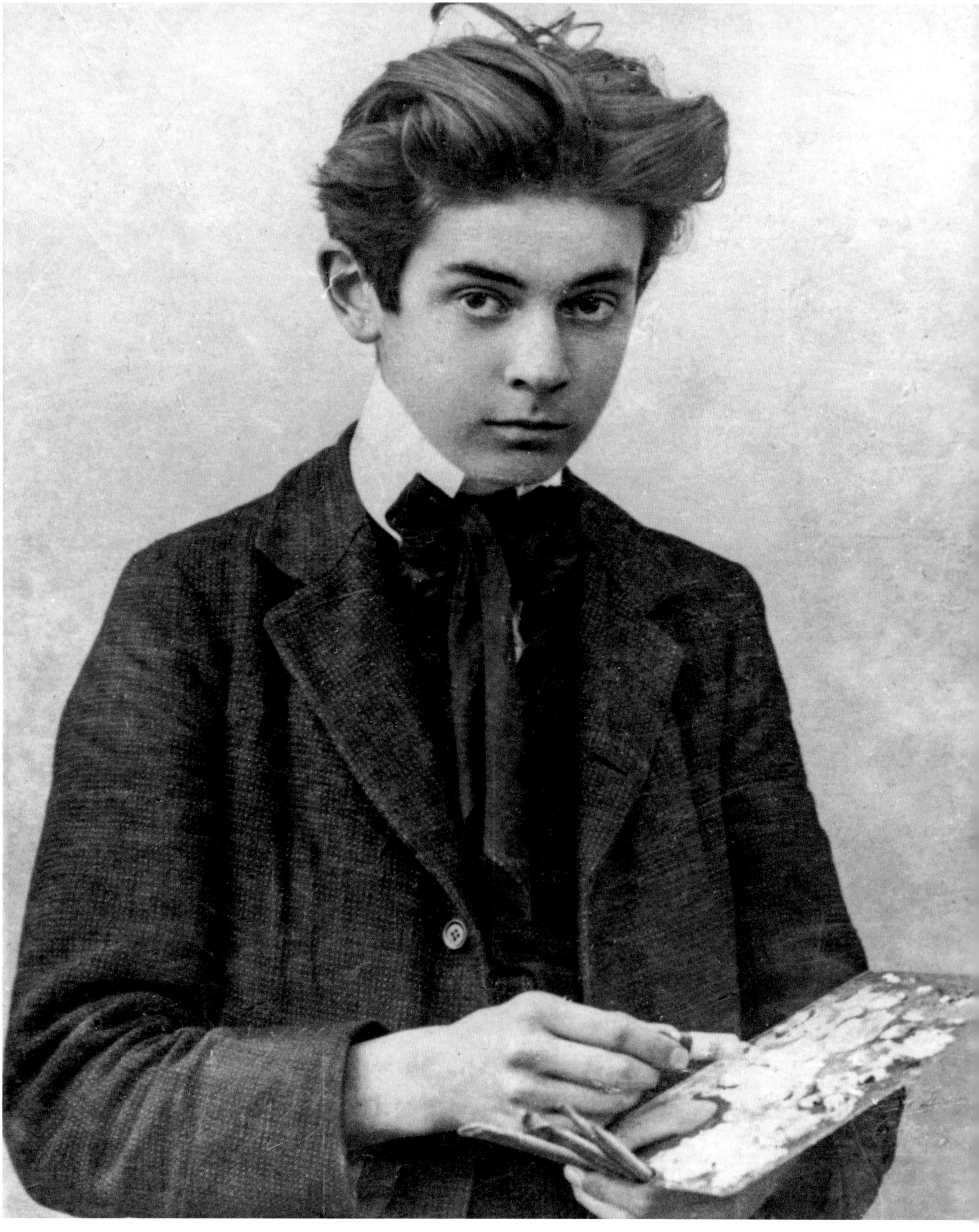

Egon Schiele – "A Nice Young Man from a Respectable Middle-Class Family"

Jane Kallir

Fig. 1
UNKNOWN PHOTOGRAPHER
Egon Schiele as a first-year student at the Vienna Academy of Fine Arts, 1906
Private collection

Fin-de-siècle Viennese intellectuals were obsessed with female sexuality. This obsession colored the work of such disparate figures as Sigmund Freud and Gustav Klimt, Otto Weininger and Oskar Kokoschka, Arthur Schnitzler and Egon Schiele. And yet, even within this context, Schiele's depictions of women have always been considered exceptionally transgressive. Obscenity charges first emerged in 1910, when fourteen of the artist's drawings were removed by the police from an exhibition in Prague,[1] and continued with Schiele's imprisonment on a morals complaint in 1912. Later, Kokoschka repeatedly dismissed his competitor as a "pornographer."[2] The contention that Schiele's erotica served commercial rather than artistic ends was repeated by others and eventually handed down to present-day critics.[3] Even today, many assume that the artist must have been emotionally disturbed; that the "mangled" bodies in his paintings and drawings were expressions of a "mangled soul."[4]

In fact, Schiele was probably the most "normal" of his colleagues. Unlike Alfred Kubin, he never attempted suicide or suffered a nervous breakdown. He did not, like Kokoschka, commission an anatomically correct replica of an ex-girlfriend and then take the doll out on dates. Nor was Schiele anywhere near as promiscuous as Klimt. Schiele was essentially a serial monogamist, with a regrettable tendency to cheat. What distinguishes Schiele from his colleagues is that he was the youngest in the group. Scarcely twenty when he executed his "breakthrough" Expressionist paintings, he was in many respects still an adolescent; his artistic abilities far outpaced his emotional development. The hallmarks of Schiele's work—metaphysical questioning and a preoccupation with sex—are typical of late adolescence.[5] The artist was tormented by these issues in his early twenties, but then, with age, he mellowed. Those who consider Schiele's interests aberrant fail to take into account his relative youth and exceptional creative precocity, which made it possible for him to express feelings older artists generally repress.

Also often overlooked are the sexual mores of *fin-de-siècle* Vienna, which condoned behavior that would today be intolerable. Because they were deemed unfit to marry until they had established themselves professionally, bourgeois young men were encouraged to "sow their wild oats" with various readily available lower-class women (the *süße Mädel* immortalized by Schnitzler). It has been estimated that 90% of Viennese males frequented prostitutes,[6] the majority of whom were minors.[7] A distinction was made between such "inherently wanton" children and bourgeois girls, who were not allowed to know anything about sex. Only members of the latter group qualified as marriage material, and bachelors often "reserved" their brides when they were still children. Such was the case with Egon Schiele's father, Adolf.

Adolf Schiele met his future wife, Marie Soukup, in 1874, when he was twenty-three and she twelve. They married five years later. While Marie at seventeen still played with dolls, [8] her husband evidently had already contracted syphilis.[9] The illness blackened their marriage from start to finish. Probably infected by Adolf, Marie suffered two or three stillbirths in a row.[10] The first infant to survive, Elvira, was born in 1883 and died of meningitis (a common complication of congenital syphilis) at the age of ten. Another daughter, Melanie, was born in 1886, followed by Egon in 1890, and a final daughter, Gertrude (known as Gerti), in 1894. In 1904, when Egon was fourteen, Adolf died following a protracted descent into syphilitic madness.

Adolf's death had an enormous impact on Egon. It toppled the family from its former middle-class station and put them at the mercy of better-off relatives. Deprived of a paternal role model just when he was going through puberty, Egon later sought father substitutes in patrons like Arthur Roessler.[11] The syphilitic curse established a visceral connection between *Eros* and *Thanatos* that reverberated through much of the artist's oeuvre. Finally, as the sole surviving male in a family of females, Schiele (like Klimt but unlike Kokoschka) would always be at ease in the company of women.

Young Egon readily dominated his mother and two sisters. After Adolf's death, Marie's relatives expected the boy to support his family, but he convinced his mother to let him enter the Vienna Academy of Fine Arts. He and Gerti joined forces against their more responsible older sister, who had gone out and gotten a job. To her two siblings, Melanie was "the dragon."[12] Egon also bullied Gerti. Though she suffered from trains sickness, he persuaded her to accompany him on long exploratory rail journeys. In the mornings, he woke her with a clock in his hand. At the count of three, she had to be up and ready to pose.[13]

All Schiele's family members posed for him during his years at the Academy (1906–09), but Gerti was his favorite (cat. 17). A sometime model for the Wiener Werkstätte, she had a professional flexibility well attuned to her brother's needs. She readily assumed multiple guises: ingénue or harpy; innocent or seductress. Because Gerti frequently posed nude (cat. 134), conjectures about incest have colored discussions of her relationship with Egon.[14] However, it seems unlikely that they had any overt sexual contact. For each sibling, the other was undoubtedly the first intimate companion of the opposite sex, and Gerti was a more pliable, less intimidating model than a stranger would have been. During the period when they worked together most closely (through 1910), Schiele was not ready for a full-fledged romantic relationship.[15] His collaboration with his sister was probably not a sexual liaison in its own right, but rather a means to evade such a liaison.

Although it appears Schiele impregnated one of his models in the spring of 1910,[16] the earliest evidence of a protracted sexual encounter dates to the end of that year. It is then that two models, known as the "black-haired girls," begin to appear regularly in his work (cat. 3, 56, 123). Probably both were prostitutes. Modeling and prostitution were at the time kindred occupations, in that each entailed disrobing in exchange for payment. Several explicit drawings indicate that the artist had a sexual relationship with at least one of the "girls," lasting into 1912 (Kd 961–71, 1158a). Like Klimt, who regularly slept with his models, Schiele here blurred the line between the professional and the personal.

But Schiele differs from Klimt in that his depictions of the "black-haired girls" and of his next model/lover, Valerie (Wally) Neuzil (cat. 96, 97, 99, 127), are not simple projections of male lust. There is a visible interaction in these works, between artist and model: sometimes confounding or anxious, hostile or affectionate; and always probing, questioning the mysteries of sexual attraction and repulsion. Schiele was hardly a feminist, but few male artists, before or since, have so overtly acknowledged female sexual autonomy. By willfully violating the aesthetic devices that had traditionally been used to pacify and objectify representations of the female nude, he unleashed the power of the feminine "other" and thereby

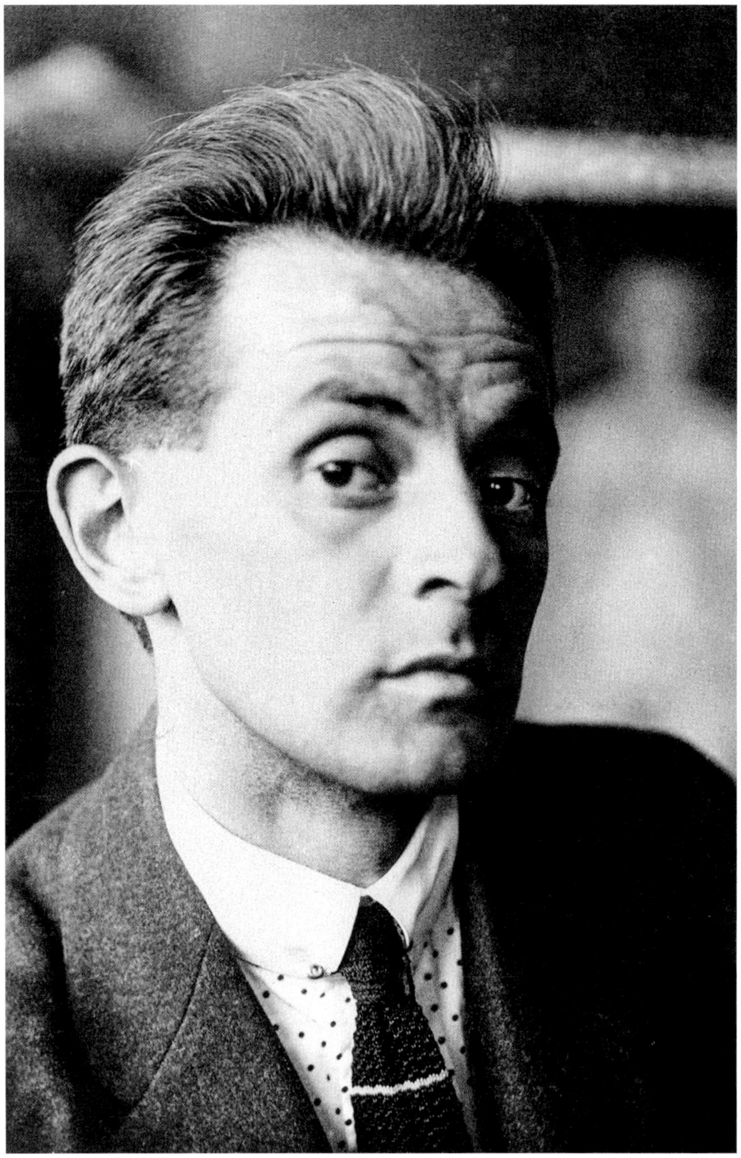

Fig. 2
UNKNOWN PHOTOGRAPHER
Egon Schiele, 1918
Private collection

called into question the efficacy of rational masculine control. To this day, some heterosexual men feel threatened by Schiele's Expressionist nudes. Whereas Klimt kept an emotional distance from his lovers, even when they bore his children, Schiele's involvement with Wally deepened over time. In 1911, (when they first met) she can scarcely be distinguished from the other models in his work. By 1912, not only had she developed a distinctive persona, but Schiele began to depict her in proper portraits. The best known of these (Kp 234) was paired with a self-portrait (Kp 233), as if to seal the couple's commitment to one another. More than just a model or casual sexual partner, Wally was Schiele's willing creative collaborator and steady companion. Proud of "her queenly bearing," [17] he enjoyed showing her off. By openly cohabiting with his lover, Schiele breached the implicit boundary between the privacy of the studio and the public arena.

Klimt's philanderings were discrete, even in liberal Vienna. Schiele, however, took Wally with him to the far more conservative provincial towns of Krumau (where they were evicted from their lodgings after just a few months)[18] and Neulengbach (where the artist was arrested in 1912 for "corrupting the morals" of minors).[19] Schiele's troubles in both places stemmed from a degree of naiveté. His dalliances with Wally and the "black-haired girls" were, after all, well within the range of then permissible behavior. His erotic drawings were avidly collected by any number of respectable older men. But Schiele did not understand that there was a difference between the "inherently wanton" girls of the Viennese streets and the bourgeois children of Neulengbach, or that extramarital liaisons, though common, had to be kept under wraps. He did not understand that drawings which could be traded privately among adult males could not be openly displayed. He believed that as an artist he was exempt from the rules of society at large, and that "even the erotic work of art is sacred."[20]

Nevertheless, Schiele saw himself as "a nice young man from a respectable middle-class family."[21] Unlike Kokoschka, who relished the role of *Spießerschreck* (bogeyman of the bourgeoisie), Schiele was not an intentional rebel. Vocally protesting what he perceived as martyrdom, he nonetheless felt chastened by the prison experience. And while he thought he had special license to pursue a libertine lifestyle, Schiele did not grant the same latitude to the women in his life. When Gerti became involved with his friend, the artist Anton Peschka, Egon confidently assured their mother that Peschka would not "pick the plant before it is ripe." "Gerti," he continued, "would be a base person in my eyes if she succumbed to such molestation."[22] (Lofty sentiments notwithstanding, Gerti married Peschka roughly a month before the birth of their son, Anton Jr., in December 1914.) Schiele evidenced a similar prudery with regard to Melanie. Though fascinated artistically by lesbian subject matter (cat. 91, 93), he was disgusted by the idea that his older sister might be indulging in similar behavior. "Her female life partner has destroyed her in a vulgar fashion," Schiele proclaimed. "I believe she is on the road to ruin."[23]

As a model, Wally was too sexually available, too lowly in social station, to be a serious marriage prospect. Schiele would, in the end, choose someone more "favorable"[24]: Edith Harms, the daughter of a bourgeois railway machinist (cat. 37). Edith insisted that Egon break completely with his lover so their marriage could have a clean start. But Schiele, like many bourgeois men, wanted to eat his cake and have it too: presumably behind Edith's back, he made Wally a written proposition, wherein he obligated himself to take an annual holiday with her.[25] She rejected this proposal out of hand and never again saw the artist.[26] The works executed around the time of Schiele's breakup with Wally, and on into the first months of his marriage, reflect a difficult transition (cat. 102). The ecstatic union of body and soul trumpeted in some of his earlier erotic works has been dashed by the discomfiting realties of actual human relationships.

Schiele proved to be a surprisingly closed-minded, authoritarian husband. Shortly before his marriage in June 1915, he had been drafted into the Austrian army, and he insisted that Edith accompany him to basic training in Prague. She, who had never ridden a train by herself, now whiled away the lonely hours in a hotel room and was berated by her husband if she dared talk to another man. The same thing, more or less, happened when Schiele was later sent to a military installation in the remote village of Mühling. Edith was by herself all day, far from family and friends, "My nerves are sick," she confided to her diary. "Nowhere do I find understanding, and this hurts me so."[27]

By the time Egon and Edith returned to Vienna in early 1917, their marriage had settled into a familiar pattern, shaped by the age-old double standard. Edith may have ruled in the home, but she had little to do with her husband's professional activities. "E[gon] certainly loves me in his own way," she lamented, "but he does not want to share the least thought with me."[28] From the outset, Edith had been reluctant to pose nude (cat. 129, 130), and now, for the first time, Schiele was able to afford a steady supply of professional models. Regardless of whether he was unfaithful to Edith (as has been suggested),[29] his studio life and his domestic existence had split from one another. This split manifested itself as well in his paintings and drawings of women. Schiele's portraits, deepened by his experiences of marriage, became more insightful (cat. 40, 41, 42, 43), while the nudes grew more remote. Though disruptive pictorial elements occasionally surface in his depictions of models, these images are less confrontational, more objectified, than the earlier erotic work (cat. 10, 128, 131, 132).

Reclaiming his bourgeois birthright, Schiele in the last two years of his life produced art that was comparatively realistic, more in keeping with established convention. Many subsequent observers have been disappointed by this evident loss of youthful verve. On the other hand, however, Schiele in 1917 and '18 was at his peak artistically, able to capture his subjects with perfect, nearly unbroken lines. Critics may praise the audacity of the artist's Expressionist period, but collectors have always been attracted to the precision and beauty of the later work. We will never know what Schiele might have achieved had he (along with Edith) not died of the Spanish influenza in 1918. As the art historian Hans Tietze observed, the artist "expended all his vitality racing across a narrow space."[30] Encompassing the arc from adolescence to adulthood, Schiele's oeuvre is complete.

1 Irmgard Hutter, "Gütersloh: Die ersten zwanzig Jahre," in: Heribert Hutter (ed.), *A.P. Gütersloh: Zum 100. Geburtstag*, Vienna 1987, pp. 40–45.
2 Oskar Kokoschka, "Drei Fabriken fälschen meine Bilder," in: *Der Spiegel*, October 24, 1966, p. 172. – Wolfgang G. Fischer, "Egon Schiele's Rise to Posthumous Fame," in: Jane Kallir, *Egon Schiele: The Complete Works,* New York 1990, p. 253.
3 Heinrich Benesch, *Mein Weg mit Egon Schiele*, New York 1965, p. 27. – Robert Jensen, "True Confessions?" in: *Print Collectors' Newsletter*, March–April 1995, p. 28.
4 Klaus Albrecht Schröder, *Egon Schiele: Eros and Passion*, New York/Munich 1999, p. 50.
5 See Peter Blos, *On Adolescence: A Psychoanalytic Interpretation*, New York 1962.
6 Alexander Sixtus von Reden and Josef Schweikhardt, *Eros unterm Doppeladler: Eine Sittengeschichte Altösterreichs*, Vienna 1993, p. 23.
7 Sander L. Gilman, *Difference and Pathology: Stereotypes of Sexuality, Race, and Madness*, Ithaca, N.Y. 1985, p. 41.
8 Anton Peschka, Jr., *Die Wahrheit über Egon Schiele* (unpublished manuscript), pp. 15–16.
9 Kallir 1990 (see note 2), p. 27.
10 Ibid., p. 38, note 8.
11 Schieles's earliest group of patrons included, in addition to Arthur Roessler, potential father figures such as Heinrich Benesch, Oskar Reichel, and Carl Reininghaus. Schiele's expectation of paternal financial and emotional support from these men occasioned numerous spats.
12 Peschka (see note 8), pp. 29, 142.
13 Christian Nebehay, *Egon Schiele, 1890–1918: Leben, Briefe, Gedichte,* Salzburg/Vienna 1979, p. 22, note 28.
14 Alessandra Comini, *Egon Schiele's Portraits*, Berkeley 1974, p. 14
15 Other than Gerti, Schiele's principal nude models in 1910 were males (probably his friends Erwin Osen and Max Oppenheimer) and the patients of the gynecologist Erwin von Graff. See Jane Kallir, *Egon Schiele's Women*, New York/Munich 2012, pp. 68–70, 87–88.
16 Ibid., p. 88.
17 Peschka (see note 8), p. 136.
18 Krumau (today Cesky Krumlov in the Czech Republic) was the birthplace of Schiele's mother and one of the artist's favorite haunts.
19 For a detailed discussion of the "prison incident," see Kallir 1990 (see note 2), pp. 127–137
20 Nebehay 1979 (see note 13), #251 (translated by Jane Kallir).
21 Arthur Roessler, *Erinnerungen an Egon Schiele*, Vienna 1948, pp. 25–26 (translated by Jane Kallir).
22 "... die Pflanze vor der Reife knicken wollte, und Gerti würde die gemeine Person in meinen Augen sein, so sie diese Berührung erdulden würde," letter from Egon to Marie Schiele, March 31, 1913, in Nebehay 1979 (see note 13), #483 (translated by Jane Kallir).
23 "Ich glaube ihre Lebensgefährtin hat sie auf ganz gemeine Art zu Grunde gerichtet; sie ist glaube ich am Wege nach dem Untergang," ibid.
24 Ibid., #772.
25 Kallir 1990 (see note 2), p. 178.
26 Wally volunteered as a Red Cross nurse during World War I and died in Dalmatia of scarlet fever in 1917.
27 Edith Schiele, diary entry, August 21, 1916 (translated by Fanny Kallir).
28 Ibid., April 16, 1918 (translated by Fanny Kallir).
29 Kallir 1990 (see note 2), p. 244, note 60.
30 Hans Tietze, "Egon Schiele," in: *Die bildenden Künste*, vol. 2, no. 5, 1919, pp. 99–100 (translated by Frank Whitford).

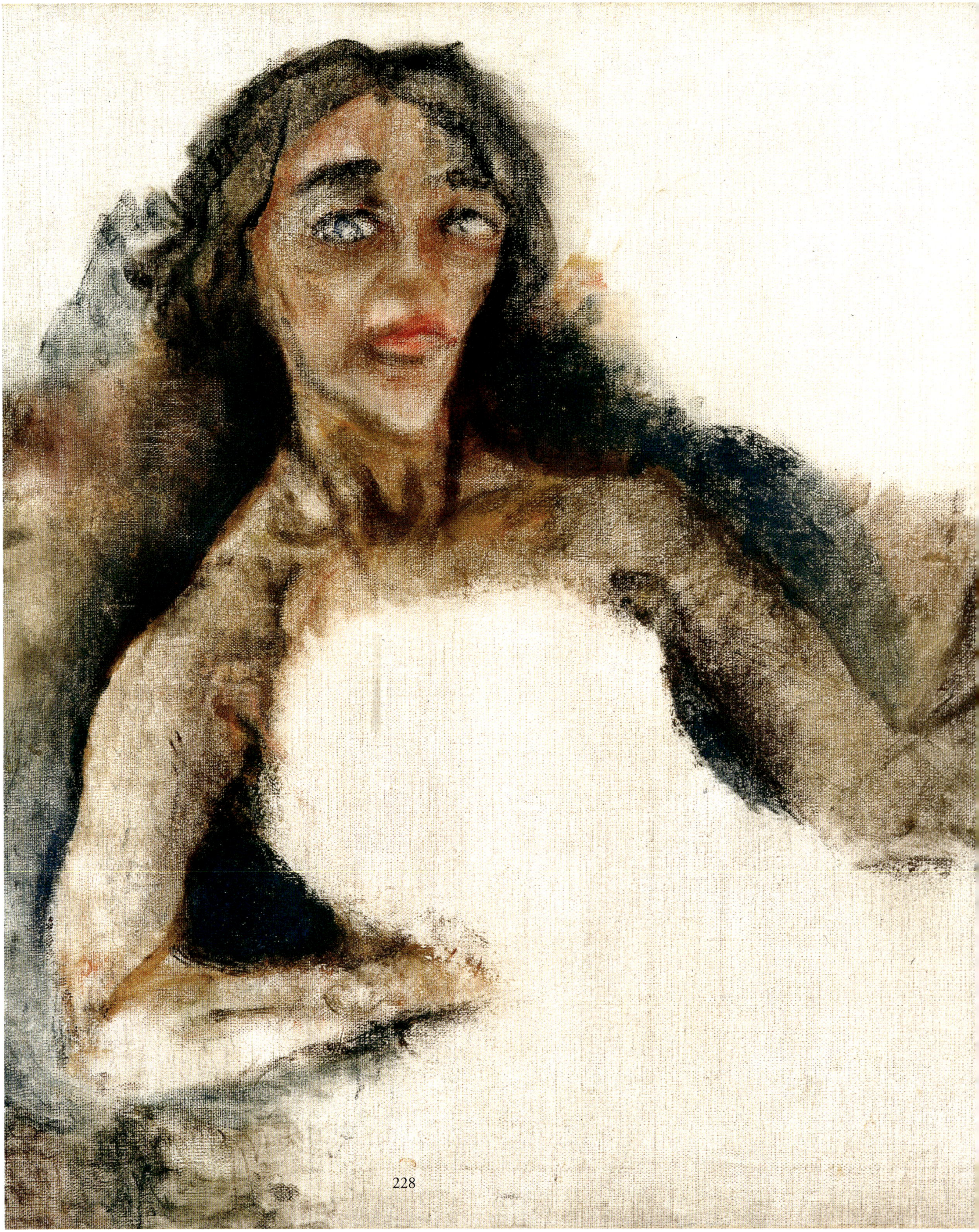

Oskar Kokoschka – Chief Savage and Pathetic Pageant of Folds

Mateusz Mayer

Fig. 1
OSKAR KOKOSCHKA
Bertha Eckstein-Diener, 1910
museum moderner kunst stiftung ludwig wien, Vienna

In early twentieth-century Vienna, Oskar Kokoschka (1886–1980) earned himself the not entirely unflattering nickname "chief savage."[1] His contributions to the Vienna Kunstschau exhibitions in 1908 and 1909 were heavily criticized by the press, his portraits and plays were controversial, and his shaved head was radical (fig. 2). His early artistic activities came at the highpoint of an increasing alienation of the sexes due to restrictive bourgeois sexual morality. This resulted in an atmosphere of discomfiture regarding all things sexual, as modernist literature characterized the turn-of-the-century woman as a man-eating nymphomaniac, licentious seducer, or adored hetaera, and—in the form of Judith or Salome—as an expression of the male fear of castration. This mood had a marked influence on the "chief savage" Kokoschka.

In the intellectual climate of turn-of-the-century Vienna, the image of women conveyed both directly and indirectly to Kokoschka, who had been admitted to the School of Applied Arts in 1904, was one of "backwardness." For example, in 1907, at the age of twenty-one, he wrote: "175–186 cm above the ground, hats go for walks, and clothes 15 cm lower, falling in folds as if they were alive, and everywhere all the folds are governed by the same monotonous theatrical law, and I shall buy myself a false red beard to put between hat and clothes so as to disrupt this pathetic pageant of folds."[2] Kokoschka makes a sweeping generalization about women on account of their sex, denying them any individuality and, remarkably, disregarding their faces. In so doing he was echoing the words of Otto Weininger, according to whom women were "soulless" and possessed "neither a sense of self nor individuality, personality nor freedom, character nor will."[3] Kokoschka's remarks also correspond with those of Adolf Loos that women "preferred ornamental and colorful effects" in their clothing and were "greatly underdeveloped" compared to men.[4] Kokoschka's observation thus coincided with the negative stigmatization of women inherent in Vienna's patriarchal social structure and reflected his generation's attitude to women.

Despite his convictions, the young Kokoschka in no way managed to disrupt the "pathetic pageant of folds." On the contrary, as early as 1907 he stated that interpersonal relations only caused "torment." In later letters to Alma Mahler he further emphasized how difficult it was for him "to become wholly one with another person," as he had "passionately refused all ties in the past" and had "never before experienced physical happiness."[5] This sexual disinterest at the time might also have been an attempt to come to terms with the misogynistic tendencies of his day. Indeed, it would be no surprise if the dangerously seductive femme fatale, so popular in literature and art, unsettled a "pubescent boy" with his "tragedies still undigested,"[6] as Kokoschka saw himself. To that extent he was not unlike his contemporaries: Hugo von Hofmannsthal, for example, is said to have stated that Arthur Schnitzler's writings made him "afraid of women."[7]

It has therefore been suggested that Kokoschka's *Temptation of Saint Anthony* (fig. 3) should be interpreted as an expression of his misogynistic attitude.[8] The story of the saint is basically consistent with Otto Weininger's theory, which reduced women to their sexuality and elevated men to the status of intellectual geniuses. Women are seen purely as sensuous beings whose libidinous aim is to throw men off balance. Weininger argued that man must overcome his own sexuality for that reason, claiming that "the rejection of sexuality is merely the death of the physical life to put in its place the full development of the spiritual life."[9] In fact, Kokoschka later commented in his autobiography that "the erotic advance of the female principle put my hard-won equilibrium in jeopardy,"[10] which would appear to confirm his youthful asceticism and the fact that for him women were not an inspiration but an obstacle.

It is highly likely that this negative connotation after 1907 was considerably enhanced by Kokoschka's unsuccessful courting of his fellow student Lilith Lang.[11] The legendary success of his idol Gustav Klimt as a womanizer will no doubt have frustrated him even further. He also spoke enviously and disdainfully of his artistic rival Egon Schiele, who was always surrounded by "scores of women," something that had already been his "Malheur" as a student at the Academy of Applied Arts.[12] Karl Kraus and Adolf Loos, with whom Kokoschka struck up acquaintanceships around 1908 or 1909, were very much on a par with Klimt and Schiele in this regard. Loos, for instance, had several affairs, married three times, and in 1928 was even involved in a moral scandal.[13]

By contrast, the young Kokoschka usually avoided any involvement with affairs of the heart. His description of an encounter with a "[snake] dancer [...] not dissimilar to her giant snake," whose room he left promptly on discovering that she was a prostitute, brings to mind Franz von Stuck's painting *The Sin*.[14] During a trip to Switzerland financed by Loos in 1910, he felt so sexually threatened by Bertha Eckstein-Diener (WE 39; fig. 137) that he escaped through a window one night leaving her portrait unfinished.[15] The commission to paint the actress Tilla Durieux, obtained through Paul Cassirer in Berlin (WE 54), also remained unfinished, as he recalls, on account of her great "seductive art." In this instance he left behind both the painting and his box of paints.[16] It is not unlikely, therefore, that the young Kokoschka saw most women as terrifying seductresses and sexual desire as a threat to men.

While the young Kokoschka thus tried to avoid female eroticism as much as he could in real life, Karl Kraus's circle made the observation that "the fantasy of the chaste [...] is nurtured continuously by images of sin. The greater the virtue, the stronger the desire becomes."[17] It is possible, therefore, that, despite (or rather because of) his own asceticism, in his early creative period, Kokoschka attempted to compensate for his own sexual inexperience through his art. He noted retrospectively in his autobiography that "an inner voice with ideas connected with the female sex" plagued him like a "lonely man in the wilderness."[18] In that context, the female nude no doubt offered him the possibility of approaching the opposite sex from a passive position. It is interesting to note, however, that Kokoschka's nudes do not arouse desire, nor do they idealize the female body in the academic tradition (cat. 133, 135–139). Instead, Kokoschka is fascinated by the movement of the body or tries to portray the inner psyche, which in some cases might even provoke revulsion. The overly grotesque Berlin prostitutes drawn in 1910

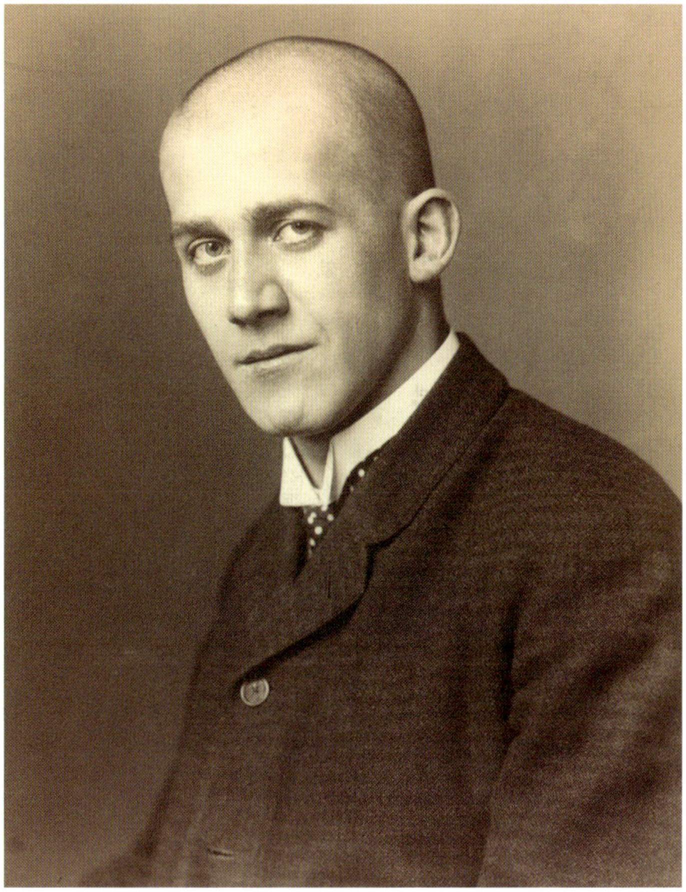

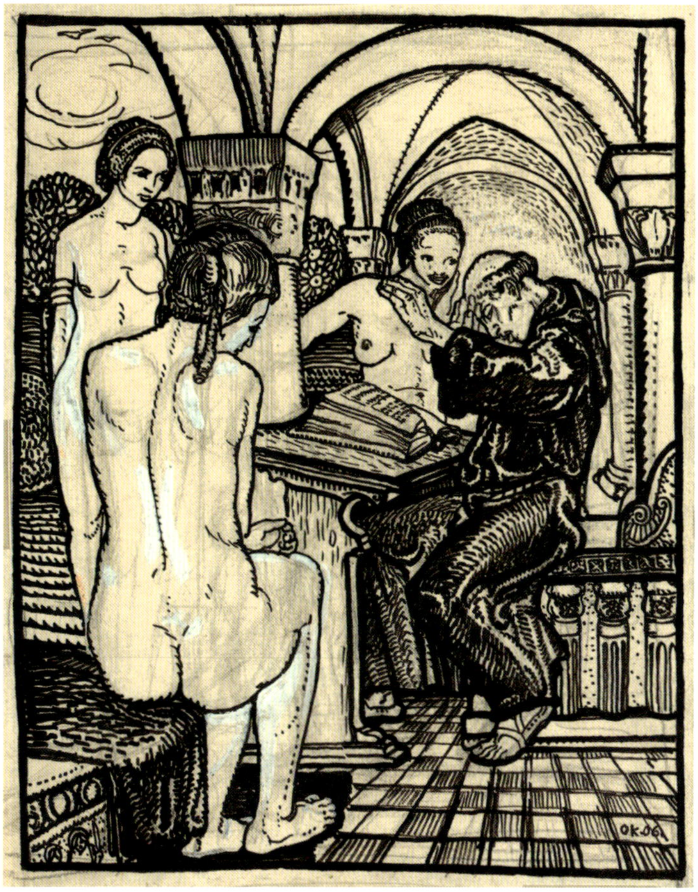

Fig. 2
WENZEL WEIS
Oskar Kokoschka with Shaven Head, 1909
Österreichische Nationalbibliothek, Bildarchiv und Grafiksammlung, Vienna

Fig. 3
OSKAR KOKOSCHKA
Temptation of St. Anthony, 1906
Wien Museum, Vienna

(fig. 5), for example, draw attention to the devastating effects of their trade and may be seen as a warning. Kokoschka's nudes are therefore in stark contrast to the erotic and sensuous connotations of Klimt's nudes and Schiele's explicit erotic depictions mined from his own sexual experience.

On the other hand, Kokoschka's sexual inexperience particularly stimulated his interest in painting adolescent girls (cat. 69, 70, 72), who not only moved more naturally than adult models but had also not yet developed their sexually aggressive potential.[19] Kokoschka's fascination with the prepubescent eroticism of girls is in line with the contemporary interest in the *Kindweib* (or "nymphet") discussed in the writings of Frank Wedekind, Sigmund Freud, and Fritz Wittels.[20] In 1898, Peter Altenberg also issued the expressive appeal: "Artists, poets, do you not yet realize that the nascent woman is closer to you than the grown one? [...] The world of the finished is useful! But the world of the unfinished is beautiful!"[21] Whereas Altenberg had a notorious predilection—shared incidentally with Adolf Loos—for young girls, Kokoschka's fascination with adolescent girls, which continued until his Dresden years (cat. 73, 74), was limited to the role of the haptically observing artist, without any of the erotic undertones present in some of Schiele's depictions of nude girls (cat. 123).[22]

It is also worth noting that before he left the School of Applied Arts in 1909, Kokoschka still regarded himself as a "boy." He escaped, particularly in his graphic works for the Wiener Werkstätte, to a certain extent into a fairy-tale world that was still completely influenced by the Secessionist formal canon. This was also the driving force behind his book *The Dreaming Youths*, which was commissioned in 1908 by the Wiener Werkstätte and could be seen as a response to public morality and prudish sentiment with regard to

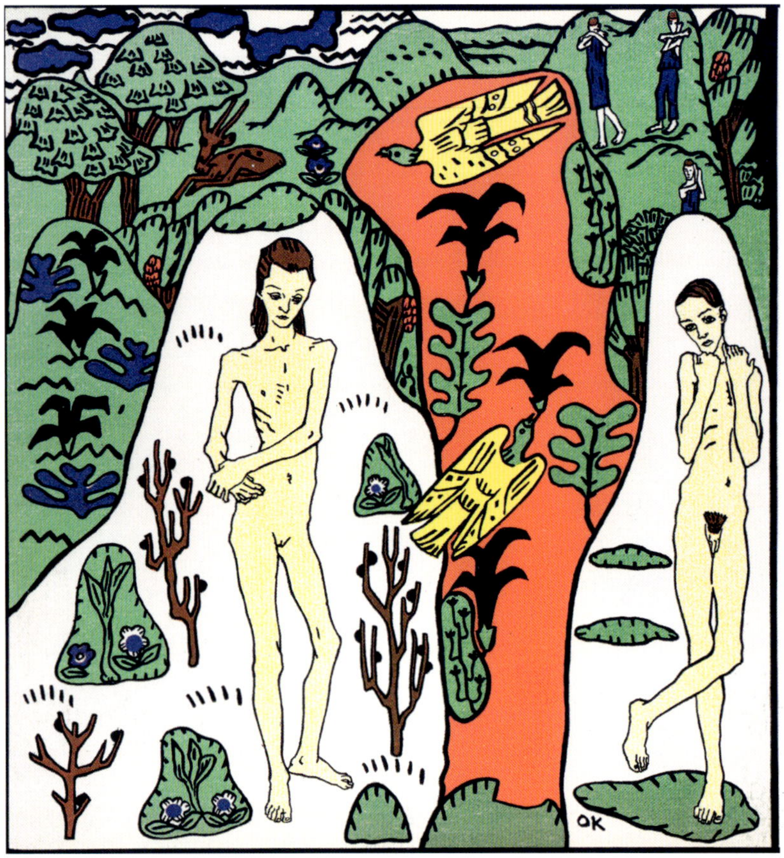

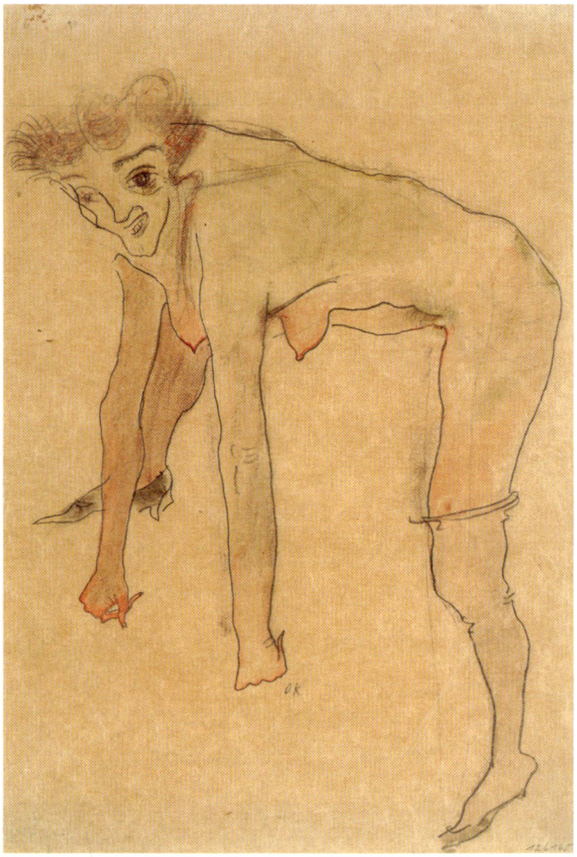

emerging sexuality.[23] Above all, it expresses Kokoschka's personal frustration and pubescent attitude to his own sexuality, linked to his rejection by Lilith Lang. In the last illustration in the book (fig. 4), the shy, distant posture of Kokoschka's naked self-image emphasizes his great discomfort toward the girl.

Just a year after the book was published, the transfigured fairy-tale world gave way to a dramatic and decidedly expressionistic style. *Running Amok* (fig. 6), drawn in 1909, with the initials L[ilith]. L[ang] and O[skar].K[okoschka] tattooed on the figure's lower arm communicates Kokoschka's explicit frustration with regard to Lilith. Hans Tietze also noted that here the "misunderstood man" sees himself "besieged by the burning lust of women," referring to the three female figures in the background.[24] This drawing clearly illustrates Kokoschka's internal conflict associated with his sexual longing for Lilith, her rejection, and the simultaneous attempt to escape female temptations. It is therefore hardly surprising that the war of the sexes played an essential role and took on autobiographical features in Kokoschka's early work. The most controversial result of this was *Murderer, Hope of Women*, a play performed at the second Vienna Kunstschau in 1909, and announced by a much acclaimed poster (fig. 7). In this drama, the subject of which is the struggle between the sexes for social supremacy, warriors arrive at a fortress ruled by women. The situation soon escalates from the sexual tensions between the sexes. When the man orders that the woman be branded with his mark, she stabs him and locks him in the dungeon. Soon after, the woman's desire awakens and, in a state of arousal, she goes to see the imprisoned warrior. The moment she touches him expectantly, she loses all her strength, while the man regains his vitality through her death and proceeds to slay all the remaining characters in the play.[25]

Fig. 4
OSKAR KOKOSCHKA
The Girl Li and I, from the cycle *The Dreaming Boys,* 1908
Private collection

Fig. 5
OSKAR KOKOSCHKA
Female Nude in Stockings, 1910
Kunsthaus Zug, Stiftung Sammlung Kamm, Zug

Fig. 6
OSKAR KOKOSCHKA
Running Amok, 1909
Private collection

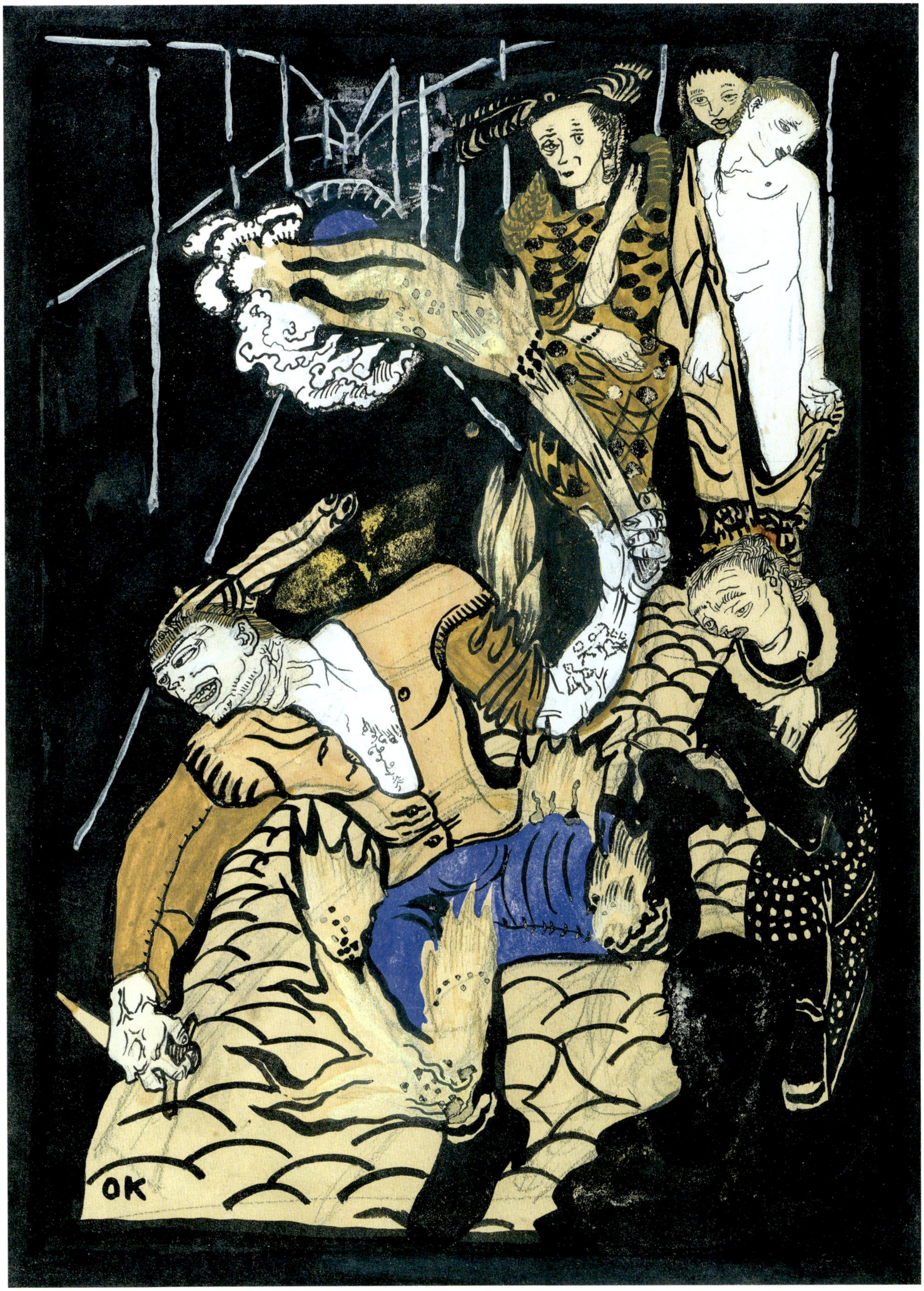
OK

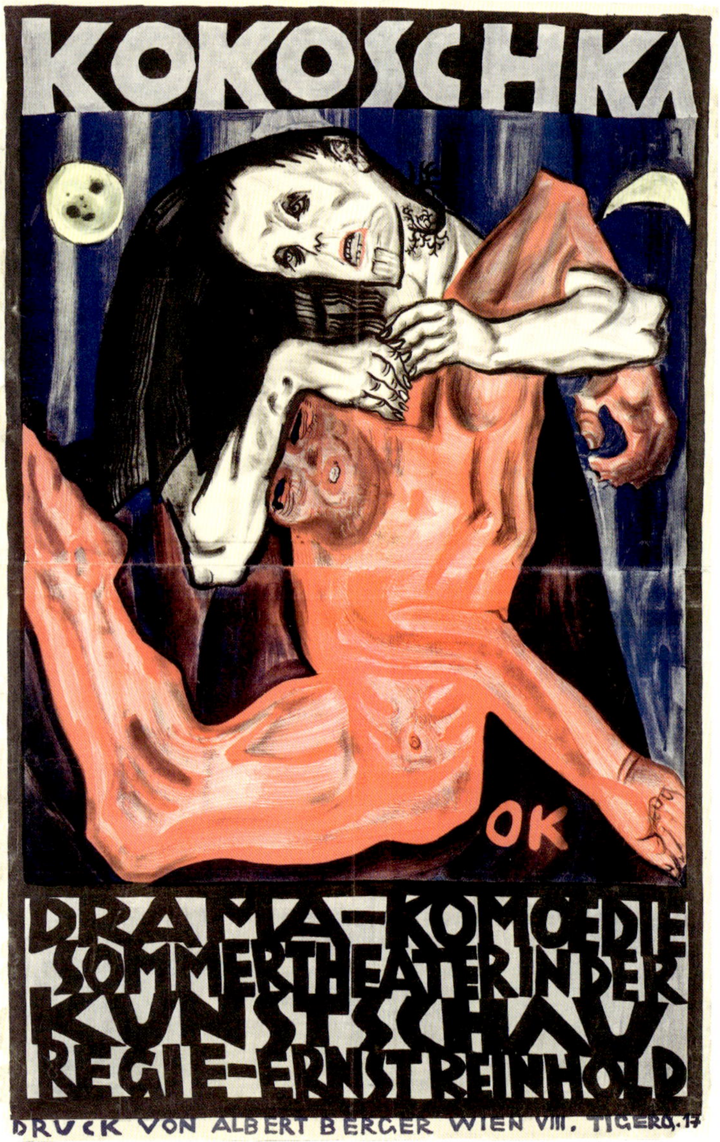

Fig. 7
OSKAR KOKOSCHKA
Poster for the *Internationale Kunstschau*, 1909
MAK – Österreichisches Museum für angewandte Kunst/ Gegenwartskunst, Vienna

On one level, the play is an autobiographical reckoning following Kokoschka's unhappy experience with Lilith. This is indicated by the fact that in his illustrations for the Berlin magazine *Der Sturm*, the leading male character has the artist's own facial features (WS 315–318; fig. 8; p. 145, fig. 3). At the same time, it is clear that the play is influenced by the anti-feminist tone in the writings of contemporary authors, as was the case with Wedekind and the murder of Lulu in his *Pandora's Box*, Weininger, who compares sexual union with murder, Sigmund Freud, who described the latent aggression in sexual relations and penis envy in women, and Arthur Schopenhauer, whose theory of sexual love as touching life and death Kokoschka appears to have taken literally.[26] The play not only reflects the spirit of his age, but also falls in line with Loos's comment from 1902, according to which the arousal of love was the "only weapon currently possessed by women in the battle of the sexes" and "their craving to excite man's desire was their hope."[27] This might explain why Kokoschka dedicated the printed version of his drama to his friend Loos and later claimed that with his play he sought to capture his idealized image of the sexes, in which he was the "stronger" one.[28]

This battle between the "stronger" and "weaker" sex remained omnipresent in Kokoschka's writ-

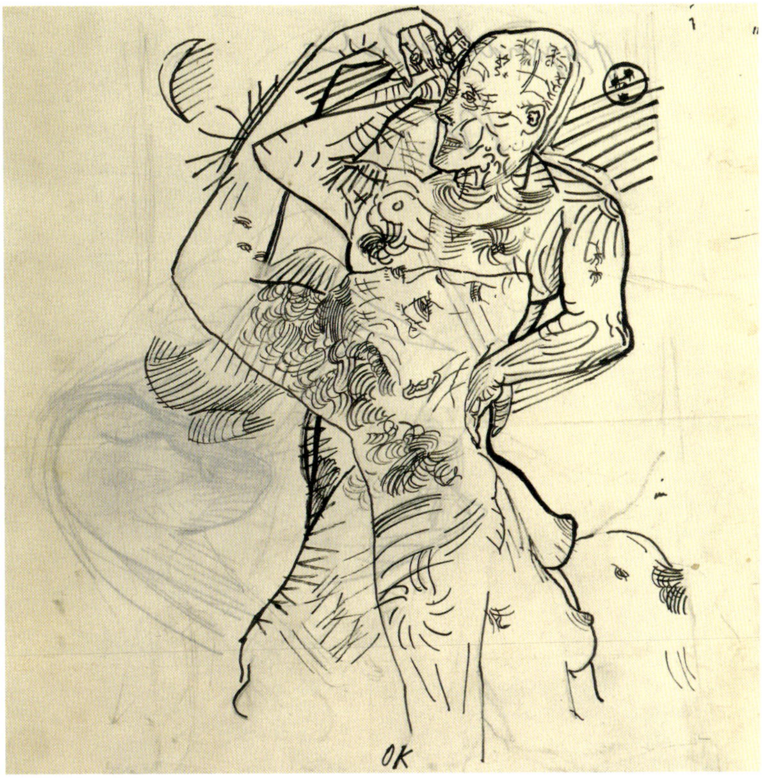

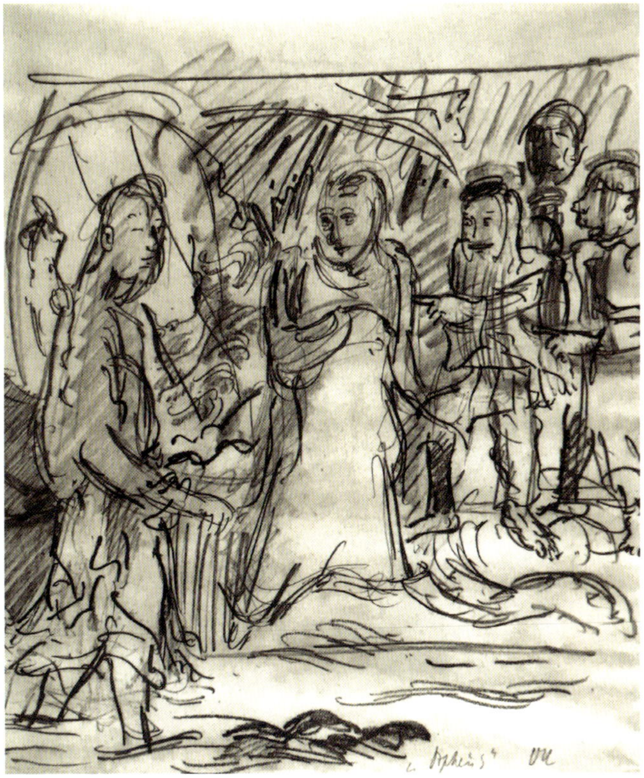

Fig. 8
OSKAR KOKOSCHKA
Murderer, Hope of Women II, 1910
Kunsthaus Zug, Stiftung Sammlung Kamm, Zug

Fig. 9
OSKAR KOKOSCHKA
Orpheus and Eurydice, 1918
Kunsthalle Bremen

ings. In his 1909 play *Curiosum*, later renamed *Sphinx and Strawman*, the leading male character, Herr Firdusi, shoots himself because of his wife's unfaithfulness. In *The Burning Bush* (1911) the woman kills her lover, while in *Orpheus and Eurydice* (1915–18, see fig. 9) the ghost of Eurydice kills Orpheus. Scholars have connected these writings with Arthur Schopenhauer and August Strindberg, whose works convey the idea that women lack both spirit and understanding and that, as a consequence, they can be shaped by man.[29] Kokoschka takes up these ideas by giving the woman a soul borrowed from the man, with which she can attract other lovers and torment the man who has originally given her his soul.

This image of women, which appears strange today, clearly fits with Kokoschka's personal view, as can be seen in his conflictual relationship with Alma Mahler, widow of the composer Gustav Mahler, with whom he eventually also experienced "physical happiness" between 1912 and 1915.[30] In his letters, for example, he notes that in Alma's memories he is constantly discovering other people who had been happy with her before him, and that he would like to scrape out of her brain the ideas alien to her.[31] He admits having tried to "eject" these memories from her mind and having made the mistake of "mixing up rudimentary memories and facts about other people" with her own "living being" instead of separating them from ideas and assertions that had accrued to her.[32] It is therefore hardly surprising that in 1915, after Alma had left Kokoschka for Walter Gropius, she wrote that she never wanted to see him again because he had "almost destroyed [her] mind."[33]

This once again reveals interesting parallels with the attraction that the archetypal nymphet exerted on the likes of Loos, Kraus, and Altenberg. Loos's marriages in particular reflected his wish to pick out young and emotionally and sexually naïve women whom he could shape according to his (male) fantasies.[34] Characteristically, Loos noted that women had only one longing, namely "to assert themselves next to a tall, strong man."[35] This is in keeping with the bourgeois ideology of dominance of man, who determines the idealized status and social function of a woman. Kokoschka, who was supported, encouraged, and decisively influenced by Loos, also tried to impose this ideal of the *Kindweib* on Alma. He frequently referred to his much older lover as "little girl," who, in spite of all her various talents, did not know what she was doing.[36] Ironically, Alma too, in her role as muse, felt coerced to treat the artists she inspired as children. She later said that she had loved the "ill-bred, stubborn child" in Kokoschka and also her future husband Franz Werfel "like one loves a man-child."[37] The sexual roles appear to have been inverted here. Kokoschka's ambivalent relationship with Alma is also illustrated by the fact that he loved her "like a child, like a mistress, like my wife and sister and mother."[38] Alma could not (and did not want to) play this role, hence her constant refusal to marry him and the abortion of his child. Kokoschka's image of women was too much at odds with her own image of herself. As Gustav Mahler's widow she enjoyed high social and, above all, independent status, while Kokoschka tried to undermine this very independence and love of freedom, ultimately leading to the termination of their relationship.

The conflictual relationship is reflected in Kokoschka's art. He addressed the emotional turmoil in double portraits and numerous drawings and graphics (p. 21, fig. 4). The fateful love-hate relationship is illustrated, for example, by the original title of *Tristan and Isolde* for his major work *The Tempest* (p. 21, fig. 5). In this context, Kokoschka's illustrations for *Bach Cantata* (cat. 100, 101) are also significant, showing Alma holding him captive in a grave.[39] In 1918, after being seriously wounded in the war and finding a new home in Dresden, he also sought to deal with their break-up. He commissioned a life-size doll based on Alma made according to his precise instructions, drawings, and a study in oil (cat. 143), which was to serve him as a model.[40] Alma wrote in her autobiography that he now finally had her as he wanted her to be, an "obedient, submissive tool."[41] To some extent, the doll's silence helped him to "conquer" (at least artistically) the self-confident mistress who was no longer reachable for him in reality.

This "conquest" of Alma and his processing of the failed relationship coincided with a normalization of Kokoschka's image of women. As he frequently reported to his parents, Kokoschka had relationships with several women in Dresden, among whom Anna Kallin in particular proved to be a faithful partner (cat. 45, 46).[42] In spite of his considerable jealousy, he appeared to achieve with her what he had been unable to do with Alma. As paintings like *The Slave Girl* (cat. 110) show, she fitted his image of women and played the role of the erotic mistress. Whereas he had pestered Alma to marry him, however, his attitude had now changed significantly. He informed his mother, who was worried that he might marry one of his numerous mistresses in haste, that he was in any case "engaged to his imagination" and that he did not need any "good or bad" matches. "Such matches are for post office clerks, bourgeois, ephemeral people. I am an adventurer."[43] Yet his patriarchal world view shaped by Loos remained unchanged, as emerges in his comment that he wanted to travel with Anna to the Middle East to be her "patriarch."[44]

Kokoschka's image of women thus underwent a remarkable change. It should be pointed out that his investigation of sexual matters represented only a part of his diverse oeuvre and occupied him only for a certain period of time. The unsettling diversity of popular images of women and sexual theories at the turn of the century caused an internal conflict in the young Kokoschka, between sexual desire and his rejection of "threatening" sexual lust. Unlike Egon Schiele and his circle of friends around Adolf Loos and Karl Kraus, Kokoschka initially had no opportunity to develop an assured sexual identity through positive experiences of love. The uncertainty gnawed at him from within, and the unknown made him insecure. This inner unrest was ultimately reflected in his works, although Kokoschka's uncompromising analysis of the human psyche and his radical theatrality soon set him apart from the Secessionist tradition, which aestheticized daily life and avoided personal sentiments. For Kokoschka, the latter in particular were central. This permits a deep insight into the artist's psyche, which, as with many of his contemporaries, was torn between morality and desire. It was only after the failure of his relationship with Alma Mahler and the processing of his inner conflicts, combined with the positive experience with Anna Kallin, that the "chief savage" Kokoschka was able to successfully come to terms with women's "pathetic pageant of folds." When he left Dresden in 1924, he was much more self-assured, and other subjects, particularly urban and rural landscapes, became more important for him. He was not to wed, however, until 1941.[45]

1 Ludwig Hevesi, *Altkunst – Neukunst*, Vienna 1909, p. 313.
2 Kokoschka to Erwin Lang, winter 1907, in: Oskar Kokoschka, *Oskar Kokoschka Letters 1905–1976*, (translated by Mary Whittall), London 1992, p. 12.
3 Otto Weininger, *Geschlecht und Charakter*, Vienna 1903, p. 269.
4 Adolf Loos, "Damenmode," in: *Dokumente der Frauen*, vol. 6, no. 23, March 1, 1902, pp. 660–64, here p. 663.
5 Kokoschka to Alma Mahler in July 1912 and January 1913, in: Kokoschka [transl. Whittall 1992] (see note 2), pp. 30, 34.
6 Kokoschka [transl. Whittall 1992] (see note 2).
7 Quoted in Nike Wagner, *Geist und Geschlecht: Karl Kraus und die Erotik der Wiener Moderne*, Frankfurt/M. 1982, p. 32.
8 Claude Cernuschi, *Re/Casting Kokoschka*, Madison WI 2002, pp. 82–83; other examples of similar interpretations of this theme in Bram Dijkstra, *Idols of Perversity: Fantasies of Feminine Evil in Fin-de-siècle Culture*, Oxford/New York 1986, pp. 253–56.
9 Weininger 1903 (see note 3), pp. 456, 458.
10 Oskar Kokoschka, *My Life*, (translated by David Britt), London 1974, p. 26.
11 See Alfred Weidinger, *Kokoschka: Träumender Knabe – Enfant Terrible*, (exh. cat. Belvedere Vienna), Vienna 2008, pp. 108–109.
12 Ludwig Goldscheider, *Kokoschka*, Cologne 1970 [1963], p. 10.
13 See Adam Brandow, *Modern Façades, Anti-modern Interiors: The Ambivalence of Adolf Loos's Vision of Modern Womanhood*, diss., Bard Graduate Center, New York 2010. – Christopher Long, *Der Fall Loos*, Vienna 2015.
14 Kokoschka 1974 (see note 10), pp. 54–55; for equating of woman with snake, see Dijkstra 1986 (see note 8), pp. 305–13.
15 See Heinz Spielmann, *Oskar Kokoschka: Leben und Werk*, Cologne 2003, p. 94.
16 Kokoschka [transl. Britt 1974] (see note 10), pp. 101–102.
17 Lucianus [Karl Hauer], "Erotik der Keuschheit," in: *Die Fackel*, no. 192, January 1, 1906, pp. 8–14, here p. 10.
18 Kokoschka [transl. Britt 1974] (see note 10), p. 26.
19 Weidinger 2008 (see note 11), pp. 62–66; see also Elana Shapira, "An Early Expressionist Masterpiece: Oskar Kokoschka's *Children Playing* from 1909," in: *Zeitschrift für Kunstgeschichte*, vol. 64, no. 4, 2001, pp. 501–36.
20 See Avicenna [Fritz Wittels], "Das Kindweib," in: *Die Fackel*, no. 230–231, July 15, 1907, pp. 14–33. – Sigmund Freud, *Three Essays on the Theory of Sexuality*, Vienna 1905. – Frank Wedekind, *Frühlings Erwachen*, Zurich 1891.
21 Peter Altenberg, "Der Zeichner Fidus," in: *Wiener Rundschau*, no. 3, December 15, 1898, p. 68.
22 Weidinger 2008 (see note 11), pp. 62f.
23 See Werner J. Schweiger, *Der junge Kokoschka*, Vienna 1983, pp. 59–60. – Weidinger 2008 (see note 11), pp. 74–100. – Helen O. Borowitz, "Youth as Metaphor and Image in Wedekind, Kokoschka and Schiele," in: *Art Journal*, vol. 33, no. 3, 1974, pp. 219–25.
24 Hans Tietze, "Oskar Kokoschka," in: *Zeitschrift für bildende Kunst*, vol. 53 [N.F. 29], 1918, p. 85.
25 See Alice Strobl/Alfred Weidinger, "Oskar Kokoschka: Mörder, Hoffnung der Frauen oder Der Todehaß der Geschlechter," in: Achim Gnann (ed.), *Festschrift für Konrad Oberhuber*, Milan 2000, pp. 402–14. – Claude Cernuschi, "Pseudo-Science and Mythic Misogyny: Oskar Kokoschka's Murderer, Hope of Women," in: *The Art Bulletin*, vol. 81, no. 1, 1999, pp. 126–48. – Barbara Eschenburg, "Anima, süße Anima," in: *Kokoschka und Dresden* (exh. cat. Staatliche Kunstsammlungen Dresden/Belvedere Vienna), Leipzig 1996, pp. 51–60.
26 See Strobl/Weidinger 2000 (see note 25). – Cernuschi 1999 (see note 25). – Eschenburg 1996 (see note 25).
27 Loos 1902 (see note 4), p. 661.
28 See Henry Schvey, *Oskar Kokoschka: The Painter as Playwright*, Detroit 1982, p. 34.
29 Eschenburg 1996 (see note 25).
30 For a detailed study of the relationship, see Alfred Weidinger, *Kokoschka und Alma Mahler: Dokumente einer leidenschaftlichen Begegnung*, Munich 1996.
31 Kokoschka to Alma Mahler in May 1912, in: Kokoschka [transl. Whittall 1992] (see note 2), p. 26.
32 Kokoschka to Alma Mahler in January 1913, in: ibid., p. 34.
33 Alma Mahler to Walter Gropius in June 1915, quoted in Reginald Isaacs, *Walter Gropius*, Berlin 1983, vol. 1, p. 146.
34 Brandow 2010 (see note 13), pp. 49–58.
35 Loos 1902 (see note 4), p. 660.
36 Kokoschka to Alma Mahler in April 1912, in: Kokoschka [transl. Whittall 1992] (see note 2), p. 22.
37 Alma Mahler-Werfel, *Mein Leben*, Frankfurt/M. 1960, pp. 59, 128.
38 Kokoschka to Alma Mahler in November 1912, in: Kokoschka [transl. Whittall 1992] (see note 2), p. 33.
39 See Weidinger 1996 (see note 30), pp. 45–52.
40 For discussion of the doll, see Klaus Gallwitz (ed.), *Oskar Kokoschka und Alma Mahler: Die Puppe* (exh. cat. Städtische Galerie im Städel, Frankfurt/M. 1992) Frankfurt/M. 1992. – Eschenburg 1996 (see note 25). – Weidinger 1996 (see note 30), pp. 89–92. – Peter Gorsen, "Kokoschka und die Puppe: Pygmalionistische und fetischistische Motive im Frühwerk," in: Erika Patka (ed.), *Oskar Kokoschka. Symposion*, Salzburg 1986, pp. 187–202.
41 Mahler-Werfel 1960 (see note 37), p. 130.
42 See Spielmann 2003 (see note 15), pp. 205–206.
43 Kokoschka to his brother Bohuslav in early summer 1922, in: Oskar Kokoschka, *Briefe II: 1919–1934*, Düsseldorf 1985, p. 47.
44 Kokoschka to Anna Kallin in October 1921, in: ibid., p. 34.
45 In 1941, as a 55-year-old, he married the 26-year-old law student Olda Palkovská.

Author Biographies

Agnes Husslein-Arco, director of the Belvedere in Vienna since 2007, is an art historian and curator of numerous exhibitions on classical Modernism and contemporary art. She is also the author and editor of several academic publications. She studied art history and archeology at the University of Vienna, the Sorbonne, and the École du Louvre in Paris, and obtained a PhD from the University of Vienna. In 1981 she opened the Viennese branch of Sotheby's, which she managed until 2000. From 1988 onwards, she was also managing director of the Sotheby's branches in Budapest and Prague. In the 1990s, Agnes Husslein-Arco was director of European Development at the Solomon R. Guggenheim Museum in New York, from 2001 to 2003 director of the Rupertinum in Salzburg, and from 2003 to 2005 founder-director of the Museum der Moderne Salzburg. From 2002 to 2004, she organized the foundation of the Carinthian Museum of Modern Art.

Jane Kallir is co-director of the Galerie St. Etienne in New York and known as the international Schiele expert. She studied at Brown University and curated numerous exhibitions for museums throughout Europe, the United States and Asia, including the National Gallery of Art in Washington D.C., the Indianapolis Museum of Art, the San Diego Museum of Art and the Belvedere in Vienna. She wrote over fifteen books on early twentieth-century Austrian Art and is the author of the first comprehensive catalogue raisonné of Egon Schiele's paintings and drawings.

Eric Kandel is University Professor and Kavli Professor at Columbia University in New York and a Senior Investigator at the Howard Hughes Medical Institute. He is founding director of the Center for Neurobiology and Behavior at the College of Physicians and Surgeons of Columbia University, and recipient of the 2000 Nobel Prize in Physiology or Medicine for his work on memory storage in the brain. He is the author of the book *The Age of Insight: The Quest to Understand the Unconscious in Art, Mind, and Brain, from Vienna 1900 to the Present* (2012) and author of numerous publications on neural science.

Mateusz Mayer studied history of art at the University of Vienna and the University of Cambridge, where he received the Brancusi Grant in 2014. His academic interests focus on Central European art around 1900 as well as the Early Modern period. Between 2014 and 2015, he was curator assistant at the Belvedere's department of nineteenth- and twentieth-century painting. Prior to this, he was involved in the refurbishment of the Kunstkammer of the Kunsthistorisches Museum in Vienna and worked as a museum assistant at Klosterneuburg Abbey.

Alfred Weidinger, since 2007 at the Belvedere, head curator and deputy director, previously curator and deputy director of the Albertina. Research focuses: art and photography of the classic Modernist period, Actionism, feminism, and three-dimensional art. He recently organized the retrospective "Peter Weibel – Media Rebel." Publications include the catalogue raisonné of the paintings of Gustav Klimt (Munich/New York 2007) and the annotated catalogue raisonné of Oskar Kokoschka's drawings and watercolors (vol. 1, Salzburg 2008).

Luisa Ziaja is an art historian, lecturer and since 2013 curator for contemporary art at the Belvedere/21er Haus. Prior to this, she curated numerous exhibitions on the relationship between art, society, and contemporary history including *Recollecting. Looted Art and Restitution* (2008, MAK Vienna), and was an assistant curator at the Generali Foundation from 2001 to 2004. She was a lecturer at several local and international universities and has been co-director of the postgraduate program in exhibition theory and practice ecm at the University of Applied Arts Vienna since 2006. She is the author and co-editor of catalogs and anthologies on contemporary art, curating, and art and exhibition theory.

Picture credits

p. 123: Akademie der bildenden Künste Wien, Kupferstichkabinett; pp. 22 (fig. 6), 17, 58, 84 (cat. 29), 87, 92, 101, 111 (cat. 50), 122, 126, 148, 206, 208: Albertina, Vienna; p. 20 (fig. 3): Alte Pinakothek, Munich, Germany/Bridgeman Images; p. 143: Archiv der Autorin; pp. 24, 29: Archiv Eric Kandel; pp. 22 (fig. 7), 33 (fig. 4), 40, 44 (fig. 19), 45, 108 (fig. 6, 7), 151, 175 (fig. 4), 214 (fig. 5), 232 (fig. 4): Archiv Alfred Weidinger; pp. 27, 30, 38, 39 (fig. 11), 63, 71, 79, 84 (cat. 28), 89, 94, 95, 97, 120, 121, 139, 144, 156, 163, 166, 167, 173, 202, 207, 210, 217, 218: Belvedere, Vienna; p. 215 (fig. 7): bpk | Bayerische Staatsgemäldesammlungen; pp. 53, 56, 124, 214 (fig. 4): bpk | The Metropolitan Museum of Art; p. 109: bpk | The Metropolitan Museum of Art | Schecter Lee; p. 108 (fig. 4): bpk | Museum der bildenden Künste, Leipzig; p. 225: Alessandra Comini; pp. 86 (cat. 32), 154, 186 (cat. 118): Coninx-Stiftung, Zürich; p. 137: Detroit Institute of Arts, USA / Bridgeman Images; pp. 65, 156, 177: © Erich Lessing; pp. 99, 134 (cat. 76), 138, 140, 141 (cat. 8): © Fondation Oskar Kokoschka, Vevey/2015, ProLitteris, Zürich; p. 201: © Fondation Pierre Gianadda, photo: Foto Heinz Preisig, Sion; pp. 50, 51, 68 (cat. 11), 74, 77, 86 (cat. 31), 88, 93 (cat. 39), 107 (fig. 5), 111 (cat. 51), 112 (cat. 52), 113, 116, 118, 125, 127, 128, 129, 133, 146, 150, 155, 157, 159, 180, 181, 184 (cat. 116), 185, 187, 188, 192, 194, 195, 198, 203, 204, 222: Galerie St. Etienne, New York; p. 233: Galerie und Auktionshaus Wolf Dietrich Hassfurther, Vienna; p. 169: Galerie Zlatá husa; p. 25 (fig. 10): Galleria degli Uffizi, Florence/ Bridgeman Images; p. 110: Galleria Nazionale d'Arte Moderna, Rome/De Agostini Picture Library/A. Dagli Orti/Bridgeman Images; p. 91: Collection of the Gemeentemuseum Den Haag; p. 41 (fig. 14): Digital image courtesy of the Getty's Open Content Program; pp. 39 (fig. 12), 172: KHM-Museumsverband; p. 105: KODE - Art museums of Bergen, Rasmus Meyers Collection, photo: KODE/Dag Fosse; p. 106: Kunsthalle Bremen - Der Kunstverein in Bremen, photo: Lars Lohrisch; p. 136: Kunsthandel Giese & Schweiger, Vienna; pp. 62, 232 (fig. 5), 235: © Kunsthaus Zug, Albert Frommenwiler; p. 168: © Kunsthaus Zürich; p. 21 (fig. 5): Kunstmuseum, Basel, Switzerland/De Agostini Picture Library/M. Carrieri/Bridgeman Images:); p. 69: Kunstmuseum Moritzburg Halle (Saale) photo: Klaus E. Göltz; pp. 2, 183: © Kunstmuseum Solothurn, Dübi-Müller-Stiftung, 1980; pp. 80, 98, 100, 131, 132, 134 (cat. 75), 162, 170: Kupferstich-Kabinett, Staatliche Kunstsammlungen Dresden, photo: Herbert Boswank; p. 130: Lehmbruck Museum, Duisburg, photo: Bernd Kirtz; p. 82: LENTOS Kunstmuseum, photo: Reinhard Haider; pp. 20 (fig. 2), 21 (fig. 4), 23, 42, 48, 52, 54, 117, 119, 161, 199: Leopold Museum, Vienna; p. 209 (cat. 142): Leopold Privatsammlung; p. 32: photo Les Arts décoratifs, Paris/Jean Tholance; p. 234 : © MAK/Georg Mayer; p. 219 (fig. 10): Henri Matisse, Harmonie Rouge, 1908 © Succession H. Matisse/Bildrecht, Vienna, 2015; pp. 25 (fig. 11), 174: Musée d'Orsay, Paris/Bridgeman Images; p. 44 (fig. 18): Musée Rodin, Paris/akg-images; p. 215 (fig. 6): © Musees Royaux des Beaux-Arts de Belgique, Brussels, Belgium/Peter Willi/Bridgeman Images; p. 141 (cat. 84): Museum der Moderne Salzburg; pp. 164, 165: Museum für Kunst und Gewerbe Hamburg; p. 228: © museum moderner kunst stiftung ludwig wien; p. 18: © Museum of Fine Arts, Boston; pp. 73, 75: © 2015, Digital image, The Museum of Modern Art, New York/Scala, Florence; p. 214 (fig. 3): National Gallery of Art, Washington DC, USA/Bridgeman Images; p. 103: National Gallery of Canada, Ottawa, photo © NGC; p. 70: National Gallery, London, UK/Bridgeman Images; p. 67: Oskar Kokoschka, Alma Mahler, 1912, The National Museum of Modern Art, Tokyo, © Bildrecht, Vienna, 2015; pp. 26 (fig. 12), 55, 68 (cat. 12), 76, 78, 90, 182, 189, 190: Neue Galerie, New York; p. 114: NordseeMuseum. Nissenhaus Husum; pp. 8, 11, 13, 15, 231 (fig. 2): ÖNB/Vienna; p. 41 (fig. 15): Petit Palais, musée des Beaux-Arts de la Ville de Paris/Bridgeman Images; p. 160: © James Prinz Photography; p. 37: Private Collection/Bridgeman Images; p. 96: Private Collection, London; p. 28: Private Collection/© Look and Learn/Bernard Platman Antiquarian Collection/Bridgeman Images; pp. 35, 175 (fig. 5): Private Collection/The Stapleton Collection/Bridgeman Images; pp. 57, 115, 153, 191, 196, 197, 200, 205: Richard Nagy Ltd., London; p. 171: Saint Louis Art Museum; p. 193: Sammlung Deutsche Bank; p. 49: Sammlung E. W.K., Bern; p. 93 (cat. 40): photo: Pixelstorm; p. 209 (cat. 143): Caroline Schmidt Fine Art LLC, photo: Matthew Hollow; p. 135: Sotheby's; p. 36: © Staatliche Kunstsammlungen Dresden/Bridgeman Images; p. 145: © photo: Staatsgalerie Stuttgart; p. 219 (fig. 11): Tel Aviv Museum of Art, Mizne-Blumental Collection, photo: Elad Sarig; p. 85: Toyota Municipal Museum of Art; p. 31: © Trustees of the British Museum; p. 14 (fig. 9): Universitätsbibliothek der Universität Wien, Fachbibliothek des Instituts für Zeitgeschichte; p. 14 (fig. 12): Verein für Geschichte der ArbeiterInnenbewegung, Vienna; pp. 4, 72: photo: Medienzentrum, Antje Zeis-Loi/Von der Heydt-Museum Wuppertal; pp. 81, 112 (cat. 53), 149, 152, 186 (cat. 119), 231 (fig. 3): Copyright Wien Museum; pp. 14 (fig. 10, 11), 33 (fig. 5), 213: Wienbibliothek im Rathaus, Druckschriftensammlung; pp. 83, 184 (cat. 115): W&K – Wienerroither & Kohlbacher; p. 34: www.akantiek.nl/shunga.13.htm;

For the works of Oskar Kokoschka: © Fondation Oskar Kokoschka/ Bildrecht, Vienna, 2015

If in spite of our thorough research any individual illustrations have not been correctly attributed or acknowledged, we offer our apologies and would appreciate any information that will allow us to rectify the matter in future editions.

Catalogues raisonné (abbreviations)

AS
Alice Strobl, *Gustav Klimt. Die Zeichnungen 1878–1903*, Salzburg 1980; Alice Strobl, *Gustav Klimt. Die Zeichnungen 1904–1912*, Salzburg 1982; Alice Strobl, *Gustav Klimt. Die Zeichnungen 1912–1918*, Salzburg 1984; *Alice Strobl, Gustav Klimt. Die Zeichnungen. Nachtrag 1878–1918*, Salzburg 1989

AW
Alfred Weidinger (ed.), *Gustav Klimt*, Munich 2007

Kd / Kp
Jane Kallir, *Egon Schiele: The Complete Works*, New York 1998

WE
Johann Winkler/Katharina Erling, *Oskar Kokoschka. Die Gemälde, 1906–1929*, Salzburg 1995

WS
Alfred Weidinger/Alice Strobl, *Oskar Kokoschka. Die Zeichnungen und Aquarelle 1897–1916*, Salzburg 2008

WW
Hans M. Wingler/Friedrich Welz, *Oskar Kokoschka. Das druckgrafische Werk*, Salzburg 1975

Colophon

This catalogue has been published in conjunction with the exhibition *The Women of Klimt, Schiele and Kokoschka*, held at the Belvedere, Vienna, from October 22, 2015 to February 28, 2016.

Director: Agnes Husslein-Arco
Curators: Jane Kallir, Alfred Weidinger
Curatorial Assistants: Mateusz Mayer, Markus Fellinger, Katharina Lovecky

Belvedere
Prinz Eugen-Straße 27
1030 Vienna
www.belvedere.at

Publication
Editors: Agnes Husslein-Arco, Jane Kallir, Alfred Weidinger
Graphic Design: Peter Baldinger, Vienna
Translation German – English: Andrew Horsfield, Lisa Rosenblatt, Nick Somers
Proofreading: Betti Moser
Production: Andrea Cobré, Prestel Verlag, Munich
Printing and binding: GRASL FairPrint, Bad Vöslau

Prestel Verlag, Munich
A member of Verlagsgruppe Random House GmbH
Neumarkter Strasse 28
81673 Munich
Tel. +49 (0)89 4136-0
Fax +49 (0)89 4136-2335

www.prestel.de

Prestel Publishing Ltd.
14-17 Wells Street
London W1T 3PD
Tel. +44 (0)20 7323-5004
Fax +44 (0)20 7323-0271

Prestel Publishing
900 Broadway, Suite 603
New York, NY 10003
Tel. +1 (212) 995-2720
Fax +1 (212) 995-2733

www.prestel.com

Library of Congress Control Number is available; British Library Cataloguing-in-Publication Data: a catalogue record for this book is available from the British Library; Deutsche Nationalbibliothek holds a record of this publication in the Deutsche Nationalbibliografie; detailed bibliographical data can be found under: http://www.dnb.de

Printed in Austria

FSC
www.fsc.org
MIX
Papier aus verantwortungsvollen Quellen
Paper from responsible sources
FSC® C011912

Verlagsgruppe Random House FSC® N001967
printed on the FSC®-certified paper Gardamatt

ISBN 978-3-7913-5494-1 (English trade edition)
ISBN 978-3-902805-80-5 (English museum edition)
ISBN 978-3-7913-5495-8 (German trade edition)
ISBN 978-3-902805-79-9 (German museum edition)